26th International Workshop on Intelligent Computing in Engineering (EG-ICE 2019)

Leuven, Belgium
30 June – July 2019

Editors:

Philipp Geyer
Karen Allacker
Mattias Schevenels
Frank de Troyer
Pieter Pauwels

ISBN: 978-1-5108-9021-3

Printed from e-media with permission by:

Curran Associates, Inc.
57 Morehouse Lane
Red Hook, NY 12571

Some format issues inherent in the e-media version may also appear in this print version.

Printed by Curran Associates, Inc. (2019)

For permission requests, please contact the European Group For Intelligent Computing in Engineering (eg-ice) at the address below.

European Group For Intelligent Computing in Engineering (eg-ice)
c/o Andre Borrmann
Arcisstrasee 21
80333 Munich
Germany

Phone: 498928-925117
Fax: 498928-948789

anything@eg-ice.org

Additional copies of this publication are available from:

Curran Associates, Inc.
57 Morehouse Lane
Red Hook, NY 12571 USA
Phone: 845-758-0400
Fax: 845-758-2634
Email: curran@proceedings.com
Web: www.proceedings.com

TABLE OF CONTENTS

SESSION 5: BIM AND ENGINEERING ONTOLOGIES II

SESSION 6: MONITORING AND CONTROL ALGORITHMS IN ENGINEERING I

SESSION 7: MONITORING AND CONTROL ALGORITHMS IN ENGINEERING II

SESSION 8: ADVANCED COMPUTING IN ENGINEERING

SESSION 9: COMPUTER SUPPORTED CONSTRUCTION MANAGEMENT

Organizers/Committees

Workshop Chairs

Philipp Geyer
Karen Allacker
Mattias Schevenels
Frank de Troyer
Pieter Pauwels

Local Organizing Committee, KU Leuven

Sundaravelpandian Singaravel, Manav Mahan Singh, Muhannad Delwati
Architectural Engineering Division, Department of Architecture

The Scientific Committee

Search:

Member	Affiliation
Markku Heinisuo	Tampere University of Technology
Yaqub Rafiq	University of Plymouth
Jamal A. Abdalla	American University of Sharjah
Esther Adhiambo Obonyo	Pennsylvania State University
Burcu Akinci	Carnegie Mellon University
Karen Allacker	KU Leuven
Robert Amor	University of Auckland
Chimay Anumba	University of Florida
Burcin Becerik-Gerber	University of Southern California
Jakob Beetz	RWTH University of Aachen
Mario Berges	Carnegie Mellon University
André Borrmann	Technical University of Munich
Stefan Boeykens	KU Leuven
Frédéric Bosché	Heriot-Watt University
Manfred Breit	University of Applied Sciences FHNW
Ioannis Brilakis	University of Cambridge

Member	Affiliation
Hubo Cai	Purdue University
Jack C.P. Cheng	Hong Kong University of Science and Technology
Symeon Christodoulou	University of Cyprus
Frank de Troyer	KU Leuven
Pieter de Wilde	University of Plymouth
Bernd Domer	University of Applied Sciences Geneva
Semiha Ergan	New York University
Esin Ergen	Istanbul Technical University
Martin Fischer	University of Stanford
Ian Flood	University of Florida
Adel Francis	ETS Montreal
Renate Fruchter	Stanford University
James Garrett	Carnegie Mellon University
David Gerber	University of Southern California
Philipp Geyer	KU Leuven
Mani Golparvar	University of Illinois at Urbana-Champaign
Ewa Grabska	Jagiellonian University
Carl Haas	University of Waterloo
Amin Hammad	Concordia University
Timo Hartmann	Technical University of Berlin
Patrick Hsieh	National Taiwan University
Raymond Issa	University of Florida
Farrokh Jazizadeh	Virginia Polytechnic Institute and State University
Vineet Kamat	University of Michigan
Peter Katranuschkov	Technical University of Dresden
Arto Kiviniemi	University of Liverpool
Christian Koch	Bauhaus University Weimar
Markus König	Ruhr University of Bochum
Bimal Kumar	Glasgow Caledonian University
Debra Laefer	New York University
Kincho H Law	University of Stanford
SangHyun Lee	University of Michigan
Fernanda L Leite	University of Texas at Austin
Haijiang Li	Cardiff University

We are very pleased to host the International Workshop of the European Group for Intelligent Computing in Engineering in 2019 in Leuven, a beautiful university town in the vicinity of Brussels, Belgium. The event brings together international experts working on the application of computer science to engineering activities. The workshop is intended to be a high-quality, small-scale event focusing on exchange of knowledge and ideas through intensive discussion. This is supported by the single-track workshop style of the meeting. Although the workshop is particularly dedicated to the application of computer science to challenges in the AEC industry, it is open for experts in neighbouring fields, such as mechanical engineering, geodesy, and informatics, thus fostering interdisciplinary collaboration. We received 55 abstracts from authors from 12 different countries not only in Europe but also including United States, Canada, Singapore and Hongkong. 38 papers have been accepted by the International Scientific Committee, based on a two-phase review process. We are looking forward to the presentation of these papers during the workshop. The corresponding extended abstracts are contained in this booklet; the full papers are available in electronic form online at http://ceur-ws.org.

We wish our guests a successful participation in the workshop and a pleasant stay in Leuven.

Philipp Geyer, Karen Allacker, Mattias Schevenels, Frank de Troyer

KU Leuven

Pieter Pauwels

Ghent University

Leuven, June 30, 2019

Semantic Segmentation of Images of Building Facilities

Thomas Czerniawski, M.S., PhD student, Fernanda Leite, Ph.D., P.E., Associate Professor
The University of Texas at Austin, USA
tczernia@utexas.edu

Abstract. Scan-to-BIM is the process of converting a 3D reconstruction into a building information model (BIM). The process has two parts: (1) sorting subsets of the reconstruction into classes (semantic segmentation) defined by a BIM taxonomy and (2) identifying geometric parameters describing each class instance. Here we demonstrate the ability of deep learning artificial neural networks to semantically segment images of building facilities. We found this deep learning approach capable of simultaneously recognizing: ceiling, wall, plumbing, duct, door, floor, and stairs classes. This semantic scope surpasses state-of-the-art building system recognition methods and represents progress towards comprehensive BIM creation.

1. Introduction

Building information models (BIM) enable simulation, automation, and information sharing. However, building owners do not invest in creating and maintaining BIMs for most of their existing building facilities (Edirisinghe et al., 2016, Shen et al., 2016, Mayo et al., 2012, Giel and Issa, 2015). In order to make the adoption of BIM easier, researchers have been automating parts of BIM creation by applying computer vision (Lee and Lu, 2017, Fathi et al., 2015, Pătrăucean et al., 2015, Volk et al., 2014, Xiong et al., 2013, Musialski et al., 2013, Huber et al., 2011, Tang et al., 2010, Brenner, 2005). The process begins by digitizing existing facilities using reality capture technologies including laser scanners and range cameras. Information from the digital reconstructions is used to automatically generate objects in a BIM as defined by an object class label (e.g. wall, door, window, and column) and parameters (e.g. height, elevation, and relationships). This technical challenge has two parts.

(1) Sorting subsets of the spatial data into classes defined by a BIM taxonomy.
(2) Identifying geometric parameters describing each class instance.

Associating subsets of the input raw spatial data with a BIM taxonomy creates semantic interoperability between the raw spatial data and the computational/algorithmic design software generating the BIM. For this purpose, object recognition algorithms are used. Published work will typically focus on recognizing one type of object category such as plumbing (Ahmed et al., 2014), partition walls (Hamledari et al., 2017), building facades (Oskouie et al., 2017), or a limited number of categories together such as walls, floor, doors, and windows (Quijano and Prieto, 2016, Bassier et al., 2016, Ochmann et al., 2016, Anagnostopoulos et al., 2016, Mura et al., 2016). Researchers have yet to combine and scale existing methods to achieve comprehensive BIM creation because the diversity of objects and systems encountered in buildings far exceeds the scope of existing recognition models.

Emerging deep learning methods demonstrate a level of versatility that has the potential to greatly increase the scope of building system focused recognition. This paper presents a deep learning based object recognition method that successfully recognizes: ceiling, wall, plumbing, duct, door, floor, and stairs classes. This collection of building classes surpasses in size and diversity the state-of-the-art in the building systems literature.

2. Related Work

Several review articles covering the automated generation of BIMs have been published (Lee and Lu, 2017, Fathi et al., 2015, Pătrăucean et al., 2015, Volk et al., 2014, Xiong et al., 2013, Musialski et al., 2013, Huber et al., 2011, Tang et al., 2010, Brenner, 2005). Deep learning approaches are noticeably absent. Research in deep learning applied to computer vision has experienced success processing both 2D and 3D data (Krizhevsky et al., 2012, Qi et al., 2016a, Dai et al., 2017, Qi et al., 2016b). Although datasets used to train these emerging deep learning algorithms are not specifically building systems focused, there is some overlap. For example, of the 20 classes involved in the ScanNet Benchmark Challenge[1], the relevant to BIM include: door, floor, wall, and window. Despite this lack of BIM taxonomy coverage, these other datasets enable transfer learning (Pratt, 1993, Pan and Yang, 2010). Transfer learning is the process of reusing a model trained for one task as the starting point for a model on a second task. Deep learning requires algorithms to be trained on these large annotated datasets, but then they can be fine-tuned on building system focused specialty datasets such as 3DFacilities (Figure 1) (Czerniawski and Leite, 2018).

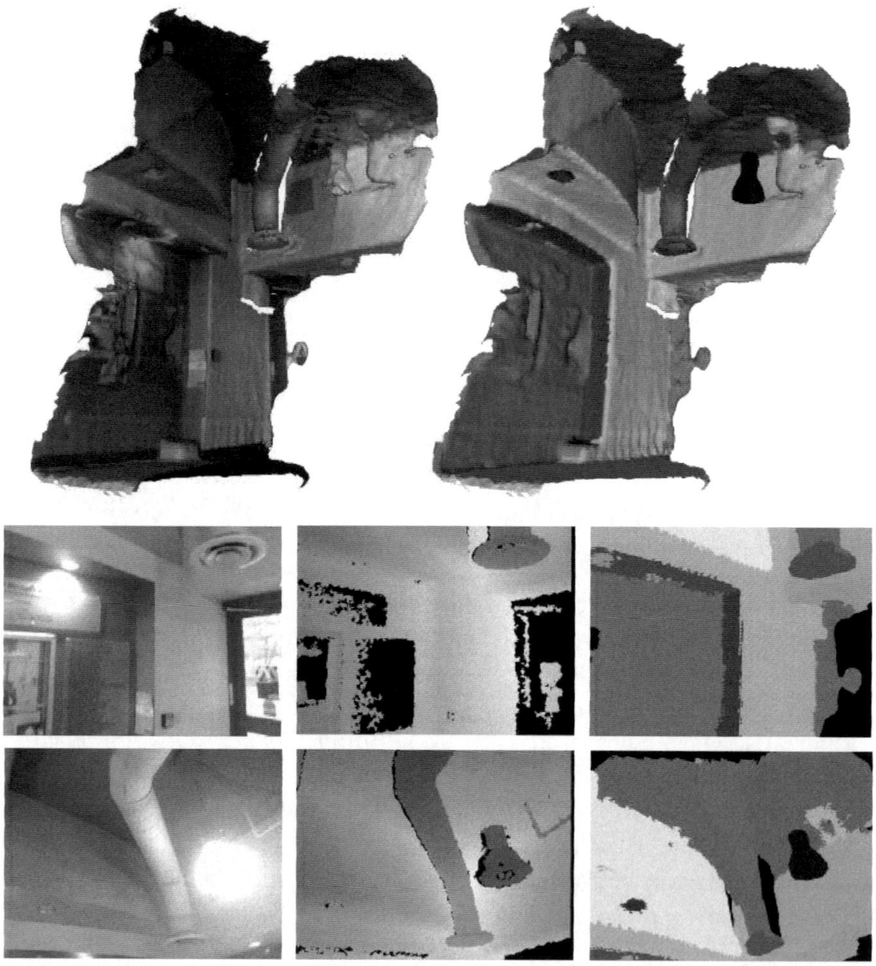

Figure 1: Example of data provided in the 3DFacilities dataset; 3D reconstruction with color texture (scan); 3D reconstruction annotated with instance-level category labels (scan); 2D image color (frame); 2D image depth (frame); 2D image annotated with instance- level category labels (frame)

[1] http://kaldir.vc.in.tum.de/scannet_benchmark/

3. Methodology

Here we implement a deep learning artificial neural network as a supervised machine learning algorithm. In addition to the network architecture, the implementation required training data and computational resources.

3.1 Training Data

Since its initial submission to EG-ICE in 2018 (Czerniawski and Leite, 2018), 3DFacilities (Figure 1) has grown to over 25,000 RGB-D frames and 110 3D reconstructions. Each individual RGB-D frame and each reconstruction have an associated annotation file where each pixel and vertex, respectively, have been categorized into one of 19 different building element categories. The instance count distribution in Figure 2 counts the number of physical building components represented in the dataset. 3DFacilities is a relatively small specialty dataset. Therefore, we make use of two additional datasets, MS-COCO (Lin et al., 2014) and VOC 2012 train_aug + trainval (image segmentation datasets) (Everingham et al., 2010) and transfer learning as described in Section 3.3.

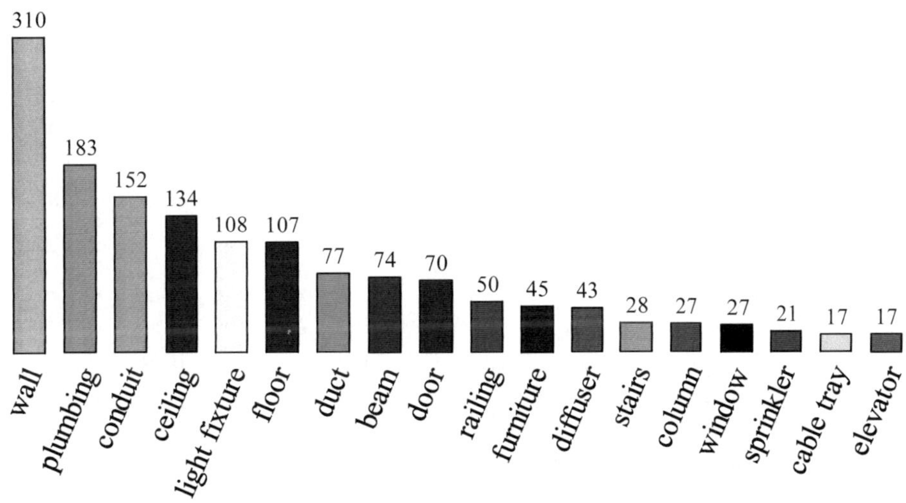

Figure 2: Instance count for each of the 18 categories in 3DFacilities

3.2 Programming Environment

The computing demand of training deep neural networks necessitates the use of high-performance computing. The Texas Advanced Computing Center (TACC) designs and operates some of the world's most powerful computing resources. Stampede2 is the flagship supercomputer at The University of Texas at Austin's TACC and provides high-performance computing capabilities to thousands of researchers across the U.S. It entered full production in Fall 2017 as an 18 petaflop system (TACC, 2018). The neural network is trained using compute nodes on Stampede2.

Although it is possible to code deep learning algorithms from scratch, there are several open-source libraries available. Tensorflow is an open source software library for high-performance numerical computation. It is written in Python, C++, and CUDA. Originally developed by researchers and engineers from the Google Brain team within Google's AI organization, it comes with strong support for machine learning and deep learning (Abadi et al., 2016). Tensorflow was chosen as the development environment because of its supportive online community and its availability on TACC resources.

3.3 Semantic Image Segmentation

The specific neural network architecture we used is called DeepLab (Chen et al., 2014, Chen et al., 2018a, Chen et al., 2017, Chen et al., 2018b). DeepLab is a state-of-the-art deep learning model for semantic image segmentation, where the goal is to assign semantic labels to every pixel in the input image. DeepLab, along with its variations, currently performs amongst the top performing algorithms on the PASCAL VOC Challenge leaderboard (Everingham et al., 2018). PASCAL VOC is a standard recognition dataset and benchmark with detection and semantic segmentation challenges (Everingham et al., 2010). DeepLab is an especially attractive option for semantic segmentation because of its availability in the Tensorflow research model repository.

Data Preprocessing

Annotations from 3DFacilities must be converted into 8-bit images where the value of each pixel corresponds to the pixel's class. There is no input image size requirement as the network architecture is fully convolutional.

3DFacilities was split into a training set and a validation set using an algorithm that optimized for similarity between the pixel class distributions of both sets. This is so the neural network is validated on a dataset that has the same distribution as the dataset it is trained on. In an effort to reduce data dependence between the training and validation sets, sequences of 20 frames were used as inseparable units.

Neural Network Training

3DFacilities is a relatively small training dataset for deep learning. It is, nonetheless, possible to use the dataset to successfully train neural networks because of a technique called transfer learning. Transfer learning is a machine learning method where a model trained on one dataset is reused as the starting point for a model fine-tuned on a second dataset. This is a common approach given the vast compute and time resources required to develop datasets and neural network models.

The DeepLab implementation used by this research uses as its foundation MobilenetV2 (Sandler et al., 2018) that has been trained on ImageNet (Russakovsky et al., 2015) (an image classification dataset). The entire DeepLab implementation was then pre-trained on MS-COCO (Lin et al., 2014) and VOC 2012 train_aug + trainval (image segmentation datasets) (Everingham et al., 2010). The final layer of the neural network was replaced in order to account for the different semantic classes of 3DFacilities. The neural network was fine-tuned on 3DFacilities using the Tensorflow Momentum Optimizer for nearly 75 epochs at a learning rate of 0.0001 (Figure 3). For comparison, the learning rate used to pre-train on PASCAL VOC was 0.007. Total loss is a measure of classification error and is calculated using softmax cross-entropy.

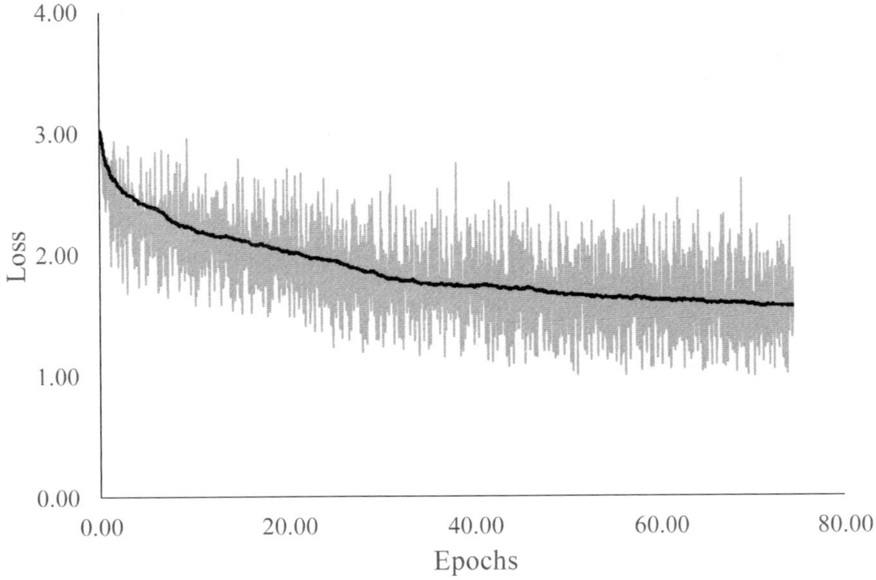

Figure 3: Deeplab fine-tuning on 3DFacilities, total loss vs. epochs

4. Results and Discussion

4.1 Semantic Image Segmentation

Example segmentations created by the DeepLab network can be seen in Figure 5. The neural network limits its pixel classifications to the following seven classes: ceiling, wall, plumbing, duct, door, floor, and stairs. It does not assign the following 12 classes: furniture, window, column, beam, railing, light fixture, elevator, diffuser, fire sprinkler, cable tray, conduit, and background. Comparing these results to the pixel class distribution in Figure 4, it is apparent the neural network has a bias for classes that occur more frequently in the training dataset and ignores those classes that occur less frequently.

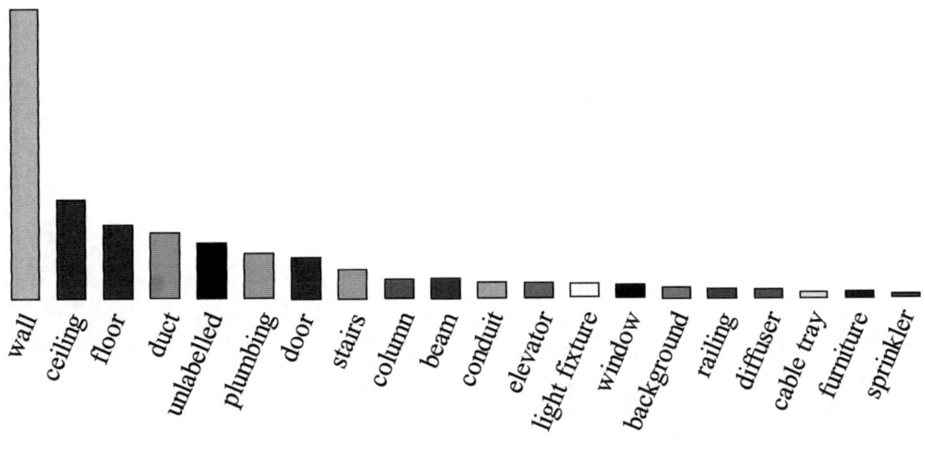

Figure 4: Pixel class distribution of 3DFacilities, horizontal axis is individual frames of 3D Facilities, and vertical axis is percentage of pixels in frame per class

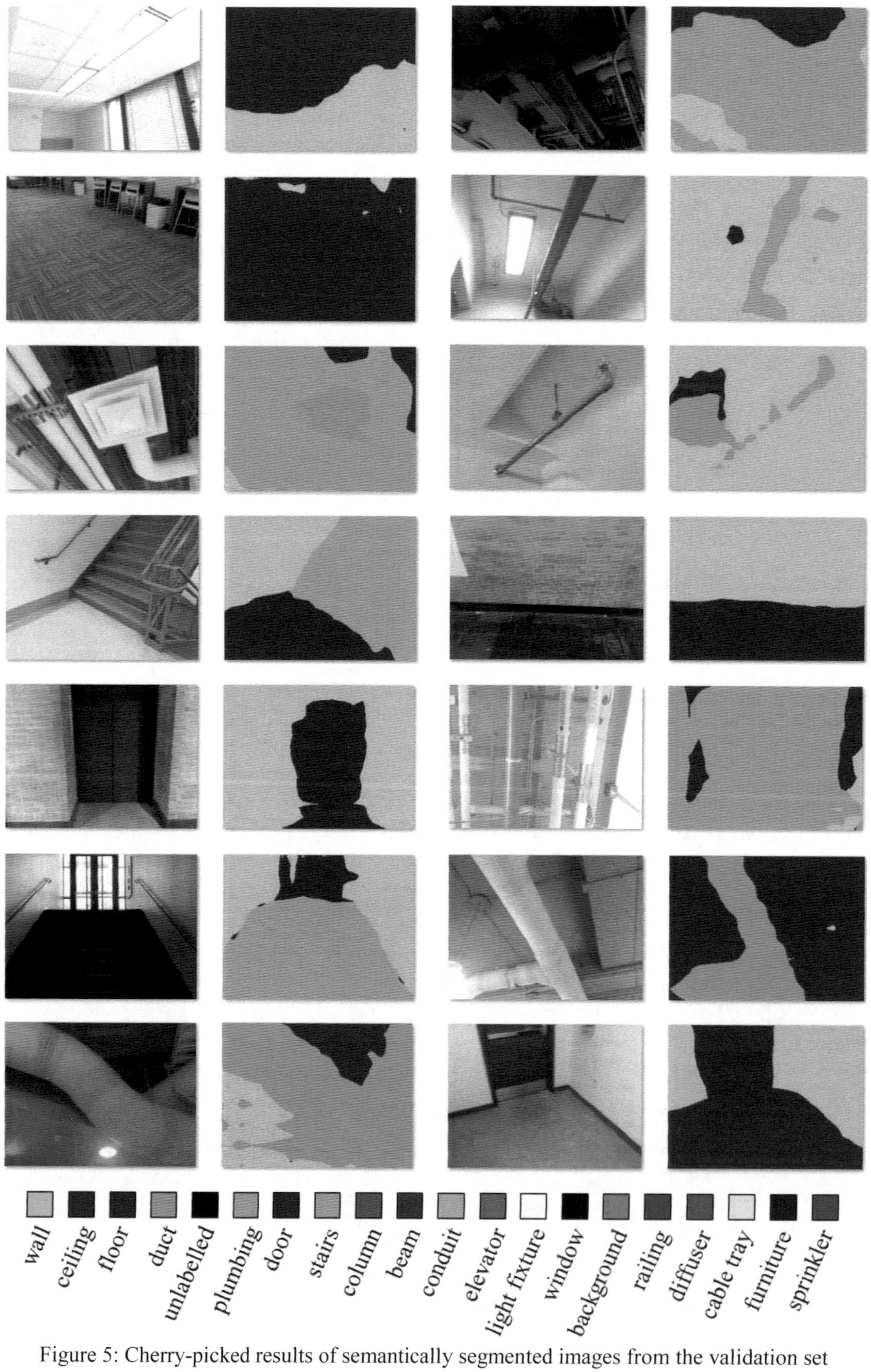

Figure 5: Cherry-picked results of semantically segmented images from the validation set

The seven classes provide partial semantic coverage of the BIM taxonomy as described in Tables 1 & 2 using Uniformat and Revit Families. Uniformat is a standard for classifying construction information in the U.S. and Canada endorsed by the American Society for Testing and Materials (ASTM). It classifies information based on functional elements or parts of a facility characterized by their function. Autodesk Revit is a prominent building information modeling software for people in the building industry. Components in Revit are categorized into families, which are groups of elements with a common set of properties.

Table 1: Top three levels of the UNIFORMAT classification system associated with Semantic Class Outputs from Neural Network

Level 1 **Major Group Elements**	**Level 2** **Group Elements**	**Level 3** **Individual Elements**
B SHELL	B10 Superstructure	B1010 Floor Construction
C INTERIOR	C10 Interior Construction	C1010 Indoor partition C1020 Interior Doors
	C20 Stairs	C20 Stairs
	C30 Interior Finishes	C3030 Ceiling Finishes
D SERVICES	D20 Plumbing	D20 Plumbing
	D30 HVAC	D3040 Distribution Systems

Table 2: Example Standard Families in Autodesk Revit Associated with Semantic Class Outputs from Neural Network

Included System Families		
• Ceilings • Ducts	• Floors • Pipes	• Stairs • Walls
Loadable Families		
Architectural Families	**Structural Families**	**MEP Systems Families**
• Doors • Furniture • Railings • Windows	• Columns • Framing • Trusses	• Conduit • Duct • Fire Protection • Lighting • Plumbing

4.2 Conclusions and Future Work

Scan-to-BIM involves segmenting 3D reconstructions into parts to conform to a BIM taxonomy. The set of seven classes successfully segmented by the neural network presented in this paper represents a substantial increase in semantic scope for recognition methods as compared to the state-of-the-art in the building systems literature.

Class Balancing

The neural network has a tendency to assign classes which are most dominant in the 3DFacilities dataset. In an effort to encourage the neural network to assign classes which appear less frequently in the 3DFacilities dataset, a modified loss function and a variable data feeder will be tested. Final image segmentation performance will be evaluated using standard metrics (mean IoU) (Shelhamer et al., 2017).

Incorporating Additional Data Channels

In an effort to improve semantic segmentation further, two additional inputs should be introduced to the segmentation system: a depth channel and inertial measurement unit (IMU) data. Since these two input types are relatively uncommon as compared to RGB input channels, incorporating them will be a challenge.

Uncertainties include: modifying the DeepLab architecture and cross-modality (Gupta et al., 2016) "warm-starting" with pre-trained parameters from standard DeepLab. The Slim Tensorflow interface provides functions that can be used to "warm start" training algorithms by using pieces of pre-existing model checkpoints[2].

Identifying Geometric Parameters for Class Instances

Combining segmentation results for the 2D data in order to segment the 3D reconstruction can be performed using a multi-view classification process (Pham et al., 2018, Qi et al., 2016b). Then work can begin on identifying geometric parameters describing each class instance.

References

ABADI, M. I., BARHAM, P., CHEN, J., CHEN, Z., DAVIS, A., DEAN, J., DEVIN, M., GHEMAWAT, S., IRVING, G., ISARD, M., KUDLUR, M., LEVENBERG, J., MONGA, R., MOORE, S., MURRAY, D. G., STEINER, B., TUCKER, P., VASUDEVAN, V., WARDEN, P., WICKE, M., YU, Y. & ZHENG, X. 2016. Tensorflow: a system for large-scale machine learning. *12th USENIX symposium on operating systems design and implmentation.* Savannah, GA.

AHMED, M. F., HAAS, C. T. & HAAS, R. 2014. Automatic detection of cylindrical objects in built facilities. *Journal of Computing in Civil Engineering,* 28, 04014009.

ANAGNOSTOPOULOS, I., PĂTRĂUCEAN, V., BRILAKIS, I. & VELA, P. Detection of walls, floors, and ceilings in point cloud data. Construction Research Congress 2016, 2016. 2302-2311.

BASSIER, M., VERGAUWEN, M. & VAN GENECHTEN, B. Automated semantic labelling of 3D vector models for scan-to-BIM. Proceedings of the 4th Annual International Conference on Architecture and Civil Engineering (ACE2016), 2016. 93-100.

BRENNER, C. 2005. Building reconstruction from images and laser scanning. *International Journal of Applied Earth Observation and Geoinformation,* 6, 187-198.

CHEN, L.-C., PAPANDREOU, G., KOKKINOS, I., MURPHY, K. & YUILLE, A. L. 2014. Semantic image segmentation with deep convolutional nets and fully connected crfs. *International Conference on Learning Representations (ICLR).* San Diego, CA.

---

[2] https://github.com/tensorflow/tensorflow/tree/master/tensorflow/contrib/slim

CHEN, L.-C., PAPANDREOU, G., KOKKINOS, I., MURPHY, K. & YUILLE, A. L. 2018a. DeepLab: Semantic Image Segmentation with Deep Convolutional Nets, Atrous Convolution, and Fully Connected CRFs. *IEEE Transactions on Pattern Analysis and Machine Intelligence,* 40, 834-848.

CHEN, L.-C., PAPANDREOU, G., SCHROFF, F. & ADAM, H. 2017. Rethinking atrous convolution for semantic image segmentation.

CHEN, L.-C., ZHU, Y., PAPANDREOU, G., SCHROFF, F. & ADAM, H. 2018b. Encoder-decoder with atrous separable convolution for semantic image segmentation.

CZERNIAWSKI, T. & LEITE, F. 3DFacilities: annotated 3D reconstructions of building facilities. Workshop of the European Group for Intelligent Computing in Engineering, 2018. Springer, 186-200.

DAI, A., CHANG, A. X., SAVVA, M., HALBER, M., FUNKHOUSER, T. A. & NIEßNER, M. ScanNet: Richly-Annotated 3D Reconstructions of Indoor Scenes. CVPR, 2017. 10.

EDIRISINGHE, R., KALUTARA, P. & LONDON, K. An investigation of BIM adoption of owners and facility managers in Australia: institutional case study. COBRA 2016, 2016. Royal Institution of Chartered Surveyors, 1-10.

EVERINGHAM, M., GOOL, L. V., WILLIAMS, C. K., WINN, J. & ZISSERMAN, A. 2018. *Segmentation Results: VOC2012: Leaderboard* [Online]. Available: http://host.robots.ox.ac.uk:8080/leaderboard/displaylb.php?challengeid=11&compid=6 [Accessed 10/20/2018].

EVERINGHAM, M., VAN GOOL, L., WILLIAMS, C. K. I., WINN, J. & ZISSERMAN, A. 2010. The Pascal Visual Object Classes (VOC) Challenge. *International Journal of Computer Vision,* 88, 303-338.

FATHI, H., DAI, F. & LOURAKIS, M. 2015. Automated as-built 3D reconstruction of civil infrastructure using computer vision: Achievements, opportunities, and challenges. *Advanced Engineering Informatics,* 29, 149-161.

GIEL, B. & ISSA, R. R. 2015. Framework for evaluating the BIM competencies of facility owners. *Journal of management in engineering,* 32, 04015024.

GUPTA, S., HOFFMAN, J. & MALIK, J. 2016. Cross modal distillation for supervision transfer. *Computer Vision and Pattern Recognition (CVPR).* Las Vegas, NV.

HAMLEDARI, H., MCCABE, B. & DAVARI, S. 2017. Automated computer vision-based detection of components of under-construction indoor partitions. *Automation in Construction,* 74, 78-94.

HUBER, D., AKINCI, B., ADAN, A., ANIL, E., OKORN, B. & XIONG, X. 2011. Methods for automatically modeling and representing as-built building information models. *NSF Engineering Research and Innovation Conference.* Atlanta, Georgia.

KRIZHEVSKY, A., SUTSKEVER, I. & HINTON, G. E. Imagenet classification with deep convolutional neural networks. Advances in neural information processing systems, 2012. 1097-1105.

LEE, S. & LU, Q. 2017. Image-Based Technologies for Constructing As-Is Building Information Models for Existing Buildings. *Journal of Computing in Civil Engineering,* 31, 4017005.

LIN, T.-Y., MAIRE, M., BELONGIE, S., HAYS, J., PERONA, P., ROAMANAN, D., DOLLÁR, P. & ZITNICK, C. L. 2014. Microsoft COCO: Common Objects in Context. *European Conference on Computer Vision (ECCV).* Zurich, Switzerland: Springer, Cham.

MAYO, G., GIEL, B. & ISSA, R. R. 2012. BIM use and requirements among building owners. *Computing in civil engineering (2012).*

MURA, C., MATTAUSCH, O. & PAJAROLA, R. Piecewise-planar Reconstruction of Multi-room Interiors with Arbitrary Wall Arrangements. Computer Graphics Forum, 2016. Wiley Online Library, 179-188.

MUSIALSKI, P., WONKA, P., ALIAGA, D. G., WIMMER, M., GOOL, L. & PURGATHOFER, W. 2013. A Survey of Urban Reconstruction. *Computer Graphics Forum,* 32, 146-177.

OCHMANN, S., VOCK, R., WESSEL, R. & KLEIN, R. 2016. Automatic reconstruction of parametric building models from indoor point clouds. *Computers & Graphics,* 54, 94-103.

OSKOUIE, P., BECERIK-GERBER, B. & SOIBELMAN, L. 2017. Automated recognition of building façades for creation of As-Is Mock-Up 3D models. *Journal of Computing in Civil Engineering,* 31, 04017059.

PAN, S. J. & YANG, Q. 2010. A survey on transfer learning. *IEEE Transactions on knowledge and data engineering,* 22, 1345-1359.

PĂTRĂUCEAN, V., ARMENI, I., NAHANGI, M., YEUNG, J., BRILAKIS, I. & HAAS, C. 2015. State of research in automatic as-built modelling. *Advanced Engineering Informatics,* 29, 162-171.

PHAM, Q.-H., HUA, B.-S., NGUYEN, D. T. & YEUNG, S.-K. 2018. Real-time Progressive 3D Semantic Segmentation for Indoor Scene. arXiv.

PRATT, L. Y. Discriminability-based transfer between neural networks. Advances in neural information processing systems, 1993. 204-211.

QI, C. R., SU, H., MO, K. & GUIBAS, L. J. 2016a. PointNet: Deep Learning on Point Sets for 3D Classification and Segmentation. *arXiv preprint arXiv:1612.00593.*

QI, C. R., SU, H., NIEßNER, M., DAI, A., YAN, M. & GUIBAS, L. J. Volumetric and multi-view cnns for object classification on 3d data. Proceedings of the IEEE conference on computer vision and pattern recognition, 2016b. 5648-5656.

QUIJANO, A. & PRIETO, F. 2016. 3D Semantic modeling of indoor environments based on point clouds and contextual relationships. *Ingeniería,* 21, 305-323.

RUSSAKOVSKY, O., DENG, J., SU, H., KRAUSE, J., SATHEESH, S., MA, S., HUANG, Z., KARPATHY, A., KHOSLA, A., BERNSTEIN, M., BERG, A. C. & FEI-FEI, L. 2015. ImageNet Large Scale Visual Recognition Challenge. *International Journal of Computer Vision,* 115, 211-252.

SANDLER, M., HOWARD, A., ZHU, M., ZHMOGINOV, A. & CHEN, L.-C. 2018. MobileNetV2: Inverted Residuals and Linear Bottlenecks. *Computer Vision and Pattern Recognition (CVPR).* Salt Lake City, UT.

SHELHAMER, E., LONG, J. & DARRELL, T. 2017. Fully Convolutional Networks for Semantic Segmentation. *IEEE Transactions on Pattern Analysis and Machine Intelligence,* 39, 640-651.

SHEN, L., EDIRISINGHE, R. & YANG, M. An investigation of BIM readiness of owners and facility managers in Singapore: institutional case study. CIB World Building Congress, 2016.

TACC, O. O. T. V. P. F. R. 2018. *STAMPEDE2: TACC'S flagship supercomputer* [Online]. Texas Advanced Computing Center (TACC). Available: https://www.tacc.utexas.edu/systems/stampede2 [Accessed 10/21/2018 2018].

TANG, P., HUBER, D., AKINCI, B., LIPMAN, R. & LYTLE, A. 2010. Automatic reconstruction of as-built building information models from laser-scanned point clouds: A review of related techniques. *Automation in Construction,* 19, 829-843.

VOLK, R., STENGEL, J. & SCHULTMANN, F. 2014. Building Information Modeling (BIM) for existing buildings — Literature review and future needs. *Automation in Construction,* 38, 109-127.

XIONG, X., ADAN, A., AKINCI, B. & HUBER, D. 2013. Automatic creation of semantically rich 3D building models from laser scanner data. *Automation in Construction,* 31, 325-337.

A product-centric approach for assessing the energy performance of solution for building renovations

Christoph Bindal-Gutsche, Timo Hartmann
Technical University Berlin, Germany
christoph.gutsche@tu-berlin.de

Abstract: Considering that 35% of the buildings in the EU are over 50 years old, the renovation of buildings represents a substantial potential for energy savings. The EU estimates that improvements in the energy efficiency of buildings could lead to a reduction of energy consumption in the order of 5 - 6% and a reduction of CO2 emissions of 5% (European Commission, 2019). Building energy performance is the basis to make any decision to enhance the energy efficiency of a building. Unfortunately, building energy performance models are rarely used in building design, commission and operation. The process is very time consuming, costly and labor intensive. Furthermore, the delivery of the results takes too long. Within our approach, we present a method how to build energy models only by changing elements of existing building energy models. This paper presents an energy simulation approach that allows designers to evaluate the performance of a combination of different energy savings products that are available on the market

Keywords: Building Energy Model (BIM), Product-centric simulation, Building renovation, energy-efficient buildings

Introduction

According to Buildings Performance Institute Europe, 40% of the energy consumed and 36% of CO2 emissions in the European Union are related to buildings (European Commission, 2019). Considering that 35% of the buildings in the EU are over 50 years old, the renovation of buildings represents a substantial potential for energy savings. The EU estimates that improvements in the energy efficiency of buildings could lead to a reduction of energy consumption in the order of 5 - 6% and a reduction of CO2 emissions of 5% (European Commission, 2019). Moreover, the renovation of the building stock is the most viable solution to reduce energy consumption and CO2 emissions (Nägeli, Camarasa, Jakob, Catenazzi, & Ostermeyer, 2018, p. 444).

Renovation strategies are required to find existing energy saving products that can be installed to achieve energy efficient renovation. The energy use of buildings depends to a significant extent on how the various elements of a building work together as systems, rather than depending on efficiencies of the individual devices (Harvey, 2009, p. 140). To obtain a good renovation strategy in terms of improving the energetic values of the building, models for analyzing and predicting the energy balance are suitable.

Unfortunately, building energy performance models are rarely used in building design, commission and operation. The process is very time consuming, costly and labor intensive. Furthermore, the delivery of the results takes too long. Also, the quantitative results are difficult to reproduce or to compare to each other (Vollaro, et al., 2014, p. 87). Most of the time, building energy models are generated based on building information models. These generated models are often inaccurate and difficult to make established statements. Nevertheless, building energy performance assessment is necessary to ascertain the efficiency of energy use in buildings. Moreover, it is the basis to make any decision to enhance the buildings energy efficiency.

In our approach, we want to present a method how to build energy models by changing elements of the building model. Based on Building Energy Models from real construction projects, we want to show the energetic effects by changing the elements for renovation within the model. As input variables, we use weather conditions, building description and building component descriptions. The inputs for component description include the elements of the building, for example façade elements or windows. Within our approach, we take these building elements as the basis for the simulation. The improvement of the building elements has the advantage of being simple to model. Moreover, it provides important information to support development of energy efficiency buildings or to justify investments (Borgstein, Lamberts, & Hensen, 2016, p. 477). Laying the focus on the renovation products, we present the different energy performances for building renovations. Accounting the properties of the structures can allow an accurate modelling procedure that reflects the building energy consumption based on the different product values. Analysis of buildings can lead to correctly estimate the building energy performance. However, this type of analysis is often limited to simple technological upgrades and assume, that the environmental conditions were identical before and after renovation.

We want to show a proceeding to simulate the whole building energy changes based on different design strategies. To overcome the uncertainties with respect to building renovation, this paper presents an energy simulation approach that allows designers to evaluate the performance of a combination of different energy savings products that are available on the market.

We do the energetic simulation with the help of EnergyPlus. This software simulates almost all types of buildings with there elements. In addition to that, EnergyPlus runs building energy simulations based on their components. The Building Energy Data will come from real demonstration cases, which are in three different countries in European Communion. We will start with three Energy Models to test our approach.

These results are then employed to point possible energy saving potentials, and to benefit the decision-making process leading to more sustainable and cost-effective projects. This paper refers to the EU collaborative research project called P2Endure. This project focused the practical development and implementation of Plug-and-Play solutions and tools for deep renovation projects of residential as well as public building (P2Endure, 2019).

1. Optimization and energy model in construction projects

Determining and predicting the energy consumption is a critical and equally important input for planning and controlling the energy performance of a building (Xiaoshu, Tao, Charles J., & Martti, 2015). A detailed and accurate building energy model thus provides an outlook on the expected energy values of the building (Arayici, et al., 2011). These energy values are the basis for the selection and use of various building elements in accordance with the requirement to achieve energy target values. Various design options can be compared against each other during the planning phase in order to find the optimal solution for the construction of a building. Creating building energy models requires significant effort. However, the need for such models is increasing (Giannakis, Lilis, Kontes, & García-Fuentes, 2015). There are also numerous publications in the literature that focus on the creation of building energy models. The focus, then as now, is the generation of energy models from existing building models. One of the first efforts for a transformation into energy models are already more than two decades old. Earlier applications of the Lawrence Berkeley National Laboratory (LBNL) started to extract rudimentary geometries of building elements from instances of building information models and converting them into an Input Data File (IDF) for EnergyPlus (Hitchcock & Wong, 2011). Olof Granlund Oy, a building service company from Finland, developed middleware software more than 20 years ago, which can convert elements from a building model to an IDF format without requiring the user to have detailed knowledge of the elements (Karola, et al., 2001). The Architecture, Engineering, Construction, Owner Operator, Phase 1 (AECOO-1) Years later, Testbed started the attempt to optimize the data exchange during the development phase of a building in order to reduce costs and improve the Building Performance Energy Analysis (BPEA). The BPEA thread focused on defining and documenting data exchange requirements for early design energy analysis (Hitchcock & Wong, 2011). New applications, such as the Green Building Web Services, convert special gbXML descriptions of the building into data formats that can be loaded by the EnergyPlus software, among others. Object-oriented frameworks for the optimization of green buildings have been developed (Wang, Jing, Zhang,

& Zhao, 2009) and also optimization processes to develop a collaborative design framework (Bleiberg & Shaviv, 2007). Component-oriented frameworks were presented to facilitate multi-disciplinary design optimization (Geyer, 2009).

At the European level, various research projects have devoted themselves over the past few years to optimizing the planning, implementation and control of construction projects. Holisteec, a H2020 funded research project, developed a Building Information Model (BIM) based collaborative software platform with the aim of designing, implementing and controlling building plans after completion of the construction project. Holisteec aims to improve the overall process efficiency, cooperation and conflict resolution of all participants. At the same time, life cycle costs and errors in planning and execution are to be reduced. Another research project, which should be mentioned, is eeEmbedded. This project was also funded by the European Commission within the framework of H2020. Similar to Holisteec, a cooperative BIM-based simulation platform was developed. In addition to that, a holistic building design methodology, an energy system information model and an integrated information management concept for the design of energy-efficient buildings were presented. Within the project, knowledge-based templates were presented, which enable energy simulations already in the early project phases. Finally, Design4Energy, also a H2020 project, should be mentioned. The aim of this project was to develop methods to simulate future energy values of buildings. The baseline of this procedure are energy attributes of buildings, neighborhood energy systems, result-related parameters, Energy simulation tools as well as current consumer usage parameters.

The process of product-centered representation for evaluating the energy efficiency of buildings has common features regarding this research. The present work is also focusing on optimizing the existing process for the evaluation and controlling of energy values. Our proposal also uses defined building model values or values of the building elements contained therein. On the other hand, our process, focuses on the exchange of elements from existing building models. We show a procedure with the help of which the simulation of different renovation options with one and the same building model.

2. Case study

In this section, we present the process of the product centric approach for assessing the energy performance of building renovations. We describe the structure of the buildings elements as well as the exchange of elements between the building energy models. Before we discuss the product centric approach, we start with a brief introduction about the demonstration case, which we use within this paper.

The case study for testing and demonstrating our approach, is a real existing building located in Warsaw, Poland. The case study is a two storey kindergarten, which was constructed in 1965. The building volume is 2712 m^3. Through a deep retrofitting procedure, the energy consumption of the building, especially for heating, are to be reduced. Therefore, the plan is to install new windows as well as a new Plug-and-play façade. To monitor the renovation process, a building energy model was created. Within this paper, we use this energy model to demonstrate the aim of our approach.

Based on the demonstration project in Warsaw, the design exchange was performed by two entity classes and parameters, windows and panels. First, the old windows of the kindergarten will be replaced by new windows in the course of the renovation project. The new windows have values specified by the manufacturer. The size and number of the windows will remain the same after the renovation. The old windows had single glazing. The new windows will be double or triple glazed. The windows can also be rotated around their own axis. The interior and exterior glazing have different parameters in terms of light transmittance. By rotating the windows, the amount of light entering the room can be reduced, thus reducing the amount of light in summer. Table 2 presents the values of the old window, while table 3 demonstrate the new windows, that will be integrate as part of the renovation process.

Table 1: Window objects from the original building energy model

Field	Units	Obj. 1	Obj. 2	Obj. 3	Obj. 4
Name		V06_ Window_PVC	V07_ Window_PVC	V08_ Window_PVC	V09_ Window_PVC
U-Factor	W/ m²K	1,5	1,5	1,5	1,5
Solar Heat Gain coefficient		0,7	0,7	0,7	0,7

Table 2: New values of the windows, which will be integrate into the original building energy model

Field	Units	Obj. 1	Obj. 2	Obj. 3	Obj. 4
Name		V09_ Window_PVC	V10_ Window_PVC	V03_BGTec	V08_ Window_PVC
U-Factor	W/ m²K	0,9	0,9	0,9	0,9
Solar Heat Gain coefficient		0,53	0,53	0,27	0,53

Second, Plug-and-Play external façade panels will be installed. The façade values are also specified by the manufacturer. Table 3 presents the values of the external panel according to the manufacture. The façade consists of several elements with different characteristics. The left side on figure 1 indicates the installation of the new façade. A panel installation shaft connects the whole panel with the extemal wall. The right side of figure 1 presents a schematic illustration of the façade with the individual elements described in Table 3.

Table 3: Attributes and values of the new panel

Material	Density [kg/m³]	Thickness s[mm]	Λ [W/mK	R [m²K/W]	Diff. - Wid
Structure of the field area Air passage warm side Rsi 0.13					
Mineral wool 04	20	50	0.040	1.250	1
Fermacell gipsum fibre	1150	Dez 50	0.320	0.039	13
Vapour break	1100	0.2	0.2	0.1	100000
Mineral wool 035	50	200	0.035	5.714	1
Fermacell Powerpanel	950	15	0.3	0.05	40
Light mortar LM 21	700	10	0.21	0.048	15/35
Air passage cold side Rse 0.04					

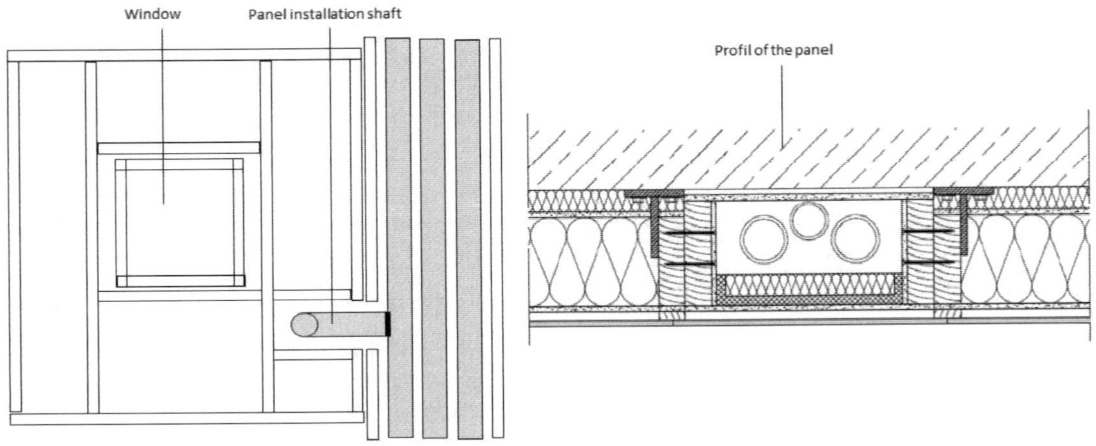

Figure 1: Construction plan of the external facade

In our approach, we use EnergyPlus to perform the simulation of the buildings energic values. EnergyPlus is an energy simulation code with a modular structure. It uses the IDF data format for input data. IDF consists of architectural- and mechanical design elements. Space boundaries, shading and thermal view are part of the architectural design. These design features are important to build to geometry for the IDF file. The architectural design consists of thermal properties of construction material. These construction properties are also needed for the IDF file to run the energetic simulation (National Renewable Energy Laboratory (NREL), 2019).

3. Product centric assessement process

We classify our process into three overall process phases. At the end of a process step, results are generated that serve as input parameters for the following sections. Within the first phase, we define the building elements. Each element is defined by attributes. These attributes are product specific. Based on these specific attributes for describing the building classes, we can build types of products. We then classify these product types into product classes in the product class layer. The sum of the elements of all product classes is the description of the building energy model.

In the second phase, the simulation of the building energy model takes place. The outcome of the second process step are the simulated energetic values based on the chosen renovation options. These values are the input for the third and last phase. Here, the visualization of the energetic values takes place. Within this paper, we want to focus on the process steps one and two. The third phase is not part of the scope. Below, we describe the process steps 1 and 2 in more detail. Figure 2 presents the overall process with the three internal process steps.

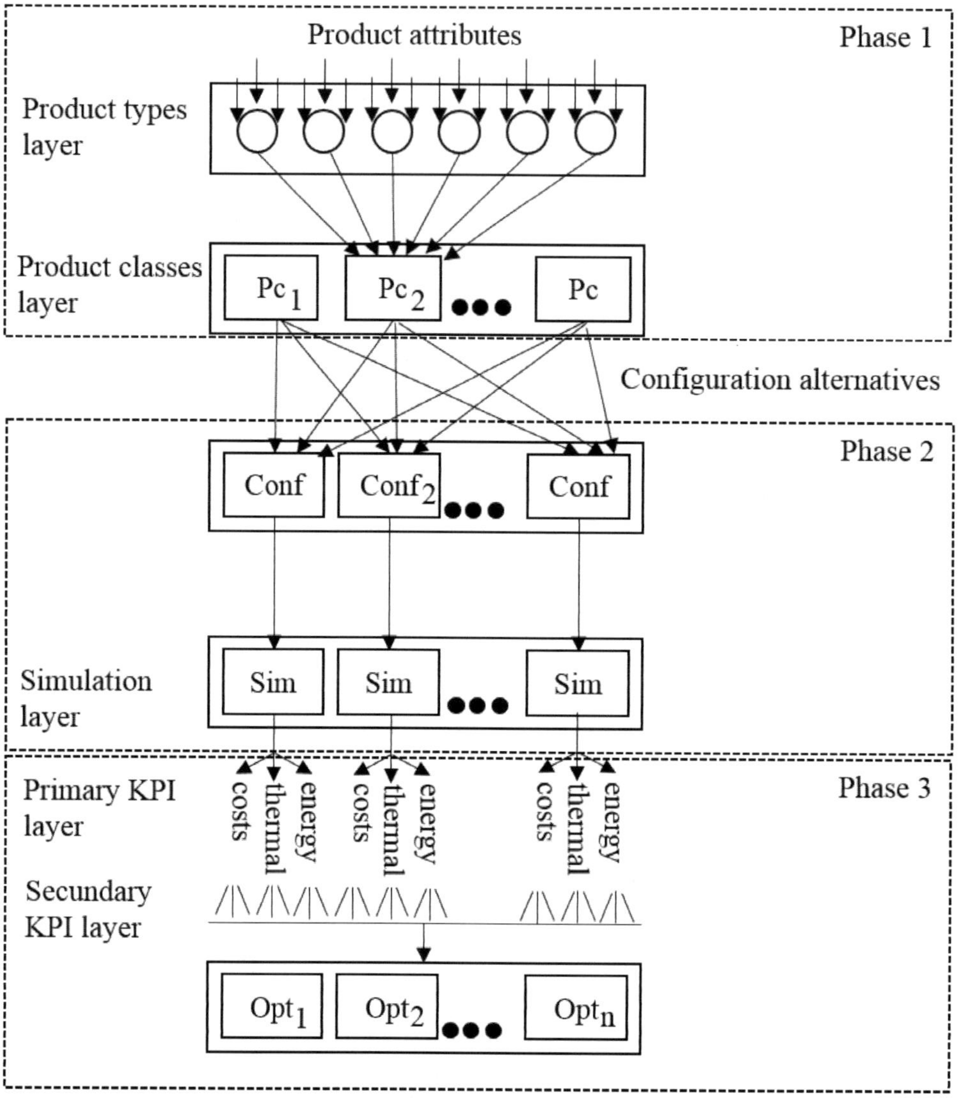

Figure 2: Overall process where we build product classes based on attributes (phase 1), run the simulation based on the chosen renovation option (phase 2) and present the results (phase 3).

As shown in Figure 2, multiple simulations are required to determine the best selection of design options. In the traditional approach, different energy models with integrated renovation elements must be created and then tested through an energy simulation program (e.g. EnergyPlus). Our approach preserves the existing energy model. Only the elements to be renovated are replaced by new components. This replacement does not take place in EnergyPlus. For this we use an algorithm developed by us, which changes the file of the energy model according to the design options. Components that need to be renovated are replaced by the same types.

Process step 1

In the first process step we define the classes of products. Following our case study, we describe the class definition using the example of windows and facades. To define product classes, attributes are required to describe the properties of the class. Here, we adapt the respective class descriptions for building elements of EnergyPlus. Figures 3 illustrate the structure of the product classes façade and window.

```
Material:[
 {
   "Name" :"",
   "Roughness":" ",
   "Thickness":"",
   "Conductivity":"",
   "Density":"",
   "Specific_Heat":"",
   "Thermal_Absorptance":" ",
   "Solar_Absorptance":" ",
   "Visible_Absorptance":" "
 },
]
```

```
[
 {
   "Window":{
   "U-Factor":" ",
   "Solar Heat Gain Coefficient":" ",
   "VisibleTransmittance":" "
 },
 "WindowMaterial:GlazingSystem":{
   "Name":" ",
   "Optical Data Type":" ",
   "Window Glass Spectral Data Set Name": " ",
   "Thickness":" ",
   "VisibleTransmittance (*)":" ",
   "Incidence":" ",
   "Conductivity":" "
  },
 }
]
```


Figure 3: Description of the attributes for the renovation product class Material and Window

According to figure 3, we illustrate the groups of parameters necessary for the creation of the facade and window classes. On the left of figure 3, a façade element is shown. A facade consists of one or more material elements. In figure 3, an example of a facade panel with only one material is shown. Accordingly, a parameter group is sufficient to describe the material of the facade. If the facade consists of several elements, a parameter group is used for each element to describe it. This n-number of the describing parameter groups are combined in the entire façade element class. The Windows class consists of two parameter groups. The first group describes the properties of the window. The second group describes the glazing system.

The parameters shown in Figure 3, are without values. These values will be added according to the properties of the respective facades or windows. The parametric description of the classes completes the first phase of the process. At the same time, the product classes describe also the interface for the second phase of the process.

Process step 2

This second phase of the process is characterized by three internal process steps. In the first process step, the as-is building energy model is analyzed regarding the building elements to be renovated. According to the renovation plan described in chapter 3, all windows are replaced by new double-glazed windows. For the analysis, we developed a context-dependent algorithm to examine the building energy model according to the classes to be replaced.

```
! ===================== GAP - MATERIAL GLASS =====================
WindowMaterial:SimpleGlazingSystem,
 V07_Window_PVC_2350x2250_Win (10mm), ! Name
 1.5,          ! U-Factor
 0.7,          ! Solar Heat Gain Coefficient
 ;             ! Visible Transmittance (*)

! ===================== GAP - MATERIAL FRAME =====================

! ======================= GAP - CONSTRUCION ======================
Construction,
 H06_Window,     ! Name
 V07_Window_PVC_2350x2250_Win (10mm); ! Outside Layer
```

Figure 4: Presentation of the class window within the building energy model. To cut out the old window, construction parameters also needs to be included

Figure 4 shows an excerpt from the energy model. In order to completely remove the old windows, the construction feature must also be removed. Figure 4 shows the properties required to replace the windows. "GAP-MATERIAL-GLASS" describes the properties of the glass used in the existing building. In addition to these parameters, the "GAP-CONSTRUCTION" properties must also be considered and adapted or replaced. The parameters for "GAP-MATERIAL FRAME" are not considered within our model.

After the data has been removed from the model, the second internal process step starts. The instances of the new windows are inserted. At the moment we arrange the new values at the end of the building energy model. The placement of these elements is not decisive for EnergyPlus. After the new elements have been inserted, the third process step, the new simulation of the energy model, can start. The results of this simulation are the input values for the third phase of our proposed process.

4. Results and outlook

Section 5 presents the method behind the product centric exchange of elements in building energy models and describes the process of finding, adding or replacing construction objects in the model. Within this section, we describe the outcome of our product centric approach. Therefore, we compare the energic consumptions of the different renovation options.

Table 4 shows the outcome of the energy simulation based on the performance parameter "Total Site Energy", "End Uses" and "Energy Use Summary". We compare these parameters with four different renovation option. The baseline for further considerations is the building energy model of the demonstration project in Warsaw. The energetic values of the performance parameters describe the situation before any kind renovation activity takes place. Our product centric approach allows use, to add and remove building elements within the as-is building energy model. Within table 4, we present the energetic values of the building energy model with a) additional external facades, b) new window, c) external façade as well as new window. To compare the different design options, we also present the energetic values of the as-is building energy model.

The first renovation option describes the integration of an external façade element. The energetic values are significantly improved by adding the new construction element. For example, the value for Total Energy decreases from 211325.3 to 161776.79. In option b) we replaced the old windows of the building with new ones. The panels from option a) are not integrated. A significant reduction in energy consumption is also noticeable. In option c) we added the external panels as well as the new windows. Compared to the renovation options a), b) and the as-is building energy model, Option c) is the best solution for renovation in terms of energy consumption.

Table 4: Comparison the energetic results bases on different products (renovation options) within the building energy model

Performance parameters		As-is building energy model	a) Model with external facade panels	b) Model with new windows	c) Model with new window and external facade panels
Total Site Energy	Total Energy in [kWh]	211325.30	161776.79	206728.27	151861.20
	Energy Per Total Building Area [kWh/m2]	154,05	91,53	150,70	85,92
	Energy Per Conditioned Building Area [kWh/m2]	166.22	97.05	162.60	91.10
End Uses	District heating [kWh]	179243.29	123207.33	174646.26	113291.74
Energy Use Summary	Total [kWh]	211325.47	161776.92	206728.43	151861.32

Table 5 visualize the energetic outcome of the three renovation options as well as the energy values of the as-is building energy model.

Table 5: Visualisation of the energetic comsumption based on different products within the energy model

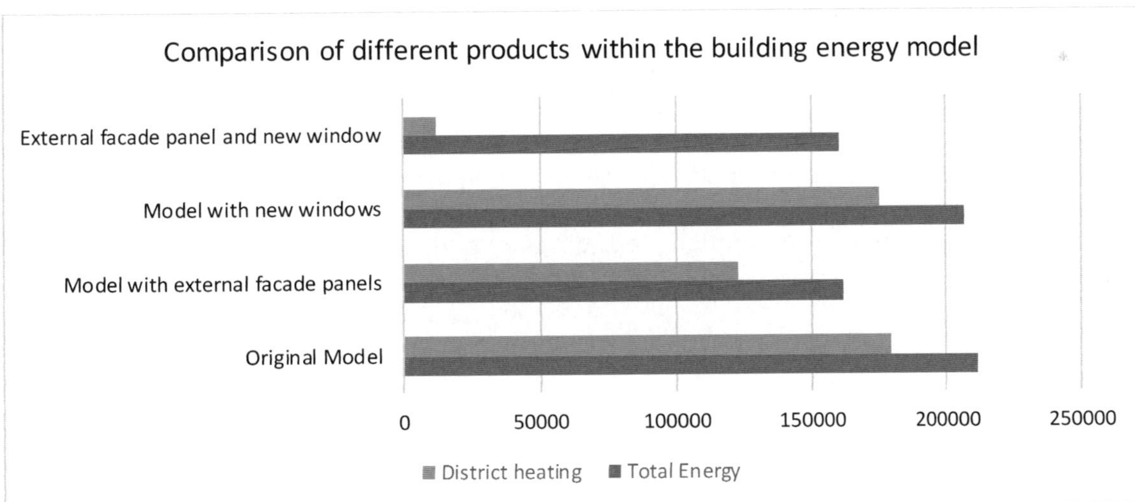

Based on the results, we can demonstrate the benefits of our approach. With the process of our approach, we only change elements of the energy model, not the whole model. Therefore, we enable a fast and comparable way of simulating and displaying energy data. The as-is energy model serves as the baseline for the further simulation of the different renovation options.

Within this paper, only windows and panels are considered as renovation options. Based on Tables 4 and 5, however, we demonstrate the benefits of our approach. The exchange of individual elements of an energy model under the assumption that all other elements of the building energy model, which are not affected by the exchange, remain unconsidered, enables a precise prediction of the energetic results of different renovation options.

Using a short application example, we want to propose a possible outlook of our approach.

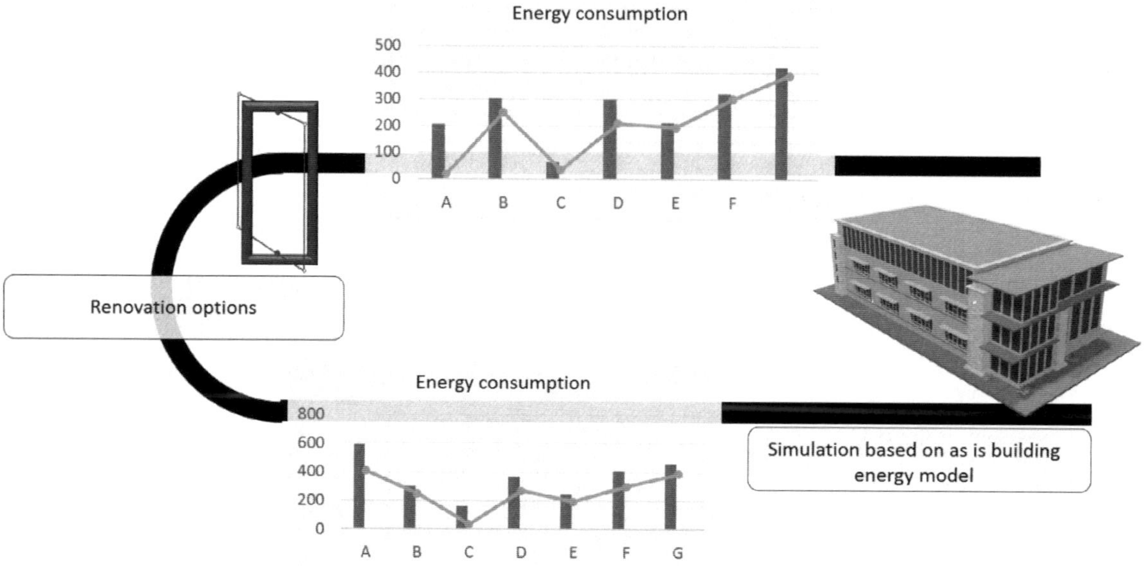

Figure 5: Preparing of energy consumption forecasts based on product centric data exchange within the building energy model

Figure 5 shows a possible operation process. We integrate our product centric data exchange approach into an application, which presents the outcome of the simulation results of the different renovation options. The potential user group can be reached from a homeowner with a single renovation project up to a municipality, who wants to renovate various buildings with nearly same construction features.

Based on the initial values, the software simulates and represents energetic values of the as-is building energy model. The user will get the initial energetic values of the building as the baseline for the further suggestions. As a second process step, building elements according to his renovation project can be add or replaced. Based on the design decision, the energy values are simulated and displayed again. Consider that, our approach can offer an energetic comparison and prediction of energetic values. The forecast of building energy consumptions regarding various renovation options can improve the outcome energy results and reduce unforeseen costs.

5. Conclusion

The paper presents a procedure to close the existing gap in the representation of building energy models in renovation projects. The procedure focuses on a product-centered approach. Renovation products can be exchanged within the existing energy model of the object to be renovated. Thus, various design options can be analyzed without having to create new energy models. Within the work we have demonstrated this approach by replacing window elements and adding new external facades. The intention of this work is to present a variant in order to make the optimal decision between building design and energy target values already during the planning of renovation projects. At the same time, this work would like to support future research efforts with a focus on product-centred assessment. On the other side, this paper wants to motivate for future research in the field of product centered assessment of the energy performance, especially in renovation projects. During the coming months we will continue to expand our process and be able to map more product types, such as HVAC systems, through our product-centered process.

Funding: This research was funded by the European Union's Horizon 2020 research and innovation program grant number 723391.

References

Arayici, Y., Coates, S., Koskela, L. J., Kagioglou, M., Usher, C., & O'Reilly, K. (2011). Technology adoption in the BIM implementation for lean architectural practice. *Automation in Construction*, 189-195.

Bleiberg, T., & Shaviv, E. (2007). Optimization for enhancing collaborative design. *Proceedings: Building Simulation*, 1698-1705.

Borgstein, E., Lamberts, R., & Hensen, J. (2016). Evaluating energy performance in non-domestic buildings: A review. *Energy and Buildings*(128), 734-755.

Echenagucia, T. M., Capozzoli, A., Cascone, Y., & Sassone, M. (2015). The early design stage of a building envelope: Multi-objective search through heating, cooling and lighting energy performance analysis. *Applied Energy*(154), 577–591.

European Commission. (2019, March 04). *Energy Performance of Buildings*. Retrieved from https://ec.europa.eu/energy/en/topics/energy-efficiency/energy-performance-of-buildings

Geyer, P. (2009). Component-oriented decomposition for multidisciplinary design optimization in building design. *Advanced Engineering Informatics, 23*(1), 12-31.

Giannakis, G. I., Lilis, G. N., Kontes, G., & García-Fuentes, M. Á. (2015). A methodology to automatically generate geometry inputs for Energy Performance Simulation from IFC BIM models. *Building Simulation Conference.* Hyderabad, India.

Harvey, D. (2009). Reducing energy use in the buildings sector: measures, costs, and examples. *Energy Efficiency*, 139–163.

Hitchcock, R. J., & Wong, J. (2011). Transforming Ifc Architectural view BIMs for Energy Simulation: 2011. *Proceedings of Building Simulation: 12th Conference of International Building Performance Simulation Association*, (pp. 1089-1095). Sydney.

Karola, A.; Lahtela, H.; Hänninen, R.; Oy, O. G.; Hitchcock, R.; Chen, Q.; Dajka, S.; Hagström, K. (2001). BSPRO COM-SERVER– Interoperability between software tools using industry foundation classes. *Seventh International IBPSA Conference*, (pp. 747-754). Rio de Janeiro, Brazil.

May, G., Barletta, I., Stahl, B., & Taisch, M. (2015, July). Energy management in production: A novel method to develop key performance indicators for improving energy efficiency. *Applied Energy*(149), pp. 46-61.

Nägeli, C., Camarasa, C., Jakob, M., Catenazzi, G., & Ostermeyer, Y. (2018). Synthetic building stocks as a way to assess the energy demand and greenhouse gas emissions of national building stocks. *Energy & Buildings*(173), : 443-460.

National Renewable Energy Laboratory (NREL). (2019, May 30). *EnergyPlus*. Retrieved from https://energyplus.net

P2Endure. (2019, April 03). *P2Endure: Plug-and-Play Product and Process Innovation for Building Deep Renovation*. Retrieved from https://www.P2Endure-project.eu

Vollaro, R. D., Guattari, C., Evangelisti, L., Gori, P., Battista, G., & Carnielo, E. (2014). Building energy performance analysis: A case study. *Energy and Buildings*(87), 87-94.

Wang, J.-J., Jing, Y.-Y., Zhang, C.-F., & Zhao, J.-H. (2009). Review on multi-criteria decision analysis aid in sustainable energy decision-making. *Renewable and Sustainable Energy Review, 13*(9), 2263-2278.

Xiaoshu, L., Tao, L., Charles J., K., & Martti, V. (2015). Modeling and forecasting energy consumption for heterogeneous buildings using a physical–statistical approach. *Applied Energy, 144(C)*, 261-275.

Extended Abstract - Semantic query languages for knowledge-based web services in a construction context

Jeroen Werbrouck[a,b], Madhumitha Senthilvel[a], Jakob Beetz[a], Pierre Bourreau[c], Léon van Berlo[d]

[a] RWTH Aachen University, Germany
[b] Ghent University, Belgium
[c] Institut pour la Transition Energétique Nobatek/Inef4, France
[d] Netherlands Organisation for Applied Scientific Research TNO, the Netherlands

werbrouck@caad.arch.rwth-aachen.de

1. Introduction

Building Information Modelling (BIM) has proven itself an extremely valuable asset for the construction industry, in terms of design, planning, rule checking and collaboration. However, a lot of fragmentation persists; each of the many stakeholders involved in a project has different methods and different software tools that need to exchange information. Conversion to standard exchange formats such as the Industry Foundation Classes (IFC) enables such cross-domain communication only partly.

Over recent years, the use of web technologies in the building industry has been gaining momentum, considered promising mechanisms for reaching a more interoperable BIM practice. Specifically, this relates to (1) cloud-based applications, and (2) Linked Data and Semantic Web technologies. Cloud-based initiatives for streamlining collaboration in building projects have known a long history. Spanning nearly two decades, they go from the (discontinued) frameworks in the early 2000s IMSvr (Hietanen, 2002) and BLIS/SABLE (BLIS-project, 2002; Kiviniemi et al., 2005) to the more recent and popular model server BIMserver (Beetz et al., 2010), and the recently introduced concept of "BIM bots" (van Berlo, n.d.). These projects are all based on collaboration and exchange through IFC. However, IFC only spans certain disciplines and offers limited interoperability with domains that are not covered in the schema. Such interoperability can be provided by adopting Linked Data technologies.

The idea that the application of Linked Data concepts could seriously enhance interoperability and collaboration has been documented multiple times already (Beetz et al., 2005; Pauwels et al., 2017; Pauwels and Terkaj, 2016; Rasmussen et al., 2017), and several research projects are currently working on making Linked Data-based BIM more mature. With the use of the Linked Data standard RDF (Resource Description Framework)[1], it is possible to construct dedicated vocabularies for each related sub-discipline, connected with one another in a neutral format and without information loss. An additional advantage of such Linked Data vocabularies over traditional, monolithic, domain-specific information models such as IFC is their modularity, which increases the flexibility to address domain specific and local challenges.

In order to combine both topics, the threshold for developing Linked Data applications needs to be lowered (Verborgh, 2018). Web applications need to communicate in an efficient way, to enable the interoperability and automation potential given by these technologies. The W3C standard for creating, querying and updating Linked Data databases is SPARQL[2]. SPARQL has proven to be a very powerful querying language, but it is also known to be cumbersome

[1] https://www.w3.org/RDF/, W3C
[2] https://www.w3.org/TR/sparql11-query/, W3C

and a threshold for developers that do not have a lot of experience with Linked Data triples. To overcome these issues, initiatives such as GraphQL-LD (Taelman et al., 2018) and HypergraphQL[3] rely on the API querying language GraphQL[4], but extend it with Linked Data querying functionality, so it is possible to fetch the necessary data from the distributed RDF building model. The advantage of these initiatives is that no real Linked Data knowledge is needed to develop a service that makes nevertheless use of its core principles: GraphQL is flexible and clearly structured, designed to build client applications, their data requirements and interactions; the query response being structured according to the widely used JSON-format.

2. Methodology

In this paper, we investigate the use of existing open-source GraphQL-based solutions for querying the semantic web; HyperGraphQL and GraphQL-LD. Firstly, an overview is given about some past and present frameworks for cloud-based collaboration in construction, based on IFC. Then, recent developments regarding Linked Data for the building industry are outlined, followed by a brief discussion on Semantic Web query languages. A comparison is made between the solutions proposed by HyerGraphQL and GraphQL, according to different criteria, with a focus on schema versus schemaless deployment, the use of intermediary servers, type querying and the need for updating functionality. Whenever deemed relevant, example use cases are implemented for clarification and comparison.

3. Outcomes

This comparison results in a table that compares the discussed GraphQL approaches with one another and with SPARQL. Because different use cases are possible, the application of a query language can differ depending on scenario: communication between web-applications and databases is different from retrieving information from fixed datasets. Because GraphQL-LD uses a serverless and schemaless deployment, it is considered more flexible to implement in web applications. However, for querying specific datasets for specific data patterns, HyperGraphQL offers a good way of exposing certain data and hide other. The outcomes of this comparison will serve as an input for further development of Linked Data based solutions for collaboration in building projects, to come a step closer to the use of interoperable web-tools in practice.

4. Acknowledgements

The authors would like to acknowledge the support by both the BIM4REN project, which has received funding from the European Union's Horizon 2020 Research and Innovation Program under grant agreement No 820773 and the UGent Special Research Fund (BOF).

References

Beetz, J., van Berlo, L., de Laat, R., van den Helm, P., 2010. BIMserver. org–An open source IFC model server, in: Proceedings of the CIP W78 Conference. p. 8.

[3] https://www.hypergraphql.org/, Semantic Integration Ltd.
[4] https://facebook.github.io/graphql, Facebook Inc.

Beetz, J., Van Leeuwen, J.P., De Vries, B., 2005. An ontology web language notation of the industry foundation classes, in: Proceedings of the 22nd CIB W78 Conference on Information Technology in Construction. Technical University of Dresden, p. 670.

BLIS-project, 2002. BLIS Building Lifecycle Interoperable Software. URL http://www.blis-project.org/index2.html.

Hietanen, J., 2002. BLIS review: IMSvr. BLIS.

Kiviniemi, A., Fischer, M., Bazjanac, V., 2005. Integration of multiple product models: Ifc model servers as a potential solution, in: Proc. of the 22nd CIB-W78 Conference on Information Technology in Construction.

Pauwels, P., Terkaj, W., 2016. EXPRESS to OWL for construction industry: Towards a recommendable and usable ifcOWL ontology. Automation in Construction 63, 100–133.

Pauwels, P., Zhang, S., Lee, Y.-C., 2017. Semantic Web Technologies in AEC Industry: A Literature Overview. Automation in Construction 73, 145–165.

Rasmussen, M., Pauwels, P., Lefrançois, M., Schneider, G.F., Hviid, C., Karlshøj, J., 2017. Recent Changes in the Building Topology Ontology, in: LDAC2017-5th Linked Data in Architecture and Construction Workshop.

Taelman, R., Vander Sande, M., Verborgh, R., 2018. GraphQL-LD: Linked Data Querying with GraphQL, in: ISWC2018, the 17th International Semantic Web Conference.

van Berlo, L., n.d. bimbots.org - Automate your work with BIM Bots. URL http://bimbots.org.

Verborgh, R., 2018. Designing a Linked Data Developer Experience. URL https://ruben.verborgh.org/blog/2018/12/28/designing-a-linked-data-developer-experience/.

Semantic query languages for knowledge-based web services in a construction context

Jeroen Werbrouck[a,b], Madhumitha Senthilvel[a], Jakob Beetz[a], Pierre Bourreau[c], Léon van Berlo[d]

[a] RWTH Aachen University, Germany
[b] Ghent University, Belgium
[c] Institut pour la Transition Energétique Nobatek/Inef4, France
[d] Netherlands Organisation for Applied Scientific Research TNO, the Netherlands

werbrouck@caad.arch.rwth-aachen.de

Abstract. Since the early 2000s, different frameworks were set up to enable web-based collaboration in building projects. Unfortunately, none of these initiatives was granted a long life. Recently, however, the use of web technologies in the building industry has been gaining momentum again, considered some promising technologies for reaching a more interoperable BIM practice. Specifically, this relates to (1) Linked Data and Semantic Web technologies, and (2) cloud-based applications. In order to combine these into a network of interlinked applications and datastores, an agreed-upon mechanism for automatic communication and data retrieval needs to be used. Apart from the W3C standard SPARQL, often considered too high a threshold for developers to implement, there are some recent GraphQL-based solutions that simplify the querying process and its implementation into web services. In this paper, we review two recent open source technologies based on GraphQL, that enable to query Linked Data on the web: GraphQL-LD and HyperGraphQL.

1. Introduction

Building Information Modelling (BIM) has proven itself an extremely valuable asset for the construction industry. However, a lot of fragmentation persists, due to the large number of stakeholders in a typical construction project, each one relying on specialized software packages that often use proprietary formats. This fragmentation makes it difficult to exploit the full potential of digitisation in the building industry. To improve interoperability, the Industry Foundation Classes (IFC)[1] are the international standard for exchange of construction-related data. However, because the IFC schema includes an enormous amount of classes and properties, software vendors almost never implement it completely; obviously, in most cases only the subsets that are relevant to the tool's purpose are considered. Additionally, the conversion process from native formats to IFC files is seldom watertight, making the ideal scenario of lossless information flow very difficult, if not impossible to achieve (Kiviniemi et al., 2005; Shafiq et al., 2018). Interoperability and interdisciplinarity become even more complicated when dealing with disciplines that are not taken into account in the IFC schema. These are mainly areas that relate to parts of the Building Life Cycle (BLC) that are not directly involved with construction itself, e.g. heritage conservation, Facility Management and implementation of GIS data (Geographic Information Systems).

To tackle at least some of these challenges, there have been a number of initiatives to make the construction industry more web-based, using web technologies for improved collaboration and interdisciplinary crossovers. Specifically, this relates to (1) the use of cloud-based, interconnected services (Afsari et al., 2016; Beetz et al., 2010b; Kiviniemi et al., 2005) and (2)

[1] http://www.buildingsmart-tech.org/specifications/ifc-overview

the use of Semantic Web technologies based on the Resource Description Framework (RDF)[2] (Beetz et al., 2005; Pauwels et al., 2017). Instead of 'monolithic' software suites that claim to encompass the entire BLC, cloud-based, service-oriented BIM applications dedicated to a single purpose are considered much more agile, since their modularity allows easy extension and custom chaining of tools. Recently, this service-oriented concept was re-introduced as 'BIM bots' (van Berlo, n.d.). As demonstrated by the recent Solid (Social Linked Data) framework (Mansour et al., 2016), these topics are tightly connected and do not only apply to the building industry, but to virtually all disciplines that are concerned with data exchange.

The combination of improvements in web infrastructure with current web technologies and their implementations for the building industry might provide the right receipt for the setup of a Linked Data-based descendant of the earlier frameworks such as IMSvr (Hietanen, 2002) BLIS/SABLE (BLIS-project, 2002; Kiviniemi et al., 2005) or the BIMserver (Beetz et al., 2010b). As in these frameworks, the most appropriate service for a specific task could be chosen out of a network of interconnected online tools. The main difference would be, however, that in this context the service fetches the data by requesting it from the distributed RDF building model rather than from an IFC file on a central server. Such approach is being actively pushed in the web community by initiatives such as Solid (Mansour et al., 2016) and OSLC (OASIS Open Project, n.d.). This way, not only BIM data from within the framework's software pool can be integrated, but also the immense stack of open data on the web, including non-BIM related information about geology, weather data, historic data etc.

For such a network of connected web services and data pods to exchange information efficiently and unambiguously, they need to make use of international standards. Therefore, an essential part for a successful set up of a Linked Data-based network of BLC-oriented services is to identify possible solutions for data exchange. A starting point is the W3C standard for querying Linked Data, SPARQL (SPARQL Protocol and RDF Query Language)[3]. However, SPARQL is often considered too high a threshold for software developers (Taelman et al., 2018b; Verborgh, 2018). Recently, a number of initiatives were launched for making Linked Data querying more accessible, by extending the GraphQL query language (Facebook Inc., 2016) to encompass Linked Data as well (Taelman et al., 2019): proprietary solutions such as Stardog and TopBraid, and open source technologies such as HyperGraphQL (Semantic Integration Ltd., n.d.) and GraphQL-LD (Taelman et al., 2018b). In this paper, we discuss the main differences between HyperGraphQL and GraphQL-LD, as these are open source solutions.

In the following sections, we first review existing concepts for cloud-based collaboration in construction projects, based on IFC (Section 2.1). This is followed by a brief introduction to Linked Data (Section 2.2), after which some characteristics of semantic web query languages are discussed (Section 2.3). Finally, they are compared according to multiple criteria, illustrated by some exemplary queries on a Linked Building Project (Section 3).

2. Related Work

2.1 IFC Model Servers

In the past, numerous methods have been explored for facilitating a collaborative platform for working with shared IFC models. File-based exchange between stakeholders gave rise to

[2] https://www.w3.org/RDF/, W3C, accessed 25/03/2019
[3] https://www.w3.org/TR/sparql11-query/, W3C, visited 15/12/2018

numerous problems including failure to handle IFC complexity and facilitate flexible data access. To combat these challenges, one of the potential solutions suggested was the use of Model Servers. Model Servers act as a database with a set of server applications that provide multi-user database management and also allow the use of IFC as the underlying database structure. A Model Server environment offers considerable advantages over file-based exchanges. For example, they provide flexibility for a multi-disciplinary management, scalability for larger projects, and more (Jørgensen et al., 2008).

Some notable initiatives in Model Server development are the BLIS/SABLE project, IMSvr, BIMServer, and BIMSie. SABLE aimed at increasing the interoperability application through semantic model sharing using SOAP. (BLIS-project, 2002). Its outputs were distinct domain specific APIs which handle the information exchange required by client applications for the respective domains. These relate to the BLIS views (Kiviniemi et al., 2005). On the other hand, in the IMSvr project, a combination of relational databases based on the IFC EXPRESS schema and a XML SOAP API was developed to expose server functionality. These initiatives were aimed at the entire organisation of BIM workflows through web technologies. However, real-world datasets proved much too complex and large for the web-technologies that were used back in the days; these were not able to extract and process multiple partial models for different construction-related tasks, with high computational demands, and requiring quick access to different data sources that contain disparate data. While these initiatives are now discontinued, the experiences gained in the projects and the results were constructive in developing future practices such as MVDs and IDM, which now form some of the basic concepts of IFC.

Two more recent Model Server developments, BIMServer and BIMSie, are currently being adopted by a wider community. BIMServer is based on a flexible model based layers including the model schema defined in ISO 10303 EXPRESS which in turn is used to generate a Meta Object Facility (MOF) described as an XML Metadata Interchange (XMI) model. Beyond these layers, BIMServer also facilitates user operations for management of data. Querying and filtering of data, user management and access rights are some of the possible operations in the current implementation (Beetz et al., 2010a). The BIMSie project furthered the BIMServer project through standardisation of a web services API for online BIM services. Such API standardisation enables machine-to-machine exchange of BIM data and stimulates innovation towards broader implementation of BIM bots. BIMSie is as protocol independent as possible and supports JSON and SOAP (van Berlo, 2013).

With the years, distributed, service-oriented architectures became more mature, allowing to establish chains of processes that connect different services over the globe. These chains of connected tools rely on advances in network technologies, which allow data exchange to take place at an unseen rate. At the same time, more and more sectors are adopting semantic web technologies (Berners-Lee et al., 2001), which allow to link individual statements (data at the smallest possible scale) with one another over the web. This happens in a way that this data can be uniquely identified all over the world, by both humans and digital actors, based on RDF.

2.2 Linked Data and the Building Industry

In the Linked Data technology stack, information is represented through the use of so-called triples, which resemble basic sentences with a subject, a verb (predicate) and an object. Each of these tree is denoted with a Uniform Resource Identifier (URI), which gives it a unique and universal context within the world wide web. This way, a data item can be referred to even if it is not stored on the same server, and can in turn refer to other data somewhere on the web, thus actively contributing to a global graph of Linked Data. Furthermore, domain models can be developed with rules and taxonomies for certain disciplines. When distributed data makes use of such domain models ('ontologies' or 'vocabularies'), the 'semantic' in Semantic Web starts to make sense.

The idea that the application of Linked Data concepts could seriously enhance interoperability and collaboration in the AECO Industry (Architecture, Engineering, Construction, Operation) has been documented multiple times by now (Beetz et al., 2005; Pauwels et al., 2017; Pauwels and Terkaj, 2016; Rasmussen et al., 2017). With the use of Linked Data, it is possible to construct vocabularies for each related sub-discipline, connected with one another in a neutral format. This allows applications that are concerned with different aspects of the built environment to connect and exchange information without information loss. Furthermore, since vocabularies contain the information to interpret the data in a semantic way, automatic reasoning and rule checking comes within reach (Pauwels et al., 2017). With this in mind, several research projects are currently working on making Linked Data-based BIM more mature. The setup of a Linked Data-based version of IFC was first proposed in (Beetz et al., 2005) and has resulted in a buildingSMART-approved version ifcOWL (Pauwels and Terkaj, 2016). However, as ifcOWL covers the entire EXPRESS schema, it is a very large schema and therefore not flexible to deal with topics that are not covered in the IFC standard. The W3C Linked Building Data Working Group therefore targets the development of more modular vocabularies that each address a specific building-related topic (Rasmussen et al., 2017). The main advantage of such modular Linked Data vocabularies over traditional, monolithic, domain-specific information models such as the IFCs is their modularity, which increases the flexibility to address domain specific and local challenges.

2.3 Semantic Web Query Languages

As mentioned in Section 1, the W3C standard for creating, querying and updating Linked Data databases is SPARQL. SPARQL has proven to be a very powerful querying language, but it is also known to be cumbersome and a threshold for developers that have limited experience with Linked Data. To overcome these issues, initiatives such as GraphQL-LD and HypergraphQL rely on the API querying language GraphQL, but extend it with Linked Data querying functionality, making it possible to fetch the necessary data from the distributed RDF datasets by formulating simple GraphQL queries. The advantage of these initiatives is that no real Linked Data knowledge is needed to develop a service that makes nevertheless use of its core principles: GraphQL is flexible and clearly structured, designed to build client applications, data requirements and interactions.

'Plain' GraphQL is both a query language and a specification. It focuses on minimising and optimising data loads over the web, by connecting to a GraphQL API. Essential within GraphQL is a *schema* that describes *types*, their attributes (*fields*) and the relationships of those fields to other types or datatypes. In this perspective, the reference to graphs becomes obvious: there are nodes (the types) and edges (the fields) that point to other nodes. Note that the data structuring only happens in the schema, and therefore lacks the uniqueness of data and relationships in Linked Data graphs. Nevertheless, this structure allows to describe data in a linked and coherent way, and to query, update (*mutate*) and delete information.

As for developers, GraphQL as a query language is much more widely adopted than SPARQL. This is explained by the fact that the semantic web service stack is still quite small compared to services that use non-RDF databases, and that the learning curve for semantic web technologies such as SPARQL is still quite steep (Verborgh, 2018). In GraphQL, querying happens in a more straightforward and 'cleaner' way: essentially, both GraphQL queries and their results are 'tree-like' queries, which make them easier to understand compared to SPARQL, which aims to query full graphs with a universal context. A comparison between a GraphQL query and a similar SPARQL query (with context) is given in table 1.

Table 1: GraphQL and SPARQL query

{
architect {
name
friends {
name
}
}
}
	PREFIX ex: <www.example.com/buildingteam#>
	PREFIX foaf: <http://xmlns.com/foaf/0.1/>
	
	SELECT ?name ?friendname
	WHERE {?person a ex:architect .
	?person foaf:name ?name .
	?person foaf:knows ?friend .
	?friend. foaf:name ?friendname .}

While there is essentially no relationship between GraphQL and SPARQL, a GraphQL query might be extended by some dictionary that relates the used concepts to a universal identification. This is exactly what happens in the semantic web extensions to GraphQL that will be discussed and compared in the next section: GraphQL-LD and HyperGraphQL.

3. Comparison

In this section, GraphQL-LD and HyperGraphQL are compared according to multiple criteria:

- Schema use
- Updating functionality
- Intermediary servers
- Federated querying
- Type querying
- Reverse querying

Whenever relevant, construction-related queries are used as illustrations. The sample dataset is a Linked Building Data (LBD) model of the CAAD chair at RWTH Aachen. This dataset was previously prepared for Linked Data queries by converting the original IFC file to its LBD equivalent, using the main LBD vocabularies BOT (Rasmussen et al., 2017), BuildingElement and PROPS. This conversion was done using the IFCtoLBD[4] converter (Bonduel et al., 2018).

3.1 GraphQL Schema

Semantic meaning in GraphQL is limited to the schema that is used. However, when extended with a mapping that relates the necessary definitions to a universal context, it can be used to also query RDF graphs. HyperGraphQL and GraphQL-LD implement this context differently.

The HyperGraphQL approach is closely related to the original GraphQL specifications. As with GraphQL, HyperGraphQL uses a schema that determines which data can be queried and which cannot. Each type and relationship in the schema is mapped to a URI that extends it to a universal context. Further on, both the type itself and its fields need to point to a specific service that needs to be queried.

[4] https://github.com/jyrkioraskari/IFCtoLBD, accessed 30/03/19

In contrast with HyperGraphQL, GraphQL-LD does not require a schema to be defined. In fact, it uses only the syntax of GraphQL to provide a streamlined querying experience, but 'under the hood', this query is translated to a SPARQL query, making use of a JSON context that maps the GraphQL definitions to URIs. The outcome of this GraphQL-to-SPARQL translation[5] is then used to perform a 'classic' SPARQL query. Results are presented in a tree-like structure[6], similar to a GraphQL response.

Both approaches have their benefits and disadvantages. Using a schema, HyperGraphQL provides a formal mechanism of projecting RDF data via a 'GraphQL lens', thereby affecting how clients can access certain data. On the one hand, this allows for fine-grained mapping of definitions to the services that are queried. On the other hand, this introduces some rigidness in the schema definition, as at the moment a class can only be mapped to one service[7]. The decision to only use a JSON-LD context and no schema enables a more flexible approach and allows to query the endpoint as a SPARQL query would, without restrictions on which data can be queried and which cannot. This means it also does not support (nor does it need) GraphQL schema introspection, which allows to see what kind of queries are supported: as all exposed data can be queried with GraphQL-LD, such introspection feature is superfluous.

3.2 Updating

Updating databases with GraphQL happens with so-called mutations. These allow to create, update and delete data. Similarly, SPARQL defines INSERT and DELETE; combining the two can be regarded as updating. This being said, at the moment of writing, neither GraphQL-LD nor HyperGraphQL supports mutations. When imagining a network of connected, interacting tools and online datastores owned by different stakeholders, updating is an essential prerequisite for enabling automatic communication. For now, regarding updating graph data on the web, developers are limited to either SPARQL queries or software libraries that hide SPARQL's complexity, offering simple functionality to manipulate data (e.g. rdflib, rdflib.js, LDflex).

3.3 Intermediaries

As mentioned in Section 3.1, the setup of HyperGraphQL requires the setup of an intermediary server, combining the provided schema and the Linked Data services defined in the configuration file to expose a GraphQL endpoint. The parameters for this intermediary service are given by a configuration file that points to the schema, the server port to use and the information required to identify the right services (graphs). Consequentially, when one needs to change the services to be queried, a new configuration file should be made, the schema types should be changed to point towards the new service, and one should run a new server.

GraphQL-LD, in contrast with the above approach, works serverless; as it is part of the Comunica framework (Taelman et al., 2018a), it can be embedded right into the application code or executed independently via the command line. This is quite an advantage in terms of ease-of-use for developers, and offers more flexibility for querying multiple services.

3.4 Data Federation

Both approaches allow to query multiple services. The main difference is that in HyperGraphQL, these services need to be defined in a configuration file before setting up the

---

[5] https://github.com/rubensworks/graphql-to-sparql.js, accessed 28/03/19

[6] https://github.com/rubensworks/sparqljson-to-tree.js, accessed 28/03/19

[7] https://www.hypergraphql.org/documentation/, accessed 30/03/19

intermediary server, while GraphQL-LD adds them dynamically before it carries out the query. Due to this implementation in Comunica, GraphQL-LD also allows to query graph data on the web that is not exposed through a SPARQL endpoint, such as regular Turtle graphs that are stored as documents. On the other hand, HyperGraphQL provides the functionality to query other, remote HyperGraphQL services on the web.

3.5 Querying by Type

An advantage of HyperGraphQL's usage of a schema, is that it automatically detects what can be queried as a type, and what is a property. This is then used by the intermediary server to automatically append to each type a 'GET' and a 'GET_BY_ID' extension, allowing to query items respectively by type (Fig. 1) or by URI (Fig. 2). A disadvantage is that a type should be stated explicitly in the graph, which is not always the case. For example, it cannot derive the results for *INST:Storey1 bot:hasSpace INST:Space1*, when in the graph it is not explicitly stated that *INST:Space1 a bot:Space.*

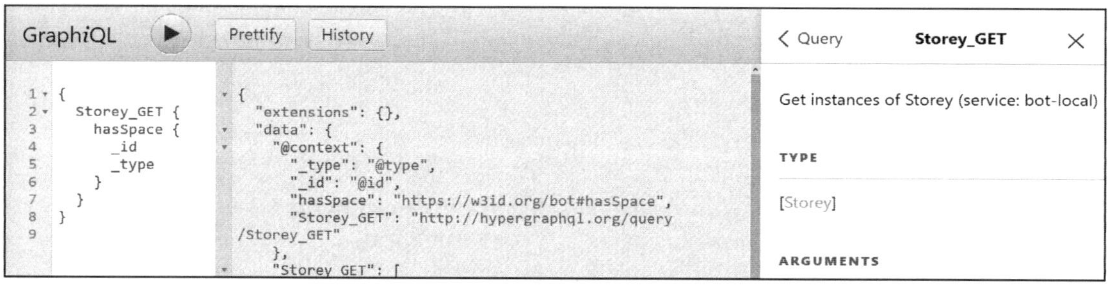

Figure 1: HyperGraphQL query to retrieve all instances of bot:Storey, by using Storey_GET. The introspection schema can be expanded in the GraphiQL interface.

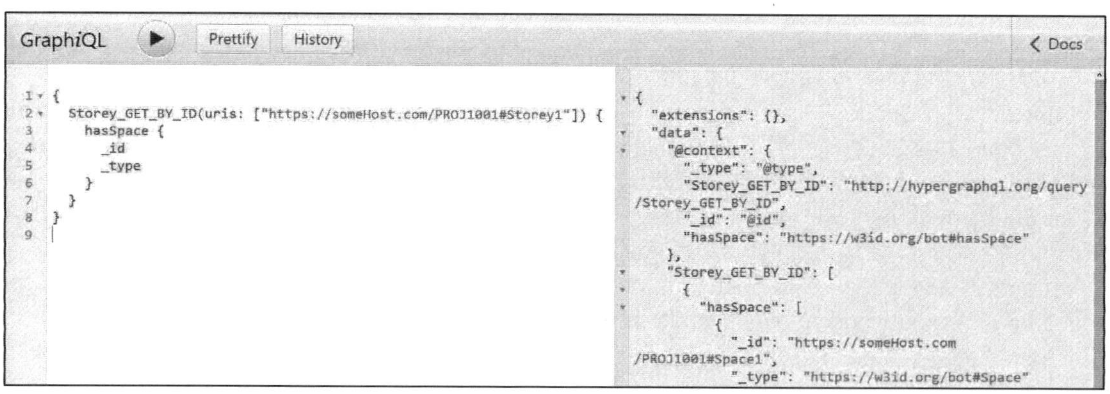

Figure 2: HyperGraphQL query to retrieve the instances of bot:Space of one specific instance of bot:Storey, by using Storey_GET_BY_ID.

Another point is that, as far as we know, it is currently not possible to map relationships to more than one schema type: for example, if the field 'hasSpace' is mapped to the type Space, we cannot make it apply to something which is an instance of type Kitchen, although this might be a subtype of Space. During the setup of our HyperGraphQL schema, any attempts to construct a GraphQL UNION type to solve this, failed. In RDF, on the contrary, a resource can be an instance of bot:Space and dogont:Kitchen at the same time. Since GraphQL-LD is in fact a translation of a GraphQL query to SPARQL, such multiple type assignments are no real issue.

GraphQL-LD is mainly focused on predicates, i.e. on querying by the relationships between nodes. Therefore, when querying for specific classes, a workaround is needed. The user should then include a '_' argument in the query and define 'a' in the context, referring to 'rdf:type'. The corresponding query is then *a(_:Storey)*. As an illustration, in Table 2, we define a more complex query for GraphQL-LD, that searches for the first 10 furniture elements of simple type "Stuhl (2): Stuhl (CIP-Pool)", and the bot:Space where this chair is located. The query contains limitation, type querying and value querying. Some tricks are necessary to get the URI of the furniture as well, since the translation from GraphQL-LD to SPARQL only takes the fields without curly braces as SPARQL variables. This results in a somewhat cumbersome 'double' query for 'containsElement'. This query has no equivalent in HyperGraphQL, since a 'reverse' context is used for backwards querying.

Table 2: Full GraphQL-LD query example

Context	{ "Element": "https://w3id.org/bot#Element", "Furniture": "https://w3id.org/product/Furnishing#Furniture", "containsElement": "https://w3id.org/bot#containsElement", "containedInZone": {"@reverse": "https://w3id.org/bot#containsElement"}, "simpleType": "https://w3id.org/props#type_simple", "a": "http://www.w3.org/1999/02/22-rdf-syntax-ns#type", "simpleName": "https://w3id.org/props#nom_simple" }
Query	{ containsElement containsElement (first:10) { a(_:Furniture) simpleType(_:"Stuhl (2): Stuhl (CIP-Pool)") containedInZone{ simpleName } }}

SPARQL translation (prefixed)	SELECT ?containsElement ?containsElement_containedInZone_simpleName
	WHERE { ?b1 bot:containsElement ?containsElement.
	{SELECT * WHERE {
	?b1 bot:containsElement ?containsElement.
	?containsElement a furn:Furniture;
	props:type_simple "Stuhl (2): Stuhl (CIP-Pool)".
	?containsElement_containedInZone bot:containsElement ?containsElement;
	props:nom_simple ?containsElement_containedInZone_simpleName.
	} LIMIT 10 }
	}

Results	[0:{"containsElement":[{"value":"https://www.hackathon.org/caadchair#furniture_bb4d-87cf-d8a0"} {"containedInZone":[{"simpleName":[{"value":"Hiwis"}]}]}]} 1:{"containsElement":[{"value":"https://www.hackathon.org/caadchair#furniture_f879-4af7-88b5"} {"containedInZone":[{"simpleName":[{"value":"CIP-Pool"}]}]}]} 2:{...}]

The queries in Fig. 1, 2 and Table 2 also show that both approaches allow to define arguments in a query. While in HyperGraphQL, this might be used to specify the subject of the query itself (by the GET_BY_ID extension), GraphQL-LD is currently limited to relationships with objects.

3.6 Other

GraphQL-LD supports the use of an '@reverse' keyword in the JSON context (see Table 2). Practically, this means it allows to query both relationships 'hasSpace' and 'spaceOf. This functionality enables 'backwards querying', although the results will still be shown as a tree.

Note that this does not mean any reasoning is used to determine an 'InverseOf' relationship; this is supposed to be handled at the side of the SPARQL endpoint.

Similarities between both approaches are, amongs others, the functionality to specify limit and offset arguments, to set variables, to include aliases and set (inline) fragments.

3.7 Summary

In the above section, some large and small differences between two GraphQL-based approaches for querying linked data on the web were laid out. Table 3 shows the differences and similarities according to various parameters. SPARQL is also added to the comparison as a reference.

Table 3: Comparing different approaches for querying Linked Data on the Web

	GraphQL-LD	**HyperGraphQL**	**SPARQL**
Updating graphs	No	No	Yes
Schema and Introspection	No	Yes (+ introspection)	No
Intermediary server	No	Yes	No
Federated service querying	Yes	Yes	Yes
Reverse querying (O-P-S)	Yes	No	Yes

Both approaches have their application domain: using HyperGraphQL, querying fixed datasets (e.g. DBpedia.org or local multi-models) becomes more user friendly and uniform with a subset predefined set of types and fields. Therefore, we consider it mainly suitable for the setup of fixed endpoints to retrieve data from large, open databases.

On the other hand, GraphQL-LD seems to be more flexible regarding switching between endpoints, because of its serverless end schemaless deployment. If the goal is to simplify the development of Linked Data-based applications, the implementation of GraphQL-LD certainly takes less time and is more straightforward.

Because both initiatives have started rather recently, we hope the developers continue to work on their refinement, possibly implementing the option for applications to change the distributed datasets they communicate with, using a simple 'mutation'.

4. Conclusion

In this paper, an overview was given to some past and current frameworks for cloud-based collaboration in the AECO industry. Considering the upcoming of Linked Data and advancement in network technologies, the basic concepts of these early projects could be re-implemented in a Semantic Web based framework. Different solutions for communication between the services in such a framework and the distributed data these services use, were presented and compared. In context of a Linked Data based ecosystem, and in terms of a straightforward implementation, GraphQL-LD seems the most flexible choice.

Determining how tools within a framework can communicate is the first step in the development of a testing environment that consists of multiple modular services. The next steps will be the categorisation of such tools, by configuring a Linked Data 'use case ontology', that allows to express multiple steps within a certain use case, and link at the same time the exchange requirements and data validation shapes (e.g. using mvdXML or SHACL) to the different modules. With this in mind, we hope to come one step closer to a web-based, interdisciplinary and interoperable building industry.

5. Acknowledgements

The authors would like to acknowledge the support by both the BIM4REN project, which has received funding from the European Union's Horizon 2020 Research and Innovation Program under grant agreement No 820773 and the UGent Special Research Fund (BOF).

6. References

Afsari, K., Eastman, C.M., Shelden, D.R., 2016. Cloud-based BIM data transmission: current status and challenges, in: ISARC. Proceedings of the International Symposium on Automation and Robotics in Construction. Vilnius Gediminas Technical University, Department of Construction Economics, p. 1.

Beetz, J., de Laat, R., van Berlo, L., Helm, P. van den, 2010a. Towards an Open Building Information Model Server, in: Proc. of the 10th International Conference on Design & Decision Support Systems in Architecture and Urban Planning.

Beetz, J., van Berlo, L., de Laat, R., van den Helm, P., 2010b. BIMserver. org–An open source IFC model server, in: Proc. of the CIP W78 Conference.

Beetz, J., Van Leeuwen, J.P., De Vries, B., 2005. An ontology web language notation of the industry foundation classes, in: Proceedings of the 22nd CIB W78 Conference. Technical University of Dresden, p. 670.

Berners-Lee, T., Hendler, J., Lassila, O., 2001. The semantic web. Sci. Am. 284, 34–43.

BLIS-project, 2002. BLIS Building Lifecycle Interoperable Software. http://www.blis-project.org/index2.html.

Bonduel, M., Oraskari, J., Pauwels, P., Vergauwen, M., Klein, R., 2018. The IFC to Linked Building Data Converter-Current Status, in: 6th Linked Data in Architecture and Construction Workshop. pp. 34–43.

Facebook Inc., 2016. GraphQL. Working Draft. https://graphql.github.io/graphql-spec/draft/

Hietanen, J., 2002. BLIS Review: IMSvr. BLIS. http://www.blis-project.org/

Jørgensen, K.A., Skauge, J., Christiansson, P., Svidt, K., Sørensen, K.B., Mitchell, J., 2008. Use of IFC Model Servers Modelling. Aalborg University.

Kiviniemi, A., Fischer, M., Bazjanac, V., 2005. Integration of multiple product models: IFC model servers as a potential solution, in: Proc. of the 22nd CIB-W78 Conference on Information Technology in Construction.

Mansour, E., Sambra, A.V., Hawke, S., Zereba, M., Capadisli, S., Ghanem, A., Aboulnaga, A., Berners-Lee, T., 2016. A Demonstration of the Solid Platform for Social Web Applications, in: Proc. of the 25th International Conference Companion on World Wide Web. International World Wide Web Conferences Steering Committee, pp. 223–226.

OASIS Open Project, n.d. OSLC - Open Services for Lifecycle Collaboration. URL https://open-services.net/

Pauwels, P., Terkaj, W., 2016. EXPRESS to OWL for construction industry: Towards a recommendable and usable ifcOWL ontology. Autom. Constr. 63, 100–133.

Pauwels, P., Zhang, S., Lee, Y.-C., 2017. Semantic web technologies in AEC industry: A literature overview. Autom. Constr. 73, 145–165.

Rasmussen, M., Pauwels, P., Lefrançois, M., Schneider, G.F., Hviid, C., Karlshøj, J., 2017. Recent changes in the Building Topology Ontology, in: LDAC2017-5th Linked Data in Architecture and Construction Workshop.

Semantic Integration Ltd., n.d. HyperGraphQL. https://www.hypergraphql.org/

Shafiq, M.T., Matthews, J., Lockley, S., Love, P.E., 2018. Model server enabled management of collaborative changes in building information models. Front. Eng. Manag. 5, 298–306.

Taelman, R., Van Herwegen, J., Vander Sande, M., Verborgh, R., 2018a. Comunica: a modular SPARQL query engine for the web, in: International Semantic Web Conference. Springer, pp. 239–255.

Taelman, R., Vander Sande, M., Verborgh, R., 2019. Bridges between GraphQL and RDF.

Taelman, R., Vander Sande, M., Verborgh, R., 2018b. GraphQL-LD: Linked Data Querying with GraphQL, in: ISWC2018, the 17th International Semantic Web Conference.

van Berlo, L., 2013. BIM Service interface exchange (BIMSie). https://www.nibs.org/page/bsa_bimsie

van Berlo, L., n.d. bimbots.org - Automate your work with BIM Bots. http://bimbots.org.

Verborgh, R., 2018. Designing a Linked Data Developer Experience.
https://ruben.verborgh.org/blog/2018/12/28/designing-a-linked-data-developer-experience/

A Quantitative Comparison of Adaptive Reuse Strategies of Residential Towers in Northern Climates

Sheida Shahi, Carl T. Haas, Philip Beesley
University of Waterloo, Canada
sshahi@uwaterloo.ca

Abstract. Tall concrete structures with cantilevered balconies have prevailed as the main type of multi-family housing construction in Canada since the 1950s. Within aging residential structures, balcony degradation is a prominent contributor to overall performance. This includes high levels of structural failures, low energy performance, and inefficient use. Some common strategies for improvements to balconies in residential towers include structural reconstruction, thermal insulation, enclosure of balconies, and reconstruction of guards. While these strategies can greatly improve existing conditions of residential towers, there is opportunity for anticipating the future needs of dense urban environments through adaptive reuse of residential balconies. This project analyses balcony adaptive reuse strategies focusing on structural and environmental refurbishment as well as spatial conversion in terms of various performance metrics. The goals of this project are to investigate methods for analysing existing buildings for their potential adaptive reuse at the scale of the balcony and optimize decision making through developing an index for adaptability.

1. Introduction

Concrete cantilevered balconies in Canada first emerged during the economic and population boom of the mid 20th-century. This boom gave rise to a large number of high-rise housing neighbourhoods across the country, with significant concentrations in Southern Ontario. From the 1950's, the balcony became a common feature of the residential tower in the City of Toronto. The next wave of concrete multi-family construction followed in the form of high-rise condominium ownership in the 1970's and lasted for 10 years (Rosen, Walks, 2015). From the 1960's to the late 1970's, there was an increase in the popularity in the use of balconies in residential buildings. The use of balconies was minimized in the 1980's and 1990's with most towers being built in this era having 0% to 20% of their facades covered with balconies. The balcony proliferation patterns of the 1970's, with high numbers of towers possessing 40% to 100% of balcony coverage and minimal buildings with no balconies at all, have been ongoing from the late 1990s onwards. The next wave of popularity was brought on by Toronto's on-going condo boom (Figure 1). During this time, cantilevered balconies gained more momentum in tall buildings, and played an important role in the housing market (Figure 1).

More than 22,000 residential units were built within the City of Toronto in 2018, and this is expected to increase yearly to about 30,000 in 2020 (Dingman, 2018). Out of these, 60-80% of balconies are expected to be cantilevered. This marks Toronto as the largest condominium, and cantilevered balcony market, in North America (Lehrer, Keil & Kipfer, 2010). The future development of the residential tower is assured and supported by a 30% population increase expected by 2050 in the Greater Toronto Area (Hoornweg, Pope, 2014), the ongoing popularity of apartment unit ownership, and the provincial plan for future development (Lehrer, Keil & Kipfer, 2010) (Rosen, Walks, 2015).Currently, with shrinking unit sizes and despite the rising expense of cantilevered balcony construction, the balcony continues to remain an attractive feature of dense urban living. Through the last several decades, many changes have affected the form, context and use of concrete residential towers. From the 1950s onwards, planning and cultural changes have varied the form and context of the concrete residential towers from towers-in-the-park, dominant in the 20th century, to contemporary urban point towers and tower-podiums. (Rosen, Walks, 2015).

1970s: 40% Balconies   1970s: 60% Balconies   1970s: 80% Balconies   1970s: 100% Balconies

Percentage of Balcony Coverage in Residential Towers Built in the 1970s.

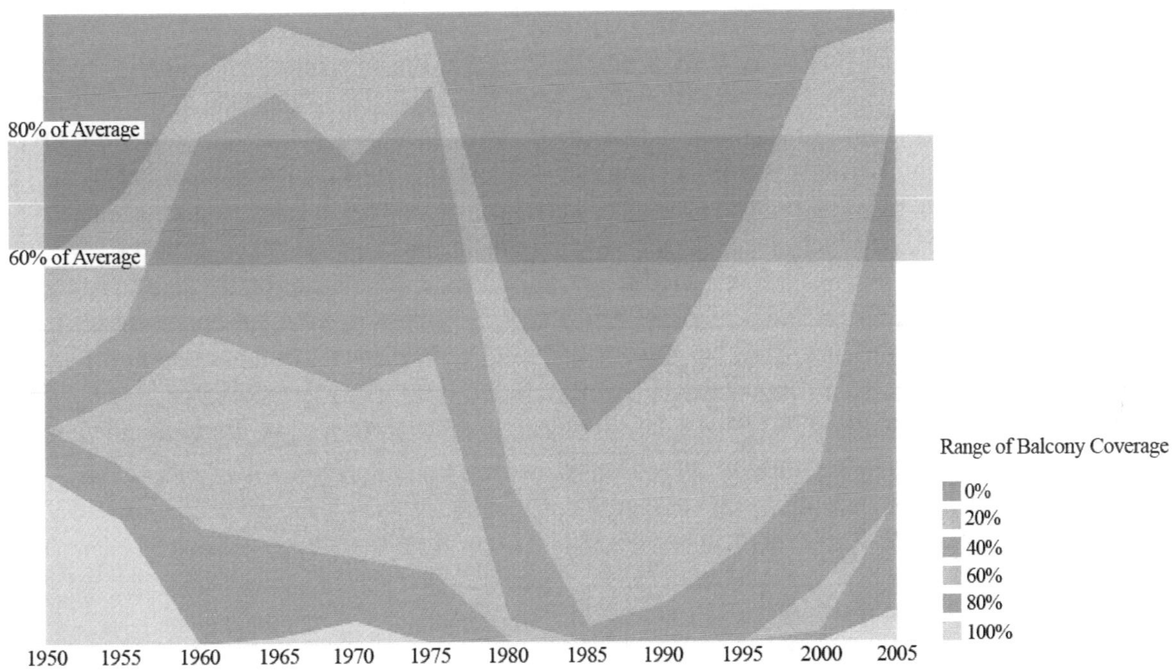

Figure 1: Percentage of Balcony Coverages in Residential Towers built from the 1950s to the 21st Century Across the Greater Toronto Area. (ACO Toronto 2016).

Currently, most of 20th century high-rise concrete towers have reached the end of their first lifecycle in terms of structural integrity, environmental performance, and contextual relevance. Meanwhile, limited improvements have been made in terms of structural integrity and environmental performance of balconies in residential towers. Multi-family towers are typically rigid in structure and therefore limited in use, making them prone to obsolescence (Kesik, 2009). Building obsolescence is directly related to shortcoming of designing prescribed housing arrangements and their limited life cycles, causing about 60% of all building demolitions in North America (Ross et al., 2016) (Chen, D. A., Klotz & Ross, 2016). Therefore, the obsolescence and redundancy of existing dated residential building stock is identified as a critical issue for sustainable development (Manewa et al., 2016). Meanwhile, balcony degradation is a prominent factor in aging multi-family housing including high levels of structural failures, low energy performance, and inefficient use (Kesik, 2009).

Structural failures for weather exposed concrete of balconies include concrete spalling, cracking and rust of reinforcements. The exposure of both sides of the concrete to the weather, and the stagnation of water on balconies result in balconies deteriorating more quickly as compared to vertical surfaces of buildings. Environmental performance issues in 20th century housing are also common due to aging envelope systems and lack of insulation (Kesik, 2009). While similar designs and construction methods have prevailed in concrete construction of the cantilevered balcony over the decades, it is anticipated that recent and new construction will face similar problems and shortcomings in the future. Therefore, it is important to consider adaptive reuse strategies that address the limitations of current and common balcony systems as an alternative to demolition, a tool for revitalizing aged multi-family housing, reducing energy consumption and improving life cycle of existing building stock.

Strategies for Adaptive Reuse

Strategies currently in practice for improving conditions of existing balconies are closely tied to improving the overall conditions of residential towers (Leblanc, 2012). Immediate and common strategies for improvements include structural and aesthetic remediation of balconies. More intrusive strategies involve addressing thermal issues. Thermally insulating the building envelope and permanently enclosing balconies are proven to increase environmental performance and minimize occupant health risks from the reduction of thermal bridging at the balcony (Hensel, 2013) (Tower Renewal Partnership, 2017). Strategies extracted from case study analysis can be divided in to the two categories of refurbishment and spatial conversion. Primarily, environmental and structural refurbishment strategies that aim at improving the current condition of residential towers highlighted in this research include: 1) Restructuring of the balcony slab and guards, 2) Extension of glazing, 3) Re-cladding, 4) Enclosing balconies and 5) Insulating balconies. Secondary strategies, categorized as spatially restructuring, have also been highlighted that aim at improving urban relevance, spatial use, and occupant comfort aside from addressing environmental and structural issues. These strategies include: 1) Addition, 2) In-setting, 3) Layering and 4) Extension of balconies.

2. Objectives and Methodology

There are multiple guidelines and models developed for evaluating a building for its adaptive reuse potential (Conejos, Langston & Smith, 2015). Currently, no formal and structured process exists for evaluating, quantifying, and comparing benefits of altered adaptive reuse designs for residential balconies (Gosling et al., 2013). The objective of this research is to develop a methodology for improving decision making in adaptive reuse of residential balconies. Focusing on adaptive reuse of balconies in multi-family residential buildings, a comparison model is developed based on simulation and analysis of multiple adaptive reuse strategies.

Ten balcony adaptive reuse strategies are identified from case study analysis. Each strategy is analysed regarding environmental, life cycle and cost benefits metrics in comparison to the existing building base case. A BIM platform is used to study relationships of strategies by simultaneous analysis of multiple criteria (Peters, 2018). The results are categorized in an index score system for adaptability, in order to create a basis for understanding the implications of adaptive reuse strategies. 6D BIM models of each strategy is developed in Revit®, including detailed information regarding construction phase, cost and life cycle phasing. Models include information of existing conditions and alterations as part of the adaptive reuse strategy for accurate analysis. Various simulation software is used to measure the following parameters: 1) Energy use, 2) Thermal comfort, 3) Daylighting, 4) Natural Ventilation, 5) Systems performance, 6) Life cycle analysis, 7) Cost and 8) Constructability. This paper focuses on highlighting results from life cycle analysis simulation and calculations.

Structural and Environmental Refurbishment

Restructuring is an immediate and common strategy for improvements to the general condition of residential towers is through the remediation of the balcony structure and railings of balconies. This strategy is one of the least intrusive and is most common across the City of Toronto. Re-glazing involves the replacement of windows or increasing the amount of glazing is a strategy to improve environmental performance of the envelope, increase daylighting and ventilation. Re-cladding involves the restructuring the building envelope to increase the environmental performance and to eliminate tenant health hazards primarily include thermally insulating the envelope in order to improve building performance and the elimination of thermal bridging in the balconies. This strategy is common as complimentary to other strategies, including re-glazing and enclosing. Enclosing the balcony is a strategy to protect the balcony from the environment while not thermally mediating the balcony space as part of the interior. Enclosing of the balcony is often a stand-alone strategy aimed at improving the spatial qualities of the balcony by providing more weather-protected living space, while at the same time beginning to mediate the interior space through a layered approach. Lastly, insulating balconies and creating a unified enclosure over the building façade can increase thermal performance and occupant comfort and the reduction of mold and health hazards (Kesik, 2009). Thermally over-cladding the envelope and permanently enclosing balconies as a solution, will strengthen the thermal boundary of the building creates a rigid boundary. This approach contributes to a mainstream and traditional environmental division (Figure 2).

Spatial Conversion

The following strategies are aimed at larger scale conversions of balconies and the building envelope. These strategies address spatial concerns of residential towers including densification and rearrangement, as examples. Addition of balconies typically requires additional structural support, and reconstruction of the building envelope to include openings. Interior modifications are also common as the relation between the interior and exterior changes. While addition of balconies is common as part of more complex adaptive reuse of towers that involves various strategies, relocation of balconies can be a resultant strategy from extension or interior modifications of the building. In-setting of the balcony, while not common due to financial justification, considers the development of balconies from already existing interior spaces. Layering of the balcony is often made possible through extension of the balcony and the introduction of different layers to the building envelope to create mediating spaces, such as winter gardens, and as a strategy to better control the environment. Outward extension involves a complete spatial and structural reconfiguration of the balcony and is a result of densification requirements and often a reconfiguration of interior spaces to add more units, as examples (Figure 3).

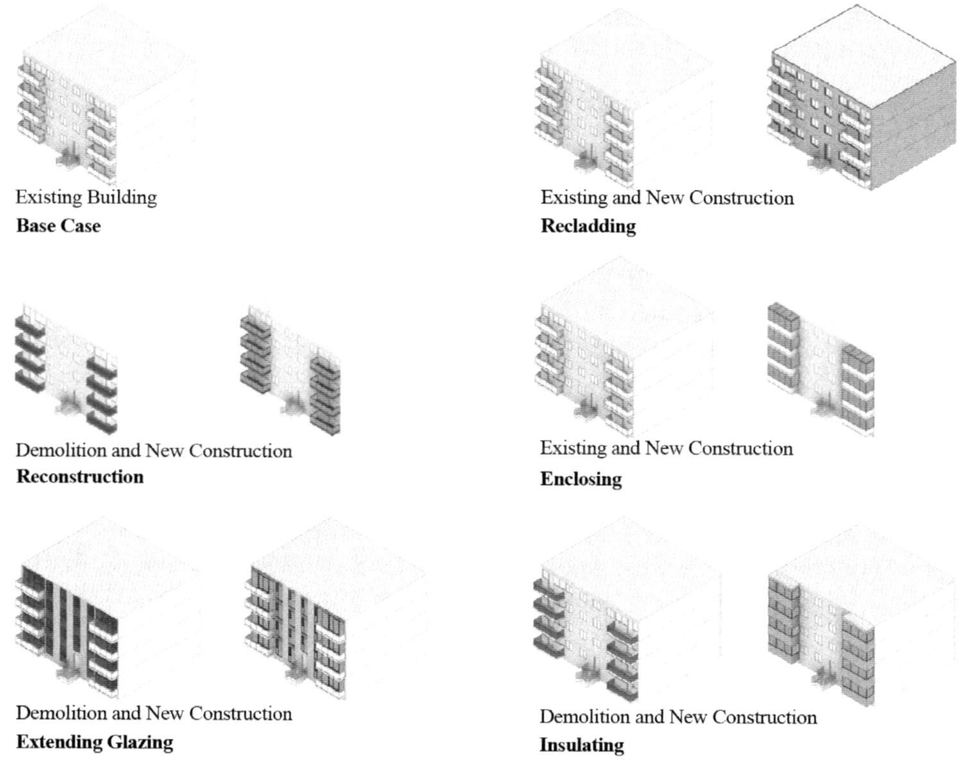

Figure 2: 6D BIM Models of Structural and Environmental Refurbishment Strategies

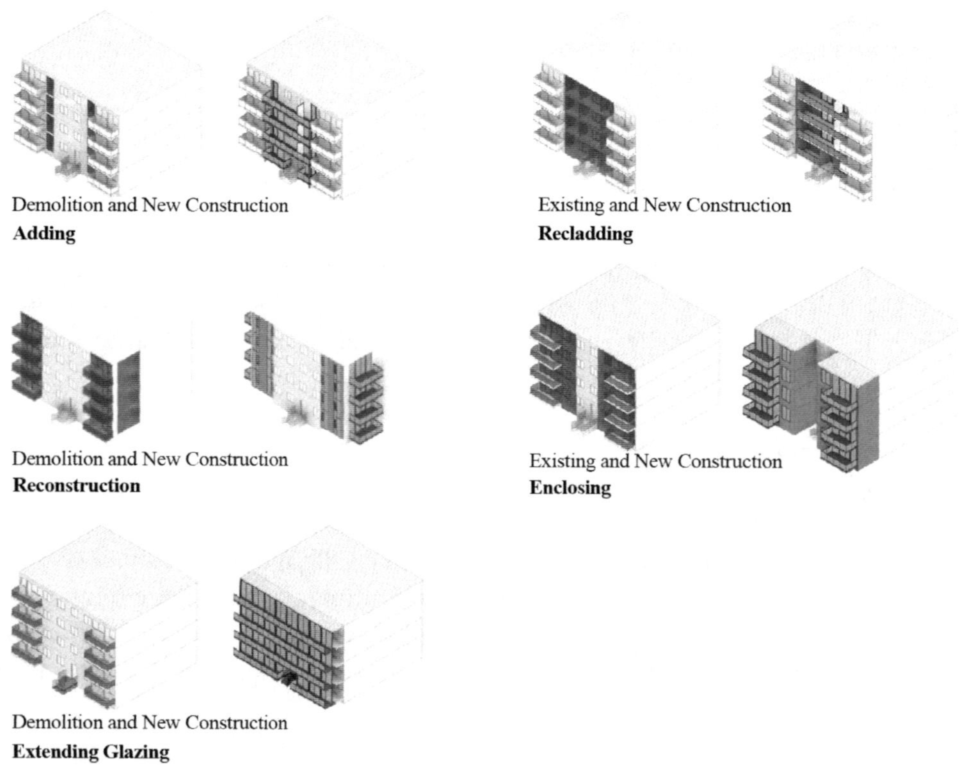

Figure 3: 6D BIM Models of Spatial Conversion Strategies

BIM Integration with Simulation

The integration of BIM and Building Performance Simulation (BPS) tools can facilitate the development of holistically efficient and sustainable structures through the simultaneous analysis of multiple parameters (Krygiel, 2008) (Chen, S., 2018). BIM and BPS processes are being increasingly integrated to analyze and predict various performance measures while communicating through images and analyzed data (Attia et al., 2012). Simulations evaluate and analyze various performance metrics with an objective to advance understanding regarding the various factors influencing design strategies and facilitate optimized decision-making (Attia et al., 2012) (Peters, 2018). The integration of simulation tools with BIM in this manner is proven to be beneficial from preliminary stages of a design process (Chen, 2018).

BIM integration with BPS has been made possible through easy exchange between BIM software and simulation tools. As an example, Autodesk Revit® includes built-in BPS software and multiple plugins from Autodesk and other developers that provide extended simulation capabilities. Insight, Autodesk Revit®'s built-in environmental simulation tool uses integrated EnergyPlus® engines to simulate a building's energy cost range, lighting analysis, solar analysis and insolation ranges. Autodesk Revit® also hosts other simulation plugins including Autodesk CFD® for ventilation and air flow simulation, and Robot Structure Analysis®, for structural performance, as examples. Independent software, such as Sefaira® for energy, daylighting and systems simulation, also have BIM plugins that allow a seamless flow of data between their tools and BIM models. In this process, the plugins easily communicate geometric and contextual data to simulation engines, and analysis results are either transferred back and visualized in the BIM software (Chen, 2018) , or are housed and organized as iterations on the cloud, in the case of Sefaira®.

Application of simulations in BIM includes the abilities to find relationships, map similarities and differences, and be able to organize results efficiently by correlating geometry and performance. These relationships can be studied by simultaneous analysis of multiple criteria including energy, thermal comfort, daylighting, direct sunlight and shadow, ventilation, and acoustics as examples (Peters, 2018). There have been increasing efforts in improving the integration, interoperability and communication of simulation tools. A tool for McNeel's Rhino® Grasshopper is being developed by Burrohapold as a 'Smart Building Analyzer' that can simulate and analyze energy use, thermal comfort, daylighting, acoustics, security, fire safety and circulation simultaneously. Through simulation and visualization, and working at a multidisciplinary boundary, a comprehensive tool like this can create a precedent for improved accessibility and integration of simulation tools in all stages of a project (Peters, 2018).
The future of simulation is rooted in development of comprehensive tools that aside from measuring energy and carbon, can also begin to predict occupant centric measures including productivity, health, wellbeing and happiness. The applicability of simulations in the design process is encouraged by the move away from static two-dimensional drawings to the integrated use of accurate and live building information models for design and documentation. Since simulation is optimized with multi-disciplinary knowledge and improvements in collaboration, BIM is therefore a great starting point for its proliferation. New and integrated tools, and immersive simulation and visualization capabilities, with ability to customize codes allows the participation of users in the development and customization of tools within BIM (Azhar, Brown, 2009)(Sinha et al., 2013) (Peters, 2018).

3. Results and Analysis

BIM can be used to conduct accurate Life Cycle Analysis (LCA) and can assist in better understanding life cycle of projects in design, construction, maintenance, and operation stages of a building (Park, Kim & Cho, 2017). Performing a comprehensive LCA can be challenging due to the effort required to gather and input necessary data, the volume of information required to process a correct evaluation, and the management of changes over the various phases of a project (Finnveden et al., 2009). There are many LCA tools for BIM that are effective in overcoming these challenges and are validated for accuracy, including GaBi® and Tally® amongst others (Wu, Issa, 2015). Tally® is an integrated tool within Autodesk Revit®, and through an interface for matching existing BIM data with LCA databases in Tally®, allows for an integrated calculation of LCA that can be updated in real-time to geometry and material changes.

The main metrics for LCA are analyzed in this study and include Global Warming Potential (GWP) and Primary Energy Demand (PED). GWP measures greenhouse emissions including carbon dioxide and methane. Increases in greenhouse emissions increase the radiation emitted by the earth leading to increased temperatures negatively affecting ecosystems, health and resources. PED measures the total amount of energy extracted for use, and measures energy resource use excluding environmental impacts. The various life cycle stages considered in Tally® calculations include product, maintenance and replacement, end of life and potential of reuse after life of building, including energy recovery and material recycling, referred to as Module D (Cays, 2017) (De Wolf, Pomponi & Moncaster, 2017). Lastly, information regarding operational energy is input manually for calculation by Tally®. Required operational energy data includes energy use intensity (kWh/m2/year) and total electricity demand (kWh). The energy use information for each strategy is gathered through Sefaira® energy analysis. The effects of GWP for product, construction, use, end-of-life and Module D are represented for each strategy compared to GWP for OE (Operational Energy) in Figure 4. GWP and PED are calculated for various life cycle stages of the base building and adaptive reuse strategies, ranging from raw building materials to final disposal. The sums for the estimated 60-year life of the building are combined in Figure 5.

The results for life cycle analysis of the base case strategy and the ten adaptive reuse strategies can be summarized as follows. The base case is estimated to have a total global warming potential of 3,213,745 kgCO2eq and a primary energy demand of 65,322,390 MJ. Adaptive reuse strategies of re-glazing, re-cladding, insulating, and in-setting show reductions in GWP and PED as compared to the base case over the life cycle of the building. While adding and in-setting demonstrate 16% and 17% improvements in GWP respectively, the effect of insulating is 10%. Enclosing, relocating, layering and extending show a negative effect on life cycle impacts. Layering has the highest negative GWP and PED impact at 3%.

As described earlier, life cycle analysis is only one dimension of the adaptability index being developed. The results of the comprehensive analysis index for enclosing and layering strategies are compiled and summarized in an Adaptability Index Tool Interface for comparison of the performance and evaluation of all the strategies under study, as examples (Figure 6). The LCA analysis is thus illustrated in that broader context.

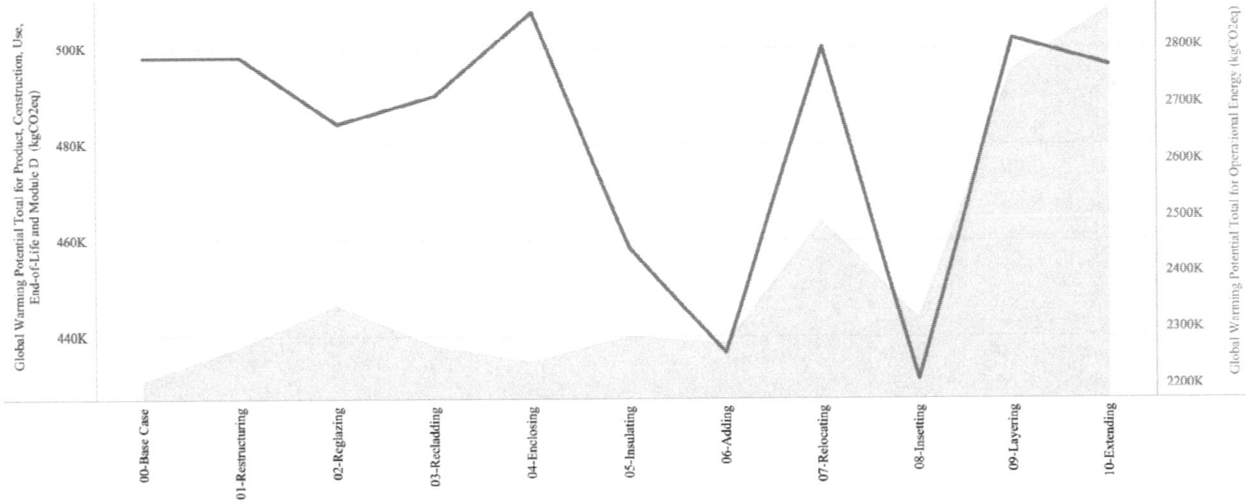

Figure 4: GWP for Product, Construction, Use, End-of-Life and Module D is represented for each strategy (line) in comparison GWP for Operational Energy (area) (kgCO2eq)

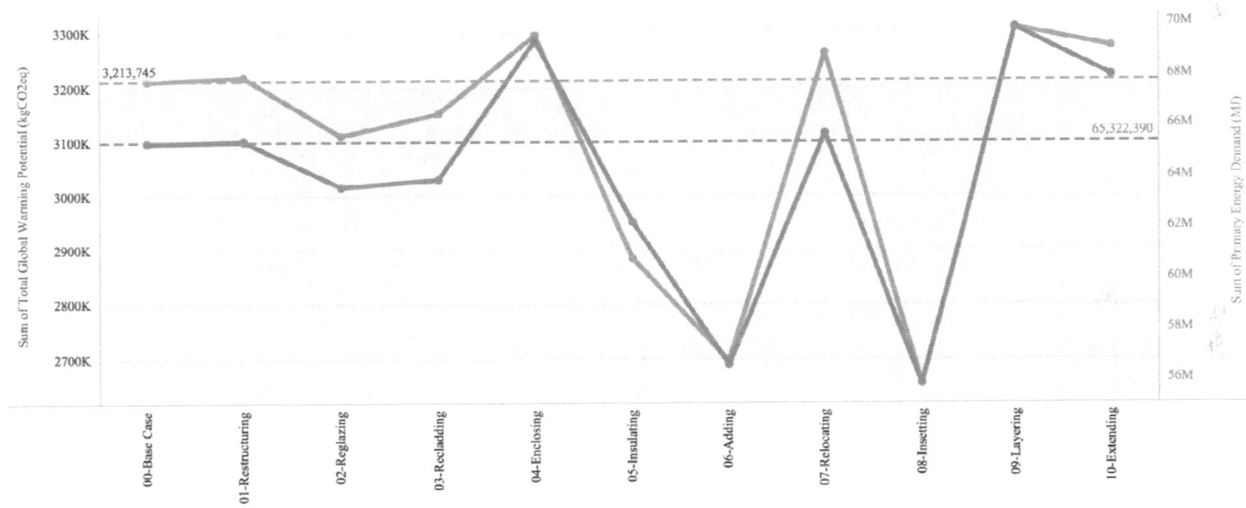

Figure 5: Sum of Primary Energy Demand Total (MJ) and Sum of Global Warming Potential Total (kgCO2eq) for Base Case and Adaptive Reuse Strategies. The dotted orange and grey lines represent the corresponding base case values. Strategies that fall below the orange line show improvements in primary energy demand. Strategies that fall below the grey line show improvements in total global warming potential.

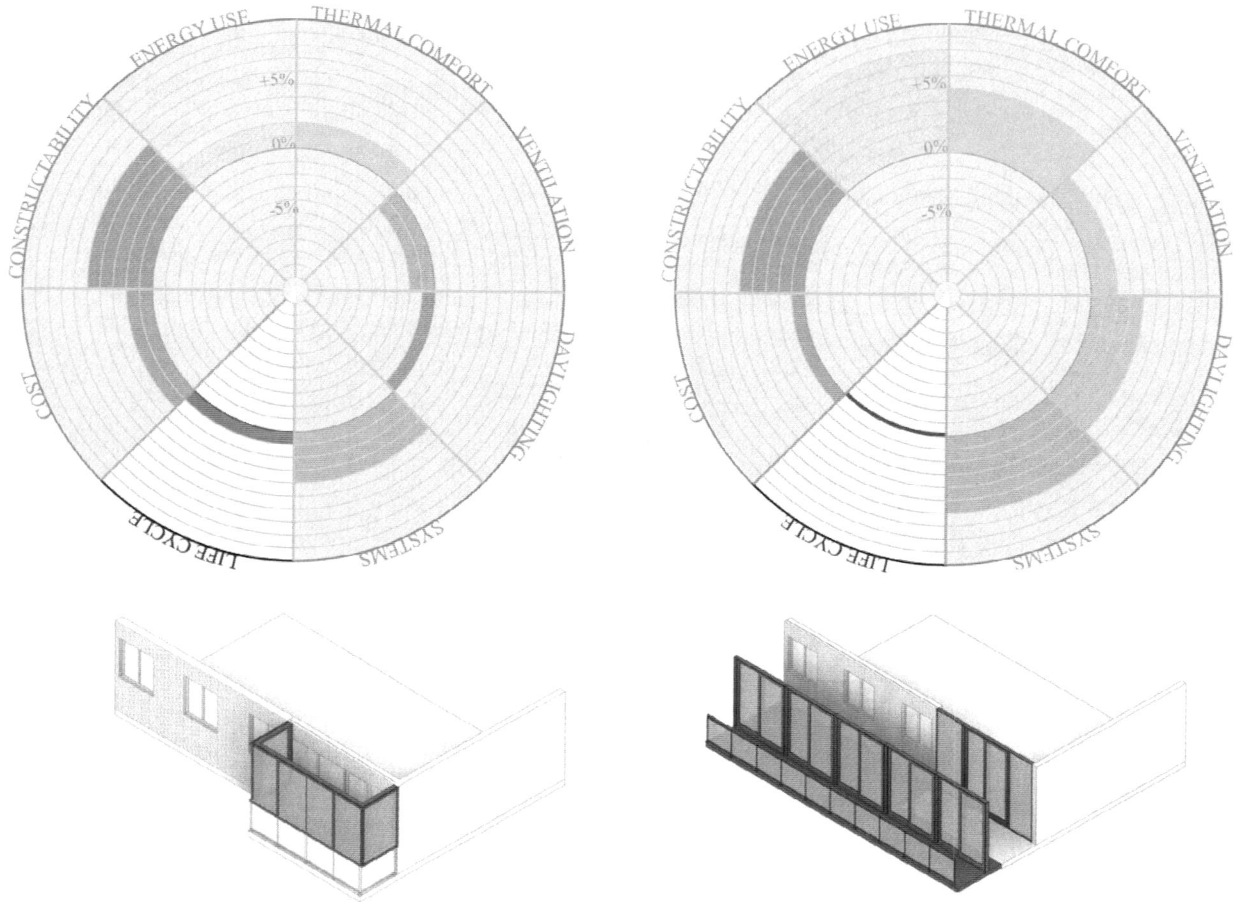

04 – Enclosing 09 – Layering

Figure 6: Adaptability Index Tool Interface Example for Enclosing and Layering, Summarizing Performance Results

4. Conclusion and Future Work

A quantifiable comparison of balcony adaptive reuse strategies evaluates the success of their overall performance and demonstrates environmental as well as economic justifications for future adaptive reuse projects. With the developed comparative metrics, it is possible to understand the strengths, weaknesses and possibilities of each strategy. Identifying advantages and disadvantages facilitates a timely analysis of the success of existing adaptive reuse projects. A thorough comparative tool also enables the determining of best possible options as a design tool for new residential adaptive reuse projects. This enables limited analysis requirements in the early design stages of a project. Challenges for accurate implementation of the tool includes gathering quality data of existing buildings and accurate documentation of components for simulation. The future development of this comparative tool will benefit from more extensive case study analysis, data collection and more complex interdisciplinary efforts.

References

Attia, S., Hensen, J.L.M., Beltrán, L. & De Herde, A. 2012, "Selection criteria for building performance simulation tools: contrasting architects' and engineers' needs", *Journal of Building Performance Simulation,* vol. 5, no. 3, pp. 155-169.

Azhar, S. & Brown, J. 2009, "BIM for Sustainability Analyses", *International Journal of Construction Education and Research,* vol. 5, no. 4, pp. 276-292.

Cays, J. 2017, "Life-Cycle Assessment: Reducing Environmental Impact Risk with Workflow Data You Can Trust", *Architectural Design,* vol. 87, no. 3, pp. 96-103.

Chen, D.A., Klotz, L.E. & Ross, B.E. 2016, "Mathematically Characterizing Natural Systems for Adaptable, Biomimetic Design", *Procedia Engineering,* vol. 145, pp. 497-503.

Chen, S. 2018, "Use of neural network supervised learning to enhance the light environment adaptation ability and validity of Green BIM", *Computer-Aided Design and Applications,* vol. 15, no. 6, pp. 831-840.

Conejos, S., Langston, C. & Smith, J. 2015, "Enhancing sustainability through designing for adaptive reuse from the outset", *Facilities,* vol. 33, no. 9, pp. 531-552.

De Wolf, C., Pomponi, F. & Moncaster, A. 2017, "Measuring embodied carbon dioxide equivalent of buildings: A review and critique of current industry practice", *Energy & Buildings,* vol. 140, pp. 68-80.

Dingman, S. 2018, February 12, -last update, *Toronto condo numbers set new records*. Available: https://www.theglobeandmail.com/real-estate/toronto/toronto-condo-numbers-set-new-records/article37959424/ [2018, July 28].

Finnveden, G., Hauschild, M.Z., Ekvall, T., Guinée, J., Heijungs, R., Hellweg, S., Koehler, A., Pennington, D. & Suh, S. 2009, "Recent developments in life cycle assessment", *Journal of environmental management,* vol. 91, no. 1, pp. 1-21.

Gosling, J., Sassi, P., Naim, M. & Lark, R. 2013, "Adaptable buildings: A systems approach", *Sustainable Cities and Society,* vol. 7, pp. 44-51.

Hensel, M., author. 2013, *Performance-oriented architecture: rethinking architectural design and the built environment,* Wiley, Chichester, West Sussex.

Hoornweg, D. & Pope, K. 2014, "Socioeconomic Pathways and Regional Distribution of the World's 101 Largest Cities".

Kesik, T.J., 2009, *Tower renewal guidelines for the comprehensive retrofit of multi-unit residential buildings in cold climates,* Daniels Faculty of Architecture, Landscape, and Design, University of Toronto, Toronto.

Krygiel, E., 2008, *Green BIM: successful sustainable design with building information modeling,* Wiley Pub, Indianapolis, Ind.

Leblanc, D. 2012, "' Re- skinning' the skyscape", *The Globe and Mail (Index-only),* pp. G.4.

Lehrer, U., Keil, R. & Kipfer, S. 2010, "Reurbanization in Toronto: Condominium boom and social housing revitalization", *disP - The Planning Review,* vol. 46, no. 180, pp. 81-90.

Manewa, A., Siriwardena, M., Ross, A. & Madanayake, U. 2016, "Adaptable buildings for sustainable built environment", *Built Env Proj and Ass Man,* vol. 6, no. 2, pp. 139-158.

Park, J., Kim, K. & Cho, Y.K. 2017, "Framework of automated construction- safety monitoring using cloud-enabled BIM and BLE mobile tracking sensors. (building information model) (Bluetooth low-energy) (Report) (Author abstract)", *Journal of Construction Engineering and Management,* vol. 143, no. 2.

Peters, B. 2018, "Defining Environments: Understanding Architectural Performance through Modelling, Simulation and Visualisation", *Architectural Design,* vol. 88, no. 1, pp. 82-91.

Rosen, G. & Walks, A. 2015, "Castles in Toronto's Sky: Condo-ism as Urban Transformation", *Journal of Urban Affairs,* vol. 37, no. 3, pp. 289-310.

Ross, B.E., Chen, D.A., Conejos, S. & Khademi, A. 2016, "Enabling Adaptable Buildings: Results of a Preliminary Expert Survey", *Procedia Engineering,* vol. 145, no. Complete, pp. 420-427.

Sinha, S., Sawhney, A., Borrmann, A. & Ritter, F. 2013, "Extracting information from building information models for energy code compliance of building envelope", *RICS COBRA Conference 2013,* pp. 10-12.

Tower Renewal Partnership 2017, *Thermal Comfort; Cooling in Apartment Towers*, Tower Renewal Partnership, Toronto, Canada.

Wu, W. & Issa, R.R. 2015, "An integrated green BIM process model (IGBPM) for BIM execution planning in green building projects" in *Building Information Modeling: Applications and Practices*, pp. 135-165.

Information Extraction to Support Automation of Navigation through 3D Models during Collaborative Design Sessions

Lucian Constantin Ungureanu, Timo Hartmann
Technical University of Berlin, Germany
l.ungureanu@tu-berlin.de

Abstract. This paper explores the possibility of creating a voice-based interface to support collaborative design sessions. The main purpose is to automate changes of viewpoints for 3D models based on ongoing design conversations. We employ a design science research methodology and propose a framework to support this task. Within the structure of the framework, we propose three main components for (1) information filtering, (2) information extraction and (3) domain knowledge encapsulation. A small-scale implementation on two transcripts of real-world design sessions allows us to assess the performance of the components. The classifier for information filtering performs well for identifying the speaker turns not related to viewpoint changes of the 3D model, while additional work needs to be done to reduce the rate of false positives. It also reveals various future research directions.

1. Introduction

Creative design is often seen as a result of collaboration rather than an expression of isolated genius (*Jones, 1983*). Practitioners and researchers in the architecture, engineering and construction (AEC) field embraced this perspective. Consequently, this philosophy shaped the design and engineering thinking in the AEC field, where collaborative and coordinative design sessions represent the manifestation of this perspective. While collaborative design sessions require a strong commitment of all participants towards achieving a design goal (*Chiu, 2002*), coordinative design sessions aim at identifying issues and to define resolution pathways for these (*Mehrbod et al., 2019*).

During such sessions, creativity is enhanced by using various design artefacts. Designers interact with design artefacts and use these to support communication (*Perry and Sanderson, 1998*). Examples of such artefacts are drawings, sketches, and virtual representations such as 3D models (*Perry and Sanderson, 1998*). Most of these artefacts represent visual aids. These visualizations are meant to enhance communication, coordination and collaboration (*Leite et al., 2016; Dossik and Neff, 2011*). Computers started to play an essential role during such sessions, especially considering the high adoption rate of building information modelling (*Golparvar-Fard et al.,2013*). The use of 3D models to support collaboration and communication has been widely adopted. For example, a survey conducted in the U.S. (*Leite et al., 2016*) reported that 3D models represent the most commonly used form of visualization, with a score of 95%. Moreover, technological tools are supposed to "stimulate, cause or assist" creativity (*Achten and Beetz, 2009*). A review of collaborative design studies (*Achten and Beetz, 2009*) reported that 40% of the studies focus on technological aspects, a conclusion also enforced by later studies (*Dossik and Neff, 2011*). At the same time, the static nature of 3D representations does not allow for a natural interaction with the virtual artefacts (*Dossik and Neff, 2011*).

In practical settings, designers expect to be able to points to (gesture), talk about (speech) or sketch on (sketching) (*Perry and Sanderson, 1998*). When it comes to gesture and sketching, emerging technologies such as touch-based hardware are possible alternatives towards a more natural designer-artefact interface. Various studies (*Kim and Maher, 2008; Gu et al., 2011*) started investigating the effect of tangible interfaces on design creativity. A study comparing gesture-based communication with sketching-based communication (*Eris et al., 2014*) highlight that speech is the main communication channel, while gesture and sketching represent secondary means of communication. To our knowledge, speech-augmented designer-artefact interaction does not currently represent a mature research area.

This paper investigates the possibility to automatically extract information from design communications to automatically change viewpoints in 3D models. During design sessions, participants naturally communicate their ideas, intentionally referring to some detail of the design. However, navigating a 3D model to find a viewpoint that shows this detail is a tedious task. Moreover, most of the times, participants in such sessions do not have the required skill set to quickly change a 3D model's viewpoint. A natural language interface between participants and computer might represent a good alternative. However, contemporary voice assistants are intrusive as they require formalised queries.

In this study, we are looking at automating the extraction of viewpoints-related information out of natural human-to-human conversations. To this end, we propose a framework which combines ontological modelling of domain-specific knowledge and the use of probabilistic models to support information filtering and extraction from natural language conversations.

The paper continues with a more detailed overview of state-of-the-art possibilities to interact with digital design artefacts. The paper then introduces the steps we followed to conduct this research as well as the framework we proposed to solve the problem of automatically changing the viewpoints of 3D models. Moreover, we present the implementation of the proposed framework using the transcripts of two real-world design meetings. The implementation is followed by the evaluation of various parts of the framework and discussions of the current status of the framework, where we propose various scenarios for future development. Finally, we present a summary of our findings, limitations and future research in the conclusion section.

2. Human-Computer Interfaces in Design

Human-Computer interfaces usually require a set of input and output devices. Input devices allow a user to provide a set of commands which are translated in specific machine-interpretable actions. The user accesses the results of the provided commands using output devices. Keyboard and mouse represent the most common input devices, while screens represent the most common output devices. Early research in the field of computer-aided design aimed to assess the human performance while using machines for design tasks (Cuomo and Sharif, 1989) emphasising the need of training to improve the human performance, while more recent research start focusing on the need of designing better interfaces aiming at a more natural and intuitive way of interacting with machines (Turk, 2014).

To this end, the research community highlighted that multi-modality is an inherent characteristic of human communication (Turk, 2014). Aiming to move away from the keyboard-mouse-based input interface, the research community started exploring various interfaces which will allow the humans to provide input through gesture, sketching and speaking. When it comes to design, the purpose is to allow the computers to meaningfully support the design process without hindering creativity.

On one hand, as a result of the rapid technological development, gesture and sketch-enable technologies are slowly integrated into the design process. Studies show that these tangible interfaces increase creativity (Kim and Maher, 2008; Gu et al., 2011). On the other hand, there is a huge gap in the use of speech-based interfaces during collaborative design sessions. Most of the previous research focused on developing voice-based input interfaces with a limited number of voice-based commands which allow users to access various CAD-software functionality such as modelling geometrical primitives (Chu et al., 1997; Kou and Tan, 2008; Xue et al., 2009; Kou et al., 2010) or accessing information linked to 3D elements (Xue et al., 2010, Behera and McKay, 2017). A limitation of the proposed systems is that users always need to remember what they can ask the computer. Additionally, expanding the repository of available commands is very difficult. Finally, these commands are highly structured and disrupt the natural course of design conversations. Advanced approaches which make use of the current state of the art natural language techniques are still missing, but moreover, there is a lack of understanding the specificity of the natural language conversations used in design-related situations. This paper employs a design science research method which aims at laying the foundation for the development of non-intrusive voice-based interfaces, with the main goal of changing the 3D models' viewpoints based on information extracted out of natural language conversations held by the practitioners during collaborative and coordinative sessions.

3. Research Method and Framework Description

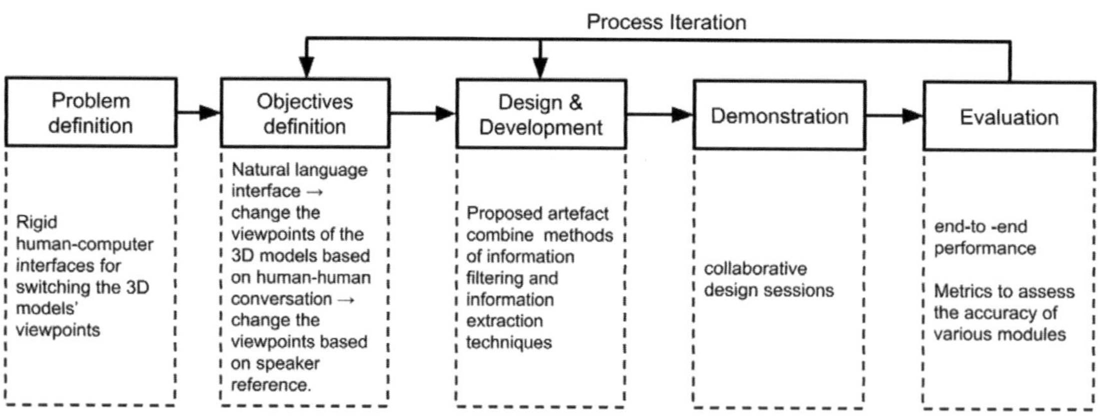

Figure 1-Design Science Research Method with Problem-Centred Initiation

This paper employs a design science research method following the framework proposed by Peffer et al. (2007). Figure 1 presents the problem-centered research method which consists of five main components. Extracting the right information of out human-to-human conversations is a challenging task mainly because there is no distinction between commands-related conversation and background conversation (messy talk). The objective of the current paper is to develop a system that will extract the information related to various parts of the product to be designed and perform operations such as zoom in or isolate the parts mentioned by designers.

For example, when designers exchange design ideas about the first floor, the operation expected from the system is to isolate the first floor as shown in Figure 2.

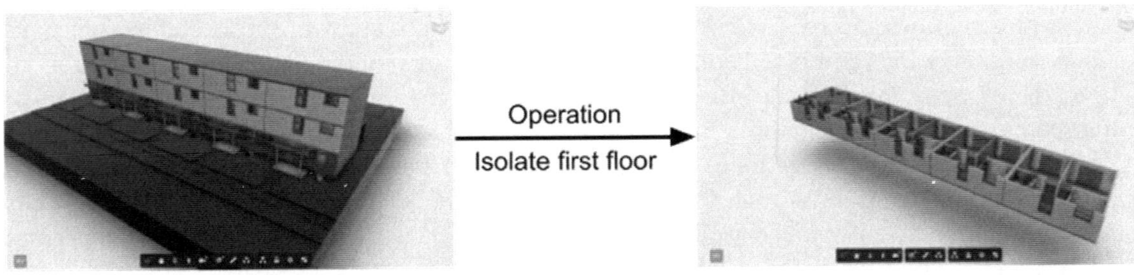

Figure 2-Possible 3D model's viewpoint operation

Figure 3 presents the proposed framework. Within this framework, we distinguish three major components, namely: (1) information filtering, (2) information extraction, and (3) domain knowledge base. Information filtering represents the process of removing data from an incoming stream with the sole purpose of keeping the information relevant for a task (*Belkin and Croft, 1992*). Information retrieval represents the process of extracting the information required to perform a task. Both, information filtering and information retrieval are contexts sensitive. In our framework, this gap is addressed using the third component – domain knowledge.

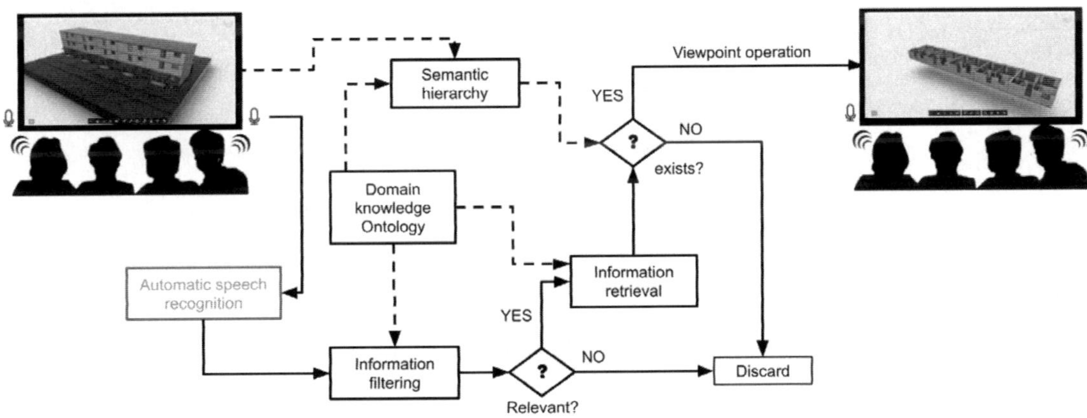

Figure 3-Artefact framework

To develop this system, we use a dataset of recordings of design conversations. We aim at extracting specific information for viewpoint changes for this dataset. As design conversations are unstructured, we structure the cleaning process in two subtasks: (1) automatic detection of those utterances and natural language constructs not related to viewpoints changes and (2) a manual cleaning necessary as preparation for the information extraction. For the automatic detection of task-related constructs, we explore the use of probabilistic classifiers. A classifier can identify constructs not related to any viewpoint operations and discard these. To support information filtering and information extraction, we built an ontology. This ontology aims to capture the knowledge related to the project breakdown. The central assumption we make is that participants use domain-specific named concepts during conversations. We use the error rate to individually evaluate the proposed components for information filtering and information extraction to conduct an end-to-end validation of the entire framework.

For a small-scale practical implementation of the framework, we used the transcripts of two architectural meetings recorded by the Design Thinking Research Group (Llyod et al. 2005). These meetings are part of an effort to design a crematorium and were recorded in their natural setup. Both meetings combined consist of 2318 speaker turns and almost four hours of recorded time. Three participants were involved during the first meeting (A1) and five participants for the second meeting (A2). In both meetings, a researcher was present as an observer. During the design sessions, participants focus on designing various parts of the crematorium while using paper-based drawing to visualize various parts of the design. At this point, it is worth mentioning that no computer-based artefacts were used during these sessions. In this paper, we address the issue of information filtering and information extraction supported by an ontology created for the crematorium domain.

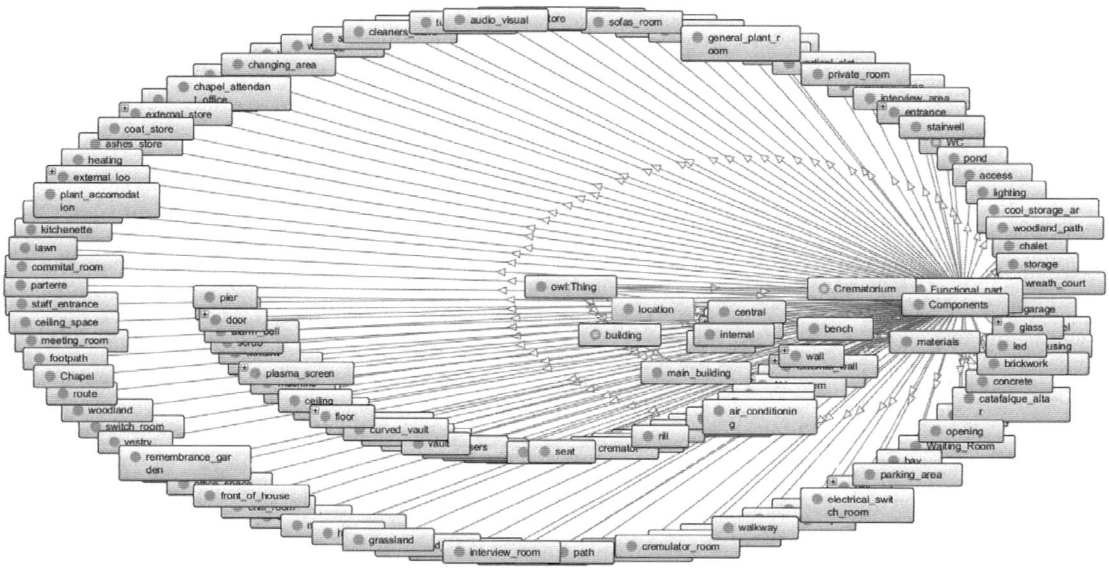

Figure 4-Crematorium Ontology

Figure 4 presents the crematorium-related domain concepts included in the ontology. The ontology has concepts *functional parts (*which include concepts such as *waiting room* or *chapel* which describe the functional aspects of a crematorium project), components (which included concepts such as *wall* or *roof*), locations (which include concepts such as *back* or *top*), and materials (which include concepts such as *concrete*). These concepts were used to automatically label speaker turns which contain these concepts. For the information filtering, we prepared the transcripts for a binary classification problem, where a new feature was created to indicate if a specific speaker turn is or is not a possible candidate for a viewpoint change, mainly based on content related to the ontological concepts. After labelling 541 speaker turns were labelled as related, while 1777 were labelled as not related. In preparation for the classification, we performed additional cleaning tasks such as remove numbers, stop words, and punctuation, steaming and characters case folding from upper to lower case. After cleaning, a document term matrix was created. In a document-term matrix, the number of rows is equal to the number of documents while the number of columns is equal to the number of unique terms in the dataset. For our implementation, the number of rows is equal to the number of turns (2318) and the number of columns corresponds to 2224 unique terms. Each term is weighted based on its frequency on each turn. For the classification, 75% of the dataset was used for training and the other 25% were used for testing. Within the training subset, 1320 turns correspond to negative class and 418 turns correspond to the positive class. Within the testing subset, 457 turns correspond to negative class and 123 turns correspond to the positive class. We implemented a simple Naïve Bayesian classifier for which we disabled the Laplace smoothing (Laplace = 0).

For the information extraction, we implemented a natural language parser and we extracted the noun phrases (NP) from each turn. These phrases were once again filtered, using pattern matching to keep only those which are part of the crematorium ontology. The performance of the information filtering module depends on the language used during design and on the concepts captured in the ontology. When it comes to language use, one of the major concerns relates to syntactic ambiguity. Syntactic ambiguity means that a sentence can have more than one parse trees, which means that some parts can have multiple syntactic roles within the uttered sentence. As mentioned previously, those concepts captured in the ontology must reflect the structure of the design artefact (e.g. 3D models). For an in-depth analysis, we can consider the following sentence extracted from the transcripts.

"*Basically we're arriving in the new car park in this area and from the car park we'll enter the building through a waiting area*".

The syntactic parser identifies the following items as noun phrases: "*we*", "*the new car park*" "*this area*", "*the car park*", "*we*", "*the building*", "*a waiting area*". Using the concepts included in the ontology, the following terms are extracted after filtering: "*building*", "*waiting area*", "*car park*". We notice that the quantifier "*new*" used by the speaker to make a separation between the existing car park and the new car park is missing.

4. Evaluation and Discussions

The results of the classifier indicate a sensitivity of 53.91% and a specificity of 94.42%, with a balanced accuracy of 74.16%. The classifier performs well in terms of identifying those turns not related to viewpoint changes. The true positive rate is low, and future efforts should focus on improving this and reducing the false positive rate as these correspond to turns related to viewpoint changes. Moreover, one limitation of the current exploration is given by structuring the conversations on speaker turns. This approach does not capture the real behaviour of the speaker. Segmentation of the speaker turns in small units called utterances must be employed in this direction. Moreover, experimentation with other classification methods should be the subject of future studies, especially with those which perform well on short text classification.

The use of natural language processing techniques, such as parts of speech tagging and syntactic parsing, is usually computationally intensive. In this direction, the use of the classifier to discard the turns not related to viewpoints helped to reduce the workload for a such as task. For an utterance such as "*basically we're arriving in the new car park in this area and from the car park we'll enter the building through a waiting area*" the extracted parts will be [*"car park", "car park", "building", "waiting area"*]. "*car park*" and "waiting area" represent specific parts which can be easily identified, and the system can perform operations such as isolating or zooming in. When it comes to the concept "building" it is not clear to what building the speaker refers to. A limitation of this study is that it is not considering the relationships defined in the ontology. A relationship such as "*crematorium*" has some "*waiting room*", "*waiting room*" has some "*wall*", "*wall*" has some "*window*" will allow us to identify when the speaker refers to "*that specific window which is part of the wall which is part of the waiting room*", and not to another window.

Ontologies also play an important role in improving the performance of the voice assistants such as Alexa or Siri. Most of the voice assistants make use of WikiData repository which is mainly built for general purpose tasks. Design is a very specialized activity for which repositories such as WikiData do not manage to capture all required knowledge.

One major limitation of both components proposed for information filtering and information extraction is that it covers only those situations where the speaker directly refers to the thing, without considering that the speaker might refer to a thing using various expressions such as "*this*" or "*it*". Future studies will aim to investigate the use of coreferential expressions in design conversations. Moreover, future efforts will focus on creating an instantiation of the proposed artefact for the purpose of end-to-end testing. Moreover, any operation leading to the change of viewpoints in 3D models need to clearly identify the input data required to be performed. Making the operation indicated in Figure 2 requires additional domain knowledge such as knowing which elements are part of level 1. This points out toward the fact that the ontology needs also to capture knowledge related to the semantic hierarchy of the 3D models.

5. Conclusions

The current paper proposes an artefact which aims to address the gap of voice-based interfaces in collaborative design sessions. This research follows the design science methodology with the aim of creating a framework to solve the above-stated problem. Precisely, the framework aims to analyse the participants' conversations with the purpose of filtering and extracting information related to the viewpoints of the 3D models. For the filtering task, we proposed the use of a classifier, while information extraction relies on natural language processing techniques such as syntactic parsing.

A small-scale implementation was performed using the transcript of two real-world design sessions. The design science research method proposes an iterative approach to develop the framework. Each iteration reveals various aspects which need to be addressed by future research. In the case of our implementation, the classifier proposed for information filtering performs well for the classification of the true negatives (turns not related to 3D models' viewpoints). The performance of the classifier on true positives indicates that future research should focus on reducing the false positives, aim to capture the real speakers' behaviour by segmentation of the transcript in small utterances, and exploring the performance of various classification methods especially focusing on short text classification. Implementation of the information extraction module indicates that future research should focus on making better use of the knowledge encapsulated in the ontologies.

References

Achten, H. and Beetz, J., 2009, September. What happened to collaborative design?. In *Proceedings of the eCAADe Conference* (pp. 357-366).

Behera, A.K. and McKay, A., 2017, September. Designs that talk and listen: Integrating functional information using voice-enabled CAD systems. In Proceedings of 2017 25th European Signal Processing Conference. Leeds.

Chiu, M.L., 2002. An organizational view of design communication in design collaboration. *Design studies*, *23*(2), pp.187-210.

Chu, C.C.P., Dani, T.H. and Gadh, R., 1997. Multi-sensory user interface for a virtual-reality-based computer-aided design system. Computer-Aided Design, 29(10), pp.709-725.

Cuomo, D.L. and Sharif, J., 1989. A study of human performance in computer-aided architectural design. International Journal of Human-Computer Interaction, 1(1), pp.69-107.

Dossick, C.S. and Neff, G., 2011. Messy talk and clean technology: communication, problem-solving and collaboration using Building Information Modelling. *The Engineering Project Organization Journal*, *1*(2), pp.83-93.

Eris, O., Martelaro, N. and Badke-Schaub, P., 2014. A comparative analysis of multimodal communication during design sketching in co-located and distributed environments. *Design Studies*, *35*(6), pp.559-592.

Golparvar-Fard, M., Tang, P., Cho, Y.K. and Siddiqui, M.K., 2013. Grand challenges in data and information visualization for the architecture, engineering, construction, and facility management industries. Computing in Civil Engineering (2013), pp.849-856.

Gu, N., Kim, M.J. and Maher, M.L., 2011. Technological advancements in synchronous collaboration: The effect of 3D virtual worlds and tangible user interfaces on architectural design. *Automation in Construction*, *20*(3), pp.270-278.

Jones, J.C., 1983. Continuous design and redesign. *Design Studies*, *4*(1), pp.53-60.

Kim, M.J. and Maher, M.L., 2008. The impact of tangible user interfaces on spatial cognition during collaborative design. *Design Studies*, *29*(3), pp.222-253.

Kou, X.Y. and Tan, S.T., 2008. Design by talking with computers. Computer-Aided Design and Applications, 5(1-4), pp.266-277.

Kou, X.Y., Xue, S.K. and Tan, S.T., 2010. Knowledge-guided inference for voice-enabled CAD. Computer-Aided Design, 42(6), pp.545-557.

Leite, F., Cho, Y., Behzadan, A.H., Lee, S., Choe, S., Fang, Y., Akhavian, R. and Hwang, S., 2016. Visualization, information modeling, and simulation: Grand challenges in the construction industry. *Journal of Computing in Civil Engineering*, *30*(6), p.04016035.

Lloyd, P., McDonnell, J., Reid, F., Luck, R., 2005. DTRS7-Dataset from 7th design thinking research symposium, http: //design.open.ac.uk/dtrs7

Mehrbod, S., Staub-French, S., Mahyar, N. and Tory, M., 2019. Characterizing interactions with BIM tools and artifacts in building design coordination meetings. *Automation in Construction*, *98*, pp.195-213.

Peffers, K., Tuunanen, T., Rothenberger, M.A. and Chatterjee, S., 2007. A design science research methodology for information systems research. *Journal of management information systems*, *24*(3), pp.45-77.

Perry, M. and Sanderson, D., 1998. Coordinating joint design work: the role of communication and artefacts. *Design studies*, *19*(3), pp.273-288.

Turk, M., 2014. Multimodal interaction: A review. Pattern Recognition Letters, 36, pp.189-195.

Xue, S., Kou, X.Y. and Tan, S.T., 2009. Natural voice-enabled CAD: modeling via natural discourse. Computer-Aided Design and Applications, 6(1), pp.125-136.

S. Xue, X. Y. Kou & S. T. Tan (2010) Command Search for CAD System, Computer-Aided Design and Applications, 7:6, 899-910

Minimized communication protocol based on a multi-LOD meta-model for adaptive detailing of BIM models

Ata Zahedi[1], Jimmy Abualdenien[2], Frank Petzold[1], André Borrmann[2]
[1]Chair of Architectural Informatics, Technical University of Munich, Germany
[2]Chair of Computational Modeling and Simulation, Technical University of Munich, Germany
ata.zahedi@tum.de , jimmy.abualdenien@tum.de (Lead author email address)

Abstract. A continuous generation and evaluation of design variants characterize the conceptual architectural design stages. Variants comparison is a crucial process for making design-detailing decisions. Objectifiable criteria, including results of simulations and analysis, used for evaluation and comparison of design variants can legitimize decisions as the design process proceeds. A major challenge today is the management of design information and collaboration among several actors in a building project. Yet, a large portion of the Architecture, Engineering and Construction (AEC) industry deals with conventional methods to exchange design information. The growing use of building information models is promising but even the most recent developments and practices still rely heavily on human-readable protocols and issue management systems. Considering the potential of schematized computer-readable communications to be analyzed and used for future references and case-based reasoning systems. This paper proposes a novel minimized communication protocol that aims to introduce a computer-readable, yet adaptive universal method which works on schematized information exchange requirements (templates) for different use cases. The concept is demonstrated using an example scenario.

1. Introduction

While the building sector alone consumes around 50% of all the materials obtained from the earth, the architecture, construction, and engineering (AEC) industry still fall greatly behind other advanced industries, such as automotive industry in terms of efficiency and productivity (Hegger *et al.*, 2012). The early conceptual architectural design stages comprise a highly creative process that is characterized by a continues endeavor for the creation of variants, evaluating their performance, and a progressive detailing of their components. Decisions taken in the early stages have a significant influence on the performance and costs of the developed solution. Typically, decisions about the building's envelope, shape and façade are made in a short period of time mostly based on the architect's empirical knowledge, generic values, or rules of thumb (Attia *et al.*, 2012). Since the use of analytical tools requires a mostly completed and very detailed model, the application of simulation tools in the early stages, including the assessment of different design options, is not fully attainable.

Today, the use of digital building models for the design, construction, and operation of buildings is already a hot trend in the building industry. Building Information Modelling (BIM) plays an important role in the construction industry resulting in a significant modernization of the working procedures (Borrmann *et al.*, 2018). However, the use of BIM in the early design stages is difficult to master since this method requires more planning effort and leads to highly detailed designs, which are not necessarily apt for these early stages (Azhar, 2011). Nevertheless, certain potential lies in the direct reuse of data held by digital models for diverse analysis and simulation tasks, e.g. the structural analysis or the energy performance simulation (Borrmann *et al.*, 2018). To address this gap, the research project EarlyBIM (FOR2363)[1], funded by the 'Deutsche Forschungsgemeinschaft' (DFG), is dedicated to the development of strategies and methods for adaptively detailing the partially incomplete and vague design

[1] https://for2363.blogs.ruhr-uni-bochum.de

models in order to assess and compare different design options. This paper proposes an upgrade for our adaptive minimized BIM-based protocol for communication between architects and various specialist planners (domain experts) in the design stages (Zahedi and Petzold, 2018b).

2. State of the Art

2.1 The Design Process in the Early Design Stages

As the building design evolves, many aspects of the design desire different domain-experts to evaluate and comment on them. Among the challenges during the early design phases are the incompleteness of input information and immensity of design decisions regarding numerous variations of design parameters. Moreover, since one way to overcome the gap between data requirements of simulation tools and model quality (degree of detailing and abstraction) in conceptual design is to simplify simulation engines and make assumptions, hence the leading results may appear to be exact but then again are uncertain. Studies show that the AEC professionals become so occupied with managing design information, including manually integrating and coordinating domain-specific design information and representations that, in the end, they manage to create only few design alternatives (Flager *et al.*, 2009).

Another way to close the gap is to decide on and fill in the missing data. This pretty much means passing through the conceptual design and reaching into more detailed design. Moreover, the architect (other than having a knowhow) is not and should not be an expert in all aspects of design. The alternative according to the adaptive detailing concept is to suggest and provide proper detailing, corrections and modifications from domain-expert to the architect. Nonetheless, without the architect's approval, no change will be recognized. These suggestions and modifications received from the domain-experts are referred to as ***Feedback*** (Zahedi and Petzold, 2018a).

Exploring different paths and developing several design variants is a fundamental recurrent feature in the creative activity of building design. Every building design task/activity starts with some requirements demanded by the client, followed by some city restrictions and regulations. As the planning activity moves forwards, more suitable and preferred variants are explained in more detail while other drafts are rejected or discarded. Proper management of design variants and avoiding data redundancies has been a topic of many researches. Mattern & König (2018) introduced so called option categories to organize the possibilities that evolve in design process. Furthermore, the authors suggested graph models to manage interdependencies within different design variants. Nevertheless, due to complex situations and restrictions, the authors suggest that the creation of invalid combinations are to be avoided (Mattern and König, 2018). This paper aims to utilize the concept as mentioned above later on in its backend system during the temporal development between options and design variants.

2.2 BIM Collaboration Format (BCF)

There exists strong evidence in the literature that knowledge, especially in complex projects, is a socially attained phenomena. In other words, obtaining appropriate information for better decision-making in early design stages could be achieved by integrating as many domain-experts as early as possible in the design process (Kvan, 2000). Turk (Turk, 2000) argued that based on speech act theory (Searle *et al.*, 1980) the primary goal of communication is requesting and fulfilling commitments (between participants) rather than just exchanging information. In other words, when the structural engineer advises to the architect that the supporting columns are too far apart, besides the information exchange he is trying to commit the architect to fix it.

Taking into account the significance of internal communications in building design, the buildingSMART organization (formerly known as International Alliance for Interoperability - IAI) introduced an open standard called BIM Collaboration Format (BCF) to enable BIM-based workflow and communication between different software tools. Through BCF, actors create topics (e.g. issues, proposals, change requests) that comprise various types of communication information (e.g. type, description, comments, screenshots and viewpoints inside model) addressed in BIM data models. This way only topics and not the entire bulky BIM models will be exchanged between different BIM authoring tools. In 2014, BCF-V2 was equipped with a RESTful API and the possibility to exchange machine-readable topics, using so called BIM-Snippets. Example of a BIM-Snippet could be a partial IFC file (buildingsmart-tech.org, 2019)

There's no doubt that BCF is a well-established and -supported communication protocol that is vendor-neutral and opensource. Almost all commercial BIM software have implemented BCF in their systems too. However, BCF XML is dominantly used for grasping human-readable data regarding issue management. Even though BCF v2.1 is capable of encompassing so-called BIM-Snippets to encapsulate schematized arbitrary data, BCF is still mostly used to address human-readable issue management in AEC and examples of implementing BIM-Snippets are not yet commonly introduced. The authors of this paper, while not arguing the reputation and usefulness of BCF, merely intend to present another approach for BIM-based communication workflow and structured dialogue in early stages of design. A machine-readable structured dialogue between project participant could help the AEC industry with its fragmented nature to learn from various projects and communications. Nevertheless, aiming for computer-readable communications does not necessarily eliminates the need for social interactions. Still, in our protocol, there is room for comments and freestyle text and explanations. However, since the AEC industry is fragmented with many small and medium-size companies, and in most cases, collaborations between companies are limited to the duration of one project, we believe that being able to learn from the partnerships and communications of various building projects might be of great help to improve this less advanced industry.

3. Multi-LOD Meta-Model and Adaptive Requirements Template

A major challenge for using BIM-authoring tools in the early design stages is that despite the insufficient information available in these stages, a BIM model appears precise and certain, which can lead to false assumptions and model evaluation. Additionally, although the Level of Development (LOD) (BIMForum, 2019), is a well-known concept that describes the quality and quantity of the information contained within a BIM model, the currently available specifications are informal, textual descriptions and graphical illustrations.

To define the different component types' LOD requirements in a formal manner, Abualdenien & Borrmann (Abualdenien and Borrmann, 2019) have introduced a multi-LOD meta-model. As illustrated in Figure 1, the meta-model consists of two layers: (1) the *data-model level* to define the component types' LOD requirements, and (2) and the *instance level* to represent the actual building components as well as their relationships. The data-model level facilitates the definition of various component types, such as *wall*, *window*, *and slab*. Each component type is associated with multiple LOD definitions and linked to an Industry Foundation Classes (IFC) (buildingSMART, 2019) class, which makes it possible to use the rich geometry representations and test with real-world building models. An LOD definition includes a geometry representation, *BoundingBox* as an example, as well as geometric and semantic properties, which are assigned to a vagueness type and maximum percentage. The explicit specification of vagueness to the LOD requirements facilitates a model's analysis and supports informed decision-making in the early design stages. The instance level, on the other hand, represents the building components and maps their properties as well as geometry representation to the requirements defined at the data-model level.

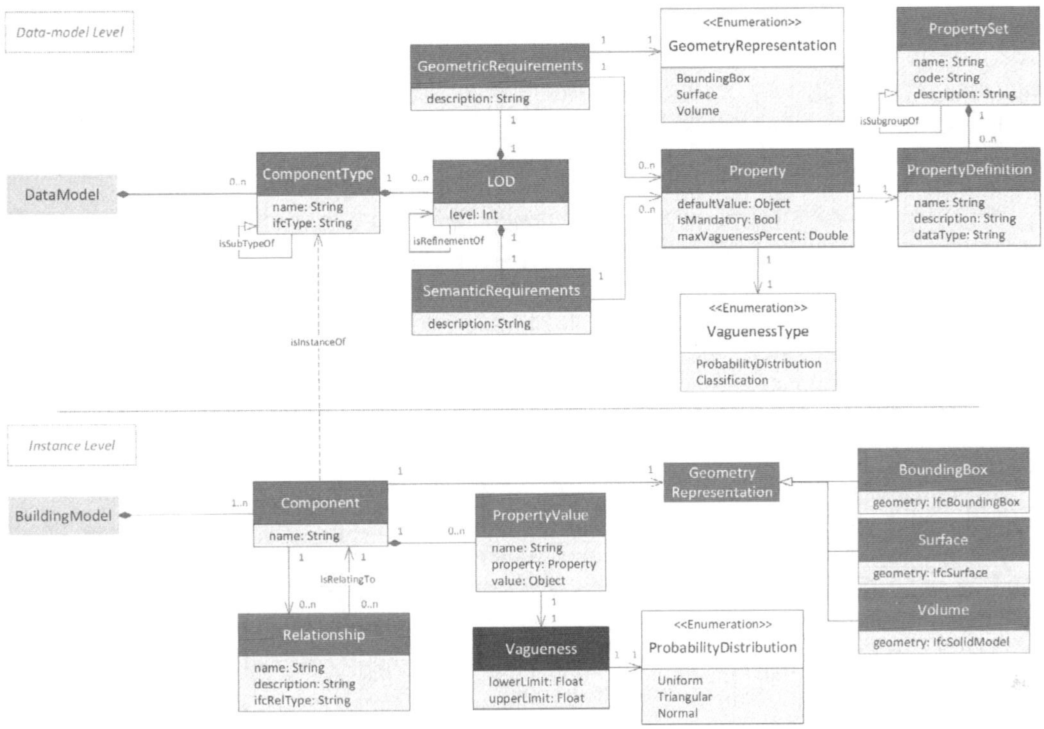

Figure 1: Multi-LOD meta-model (Abualdenien and Borrmann, 2019)

Besides communicating the information vagueness to the project's participants, a major benefit of defining the requirements at the multi-LOD meta-model is to formalize the vague input used by the different analysis tools. Accordingly, the domain experts collaborate to alleviate the impact of the information vagueness. As demonstrated in Figure 2 and 3, the concept is implemented as a web-server with a user interface (UI) providing the possibility for managing and checking exchange requirements between different domains (Abualdenien and Borrmann, 2019). These exchange requirements defined on the multi-LOD meta-model are used as the basis for the *aLODx* templates that are used in communication protocol proposed in this paper (please refer to Section 4). Accordingly, depending on the analysis type and the design stage, which contains diverse levels of development for the different component types, every domain-expert specifies a list of building components in addition to a set of properties.

4. Adaptive Minimized Communication Protocol Based on BIM

In a general sense, any request for analysis during early design stages could yield to three possible outcomes as following:

1. The design model is extremely immature and therefore not capable of analysis.

2. Some geometrical details or semantical information which are expected to be present in the model are missing. In this case, the analysis might be performed with simplification of simulation tools (or making assumptions regarding the missing input data) or the domain-expert reports the missing information to the architect as this information is required to carry on with the analysis.
3. The analysis could be performed, and the results will be presented to the architect.

Making design decisions requires knowledge and experience in various domains; hence, the architect confronts multiple challenges while overcoming the lack of information by making estimations. Therefore, the early domain-experts involvement facilitates evaluating the consequences of the design decisions as well as provides the required assistance by providing design suggestions/options.

This paper differentiates design *variants* and *options*. The term variants are given to the design models developed by the architect, whereas options represent the feedback and suggestions provided by the different experts. The options are to be used (accepted or rejected) by the architect as a source of inspiration, suggestion, or a possible solution provided by a domain-expert. It is important to note that throughout the design process, the architect is the team leader and the only responsible for creating and modifying the design model/variants. At the same time, the architect is the team member who is liable for updating the design state and approving the final decisions.

To support communication among the project participants in a means of structured dialogue, the authors propose establishing a Common Data Environment (CDE). Besides formalizing the communication, the proposed approach makes it possible to share bulk product and model data, as well as facilitating proposing design options to the architect for further detailing the available design variants. The proposed design options, so-called "feedback", which are provided by the domain-expert, consist of the following responses:

- report on the missing details in the design model
- possible options that could serve to fulfill the shortcomings in the design model
- the results of analysis or simulations when each of those options is selected

The proposed communication protocol focuses on staying as minimized and lite as possible, which means avoiding to send back and forth any actual digital BIM files. Even partial models (as options) will rest on the CDE, and the protocol will only inhale their links and globally unified IDs (*GUID*). In the case of updating/suggesting attributes and properties for already existing building components in the digital design model, these alphanumerical values will be included in the messages. But in the case of creating/suggesting new building components/objects, they will be only referred/linked to inside the messages.

The proposed communication system is consisting of two parts. One part would be an issue tracking system or so-called ticketing system. Via this part, just like any other ticketing system, requests and responses will be managed, and their progress will be controlled. Priorities can be set for each ticket, and their responsive person can also be traced back. Various tags can be assigned to tickets which makes the coordination and communication more seamless and transparently traceable. The other part would serve and inhale the essence of the feedback provided by various consultants and domain experts. In the next section, the method/function called "feedback" will be defined.

4.1 Feedback Function

This universal method based on its use case will receive different arguments. This adaptive feedback function along with its' arguments are explained one by one as follows:

Feedback (actionType, optionGroupID, GUID, aLODx, objectID, propertyID, value, rating)

actionType: The first argument is called *actionType*. It represents the use case of the feedback function. Possible *actionTypes* are *missingObject, missingObjectProperty, createNewObject, deleteObject, updateObjectProperty*. *missingObject* is to report for some building components that are missing overall (e.g., all the openings are missing). *missingObjectProperty* refers to an attribute required for a building component that is unfilled. *createNewObject* refers to a newly created building component (probably as part of an option) by the domain-expert which will have a GUID that is unique and will be used to refer later on in the protocol. *deleteObject* refers to an unnecessary building component to be deleted by the architect. *updateObjectProperty* is used to suggest a value to fill in missing property.

optionGroupID: This argument is used to group multiple suggestions. The proposed details could either be individually suggested, or they could be part of a package all sharing the same *optionGroupID*. To preserve the consistency and effectiveness of the suggested option, packaged suggestions should be treated (accepted or rejected) as a whole and not individually.

GUID: This argument refers to the Globally Unique ID of a particular building component inside a given BIM model on the CDE. In case the *actionType* in the feedback function is *missingObject*, then this argument (*GUID*) would be the unique id of the building component that contains the missing objects. Like with the example of all the openings being absent, then this GUID could be the Building's GUID. But when the *actionType* is *createNewObject* then this argument will be the GUID of the temporarily newly created object that is suggested to the architect by the domain-expert. With the *missingObjectProperty* and *updateObjectProperty* as *actionType*, then this argument is the *GUID* of the building component that accordingly has a missing property, or a new value is suggested for its absent property. Finally, when the *actionType* is *deleteObject* then this argument is the GUID of the building component, which is recommended for deletion by domain-expert.

aLODx, objectID, propertyID: In each design stage, the individual demand detailed requirements when exchanging building models. The presence of these requirements is crucial to perform model analysis, such as Life Cycle Assessment (LCA) and Structural Analysis. To support this kind of information exchange, the defined components and their LOD requirement at the multi-LOD meta-model (explained in Section 3), which are intended for a particular analysis, are called aLODx. This way, the requirements for a specific analysis are formulized. Inside the proposed concept, an aLODx serves as an adaptive lookup table (using ObejctID & PropertyID) that both the architect and the domain expert will refer to when they are communicating with each other. Accordingly, they can both be sure about what type of building a component (object) and what sort of attribute (property) they are talking about.

The requirements demonstrated in Figure 2 represent an example of the scheme (aLODx) of the properties required from the structural analysis specialists in the authors' research group. Using this screen, the domain-experts are capable of defining the property sets that are expected to be present in the exchanged model to perform their analysis. For each of the defined the properties, it is possible to specify the property's details as well as assigning a corresponding set of disciplines, including structural analysis (SA), operational energy (OE), and embodied energy (EE).

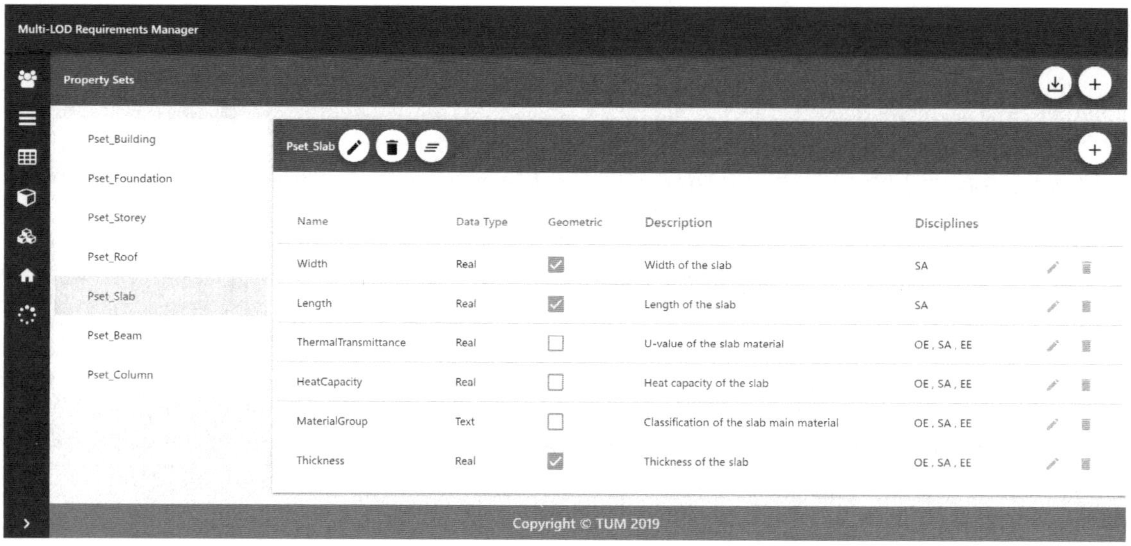

Figure 2: Prototype: property sets screen (Abualdenien and Borrmann, 2019)

After defining the exchange requirements, the corresponding component types are defined and mapped to their properties. Figure 3 illustrates the *FloorSlab* component type's details screen. The *General* tab defines the component name, IfcType, and description. Whereas the second tab *Requirements* facilitates the association of properties at every LOD, including a specification of the vagueness type and percentage.

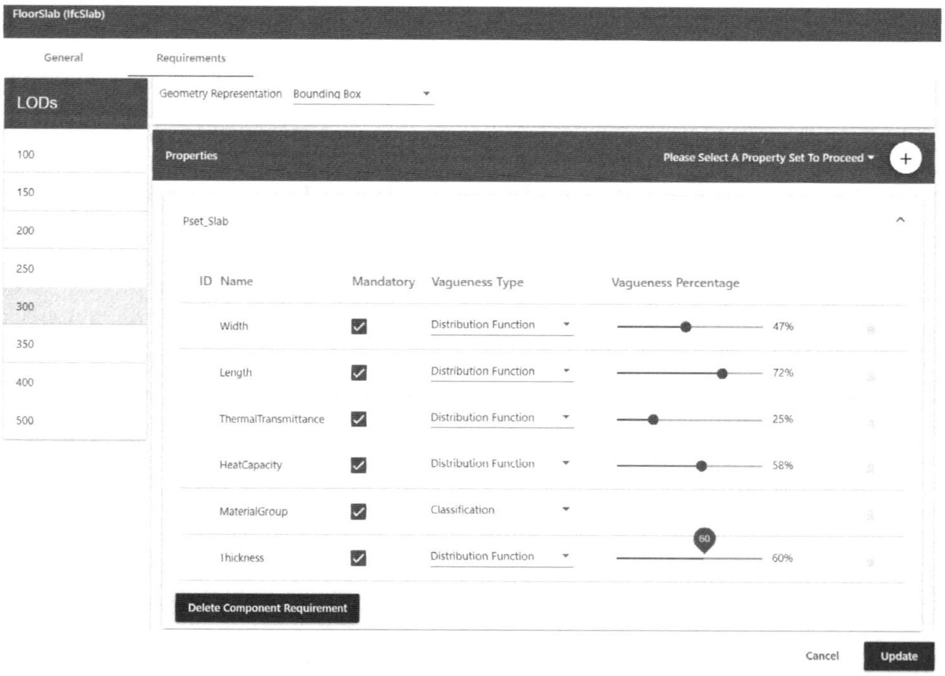

Figure 3: Prototype: component type details screen (Abualdenien and Borrmann, 2019)

value: This argument, if present depending on the actionType, will inhale the suggested values in the form of different options for the architect. Through the demonstrative example in the next section, the use of this argument will be more clarified.

rating: This new argument represents the normalized evaluation or rating/grade of the suggested option according to its performance with respect to the (based on the result of the) requested analysis. For example, this rating could be a number between 1 to 5, while 5 being the best.

5. Case Study: Structural Analysis in the Early Design Stages

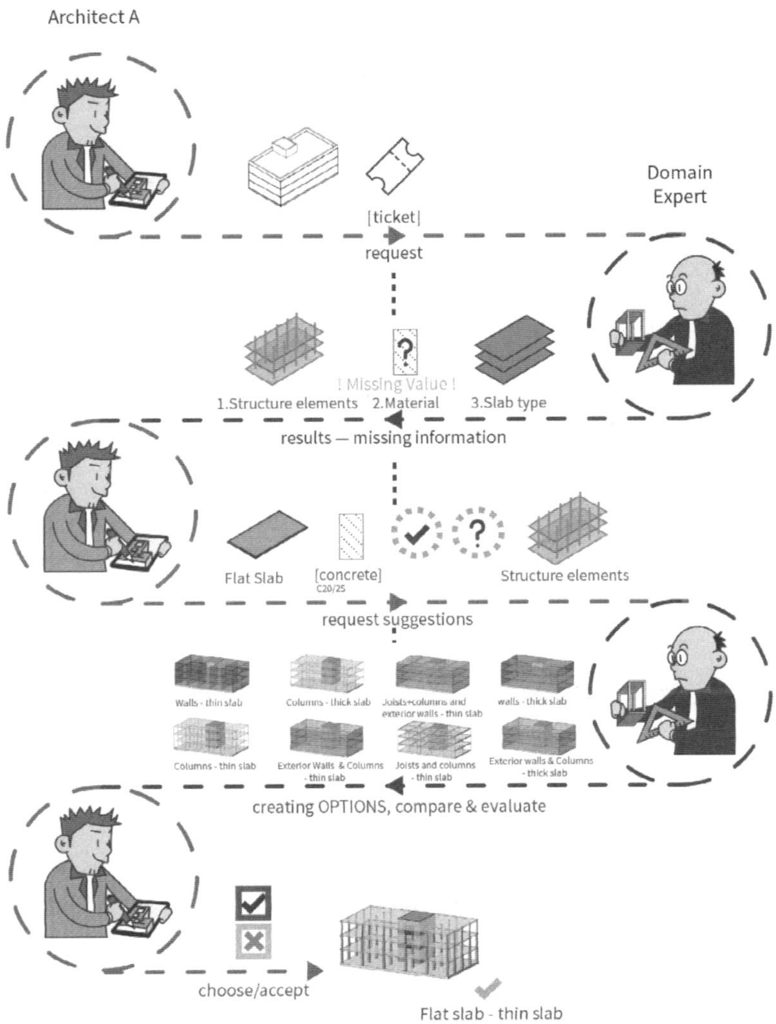

Figure 4: Demonstrative example using Structural analysis

Figure 4 demonstrates an example of the communication in case of structural analysis. Upon requesting for analysis, a ticket will be issued which clarifies the scope of analysis. The domain-expert, as the recipient of this ticket (following the link to the CDE) checks the model against the requirements and sends the architect a feedback regarding the missing details. In this simplified example slab type, main material group and structural elements are missing. The architect decides for flat slab and concrete but asks the structural engineer in return to give him options regarding the formation and possible types of structural elements. The structural engineer will provide three option, one with the mainly interior walls, one with exterior walls as load-bearing with columns and bars (joists), and the other with mainly columns and bars.

Furthermore, the structural engineer also provides the options with ratings according to their structural performance. At the same time, the architect may have also other criteria in mind for making design decisions, such as spatial layout flexibility or preferred window-to-wall ratio & etc. This makes the point again clear that he is the only responsible team leader to make design decisions.

With regard to our minimized communication protocol, the feedback function will be used in two stages and in multiple forms. At first it is used to report the missing details, namely in this example *missingObjectProperty* and *missingObject* as *actionType* are used in multiple instances. In the next round as the structural expert proposes options, *createNewObject* is used and various components (objects) are being created (temporarily) as part of a packaged option. All new objects within an option will share the same *optionGroupID*, but each will be referred to by their unique ID (*GUID*). Figure 5 shows the demonstration of the feedback function in the case of creating new columns.

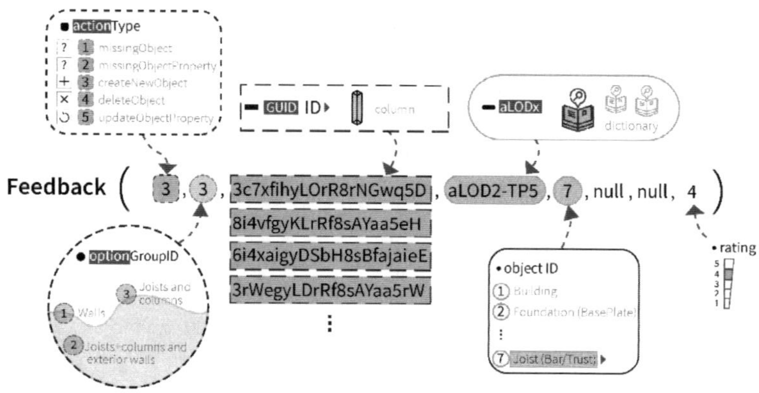

Figure 5: Feedback function explained

6. Conclusions

This paper introduced a BIM-based minimized communication protocol that is based on a meta-model approach for defining exchange requirements for the different component types at multiple LODs. The protocol enhances the collaboration and transparency of communication during the important early phases of design. This BIM-based communication protocol is built on schematized information requirements that are adaptively defined by domain-experts for the different analysis types and building project types using the multi-LOD meta-model. The protocol's aim is to store the history of these communications and use this accumulated data for supporting decision making in future use cases. By means of this minimized protocol, computer-readable communications take place, which can be filtered and analyzed for future use cases. Using this protocol, all communications, variant evaluations, and decision-making will be documented and traceable afterward for further use cases.

7. Acknowledgments

We gratefully acknowledge the support of German Research Foundation (DFG) for funding the project under grant FOR 2363.

8. Reference list

Abualdenien, J. and Borrmann, A. (2019) 'A meta-model approach for formal specification and consistent management of multi-LOD building models', *Advanced Engineering Informatics*, pp. 20–42.

Attia, S. *et al.* (2012) 'Simulation-based decision support tool for early stages of zero-energy building design', *Energy and Buildings*, 49, pp. 2–15.

Azhar, S. (2011) 'Building information modeling (BIM): Trends, benefits, risks, and challenges for the AEC industry', *Leadership and management in engineering*, 11(3), pp. 241–252.

BIMForum (2019) *LOD | BIMForum: Level of Development Specification*. Available at: https://bimforum.org/lod/ (Accessed: 3 April 2019).

Borrmann, A. *et al.* (2018) 'Building Information Modeling: Why? What? How?' in *Building Information Modeling:* Springer, pp. 1–24.

buildingSMART (2019) *IFC Introduction - buildingSMART,* 3 April. Available at: https://www.buildingsmart.org/about/what-is-openbim/ifc-introduction/ (Accessed: 3 April 2019).

buildingSMART (2019) *Open BIM Collaboration Format (BCF) intro*. Available at: http://www.buildingsmart-tech.org/specifications/bcf-releases (Accessed: 3 April 2019).

Flager, F. *et al.* (2009) 'Multidisciplinary process integration and design optimization of a classroom building', *Journal of Information Technology in Construction*, 14(14), pp. 595–612.

Hegger, M. *et al.* (2012) *Energy manual: sustainable architecture*: Walter de Gruyter.

Kvan, T. (2000) 'Collaborative design: what is it?' *Automation in Construction*, 9(4), pp. 409–415.

Mattern, H. and König, M. (2018) 'BIM-based modeling and management of design options at early planning phases', *Advanced Engineering Informatics*, 38, pp. 316–329.

Searle, J.R. *et al.* (1980) *Speech act theory and pragmatics*. (10): Springer.

Turk, Z. (2000) 'Communication workflow approach to CIC', in *Computing in Civil and Building Engineering (2000)*, pp. 1094–1101.

Zahedi, A. and Petzold, F. (2018a) 'Seamless integration of simulation and analysis in early design phases', in *Proceedings of the 6th IALCCE Conference*, pp. 2007–2015.

Zahedi, A. and Petzold, F. (2018b) 'Utilization of Simulation Tools in Early Design Phases Through Adaptive Detailing Strategies', in *Proceedings of the 23rd CAADRIA, Beijing, China, 17-19 May 2018*, pp. 11–20.

Influence of building parameters on thermal mass modification with phase-change materials: numerical study based on design of experiments

Gilles Baudoin, Geoffrey van Moeseke
Université catholique de Louvain (UCLouvain), Belgium
gilles.baudoin@uclouvain.be

Abstract. Phase-change materials (PCM) offer new opportunities to modify thermal mass. The energy savings due to thermal mass modification, with or without PCM, may significantly vary between the studies reported in the literature. This has shown the interest to systematically study the effect of enhanced thermal mass on different buildings. This study investigates the influence of eight building parameters on the benefits of using three different PCM-panels, by simulating a test-cell based on an office building in a temperate climate. Our results showed that the building parameters strongly influenced the energy savings through use of PCM. The main building parameters influencing the potential benefits were the initial thermal mass and the parameters related to solar heat gain.

1. Introduction

Recently, researchers have shown an increased interest in phase-change materials (PCM) to modify thermal mass in the building sector (see the review articles of Soares et al. (2013) and Kalnæs et al. (2015)). PCM offer indeed an opportunity to increase the thermal mass effect on a given temperature range.

The potential benefits of PCM-enhanced building components can be affected by their properties, by the climate and by the building under investigation. Comparisons between studies have not always been straightforward due to different uses of key performance indicators (KPI), the parameters concerning thermal mass modification and the building under study (Verbeke et al. (2018) and Saffari et al. (2017)). More specifically, for the use of PCM in Cfb climates, Soares et al. (2014) obtained annual energy savings for cooling and heating needs of about 16 kWh/m^2 and Alam et al. (2014) 20 kWh/m^2. Saffari et al. (2017), considering the HVAC system efficiency of a typical office building and with less PCM quantity, achieved savings of less than 1 kWh/m^2. In a previous study (Baudoin et al., 2018), we also obtained relatively low gains of about 2 kWh/m^2. Could the different buildings under investigation explain the difference of energy savings? To the best of our knowledge, the influence of building parameters on the potential benefits of thermal mass modification with PCM has never been systematically studied.

This study aims to quantify the effect of the building parameters on the potential benefits of modifying thermal mass with PCM. Annual cooling and heating energy needs were used as KPI for the Belgian climate. Starting from a previous study (Baudoin et al., 2018), the effect of eight building parameters were tested on the use of three different PCM-panels. PCM_{cool} was a panel specifically designed to minimise cooling energy needs, PCM_{heat} to minimise heating energy needs and PCM_{tot} was a non-specific one. The eight building parameters investigated were wall insulation (WI), window insulation (WDI), solar heat gain coefficient (SHGC), heat recovery percentage (HR), free-cooling rate (AFR), air leakage (ALE), orientation (OR) and initial thermal mass (TM).

The results of this study showed that the building parameters strongly influenced the energy savings resulting of PCM use. For the PCM-panel based on PCM_{tot}, the energy savings for cooling varied from zero to 16.40 kWh/m^2. The energy savings for heating varied from a negative effect of -0.41 to a positive effect of 3.96 kWh/m^2. The main building parameters influencing the potential benefits were the initial thermal mass (TM) and the parameters linked to solar heat gain, i.e. the solar heat gain coefficient (SHGC) and the orientation (OR). Interestingly, higher energy savings could be achieved using PCM_{tot} instead of PCM_{cool} or PCM_{heat}. This suggested that the optimum combination of PCM parameters to minimise the energy needs for cooling or heating would depend on the studied parameters of the building.

This study gave new insight to understand the discrepancies between authors. Knowing the effect of the building parameters on the potential benefits also allowed (i) to identify the building for which it is the most beneficial to modify thermal mass and (ii) to identify the boundaries of the potential benefits of modifying thermal mass with PCM.

2. Method

Annual dynamic building simulations were done for a simplified test-cell based on an office building, using EnergyPlus 8.8.0. For 50 combinations of building parameters, a case with and without phase-change material properties were compared to obtain the potential gains of using PCM on energy needs for cooling ΔE_{cool} and heating ΔE_{heat}. The 50 combinations of building system parameters were selected based on design of experiments and one metamodel was constructed for ΔE_{cool} and one for ΔE_{heat}. The metamodel linked the energy savings with the eight building parameters in the form of a second order polynomial function. Three different PCM-panels were tested: PCM_{cool}, a panel specifically designed to minimise cooling energy needs, PCM_{heat}, to minimise heating energy needs and PCM_{tot}, a non-specific one. For pre- and post-processing with EnergyPlus, python jupyter notebook was used with the eppy package (Figure 1). The JMP Pro 14.1.0 software was used as support for the design of experiment part and to build the metamodel.

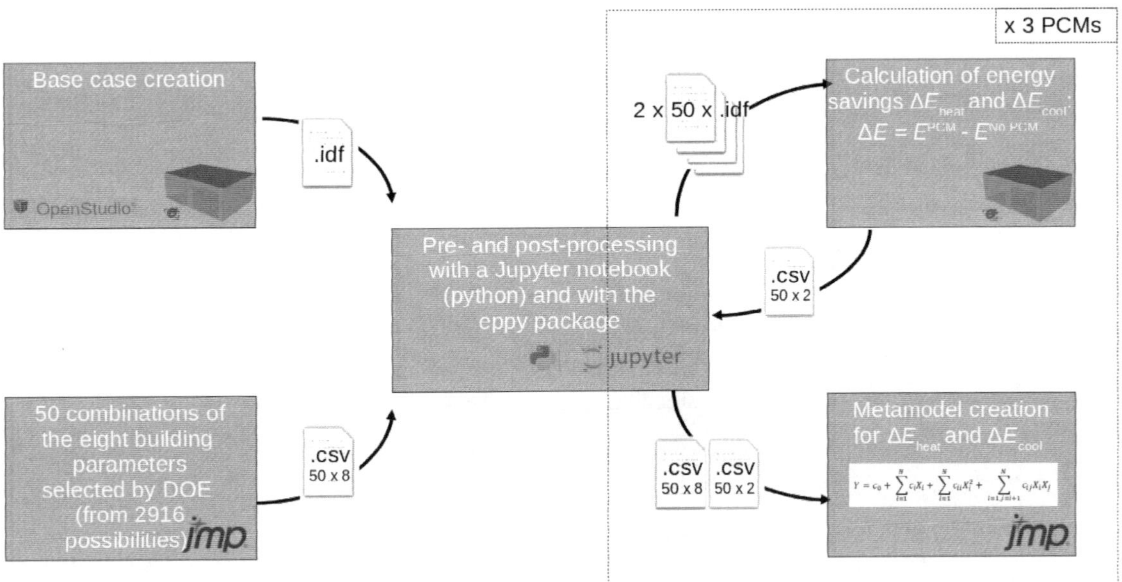

Figure 1: Computational workflow.

2.1 Test-cell

The test-cell dimensions were based on the model specified in ASHRAE (2007) 140 standard (Figure 2.a), as previously used in similar studies. Annual cooling and heating energy needs E_{cool} and E_{heat} were used as KPI for the Belgian climate. The surface with the windows had outdoor boundary condition and the other surfaces were defined as internal surfaces with an adiabatic boundary condition. The surface compositions are given in Table 1, in which two compositions are given for the internal floor/ceiling: one for the *lightweight* case and one for the *heavyweight*. The selection of one composition was based on the building parameter TM. More details about envelope composition and test-cell loads can be found in the appendix of Baudoin et al. (2018).

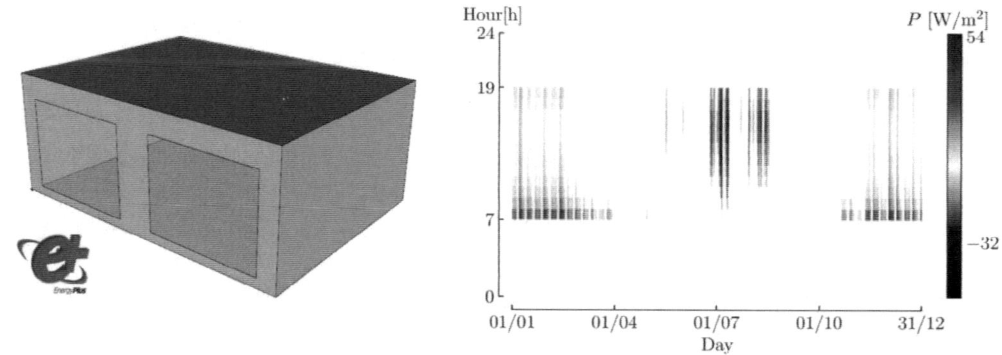

Figure 2: (a) Test-cell based on ASHRAE Standard 140. (b) Hourly energy needs for the base case with the ideal HVAC system.

Heat recovery system, diurnal and nocturnal free cooling were implemented in a simplified way using the Ideal-LoadsAirSystem object in EnergyPlus. The free cooling was based on difference in air-dry bulb temperature and the outside airflow was allowed to increase up to the number of air changes per hour defined by the building parameter AFR. For night cooling, the temperature was allowed to decrease up to 20.0°C.

Table 1: Test-cell envelope composition. The thickness of the Fiberglass quilts-1 varied between the simulations. The internal floor/ceiling was either the heavy one or the light one depending on the thermal mass parameter.

		Thickness [m]	λ [W/mK]	Density [kg/m^3]	Specific heat [kJ/kgK]
Internal floor/ceiling (heavy)	Carpet	0.008	0.06	200	1300
	Cement screed	0.06	0.93	1900	1000
	Reinforced concrete	0.04	1.7	2400	1000
	Precast concrete slab	0.16	1.23	1870	1000
	Plaster	0.01	0.52	1300	1000
Internal floor/ceiling (light)	Wooden floor	0.014	0.13	525.0	1880.0
	OSB	0.015	0.15	600.0	1880.0
	Wood and mineral wool	0.230	0.05	125.0	1048.0
	Plaster 2	0.012	0.25	800.0	840.0
Internal wall	Plasterboard	0.012	0.35	900	1000
	Mineral wool	0.06	0.05	35	1030
	Plasterboard	0.012	0.35	900	1000
External wall	Wood siding-1	0.009	0.14	530	900
	Fiberglass quilt-1	0.16	0.04	12	840
	Plasterboard-1	0.012	0.16	950	840

The set point temperature T_{th} was based on the operative temperature T_{op} and set to 20.0 °C for heating and 26.0 °C for cooling. The weather data used came from the International Weather for Energy Calculation (IWEC) data file, which is a typical weather file for building energy simulation for Uccle in Belgium.

For the set of parameters corresponding to the base case studied in Baudoin et al. (2018), the annual heating energy need was 5.11 kWh/m^2 and the annual cooling energy need was 3.35 kWh/m^2. For this base case, the distribution of power loads varied between heating and cooling (Figure 2.b). By using PCM_{heat}, the saving in term of E_{heat} was 1.13 kWh/m^2 and by using PCM_{cool}, the saving in term of E_{cool} was 1.45 kWh/m^2.

2.2 PCM simulation

A 2 cm thick PCM-panel with an exchange surface of 1 m^2 /m$^2_{floor}$ was added as an internal mass object in the test-cell. This approach allowed to consider the addition of PCM properties regardless of its position in the test-cell. The PCM-panel was directly in contact with the inside environment. For the base case, no phase-change properties were used for this panel. It allowed to separate the sensible contribution of the panel from its latent contribution on the energy savings.

The properties of the PCM-panel were based on DuPont Energain PCM. This product comes as an aluminium-laminated panel, containing a copolymer and paraffin wax compound. The latent heat is 110 kJ/kg, the density 855 kg/m^3 and the specific heat 2500 J/kgK. In this study, the thermal conductivity value was assumed not to vary between the solid and liquid phase, and was set to 0.16 W/mK.

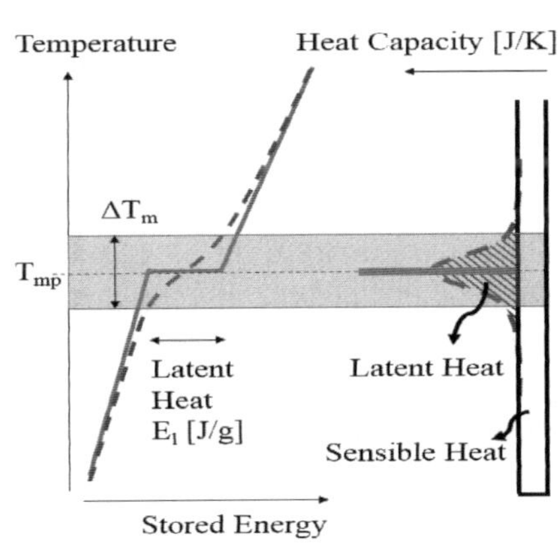

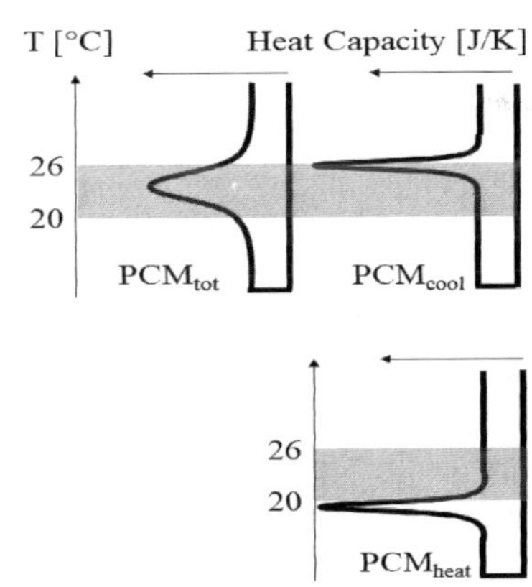

Figure 3: (a) PCM properties in the Enthalpy/Temperature curve and the associated heat capacity. Ideal behaviour (green) and quasi-ideal behaviour (red dotted line). (b) Conceptual comparison of the three PCM used in this study: PCM_{tot}, PCM_{cool} and PCM_{heat}.

The PCM behaviour was considered as quasi-ideal, i.e. no hysteresis, nor sub-cooling effects were included. The main properties of a quasi-ideal PCM are the melting-peak temperature T_{mp}, the melting temperature range ΔT_m and the latent heat E_l (Figure 3.a). An ideal solid-liquid PCM would melt and solidify at T_{mp} and the latent heat would be stored and released at this temperature. The three different PCM studied only differed in their melting-peak temperature T_{mp} and their melting temperature range ΔT_m (Figure 3.b). PCM_{cool} was a panel designed to minimise cooling energy needs, PCM_{heat}, to minimise heating energy needs and PCM_{tot} was a non-specific one. The sensible heat of the PCM-panel was about 21 kJ/Km^2 and the additional thermal energy storage due to the PCM latent heat was about 940 kJ/m^2 (261 Wh/m^2).

2.3 Experimental design

Design of experiments was used to select the various combinations of building parameters (Table 2). The following parameters were investigated as continuous variable: wall insulation (WI), window insulation (WDI), solar heat gain coefficient (SHGC), heat recovery percentage (HR), free-cooling rate (AFR) and air leakage (ALE). The values of the parameters were directly changed in the EnergyPlus file by using the eppy python package in a python jupyter notebook. For the wall insulation, the thickness of the insulation layer was changed to match the given wall insulation. The two following parameters were investigated as categorical variable with two levels: the orientation (OR) and the thermal mass (TM). The orientation could be either *south* or *north* and the thermal mass was characterised as *heavy* or *light*. The heavy case had a ceiling/floor described as heavy in Table 1, and the light case had the light ceiling/floor.

Table 2: List of parameters and their simulated value boundaries: low and high values with a comparison of a set of value from a previous case study.

Parameter	Symbol	Low value	High value	Case study value
Wall insulation (W/m2K)	WI	0.15	2.00	0.25
Window insulation (W/m2K)	WDI	0.80	3.00	1.50
Solar heat gain coefficient	SHGC	0.20	0.70	0.62
Heat recovery percentage (%)	HR	0	100	79
Free-cooling rate (ACH)	AFR	0	4	2
Air leakage rate (ACH)	ALE	0.03	0.50	0.03
Orientation	OR	north	south	north
Thermal mass	TM	heavy	light	heavy

The JMP Pro 14.1.0 software was used as support for the design of experiment part and to build the metamodel. Based on a D-optimal criterion, 50 combinations of building system parameters were selected with a custom design. Compared to classical design, the custom design allowed to avoid specific features related to no deterministic experiences. For example, a classical design would produce a number of repetition of the same set of building parameters. The D-optimal criterion allowed to get the best approximation of the coefficients of the building parameters in the metamodel.

For these 50 combinations of building system parameters, a case with and without phase-change material properties were compared to assess the influence of using PCM on energy needs for cooling ΔE_{cool} and heating ΔE_{heat}. Based on these data, a metamodel was built to link the energy savings with the eight building parameters in the form of a second order polynomial function:

$$Y = c_0 + \sum_{i=1}^{N} c_i X_i + \sum_{i=1}^{N} c_{ii} X_i^2 + \sum_{i=1,j=i+1}^{N} c_{ij} X_i X_j$$

where Y represents the output value (ΔE_{cool} or ΔE_{heat}) and X represents the N building parameters considered. The interaction term X_iX_j of the two categorical variables OR*TM was not considered. The c's are the coefficients of terms in the polynomial function.

3. Results and discussion

3.1 PCM_{tot} case

For the 50 combinations of building system parameters, the values of ΔE_{cool} and ΔE_{heat} were calculated for the PCM-panel based on PCM_{tot}. Depending on the set of building system parameters, the energy savings for cooling varied from zero up to 16.40 kWh/m^2. The energy savings for heating varied from a negative effect of -0.41 to a positive effect of 3.96 kWh/m^2.

These results confirmed that the potential benefits which could be achieved were generally higher for cooling than for heating. In our previous study, the potential energy needs for heating and cooling were of the same order of magnitude by using PCM_{heat} 1.13 kWh/m^2 and PCM_{cool} 1.45 kWh/m^2. It is worth noting that the same order of magnitudes than Soares et al. (2014) and Alam et al. (2014) could be achieved only by changing the building parameters, with the same PCM-panel properties and the same weather data file.

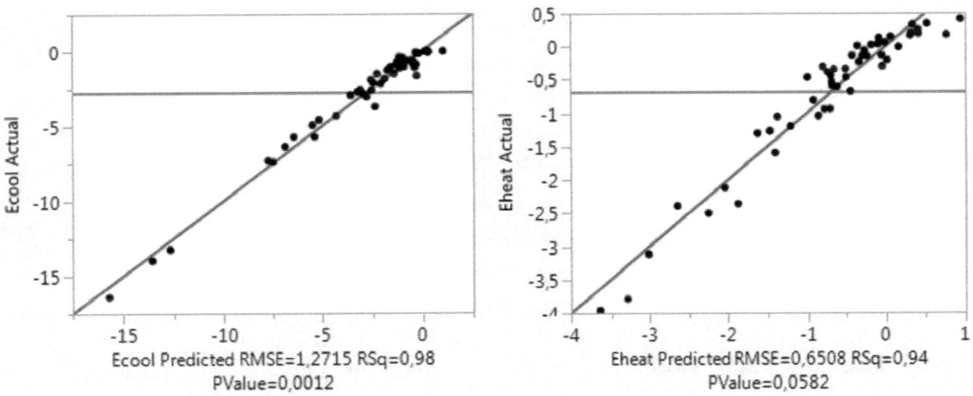

Figure 4: Comparison of the calculated values with EnergyPlus and the predicted values with the metamodel for ΔE_{cool} (left) and ΔE_{heat} (right). The blue line corresponds to the mean.

The calculated values were compared to the predicted values by the metamodel (Figure 4). The R^2 was of 0.98 for the function of ΔE_{cool} and 0.94 for the function of ΔE_{heat}. The solar heat gain coefficient (SHGC), the thermal mass (TM) and the orientation (OR) played a major role on the potential benefits of using PCM on energy needs (Figure 5). The table shows the minimum p-value among the p-values for that effect on ΔE_{cool} and ΔE_{heat}. The p-value was linked to the effect test, which tested the null hypothesis that the coefficient c associated to the effect is zero. The associated coefficients for the metamodel for ΔE_{heat} were estimated to – 1.27 for TM (heavy to light case), -0.88 for OR (north to south case) and -1.70 for SHGC. For the ΔE_{cool} metamodel, the associated coefficient were -3.01 for TM (heavy to light case), -2.77 for OR (north to south case) and -7,63 for SHGC.

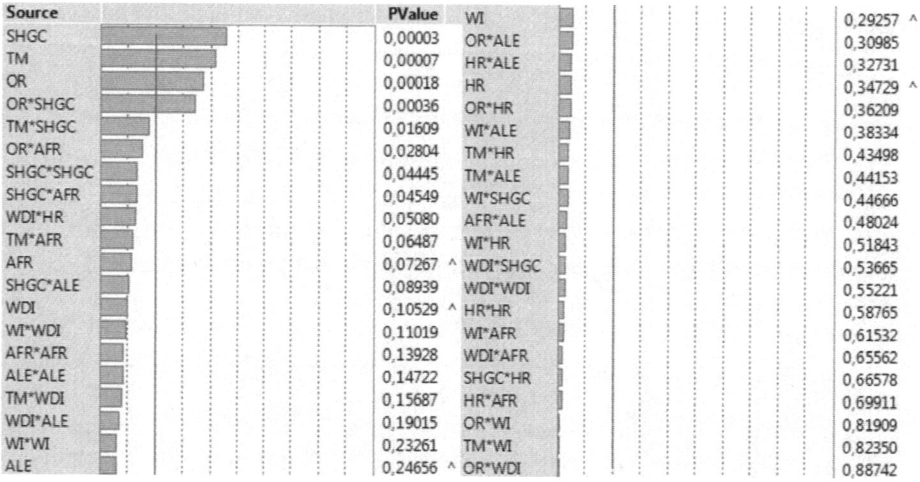

Figure 5: Effect tests of the coefficients associated with the main and second order effect of the eight building parameters for the PCM_{tot} case.

3.2 PCM_{cool} and PCM_{heat} cases

The same sets of calculation were conducted for the PCM-panel with PCM_{cool} and PCM_{heat}. Interestingly, higher savings of energy needs could be achieved using PCM_{tot} instead of PCM_{cool} (11.89 kWh/m^2 of achievable savings for ΔE_{cool}) or PCM_{heat} (3.61 kWh/m^2 of achievable savings for ΔE_{heat}). In addition to the parameters related to solar gains and the thermal mass, the heat recovery percentage (HR) had a role to play in the case of PCM_{heat} (Figure 6). The associated coefficient was -1.08. This means that, assuming no interactions and no second order effect, ΔE_{heat} would unexpectedly increase by -1.08 from a case without heat recovery (0%) to a case with an ideal heat recovery system (100%).

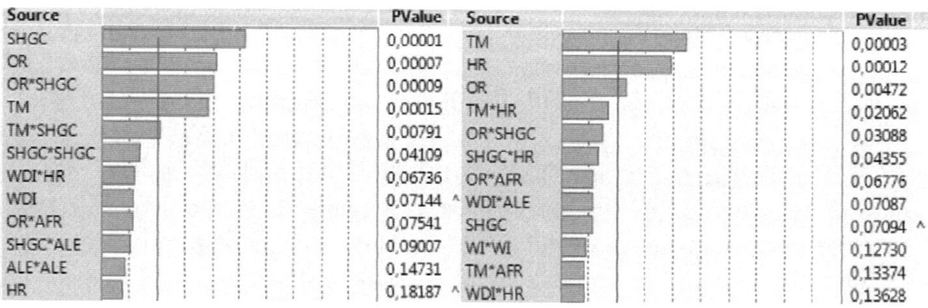

Figure 6: Effect tests of the coefficients associated with the main and second order effect of the eight building parameters for the PCM_{cool} case on ΔE_{cool} (left) and for the PCM_{heat} case on ΔE_{heat} (right).

3.3 Limitations of the model

The two categorical variables seemed to have a major influence on the energy needs. However, due to their categorical properties and the two levels studied, the influence of these parameters could not be analysed in details (Figure 7). It would be interesting to know intermediate values between the two extremes ones. For the thermal mass, the categorical variable could be turned into a continuous one. This could be done by considering the energy capacity of the thermal mass and the speed of (un)loading.

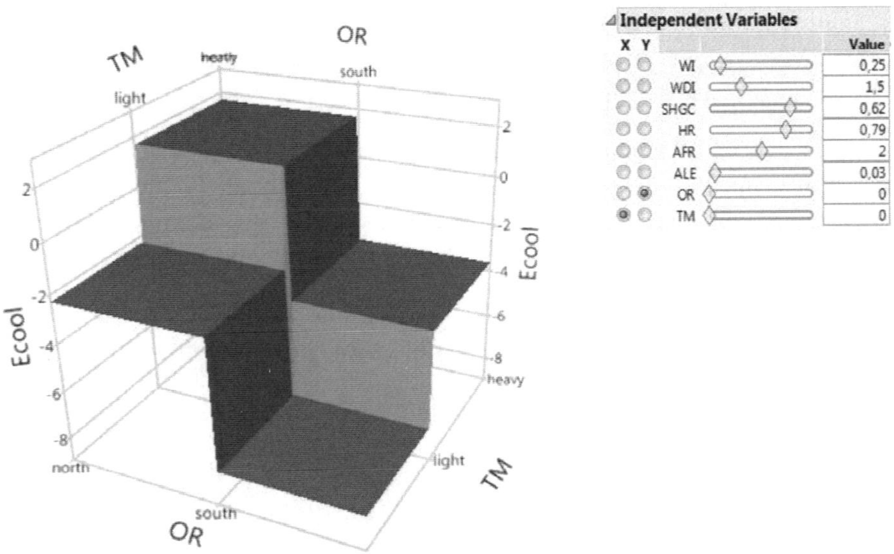

Figure 7: Influence of the two categorical variables on ΔE_{cool} for a given set of the six continuous variables.

The model had limitations for accurate predictions. For example, considering PCM_{heat} with the same set of parameter as in our previous study, a saving in term of ΔE_{heat} of 0.73 kWh/m^2 was calculated with the metamodel instead of 1.13 kWh/m^2. The experimental design was chosen with a D-optimal criterion, which optimises the approximation of the coefficients of the building parameters, instead of an I-optimal criterion, which optimises the predictions of the metamodel. Further studies should also consider using other metamodels than the polynomial one (Van Gelder et al., 2014)) and using other experimental designs, more appropriated to computer experiments such as the space-filling design (Simpson et al., 2001).

Some parameters seemed to have no or small effects compared to what could have been expected. In a previous study, but with another key performance indicator, Evola et al. (2013) showed that the free-cooling rate (AFR) has a positive influence on the potential benefits for cooling. In our model, AFR determined the maximum rate for diurnal free cooling and nocturnal free cooling. For further investigations, the diurnal and nocturnal free cooling could be studied separately. In addition, a non-linear effect of the free-cooling rate was observed to have a potential negative influence. It could be explained by the low cooling energy with high AFR, which could affect the validity of the built metamodel.

4. Conclusion

This study investigated the influence of eight building parameters on the energy needs savings for cooling and heating. The case study was a test-cell based on an office building in the Belgian climate. The three main results of this study were:

1. The building parameters strongly influenced the energy savings due to PCM use. For the PCM-panel based on PCM_{tot}, the energy savings for cooling varied from zero up to 16.40 kWh/m2.
2. The achievable savings could be higher for cooling than for heating. The energy savings for heating varied from a negative effect of -0.41 to a positive effect of 3.96 kWh/m2.

3. The main building parameters influencing the potential benefits were the initial thermal mass (TM) and the parameters linked to solar heat gain, i.e. the solar heat gain coefficient (SHGC) and the orientation (OR).

Interestingly, it was also observed that higher savings of energy needs could be achieved with PCM_{tot} instead of using PCM_{cool} or PCM_{heat}. This suggested that the optimum combination of PCM parameters to minimise the energy needs for cooling or heating would depend on the studied parameters of the building.

These results gave new insight (i) to identify the building for which it is the most beneficial to modify thermal mass and (ii) to identify the boundaries of the potential benefits of modifying thermal mass with PCM.

The findings presented here provide a starting point for further examination of the influence of building parameters on thermal mass modification with PCM. The further studies could investigate in more details the influence of the initial thermal mass by changing it from a categorical variable to a continuous one. In addition to the energy capacity of the thermal mass, the loading and unloading speed could also be taken into consideration. This could be done by considering the exchange surface with the internal environment. The impact of the free-cooling rate (AFR) could also be studied in more details. In this study, the same parameter defined the maximum rate for diurnal and nocturnal free cooling. The two effects could be studied separately. Other building parameters could be added to the study: the occupation pattern (e.g. residential) and the set point temperature. Concerning the design of experiments method, the use of experimental designs, better adapted to computer experiments (e.g. space-filling design), could be studied in more details. The metamodel could also be built by using more complex form than the second order polynomial function.

Acknowledgement

FEDER (le Fonds europééen de développement régional) and Wallonia have funded this research project in the framework of operational programme Wallonie-2020.EU. The authors would like to thank C. Rasse from the SMCS (Support en Méthodologie et Calcul Statistique) for her precious advices in the field of design of experiments.

References

Alam M., Jamil H., Sanjayan J. and Wilson J. (2014), Energy saving potential of phase change materials in major Australian cities, Energy and Buildings, 78: 192-201.

Baudoin G. and van Moeseke G. (2018). Phase Change Materials in Buildings: Combined Optimisation of Melting-Peak Temperature and Melting Temperature Range. 4th Building Simulation and Optimization Conference, Cambridge UK.

Evola G., Marletta L. and Sicurella F. (2013), A methodology for investigating the effectiveness of PCM wallboards for summer thermal comfort in buildings, Building and Environment, 59: 517-527.

Kalnæs S. E. and Jelle B. P. (2015), Phase change materials and products for building applications: A state-of-the-art review and future research opportunities, Energy and Buildings, 94: 150-176.

Saffari M., de Gracia A., Fernández C. and Cabeza L. F. (2017), Simulation-based optimization of PCM melting temperature to improve the energy performance in buildings, Applied Energy, 202: 420-434.

Saffari M., de Gracia A., Ushak S. and Cabeza L. F. (2017), Passive cooling of buildings with phase change materials using whole-building energy simulation tools: A review, Renewable and Sustainable Energy Reviews, 80: 1239-1255.

Simpson T. W., Poplinski J. D., Koch P. N. and Allen J. K. (2001), Metamodels for Computer-based Engineering Design: Survey and recommendations, Engineering with Computers, 17(2): 129-150.

Soares N., Costa J. J., Gaspar A. R. and Santos P. (2013), Review of passive PCM latent heat thermal energy storage systems towards buildings' energy efficiency, Energy and Buildings, 59: 82-103.

Soares N., Gaspar A. R., Santos P. and Costa J. J. (2014), Multi-dimensional optimization of the incorporation of PCM-drywalls in lightweight steel-framed residential buildings in different climates, Energy and Buildings, 70: 411-421.

Van Gelder L., Das P., Janssen H. and Roels S. (2014), Comparative study of metamodelling techniques in building energy simulation: Guidelines for practitioners, Simulation Modelling Practice and Theory, 49: 245-257.

Verbeke S. and Audenaert A. (2018), Thermal inertia in buildings: A review of impacts across climate and building use, Renewable and Sustainable Energy Reviews, 82: 2300-2318.

Statistical decision assistance for determining energy-efficient options in building design under uncertainty

Singh, M.M., Geyer P.
KU Leuven, Belgium
manavmahan.singh@kuleuven.be

Abstract. Designers need to compare numerous design options in the process of designing an energy-efficient building. There are two impediments in this process, first probabilistic prediction of energy requirement at an early stage of design with uncertain design parameters and, second, selecting a design option based on the probabilistic energy prediction. The paper presents an integration of machine learning energy prediction model with building information modelling (BIM) tool to make probabilistic energy prediction, *i.e.* ranges of values. Wilcoxon rank-sum test is useful in this situation, which is capable of comparing alternatives based on probabilistic energy predictions. The tool has been developed to extract information from the BIM model, make probabilistic energy prediction using the Monte Carlo method, and perform statistical analysis. It has been found that BIM integrated machine learning model can make energy prediction of six design alternatives in 30-35 seconds with no additional modelling efforts. Higher uncertainty in the design parameters will result in larger uncertainty in the energy prediction, and the test may not be able to suggest the better option even using statistical comparison. This will require the more precise value of design parameters, *i.e.* reduced uncertainty. Different uncertainty levels in the design parameters have been tested to which extent they are sufficient to make a selection of the energy-efficient option. It is observed that uncertainty levels that are suitable for decision-making depend on the combination of design options to be compared. It is possible to differentiate among alternatives with high uncertainty in the design parameters if they are entirely different else more precise definition of the design parameters is required. This research provides a method to select a better option among the developed options based on energy performance at the early stage of design.

1 Introduction

It has been a challenging endeavour for designers to develop an energy-efficient design to meet the demand for low energy use buildings. The first step in this endeavour to design a building envelope which results in lower energy loads, *i.e.* heating and cooling load (Jin and Jeong, 2014; Méndez Echenagucia *et al.*, 2015). A designer develops several design options for building envelope which needs to be evaluated for the energy performance. The design of the building envelope takes place at the early stage of design, which offers several challenges for energy performance evaluation. But, the decision-making at the early stage enhances the performance of building with a lesser cost of change (MacLeamy, 2004). Thus, it is imperative for a designer to make informed decisions at an early stage of design from an energy-efficiency perspective.

There are two primary challenges for informed decision-making at the early stage for energy-efficient design. First, make probabilistic energy performance prediction of the design options with uncertain design parameters and, second, use the probabilistic prediction to identify better solutions. Since, a number of design parameters influencing the energy loads are uncertain at the early stage of design (Tian *et al.*, 2018), the probabilistic energy is estimated by simulating a large number of energy models (Van Gelder, Janssen and Roels, 2014). This utilises a Monte Carlo method to generate random samples of uncertain design parameters. The random samples are used with the design information (certain design parameters) to create energy models. Since the simulation of a large number of energy models using conventional energy simulation tools such as EnergyPlus or TrnSys is time-consuming, the use of machine learning models is suggested in previous research works (Van Gelder, Janssen and Roels, 2014; Schlueter and Geyer, 2018; Singaravel *et al.*, 2018).

The energy performance of a design option is predicted using this approach, as probabilistic heating and cooling loads. The probabilistic heating and cooling loads will be a range of values; thus, it is not possible to compare the design options using quantitative comparison. The paper proposes the use of statistical method, Wilcoxon rank sum test, to assess whether two design options are significantly different from each other (Mann and Whitney, 1947). Based on the level of uncertainty in the design parameters, it may or may not be possible to draw the difference between two options. If options are indifferent against each other, reduction of the uncertainty in the design parameters is required. In this paper, this approach has been tested by reducing the uncertainty in the design parameters and its effect on the option selection. The objective of this research is to:

1. Perform quick probabilistic energy prediction to consider design uncertainty in decision making using building information modelling (BIM) with an integrated machine learning model.

2. Assist decision-making based on probabilistic energy prediction results using a statistical test for comparison with different levels of uncertainties in the design parameters. Assist means in this context to provide the designer with information if a decision between two design options is possible or if more information is required.

2 Literature review

The energy performance analysis tools offer limited integration with the design process due to the need for extensive modelling efforts and high computational time (Schlueter and Geyer, 2018). There have been few attempts to integrate energy prediction tools with the design process by the integration of BIM model with energy models (Ahn *et al.*, 2014; Negendahl, 2015). However, the challenges of the early stage of design are not well addressed. To perform quick energy predictions, integrating energy prediction model with the design process will be of paramount importance, which is possible with an integrated BIM tool. The component-based machine learning (CBML) model are developed to allow better integration with multi-level-of-detail (multi-LOD) BIM approach and extensibility to complex design cases (Geyer and Singaravel, 2018). The concept of CBML is based on the decomposition of design artefact and engineering knowledge and predicting the intermediate parameters such as heat flows before predicting the zone heating and cooling load. The use of deep learning technologies for the second generation of models improves this capability (Singaravel *et al.*, 2018). However, energy prediction using CBML at the early stage of design is performed after generating the building elements using rules (Geyer, Singh and Singaravel, 2018). Thus, it becomes a simplified representation of the building energy model, which will have a similar limitation as to the developed CBML.

One challenge of energy prediction at an early stage of design is uncertain design parameters. This issue makes the energy performance prediction process more complicated. Gelder et al., (2014) has proposed the use of probabilistic prediction of energy performance with uncertain information using the Monte Carlo method and engineering surrogate models. The probabilistic estimation of energy performance with uncertain inputs is possible with the use of time-efficient meta-models and machine learning models (Van Gelder, Janssen and Roels, 2014; Singaravel *et al.*, 2018). However, the energy prediction model needs to be integrated with BIM tool to streamline the energy prediction process with design.

The decision-making exercise for building design is very complex, which involve assessment of building based on several contradicting performance measures such as energy consumption and thermal comfort etc. The simulation tools are used in assessing the building on these performance measures and assist in selecting a better option (de Wilde, Augenbroe and van der Voorden, 2002; Wilde and Voorden, 2004). The problem gets compounded with the inherent uncertainty in the design parameters. Thus, it is required to perform multi-criteria decision-making based on the probabilistic distribution of the performance measure (Hopfe, Augenbroe and Hensen, 2013; Rezaee *et al.*, 2015). However, the use of simulation or computation tool for decision-making requires much more efforts for collaboration among the designers and engineers (Alsaadani and Bleil De Souza, 2016). The researchers suggested using the simulation results to provide meaningful insights which assist the designers in the design process (Bleil de Souza and Tucker, 2015).

Wilcoxon rank sum test is used to test whether the randomly selected value from one sample is statistically different from a randomly selected value from another sample (Mann and Whitney, 1947; Corder and Foreman, 2014). This test is a non-parametric alternative to the two-sample t-test. Thus it is applied when the samples are not normally distributed. The method is used in quite widely used in other domain such as medicine, bio-informatics and environmental engineering (Gauthier and Hawley, 2007) but rarely used for building design application (Hu, 2019).

3 Research methodology

The research methodology is described in two parts: First, integrated tool for quick energy prediction and, second, statistical analysis to differentiate among options.

3.1 Probabilistic prediction of energy performance using BIM-integrated ML methods

CBML model is developed based on the decomposition of an energy prediction model to a building element level (Geyer and Singaravel, 2018). The element level model first predicts the heat flow for each building component - walls, floors, roof, window and ground floor. The heat flow is supplemented with the other information such as operating hours, internal heat gains and infiltration to predict the heating or cooling load at zone level, which is summed up for building level. So, the energy load prediction requires the information to be present in the BIM model at building component level. At the early stage of design, the designer develops a mass model representing the external envelope of the building. But there is no information present about building element at the early stage of the design and need to be generated using assumptions. The building elements are created using the one-zone-per-floor method described in Geyer et al., (2018) (Geyer, Singh and Singaravel, 2018) as shown in Figure 1.

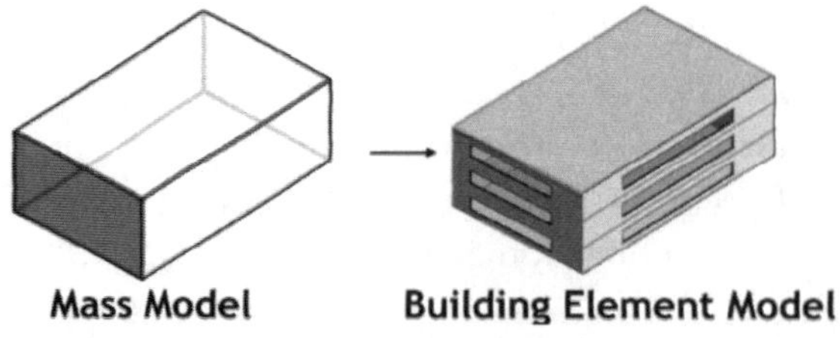

Figure 1. Generation of building elements in the mass model using the rules (Geyer et al., 2018)

After creating the building elements, namely walls, floors and roof, the geometrical parameters for these elements are certain and extracted from the BIM model (data extraction). The uncertain design parameters such as technical specifications, window construction and operational design parameters are provided using user inputs, as mentioned in Table 1. For the uncertain design parameters, the Monte Carlo method is used to generate a number of random combinations. It will result in the same number of energy models to be evaluated using a machine learning model. After this step, the data is passed to CBML for energy load predictions and results are integrated back to the BIM model.

Table 1. Data collection for the CBML model

Information	Type	Source
Geometrical parameters for wall, roof, floors and roof	Certain	BIM model (Data extraction)
Technical specifications parameters[1]	Uncertain	User input form (Monte Carlo method)
Window construction parameters[2]		
Operational design parameters[3]		

[1]Technical specifications parameters – u-value of wall, floor, roof and infiltration

[2]Window construction parameters – the window to wall ratios in each direction, u-value and g-value of windows

[3]Operational design parameters – internal heat gains and operating hours

In this research, newly developed CBML is used. It follows a similar component structure as in Geyer and Singaravel, 2018. The training data is enriched with more architectural design cases to get better performance of ML models. The newly developed models are tested on the design case outside of training data, and the performance of the models is described in Figure 2. The model shows the *goodness-of-fit* (R^2) 0.998 and 0.986 for heating and cooling load, respectively. Thus, the model can be used for energy load predictions.

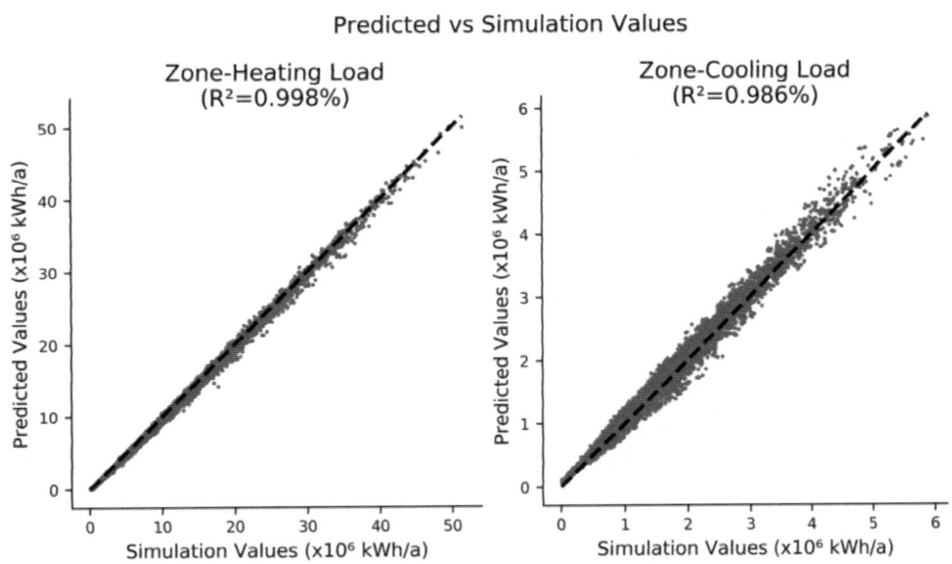

Figure 2. Performance of component-based machine learning model

The authors have developed a method integrated with a BIM authoring application to automate the process of making probabilistic energy predictions using CBML. The complete process of integration is described in Figure 3. The geometrical parameters are extracted from the BIM model, which is available as design information in the model. The remaining parameters are unknown at an early stage of the design and collected using a user input form as uncertain information. This information is passed to the CBML model to make energy predictions and integrate the results back to the BIM model.

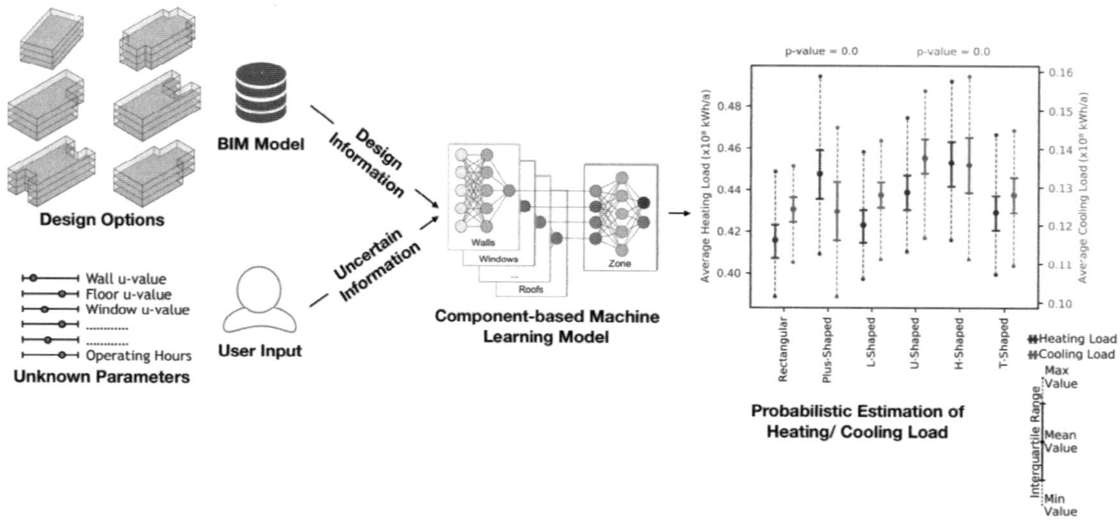

Figure 3. Probabilistic prediction of energy performance using CBML

3.2 Using statistical analysis to differentiate among options

The results are statistically analysed using non-parametric test - Wilcoxon rank sum test. Wilcoxon rank sum test is used to determine whether two independent samples selected from the population are significantly different from each other (Corder and Foreman, 2014). In this case, it is used to determine whether two design options developed by the designer differ significantly from each other concerning energy performance. If this is the case, selection and decision making is the next step of design development. Otherwise, the uncertain parameters need to be defined more precisely to differentiate among the design options. The parametric tests are not applicable as the data is not normally distributed. The probability value (p-value) is calculated for each combination of design options. The p-value is considered significant if it is less than 0.05. This p-value means we can reject the null hypothesis and state that the design options under consideration are significantly different from each other.

4 Results

The method is implemented a testcase building Tausenpfund – an average size office building in Munich. It has a rectangular floor plan with a floor area of 1200 sq. m. ($3\times14.8\times27$), distributed equally on three floors. The method is implemented on five design options developed as alternatives to rectangular floor plan building.

4.1 Integrated tool to make energy prediction using CBML model

The method based on the CBML model is integrated with BIM application Autodesk Revit to demonstrate the presented approach. The six design options are stored as conceptual masses in the application and accessed through the plugin. The successful completion of the tool allows the energy prediction and integration of energy prediction results back to the BIM model.

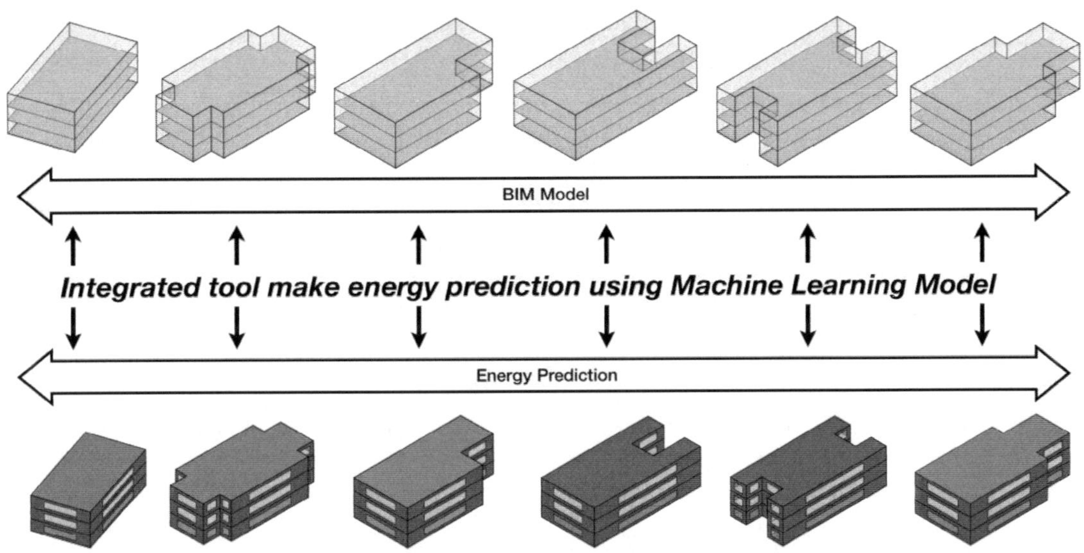

Figure 4. Integrated tool to make energy prediction using CBML model

The accuracy of the prediction is the same as the accuracy of CBML. In terms of time-efficiency, it takes 30-35 seconds to make energy prediction of six design options using 500 random samples. It means a total of 3000 energy models are evaluated in approximately 30 seconds. The process may take up to 24 hours using traditional energy simulation tools. The energy prediction is made based on the mass model and user input, which requires no additional modelling for energy prediction.

4.2 Statistical analysis to differentiate among options

Four scenarios with different level of uncertainty for input parameters are analysed to ascertain whether it is possible to make a distinction between the design options. There is a total of 15 combinations for six design options. The level of uncertainty and corresponding significant p-values for heating and cooling load is presented in Table 2 and Figure 5. The number of significant p-values is higher as the level of uncertainty decreases. With the uncertainty of ±25% in technical specification and operational design parameters and ±50% in window construction parameters, the number of significant p-values is 6 and 8 for heating and cooling load respectively for a total of 15 combinations. The number of significant p-values is 15 and 14 for heating and cooling load, respectively when the uncertainty in all the uncertain parameters is ±5%.

Table 2. Level of uncertainty in uncertain parameters

	Technical specifications parameters	Operational design parameters	Window construction parameters	No. of significant p-values (Heating Load, Cooling Load)
Scenario 1	25	25	50	6/15, 8/15
Scenario 2	5	25	50	7/15, 9/15
Scenario 3	5	5	50	13/15, 9/15
Scenario 4	5	5	5	15/15, 14/15

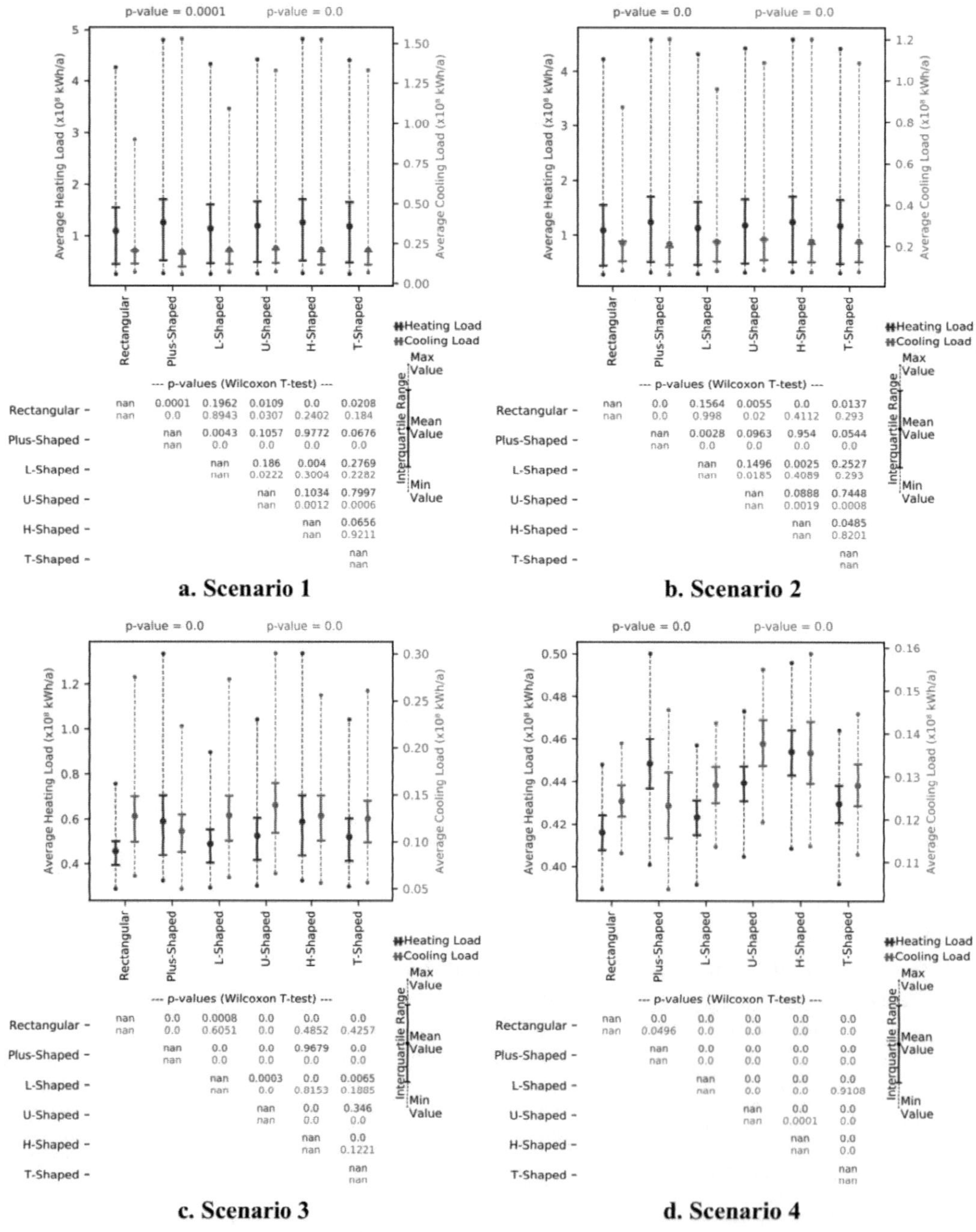

Figure 5. Energy prediction results with statistical analysis in four scenarios

5 Discussion

This paper has presented an approach of BIM integrated CBML model for probabilistic energy prediction at an early stage of design in a time-efficient way. The subsequent application of statistical analysis indicated for decision-making if two options show a significant difference in their probabilistic energy prediction of designed alternatives. The presented approach of making probabilistic estimation and statistical analysis has several limitations which are discussed in this section. The presented approach utilises CBML model, which has a limitation as all ML models, which is the applicability of models to new design cases, i.e. the generalisation. In the presented case, CBML model covers the range of design cases mentioned in the approach and energy prediction results are trustworthy. Hence, the applicability of CBML model needs to be tested extensively before using it on new design case beyond the range. A comparison of the final design configuration is recommended in this situation.

The method is only applicable to uniform floor plan buildings. The generation of building elements based on the one-zone-per-floor rule is another simplification of the energy model. On the one hand, adaptions of the method for floor plans that differ on each level are possible; however, this requires a trade-off between modelling efforts and model accuracy as well as training effort. On the other hand, such simplifications are commonly used for energy prediction at the early stage and comply with the approach of architectural design. The essential advantage of the CBML method is that it allows a higher degree of flexibility than monolithic parametric models and provides reusability of the component model and easy integration with BIM model. Flexible detail levels and creation of missing building elements are possible by generative methods.

The approach presents four scenarios with varying levels of uncertainty in the design parameters. It can be noted that the number of significant p-values increases with a lesser level of uncertainty. This fact shows the possibility of differentiating among all the options with a decreasing level of uncertainty. Also, the p-values dependent on the combination of options to be compared, so some combinations are different from each other even with a higher level of uncertainties and some are not different from each other even with precise value of design parameters. Thus, it may be possible that a designer needs to detail out one or more options before the uncertain parameters are defined more precisely.

The level of uncertainty in the design parameters is assumed to be uniformly distributed between the range of mean ± variation, however other distributions such as triangular or normal distributions are also possible which may result in lesser uncertainty in the energy prediction results. Which means the decision can be made with higher uncertainty in the design parameters. Also, if the energy prediction results are normally distributed because of another type of distribution in the design parameters, it will be possible to use a powerful parametric statistical test.

6 Conclusion

The architectural design is assisted by making a probabilistic prediction of energy performance and statistically analysing the results for decision making. The approach offers design assistance in requiring information and prioritising decisions at the early stage of design by making quick energy prediction with BIM integrated machine learning-based energy prediction model and analysing the response statistically.

The process of making energy prediction is streamlined with the use of BIM integrated machine learning model at building element level. The inherent uncertainty at the early stage of the design reflects in the energy prediction process. It requires an evaluation of several energy models for making probabilistic energy predictions. The whole process is made faster by extraction of data from the BIM model and energy predictions using CBML method. This method provides quick energy prediction results for the comparison of alternatives. In contrast to tradition energy simulation tool, the machine learning model is at least 3000 times faster. The accuracy of energy prediction is the same as the accuracy of the developed CBML mode, which is 0.998 and 0.986 (R^2 values) for heating and cooling load, respectively.

The uncertainty in the design parameters gets translated into the uncertainty in the energy predictions, which requires statistical analysis for comparison. The statistical test allows comparing the architectural design option considering the uncertainty that is present at the early stage of design. The possibility to compare the design alternatives depends on the uncertainty in the design parameters and the combination of design alternatives, as shown in the case presented in this paper. It will require a more precise definition of the design parameters to differentiate between two similar design options if the statistical comparison is not possible.

The integrated tool with BIM and CBML model offers an opportunity to address the design of energy-efficient buildings. There are some limitations of the current implementation of the approach such as simplifications of the energy model, applicability of machine learning model to new design case, uniform distribution of the design parameters and data extraction possible only for uniform floor plan buildings. It will require future research to address these limitations and to extend the applicability of the approach to more design case.

Acknowledgement

The research was funded by the Deutsche Forschungsgemeinschaft (DFG) in Researcher Unit 2363 "Evaluation of building design variants in early phases using adaptive levels of development", in Subproject 4 "System-based Simulation of Energy Flows". The computational resources and services used in this work were provided by the VSC (Flemish Supercomputer Center), funded by the Research Foundation - Flanders (FWO) and the Flemish Government – department EWI.

References

Ahn, K. U. *et al.* (2014) 'BIM interface for full vs. semi-automated building energy simulation', *Energy and Buildings*. Elsevier B.V., 68(PART B), pp. 671–678. doi: 10.1016/j.enbuild.2013.08.063.

Alsaadani, S. and Bleil De Souza, C. (2016) 'Of collaboration or condemnation? Exploring the promise and pitfalls of architect-consultant collaborations for building performance simulation', *Energy Research & Social Science*, 19, pp. 21–36. doi: 10.1016/j.erss.2016.04.016.

Bleil de Souza, C. and Tucker, S. (2015) 'Thermal simulation software outputs: a framework to produce meaningful information for design decision-making', *Journal of Building Performance Simulation*, 8(2), pp. 57–78. doi: 10.1080/19401493.2013.872191.

Corder, G. W. and Foreman, D. I. (2014) *Nonparametric statistics for non-statisticians: a step-by-step approach*. Second. Wiley.

Gauthier, T. D. and Hawley, M. E. (2007) 'STATISTICAL METHODS', in *Introduction to Environmental Forensics*. Elsevier, pp. 129–183. doi: 10.1016/B978-012369522-2/50006-3.

Van Gelder, L., Janssen, H. and Roels, S. (2014) 'Probabilistic design and analysis of building performances: Methodology and application example', *Energy and Buildings*, 79, pp. 202–211. doi: 10.1016/j.enbuild.2014.04.042.

Geyer, P. and Singaravel, S. (2018) 'Component-based machine learning for performance prediction in building design', *Applied Energy*, 228, pp. 1439–1453. doi: 10.1016/j.apenergy.2018.07.011.

Geyer, P., Singh, M. M. and Singaravel, S. (2018) 'Component-Based Machine Learning for Energy Performance

Prediction by MultiLOD Models in the Early Phases of Building Design', in *Advanced Computing Strategies for Engineering*, pp. 516–534. doi: 10.1007/978-3-319-91635-4_27.

Hopfe, C. J., Augenbroe, G. L. M. and Hensen, J. L. M. (2013) 'Multi-criteria decision making under uncertainty in building performance assessment', *Building and Environment*, 69, pp. 81–90. doi: 10.1016/j.buildenv.2013.07.019.

Hu, M. (2019) 'Does zero energy building cost more? – An empirical comparison of the construction costs for zero energy education building in United States', *Sustainable Cities and Society*, 45, pp. 324–334. doi: 10.1016/j.scs.2018.11.026.

Jin, J.-T. and Jeong, J.-W. (2014) 'Optimization of a free-form building shape to minimize external thermal load using genetic algorithm', *Energy and Buildings*, 85, pp. 473–482. doi: 10.1016/j.enbuild.2014.09.080.

MacLeamy, P. (2004) *MacLeamy Curve*. Available at: http://www.msa-ipd.com/MacleamyCurve.pdf (Accessed: 29 September 2015).

Mann, H. B. and Whitney, D. R. (1947) 'On a Test of Whether one of Two Random Variables is Stochastically Larger than the Other', *The Annals of Mathematical Statistics*, 18(1), pp. 50–60. doi: 10.1214/aoms/1177730491.

Méndez Echenagucia, T. *et al.* (2015) 'The early design stage of a building envelope: Multi-objective search through heating, cooling and lighting energy performance analysis', *Applied Energy*, 154, pp. 577–591. doi: 10.1016/j.apenergy.2015.04.090.

Negendahl, K. (2015) 'Building performance simulation in the early design stage: An introduction to integrated dynamic models', *Automation in Construction*, 54, pp. 39–53. doi: 10.1016/j.autcon.2015.03.002.

Rezaee, R. *et al.* (2015) 'Assessment of uncertainty and confidence in building design exploration', *Artificial Intelligence for Engineering Design, Analysis and Manufacturing*, 29(4), pp. 429–441. doi: 10.1017/S0890060415000426.

Schlueter, A. and Geyer, P. (2018) 'Linking BIM and Design of Experiments to balance architectural and technical design factors for energy performance', *Automation in Construction*, 86, pp. 33–43. doi: 10.1016/j.autcon.2017.10.021.

Singaravel, S. *et al.* (2018) 'Deep-learning neural-network architectures and methods: Using component-based models in building-design energy prediction', *Advanced Engineering Informatics*, 38, pp. 81–90. doi: 10.1016/j.aei.2018.06.004.

Tian, W. *et al.* (2018) 'A review of uncertainty analysis in building energy assessment', *Renewable and Sustainable Energy Reviews*, 93, pp. 285–301. doi: 10.1016/j.rser.2018.05.029.

de Wilde, P., Augenbroe, G. and van der Voorden, M. (2002) 'Design analysis integration: supporting the selection of energy saving building components', *Building and Environment*, 37(8–9), pp. 807–816. doi: 10.1016/S0360-1323(02)00053-7.

Wilde, P. de and Voorden, M. van der (2004) 'Providing computational support for the selection of energy saving building components', *Energy and Buildings*, 36(8), pp. 749–758. doi: 10.1016/j.enbuild.2004.01.003.

Future energy demands of European buildings in the framework of climate change: a scoping study

Virgilio Ciancio[1], Ferdinando Salata[1], Serena Falasca[2,3], Gabriele Curci[3,4], Iacopo Golasi[1], Pieter de Wilde[5]

[1] Department of Astronautical, Electrical and Energy Engineering - Applied Physics Area, University of Rome "Sapienza", Italy.
[2] Department of Pure and Applied Sciences, University of Urbino "Carlo Bo", Italy.
[3] Center of Excellence in Telesensing of Environment and Model Prediction of Severe events (CETEMPS), University of L'Aquila, Italy.
[4] Department of Physical and Chemical Sciences, University of L'Aquila, Italy
[5] School of Art, Design and Architecture, University of Plymouth, United Kingdom.
virgilio.ciancio@uniroma1.it

Climate change is considered an important global threat, with a significant impact on the energy performance, since buildings will be subjected to higher average outdoor temperatures. This paper explores the relative impact of global warming across the different regional climates of Europe comparing present and estimated future energy needs of a hypothetical residential house located in 19 cities characterized by different latitude and Köppen-Geiger class. Building performance simulations with EnergyPlus are performed in order to simulate the heating and cooling needs of the building and the associated CO_2 emissions in the present and in the future. The progressive increase in average temperatures in 2050 and 2080 leads to a general decrease of thermal energy request for heating and to an increase in the demand for electricity for cooling especially in the southern Europe, where high carbon intensity coefficients cause large CO_2 emissions. The resulting vicious circle can be interrupted by increasing the energy efficiency of buildings and properly converting thermoelectric power plants.

1. Introduction

The Earth is experiencing a rapid climate change whose effects are occurring with an average warming of the atmosphere happening in a relatively short period of time ("AR5 Climate Change 2013: The Physical Science Basis — IPCC,"; U.S. Global Change Research Program, 2018).

Currently, around 30% of global energy production is earmarked for end-use in the civil sector ("Energy Statistics," 2017, United Nations Statistics Division, 2018). Specifically, almost 60% of world electricity is consumed in residential and commercial buildings (Ürge-Vorsatz, n.d.). In the most industrialized countries the energy needs in buildings concern winter heating, summer cooling, domestic hot water production, lighting and household appliances (Salata et al., 2018).

Energy needs are strongly linked to local weather conditions (Ciancio, Falasca, Golasi, Curci, & Coppi, 2018), therefore it can be expected that changes in global and local weather conditions will lead in the future to an evolution of the annual energy requirement for the existing building stock (Andrić et al., 2017). Buildings will be subjected to new weather conditions that will change the needs of the civil sector in terms of primary energy required (Huang & Gurney, 2016; Lo Basso, Nastasi, Salata, & Golasi, 2017; Zhai & Helman, 2019).

The international scientific community dealing with energy demand of buildings is analysing the close relationship between climate change, energy demand and greenhouse gas emissions

(Guan, 2009) and the resulting cause-effect loop worsening this situation (Kershaw, Eames, & Coley, 2011; de Wilde & Coley, 2013). Many researchers have studied these aspects for different geographical areas. Basically, issues in this type of research can be divided into the following three points: i) the need to create weather files describing the future climate situation for each location; ii) the energy analysis of the buildings needs corresponding to future climate conditions; iii) the calculation of the modification of climate-altering gases emissions associated with increasing energy requirements (Salata et al., 2017).

On the first point, Moazami et al. worked to create a robust dataset of climatic information representing the future climatic conditions, in particular for the city of Geneve (Switzerland), according to the peculiarities of the analyzed area and to different scenarios of global warming (Moazami, Nik, Carlucci, & Geving, 2019). The UK Climate Projections 2009 are an example of the probabilistic approach that Kershaw et al. used to create, and then validate, a climate file representative of future conditions for the city of Plymouth in England (Kershaw et al., 2011). Chan has developed future hourly weather files for the city of Hong Kong and calculated an increase of up to 24% of the electricity consumption for cooling a typical building (Chan, 2011). Shen analysed future energy consumption for residential buildings in 4 US cities representing 4 different weather conditions on the North American continent, through morphing techniques and he estimated increases or decreases in the total annual energy needs according to the location (Shen, 2017). Zhai and Helman analyzed 56 combinations of climate models and emission scenarios to obtain 4 different reference climate scenarios, validated with historical data for 7 climate zones, and they were able to describe the effects of future variations on a typical building (Zhai & Helman, 2019).

Regarding the second point, Invidiata and Ghisi showed significant percentage increases (even 180%) of the annual energy needs of the buildings considered in three Brazilian cities (Invidiata & Ghisi, 2016). Xu et al. conducted similar studies in California, determining a 50% increase in the use of electricity for cooling buildings with respect to the current values (Xu, Huang, Miller, Schlegel, & Shen, 2012). Similarly, Dirks et al. considered more than 100 USA cities, counting new peaks for energy demand and claiming an increasing energy consumption for cooling up to 130%, compared to a much less marked decrease in energy needs for heating (Dirks et al., 2015). Also, in the USA, Huang and Gurney analysed 925 different locations, identifying discrepancies in energy requirements by up to 20% depending on the different use of buildings of type (Huang & Gurney, 2016). Matsuura carried out a study on energy consumption based on projections of future average temperature in 9 USA cities, determined energy increases for cooling and energy decreases for heating and suggested constructing buildings with geometries that can mitigate the negative effects of climatic variations (Matsuura, 1995). Li et al. analysed similar problems for the city of Tianjin in northern China, underlining a decrease in heating needs (Li et al., 2014).

With reference to the third point, Wan et al. studied 5 Chinese climatic areas in order to identify technological solutions able to counter balance the increase in the buildings energy needs and the consequent emission of CO_2 (Wan, Li, Pan, & Lam, 2012). Andric et al. analyzed the energy needs of 5 locations in Europe and northern Canada, determining the change in energy requirements for future climate scenarios and possible solutions to improve the insulation of the building envelope (Andrić et al., 2017).

2. Purpose of the work

Among the potentialities of computing techniques, the predictive simulation of the heat exchange phenomena between the environment and buildings allows engineers to predict future energy needs in the building sector in ever greater detail and precision. In the last few years, software simulating the energy performance of more and more detailed and complex buildings in a dynamic regime, have allowed to face the technological challenge to design increasingly more efficient buildings. Now the attention of the scientific community is shifting towards the prediction of the buildings energy resilience to changes in local climatic conditions due to global warming. In order to create weather files representative of future climate scenarios, suitable climate models must be implemented. Then, starting from historical meteorological data, annual database files can be created that can be used with dynamic simulation software for the analysis of energy performances of buildings. This is possible thanks to the computerization of knowledge provided by climatology and energy engineering.

This work aims at assessing the impact of climate change of annual energy consumption for heating and cooling across Europe of a model building, located in 19 European cities characterized by different Köppen-Geiger classification. To this end, dynamic hourly simulations were performed for each location with the EnergyPlus software, using alternatively the weather files provided with EnergyPlus for the current climate, and those relative to two future years (2050 and 2080) under a predetermined emission scenario, created for each location. In this way, it is possible to study the relative change attributable to climate change on the future energy needs of a building and on the relative carbon dioxide emissions of a building for residential use in Europe. In particular, the choice of using one and the same building allows to highlight the impact of the climate change on the energy needs across different Köppen-Geiger climate zones. A future development of this work could take into account the variation of construction types across the continent.

3. Materials and methods

In this work, the dynamic predictive software EnergyPlus was used to evaluate the energy consumption of a building alternatively located in 19 European cities, selected according to the (different) latitude and the climatic Köppen-Geiger classification (Peel, Finlayson, & Mcmahon, 2007a). Simulations were carried out on the current climate conditions and on the climate conditions of 2050 and 2080 for the 19 locations considered using weather files described in Section 3.2.

The analyzed type building was specifically designed to provide useful information during the energy analysis phase. The 3D geometry was created in SketchUp and through the OpenStudio tool it was provided as input to Energyplus.

3.1. Computation of energy needs through EnergyPlus

The EnergyPlus software was developed by the US Department of Energy (Crawley, Hand, Kummert, & Griffith, 2008) for the simulation of the entire building envelope/plant in an annual dynamic regime. EnergyPlus is an open source software that allows an in-depth analysis of all the phenomena of heat exchange affecting a building of particular architectural and plant complexity and has become a point of reference for the international scientific community studying the energy performances of the buildings (Foucquier, Robert, Suard, Stéphan, & Jay, 2013). 3D geometries can be created using SketchUp (Inc., 2018) modeling software and imported into EnergyPlus after defining with OpenStudio (Energy, 2018) the characteristics of the thermal zones on which to set up calculations for exchanges of heat with the external environment.

3.2. Weather data

The EnergyPlus software needs to load a weather file (.epw format) containing hourly weather information of a typical year for the selected location (NREL, 2018).

In this work the weather files available in the EnergyPlus database were used for the "current climate" simulations, while the "future climate" simulations are based on climate change weather files produced using the Climate Change tool World Weather file Generator (CCWorldWeatherGen). The generation of this future file weather required computational techniques based on climate models able to provide detailed meteorological information decades apart, specific to the geographic location, for the 8,760 hours of the typical year. The National Renewable Energy Laboratory (NREL) of the US Department of Energy (DOE) provides online ("Weather Data | EnergyPlus") EnergyPlus users with a comprehensive climate database that includes more than 2,100 geographic locations on all continents. The EnergyPlus database weather files were also used to create climate change weather files for 2050 and 2080 and all the 19 selected locations through the CCWorldWeatherGen tool. This tool creates a weather file starting from the current climate weather file by means of a "morphing" procedure and using the HadCM3 model output corresponding to the A2 emissions scenario (more properly, the A2 scenario family) of the IPCC Third Assessment Report. According to the IPCC definitions, such scenario family is characterized by "a very heterogeneous world with continuously increasing global population and regionally oriented economic growth" more fragmented and slower than in other scenarios (Sedac, 2019). For further details on the tool and the morphing procedure see (Jentsch, James, Bourikas, & Bahaj, 2013).

3.3. Geographic area

This study took into consideration 19 different cities of Europe. The geographical sites have been chosen according to: i) the latitude, on which the solar radiation depends; ii) the climatic classification according to Köppen-Geiger (Peel, Finlayson, & Mcmahon, 2007b). The sites selected are summarized in Table 1.

Tab. 1 – Selected cities: latitude, climatic classification e carbon intensity for electricity production.

State	City	Latitude [°]	Climatic Classification	Carbon intensity [kg(CO_2) kWh^{-1}]
Bulgaria	Plovdiv	42.0	ET	0.3701
Czech Republic	Prague	50.0	Dfb	0.3758
Denmark	Copenaghen	55.5	Dfb	0.1666
France	Bordeaux	45.0	Cfb	0.0348
France	Clemont-Ferrand	45.8	Dfc	0.0348
France	Paris	49.0	Cfb	0.0348
Germany	Berlin	52.5	Dfb	0.4249
Italy	Milan	45.5	Cfa	0.2292
Italy	Palermo	38.0	Csa	0.2292
Italy	Pescara	42.0	Cfa	0.2292
Italy	Rome	41.8	Csa	0.2292
Portugal	Porto	41.2	Csb	0.3595
Romania	Cluj-Napoca	46.0	Dfb	0.2085
Spain	Granada	37.2	BSk	0.3044
Spain	Salamanca	41.0	Bsk	0.3044
Sweden	Gothenburg	56.8	Dfb	0.0105
United Kingdom	London	51.5	Cfb	0.3888

United Kingdom	Aberdeen	56.4	Cfb	0.3888
United Kingdom	Belfast	54.5	Cfb	0.3888

It is hypothesized that the amount of carbon dioxide produced for the generation of electricity is constant over time and refers to current values (Ecometrica, 2011). The emission of carbon dioxide due to the combustion of natural gas is equal to 0.1842 kg(CO_2) · $kWh_{termico}^{-1}$.

3.4. Study building

A residential building consisting of three floors and three apartments for each floor was taken as a case study. The first floor is raised on pillars with respect to the ground; the intermediate level exchanges heat towards the outside only through its vertical infill panels; the upper floor is characterized by a flat roof. The air-conditioned interior floor area is 765.6 m^2. The height of each floor is 3 m. Two apartments have a common border area, while the third apartment totally adjoins the exterior or the landing and the stairwell that are unheated. Fig. 1 shows the plan of a plane, a 3D and the geographic orientation of the building.

Properties of materials of building envelope surfaces are summarized in Tab. 2.

The building is heated by radiators connected to a condensation boiler powered by natural gas and characterized by efficiency of 104.8% and 107.2% when the nominal power is equal to 100% and 30% respectively. Cooling takes place through split-type steam compression refrigeration systems characterized by C.O.P. equal to 3.1. To simulate the activation of the plants and calculate their energy requirements, an internal temperature has been assumed: i) greater than 18 °C, in heating; ii) less than 26 °C, in cooling. The ventilation of the rooms is natural, with a turnover equal to 0.5 hourly volumes. Internal thermal loads are assumed to be equal to 38 W m^{-2}.

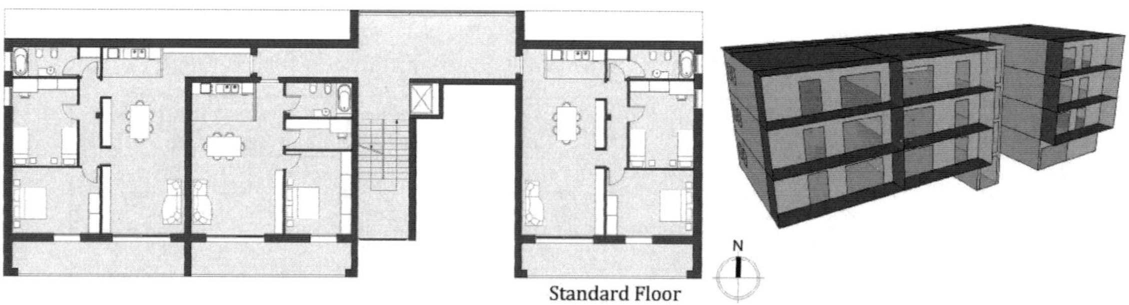

Figure 1: Analysed building: standard floor and three-dimensional representation.

Tab. 2 – Properties of building envelope surfaces.

Orientation	Type	Surface area [m^2]	Transmittance [W·m^{-2}·K^{-1}]
North	Opaque	258.6	0.273
	Glass	59.7	1.60
East	Opaque	111.6	0.273
	Glass	7.6	1.60
South	Opaque	184.5	0.273
	Glass	112.3	1.60
West	Opaque	81.0	0.273
	Glass	6.4	1.60
Horizontal	Roof	181.15	0.263
	Floor	181.15	0.343

4. Results and discussion

Figure 2 shows that the progressive increase in average monthly temperatures in all 19 locations considered in 2050 and 2080.

The few geographical locations that in 2020 present the coldest winters (such as Cluj-Napoca and Gothenburg, with average temperatures below 0°C) have milder seasons in 2050 and 2080. Some Mediterranean locations, such as Granada and Palermo, have extremely high average temperatures in the summer months (which in 2050 go well beyond 30 °C). Some cities in northern Europe (e.g. Aberdeen or Belfast) do not have large needs for summer cooling of the building as they have relatively cool summers. And since heating needs are there cut due to climate change, the annual energy needs are reduced. All this leads, in general, to a lower consumption of thermal energy for winter heating and to an increase in the demand for electricity for summer cooling through the steam compression refrigeration machines.

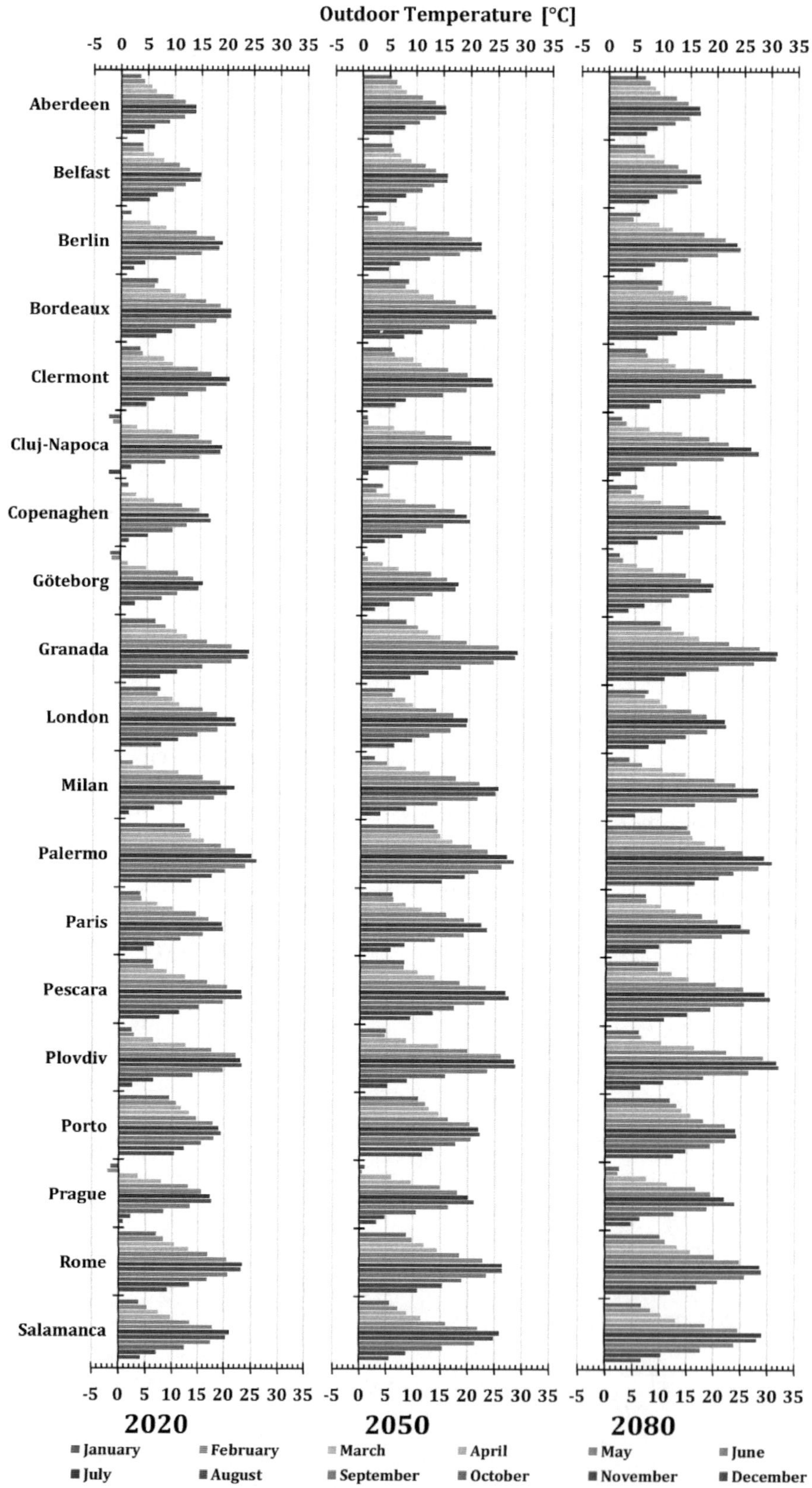

Figure 2: Mean monthly temperatures for the considered cities in years 2020, 2050, 2080.

Fig. 3 shows the energy consumption (in kWh per year) for 2020, 2050 and 2080 for both the heating and cooling of the building for each of the 19 cities.

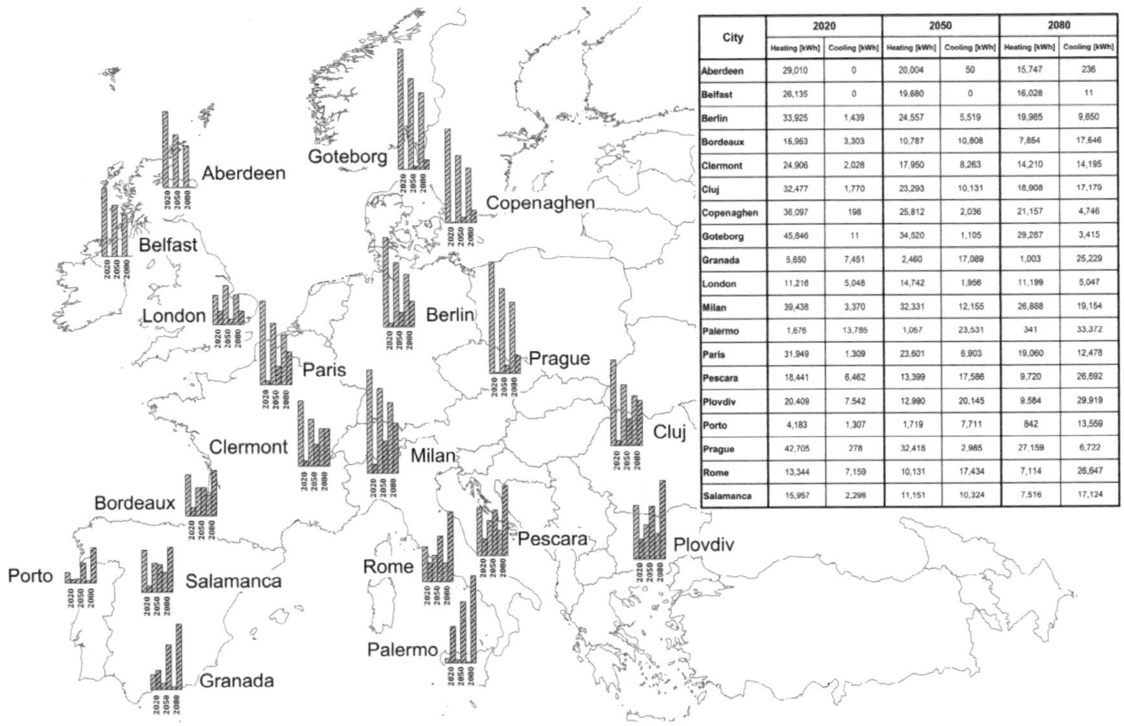

City	2020		2050		2080	
	Heating [kWh]	Cooling [kWh]	Heating [kWh]	Cooling [kWh]	Heating [kWh]	Cooling [kWh]
Aberdeen	29,010	0	20,004	50	15,747	236
Belfast	26,135	0	19,680	0	16,028	11
Berlin	33,925	1,439	24,557	5,519	19,985	9,650
Bordeaux	15,963	3,303	10,787	10,808	7,854	17,646
Clermont	24,906	2,028	17,950	8,263	14,210	14,195
Cluj	32,477	1,770	23,293	10,131	18,908	17,179
Copenaghen	36,097	198	25,812	2,036	21,157	4,746
Goteborg	45,846	11	34,520	1,105	29,287	3,415
Granada	5,650	7,451	2,460	17,089	1,003	25,229
London	11,216	5,048	14,742	1,956	11,199	5,047
Milan	39,438	3,370	32,331	12,155	26,888	19,154
Palermo	1,676	13,785	1,067	23,531	341	33,372
Paris	31,949	1,309	23,601	6,903	19,060	12,478
Pescara	18,441	6,462	13,399	17,586	9,720	26,692
Plovdiv	20,409	7,542	12,990	20,145	9,584	29,919
Porto	4,183	1,307	1,719	7,711	842	13,559
Prague	42,705	278	32,418	2,985	27,159	6,722
Rome	13,344	7,159	10,131	17,434	7,114	26,647
Salamanca	15,957	2,298	11,151	10,324	7,516	17,124

Figure 3: Annual energy consumption (kWh per year) for heating and cooling in the locations analyzed for 2020, 2050, 2080.

Annual CO_2 emissions respectively for cooling and heating the studied building are computed multiplying the annual energy consumption (in Fig. 3) for the carbon dioxide emission coefficients due to the production of electricity (fifth column of Table 1, corresponding to the national energy mix of each State) or to the stoichiometric combustion of natural gas (Fig. 4).

Figure 4 shows that there are three opposite trends in terms of annual carbon dioxide production in the future and the 19 cities can be divided into three groups according to their trend. The first large group consists of cities with a cold climate (Aberdeen, Belfast, Bordeaux, Clermont, Copenhagen, Gothenburg and Paris), where emissions tend to decrease globally; the second large group is made up of cities (Berlin, Granada, Milan, Palermo, Pescara, Plovdiv, Porto, Rome and Salamanca) where CO_2 emissions tend to increase. The behavior of these two groups can be explained as follows: i) the decrease in energy demand for heating favors the reduction of CO_2 emissions; ii) reduced cooling needs for the northern Europe locations, associated with their low carbon intensity coefficients, correspond to little carbon dioxide emissions for cooling; ii) large quantities of electricity for cooling in the cities of southern Europe, associated with their high coefficients of carbon intensity, give rise to the production of CO_2.

The third, small, group of cities is formed by Cluj-Napoca, London and Prague and shows a decrease in annual CO_2 production from 2020 to 2050 and a trend reversal from 2050 to 2080. This is because in the medium temporal term there is an important decrease in energy needs for heating in the winter months, but these savings are counterbalanced by a large increase in electricity for summer cooling.

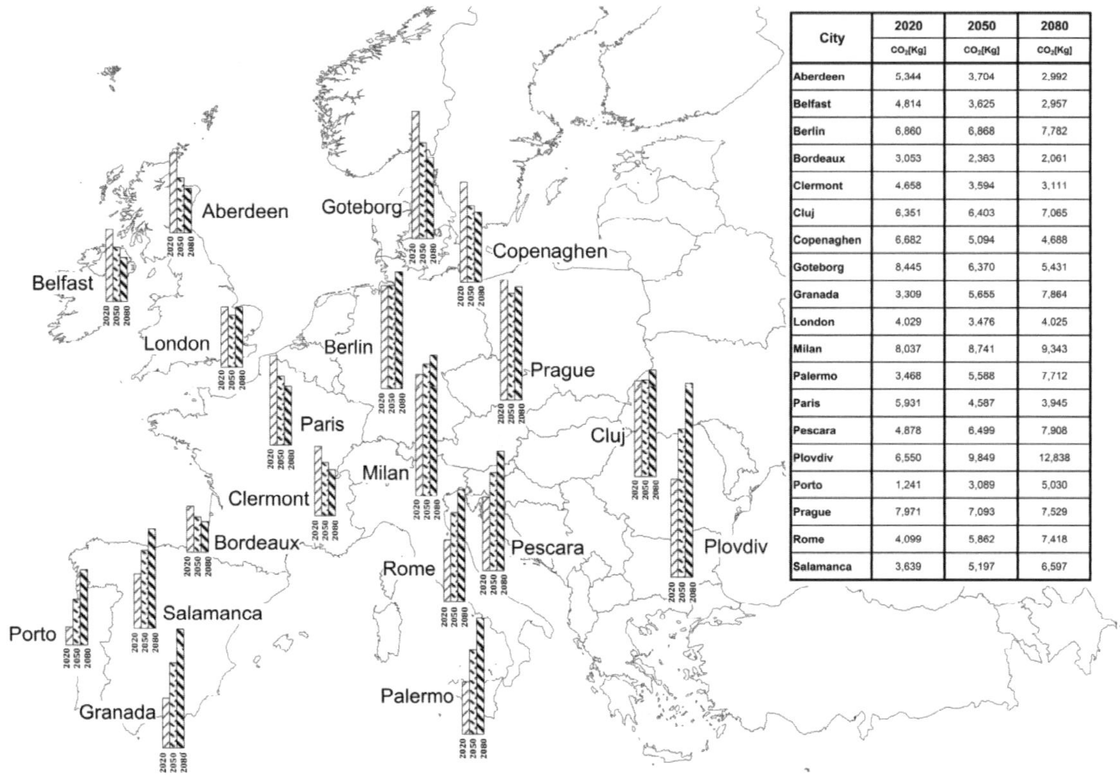

City	2020	2050	2080
	CO_2[Kg]	CO_2[Kg]	CO_2[Kg]
Aberdeen	5,344	3,704	2,992
Belfast	4,814	3,625	2,957
Berlin	6,860	6,868	7,782
Bordeaux	3,053	2,363	2,061
Clermont	4,658	3,594	3,111
Cluj	6,351	6,403	7,065
Copenaghen	6,682	5,094	4,688
Goteborg	8,445	6,370	5,431
Granada	3,309	5,655	7,864
London	4,029	3,476	4,025
Milan	8,037	8,741	9,343
Palermo	3,468	5,588	7,712
Paris	5,931	4,587	3,945
Pescara	4,878	6,499	7,908
Plovdiv	6,550	9,849	12,838
Porto	1,241	3,089	5,030
Prague	7,971	7,093	7,529
Rome	4,099	5,862	7,418
Salamanca	3,639	5,197	6,597

Figure 4: Annual carbon dioxide produced for energy needs: scenario 2020, 2050, 2080.

It can be deduced that the decrease of natural gas demand for winter heating at many sites is neutralized by the increased demand for electricity (for summer cooling). Since to date only France, Sweden and Denmark have a value of the carbon intensity related to electricity generation lower than CO_2 emissions related to natural gas combustion, the trend observed above involves the increase in the emission of greenhouse gases into the atmosphere. Therefore, it is necessary, for the purpose of climate change mitigation, to find more environmentally friendly solutions such as the conversion of large thermal power plants for electricity generation.

5. Conclusions

In the last 20 years major efforts haves been made to reduce energy consumption in the building sector, especially for private homes for residential use. The owners energetically redevelop the apartments little and very slowly and the old buildings are not replaced by more modern and efficient buildings. Long awareness campaigns have been conducted, but it is not enough. In the meantime, in fact, the global climate is undergoing major changes and the expected future warming of the Earth surface will lead to new scenarios.

Focusing on the European scene, in the next 60 years the homes will change their energy demands according to climate changes and the geographical position will play an important role in this evolution of energy needs. In fact, the energy needs linked to winter heating tend to decrease, while consumption related to summer cooling are expected to increase, especially in southern Europe. This will result in a reduction in the quantity of fossil fuels (such as natural gas) combusted for heating and, at the same time, in the increase in electricity demand used to power compression refrigeration machines. Specifically, this study highlighted how the future climate change, compared to current conditions, could lead to a decrease in the winter heating

requirement of northern European cities such as Aberdeen (-31% in 2050 and -45% in 2080), Gothenburg (-24% in 2050 and -36% in 2080) and Copenhagen (-28% in 2050 and -41% in 2080) and an increase in the summer cooling requirement of southern European cities such as Rome (+143% in 2050 and +272% in 2080), Palermo (+70% in 2050 and +142% in 2080) or Granada (+129% in 2050 and +238% in 2080). Comparing the energy demands of 2080 with the present one and taking into account all the examined European cities at the same time, the increase in energy needs for cooling will be higher than the decrease in energy needs for heating. Therefore, this would increase global energy consumption.
Assuming that the current carbon intensity coefficients are conserved in the future, European countries producing electricity mainly from fossil fuels will contribute to increasing the levels of greenhouse gases in the atmosphere, responsible for the increase in the average temperature of the earth. This vicious circle can be interrupted mainly thanks to two different strategies to be implemented on a large scale and thanks to appropriate investments: i) increasing as much as possible the energy efficiency of the existing building stock; ii) converting large thermal power plants to supply sources with reduced emissions of climate-altering species into the atmosphere (Andreani & Gasparotto, 2002; Shikama et al., 2008).

These results are the first step in a research work aiming at using optimization computational techniques such as genetic algorithms. The goals of the next steps will be the identification of the best energy efficiency upgrading of buildings in order to mitigate the effects of global warming and reduce energy demand and emissions of greenhouse gases to the atmosphere. With the definition of future scenarios on a large scale (and not only at European scale as in this study), taking into account the new energy needs of the building sector, the costs of energy sources and the modification of the energy mix for the electricity production in each nation due to climate change, the energy production sector and therefore the energy market can be reorganized.

Acknowledgements

Ferdinando Salata, Virgilio Ciancio and Iacopo Golasi have received for this research a grant on the "Progetti di Ricerca - Progetti Medi 2018" from Sapienza University of Rome.

References

Andreani, R., & Gasparotto, M. (2002). Overview of fusion nuclear technology in Europe. *Fusion Engineering and Design*, *61–62*, 27–36. https://doi.org/10.1016/S0920-3796(02)00110-2

Andrić, I., Pina, A., Ferrão, P., Fournier, J., Lacarrière, B., & Le Corre, O. (2017). The impact of climate change on building heat demand in different climate types. *Energy and Buildings*, *149*, 225–234. https://doi.org/10.1016/j.enbuild.2017.05.047

AR5 Climate Change 2013: The Physical Science Basis — IPCC. (n.d.). Retrieved February 8, 2019, from https://www.ipcc.ch/report/ar5/wg1/

Chan, A. L. S. (2011). Developing future hourly weather files for studying the impact of climate change on building energy performance in Hong Kong. *Energy and Buildings*, *43*(10), 2860–2868. https://doi.org/10.1016/j.enbuild.2011.07.003

Ciancio, V., Falasca, S., Golasi, I., Curci, G., & Coppi, M. (2018). Influence of input climatic data on simulations of annual energy needs of a building : EnergyPlus and WRF modeling for a case study in Rome (Italy)., 1–17.

Crawley, D. B., Hand, J. W., Kummert, M., & Griffith, B. T. (2008). Contrasting the capabilities of building energy performance simulation programs. *Building and Environment*, *43*(4), 661–673. https://doi.org/10.1016/J.BUILDENV.2006.10.027

de Wilde, P., Coley D., The implications of a changing climate for buildings, *Building and Environment*, 55, 2012, 1-7, https://doi.org/10.1016/j.buildenv.2012.03.014.

Dirks, J. A., Gorrissen, W. J., Hathaway, J. H., Skorski, D. C., Scott, M. J., Pulsipher, T. C., … Rice, J. S. (2015). Impacts of climate change on energy consumption and peak demand in buildings: A detailed regional approach. *Energy*, *79*(C), 20–32. https://doi.org/10.1016/j.energy.2014.08.081

Ecometrica. (2011). Electricity-specific emission factors for grid electricity. *Ecometrica*, (August), 1–22. https://doi.org/10.13044/j.sdewes.2014.02.0030

Energy, N. L. of the U. S. D. of. (2018). OpenStudio. Retrieved November 4, 2018, from https://www.openstudio.net/

Energy Statistics. (2017).

Foucquier, A., Robert, S., Suard, F., Stéphan, L., & Jay, A. (2013). State of the art in building modelling and energy performances prediction: A review. *Renewable and Sustainable Energy Reviews*, *23*, 272–288. https://doi.org/10.1016/j.rser.2013.03.004

Guan, L. (2009). Preparation of future weather data to study the impact of climate change on buildings. *Building and Environment*, *44*(4), 793–800. https://doi.org/10.1016/j.buildenv.2008.05.021

Huang, J., & Gurney, K. R. (2016). The variation of climate change impact on building energy consumption to building type and spatiotemporal scale. *Energy*, *111*, 137–153. https://doi.org/10.1016/j.energy.2016.05.118

Inc., T. (2018). SketchUp. Retrieved November 4, 2018, from https://www.sketchup.com/it

Invidiata, A., & Ghisi, E. (2016). Impact of climate change on heating and cooling energy demand in houses in Brazil. *Energy and Buildings*, *130*(2016), 20–32. https://doi.org/10.1016/j.enbuild.2016.07.067

Jentsch, M. F., James, P. A. B., Bourikas, L., & Bahaj, A. S. (2013). Transforming existing weather data for worldwide locations to enable energy and building performance simulation under future climates. *Renewable Energy*, *55*, 514–524. https://doi.org/10.1016/J.RENENE.2012.12.049

Kershaw, T., Eames, M., & Coley, D. (2011). Assessing the risk of climate change for buildings: A comparison between multi-year and probabilistic reference year simulations. *Building and Environment*, *46*(6), 1303–1308. https://doi.org/10.1016/j.buildenv.2010.12.018

Li, M., Guo, J., Tian, Z., Shi, J., Xiong, M., & Xiang, C. (2014). Future climate change and building energy demand in Tianjin, China. *Building Services Engineering Research and Technology*, *35*(4), 362–375. https://doi.org/10.1177/0143624413498245

Lo Basso, G., Nastasi, B., Salata, F., & Golasi, I. (2017). Energy retrofitting of residential buildings—How to couple Combined Heat and Power (CHP) and Heat Pump (HP) for thermal management and off-design operation. *Energy and Buildings*, *151*, 293–305. https://doi.org/10.1016/j.enbuild.2017.06.060

Matsuura, K. (1995). Effects of climate change on building energy consumption in cities. *Theoretical and Applied Climatology*, *51*(1–2), 105–117. https://doi.org/10.1007/BF00865545

Moazami, A., Nik, V. M., Carlucci, S., & Geving, S. (2019). Impacts of future weather data typology on building energy performance – Investigating long-term patterns of climate change and extreme weather conditions. *Applied Energy*, *238*(December 2018), 696–720. https://doi.org/10.1016/j.apenergy.2019.01.085

NREL. (2018). EnergyPlus - Weather Data Official site. Retrieved from https://energyplus.net/weather

Peel, M. C., Finlayson, B. L., & Mcmahon, T. A. (2007a). Updated world map of the Koppen-Geiger climate classification.

Peel, M. C., Finlayson, B. L., & Mcmahon, T. A. (2007b). Updated world map of the Köppen-Geiger climate classification. *Hydrology and Earth System Sciences Discussions*, *4*(2), 439–473. Retrieved from https://hal.archives-ouvertes.fr/hal-00298818/

Salata, F., Golasi, I., Domestico, U., Banditelli, M., Lo Basso, G., Nastasi, B., & de Lieto Vollaro, A. (2017). Heading towards the nZEB through CHP+HP systems. A comparison between retrofit solutions able to increase the energy performance for the heating and domestic hot water production in residential buildings. *Energy Conversion and Management*, *138*, 61–76. https://doi.org/10.1016/j.enconman.2017.01.062

Salata, F., Golasi, I., Verrusio, W., de Lieto Vollaro, E., Cacciafesta, M., & de Lieto Vollaro, A. (2018). On the necessities to analyse the thermohygrometric perception in aged people. A review about indoor thermal comfort, health and energetic aspects and a perspective for future studies. *Sustainable Cities and Society*, *41*(June), 469–480. https://doi.org/10.1016/j.scs.2018.06.003

Sedac Special Report on Emissions Scenarios - SRES, last access January 2019. Retrieved from http://sedac.ciesin.columbia.edu/ddc/sres/

Shen, P. (2017). Impacts of climate change on U.S. building energy use by using downscaled hourly future weather data. *Energy and Buildings*, *134*, 61–70. https://doi.org/10.1016/j.enbuild.2016.09.028

Shikama, T., Knitter, R., Konys, J., Muroga, T., Tsuchiya, K., Moesslang, A., … Nagata, S. (2008). Status of development of functional materials with perspective on beyond-ITER. *Fusion Engineering and Design*,

83(7–9), 976–982. https://doi.org/10.1016/J.FUSENGDES.2008.07.034

U.S. Global Change Research Program. (2018). Fourth National Climate Assessment, *II*, 1–470. https://doi.org/10.1016/j.pbb.2008.09.016

United Nations Statistics Division. (2018). 2018 Energy Statistics Pocketbook. *Statistics Paper Series E No. 1*, *67*, 64. Retrieved from https://unstats.un.org/unsd/energy/pocket/2018/2018pb-web.pdf

Ürge-Vorsatz, D. (n.d.). Energy End-Use: Buildings.

Wan, K. K. W., Li, D. H. W., Pan, W., & Lam, J. C. (2012). Impact of climate change on building energy use in different climate zones and mitigation and adaptation implications. *Applied Energy*, *97*, 274–282. https://doi.org/10.1016/j.apenergy.2011.11.048

Weather Data | EnergyPlus. (n.d.). Retrieved September 26, 2017, from https://energyplus.net/weather

Xu, P., Huang, Y. J., Miller, N., Schlegel, N., & Shen, P. (2012). Impacts of climate change on building heating and cooling energy patterns in California. *Energy*, *44*(1), 792–804. https://doi.org/10.1016/J.ENERGY.2012.05.013

Zhai, Z. J., & Helman, J. M. (2019). Implications of climate changes to building energy and design. *Sustainable Cities and Society*, *44*(June 2018), 511–519. https://doi.org/10.1016/j.scs.2018.10.043

Sensitivity Analysis of Door Gap Size and Solar Effect on Multi-zone Indoor Airflow CFD Simulation Using BIM

Jack C.P. Cheng [(a)], Helen H.L. Kwok [(a),*], Alison T.Y. Li [(a)], Jimmy C.K. Tong [(a)], Alexis K.H. Lau [(a)]
[(a)] Hong Kong University of Science and Technology, Hong Kong
[(b)] Ove Arup & Partners Hong Kong Ltd, Hong Kong
hlkwokab@connect.ust.hk

Abstract. Indoor airflow analysis using computational fluid dynamics (CFD) helps us study thermal comfort. Using measured data to validate CFD models can ensure the accuracy of simulations, and fine-tuning multi-zone CFD models helps further improve that accuracy. Previous studies have performed sensitivity analysis on isolated rooms to study how physical and turbulence parameters influence airflow patterns and to provide insights on models fine-tuning. However, these results do not reflect the sensitivity of multi-zone models, e.g., an office floor, which consists of zones with different mechanical ventilation and air conditioning (MVAC) layouts and are connected by doors. To investigate how multi-zone models should be tuned for higher accuracy, this study quantifies: (1) the impact that door gap sizes have on velocity variations, and (2) under different weather conditions, how much solar radiation impacts temperature distribution, using a validated CFD model of a typical office floor built with building information modeling (BIM) technology.

1. Introduction

Indoor airflow analysis using computational fluid dynamics (CFD) helps us study thermal comfort and indoor air quality (IAQ) (Nielsen 2015). Validation of CFD models using measured data is usually performed to ensure the accuracy of simulation results. When simulating airflow patterns in a multi-zone case, the model has more complicated geometry than in a single-room scenario. In a multi-zone model, the zones have different mechanical ventilation and air conditioning (MVAC) layouts. This requires applying different boundary conditions to different zones according to the MVAC layouts. Validating a CFD model often requires fine-tuning the accuracy of the model.

Previous studies would isolate rooms when performing sensitivity analysis on them to study how airflow pattern and temperature are influenced by such parameters as door openings (Kalliomaki et al. 2016) and turbulence models (Gilani et al. 2016). These results provide insights on how to fine-tune a CFD model to improve accuracy, but they cannot reflect the sensitivity of a multi-zone model of such places as an office floor, where different zones have different mechanical ventilation and air conditioning (MVAC) layouts. To investigate the sensitivity between different zones and different parameters, a multi-zone model is needed.

How indoor partitioning with doors modifies airflow patterns and pollutant dispersion has been studied in the past. The impacts that differing door sizes and types have on air velocity have been investigated (Kalliomaki et al. 2016, Lee et al. 2016). Closed doors were often assumed to be airtight in these studies. Nevertheless, the findings cannot be applied directly to a multi-zone environment, e.g., an office floor. Different MVAC settings are applied to different zones of an office floor and some of the zones may not have MVAC system installed. As these zones would not have air inlet or outlet, inside each of these zones the airflow is driven by the pressure difference between that zone and its adjacent zones. Therefore, that airflow is significantly affected by the airflows coming from those adjacent zones. Even when doors have been installed between zones and are closed, air can still travel between adjacent zones through the gaps in the doors, and that airflow needs to be taken into consideration. Hence, studying how the size of each door gap affects the velocity of air passing through that gap is necessary for improving the accuracy of multi-zone CFD simulations. When air flows from a tenant area to a corridor through a door gap, a sharp increase in velocity can be expected there. To simulate this sudden increase in velocity, first, the mesh in the door gap has to be made much finer than those in the tenant area and the corridor. This causes large variations in cell size near the door and worsens the aspect ratio of the mesh. Using a very fine mesh to conduct CFD simulations is computationally expensive, but conducting a sensitivity analysis on door gap sizes first can provide insights on how door gaps should be enlarged, in order to simulate the sharp increase in air velocity through door gaps.

The effect that solar radiation has on the temperature distribution in an indoor environment has been studied using transient CFD simulations with radiance models (Saberian and Sajadiye 2019). However, to estimate the solar heat gain for an office floor, any shading effect from the upper floors has to be considered. The CFD simulation must therefore include the whole building, making transient CFD simulations using a radiance model on an office floor computationally expensive. Another approach is to conduct steady-state CFD simulation with solar radiation on any windows that are identified as an internal heat source (Shan and Rim 2018). The solar heat load would then be deduced from the ASHRAE handbook (ASHRAE 2013). However, this approach considers neither the orientation, location, elevation of the testbed office room nor the weather conditions of the location. To properly estimate the solar heat load on the windows, both the geometry and semantic information of the model should be considered.

This study aims to address the above. It quantifies the impact of door gap size on velocity variations, and solar radiation on temperature distribution under different weather conditions, ultimately investigating how to tune a multi-zone model for higher accuracy. Essentially, this study proposes a workflow to conduct sensitivity analysis on a validated CFD model of a typical office floor using building information modeling (BIM) technology.

2. Methodology

The workflow that this study proposes is illustrated in Figure 1. BIM technology was implemented to modify the parameters for the sensitivity analysis. The illustrative example has a CFD model of a typical office floor, which was validated with field measurements (Kwok et al. in press). Figure 2 shows the BIM model of the office floor. This study used FLUENT to conduct steady-state CFD simulations (ANSYS Inc 2018). The SIMPLE algorithm was adopted for pressure-velocity coupling. A second-order upwind scheme was used for both the convection and viscous terms. An SST k-ω turbulence model was adopted. The transport equations and empirical constants used in FLUENT were the same as the original ones in Menter's paper (Menter 1994).

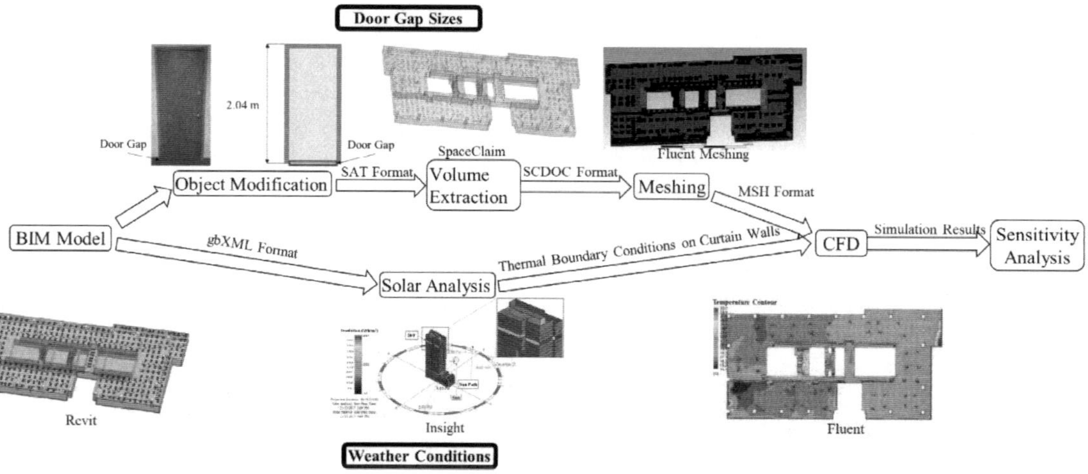

Figure 1: Workflow of Sensitivity Analysis using BIM and CFD

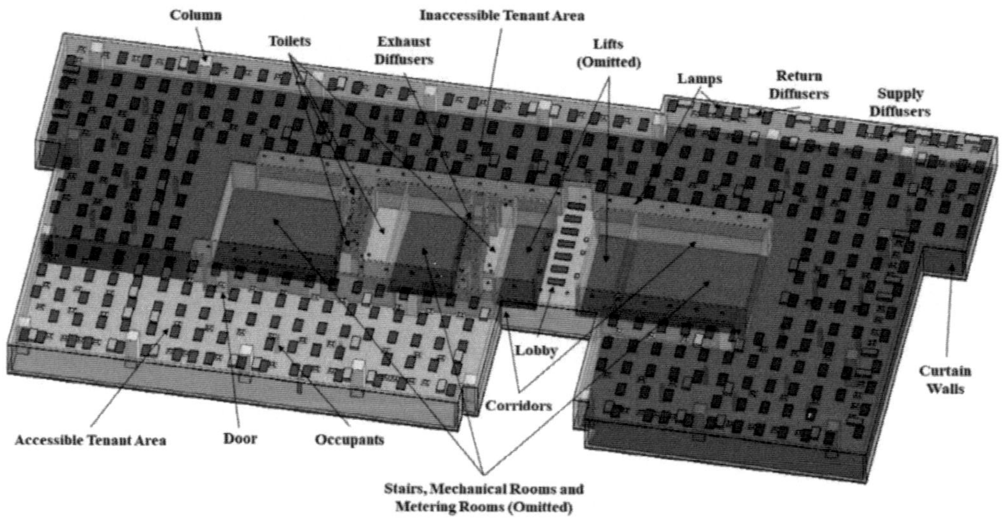

Figure 2: BIM Model of Studied Office Floor

2.1 Airflow Pattern Variation Induced by Different Door Gap Sizes

To study how to better simulate airflows through door gaps in a multi-zone model (where all doors are closed) by fine-tuning the sizes of those door gaps, vertical variations in air velocity caused by changes in door gap size were investigated. By conducting CFD simulations on different door gap sizes, the airflow passing through the door gaps was compared and determined whether a sharp increase in air velocity was present as expected. In the example, the actual size of each door gap was 1% of the height of the door panel; for the CFD simulations, the size of each door gap was varied between 1 and 5% of the height of the door panel. In turn, the size of the cells in the door gap varied with the door gap size: cell size was set to be half of door gap size at all times, in order to ensure that there was enough mesh to capture airflow through the door gap. The number of boundary layers is set to be 5 and the transitional ratio of the boundary layers is set to be 0.272. Using 3D CAD software to adjust the sizes of the door gaps, one by one, in a multi-door scenario, such as in the example (with 14 doors) would be error-prone; BIM technology provided a good alternative as it allowed all door gap sizes to be adjusted simultaneously. The study then used Revit to modified the BIM models (Autodesk Inc

2018). Doors were modeled as objects belonging to the same family, allowing the doors to have different sizes but identical material properties. Figure 3 shows one of the doors and its BIM model. The BIM models were then exported in SAT format to become part of the geometry of the model for CFD simulation.

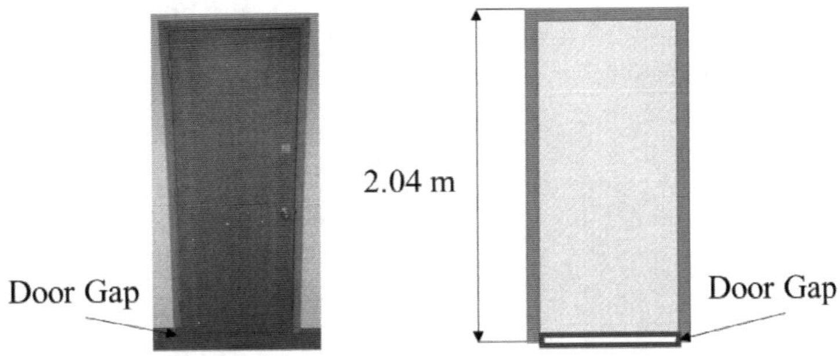

Figure 3: Actual Door (left) and BIM Model of the Door (right)

2.2 Temperature Variation Induced by Solar Radiation under Different Weather Conditions

The sensitivity analysis on how, under different weather conditions, solar radiation would impact temperature distribution on the office floor was conducted next. To simulate how much solar heat was gained and how it was distributed on the curtain walls, a solar analysis was conducted using Autodesk Insight (Autodesk Inc 2015). Autodesk Insight supports BIM-based solar analysis; its daylighting engine has been validated with measured data, and simulation results have been verified using Radiance, a popular daylighting engine. As there would be more floors above the one being studied, some of the solar radiation would be blocked or prevented from reaching its curtain walls; in other words, the solar analysis must be conducted on the entire building and not just on a particular floor. A BIM model of the whole building was used to conduct solar analysis on the exact location and orientation. The BIM model provided building geometry, orientation, location, material information, and weather data from nearby weather stations for the solar analysis. The generated 2-hour averaged insolence values on the curtain walls are inputted as heat flux boundary conditions of the curtain walls for the CFD simulations. To examine how different weather conditions affect solar radiation, the solar analysis was conducted at different times of the day (i.e. morning, noon and afternoon) and during different seasons of the year. Figures 4 and 5 show results of the solar analysis at different times of the day, and on different days of the year respectively.

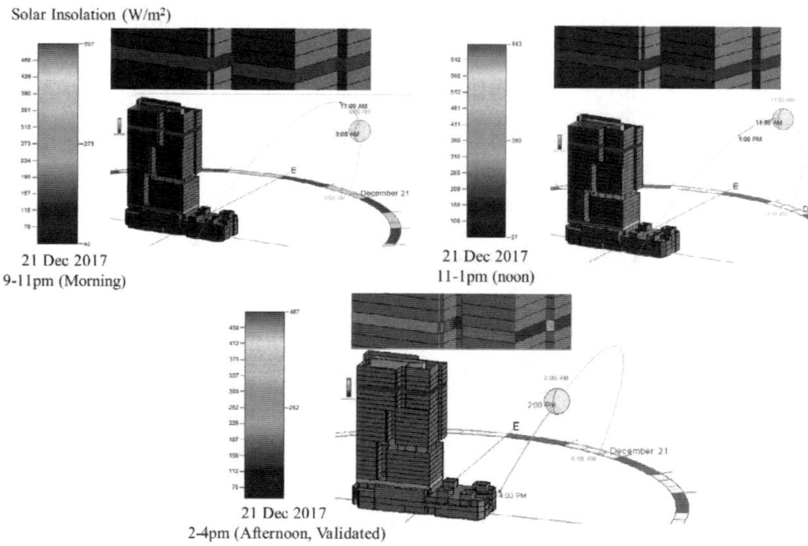

Figure 4: Solar Analysis Results at Different Times of the Day

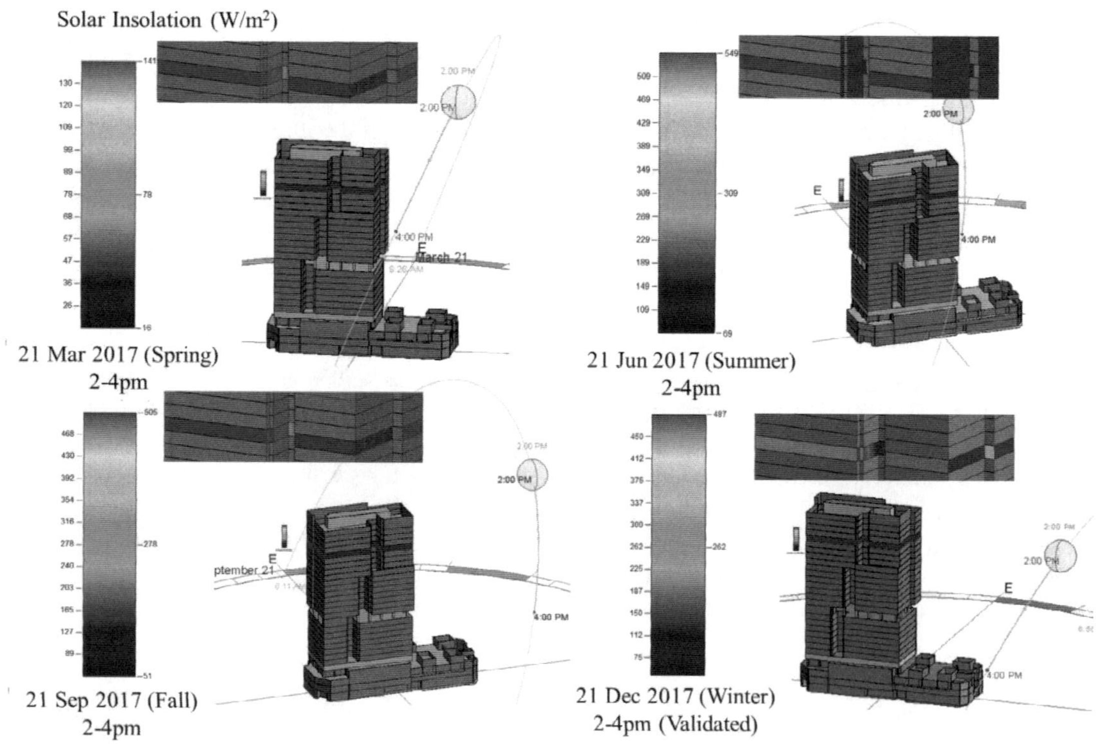

Figure 5: Solar Analysis Results in Different Days of the Year

3. Results and Discussions

3.1 Airflow Pattern Variation Induced by Different Door Gap Sizes

Figure 6 compares air velocity variations in the tenant area of the office floor at the halfway level of the door gap for different door gap sizes. When door gap size is < 3% of door height, air is trapped in the tenant area as the air velocity becomes close to zero when passing through the door gap. The velocity at the return diffuser on the right is also higher in the cases with door gap size < 3% of door height. This is because the air can only exit the tenant area via return diffusers. For the cases with door gap size > 3% of door height, a sharp increase in air velocity to > 0.6m/s was observed. This shows that the cases where door gap size > 3% of door height simulate air passing through door gap more accurately. For the region between two supply diffusers, air circulation increases as door gap size increases in general. The case where door gap size is 5% of door height has the fewest blue areas, hence the airflow here is stronger than in other cases. This implies that the 5% case has better mixing of air in the tenant area.

Figure 7 compares air velocity variations in the corridor along the centerline of the door gap for different door gap sizes. The CFD results show how air passes through door gaps in all cases. Similar to the results shown in Figure 5, only the cases with door gap size > 3% of door height are able to simulate the sharp increase in velocity. Moreover, higher air velocity is observed in the corridor in the cases where door gap size > 3% of door height than the others. Air movement is more prominent in the corridor and hence air is more thoroughtly mixed.

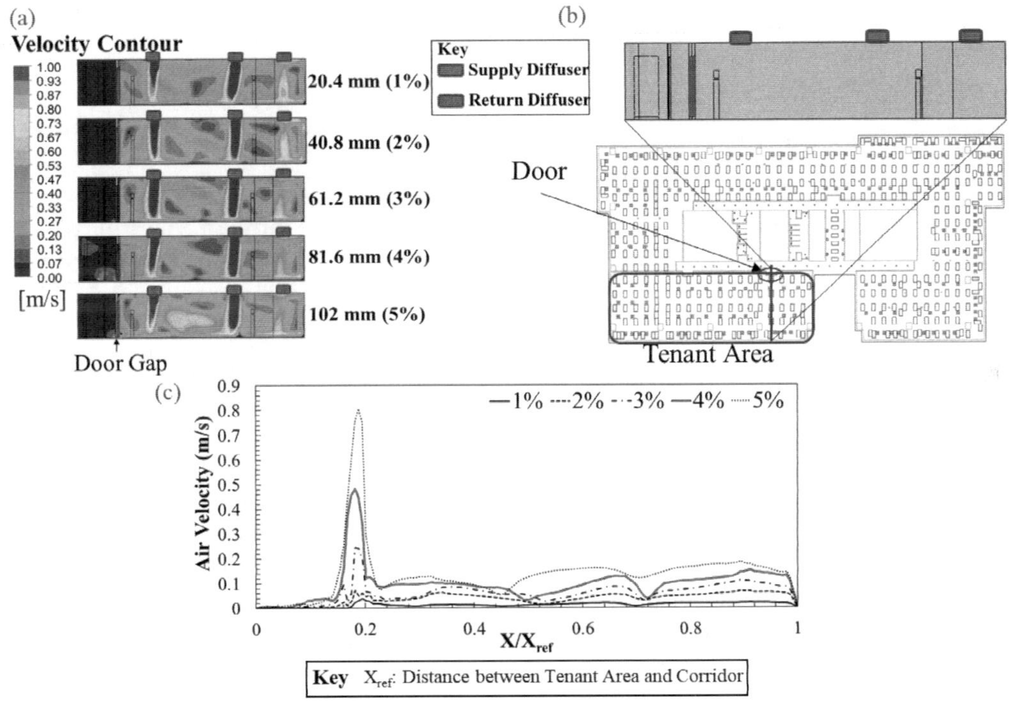

Figure 6: (a) Vertical Variations of Air Velocity for Different Door Gap Sizes in (b) Tenant Area; and (c) Comparison Different Door Gap Sizes among at the Height of the Centre of the Door Gap

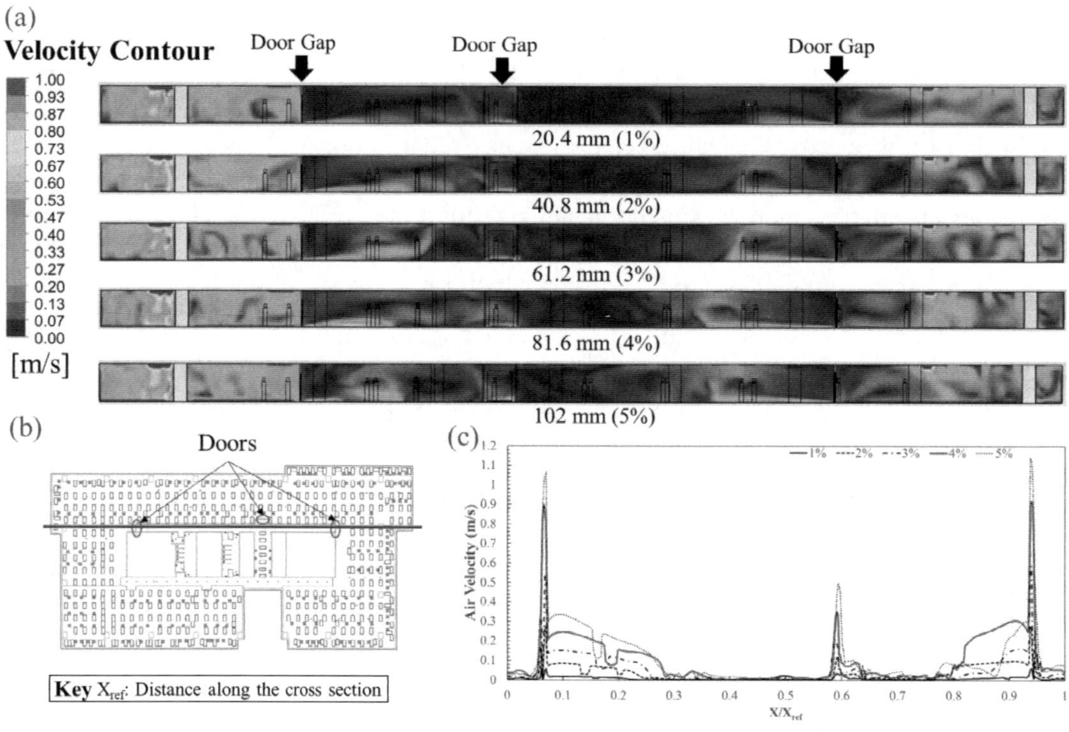

Figure 7: (a) Vertical Variations of Air Velocity for Different Door Gap Sizes in (b) Corridor; and (c) Comparison Different Door Gap Sizes among at the Height of the Centre of the Door Gaps

3.2 Temperature Variation Induced by Solar Radiation under Different Weather Conditions

Figure 8 shows the results of the temperature sensitivity analysis for solar radiation during different times of the day. The distributions of temperatures at nose level are presented. To compare the impact of solar radiation on different zones with different ventilation settings, the temperature results at P1 and P2, which are located in the tenant area and in the corridor respectively were investigated. Figures 8 (e) and 8 (f) show the normalized temperature results along the vertical direction at P1 and P2, respectively. Temperature distribution changes more significantly in the corridor than in the tenant area. As there is no MVAC system operating in the corridor, air flows to the corridor from the adjacent tenant area and lift lobby. Hence, heat is also transferred from these zones to the corridor. Since it is cooler in these zones in the 9:00-11:00 and 11:00-13:00 cases than the validated 14:00-16:00 case, the corridor also becomes cooler. In Figure 4 (f), the air is hotter near the ceiling, which is caused by the ceiling lamps.

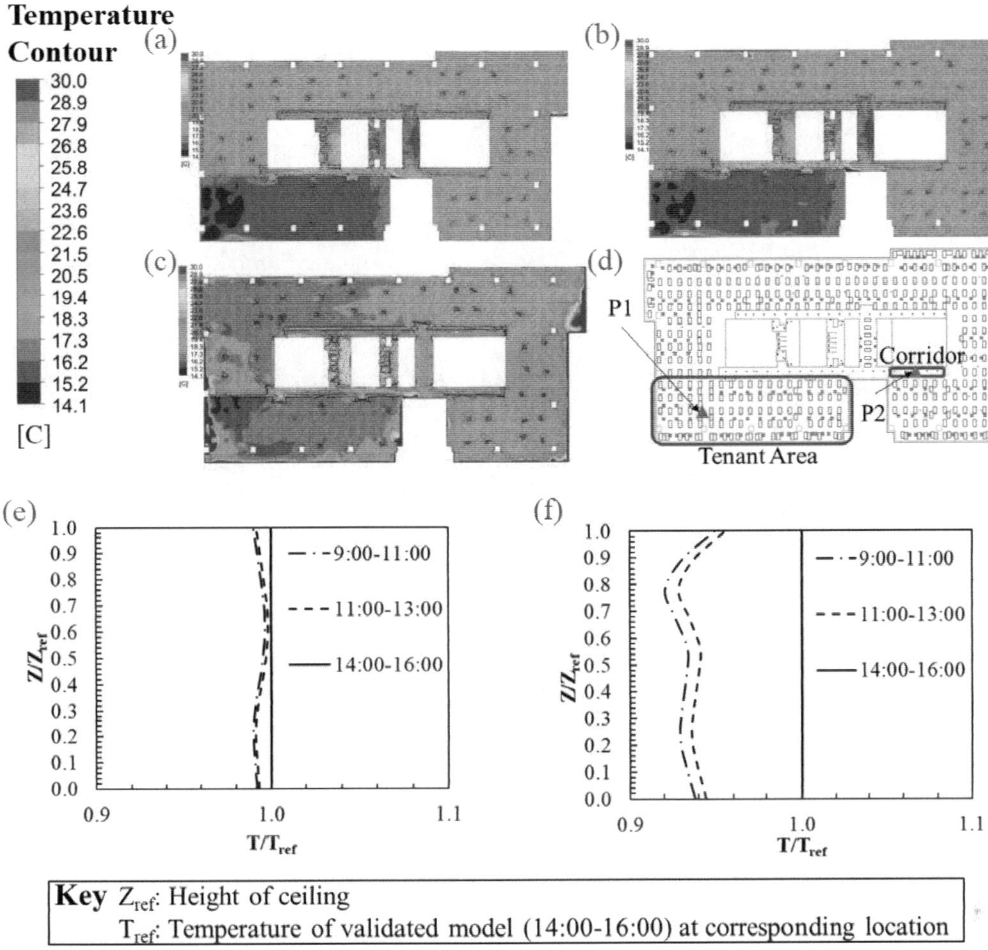

Figure 8: Temperature Distributions at Nose Level at Different Times of Day: (a) 9:00-11:00; (b) 11:00-13:00; and (c) 14:00-16:00; and Comparison of Normalized Temperature at Points Marked on (d) Floor Layout: (e) P1 in Tenant Area and (f) P2 in Corridor

To investigate the seasonal effect, Figure 9 shows temperature sensitivity analysis results for solar radiation during different days of the year. The normalized temperature results at P1 and P2 are also presented in Figures 9 (e) and 9 (f). The difference in overall temperature distribution on the floor among the cases is more significant than in the cases shown in Figure 7. The temperature variation is more substantial in regions close to the curtain walls as well as in the corridors. The toilets become hotter on the 21st of June and 21st of September. This is caused by the hot air coming from the corridor. Heat accumulation is also substantial in the two cases as solar radiation is stronger in these cases than in others. Similar to the cases of different times of the day, the corridor is more sensitive to solar heat and ceiling lamps than in the tenant area. In Figure 8 (f), peaks are formed between 0.6Z and 0.8Z in the corridor for the June 21 and September 21 cases. This is because air heated by the curtain walls near the lift lobby is hotter than the air coming from the tenant area. After entering the corridor, the hot air from the lift lobby is further heated by the ceiling lamps, thereby forming the peaks.

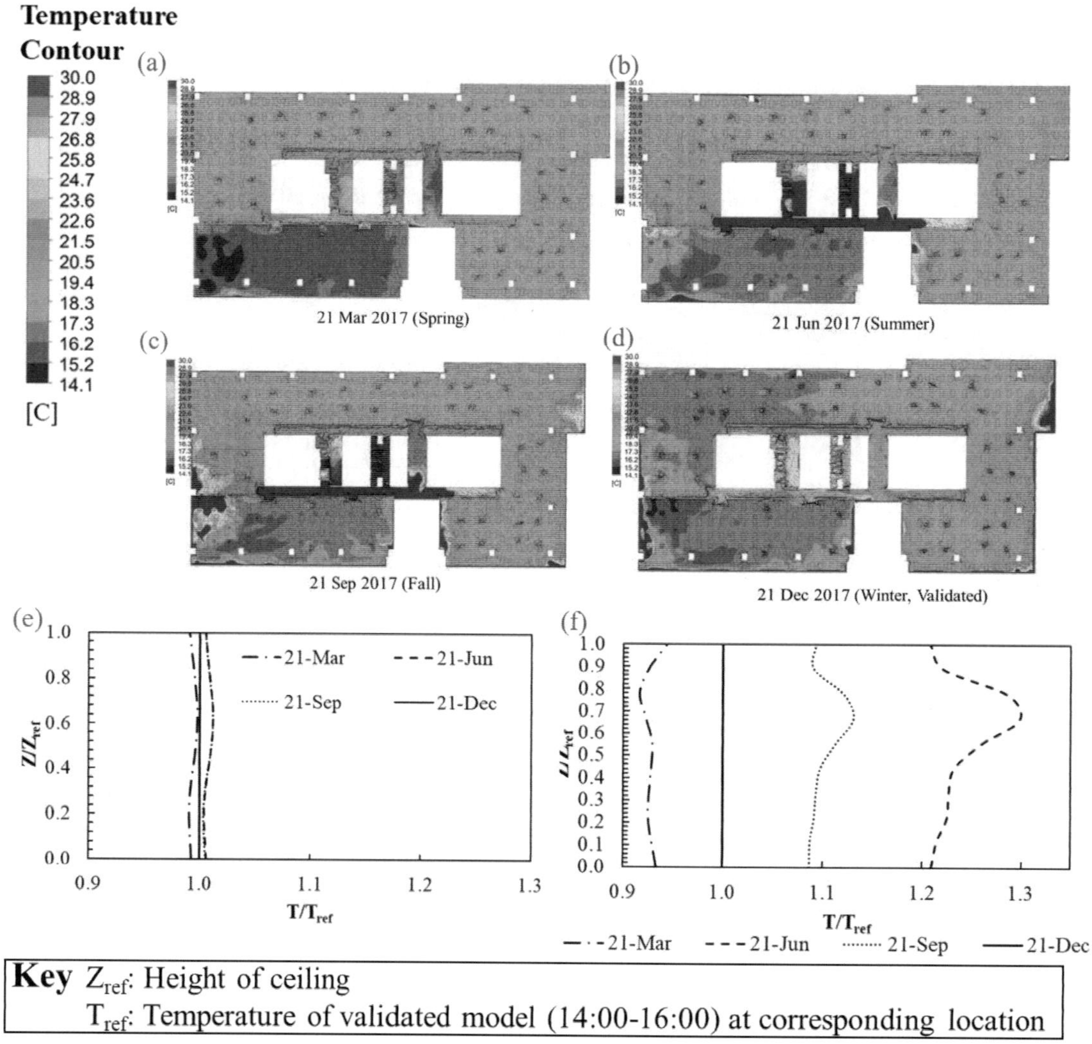

Figure 9: Temperature Distributions on Nose Level for Different Days of Year: (a) 21 Mar; (b) 21 Jun; (c) 21 Sep; and (c) 21 Dec; and Comparison of Normalized Temperature at: (e) P1 in Tenant Area and (f) P2 in Corridor

3.3 Limitations

Limitations in this study are:

1. Variability in body shapes of the office occupants was ignored. Each occupant was represented by a simplified manikin made of rectangular boxes. Airflow around the manikins was distorted.
2. The steady-state CFD simulation was conducted without occupant movements considered. The local variations in air velocity and temperature induced by movements were ignored in this study.
3. Furniture and room partitions inside the tenant areas were omitted. Hence, the deviations in airflow pattern caused by room layouts was not taken into account.

4. Conclusion and Future Study

The paper proposed a workflow to use a BIM multi-zone model to conduct a sensitivity analysis on air velocity and temperature to different door gap sizes and solar radiation under different weather conditions. The workflow was illustrated with a typical office floor. The sensitivity analysis on air velocity for different door gap sizes was conducted for door gap size of 1-5% of the door panel. The results show that a door gap size > 3% of the door panel is able to simulate the sharp increase in velocity when air is passing through the door gaps. As for the temperature sensitivity analysis results for solar radiation during different weather conditions, the zone without an MVAC system installed becomes more sensitive to solar radiation than the zone with an MVAC system operating. For future studies, how sensitive airflow is in different zones to different ventilation settings should be investigated. Moreover, how human movements, furniture and room partitions inside tenant areas alter the airflow pattern should be studied.

5. References

ANSYS INC (2018). Fluent User's Guide.

ASHRAE (2013). Handbook of Fundamentals. Atlanta: American Society of Heating, Refrigerating and Air Conditioning Engineers.

AUTODESK INC (2015). Autodesk Insight Frequently Asked Questions.

AUTODESK INC (2018). Revit.

GILANI, S., MONTAZERI, H., BLOCKEN, B. (2016). CFD simulation of stratified indoor environment in displacement ventilation: Validation and sensitivity analysis. Build. Environ. 95, pp. 299-313.

KALLIOMAKI, P., SAARINEN, P., TANG, J. W., KOSKELA, H. (2016). Airflow patterns through single hinged and sliding doors in hospital isolation rooms - Effect of ventilation, flow differential and passage. Build. Environ. 107, pp. 154-168.

KWOK, H. H. L., CHENG, J. C. P., LI, A. T. Y., TONG, J. C. K., LAU, A. K. H. (in press). Improving the Accuracy of Multi-zone Indoor Temperature CFD Simulation Under Limited Information Using Solar Analysis and BIM. CIB WBC 2019.

LEE, S., PARK, B., KURABUCHI, T. (2016). Numerical evaluation of influence of door opening on interzonal air exchange. Build Environ 102, pp. 230-242.

MENTER, F. R. (1994). 2-Equation Eddy-Viscosity Turbulence Models for Engineering Applications. Aiaa J 32, pp. 1598-1605.

NIELSEN, P. V. (2015). Fifty years of CFD for room air distribution. Build Environ 91, pp. 78-90.

SABERIAN, A., SAJADIYE, S. M. (2019). The effect of dynamic solar heat load on the greenhouse microclimate using CFD simulation. Renew Energ 138, pp. 722-737.

SHAN, W. Y., RIM, D. H. (2018). Thermal and ventilation performance of combined passive chilled beam and displacement ventilation systems. Energ Buildings 158, pp. 466-475.

Change Management Concepts for Structural Design in Early Planning Phases

Univ.-Prof. Dr.-Ing. M. Schnellenbach-Held, D. Steiner, M.Sc.
Institute for Structural Concrete, University of Duisburg-Essen, Essen, Germany
m.schnellenbach-held@uni-due.de (Lead author email address)

Abstract. Applicability and efficiency of a building design is significantly influenced by the supporting structure. Thus, a successful planning necessitates the integration of the structural engineering perspective in early phases. Additionally, the common design process is characterized by change requests that provoke interdisciplinary planning conflicts and inappropriate designs. To meet these challenges, intelligent substitution models for preliminary structural design are developed that are based on the application of engineering expert knowledge. Two methodologies are introduced for the management of design changes that are premised on the fuzzy logic-based formalization of the applied knowledge. For typical and common changes during the process, fuzzy requests are realized through temporary fuzzy sets that allow the finding of compromise solutions. Impact assessments for modifications of completed designs are enabled through extension of the applied inference systems. The presented concepts facilitate a decision support for change management and a resulting optimization of the design process.

1. Introduction

In early phases of the building planning process, the design is essentially based on creative and functional considerations. Hence, for structural assessments only few rough planning principles are allowed that commonly are simplified formulae and especially the expert experience of the structural engineers. Nevertheless, an early integration of essential structural information is of high importance for a successful design of buildings. The structural parameters are deducted from the basic specifications like the floor plan, the usage category and the building equipment that provide only few boundary conditions for the following preliminary design. Anyway, in this phase significant structural decisions are taken that entail a high influence on the further project processing and building construction (Zhang et al, 2018). The factors time and costs are significantly affected by the structural design and key aspects in the field of public construction and large-scale investments (Kim et al, 2015). Consequently, an integration of the structural design perspective in earliest possible planning phases is highly advisable (Schnellenbach-Held and Hartmann, 2003). For this purpose, the interdisciplinary collaboration of all involved planners is necessary at the same time (Oh et al, 2015; El-Diraby et al, 2017). This demands the introduction of applicable structural engineering expertise in the preliminary design stage. In addition to a useful formalization of the knowledge, its generation usually requires extensive structural analyses and simulations (Liu et al 2018). The resulting systems for the support of design decisions need to process and recommend structural solutions based on few specifications and vague parameters (Schnellenbach-Held and Albert, 2003). For this purpose, intelligent substitution models are developed that are based on development-level dependent fuzzy knowledge bases for structural design. The new approach utilizes the common intuitive engineering expertise that necessitates a specialized system of development levels as well as an applicable knowledge formalization with fuzzy logic (Steiner and Schnellenbach-Held, 2018).

In addition to the challenge of early interdisciplinary planning, the preliminary design of buildings is characterized by design modification requests from the involved planners. In principle, two differentiable kinds of demanded model parameter changes are identifiable. Typical and common adjustments occur during the design process and modifications of a completed design appear after the regular process. In the field of computer-aided decision-making, such revisions frequently provoke conflict situations that result in inappropriate designs. The ability of modification handling is realizable through applicable change management concepts. For this purpose, two basic methodologies are developed that provide a support of the decision-making process for design modification requests. For conflict situations that are induced by typical and common changes and occur during the design process, the concept of fuzzy requests allows the detection of compromise solutions. Through enhancement of the inference systems that are included in the substitution models, an impact assessment is enabled for design modifications appearing after the regular process. These methodologies enable an optimization of the building planning process through an advanced decision support. In this paper, the change management concepts for structural design in early planning phases are presented that allow the consideration of modification requests in the early design process.

2. Structural design in early planning phases

For an integration of the structural engineering perspective in early planning phases of the building design process, intelligent substitution models are developed that are based on development-level dependent expert knowledge. The applied knowledge is assigned to a specialized detailing system that consists of identified development levels for the preliminary structural design. Regarding the development of a supporting system, level dependent fuzzy knowledge bases for structural design are formulated and generated to include applicable engineering experience. For an imitation of the related decision-making process, intelligent substitution models are developed that are premised on the inference of the fuzzy knowledge bases. By means of the resulting systems, a decision support for structural preliminary design (pre-design) is realized. This enables the integration of the structural engineering perspective in early planning phases and thus an associated optimization of the building design process (Steiner and Schnellenbach-Held, 2018).

2.1 Adaptive levels of development for structural pre-design

In the common process of preliminary design and early assessments of supporting structures, the applied engineering knowledge and experience is assignable to typical levels of detailing and development (Maier et al, 2017). For a structural design, important information is premised on criteria like usability, load carrying capacity and cost efficiency of a load bearing system. Based on analyzed requirements for the included information and comprehension for structural design, an applicable configuration of Adaptive Levels of Development (ALoDs) and included parameters is developed for building models. In addition to adaptivity needs for multidisciplinary building design scenarios (Schnellenbach-Held and Steiner, 2019), the specialized perspective requires a new level system besides the numerous existing LOD specifications. The resulting level system (see figure 1) includes a basic understanding of structural engineering as well as related parameters that are necessary for the representation and further development of a supporting structure. For this purpose, five ALoDs are identified to represent applicable model states that are based on the pragmatic structural engineering comprehension. These levels are connected through transfer functions that increase the development status of the building model. The associated necessary determination of additional information is performed by the intelligent substitution models for structural pre-design that represent the implementation of the transfer functions (Steiner, 2018).

In the beginning of the design process the "ALoD 0" is defined as blackbox that provides initial parameters for global information and environmental conditions as well as the external model dimensions. Based on the ALoD 0, the subsequent floor plan development of the architect or a construction grid estimation through the substitution model "grid" are enabled. The architect-driven development results in the geometrical specification of the entire building model that is content of the "ALoD 1" enclosing the complete geometries of all components. Based on the geometric information, the common idealization of load-bearing elements is realizable through the positioning method. Alternatively, the idealized elements are inserted in the context of the grid estimation that is based on structural engineering knowledge.

In both ways, common structural positions are integrated into the model as the typical idealized elements in "ALoD 2a" that are the basis for the assessment and the design of structures with engineering expert knowledge according to conventional calculation approaches. Determination of the suitability of the structural positions is performed by the substitution model "possibility" that simulates the evaluation of structural designs based on engineering experience. For the resulting expert rating in "ALoD 2b", the possibility value is introduced that features a value range from 0,0 for "not realizable" over 0,5 for "possible" up to 1,0 for "optimal" designs. The resulting formalization of structural assessments allows the decision-making support for the design process and for the management of design modifications. The characteristic structural parameters of the selected design are determined by the substitution model "pre-design" that finalizes the preliminary dimensioning of the supporting elements. These conclusive pre-design specifications are content of the "ALoD 3" that comprises the preliminarily dimensioned structural solution and allows further analyses of the building model (Steiner and Schnellenbach-Held, 2018).

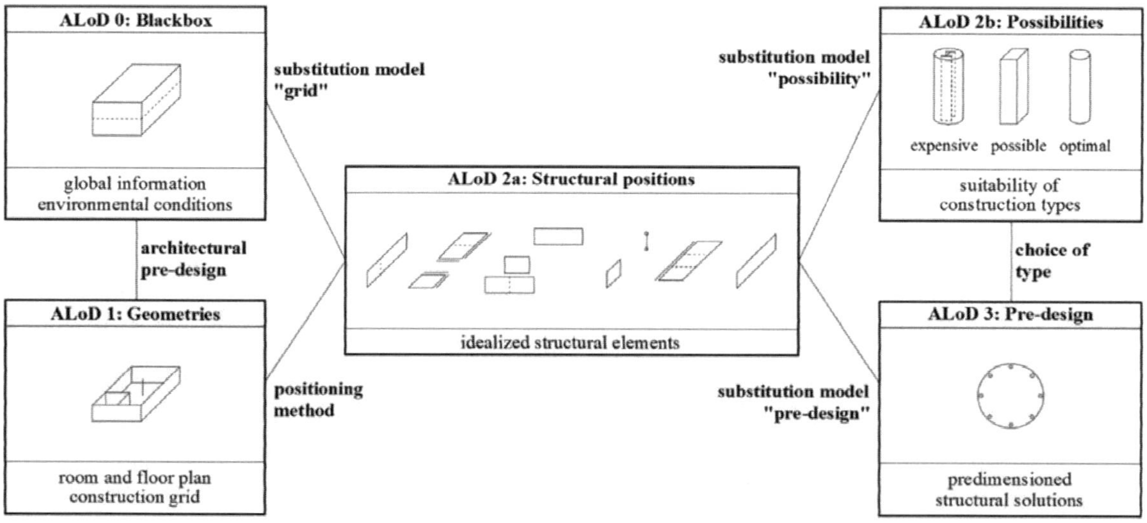

Figure 1: Development system for structural design based on Steiner and Schnellenbach-Held 2018.

2.2 Intelligent substitution models for structural pre-design

The concept of the developed intelligent substitution models is based on the application of engineering experience for structural preliminary design. Formalization of this expertise is realized using fuzzy logic-based methods that allow the application of expert knowledge and rule-based inference systems. Featuring extraordinary generalization abilities, these systems enable the imitation of human problem-solving mechanisms and reasoning competences even under most complex conditions (Steiner and Schnellenbach-Held, 2017). In the field of artificial intelligence (AI), fuzzy logic inference systems are common and well-known solutions for the simulation of decision-making processes (Schnellenbach-Held and Steiner, 2014).

Using the fuzzy approach, ALoD-dependent fuzzy knowledge bases are developed. They include applicable expert knowledge for the assessment and the structural design of load-bearing elements that is based on binding codes and directive standards as well as engineering knowledge, experience and competence. Following the formalization approach, the resulting rule bases are phrased in the Modus Ponens "if premise (lower ALoD), then conclusion (higher ALoD)" that is transparent and easy to understand (see table 1). The related decision-making processes are realized with functional TSK fuzzy inference systems that enable the evaluation of parameters for the model development through application of the engineering knowledge (Steiner and Schnellenbach-Held 2018).

Table 1: Exemplary rule for the inference systems of the substitution models

Rule		Parameter		Fuzzy set	Crisp value	ALoD
IF		Position	=		Single-span slab	ALoD 2a
	AND	Useful load	=	"small"	2,00 kN/m²	ALoD 2a
	AND	Height	=	"small"	0,20 m	ALoD 2a
	AND	Length	=	"small"	3,00 m	ALoD 2a
THEN		Possibility	=	"optimal"	1,0 –	ALoD 2b
	AND	Concrete class	=		C20: Smallest possible	ALoD 3
	AND	Reinforcement	=	"small"	6,79 kg/m	ALoD 3

Generation of the knowledge is based on parameter studies for the structural design of typical idealized positions of load bearing elements (ALoD 2a). For the configuration of the studies, adequate value boundaries and a sampling of the parameters are determined through common engineering experience. Based on the satisfaction of the required limit states according to Eurocode, the usability (ALoD 2b) and the design values (ALoD 3) of a structural element are determined. In the process, the qualification of the elements is formulated as "possible" for plannable elements and "not realizable" for infringing structures. Further determinations of the possibility are based on expert knowledge for structural ratings. As large numbers of realizable solutions occur for certain boundary conditions, optimization tasks are performed as search for the minimal approximate realization effort. The results are expressed as expert rules that are verifiable with common engineering experience. Using the additional knowledge for structural assessments, the possibility values are updated and thus a comparison basis is established for design choices and the change management. Based on the combination of the possibility progressions and the expert assessment knowledge, superordinate rules are identified that allow an estimation of construction grids with applicable and optimized structural positions (ALoD 2a). Finally, the rule bases of the inference systems are derived from the incrementally approximated functions for structural design. With the resulting substitution models, a reliable decision support is realized that enables an integration of the structural engineering perspective in early phases of the building design process (Steiner, 2018).

3. Fuzzy requests for compromise solutions

Typical and common design changes occur during the design process. Intended by the involved planners in the preliminary design of architectures, they often provoke conflict situations between the different planning disciplines. Using computer-aided decision-making processes, such changes provoke improper results that occur due to effects on assessments of the other planners. In the common real design process, these change requests are not formulated as a categorical modification by a certain value of an exact amount, but rather as an allowed fuzzy range of adjustment. Providing that these ranges indicate the preferences for different modification values, this formulation enables a compromise finding for the change induced interdisciplinary planning conflicts (Steiner and Schnellenbach-Held, 2018).

3.1 Formalization of fuzzy requests

As example, the structural engineer formulates a request for the change of a girder height using sharp values (see figure 2). The requested modification could be a crisp height increase from 60 cm to 80 cm in order to save reinforcement. As this change gives only few opportunities, there is a high risk of rejection of this request by the architect, possibly because the required clear room height is not achieved. Conversely, the request can be expressed with fuzzy values that rise from 0 at 60 cm to 1 at 80 cm. The assessment of the architect can be phrased analogously with involved preferences like falling from 1 at 60 cm to 0 at 80 cm. In doing so, the detection of an appropriate compromise solution is much more likely, as much more opportunities are given.

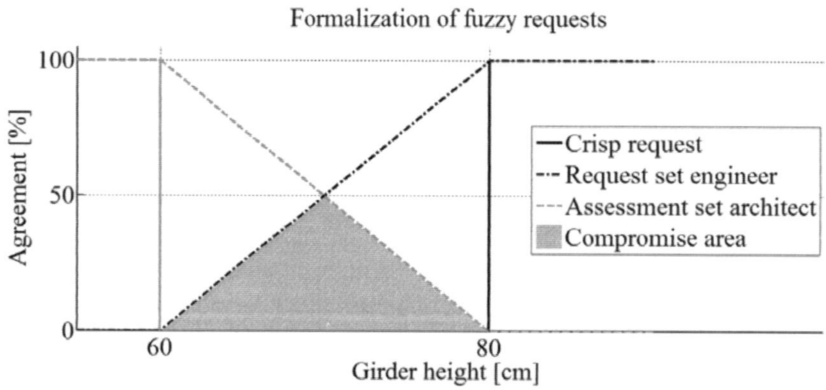

Figure 2: Formalization of change requests with fuzzy sets

The required integration of progressions in the design priorities of the different disciplines can be realized through the request formalization with fuzzy values. In accordance with ALoD 2b, the membership values of these sets conform to the possibility values that range from 0 for "unsuitable" over 0.5 for "possible" to 1 for "optimal" ratings. The resulting formalization of fuzzy requests through possibility progressions includes the allowed value ranges for the design modification as well as related preferences of the planners. The resulting concept of "fuzzy requests" is a promising approach for the management of common changes during the preliminary design of buildings. A practice-oriented modeling and support of frequently occurring interdisciplinary planning conflicts are enabled by the included computer-aided decision-making processes. This can significantly contribute to the perpetuation of continuity and integrity of the design process in early phases.

3.2 Compromise solution detection

The consideration of fuzzy requests within the developed ALoD-system and substitution models as well as the resulting complementation of the compromise finding require associated analyses based on fuzzy parameters. The extension principle according to L.A. Zadeh (Zadeh, 1965) represents a theoretical basis for the generalization of arbitrary functions to fuzzy input parameters. Considering a function with a fuzzy set as delivered argument, this principle allows the determination of membership progressions for the functional fuzzy parameters. The application of α-cuts has been proved to be helpful for the computational implementation of the extension principle (Kaufmann, 1985). For a fuzzy set, the α-cut is a crisp set of all elements that feature a membership degree μ in the confidence interval, where $\mu \geq \alpha$ is satisfied. Thereby, a discretization of the fuzzy sets is enabled. For a function with fuzzy input parameters, the determination of membership functions for result variables proved to be problematic when using α-cuts, if non-monotone mapping operators are used or the input variables are influencing each other. Therefore, various methods have been developed to specify conditions for the mapping operator and the input parameters (Wood et al, 1992; Dong and Shah, 1987).

Though, the method of α-level optimization requires no such conditions (Möller et al, 2000). This approach is based on a combination of evolutionary strategies, the gradient method and Monte Carlo simulations, hence high computational efforts are necessary in return. A further approach is the "transformation method" in a general or reduced form (Hanss, 2003). While the general transformation method is generally valid, the reduced transformation method may require monotony of the mapping operator. Based on the L-R representation, computational efforts are significantly minimized in the reduced transformation method by a reduction of calculations that are performed at the interval boundaries of α-cuts. The α-level optimization (Möller et al, 2000) and especially the transformation method (Hanss, 2003) appear to be suitable for an implementation of the extension principle using α-cuts. Based on these technologies, a methodology for fuzzy requests is developed and the decision-making support in the design process via compromise solution detection is rendered possible.

3.3 Concept of fuzzy requests in early design phases

The developed concept is based on the application of temporary fuzzy sets (see figure 3). Regarding the structural design, the fuzzy request sets are determined by the possibility substitution model. For this purpose, an incremental assessment of the possibility values is performed over the requested modification domain. Through expression of fuzzy requests with an assessed suitability for important modification values, the applied formalization can be used analogously by the other planning disciplines. Consequently, comparability of the request sets from the different planners is ensured and thus joint evaluations are enabled.

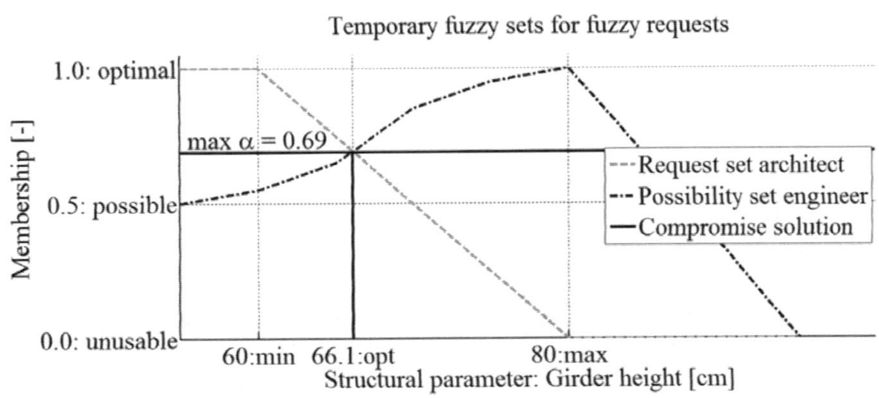

Figure 3: Detection of compromise solutions with temporary fuzzy sets

In consideration of the temporary fuzzy request sets from all design participants, the detection of compromise solutions is realizable. For this purpose, the best rated match is subsequently identified through a search algorithm that is based on the α-cut principles to find the highest possible α-value that is simultaneously valid for all included fuzzy sets. Through this α-level optimization, the most suitable modification value is determined that features the highest membership value for all involved planning disciplines. The resulting methodology of temporary fuzzy sets finally enables the integration of fuzzy requests in the design process. Thus, a computer-aided decision-making support for common multidisciplinary design changes during the process is established.

4. Substitution model extension for evaluation of design modifications

Next to the typical design changes with fuzzy requests, the current design process is characterized by further modification demands that occur after compromise detections and design selections. Such model modifications commonly result in a disproportionately high effort for the determination of remodeling needs and the redesign of the building model. Especially, the necessity to remodel limited sections or the entire load bearing system significantly influences time and costs, as the evaluation of modification impacts on the structural design involves a high complexity. Thus, the assessment of the consequences resulting from such model changes is particularly relevant for the optimization of the design process. For the determination of design modification effects, an applicable methodology is developed that is based on the engineering expert knowledge and intelligent substitution models for structural design in early phases (Steiner and Schnellenbach-Held, 2018).

4.1 Approach for the evaluation of design modifications in early phases

For this purpose, the development of fuzzy inference systems is an appropriate approach that is based on preceding knowledge analyses combined with a threshold for decision imitation. Thus, the developed methodology is premised on exploration and further application of the existing fuzzy knowledge bases. Using complementary rules that are derived from the engineering expert knowledge for parameter modifications, the processing of design changes is enabled. By extension of the mapping rules included in the substitution models, an advanced inference system is developed (see table 2 compared to table 1). The formalization of the resulting systems allows the consideration of completed structural designs as well as parameter modifications. It incorporates previous design parameters as well as the model change request for the estimation of modification effects on the applicability and design of structural elements.

The actualized possibility value of ALoD 2b that is evaluated considering the change, indicates the usability of the present structure for the modified design. Following the definition of the structural possibility, the applicability assessment is based on the interpretation of evaluated possibility values after the change. If the value exceeds a certain threshold that is inspired by the 0,5 for "possible" in the substitution model "possibility", the structure can be considered as still possible and thus a remodeling of the design is not required. In this case, the necessary adjustments of the design parameters in ALoD 3 are determined for the structural element. Otherwise, if the value falls below the threshold, the structural element must be rated as not realizable anymore and thus a model actualization in ALoD 1 and ALoD 2a is necessary or the modification has to be rejected. Thus, the assessment of model change impacts is realized through the advanced inference systems. By application of the existing knowledge bases, aspects regarding the construction, safety and economy of structural elements are integrated in the change management process. The resulting extended substitution models involve the structural engineering expert knowledge that allows the support of highly complex decision-making processes through evaluation of design modifications.

Table 2: Exemplary extended rule for modification assessment

Rule		Parameter		Fuzzy set	Crisp value	ALoD
IF		Position	=		Single-span slab	ALoD 2a
	AND	Useful load	=	"small"	2,00 kN/m²	ALoD 2a
	AND	Height	=	"small"	0,20 m	ALoD 2a
	AND	Length	=	"small"	3,00 m	ALoD 2a
	AND	Concrete class	=		C20	ALoD 3
	AND	Reinforcement	=	"small"	6,79 kg/m	ALoD 3
	AND	Height change	=	"increase"	+ 0,10 m (modification)	ALoD 2a
THEN		Possibility	=	"less"	0,5 – (– 0,5 –)	ALoD 2b
	AND	Concrete class	=		C20 still realizable	ALoD 3
	AND	Reinforcement	=	"more"	8,82 kg/m (+ 2,03 kg/m)	ALoD 3
	AND	Dead load	=	"more"	7,5 kN/m² (+ 2,5 kN/m²)	ALoD 2a

4.2 Substitution model extension

Generation of these inference systems is based on analyses of the applied engineering experience and knowledge bases that are used in the substitution models for structural design. For this purpose, the influence of parameter modifications on the structural key values is determined through sensitivity analyses. These utilize the inference systems for structural design and the included rule-based functional mapping, so that the necessary structural adjustments of the model can be determined that are reasoned by design changes. The modification impact on a structural element is evaluated through the resulting variations of the possibility in ALoD 2b and design values in ALoD 3. In addition to that, actualizations of the load transfer are considered that correspond to ALoD 2a. Thus, change impacts can be propagated to connected structural elements and consequently through the entire load bearing system. The progressions of the key parameters that are determined through the sensitivity analyses, reveal the superordinate knowledge that is applicable for the assessment of design modifications. Consequently, the resulting change management approach is based on engineering expert knowledge that includes safety, practical and economic aspects. Thus, structural engineering experience allows the support of the highly complex decision-making for the evaluation of modifications resulting in an optimization of the building design process.

4.3 Integration of learning abilities

The threshold value indicates the border point between the acceptance or rejection of a design modification. Thus, it is a key component for the imitation of underlying decision-making processes. In practice, this limit value is strongly affected by further structural engineering knowledge that is achieved through tendencies within the expert experience. Such trends can be used to further optimize the inference system for design modifications. For this purpose, the decision limit is formalized as adaptive self-learning threshold value that enables a successive inclusion of the tendencies from engineering expertise through actualizations of the limit. These adjustments are performed once the decision for the design modification is taken by the involved planners supported by the extended substitution models.

In the process, the threshold is increased, if a modification request is rejected. For the higher limit value, future modifications of the same type must produce a better suitability and thus are less likely to be recommended. Otherwise, the threshold is decreased, if a modification request is accepted. With the lower limit value, the prospective recommendation of similar design changes is more probable, as a lower possibility value is needed. Based on the training of artificial neural networks, adaptation of the threshold is performed in a softened incremental manner. This leads to a harmonization of the learning process, as strong oscillations between different choices are avoided. In doing so, the tendencies resulting from taken decisions about acceptance or rejection of design modifications are considered in the change management. Thus, the actualization of the adaptive threshold results in a successive integration of further expert experience in the decision support and an according optimization of the process.

5. Conclusions

In early phases of the building design process, an interdisciplinary planning is of high importance for the creation and modification of a building model. For an integration of the structural design perspective in the preliminary design stage, intelligent substitution models are developed. These systems are based on the application of structural engineering expert knowledge and provide a decision support for the building design development. Based on the involved knowledge formalization in fuzzy knowledge bases, methodologies for a model change management are developed that enable the consideration of the characteristic design modification requests.

During the design process, typical and common model changes often provoke conflict situations between the involved planning disciplines and lead to improper results. Using a formalization with fuzzy ranges considering the expert assessment, these modification demands are expressed as fuzzy requests enabling a compromise finding. The methodology of temporary fuzzy sets allows the integration of fuzzy requests in the early design process providing a decision support for common multidisciplinary design changes.

After the regular design process, further demands for design changes involve the modification of a completed building model, commonly resulting in disproportionately high efforts for change impact evaluation and remodeling. Based on analyses of the fuzzy knowledge bases for structural preliminary design, the inference systems of the substitution models are extended to enable an assessment of design modification effects. The resulting approach uses the engineering expert knowledge for structural design to provide a decision support for the highly complex task of processing building model modifications.

The presented change management concepts for structural design in early planning phases allow an optimization of the building design process. Therefore, continuity and integrity of the process are enhanced through decision support abilities for design modification requests. Based on the application of fuzzy methods with expert knowledge for structural engineering, the methodologies feature a high transparency and opportunities for interdisciplinary cooperation. Thus, an integration of the structural design perspective and an interdisciplinary planning are enabled to enhance the model modification processing in early design phases.

In future work, the applicability, practicability and optimization potential of the developed change management concepts are evaluated. For this purpose, practice-based and random examples for modifications of sample projects are processed by a prototypical implementation. Further development of the change management involves suggestions of model adjustments in ALoD 1 and ALoD 2a, if no usable compromise solution is detectable or the design needs to be remodeled. Following the development of the substitution model "grid", applicable modifications of geometrical model parameters can be determined through optimization tasks.

To allow an interdisciplinary assessment, these model change recommendations from the structural design perspective can be provided as options.

Acknowledgements

This project is supported by the German Research Foundation (DFG) in the context of the DFG Research Unit 2363 "Evaluation of building design variants in early phases using adaptive levels of development". We are grateful to the DFG for its support.

References

Dong, W.; Shah, H. C. (1987). Vertex Method for Computing Functions of Fuzzy Variables. Fuzzy Sets and Systems 24, pp. 65-78.

El-Diraby, T. and Krijen, T. and Papagelis, M. (2017). BIM-based collaborative design and socio-technical analysis of green buildings. Automation in Construction 82, pp. 59-74.

Hanss, M. (2003). Simulation and Analysis of Fuzzy-parameterized Models with the Extended Transformation Method. Proceedings of the 22nd NAFIPS Int. Conf., Chicago, IL, USA.

Kaufmann, A., Gupta, M.M. (1985). Introduction to Fuzzy Arithmetic: Theory and Applications. Electrical/Computer Science and Engineering Series, Van Nostrand Reinhold, New York.

Kim, J.I., Kim, J., Fischer, M., Orr, R. (2015). BIM-based decision-support method for master planning of sustainable large-scale developments. Automation in Construction 58, pp. 95-108.

Liu, H., Ong, Y.S., Cai, J. (2018). A survey of adaptive sampling for global metamodeling in support of simulation-based complex engineering design. Structural and Multi-disciplinary Optimization 57, pp. 393-416.

Maier, J.F., Eckert, C.M., Clarkson, P.J. (2017). Model granularity in engineering design – concepts and framework. Design Science, Volume 3, Cambridge.

Möller, B., Graf, W., Beer, M. (2000). Fuzzy-Tragwerksanalyse – Tragwerksanalyse mit unscharfen Parametern (in German). Bauingenieur 75, pp. 697-705.

Oh, M., Lee, J., Wan Hong, S., Jeong, Y. (2015). Integrated system for BIM-based collaborative design. Automation in Construction 58, pp. 196-206.

Schnellenbach-Held, M., Albert, A. (2003). Integrating knowledge based systems with Fuzzy logic to support the early stages of structural design (in German). Bauingenieur 11/2003, pp. 517-524.

Schnellenbach-Held, M., Hartmann, M. (2003). Using Knowledge Based Systems for Building Design in Computer Supported Cooperative Work. Darmstadt Concrete V18, Darmstadt.

Schnellenbach-Held, M., Steiner, D. (2014). Self-Tuning Closed-Loop Fuzzy Logic Control Algorithm for Adaptive Prestressed Structures. Structural Engineering International 24(2), pp. 163-172.

Schnellenbach-Held, M., Steiner, D. (2019). Structural design in early planning phases using engineering expert knowledge and intelligent substitution models. In: Proceedings of the 36th CIB W78 Conference, September 2019, Newcastle, submitted paper.

Steiner, D., Schnellenbach-Held, M. (2017). Realization of Adaptive Prestressing. In M. van Scheven & M.A., Keip & N. Karajan (eds.), Proceedings of the 7th GACM Colloquium on Computational Mechanics for Young Scientists from Academia and Industry, 11–13 October 2017, Stuttgart.

Steiner, D., Schnellenbach-Held, M. (2018). Intelligent Substitution Models for Structural Design in early BIM Stages. Publications of the Sixth International Symposium on Life-Cycle Engineering, October 2018, Ghent.

Steiner, D. (2018). Formulierung und Generierung von Expertenwissen zur Entwicklung intelligenter Ersatzmodelle für die Tragwerksplanung in frühen Entwurfsphasen (in German). Tagungsband 30. Forum Bauinformatik, 19–21 September 2018, Weimar.

Wood, K.L., Otto, K.N., Antonsson, E.K. (1992). Engineering Design Calculations with Fuzzy Parameters. Fuzzy Sets and Systems 52, pp. 1-20.

Zadeh, L. A. (1965). Fuzzy Sets. Information and Control 8, pp. 338-353.

Zhang, J., Li, H., Zhao, Y., Ren, G. (2018). An ontology-based approach supporting holistic structural design with the consideration of safety, environmental impact and cost. Advances in Engineering Software 115, pp. 26-39.

A Multi Agent Systems framework for integrating environmental parameters in the design of shell structures

Evangelos Pantazis[1], David Jason Gerber[2]

[1] Ph.D. Candidate, Sonny Astani Department of Civil and Environmental Engineering, University of Southern California, Los Angeles, California 90089. E-mail: epantazi@usc.edu
[2] Associate Professor of Practice, Sonny Astani Department of Civil and Environmental Engineering, University of Southern California, Los Angeles, California 90089. E-mail: dgerber@usc.edu

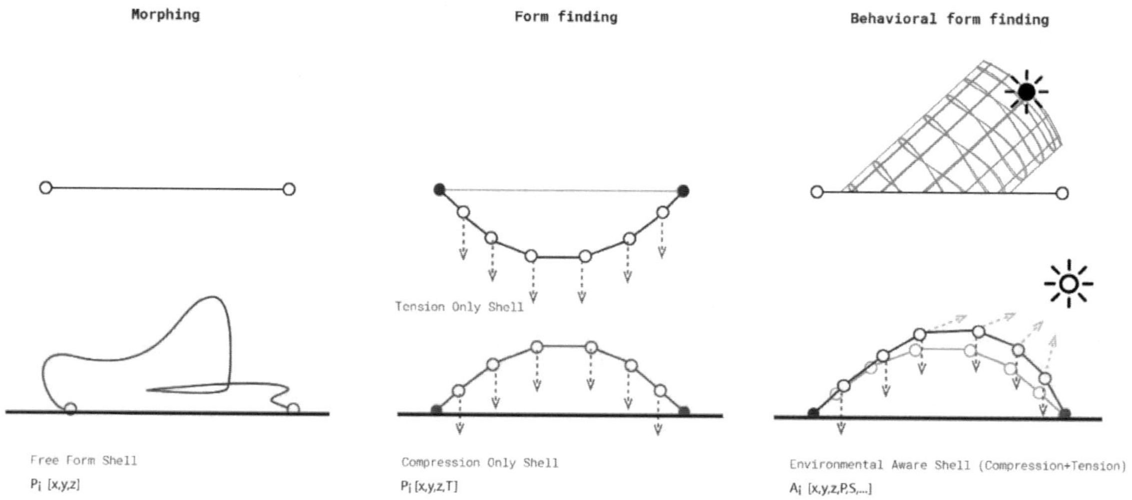

Figure 1 Illustration showing diagrammatically three different approaches towards form finding of shells. On the left. The resulting shape is the outcome of free form morphing, in the middle the shape is the outcome of applied (physical) forces and on the right the shape is the resultant of both physical and virtual (solar) forces.

1. Introduction

Design approaches based on self-organization and concepts of Multi Agent Systems (MAS) are becoming increasingly relevant in the field of architectural design. A good example is the application of agent based modelling and simulation techniques for design purposes, which can help reduce the complexity of building design(Groenewolt et al., 2018, Schwinn and Menges, 2015). The research builds upon concepts of MAS and object-oriented programming and addresses questions related to design exploration and optimization. Apart from suggesting an alternative design paradigm that expands the solution space of possible design solutions, a MAS framework can be employed in order to implement integrative planning processes, in which parameters relating to both architecture and engineering disciplines can be accounted for in the early design stage(Anumba et al., 2001). Instead of each discipline in the Architecture, Engineering and Construction (AEC) developing independent design solutions which are often times difficult to bring together for producing a coherent building design, agent based modelling offers the opportunity to combine them in an integrated loop. In such an approach each solution can be updated dynamically based on the circumstances and specific parameters of the project at stake (Macal and North, 2009).

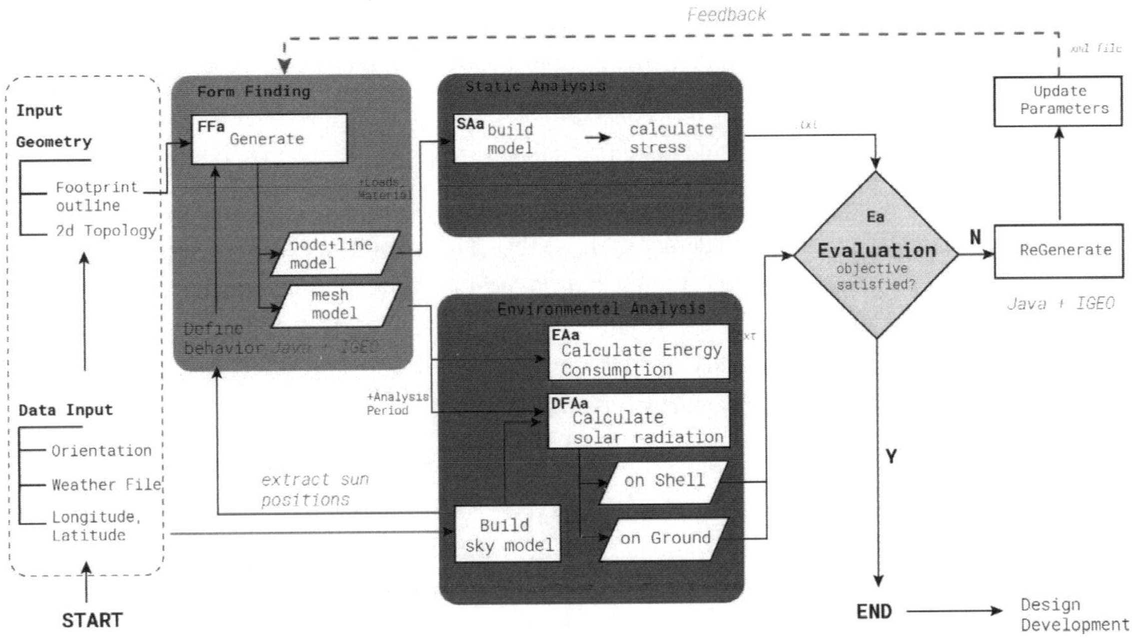

Figure 2 Flowchart diagram of the proposed behavioral form finding workflow which graphically illustrates the inputs and outputs for each agent class.

2. Background

A number of innovative physical form finding techniques were developed independently in the 20th century by practitioners such as A. Gaudi, H. Isler, F. Candela and F. Otto(Adriaenssens et al., 2014). These techniques were empirical and were driven by the motivation to create open plan spaces with large spans that were conditioned by economic and material constraints. Despite providing a more intuitive way to design structures, due to their complexity but also due to the prevalence of analytic methods for structural design, these empirical methods remained largely unexplored until recently. An increasing number of researchers working on the intersection of design and computing have started revisiting such methods from a computational perspective in an attempt to enable architects deal with hard design problems that include engineering and fabrication constraints in a more rigorous way(Kolarevic, 2004, Gramazio and Kohler, 2014).

In the last two decades a number of computational based approaches have been developed for exploring architectural form based on the concepts of form finding and optimization(Adriaenssens et al., 2014, Lachauer et al., 2010), evolutionary computation and behavioral design (Menges, 2007) as well as rule based models (Fricker et al., 2007) .Kilian, inspired by A. Gaudi hanging chain models developed one of the first digital form finding tools (Kilian, 2006). The tool was based on the hanging chain principle which was introduced by Hooke in the 17th century and demonstrated how fabrication schemas can be linked to real time form finding simulation. Piker has introduced a particle physics engine for simulating structures based on the combination of Dynamic Relaxation and the co-rotational formulation of Finite Elements Methods(Piker, 2013). Rippmann and Block introduced an interactive form finding tool based for compression only vault design which is based on graphic statics. The tool is based on Thrust Network Analysis (TNA), a method which generates possible 3d shell geometries by combining projective geometry, duality theory and linear optimization (Block and Ochsendorf, 2007).

In the field of Multi Agent Systems and Agent Based Modelling (ABM) there have been developed a number of design tools inspired by complex adaptive systems and emergent behaviours observed in nature (Bonabeau et al., 1999). These tools are driven by environmental conditions and allow behavioural modelling but have mostly focused on specific agent models such as the "boids" developed by C. Reynolds (Reynolds, 1987). Additionally, although in many disciplines MAS has been used for optimization processes in architectural design, they have been mainly used for generating designs.

More recently there has been a significant effort towards developing integrated design approaches which narrow the gap between modelling and analysis by using data to drive the design(Gerber and Lin, 2013). Yet in most cases the rationalization is happening after a design is generated and thus more research is necessary to develop tools which use local relationships and analytical data that generate models that are pre-rationalized, the aforementioned approaches have pushed the boundaries of integrated architectural design and generative design respectively. However, the former approaches have mainly emphasized in the integration of geometric and structural design (boundary condition, supports, loads etc.) but are not considering environmental parameters such as the location and/or position of the sun in the form finding process(Kilian, 2014), while the latter ones have yet to develop agent models specific to the AEC, which are relevant in the contemporary practice (Pantazis and Gerber, 2018).

3. Methodology

In this work we present the extension of a computational framework for architectural geometry, in which agents represent building elements (Pantazis and Gerber, 2018). The framework has been tested previously by the authors for developing façade designs, where the agents represented façade panels and their placing was conditioned by environmental parameters (Gerber et al., 2017). In this work the same framework is applied for the design of shell structures by incorporating environmental parameters such as the annual solar path in the form finding process. The aim is to extend existing computational form finding approaches (Rippmann et al., 2012, Piker, 2013) by introducing behaviours which allow the integration of daylight as a shaping force apart from typical forces such as gravity and tension.

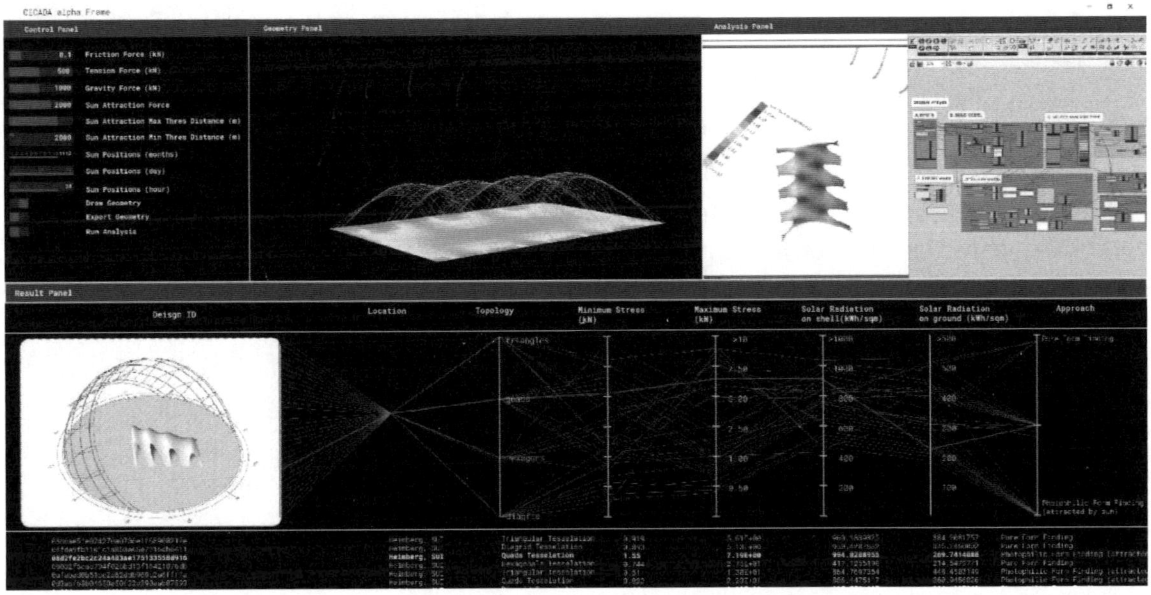

Figure 3 Graphical User Interface of the alpha version of the tool. On the top left side (control panel) are all the input parameters, in the middle is the geometry viewport and on the left is the window where we call Rhinoceros 3d and Grasshopper. In the bottom all analytical results are presented in a parallel line plot along the geometric design.

Behaviours which relate to the orientation of the site and the related solar path are described, namely a photophobic and photophilic one, in the next section along with the developed agent classes. These behaviours can be adjusted in real time in order to steer form finding away from purely form found shapes. In Figure 2 the workflow of the design approach is illustrated graphically showing the types of agents (colour of box indicates the type) and data exchanged. The designer retains control over local behaviours among the agents as well as a number of global parameters such as the initial topology of the geometry, the support condition and the environment of the agents (location, orientation).In return once the designer runs the system, different global configurations are emerging based on the behaviours and the adjustment of the initial conditions. To ensure that the design process is integrative, domain specific data and the results of external analysis (stress and solar radiation analysis) can be used as input for agent behaviours and/or can be visualized so that the designer can evaluate the design alternatives based on design performance data.

Each generated design is analysed a) geometrically (different types of meshing) b) environmentally (total annual thermal energy consumption and solar radiation) and c) structurally (Von Mises Stress analysis and displacement). The analytical results are used to evaluate the effect of different behaviours on the generated outcomes and to apply a corresponding weight on the. Figure 3 shows the developed Graphical User Interface (GUI) which allows the designer to visualize the analytical results using parallel line plots (Bostock et al., 2011)in order to help develop intuition of the trade-offs between different performance metrics(Clevenger et al., 2013).

2.1 Steering structural design of shells via applying environmental behaviours

Four different agent classes are implemented from the MAS framework (Pantazis and Gerber, 2018) namely: a generative agent class, two specialist agents classes and one evaluation agent class. A generative agent class, namely a form finding agent (FFa) is implemented which combines properties of a (physics) particle simulation such as position, velocity, gravity and tension forces with forces relating to the position of the sun in specific timestamps (solar path). Additional classes include, one specialist agent class which is tasked with the structural analysis (Structural Analysis agent) and a second specialist agent class, which is tasked with the energy analysis (Energy Analysis agent) of the generated shells. The proposed methodology is based on the following assumptions: the generative agents are represented as particles that are interconnected to represent a mesh surface. Each connection among the agents is modelled as linear elastic spring with variable stiffness which is controlled by a tension force.

Additional forces are applied on each Form Finding agent (FFa), instead of only modelling loads which are typical in existing form finding methods (i.e. gravity, dead loads and tension). Such "virtual" loads, include for instance a solar force which is modelled based on location and orientation. In this early stage of the development, two basic behaviors are implemented and tested namely a photophilic and photophobic one. The behaviors are assigned to the FFas and are used as a tool to augment the purely form found shapes. The hypothesis is that agents can attain new equilibrium states whereby applying iteratively different weighting value to the selected behavior a generated shell can be optimized not only for weight but also based on its environmental performance (i.e. increase amount of daylight availability, decrease annual energy consumption).

A photophilic behavior is defined as one where a number of positions on the solar path of a specific location exert a force on the form finding agents which steers them towards those positions, when the agents are within a distance threshold. On the contrary a photophobic behavior is defined as one where specific positions on the solar path are exerting a force that steers the agents away from these positions. For instance, depending on the longitude/latitude and orientation of the structure, the designer may assign a photophilic behavior to the positions of the sun during the morning hours which increase daylight during the operating hours of the building and a photophobic behavior to the positions of the sun during the afternoon hours which significantly increase heat gain and might negatively the total energy consumption. The photophilic/photophobic behaviors are expressed as forces on the FFa and to ensure that the behavior is not leading to undesired results, the solar attraction force is scaled according to the number of the attractor points, the distance of the point to the structure and a weight pb(w) as seen in the equation below.

$$F = \frac{\mathrm{SunAttactionForce}}{\mathrm{N(pt)}} * \mathrm{D} * \mathrm{p}b(w)$$

In order to be able, to evaluate the impact of a photophilic behavior (pb) on the design performance a weight *w* is applied to it. The weighting factors is correlated with the collected analytical results with the following heuristic function:

$$pb(w) = \frac{\mathrm{tE}(i, BaseCase) + \mathrm{tR}(i, BaseCase)}{disp(t)} - \sum (Pnlty(i))$$

The heuristic function uses the total energy consumption (*tE*), the total Radiation (*tR*) underneath the structure and the maximum displacement in order to calculate the value of the weight for the behavior. The heuristic function is used to adjust the value of the force according to the desired result. The closer to the desired analytical results a solution is compared to a base case (i.e. the purely form found case), the higher the weight of the photophilic behavior becomes.

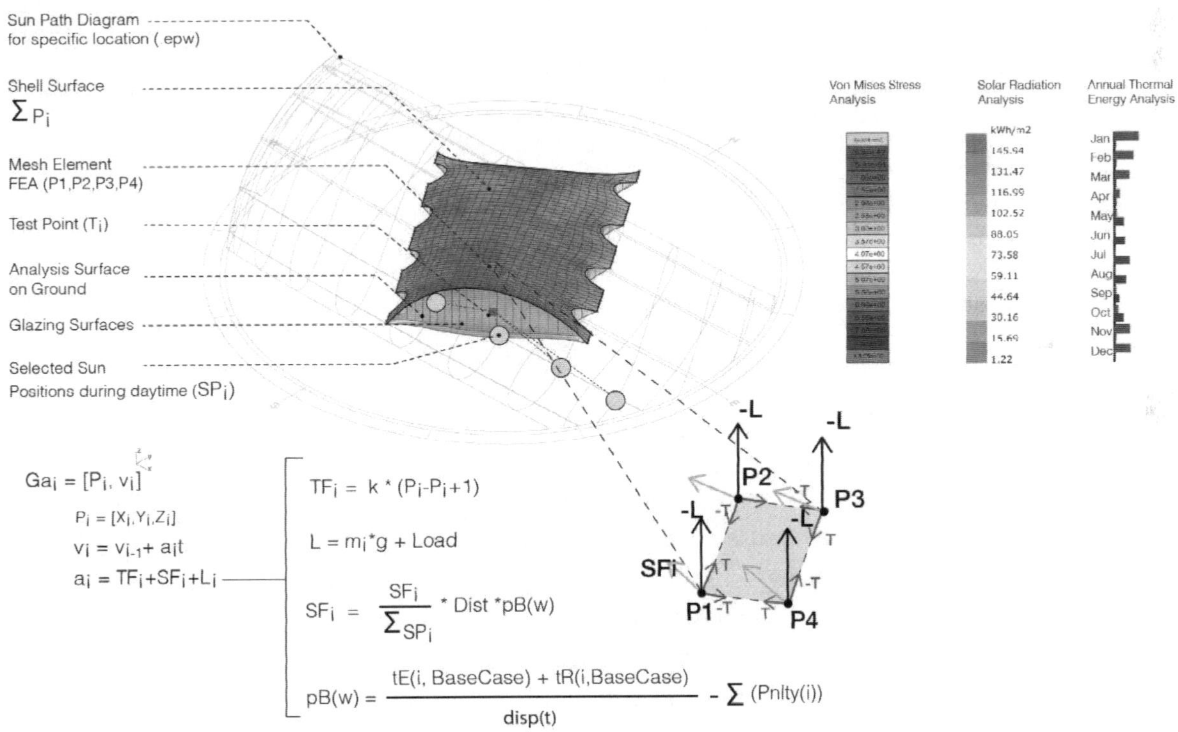

Figure 4 Experimental Design set up that describes, the environment, design parameters and the heuristic function that couples the form finding with the photophilic behavior and three different types of analysis (structural, radiation and thermal energy analysis)

A penalty is added to reduce the weight in the case that a point is moved to an undesired location. Using this heuristic function we run the system where the designer can interactively change the value of the behavior based on the assessment of the analytical results and the geometry. Once she sets a value for the behavior the systems runs for a specified amount of iterations in order to generate design alternatives which satisfy the predefined performance targets (Figure 4).

Location	Program	Span (m)	Length (m)	Type	Material	Coordinates	
A. Heimberg, Berne , CH	Sports Center	48.00	72.00	Thin Shell	Reinforced concrete	46° 47' 33.77" N	7° 35' 43.33" E
B. Düdingen, Fribourg, CH	Sports Center	48.00	54.00	Thin Shell	Reinforced concrete	46° 51' 20.35" N	7° 11' 56.88" E
C. La Tène, Neuchâtel, CH	Sports Center	48.00	72.00	Thin Shell	Reinforced concrete	47° 01' 25.21" N	7° 01' 13.20" E
D. Grenchen, Solothurn, CH	Sports Center	48.00	108.00	Thin Shell	Reinforced concrete	47° 10' 57.20" N	7° 24' 32.25" E

Figure 5 Four different shell structures designed by Isler and constructed in Switzerland (1978-1988)

4. Experimental Design

An experimental design is developed using an existing thin shell concrete structure design by H. Isler to apply and test the proposed methodology and show how such an approach can lead to quantifiable results. Isler used fabric and physical form finding to design a number of structures (Chilton and Chuang, 2017). One of the most widely applied design from Isler is that of tennis and sports halls that he has built in various locations in Switzerland (Figure 5). In this case study, a tennis hall which was built in 1978 in Heimberg, a small town in Switzerland is revisited. The thin shell structure has a span of 48 meters, a length of 72.00m and is supported in 10 points. It is made out of 100mm thick reinforced concrete, has a footprint of approx. 3000 sqm and is still being used as a sports hall. Isler developed different fabric models for one bay (48x18m) to test how different design parameters such as the fabric density and mesh orientation affect the form of the shell. A design was finally selected, scaled for 1:1 construction and multiplied according to site requirements.

The design served as an archetype for three more shell structures that were designed and built in the next decade. The shell structures are all located in Switzerland have exactly the same span but their overall length and orientation vary. The material of all structures is untreated concrete, which was cast on top of 50 mm insulation Styrofoam panels, while the rest of the envelope is single panel curtain walls.

3.1 Design Process

Although little information is publicly available for the detailed geometry of the Heimberg shell, by accessing information about the shell via and online database (www.structurae.com), one can get the basic design parameters, simulate the structure and generate a 3d model using Rhinoceros 3d and the Kangaroo Particle Physics Solver. As a first step after generating the 3d models is to simulate the existing structure and analyze it structurally. To do so we modelled the concrete material and analyzed the structure using Karamba, a finite element analysis software geared towards interactive use in the visual scripting editor Grasshopper (Preisinger and Heimrath, 2014). The same process is applied to all four structures that were designed based on the same model. Apart from modelling the structure parametrically using the Kangaroo Particle Physics Solver, an agent based model is developed in order to explore more design alternatives. The established MAS framework is used for evaluating environmental parameters in parallel to form finding. The design process can be summarized as follows:

1. Definition of typical parameters in structural design such as: *F*, the outline of the provided footprint in the form a polyline with n corners; P, as well as determine the number and type of support conditions S (n,t), , the material stiffness (E), material properties(G), and loads (L).
2. Determine the max amount of agents and the topology of their connections. This is the discretization of the given input outline and sets the initial geometric configuration of the mesh surface for the form finding. In this case we developed 4 different topological variations, namely: orthogonal topology, triangular, hexagonal and rhomboidal, but selected the rectangular one for clarity purposes.
3. Provide: the location's Longitude and Latitude (LL) of well as the orientation (O) of the structure, orientation (N,S,E,W), and the creation of a weather data (.epw file). Additionally the designer provides a generic use of the space (i.e. School, Office, Gym)
4. Develop an environmental behavior for the agent, i.e. photophilic or photophobic behavior depending on a design objective. The behavior can be simple and straightforward such as get attracted (steer towards) by selected sun positions to allow direct sunlight in the morning.
5. Apply external physical loading (self-weight, dead load) on the surface and external virtual loading (i.e. sun attraction) to derive the shape of the shell. The stiffness, weight and level of attraction of nodes are adjusted to find the equilibrium state. This is the main difference between the suggested approach and Isler's physical modelling, or computational form finding approaches. At each time step the position of the agents is updated not only based on the summation of gravity forces but also on additional ones that act upon it. By introducing specific positions of the sun as "virtual forces" we directly link environmental parameters with form finding, which was can adjust by providing "weights" for each force. In this step, the designer specifies the duration of the form finding process and the "weight" of the photophilic or photophobic behavior.
6. Once a global equilibrium is reached, and the velocity of each agent is close to 0, a NURBS geometry is generated based on the optimal force distribution, which can be directly exported to Rhinoceros 3d for further analysis

7. The generated geometry is automatically passed for structural analysis and environmental analysis using Grasshopper in conjunction with environmental simulation and analysis software which were used to model the existing structures(Preisinger and Heimrath, 2014, Roudsari et al., 2014). The results are collected and are used to inform the weight of the environmental behavior.
8. The process is repeated iteratively until the design objectives are met or the user stops the process

Information	Case A	Case B	Case C	Case D
Location (Switzerland)	Heimberg, Berne	Düdingen, Fribourg	La Tène, Neuchâtel	Grenchen, Solothurn
Span (m)	48	48	48	48
Length (m)	72	54	72	108
footprint Area (sqm)	3079.00	2266.00	3777.00	4670.00
shell area (sqm)	3253	2398	4005	4941
Structural Analysis				
max displacement [cm]	**1.38E+00**	**1.44E+00**	**1.33E+00**	2.02E+00
min Stress [kN/cm2]	1.27E+00	1.25E+00	2.82E-01	1.21E+00
max Stress [kN/cm2]	8.37E+00	8.40E+00	1.00E+01	8.70E+00
Solar Radiation Analysis				
Annual solar Radiation on shell (kwh/m2)	1131400.00	1403500.0000	1403500.00	1699900.00
Annual solar Radiation below shell (kwh/m2)	418107.5499	298344.4512	726504.195	401665.1759
Annual solar Radiation on shell /sqm	367.4569665	585.2793995	350.4369538	344.0396681
Annual solar Radiation below shell /sqm	**135.7932933**	**131.6612759**	**192.3495353**	86.00967364
Enegry Analysis				
Annual Total Thermal Energy (kW/h)	786400.1646	439080.4149	767175.4635	780620.7278
Annual Cooling Energy Needed (kW/h)	843.452221	1005.380435	28815.24791	832.444715
Annual Heating Energy Nedeed (kW/h)	777960.7124	429030.0344	738360.2156	772300.283
Annual Daylight Factor(%)	95.898399	94.843977	95.5	96.682832
Total Thermal Energy per area (kW/h/sqm)	**255.4076533**	**193.7689386**	**203.1176763**	167.1564728

Figure 6 Table with all the analytical results of the 4 different case study shell structures

Specialist agents classes are implemented for each of the performed analyses which communicate with the FFa, namely: a Structural Analysis agent (SAa) which calculates displacement and Von Mises Stress, an Energy Analysis agent (EAa) which accounts for the total thermal energy required annually for the structure and a Daylight Factor Analysis (DFAa) which accounts for the amount of sunlight on and beneath the shell structure. The input for SAa is material specifications (Concrete, 4000 ksi) section thickness, loads and support conditions. The input for the EAa and DFAa in order to be able to run the energy analysis are the following: 1) coordinates of the structure, 2) a corresponding weather file (.epw), 3) the orientation of the structure (N,S,W,E), 4) the program of the space, 5) the programmatic schedule of the space and 6) the type of glazing and some basic material properties (diffuse color, reflectance).

3.2 Results & Analysis

In Figure 6 we tabularize and compare the analytical results for each of the original Isler structures. The results indicate that the structures structurally perform identically with small differences which are due to the difference in size. However, their environmental performance is varying quite significantly depending on the case.

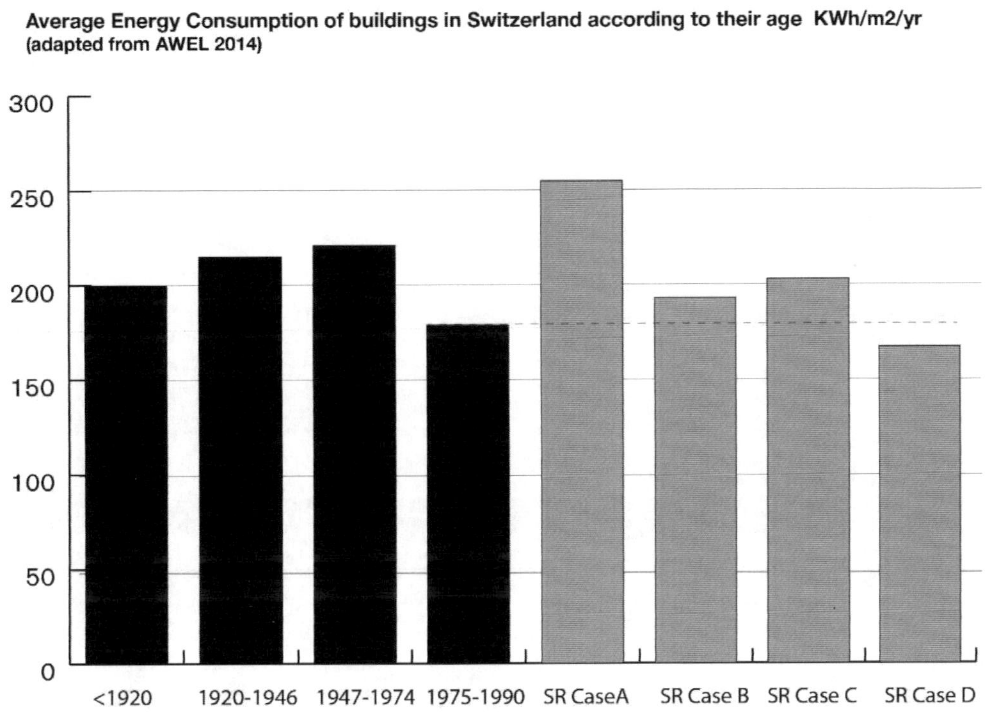

Figure 7 Comparison of simulated results (SR) with the average energy consumption of buildings in Switzerland according to the age of the Swiss building stock (adapted from AWEL 2014) KWh/m2

The annual energy consumption for instance Case D, which is the longest structure and is also oriented along a South East/North West orientation axis has the lowest average Daylight Factor. Due to the fact that the performed simulations are not based on detailed 3d models, in order to validate our results we compare them against the results of a survey from the Chair of Ecological System Design at ETH Zurich. This survey catalogs the embodied environmental impact of building stock in Switzerland since the 1920's (Ostermeyer et al., 2018). The survey lists the range of average energy consumption of buildings according their age. In Figure 7 we plot the simulated results compared to results of the survey which measures the annual energy consumption per square meter. The standard deviation between the simulated results and ones coming from the survey is calculated $\sigma = 33.7$ kWh/sqm.

In Figure 8 we use a parallel line plot to compare Case A with a subset of the behaviorally form found shapes. A photophilic behavior is applied to the structure and the system is run iteratively in order to generate new shell shapes, that perform better than the base cases in terms of Annual Thermal Energy Consumption, Daylight Factor Analysis, Displacement and Stress. The blue lines indicate the values of the four existing case studies while the red ones show design alternatives of Case Study A, after applying a photophilic behavior.

Over time the system generates alternatives that decrease the average annual consumption by 12%, increase the daylight factor analysis by 9% and increase the average solar radiation underneath the structure by 102% with regards to the base case. The amount of max displacement is increased yet is maintained within allowable thresholds (<5cm).

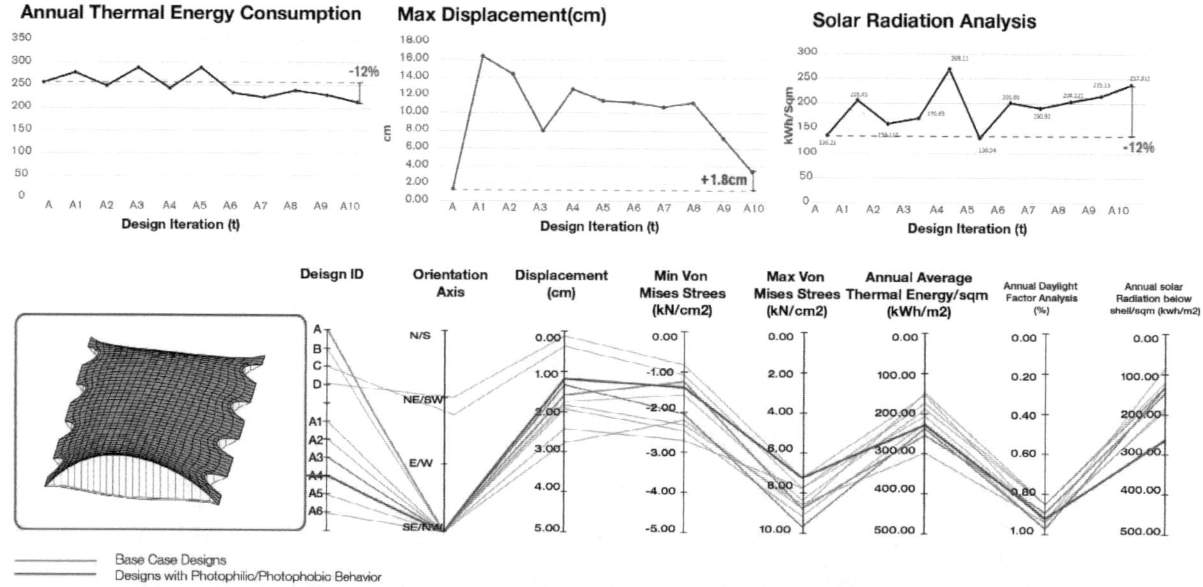

Deisgn ID	Orientation Axis	Max Displacement [cm]	min Von Mises Stress [kN/cm2]	Max Von Mises Stress [kN/cm2]	Total Thermal Energy per area (kW/h/sqm)	Annual Daylight Factor Analysis(%)	Annual solar Radiation below shell /sqm
CASE_A	SE/SW	**1.38E+00**	**1.27E+00**	**8.37E+00**	**256.407**	**85.898399**	**136.234**
CASE_A1	SE/SW	1.64E+01	2.04E-01	8.90E+00	223.213	92.793584	206.451
CASE_A2	SE/SW	1.32E+01	6.48E-02	6.31E+00	289.846	90.120658	159.112
CASE_A3	SE/SW	8.00E+00	2.04E-01	8.92E+00	253.213	89.793584	170.654
CASE_A4	SE/SW	1.12E+01	2.44E-01	**7.31E+00**	228.846	**91.120658**	**269.112**
CASE_A5	SE/SW	1.14E+01	2.04E-01	9.52E+00	223.213	92.793584	130.944
CASE_A6	SE/SW	1.12E+01	2.48E-02	1.03E+01	278.846	94.120658	201.912

Figure 8 A subset of design alternatives presented to the designer. The base case designs are marked with the blue line, while the behavioral ones are marked with red. Highlighted is a design alternative that meets the design objectives based on the available analytical metrics

4 Discussion

This work presents the application of a MAS framework for the design of shell structures which are pre-rationalized for a set of environmental objectives. The aim is to explore design alternatives that provide the same amount of light levels underneath the structure independent of their location and orientation but without affecting the structural integrity of the shells. Initial results show that by implementing a photophilic/photophobic behaviour design alternative can be generated that satisfy both structural and environmental performance targets. Unlike conventional ways of employing performance-based design approaches, the main concern of the research at this point is not solely an increase in efficiency or speed but rather in proposing an alternative form finding method which is not based on purely analytical design methods. The framework is focused in the early design stage and therefore at this stage the structural analysis is coarser and therefore is not accounting for shell bucking and creep induced failure. The reason for this is that at an early design stage the importance lies more in quickly exploring global shapes and easily evaluating to what level they meet a set of performance objectives. Once the solution space of possible design alternatives is reduced, more rigorous and detailed analysis can be performed on more refined and detailed geometries.

Despite the fact that we are interested in generating designs that perform within a specified range the focus of the work at this point is to test if a formal design method based upon MAS can extend the designers ability to explore larger solution spaces and lead to solutions, which would not be attainable conventional design and building methods.

5 References

ADRIAENSSENS, S., BLOCK, P., VEENENDAAL, D. & WILLIAMS, C. 2014. *Shell Structures for Architecture: Form Finding and Optimization,* London and New york, Taylor & Francis - Routledge.

ANUMBA, C., UGWU, O., NEWNHAM, L. & THORPE, A. 2001. A multi-agent system for distributed collaborative design. *Logistics Information Management,* 14, 355-367.

BLOCK, P. & OCHSENDORF, J. 2007. Thrust network analysis: A new methodology for three-dimensional equilibrium. *International Association for Shell and Spatial Structures,* 155, 167.

BONABEAU, E., DORIGO, M. & THERAULAZ, G. 1999. *Swarm intelligence: from natural to artificial systems,* New York, USA, Oxford university press.

BOSTOCK, M., OGIEVETSKY, V. & HEER, J. 2011. D³ data-driven documents. *IEEE transactions on visualization and computer graphics,* 17, 2301-2309.

CHILTON, J. & CHUANG, C.-C. 2017. Rooted in nature: aesthetics, geometry and structure in the shells of Heinz Isler. *Nexus Network Journal,* 19, 763-785.

CLEVENGER , C. M., HAYMAKER, J. R. & EHRICH, A. 2013. Design exploration assessment methodology: testing the guidance of design processes. *Journal of Engineering Design,* 24, 165-184.

FRICKER, P., HOVESTADT, L., BRAACH, M., DILLENBURGER, B., DOHMEN, P., RÜDENAUER, K., LEMMERZAHL, S. & LEHNERER, A. 2007. *Organised Complexity,* Frankfurt am Main,Germany, 25th eCAADe Conference Proceedings.

GERBER, D. J. & LIN, S.-H. E. 2013. Designing in complexity: Simulation, integration, and multidisciplinary design optimization for architecture. *Simulation,* 1-24.

GERBER, D. J., PANTAZIS, E. & WANG, A. 2017. A multi-agent approach for performance based architecture: Design exploring geometry, user, and environmental agencies in façades. *Automation in Construction,* 76, 45-58.

GRAMAZIO, F. & KOHLER, M. 2014. Authoring Robotic Processes. *Made by Robots,* 229, 136.

GROENEWOLT, A., SCHWINN, T., NGUYEN, L. & MENGES, A. 2018. An interactive agent-based framework for materialization-informed architectural design. *Swarm Intelligence,* 12, 155-186.

KILIAN, A. 2006. Design innovation through constraint modeling. *International journal of architectural computing,* 4, 87-105.

KILIAN, A. 2014. Steering Form. *In:* ADRIAENSSENS, S., BLOCK, P., VEENENDAAL, D. & WILLIAMS, C. (eds.) *Shell Structures for Architecture: Form Finding and Optimization.* London and New york: Taylor & Francis - Routledge.

KOLAREVIC, B. 2004. *Architecture in the digital age: design and manufacturing*, Taylor & Francis.

LACHAUER, L., RIPPMANN, M. & BLOCK, P. 2010. Form Finding to Fabrication: A digital design process for masonry vaults. *Proceedings of the International Association for Shell and Spatial Structures (IASS) Symposium*.

MACAL, C. M. & NORTH, M. J. Agent-based modeling and simulation. Winter simulation conference, 2009. Winter Simulation Conference, 86-98.

MENGES, A. Computational morphogenesis. Proceedings for 3rd International ASCAAD Conference, 2007 Alexandria,Egypt. 725-744.

OSTERMEYER, Y., NÄGELI, C., HEEREN, N. & WALLBAUM, H. 2018. Building inventory and refurbishment scenario database development for Switzerland. *Journal of Industrial Ecology,* 22, 629-642.

PANTAZIS, E. & GERBER, D. 2018. A framework for generating and evaluating façade designs using a multi-agent system approach. *International Journal of Architectural Computing (IJAC),* 16, 248-270.

PIKER, D. 2013. Kangaroo: form finding with computational physics. *Architectural Design,* 83, 136-137.

PREISINGER, C. & HEIMRATH, M. 2014. Karamba—A toolkit for parametric structural design. *Structural Engineering International,* 24, 217-221.

REYNOLDS, C. W. 1987. Flocks, herds and schools: A distributed behavioral model. *ACM SIGGRAPH computer graphics,* 21, 25-34.

RIPPMANN, M., LACHAUER, L. & BLOCK, P. 2012. Interactive vault design. *International Journal of Space Structures,* 27, 219-230.

ROUDSARI, M., PAK, M. & SMITH, A. 2014. Ladybug: A Parametric Environmental Plugin for Grasshopper to Help Designers Create an Environmentally-Conscious Design.

SCHWINN, T. & MENGES, A. 2015. Fabrication Agency: Landesgartenschau Exhibition Hall. *Architectural Design,* 85, 92-99.

Parametric Virtual Design-based Multi-Objective Optimization for Sustainable Building Design

Cunyi Cheng, Jelena Ninic, Walid Tizani
University of Nottingham, United Kingdom
evycc3@nottingham.ac.uk

Abstract. With the development of Building Information Modelling aiming for automatic, the automating of sustainability analysis will be a certain requirement in the future. Unlike the current research stream, this paper investigates a novel approach of directly linking parametric architectural models to sustainability optimization through an automatic design-through analysis workflow with the support of parametric virtual design techniques. Data required for optimization was directly extracted from architectural models and then being evaluated. After the optimization, architectural models are automatically updated with optimal parameters through parametric virtual modelling steps. A case study was carried out with optimization of daylight and energy performance for a residential building. The result demonstrates the advantages of directly using architectural models instead of energy models and the possibility of further development.

1. Introduction

With the increasing demand for sustainable building design, a practical and complete system of sustainability analysis has been gradually developed by the research community over the past years as an important step in the Building Information Modeling (BIM) design loop. Useful analysis tools have been developed and put in practice in commonly-used industrial design software such as Autodesk Insight® (AUTODESK. Autodesk Insight, 2019) for Revit (AUTODESK. Autodesk Revit, 2019), EnergyPlus® (EnergyPlus, 2019), and Autodesk Green Building Studio® (GBS) (AUTODESK. Autodesk Green Building Studio, 2019), also known as DOE-2. However, these analysis tools often involve a large amount of manual work in modeling, remodeling and adjustment. Moreover, to run sustainability analysis, two types of information are required, which are building geometry and material properties. Except for some energy analysis which could be done in a well-developed analyzing system with proper software environment (Asl, et al., 2015), common energy analyzing tools allow designers to input these two types of information separately with no constraints which could have potential risks. For example, solar and energy analysis in Autodesk Insight® is based on energy models created from conceptual masses providing basic geometry information and typed-in energy settings providing other remaining information. Where Autodesk® has recommended three common approaches for automatically generating energy models from architectural models (AUTODESK. Autodesk Revit, 2019), but the approaches are not exactly automatic. In the early design stages, where the geometries of architectural models are simple, box-shaped conceptual masses are manually created representing the geometries of target buildings and used for analysis. When the building models become more complex with large amounts of architectural elements, the energy model can only be created with a large amount of manual work to prepare the architectural model. After analysis, the effects of the building parameters on the total sustainability performance of the building will be provided individually. Then, the engineer has to make several attempts to determine an optimal solution and manually update the original model. However, this is where potential risks exist, for example, that conflicting parameters are selected for one architectural element, or the theoretically optimal result (e.g. high glass-to-wall ratio) is unrealistic or does not fit into the specific project. These two shortcomings, before and after analysis, demonstrate the limit of manual sustainability analysis. Sustainability analysis and optimization should ideally be conducted in early design stages. In later design stages, both the working load of preparing analytical model, and the impact scale of parameter change due to sustainability optimization, is significantly increased.

In recent years, many researchers have investigated different automatic approaches for sustainability designs (Wang, et al., 2006; Tuhus-Dubrow & Krarti, 2010; Evins, 2013; Hachem, et al., 2013). However, the current state-of-the-art in this field has significant limitations for practical design tasks. Most of the studies have been performed based on conceptual energy models that cannot directly be used for architectural design in the BIM design process, or based on architectural models with a limited set of parameters, which are too simple to provide critical ideas for the building's initial design. For example, Asl, et al. (2015) optimized the daylight and thermal performances of a manually predesigned building in Revit with only changing window size and window type as parameters. Backer (2017) optimized the Daylight Factor, Solar Heat Gains and Thermal Energy Losses with varying room depth, window size and building orientation for a highly simplified L-shape building. The research outcomes of these papers are therefore only a step towards parametric optimization of sustainability, which is however not detailed enough for informing an initial practical design.

In conclusion, both the official manual optimization method provided by Autodesk® and the automatic methods being explored in recent research are useful but not efficient or automated enough considering the development of higher maturity level BIM in the future. In real-design conditions, it is more reasonable to directly extract the building geometry and construction information from architectural models and use them for analysis. After optimization, the model can be automatically updated, with the optimal parameters acquired from calculation. However, since BIM has grown out of the design tools for interactive object-based parametric design (Eastman, et al., 2008), and recently developed tools enable the combination of the BIM object-based concept with parametric modelling techniques by also embedding some intelligence in the relationship between objects (Boeykens, 2012). This could be used to bridge the limitations in sustainable building optimization. Therefore, in this paper, we attempt to overcome the barrier of current software and implementation by using parametric virtual design technique. Instead of using conceptual masses to evaluate the building, by combining parametric virtual design with optimization techniques, the feasibility and efficiency of linking multi-objective sustainable analysis directly to an architectural model is investigated.

2. Methodology

In this paper, we propose an approach for the sustainable building design loop by extracting information from an architectural model, running automated optimisation of building sustainability in terms of daylight and energy performance, and updating the original model using parametric virtual design technique. The performance of this approach is explored with a predefined case study of a target building. The methodology includes parametric virtual design, energy performance assessment, sensitivity analysis and optimisation. To cover the relevant areas in the initial sustainability design, parameters of both building geometry and construction materials are considered. Prior to optimization, a sensitivity analysis is performed to decrease the range of parameters, which helps to accelerate the convergence. Then, during the optimization, similar to Generative Design (Zarzycki, 2012), possible solutions are investigated using an optimization algorithm within predefined ranges, and a range of optimal solutions is obtained through an iterative process. Then, the results are automatically applied with a parametric virtual design technique to generate an example of an optimal building model.

2.1 Linking Architectural Model and Sustainability Analysis

An obvious disadvantage of using architectural models in optimization tasks is that standard design software currently spends too much time in automatically regenerating models with large amounts of architectural elements. However, two alternative approaches can be explored to avoid this shortcoming. The first approach is by applying parametric virtual design, where a conceptual geometry model (e.g. surfaces created in Dynamo) is constructed following the same algorithm as the architectural model. In this case, these two models could change synchronously with the variation of parameters. The conceptual geometry model can be applied in the optimization process without generating an actual design model. After optimization, the same optimal architectural model can be built by directly applying the optimal parameters. This method works quickly with simple calculations, but appears to be insufficient for the analysis software, which require a large amount of specific data to finish the calculation. The second approach is to use an architectural model during the optimization, but only for the critical part instead of the whole model. This means that only instances described with the parameters relevant for the analysis will be considered, while other excess elements which are not influencing the result or not worth studying will be neglected. An example for selecting the critical parts of the model is demonstrated in the case study. This approach can be adopted for different types of buildings, such as residential and office buildings, where the most important rooms for sustainability design are normally identical, with a large amount of repetition inside the building. In this case, only simplified models appear in the optimization with limited possible variations. In this research, the second approach was explored because it is more suitable for practical applications and can integrate with 3rd-party analysis tools.

2.2 Optimization Algorithm

The optimization algorithm adopted in this research is a Genetic Algorithm, specifically the Non-dominated Sorting Genetic Algorithm-II (NSGA-II) (Deb, et al., 2002). This is a powerful multi-objective optimization tool for environmental design (Kheiri, 2018). The function of Genetic Algorithm is an improved version of Evolutionary Algorithms. As shown in Figure 1, an initial list of samples is randomly created between predefined lower and upper bounds, then a Fitness Function is used to calculate the series of initial objectives corresponding to the variables. The Fitness Function in this research is a script including steps of extracting geometry and material properties, evaluating daylight and energy performance, and exporting results for further data processing. Then, initial variables and objectives are grouped into a list and regarded as the initial generation, which is then input into a while loop for optimization. Inside the loop, new parameter values are created after crossover and mutation. The Fitness Function is applied again for generating the new generation and continued until the iteration number approaches a predefined boundary. A special advantage for NSGA-II is that the elitism samples among each child generation are compared with the last elitism before the creation of the next generation, so that the variables in the next generation will automatically be close to the value of the last elitism (Kheiri, 2018). In this case, the convergence is accelerated as the impact of useless samples among a generation is significantly decreased. The result of optimization is plotted and the best trade-off between the thermal and daylight performance is found. This is followed by a further weighted-sum optimization to optimize the Normalized Average Objective (NAO) (Qu & Suganthan, 2010) calculated from the two performances. After this, the difference between each sample in the Pareto front is compared with the optimal NAO value to select the final best result.

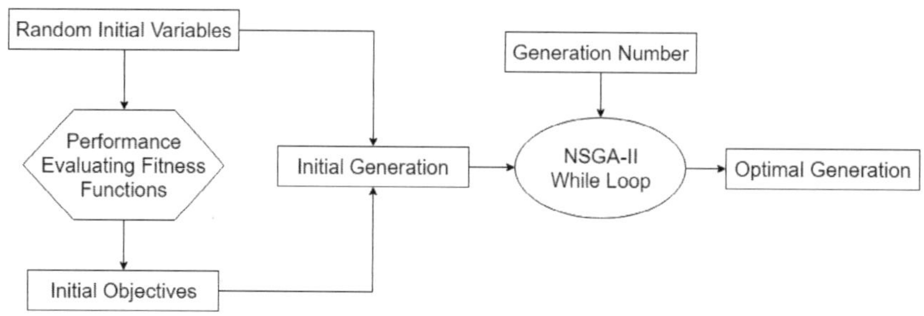

Figure 1: Workflow of NSGA-II

2.3 Daylight Simulation

The daylight simulation in this paper is evaluated by estimating the in-door lux values (lx). For the design purpose, this value needs to be high, to reduce the electricity costs spent by the lighting system. Professional 3rd-party analysing software has been used for this step. In this research, the climate environment data for location in London is used. Building properties include glass-to-wall ratio, façade orientation, glass transmittance and opaque material surface properties such as roughness. In order to be compared with energy performance, the objective Daylight Factor (DF), which is calculated based on the average in-door lux value, is introduced to the optimization system as given in the following equation:

$$DF = \frac{0.01}{n} \sum_{i=1}^{n} lx \qquad 2.3\text{-}1$$

Where:

n is the total amount of individual lx values.

2.4 Energy Analysis

In this research, the Solar Heat Gains (SHG) through glassing areas in summer and Transmission Heat Losses (THL) in winter are calculated. For the design purpose, the value of these factors needs to be lower, in order to reduce the energy consumption. SHG gives the total solar heat absorbed by the walls and transmitted by the glass (Baker, 2017).

$$H_{SHG} = \frac{A_{glass}}{A_{room}} I_t \left(\tau + \frac{\alpha U}{h_0}\right) \; [W/m^2] \qquad 2.4\text{-}1$$

Where:

I_t is the total radiation;

τ is the transmittivity of glass extracted from Revit;

α is the absorptivity of glass defined;

U is the overall heat transfer coefficient for glass extracted from Revit $W/(m^2K)$;

h_0 is the external heat transfer coefficient set as constant in this case study;

The total radiation can be calculated from direct radiation, diffuse radiation and reflected radiation.

$$I_t = I_{DN}\cos[180° - (\gamma + \zeta)] \cdot \cos(\frac{\pi}{2} - |I - d|) + I_d + I_r \qquad 2.4\text{-}2$$

$$I_{DN} = 1080 \times \exp\left[-\frac{0.21}{sin(\frac{\pi}{2} - |I - d|)}\right] \quad 2.4\text{-}3$$

$$I_d = 0.135 I_{DN} \frac{1 + cos\Sigma}{2} \quad 2.4\text{-}4$$

$$I_r = (I_{DN} + I_d)\rho_g \frac{1 - cos\Sigma}{2} \quad 2.4\text{-}5$$

Where:

I is the latitude angle at location;

d is the declination on the selected dates;

Σ is the tilt angle of surface (90° for vertical walls);

ξ is the wall azimuth angle;

ρ_g is the wall reflectivity;

Thermal Losses (TL) is the thermal energy diffused out of the building in winter when the environment temperature is lower than the room temperature, in which the Transmission Heat Losses (THL) are the most direct way. THL gives the heat directly transferred outside the building through the building envelope, including walls and glass:

$$H_{THL} = \sum_{i=1}^{n} \frac{(A_{(wall/glass),i} \cdot U_{wall})(T_{in} - T_{out})(1 + \frac{\alpha}{100})}{A_{floor,i}} \quad 2.4\text{-}6$$

Where:

U is the heat transfer coefficient extracted from wall properties in Revit W/(m^{2}K);

T_{in} is the temperature in room taken as 20 °C;

T_{out} is the temperature outside the room taken as 0 °C in winter;

α is the proportion of thermal bridges %;

Then, a normalised Thermal Factor (TF) is calculated following the general structure presented below to make a comparison with DF. After finding the pareto front between DF and TF, the final NAO could be calculated as shown:

$$N = a_1(x_1)^{b_1} \pm a_2(x_2)^{b_2} \pm a_3(x_3)^{b_3} \pm \cdots \pm a_n(x_n)^{b_n} \quad 2.4\text{-}7$$

$$TF = \frac{12.5}{H_{THL}} + \frac{50}{H_{SHG}} \quad 2.4\text{-}8$$

$$NAO = \frac{1}{TF} + \frac{1}{DF} \quad 2.4\text{-}9$$

2.5 Sensitivity Analysis

A sensitivity analysis has been carried out before the optimization is carried out in order to find the individual impact of each parameter on the final sustainable performance. During the sensitivity analysis, the target parameter is varied, while other parameters are kept constant. By doing this, the range of each parameter between predefined upper and lower bond can be reduced to a reasonable value based on the evaluated results. Since the overall range of parameters is decreased, the required number of generations for NSGA-II to reach the same optimal result is significantly reduced. As a result, the convergence of optimization is accelerated. Moreover, by comparing the resultant range of different parameters, the most influential one can be found. In conclusion, it is efficient to run a sensitivity analysis before the optimization. However, it needs to be considered that the total time cost of sensitivity analysis is significantly increased with an increasing number of parameters in the optimization task.

2.6 Parametric Virtual Design

After getting the optimal range of parameters from sustainability optimization, values are chosen and input to the script for generating building models with a parametric virtual design tool. The building model is generated based on the coordinates of several control points. An algorithm for positioning these points was developed such that the building profile is changed by adjusting predefined geometrical parameters, for example, rotation of several control points according to the orientation of one façade. Construction properties such as the insulation type and the glass type are controlled by the family type parameters of the architectural elements. Hence, the whole building, including geometric and construction parameters, is generated in a fully automatic way, by importing parametrized family instances onto a parametrically generated layout.

3. Implementation

As shown in Figure 2, following the general methodology briefly described in the previous section, the parametric virtual design and multi-objective optimization is carried out using Autodesk Revit® and its visual-programming plug-in Dynamo (Dynamo, 2019). With the support of open-source packages in Dynamo, the optimization task with the Genetic Algorithm is processed with the built-in package Optimo (Asl, et al., 2015) containing NSGA-II and the daylight performance is analyzed by the package Honeybee included in the Ladybug Tools (Mackey & Roudsari, 2017).

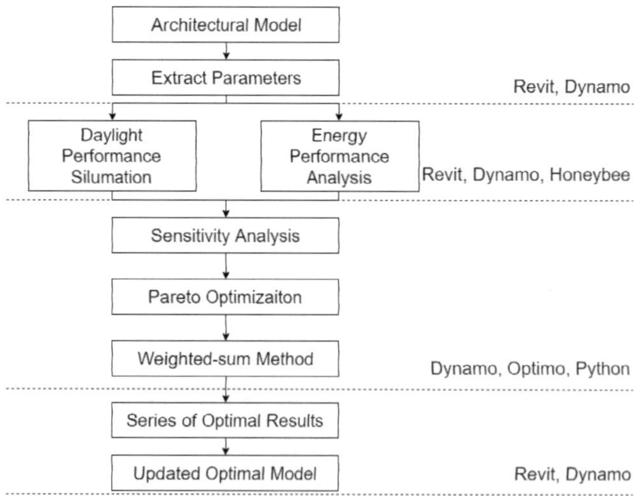

Figure 2: Workflow of the general research method

4. Case Study

A case study was carried out to investigate the feasibility and efficiency of applying sustainable optimization directly with an architectural model. The target building is a standard residential building with 12 floors as shown in Figure 3.

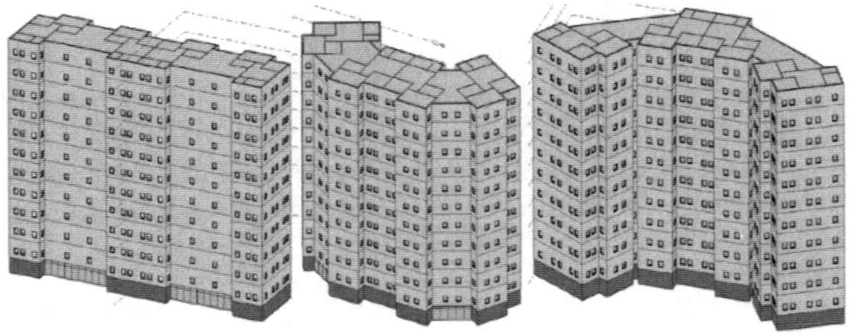

Figure 3: Visualisation of target building in different geometry

As shown in Figure 4, following the general parametric virtual design method described in previous section, the specific architectural model in this case study is generated. The algorithm performs the following steps: i) generation of initial control points and lines for one section; ii) and iii) rotations and symmetry operations for other sections; iv) generation of the reference lines and points for the architectural elements; v) generation of the initial architectural layer; and, vi) extraction of critical sections and generation of whole building.

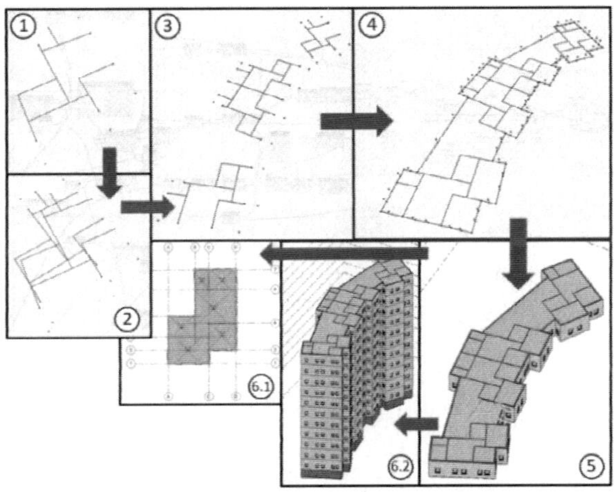

Figure 4: Demonstration of parametric virtual design process

As shown in Figure 5, the profile of each floor is identical and includes three critical parts: west, middle and east. They are three residential areas in this building that are also the focus areas in this case study. Daylight and energy consumption in the remaining areas, such as stair cases and corridors, are not considered because normally no heating/cooling would be provided, and natural lighting is not normally required in these areas.

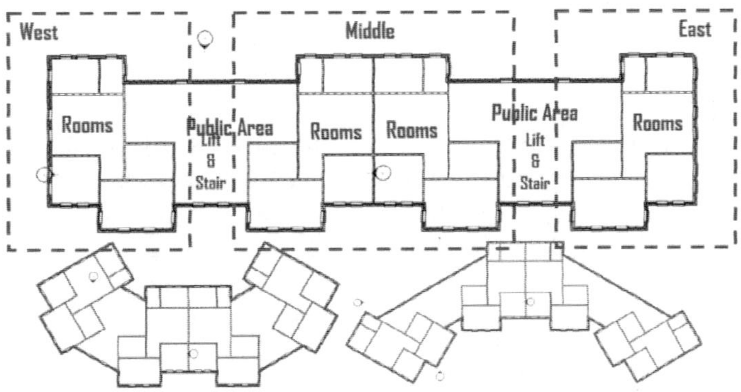

Figure 5: Target building floor plan with shape change

As mentioned in the methodology, the critical parts are then selected as the target model for optimization. The parameters for optimization in the middle critical part are shown in Table 1. The discrete variables are default settings for architectural elements and materials provided by the software. The continuous ones, are independently defined values, which are required for the sustainability performance evaluation but not provided by software. Here, the size of the windows controls the glass-to-wall ratio. Moreover, the angle to project north is used to represent the façade orientation. By doing this, we avoid the rotation of the model during the optimization process.

Table 1: Initial, filtered and final ranges for the middle critical section-Run 1

Parameters			Initial Ranges		Filtered Ranges		Final Ranges	
			Lower Bond	Upper Bond	Lower Bond	Upper Bond	Lower Bond	Upper Bond
Continuous Variable	Angle to Project North (°)		-60	60	-20	20	-9	8
	Glass Absorptivity		0.3	0.86	0.45	0.71	0.081	0.089
	Wall Surface Roughness		0	0.2	0.04	0.10	0.045	0.062
	Wall Surface Specularity		0	0.1	0.03	0.09	0.087	0.089
	Wall Surface Reflectivity		0	1.0	0.35	0.85	0.687	0.723
Discrete Variable	Glass Transmittance		0.3	0.9	0.37	0.9	0.57	0.61
	Wall Heat Transfer Coefficient		0.0876	0.1802	0.0876	0.1802	0.1056	
	Glass Heat Transfer Coefficient		1.9873	6.7018	0.39	0.81	0.36	0.48
	North Window	Width (mm)	406	915	406	915	610	
		Height(mm)	610	1220	610	1220	915	
	South Window	Width (mm)	406	915	406	915	610	
		Height(mm)	610	1220	610	1220	1220	
	East Window	Width (mm)	406	915	406	915	610	
		Height(mm)	610	1220	610	1220	915	
	West Window	Width (mm)	406	915	406	915	610	
		Height(mm)	610	1220	610	1220	915	

With these initial range of parameters, a sensitivity analysis was performed for each of the critical building parts. A filtered range of parameters has been obtained and applied to the final optimization to get the final range as also shown in Table 1. It can be observed that the optimal results for discrete variables such as glass transmittance and glass heat transfer coefficient are reasonable as the balanced point of higher daylight quality and lower SHG and TL are achieved. However, some of the continuous variables such as wall surface specularity directly converged to the upper bound, which seems unreasonable. This is because the discrete variables are all defined by the type of architectural elements, so they work like passive variables and cannot change independently. In this case, for the glass transmittance reaching the upper bound, the glass heat transfer coefficient reaching the lower bound would be the theoretically best solution. However, the type of glass satisfying these two values does not exist in practice. This is one strong advantage of directly extracting information from architectural models employing real objects, so this unrealistic scenario can be avoided. However, the obtained results for independent continuous variables were relatively valuable, since they are not limited by the practical condition. The error mentioned above could happen if all the parameters are simply used as semantic values to run an analysis without connecting them with real physical objects. The drawback of this result actually proved the advantage of directly extracting information from architectural models.

Finally, the values of objectives during convergence are plotted as DF versus TF and the optimal trade-off between these two objectives has been found. After applying a further weighted-sum optimization, figures of NAO for three critical parts are plotted. One example of the running result for the middle part of the building is shown in Figure 6.

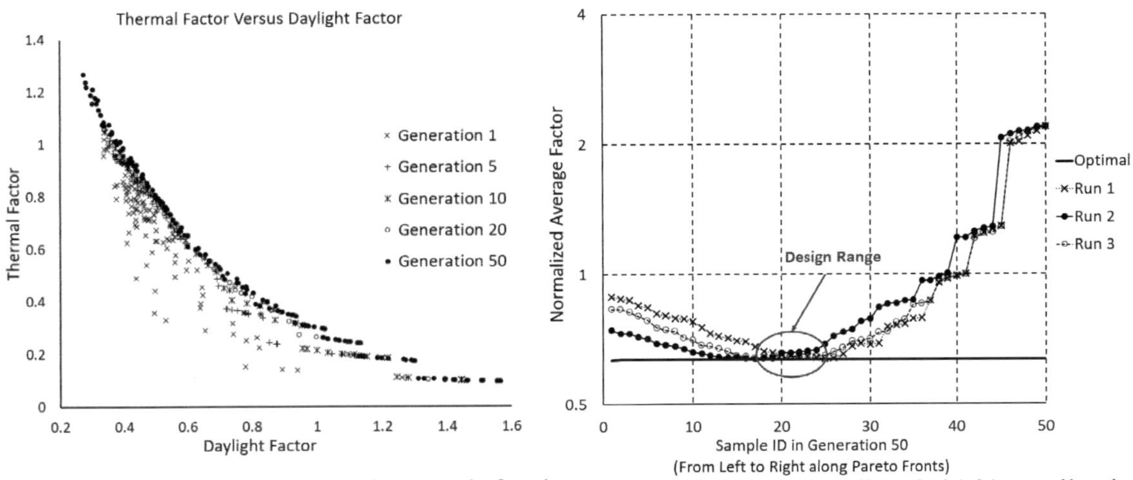

Figure 6: a) Pareto optimization result for the middle critical section-Run 1. b) Normalized optimal results for the critical middle section for 3 runs

After getting the optimal range of parameters, one combination of parameters is selected and input into the custom node for generating an optimal building.

5. Conclusion

In this paper, we proposed a design loop for multi-objective optimization of building sustainability based on the parametric virtual design approach. The methodology of this concept includes setting an automatic link between architectural models and sustainability assessment tools, optimization of sustainable performance based on the genetic algorithm and finally an automatic update of the architectural model with the determined optimal parameters. The case study presented in this paper, demonstrated the potential of the proposed methods to perform a fully automated design-through-analysis-optimization workflow. Furthermore, from the presented case study, the behavior of passive and independent variables revealed the potential risk obtaining unrealistic results when extracting the geometry and semantics from non-related sources, if the input variables are not carefully constrained. Often these constraining steps require professional knowledge and experience in environmental engineering. However, this problem could be solved by developing a method or a tool for direct use of all the information (geometry and semantics) from a single architectural project. By doing this, all the parameters, which are passive variables, are defined by a real physical property of the construction material and the element size. Even though there are limitations in the existing practical implementations, this research area has a large potential for further improvement. Firstly, the enrichment of the environmental database of the standard design tools considering the requirements of different analysis tools, will allow for more user-friendly and efficient analysis. Secondly, the programming environment associated with these tools (open-source and developer-friendly) offers the advantage for exploration of different optimization strategies, since they show different performance for different optimization problems and conditions (Kheiri, 2018). Finally, the strong functionality of parametric virtual design techniques could significantly decrease the workload for the manual update of the design models. However, developing a general algorithm for most common geometrical transformations of building forms that are compatible with the optimization tools, poses a significant challenge for future research. In conclusion, the design approach proposed in this paper has demonstrated that an automated design optimization loop based on a real design model is feasible and also offers a huge space for further developments.

References

Asl, M. R., Stoupine, A. and Zarrinmehr, S. (2015). Optimo: A BIM-based Multi-Objective Optimization Tool Utilizing Visual Programming for High-Performance Building Design. BIM - Applied, Volume 1, pp. 673-682.

Asl, M. R., Zarrinmehr, S., Bergin, M. and Yan, W. (2015). BPOpt: A framework for BIM-based performance optimization. Energy and Buildings. Energy and Buildings, Volume 108, pp. 401-412.

AUTODESK. Autodesk Insight (2019). [Online] Available at: https://insight360.autodesk.com/oneenergy [Accessed 11 April 2019].

AUTODESK. Autodesk Revit (2019). [Online] Available at: https://www.autodesk.co.uk/ [Accessed 11 April 2019].

AUTODESK. Autodesk Revit (2019). Create the Energy Model. [Online] Available at: https://knowledge.autodesk.com/support/revit-products/learn-explore/caas/CloudHelp/cloudhelp/2019/ENU/Revit-Analyze/files/GUID-A77EF18D-0EB8-47D3-A653-6370D9F1374A-htm.html [Accessed 11 April 2019].

AUTODESK. Green Building Studio (2019). [Online] Available at: https://gbs.autodesk.com/GBS/ [Accessed 11 April 2019].

Baker, N. (2017). Modelling and Analysis of Daylight, Solar Heat Gains and Thermal Losses to Inform the Early Stage of the Architectural Process. Stockholm: KTH Royal Institue of Tcchnology.

Boeykens, S. (2012). Bridging building information modeling and parametric design. In: eWork and eBusiness in Architrcutral, Engineering and Construction: ECPPM . London: Taylor and Francis Group, pp. 453-458.

Deb, K., Pratap, A., Agarwal, S. and Meyarivan, T. (2002). A Fast and Elitist Multiobjective Genetic Algorithm: NSGA-II. IEEE TRANSACTIONS ON EVOLUTIONARY COMPUTATION, 6(2), pp. 182-197.

Dynamo (2019). Dynamo BIM. [Online] Available at: https://dynamobim.org/ [Accessed 11 April 2019].

Eastman, C., Teicholz, P., Sacks, R. and Liston, K., 2008. BIM Handbook: A Guide to Building Information Modeling for Owners, Managers, Designers, Engineers, and Contractors. s.l.:Wiley and Sons.

EnergyPlus. (2019). EnergyPlus. [Online] Available at: https://energyplus.net/ [Accessed 11 April 2019].

Evins, R. (2013). A review of computational optimisation methods applied to sustainable building design. Renewable and Sustainable Energy Reviews, Volume 22, pp. 230-245.

Hachem C., Fazio, P., and Athienitis, A., (2013). Solar optimized residential neighborhoods: Evaluation and design methodology, Journal of Solar Energy, 95, 42–64.

Kheiri, F. (2018). A review on optimization methods applied in energy-efficient building geometry and envelope design. Renewable and Sustainable Energy Reviews, Volume 92, pp. 897-920.

Mackey, C. and Roudsari, M. S. (2017). The Tool(s) Versus the Toolkit. Humanizing Digital Reality, pp. 93-101.

Qu, B. Y. and Suganthan, P. N. (2010). Multi-objective evolutionary algorithms based on the summation of normalized objectives and diversified selection. Information Sciences, Volume 180, pp. 3170-3181.

Tuhus-Dubrow, D. and Krarti, M. (2010). Genetic-algorithm based approach to optimize building envelope design for residential buildings. Building and Environment, Volume 45, pp. 1571-1581.

Wang, W., Rivard, H. and Zmeureanu, R. (2006). Floor shape optimization for green building design. Advanced Engineering Informatics. Advanced Engineering Informatics, Volume 20, pp. 363-378.

Zarzycki, A. (2012). Parametric BIM as a generative design tool. Boston, ACSA.

Realistic Structural Stabilization based on Spatial Zoning

Boonstra S, Claessens DPH, Hofmeyer H, De Vries B
Eindhoven University of Technology, The Netherlands
s.boonstra@tue.nl

Abstract. An automated stabilization procedure for structural designs is presented and applied in conjunction with a building spatial zoning algorithm. The stabilization procedure can stabilize kinematic systems in a building's structural design model while taking into account structurally relevant zones within that building's spatial design. A case study shows that the presented stabilization procedure, compared to an existing stabilization technique, can find stiffer and more practical structural designs that are less sensitive to progressive collapse.

1. Introduction

Structural Design (SD) of buildings aims at the design of structural systems that are stiff, strong and stable. The strength of a structure is related to the forces at which structural components will fail. Stiffness is related to the deformations that can occur in the structure, which is important with respect to usability, sense of security, and possible load accumulations. Stability is related to any kinematic system that may develop in the structure when there are no or insufficient structural provisions to prevent such kinematics. Stability and stiffness—which influence each other—are primarily determined by the synthesis of structural components like trusses, beams, or slabs. In this work, only statically under-determinate structures are considered for stability, thus no phenomena like (local) buckling. An automated stabilization procedure is presented which can extend a structural design such that becomes stable and stiff. Moreover, the procedure can find designs that have structural redundancy, i.e. no progressive collapse occurs after one structural component fails. The automated stabilization procedure is applied in conjunction with spatial zoning, which yields a number of geometric layouts of a Building Spatial Design (BSD) that are promising for structural design. For each zoned BSD, a structural design is generated and then stabilized, from these, the most suitable structural design for a BSD can be selected.

This paper is structured as follows. In section 2 the related work and the motivation are presented. Thereafter, in section 3, the methodology behind the new stabilization procedure is explained. Next, section 4 presents a case study, in which the presented method is compared to an existing method. Accordingly, the discussion in section 5 gives critical remarks on the presented work. Finally, the conclusion and outlook are presented in section 6.

2. Related Work and Motivation

The presented work is part of a larger research project that focuses on multi-disciplinary building spatial design optimization. Within that project a toolbox has been developed (Boonstra et al.; 2018), the methods and tools in this work have been developed within its framework.

In this section, first an overview of the related work on automated structural design is given in subsection 2.1. Following that, in subsection 2.2, work on automated structural stabilization is outlined. Thereafter, in subsection 2.3, research on zoning for structural design is treated. Finally, the motivation for the presented work is explained in subsection 2.4.

2.1. Automated Structural Design

The starting point for a building structural design is usually a building spatial design. The BSD determines where the loads (e.g. live and wind loads) are located, and thus where a structure is needed. In an early example to support this process, Rafiq and MacLeod (1988) presented a method to automatically generate a structural design for a BSD. More recently, Geyer (2008) developed a method based on several design rules, that—in combination with each other—can create a large variation of structural designs. By evaluating each variation of structural design, a selection can be made for a high quality/optimal structural design. Steiner et al. (2017), on the other hand, proposed a method that integrates architectural design with structural design. This allows an architect to interactively design the building spatial design as well as the structural design simultaneously. In the toolbox, presented in (Boonstra et al.; 2018), structural designs can also be generated automatically for a BSD by using deterministic design rules that operate on the geometric entities of the BSD. As such, BSDs that are found by an optimization method can be automatically evaluated with relative ease and speed by the optimizer. The automated design methods that are mentioned above, do not explicitly take into account stability. However, stable designs are still achieved by e.g. defining design rules such that a stable structural model is guaranteed, which relies on human experience and programming. If in an unforeseen event an unstable design is generated it should be disregarded or fixed, but chances are it is considered as feasible by the automated structural design method. An automated stabilization procedure could serve to check or fix instabilities, or even become a part of an automated structural design method. Moreover, a stability check may even serve designers in detecting possible oversights in their structural design.

2.2. Automated Stabilization

Automated stabilization of a building structural design was first introduced in (Hofmeyer and Russell; 2009; Smulders and Hofmeyer; 2012). These works assume that an unstable structural design model is provided in the form of a Finite Element Method (FEM) model, stabilization is then carried out as follows. First the Global Stiffness Matrix (GSM) is generated, this system of linear equations relates the displacements of each node (discretized point) in the model to the forces in that model. A Singular Value Decomposition (SVD) is then carried out on the GSM, which is used to find the nodes that have a Degree Of Freedom (DOF)—which can be either a displacement or a rotation—that is not restrained from movement by any structure nor by any boundary condition. Once the nodes with such free DOFs are found, a search for nodes in the proximity of the free-DOF-node is performed. The found nodes serve as an anchor point, to which a stabilizing provision can be attached, e.g. a diagonal truss. More than one anchor point may exist, a selection is then based on suitability based criteria, for example if a prospected anchor point contains no free DOFs itself. This procedure is carried out in an iterative fashion until no more free DOFs are found. The above stabilization procedure has also been implemented in the toolbox of (Boonstra et al.; 2018), which is described in more detail in (Claessens; 2018).

Although stabilization with the described procedure will yield a stable design, one might ask how practical an arrangement of stabilizing provisions is but also how safe it is. Since the procedure stops directly after it stabilizes the model, there will be little to no structural redundancy. In other words, if one of the stabilizing provisions fail, the structural design is unstable again and therefore prone to collapse (Smulders and Hofmeyer; 2012). This issue is also relevant for practical design scenarios, where insufficiently redundant designs can go unnoticed.

2.3. Zoning

In a BSD, the layout that follows from its spaces may not be logical for certain building design disciplines (Hoskins; 1979). More logical layouts may follow from grouping spaces or sub-parts of spaces into zones (Björk; 1992). This is also the case for structural design. Meyer et al. (1993) and Parent et al. (2006) studied how structural engineers apply zoning to BSDs, and concluded that points of interest are the geometric continuities in a BSD and the locations where that continuity ends. Previous work on zoning for structural design by Hofmeyer et al. (2006) was extended in (Claessens; 2018; Hofmeyer et al.; 2019) for the toolbox (Boonstra et al.; 2018) by focusing on the continuities and discontinuities in a BSD. Using this extension, the amount of zoned designs can be limited to only those that have such continuity characteristics, and are thus promising for structural design.

2.4. Motivation

In this section it has been reasoned that automated structural design methods, but also designers, may benefit from an automated stabilization procedure. Such stabilization methods have been developed, but they may yield designs that are safe nor practical with respect to structural redundancy. In addition, zoning has been developed as a method to find structurally relevant zones for structural design. Here a new stabilization procedure is proposed, in which structurally relevant zones are each stabilized individually. As such, structural redundancy is taken into account more appropriately, and in a fashion that is practical from a structural point of view.

3. Methodology

In this section, first some features in the toolbox of (Boonstra et al.; 2018) are explained, where after the new stabilization procedure can be explained. These features are: The tools that can generate a structural model for a BSD in subsection 3.1; Zoning of BSDs in subsection 3.2; And, stabilization in subsection 3.3. Thereafter, in subsection 3.4, sufficient background knowledge has been supplied to introduce the new stabilization method.

3.1. From Building Spatial Design to Structural Model

This subsection gives a brief introduction into the definition of a BSD in the toolbox, a decomposition model of a BSD, and the procedure that generates a structural design model from that decomposition. For more details, the interested reader is referred to (Boonstra et al.; 2018).

Building Spatial Design. In the toolbox a BSD is primarily a collection of cuboid spaces arranged in an orthogonal grid. A space can, as such, be defined by a position vector and a dimension vector, and a BSD as a set of such pairs of vectors. BSDs in the toolbox are limited to this orthogonality so that the research for which it has been developed does not need to be distracted by complex rules, e.g. initialization and modification rules for round spaces. In the left of figure 1, an example of a BSD that can be represented in the toolbox is given.

Conformal Model. In the toolbox, the conformal model is intended to store geometric information and associate this information with the building design. This can significantly simplify queries for geometric characteristics within a BSD, e.g. T-joints, which are relevant connections

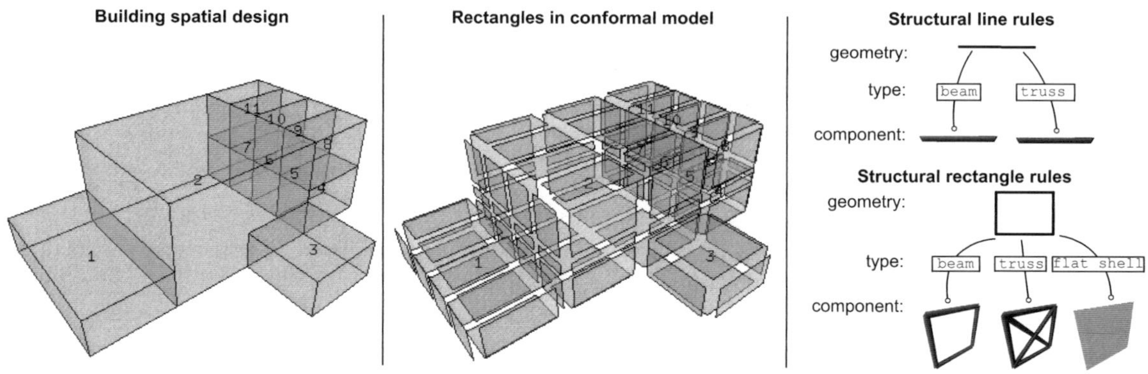

Figure 1: Left, a building spatial design; Middle, the rectangles within a conformal model; Right, examples of rectangle and line rules for structural design, trusses are indicated in blue, beams in red.

in the structural model. A conformal model is generated by considering two decompositions of a BSD. On one hand, a geometric decomposition stores all the unique non-overlapping points, lines, rectangles and cuboids that are present in the BSD's geometry. On the other hand, a building design decomposition is made, in which the points-, edges-, and surfaces of spaces and the spaces themselves are stored. Entities within these two decompositions are associated with one another. For example, a rectangle is realized by four lines and it realizes 1 or 2 cuboids, simultaneously it can be associated with 0, 1, or 2 surfaces. Such associations can be used to query information in the BSD, for example the external boundaries of a BSD are those rectangles that are associated to exactly one surface. Whereas if a rectangle were associated with two surfaces, it describes an internal boundary between spaces. The above queries are illustrated in figure 1 in the middle, which gives a visualization of the rectangles in the conformal model (of the BSD on the left) that are associated to one or two surfaces.

Structural Design Grammar. The associations between the different entities in a conformal model are convenient for a variety of concepts, one of which is the design of a structural model. For example, a rectangle can be used to define what structural component should be placed (e.g. a portal frame of beams or a flat shell). Whereas, the surface(s) that that rectangle is associated with can be used to determine the load, e.g. in case of exactly one surface association (see above) a wind load is applied. Here, a structural design grammar is a set of rules that operate on the rectangles and the lines in the conformal model. Each rectangle or line in the conformal model is supplied with such a rule. Structural components, loads, and boundary conditions are created by these rules depending on: (1) the associations that exist for that rectangle or line; And, (2) possible user specifications. On the right of figure 1 examples are given of possible structural components that can be generated using such rules. By following each rule of the grammar a structural design model is generated in a deterministic way.

3.2. Zoning

Zoning in the toolbox is achieved by using the conformal model. A zone is a collection of cuboids and is itself also defined as a cuboid. The latter is chosen for simplicity and for continuity purposes, which is what structural designs benefit from (see subsection 2.3). A zoned design is then a combination of zones, with the requirement that each cuboid in the conformal model is associated to a zone. Using the conformal model's cuboids to form zones is convenient because it is merely a combinatory task of connected cuboids that are found using the various associations within the conformal model. Additionally, through the cuboids, zones are associated with a BSD's geometry and building design information. The definition of a structural design grammar for a zoned design is then almost the same as the grammar for unzoned BSDs.

In general, the zoning algorithm searches for all the largest zones which smallest span is less than or equal to a user defined maximum span. Smaller zones are in this way excluded so that the number of found zones is relatively small. This method assumes that a suitable span length is selected for the structural system that will be generated by the design grammar. The next step in the zoning algorithm is the combination of the found zones into zoned designs. In a zoned design, zones are not allowed to overlap. When a combination of zones leaves a number of cuboids in the conformal design unoccupied and none of the remaining zones can be used to occupy them, additional zones are created. These additional zones are created for each unfinished combination by using the unoccupied cuboids. In the toolbox, the initially created zones are deemed most important and are termed primary zones, the additionally created zones are termed additional zones. The zoning algorithm, has been described in more detail in (Claessens; 2018; Hofmeyer et al.; 2019).

3.3. Stabilization of Nodes

Stabilization, similar to what is published in (Smulders and Hofmeyer; 2012), can be achieved as follows. Assuming that a possible unstable structural design model has been generated for a BSD, first a singular value decomposition (SVD) is performed for the global stiffness matrix of that SD model. The free degrees of freedom (DOFs) in the SD model are then identified as described in (Smulders and Hofmeyer; 2012). Nodes with free DOFs are iterated one by one, and for each free DOF it is assessed if a suitable anchor point, i.e. a so-called key point, is present. A key point is suitable if it is rigid in the considered DOF's direction and if it is positioned in the surface of a space (Smulders and Hofmeyer; 2012) or in the surface of a zone Claessens (2018). If a suitable key point is found, a stabilizing provision is placed. After a provision is placed, a new SVD is performed after which the nodes with free DOFs are iterated and checked for suitable key points again, this is repeated until no more free DOFs are found.

For key points, a distinction is made in the planes in which they are positioned with respect to the free DOF: in-plane or out-of-plane. If in-plane key points are available an instability can be resolved by either a diagonal truss (figure 2), or when a diagonal would intersect for example a space a portal frame of beam components can be used (figure 2). In-plane stabilization is preferred, because the DOF will then be stabilized in a more direct load path. However, when no in-plane stabilization key points are available for any of the nodes with free DOFs, out-of-plane stabilization will be applied. This type of stabilization (re)places (components with) beam components in between the free-DOF-node and the key points, also see figure 2. More information on the procedure can be found in (Smulders and Hofmeyer; 2012; Claessens; 2018).

3.4. Stabilization of Zones

Stabilizing a structural model with the procedure described in subsection 3.3 yields an SD model that is stable but does not possess structural redundancy. In real world design such redundancy is desired, therefore, it is here proposed to at least stabilize each individual primary zone in a BSD. The procedure is divided into four steps, in which patterns of structural stabilization provisions are applied to the surfaces of the zones, see figure 3. In the patterns of figure 3, each rectangle

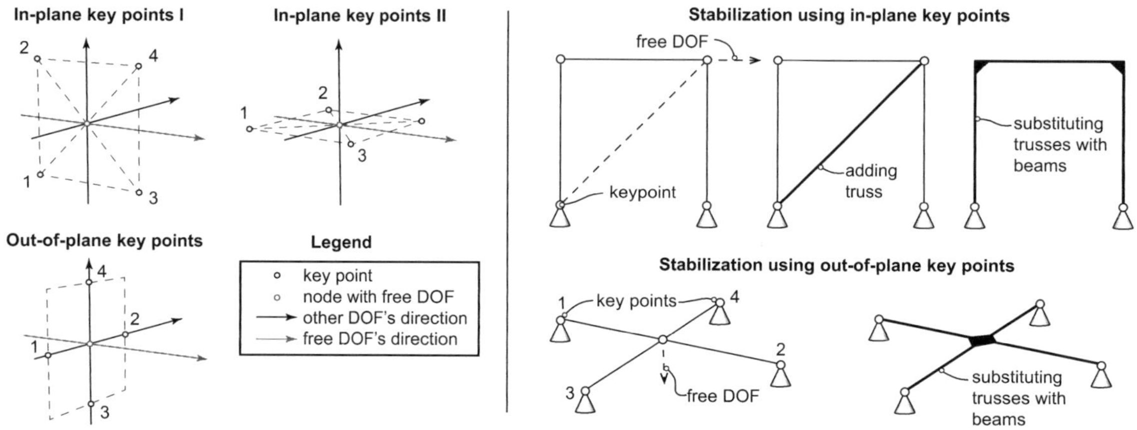

Figure 2: Left, key point positions in the conformal model for both in-plane and out-of-plane stabilization. Right, possible provisions to stabilize using either in-plane or out-of-plane key points

corresponds to a rectangle in a conformal model, all rectangles together are the complete surface of a zone (either horizontal or vertical), and to a coloured rectangle a stabilizing provision will be applied. If a stabilizing provision is applied to a rectangle, then—in the structural design grammar—its rectangle rule is assigned a diagonal truss component. If the rectangle rule has already been assigned a stable component (e.g. a flat shell), that component is maintained. The four steps in which the patterns are applied are presented in the remainder of this subsection, and they are visualized in figure 4.

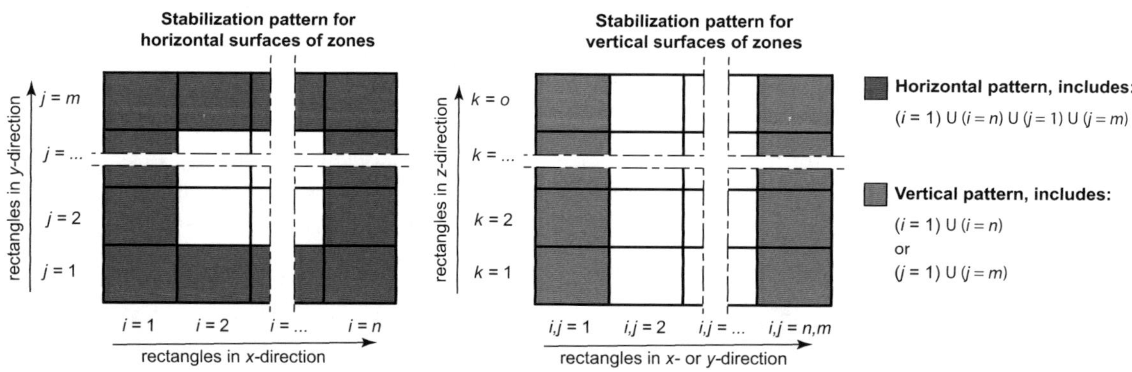

Figure 3: The two patterns of provisions, one for horizontal- and one for vertical zone surfaces.

Step 1. This step is initiated with an SVD, which is used to list the free DOFs for each node. Accordingly, the horizontal surfaces of the primary zones are listed and checked for free DOFs in geometric order (ascending in x, then y and then z-direction), if it contains a node with a free DOF the pattern for horizontal surfaces will be applied. Additionally, if it is the top surface of a primary zone, then the pattern for vertical surfaces will be applied to all vertical surfaces of that zone. Note that an SVD is carried out only once at the beginning of this step, and hereafter each primary zone will be stabilized.

Step 2. The second step is the same as the first, except that it is now performed for the additional zones and the pattern for vertical zone surfaces is not applied. The pattern for vertical zone surfaces is in this step omitted to prevent an excess of provisions in the BSD's façade.

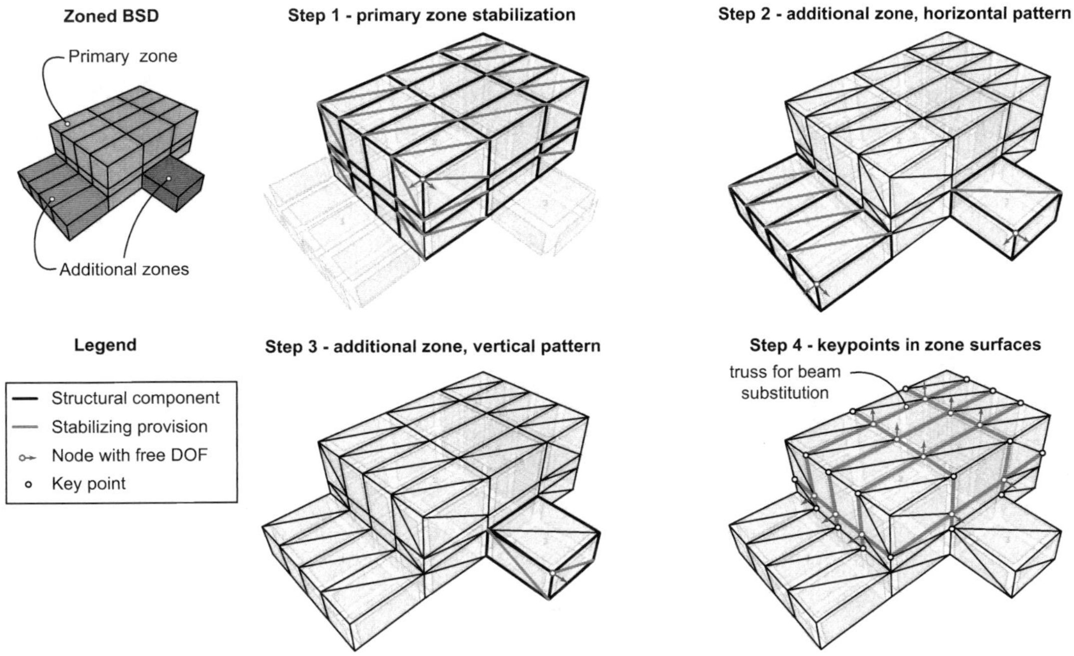

Figure 4: The provisions that may be applied by stabilization through zoning during each step for a given zoned BSD.

Step 3. Similar to the first two steps, first an SVD is used to check for free DOFs. Consequently, all horizontal surfaces of the additional zones are checked in the same geometric order that was used in steps one and two. If a node with a free DOF is contained in the top horizontal surface of an additional zone, the pattern for vertical surfaces is applied to all of that zone's vertical surfaces. If a pattern is applied, a new SVD is performed before the checks of the horizontal surfaces continues.

Step 4. In the fourth step any remaining nodes with free DOFs will be stabilized by finding key points and adding structural provisions as explained in subsection 3.3. Here, key points should be located on the surface of a zone of the considered zoned BSD. If, after the above, still free-DOF-nodes exist that do not have key points that lie on a zone's surface, also other key points are allowed.

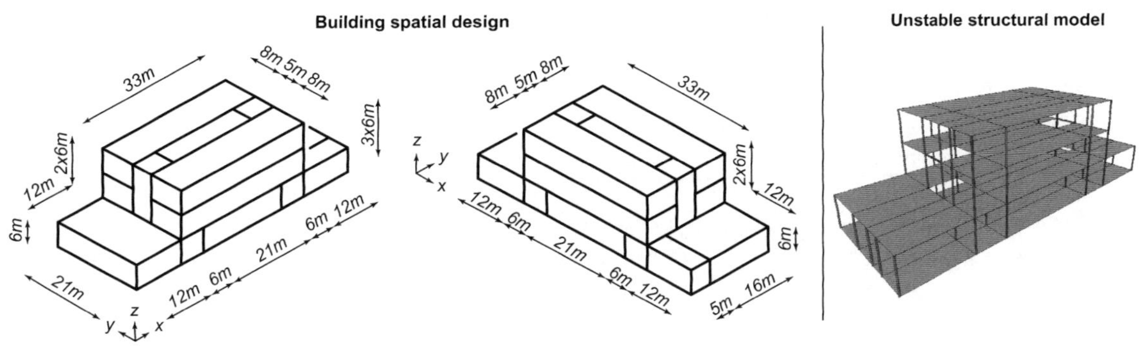

Figure 5: Left, the considered building spatial design model. Right, the structural components that will be generated by the structural design grammar for the BSD on the left.

4. Case Study

In this section, the BSD in figure 5 is subjected to a case study. The two presented methods for stabilization are applied to the BSD, i.e. stabilization of nodes via key points (subsection 3.3) and stabilization based on zones (subsection 3.4). In this section first the settings for the structural design grammar, the zoning procedure, and the stabilization procedure are given in subsection 4.1. Thereafter the results are presented in subsection 4.2.

4.1. Settings

Structural Design Grammar. The structural design grammar assigns flat shell components (elasiticity modulus $E = 3 \times 10^4\,\mathrm{N\,mm^{-2}}$, Poisson ratio $\nu = 0.30$, and thickness $t = 150\,\mathrm{mm}$) to horizontally oriented rectangles that are associated with one or two surfaces of a space. And, the grammar assigns truss components (cross sectional area $A = 5000\mathrm{mm}^2$ and elasticity modulus $E = 2.1 \times 10^5\,\mathrm{N\,mm^{-2}}$) to vertically oriented line segments that are associated to one or more surfaces of spaces. As truss components cannot transfer lateral or bending forces, the structural model is unstable, the resulting structural model is shown in the right of figure 5. Five load cases are defined, one live load case and four wind load cases. The live load acts in $-z$-direction, is assigned to all flat shell components, and has a magnitude of $5.0\,\mathrm{kN\,m^{-2}}$. A wind load case is defined in each azimuthal direction ($+x, +y, -x$, and $-y$), where for each wind load case three types of loads are applied: wind pressure ($1.0\,\mathrm{kN\,m^{-2}}$), wind suction ($0.80\,\mathrm{kN\,m^{-2}}$), and wind shear ($0.40\,\mathrm{kN\,m^{-2}}$). A wind load is applied to rectangles that are associated with exactly one space surface, where the type of wind load depends on the orientation of that rectangle. Because no structure—to which the wind loads can be applied to—exists at vertically oriented rectangles, flat shell components (elasticity modulus $E = 3.00 \times 10^{-2}\,\mathrm{N\,mm^{-2}}$, Poisson ratio $\nu = 0.30$, and thickness $t = 150\,\mathrm{mm}$) are applied in order to transfer these loads to the structure. The low stiffness of these load transferring components ensures that these components do not influence the stiffness of the building structure. As such, the load transferring components function similar to façade systems, which transfer load but do not take part in the building's structural system. Moreover, all flat shell components with a z-coordinate lower or equal to zero ($z \leq 0$) have their movement in x-, y-, and z-direction constrained at their edges. Finally, flat shell components are meshed into 10×10 flat shell elements, beam components (applied by the stabilization procedures) are meshed into 10 beam elements, and truss components are meshed into 1 element.

Zoning Procedure. For zoning, the maximum span in the structure is set to 21 m. Other settings for the zoning procedure have been omitted from this work for brevity. However, in reference to (Claessens; 2018; Hofmeyer et al.; 2019), it is noted that the large solution space of zoned designs (labeled by 'L' in their work) is used for this case study.

Stabilization As mentioned, stabilization will be performed using the two presented methods (subsection 3.3 and 3.4). Here, each method will be applied once to every zoned design that results from the zoning procedure. In order for the method that stabilizes nodes to yield a different solution for each zoned design, here, it is required that each of the used key points lies within the surface of a zone. The latter requirement has in fact proven to lead to better designs in (Claessens; 2018; Hofmeyer et al.; 2019). Both stabilization procedures have the ability to apply truss components (same as in design grammar) and beam components (width $w = 150\,\mathrm{mm}$, height $h = 150\,\mathrm{mm}$, elasticity modulus $E = 3.0 \times 10^4\,\mathrm{N\,mm^{-2}}$, Poisson ratio $\nu = 0.30$).

4.2. Results

The zoning procedure found 14 zoned designs for the BSD of the case study. Applying both methods once for each zoned design has thus yielded 28 structural models. The performances of each of those designs are compared to each other in the plot in figure 6. Plotted on the horizontal axis is the total sum of volumes of the structural components that were used to stabilize the structural model. On the vertical axis—using a logarithmic scale—is the total sum of strain energy in the structural model, which is a common measure for the stiffness: higher stiffness yields a design with less strain energy. In the plot, performances of structural designs whose nodes were stabilized are indicated with a cross, whereas a circle is used to indicate performances of SDs resulting from stabilization of zones. Moreover, a Pareto front approximation (PFA) is given by drawing a line through the non-dominated points in the plot.

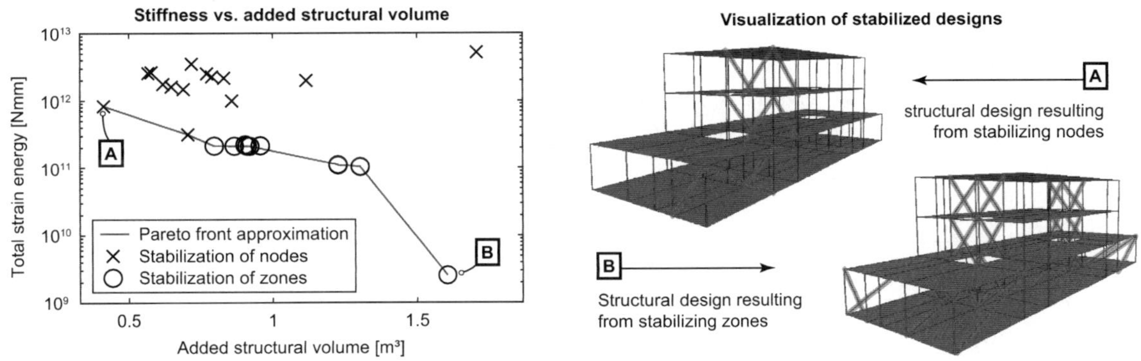

Figure 6: Left, plot with structural design performances that result from the two stabilization methods. Right, from each method one visualization of the found structural designs.

From the plot in figure 6 it can be observed that all structural designs resulting from stabilization based on zoning are on or close to the PFA, whereas the other method mostly yielded dominated solutions. Therefore, any SD resulting from the method that stabilizes zones individually can—for this case study—be regarded optimal in some sense for the contradicting objectives of stiffness and structural volume. Another observation that is made from the plot: stabilization of zones, adds more structural volume to the structural model, i.e. more material is needed. However, considering that a stiff design may allow for components to be dimensioned smaller, this additional volume could be negated. Finally, in the right of figure 6, one of the SDs is depicted for each of the two methods. Comparing these SDs, it is noticed that stabilizing each zone individually indeed requires more components, but it can also be noticed that the method will indeed provide an SD with more structural redundancy and a more organized layout.

5. Discussion

Although results are promising, critical notes can be made. First, the case study is limited, and the presented results may not generalize. Therefore, a more extensive case study should be performed to make the conclusions that were extracted from the results better grounded. Second, a rather simple pattern of stabilizing components has been used for stabilization based on zoning. In practice, more (perhaps better) patterns may be observed, and it would be interesting to also investigate other patterns. Finally, the stated hypothesis that stiff designs allow for components to be dimensioned smaller is not investigated. It would be interesting to also investigate this hypothesis in conjunction with the new zoning method.

6. Conclusion and Outlook

In this paper, a new stabilization method for structural building design is presented. The method uses a zoning procedure to find structurally promising zones within a building design, which are then used to check the structure that is enveloped by these zones for stability. As such, the stabilization procedure can find structurally redundant designs, i.e. designs that are less sensitive to progressive collapse, by placing stabilizing provisions at locations (derived form zones) that are logical from a structural point of view. A case study has shown that the proposed method is promising, as it finds designs that are stiff and structurally redundant. However, critical notes were made in the discussion, which gives an outlook onto an extended case study which includes more design scenarios and additional settings for the proposed zoning procedure.

Acknowledgements

This work is part of the TTW-Open Technology Program with project number 13596, which is (partly) financed by the Netherlands Organization for Scientific Research (NWO).

References

Björk, B. C. (1992). A conceptual model of spaces, space boundaries and enclosing structures, *Automation in Construction* **1**(3): 193–214.

Boonstra, S., van der Blom, K., Hofmeyer, H., Emmerich, M. T., van Schijndel, J. and de Wilde, P. (2018). Toolbox for super-structured and super-structure free multi-disciplinary building spatial design optimisation, *Advanced Engineering Informatics* **36**: 86–100.

Claessens, D. P. H. (2018). *Influence of spatial zoning on structural topology performance*, Master's thesis, Eindhoven University of Technology, Department of the Built Environment, Applied Mechanics and Design.

Geyer, P. (2008). Multidisciplinary grammars supporting design optimization of buildings, *Research in Engineering Design* **18**(4): 197–216.

Hofmeyer, H., Claessens, D. P. H., Boonstra, S. and de Vries, B. (2019). Effects of 3D zoning of spatial designs on the performance of structure systems, *Intelligent & informed, Proceedings of the 24th International conference of the Association for Computer-Aided Architectural Design Research in Asia (CAADRIA)*, pp. 1–10.

Hofmeyer, H. and Russell, P. (2009). Interaction between spatial and structural building design: a finite element based program for the analysis of kinematically indeterminable structural topologies, *CONVR2009, Proceedings of the 9th international conference on construction applications of virtual reality*.

Hofmeyer, H., Rutten, H. S. and Fijneman, H. J. (2006). Interaction of spatial and structural design, an automated approach, *Design Studies* **27**(4): 423–438.

Hoskins, E. (1979). Design development and description using 3D box geometries, *Computer-aided design* **11**(6): 329–336.

Meyer, S., Fenves, S. J. et al. (1993). Structural design of tall buildings knowledge acquisition study report, *Technical report*, Engineering Design Research Center, Carnegie-Mellon University, USA.

Parent, S., Rivard, H. and Mora, R. (2006). Acquisition and modeling of conceptual structural design knowledge, *Proceedings of the Joint International Conference on Computing and Decision Making in Civil and Building Engineering*, pp. 1–10.

Rafiq, M. Y. and MacLeod, I. A. (1988). Automatic structural component definition from a spatial geometry model, *Engineering Structures* **10**(1): 37–40.

Smulders, C. D. J. and Hofmeyer, H. (2012). An automated stabilisation method for spatial to structural design transformations, *Advanced Engineering Informatics* **26**(4): 691–704.

Steiner, B., Mousavian, E., Saradj, F. M., Wimmer, M. and Musialski, P. (2017). Integrated structural–architectural design for interactive planning, *Computer Graphics Forum* **36**(8): 80–94.

Integrating Railway Subdomain-Specific Data Standards into a common IFC-based Data Model

Sebastian Esser & André Borrmann
Technical University of Munich, Germany
sebastian.esser@tum.de   andre.borrmann@tum.de

Abstract

Like in many other domains in the construction industry, concepts and methods of Building Information Modeling (BIM) are becoming more and more important for the design of civil infrastructure assets. Although several data formats have been developed to capture domain-specific data, none of these schemas can be used for holistic communication and cross-domain data exchange. In this paper, we present approaches for mapping existing domain-specific data formats in a more generic schema like the Industry Foundation Classes (IFC). This offers the possibility to develop coordination models for seamless data exchange and improved communication between project stakeholders.

1. Introduction

Over the last years, the use of Building Information Modeling (BIM) related techniques has been established in the architecture, engineering and construction industry (AEC). A large number of software products is already available that helps engineers to create and validate digital models of buildings. Two critical aspects in BIM are the representation of geometric shapes and semantic attributes within a single data container as well as the seamless collaboration among several domains.

Recent efforts have pushed forward the adoption of BIM methods also in the infrastructure sector. Particularly challenging, however, is the domain of railway design and operation (Bukhsh, Hartmann, & Stipanovic, 2016). Many disciplines are involved in the design process of a railway asset, e.g., alignment design, overhead electrification, railway equipment, noise barrier design and structural asset design like bridges and tunnels. The traditional paper-based working procedures have shown to be highly error-prone and inefficient as they do not provide appropriate means for handling the complexity involving a multitude of subdomains. BIM-methods can help to overcome these issues. However, for enabling an integrated design, data exchange is required across all these sub-domains.

In recent years, a couple of data formats were developed to store, and exchange data of specific sub-domains involved in a railway design process, but they are often limited to one specific use case. An example of such a format is the data model *PlanPro* developed by German Railways for representing information about railway equipment components such as signal systems or switch controls (Maschek, Klaus, Gerke, Uminski, & Girke, 2012). For pre-design decisions as well as for maintenance and operation purposes, it is often not necessary to store an exact geometric representation of the railway equipment components. Thus, this exchange format was designed to transfer detailed semantic information and satisfies the specific needs of railway equipment design in Germany. However, there are use cases such as geometric clash detections or visualizations, which require at least a core geometric representation of each component in the three-dimensional space.

From a BIM perspective, integrating and linking domain-limited data models is required to realize a higher quality of data exchange and reduce the error-prone and often manually re-input of already generated data. This causes the need for domain-neutral and also vendor-neutral data formats such as the *Industry Foundation Classes* (IFC). This format is well-established for the exchange of building models. IFC can be used to merge data into a coordinated central model, which can then be used to perform data validation or clash detection between the components of federated submodels (Preidel & Borrmann, 2015).

In this paper, we show how domain-specific data formats can be translated into a more holistic and flexible IFC model. In detail, we compare the alignment description given in *PlanPro* with the available IFC classes to represent alignment axes an IFC model. Furthermore, we describe the opportunities how components can be placed in an IFC model. This paper also discusses the flexibility of IFC with respect to dynamic extensions by means of proxy objects and PropertySets without the need of an official schema extension for an individual domain.

The paper is structured as follows. Section 1.1 gives an overview of related work and related approaches. We will focus on the PlanPro data model as one specific data model to describe a possible mapping process of a domain-specific data schema to a more generic data framework. Two possible approaches converting alignment information and related element placement are presented in Section 2. Those approaches and their successful implementation show that it is possible to utilize well-established domain-specific data-formats in a BIM process and hence prepare the data for further analyses and simulations. We investigate some relevant classes of the input data and explain approaches to transfer them into the IFC schema. However, the proposed transformation from PlanPro to an IFC model is limited in some aspects. These issues are discussed in Section 3 and should be addressed in future research.

1.1 Related Work

In the last years, researchers and domain experts have developed a broad range of data models to carry information about civil infrastructure assets like roads and railways. These studies often put their focus on carrying semantic information and element descriptions.

Well-known data formats related to the field of railway infrastructure are *PlanPro* (Maschek et al., 2012) and RailML (Bosschaart, Quaglietta, Janssen, & Goverde, 2015). *PlanPro* was developed to exchange design data of train control systems, whereas RailML is more focused on operation issues of rail-bounded vehicles. Both of these formats are based on the Extensible Markup Language (XML), which is machine- as well as human-readable (Bray et al., 2006). For simplicity, these data models are called *Information Models* (IM) in the following sections. This term was introduced by Bukhsh, Hartmann, and Stipanovic (2016) and is used both for RailML and for PlanPro in this paper. Additionally to the development of the aforementioned formats, some initiatives investigated in ontologies and Linked-Data approaches (Turck et al., 2010). Wunsch et al. (2016) gave a comprehensive outlook on exchange requirements and possible data formats for these use cases.

Besides these separated approaches using IMs as exchange formats, Luteberget and Johansen (2018) took use of RailML to support and expand a CAD-based design application for railway safety equipment. They developed a plugin to check the compliance of their design data against national regulations at runtime. Their approach, however, is not applicable to perform cross-domain rules, which can require information for assets that cannot be modeled within RailML.

In contrast, the vendor-neutral data format Industry Foundation Classes (IFC) offers the opportunity to store detailed geometry as well as comprehensive semantic information. Initially developed in the context of building models, IFC gets more and more extended to the needs of civil infrastructure assets. Some initiatives investigated on refining the geometric descriptions for large models, i.e., for exchanging tunnel or bridge models (Vilgertshofer, Jubierre, & Borrmann, 2016). Augele (2017) worked out the similarities and differences between RailML and IFC but did not take the recent IFC extensions for civil infrastructure assets into consideration. Amann et al. (2014) focused their research on the translation of alignment models given in several data formats and proposed a common meta-model. Their model became the base for the description in the IFC data schema extension describing alignments and was added to the official schema with the version 4.1 published in summer 2016.

The contributions of the abovementioned studies are of high importance because their concepts of structuring the relevant information in a specific sub-domain are derived from domain experts' knowledge. An international standard for exchanging digital models will never be capable of all regional, local or project-specific features and requirements. Nevertheless, additional approaches are required to realize cross-domain communication and data exchange between several project stakeholders since domain-specific formats are often only supported by a minimal number of specialized applications. Thus, connecting different Information Models into a vendor-neutral and domain-neutral data format like IFC can help to overcome this problem. IFC is common in the building sector; thus, there is already a broad range of model viewer and project management applications supporting IFC import and/or export. These programs can be used for project communication for building models as well as for civil infrastructure models. Besides that, converting data from IMs into IFC makes it possible to perform cross-domain simulations like geometric clash detections between components from different domains. However, since there is no specific schema extension for railway assets in the IFC schema yet, some problems occur during the mapping process, which will be discussed afterward.

1.2 Objectives & Challenges

As shown before, IMs provide a solid base of semantic information about a specific asset. However, it is not possible to use them for cross-domain communication and simulations. Therefore, another well-established concept from the building sector can be adapted: Federated models are used to coordinate domain-specific data during the complete lifecycle of a building. This approach is already standardized by the British Standard PAS1192-2 as well as by the ISO standard 19650. Preidel and Borrmann (2015) showed the necessity of working in federated domain models and merging them into a coordinated model.

Coordination and seamless data exchange are unavoidable between all project stakeholders to optimize planning processes in the construction industry. Non-coordination of issues and design data can lead to inconsistent data. Thus, a data structure should be chosen, which is capable of all these aims. Model-based data structures for buildings are often led by a three-dimensional geometric representation and a grid-based model orientation (axes and storeys in a building). Contrary to buildings, civil infrastructure models are often line-oriented. The representation of these alignment curves is typically split into a horizontal description in the xy-plane and its corresponding gradient described by a parametric coordinate s and the height z (Markic, Schlenger, & Bratoev, 2018). Besides that, there are many cases in a design process of a civil infrastructure asset, in which the engineer must deal with a large number of semantic values but can only provide a rough estimation of the product shape. Thus, a data format for railway coordination models should be chosen, which matches the following requirements:

- A line-oriented model orientation and product placements referencing relative to a given alignment.

- Three-dimensional geometric component representations in any granularity.
- The capacity to carry semantic information assigned to components.

IFC is capable of all these requirements. Therefore, we introduce mapping processes from pure IMs into the IFC format to remedy the disadvantages of pure IMs. Especially, the strong linkage between geometric and semantic information in an IFC model enables the user to formulate complex queries against the generated model. Cross-domain problems benefit a lot from the direct integration, e.g. by accessing semantic attributes of elements in a particular area or volume (Daum & Borrmann, 2014). Design decisions often require a detailed examination of a complex geometric situation, e.g., mounting several components of different domains on one pole. Hence, linking the requirements and design options of all sub-domains should be already investigated in early design phases.

We developed a software prototype to examine the possibilities and limitations of mapping an IM into an IFC model. In the case study conducted, PlanPro was selected as origin format. The prototype supports the alignment description and the placement of signals as point-based objects along a track. Although the validation of the proposed concept is based solely on PlanPro and provides only the mapping of alignment data and signals, the strategies discussed in the next sections can also be applied for other components like switches, axle counters, or platforms.

2. Approaches

As there is an increasing number of applications supporting IFC, several options exist to implement the proposed converter from IMs into IFC models. Currently, several IFC versions are in use. Thus, a short overview regarding IFC is provided.

2.1 Industry Foundation Classes (IFC)

The *Industry Foundation Classes* (IFC) are an open, vendor-neutral data format, which is intended to transfer information among different stakeholders across the lifecycle of a built facility. IFC is mainly focused on the building sector and has many classes to describe elements from different domains like architecture, structural analysis or HVAC. Although IFC is often related to data exchange in the planning and execution phase of a project, IFC models can also be used for operation and maintenance.

With version 4.1, the classes for describing alignments were added to the official schema. These classes offer the possibility to store information about three-dimensional axes, which are the base for line-based infrastructure assets e.g., roads, rails and their corresponding structures such as bridges, tunnels or platforms. Extension projects are currently conducted by *buildingSMART* to develop the necessary extensions of the IFC data model. This includes IfcBridge, IfcRoad, and IfcRail (BuildingSMART international, 2018). A small number of authoring tools already supports the import and export of *IfcAlignment* into or from an IFC file. However, the number of applications capable to interpret *IfcAlignment* entities is low compared to a massive range of tools supporting IFC for building models.

Although there is yet no standard defined for infrastructure assets in the IFC schema, many use cases in an infrastructure planning process are already supported by IFC. The IFC data model provides flexible extension mechanisms including proxy elements and user-defined property sets, which enable the user to perform analyses and simulations on these models and allow data exchange among different stakeholders. It is possible to use the generic *IfcBuildingElementProxy* class to model components without a specific definition in the data schema. *IfcBuildingElementProxy* is derived from the abstract class *IfcProduct*. Therefore, it is capable of carrying a geometric representation as well as every other class derived from *IfcProduct*. Classes derived from *IfcProduct* can be placed inside the model using subclasses from the abstract class *IfcObjectPlacement*. A subclass of this class is the *IfcLinearPlacement* class, which places components (derived from *IfcProduct*) relatively to a given curve (BuildingSMART international, 2017).

Since IFC version 4.1, specialized classes are available to describe typical alignment curves used for civil infrastructure assets. The *IfcAlignment* class is derived from *IfcProduct* and *IfcCurve* and is used to place elements along the described curve. Figure 4 shows the relevant IFC classes used in the implementation approaches.

An international standard for exchanging digital models will never be capable of all regional, local or project-specific features and requirements. To mitigate this problem, IFC provides the concept of property sets. There are many predefined attributes (e.g., for walls, windows or beams). Additionally, it is possible to create user-defined property sets and append them to components. Thus, it is possible to extend the IFC data schema for individual requirements, while at the time the model remains interpretable by any software product that has implemented IFC reading capababilities.

In both presented approaches, an additional property set was assigned to every positioned component in the IFC model, which contains relevant attributes from the given PlanPro file. Every component in PlanPro has an individual identifier, which is stored as one property within the PlanPro property set.

2.2 Implementation strategies

Several initiatives already tried to convert existing object-oriented data structures from or into the IFC schema. Object-oriented schemas can be seen modeled as graph representations. Therefore, the main task is finding correlations between both graphs. For identifying links between IFC and CityGML entities Beetz & Borrmann (2018) made mainly use of spatial coincidences, whereas Stouffs, Tauscher, and Biljecki (2018) applied the triple graph grammar concept for these formats. The proposed mapping from IMs onto the IFC schema is rather similar to the latter approach. Both schemas have an object-oriented structure and vary in the purposes they were intended for. Thus, there is no 1:1 correlation between both graphs, but there are some classes, which can be correlated. Figure 4 at the end of this document shows possible links between both data schemas to map point-based products from PlanPro into IFC.

Figure 1 gives an overview of the investigated approaches to achieving the desired subdomain model integration. The first approach consists of pre-processing the original IM (PlanPro), then importing the resulting model into a BIM authoring tool and generating the IFC file by means of its built-in export facilities. In contrast to that, the second approach avoids applying a BIM authoring tool and instead makes use of an IFC programming library for creating a standalone conversion tool.

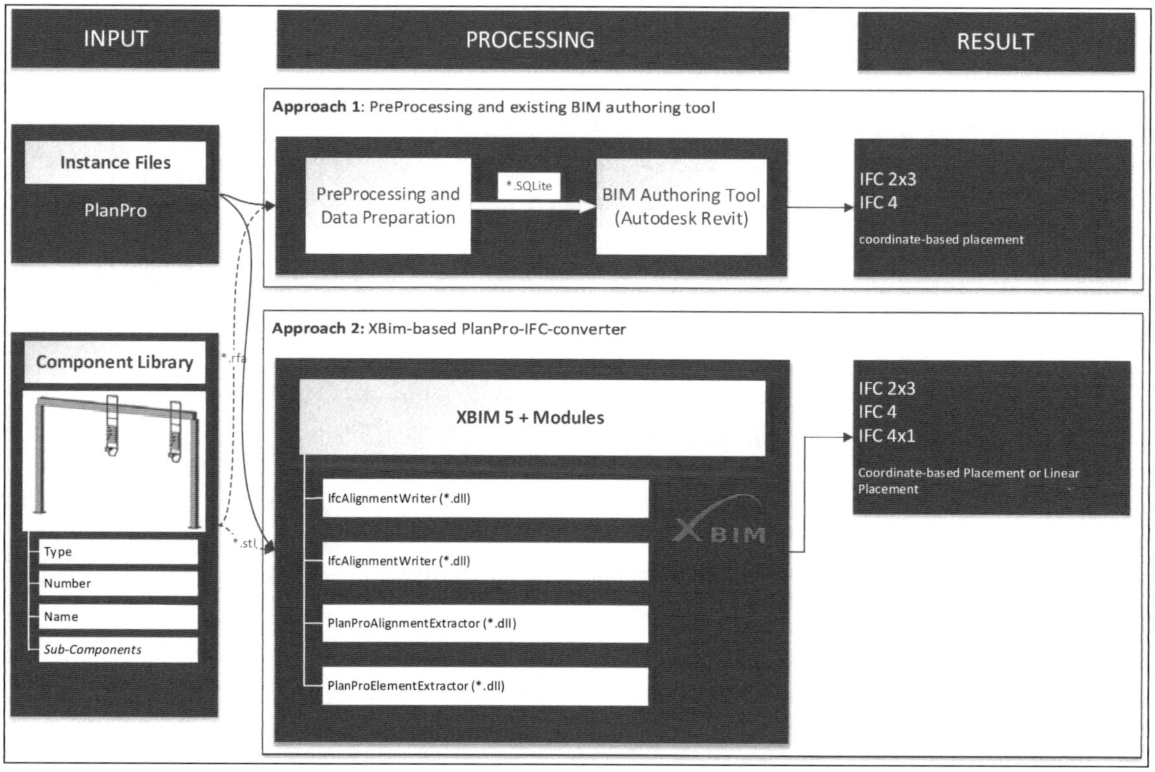

Figure 1: Different Implementation Approaches to convert Information Models into IFC Models. Approach 1 consists in pre-processing the original IM (PlanPro), then importing the resulting model into a BIM authoring tool and generating the IFC file. The second approach avoids applying a BIM authoring tool and instead makes use of an IFC programming library for creating a standalone conversion tool.

Existing BIM authoring tools offer much flexibility when creating new element groups and their respective geometry. Therefore, it is one option to use an existing application and extend it by a plugin that provides the required information in the modeling environment. For this case study, *Autodesk Revit* as a well-established BIM authoring application was selected. It has a powerful "family" editor to create new elements and can be extended using its Advanced Programming Interface (API).

A significant disadvantage of this approach is the overall dedication of BIM modeling tools for buildings and the limited support for linear infrastructure facilities. While applications like Revit organize their elements in grids and levels, civil infrastructure assets are mainly referenced to an alignment curve. Thus, Revit itself does not support the export of *IfcAlignment* Entities, but only positioning expressions in cartesian coordinate systems.

In the second approach, the framework *XBim* was selected to implement a stand-alone converter, which makes use of the IFC entities suitable to describe alignment curves. Additionally, the way of storing the placement of an individual component is addressed in detail. The next sub-sections provide an insight into the implementation process and limitations of the proposed concepts.

2.3 Product Catalogue

In the proposed concept, all available IMs are transformed into a 3D BIM representation to support coordination and informed decision making. Neither the components in *RailML* nor in PlanPro posses geometric descriptions in the form of *Boundary Representations (BRep)* or *Constructive Solid Geometry (CSG)*. For some components, however, PlanPro refers to arrangement drawings. These drawings are independent of the manufacturer, and thus can be used for vendor-neutral tendering. Because of their generic character, a component library collects the geometric shape and parameterize these representations.

Every component has a certain drawing number and can have several types. All types have a slightly similar shape. Thus, it is possible to parameterize their geometric representation. Additionally, the arrangement drawings offer some additional semantic parameters like placement rules (e.g., the required distances to overhead electrification poles), which are covered by the library as well.

The generated family library establishes the base for both approaches. Due to restrictions on publishing and sharing these arrangement drawings, the component library is not big enough to cover all possible signal types. Hence, a cuboid is used as a geometric representation for a component if there is no reference to an arrangement drawing, or the arrangement drawing was not accessible.

2.4 Using *PlanPro* Data in a BIM Authoring Tool

Since Revit is not capable of any typical alignment format yet, a preprocessing tool was developed to prepare the required data of a PlanPro model for the use inside a Revit Project. Although Revit is not intended to be a modeler for railway equipment design, the family engine and the possibility to work with large property sets make it adequately generic and suitable for the proposed converter.

All coordinates of the alignment segments in a PlanPro file are described in a world coordinate system (DB Ref as a specialized system of the well-known Gauss-Krüger-System). Since Revit cannot handle large coordinate values, a preprocessing tool translates the given world coordinates into a local project coordinate system[1] (Markič, Donaubauer, & Borrmann, 2018). In a PlanPro instance model, the placement of components is given by the track it belongs to, the station kilometer and the lateral offset to the rail axis. Revit itself cannot process this kind of placement description; thus, the preprocessing tool calculates the (projected) cartesian coordinate. Thus, the BIM authoring tool itself is mainly used to place the right family inside into the modeling environment and sets the required semantic attributes. The preprocessing approach also offers the flexibility to use the prepared data in other tools.

After finishing the modeling process, the IFC export interface of Revit was used to create the desired IFC model. Although the export interface offers the possibility to adjust some preferences (Trzeciak & Borrmann, 2018), it cannot create IFC models using *IfcAlignment* and *IfcLinearPlacement* entities.

The resulting *IFC* model in the versions 2x3 and 4 can be displayed in all common IFC viewer applications.

[1] It must be noted that this local coordinate system is still a projected one with the respective distortions that must be taken into account.

Figure 2: Resulting Revit-IFC Model in Solibri Model Checker

2.5 Using XBim Framework for a Refined IFC Model

As discussed above, the aim of mapping an existing IM into an IFC model can be solved with the first approach using existing modeling software. The resulting model contains signals with an individual geometric representation depending on the given arrangement drawings and semantic attributes. The alignment is modeled with a volumetric boundary representation as well. However, the plugin-approach leads to the loss of a direct relationship between the alignment curve and the implicit placement indication (station and axis reference) of all elements since cartesian coordinates now describe the position of any element.

The second approach remedies the disadvantage of using Cartesian Coordinates for every individual element placement. Instead, each element's position is described relative to an alignment curve in the resulting IFC model. Once the alignment curve in the xy-plane is modeled, it is possible to locate an element by a new coordinate system (s, z) in which s describes the stationing axis and z the height at a specific station s (Markic et al., 2018). With additional offset parameters in the longitudinal, lateral and vertical direction the exact component placement is defined.

To realize the second approach, we implement a direct mapping to IFC without using an existing BIM authoring tool in the toolchain anymore. Instead, the *XBim Toolkit* is employed to create the desired IFC model using *IfcAlignment* and the linear positioning concept along the alignment curve according to ISO 19148. *XBim* is an open-source framework for importing, editing and exporting IFC models and is licensed under the *CDDL Open Source License* ("xBIM Toolkit," 2019).

The required methods are split up in several modules to make the code as reusable as possible. This concept enables the developers to extend the implemented prototype for further requirements or other applications, which need similar methods. The modules *IfcAlignmentWriter* and *IfcElementWriter* are entirely decoupled from the libraries extracting data from a given PlanPro model. The modules *PlanProAlignmentExtractor* and *PlanProElementExtractor* extract the necessary data and insert suitable IFC entities into a given IFC model.

As shown in Figure 1, the created component library is used in both presented approaches. Since *Revit* families are stored in the proprietary **.rfa* format, the contained geometric and semantic data are not accessible from applications outside the Autodesk product family. Thus, an export of the geometry into the open geometry format "STereoLithography" (*STL)* was required. STL stores a given body as a triangulated boundary representation and is, therefore, an explicit geometry representation. It can easily be converted into an IFC geometry representation like *IfcTriangulatedFaceSet*.

Model View Definitions (*MVDs*) are used to define a subset of the complete IFC schema and add additional requirements such as geometric representation method or necessary attributes (Beetz, Borrmann, & Weise, 2018). The chosen IFC entities used in the standalone approach are based on the Reference View of IFC 4. Unfortunately, there is yet no official MVD for *IfcAlignment* and *IfcLinearPlacement* entities. However, the generated IFC models can be opened and visualized by several applications. We tested the alignment data with the commercial software *ProVI* (Obermeyer, 2018) and the *FZK-Viewer* (Karlsruher Institut für Technologie, 2019). The latter one is already capable of processing *IfcLinearPlacement* entities.

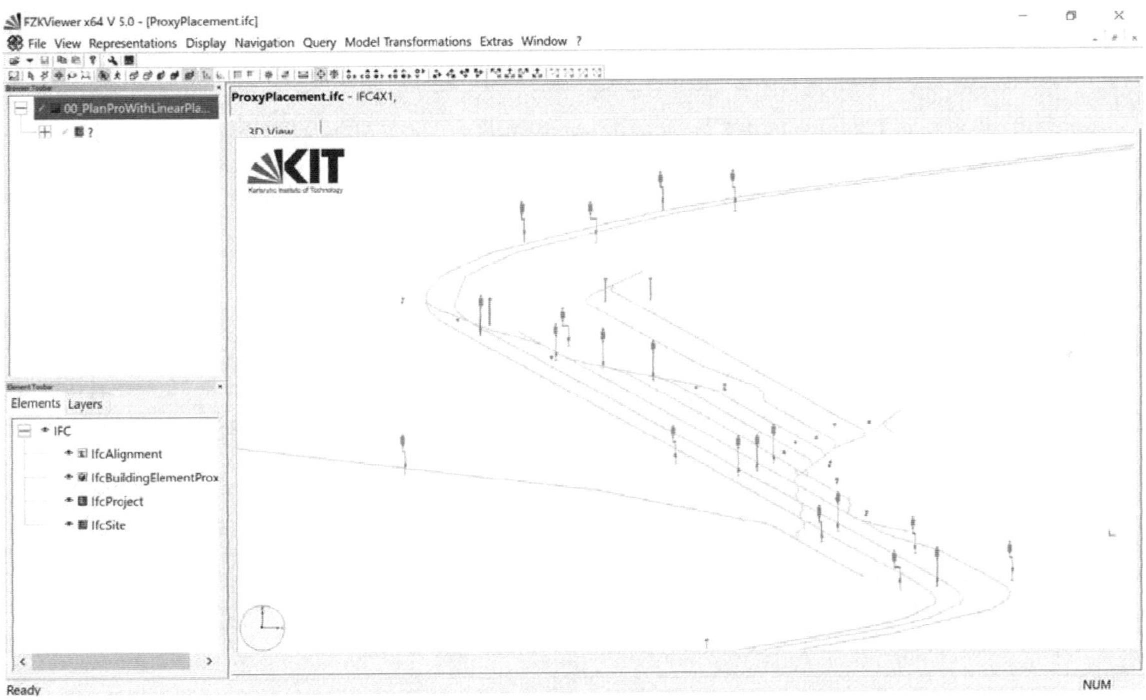

Figure 3: Resulting IFC Model based on IfcAlignment and IfcLinearPlacement

3. Discussion

The paper has presented two different approaches for integration domain-specific information models into a common model representing the overall railway project by means of the vendor neutral data format IFC. Both approaches presented the feasibility to convert domain-specific data models into an IFC model. By using the *IfcAlignment* classes as well as the *IfcLinearPlacement* concept, it is possible to set up an IFC model based in semantically powerful IMs, which uses alignment expressions for the overall project orientation. The concept of property sets enriches the data schema and provide the flexibility to adapt the model to specific needs. The presented approach of mapping semantically powerful but geometrically sparse IMs into IFC can be applied to many existing data concepts which are used for domain-specific exchange scenarios. By converting them into IFC models, it is now possible to coordinate elements and their related attributes across different domains. However, the translation and analysis of PlanPro have unveiled significant limitations: The geometric granularity of arrangement drawings can only provide an estimation of the component's shape to be built in the real world. Thus, the modeled geometry can differ from real product shape in the built environment, and this must be considered when performing simulations based on the shown IFC models. In order to use the created models on site, refinements of the used geometric representations are inevitable. In conclusion, the proposed mapping process is possible and enriches the concept of seamless collaboration and communication along different domains in a project.

IMs often provide fictive components, which do not have any geometric representation but are of high importance for the design process. Such concepts cannot be directly covered by the IFC schema yet but are depictable in an IFC model. The use of placeholder geometries like cuboids or other simple geometries is one possible solution for such issues. The obligation that every class derived from *IfcProduct* must have a *ProductRepresentation* is restrictive in that point but solvable.

User-defined property sets enrich an IFC model due to project or domain-specific requirements. However, the possible data types for property values are limited to simple numeric or textual types and Booleans. An IM can have much more specialized subclasses, which structure relevant attributes and relationships better than a simple *IfcPropertySet* can do. Thus, use cases are conceivable that could be better served with the original IM. The focus of our research was the preparation of data for project-wide communication rather than supporting advanced and specialized use cases. Another option inside the IFC schema is the use of element assemblies, which should be addressed in future research.

Due to the yet missing standardization of railway components in IFC, it is complex to define filters or to process the models in subsequent simulations. It is possible to filter specific components by their names, but the defined filters are dependent on modifiable attributes. A better approach is the detection of elements by their element type. However, the necessary changes in the implementation described in Section 2 will not have a massive impact: most of the IFC classes representing railway equipment components will probably derive from *IfcProduct*.

In summary, the proposed conversion from IMs into the IFC format can be used to utilize domain-specific information in federated models and combine those in a coordination model. However, limitations exist with respect to the granularity and expressiveness of the converted data.

4. Summary

In this paper, we showed different approaches to convert domain-specific data formats into a more generic data model. These concepts offer much flexibility when querying data in a model and using it for in cross-domain simulations.

5. Acknowledgments

This study has been performed in the frame of the RIMcomb project. We gratefully acknowledge the support of the Bavarian Research Foundation for funding this project.

References

Amann, J., Jubierre, J. R., Borrmann, A., & Flurl, M. (2014). An alignment meta-model for the comparison of alignment product models.

Augele, V. (2017). *Comparative Analysis of Building Information Modelling (BIM) and RailTopoModel/railML in View of their Application to Operationally Relevant Railway Infrastructure*. Retrieved from https://www.railml.org/en/public-relations/scientific-papers.html?file=files/download/papers/230117_TUDresdenAugele_TermPaperComparisonRailTopoModelIFCrailML.pdf

Beetz, J., & Borrmann, A. (2018). Benefits and limitations of linked data approaches for road modeling and data exchange. In *Workshop of the European Group for Intelligent Computing in Engineering* (pp. 245–261).

Beetz, J., Borrmann, A., & Weise, M. (2018). Process-Based Definition of Model Content. In *Building Information Modeling* (pp. 127–138). Springer.

Bosschaart, M., Quaglietta, E., Janssen, B., & Goverde, R. M. P. (2015). Efficient formalization of railway interlocking data in RailML. *Information Systems*, *49*, 126–141. https://doi.org/10.1016/j.is.2014.11.007

Bray, T., Paoli, J., Sperberg-McQueen, C. M., Maler, E., Yergeau, F., & Cowan, J. (2006). *Extensible Markup Language (XML)*. https://doi.org/DOI:

BuildingSMART international. (2017). Ifc 4x1 Final Documentation. Retrieved February 13, 2019, from http://www.buildingsmart-tech.org/ifc/IFC4x1/final/html/

BuildingSMART international. (2018). Infrastructure: Ongoing Projects. Retrieved July 15, 2018, from https://www.buildingsmart.org/standards/activities/

Bukhsh, Z. A., Hartmann, T., & Stipanovic, I. (2016). From analysis of information needs towards an information model of railway infrastructure. In *23rd International Workshop of the European Group for Intelligent Computing in Engineering, EG-ICE 2016*.

Daum, S., & Borrmann, A. (2014). Processing of topological BIM queries using boundary representation based methods. *Advanced Engineering Informatics*, *28*(4), 272–286. https://doi.org/10.1016/j.aei.2014.06.001

Karlsruher Institut für Technologie. (2019). KIT - FZKViewer. Retrieved February 13, 2019, from https://www.iai.kit.edu/1648.php

Luteberget, B., & Johansen, C. (2018). Efficient verification of railway infrastructure designs against standard regulations. *Formal Methods in System Design*, *52*(1), 1–32. https://doi.org/10.1007/s10703-017-0281-z

Markič, Š., Donaubauer, A., & Borrmann, A. (2018). Enabling Geodetic Coordinate Reference Systems in Building Information Modeling for Infrastructure. In *Proceeding of the 17th International Conference on Computing in Civil and Building Engineering, Tampere, Finland*.

Markic, S., Schlenger, J., & Bratoev, I. (2018). Tangible Alignment Design. In *30. Forum Bauinformatik, Weimar, Germany*.

Maschek, U., Klaus, C., Gerke, C., Uminski, V., & Girke, K.-J. (2012). PlanPro - Durchgängige elektronische Datenhaltung im ESTW-Planungsprozess. *Signal + Draht*, *104*, 22–26.

Obermeyer. (2018). ProVI: Home: Trassierungssoftware für Tiefbau, Bahnplanung, Straßenplanung, Kanal, Vermessung. Retrieved May 1, 2018, from https://www.provi-cad.de/

Preidel, C., & Borrmann, A. (2015). Seamless Integration of Common Data Environment Access into BIM Authoring Applications : the BIM Integration Framework.

Stouffs, R., Tauscher, H., & Biljecki, F. (2018). Achieving Complete and Near-Lossless Conversion from IFC to CityGML. *ISPRS International Journal of Geo-Information*, *7*(9), 355. https://doi.org/10.3390/ijgi7090355

Trzeciak, M., & Borrmann, A. (2018). Design-to-design exchange of bridge models using IFC : A case study with Revit and Allplan.

Turck, F. De, Ongenae, F., Verstichel, S., Dhaene, T., Dhoedt, B., Dings, P., … Loeve, L. (2010). Efficient data integration in the railway domain through an ontology-based methodology. *Transportation Research Part C: Emerging Technologies*, *19*(4), 617–643. https://doi.org/10.1016/j.trc.2010.10.003

Vilgertshofer, S., Jubierre, J. R., & Borrmann, A. (2016). IfcTunnel—a proposal for a multi-scale extension of the IFC data model for shield tunnels under consideration of downward compatibility aspects. In *11th European Conference on Product and Process Modelling, ECPPM 2016* (pp. 175–182). Retrieved from https://www.scopus.com/inward/record.uri?eid=2-s2.0-85016608612&partnerID=40&md5=b7dbf8d0bb46d0c0b4ddea7388a1c2c1

Wunsch, S., Lehnert, M., Krimmling, J., & Easton, J. (2016). Datenformate, -modelle und -konzepte für den Eisenbahnbetrieb. *Der Eisenbahningenieur*, (November), 8–14.

xBIM Toolkit. (2019). Retrieved February 12, 2019, from http://docs.xbim.net/

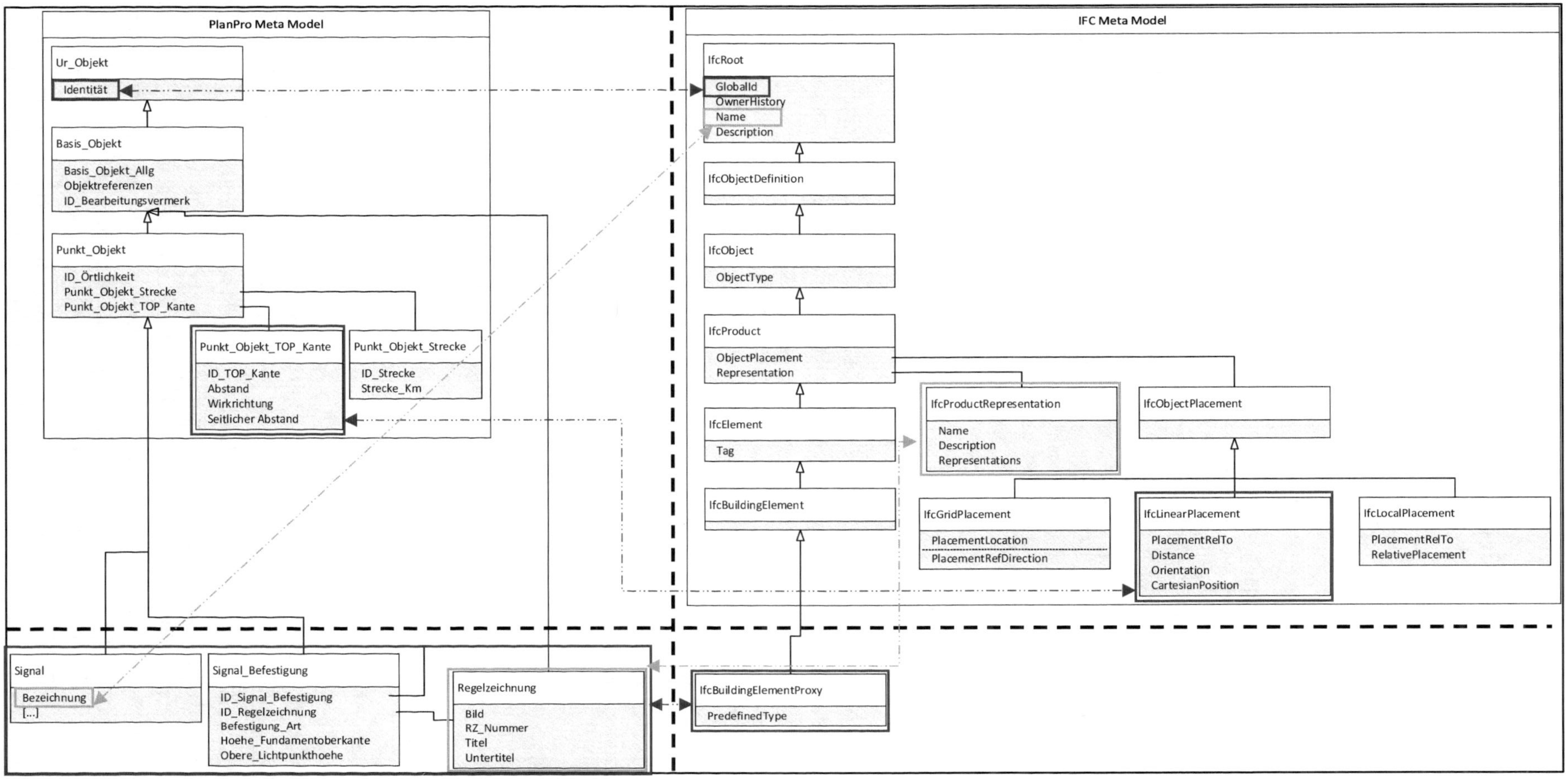

Figure 4: Possible Correlation Graphs between PlanPro (left) and IFC (right)

A semantic model of intelligent transportation systems

Mahsa Mirboland and Kay Smarsly
Bauhaus University Weimar, Germany
mahsa.mirboland@uni-weimar.de

Abstract. Intelligent transportation systems, representing core components of smart cities, combine sensing, computing, and wireless communication technologies to provide efficient and convenient mobility. Road intelligent transportation systems (ITS) have been studied in recent decades through simulation platforms that integrate computational models for various use cases, such as traffic lights control and management. However, semantic descriptions, illustrating road ITS as a whole and creating a basis for designing simulation platforms, have not been addressed. In this paper, a semantic model of road intelligent transportation systems is proposed, which describes road ITS components and architecture, serving as a formal basis for road ITS simulation platforms. Building upon the semantic model, an extension of the Industry Foundation Classes schema, facilitating ITS simulation platforms based on building information modeling, is discussed. The paper concludes with a summary, a discussion, and an outlook on potential formalization efforts.

1. Introduction

Vehicular cyber-physical systems combine physical, computing, and networking processes in vehicular environments. A vehicular cyber-physical system (VCPS) is composed of a physical subsystem, including all physical components and processes, and a computational subsystem that includes the networking processes and computational models (Legatiuk et al., 2017). As an application branch of vehicular cyber-physical systems, an intelligent transportation system (ITS) considers vehicles as intelligent VCPS components with combined on-board sensing/actuating, computing, and communication capabilities. Intelligent transportation systems constitute key elements of smart cities and increase quality of life by providing safer, greener, and more cost-effective mobility.

A road ITS refers to the land-based mode of transport that uses roads as travel routes. Road intelligent transportation systems comprise numerous elements and data-sharing processes with intermittent and temporal connections, resulting in complex and heterogeneous systems. Traffic management and fleet logistics control, road safety and maintenance management, navigation and positioning, and autonomous driving are among the most important applications of road intelligent transportation systems. To evaluate and improve road ITS performance, it is necessary to monitor road intelligent transportation systems. Therefore, simulation platforms are developed to study the performance of road ITS applications. Mitigating monitoring challenges, simulation platforms employ road ITS computational models for different use cases, aiming to investigate road ITS capabilities, potential improvements to application designs, and future mobility demands (Ghariani et al., 2014).

In recent years, simulation platforms have been employed to study different ITS mechanisms, focusing on specific use cases, e.g. traffic simulations, or global assessment of intelligent transportation systems. Boschian et al. (2011) have defined a reference model of intermodal transportation networks, describing an information management system between different modes of transport. The reference model together with a simulation module constructs an integrated structure that founds operational decision-making processes. Fernández-Isabel and Fuentes-Fernández (2015) have proposed a model-driven engineering framework to develop road ITS simulations. The framework consist of an ITS modeling language, focusing on traffic simulation and sensor networks components, and a guideline on how to obtain ITS modeling language for different simulation scenarios, e.g. traffic lights management. Datta et al. (2016) have listed challenges relevant to integrating connected vehicles into Internet of Things ecosystems, and have proposed a framework that comprises building blocks, software elements, and their operational phases and benefits. Also, the authors have discussed the implementation and interoperability of the proposed framework by mapping the semantic-based description of framework elements into standard architectures.

Despite the extensive research on simulation platforms for traffic-related applications and urban traffic management, a formal description of road intelligent transportation systems, providing a basis for simulation platform designs, has received little attention. Building information modeling (BIM), may utilize open standardized data formats, i.e. the Industry Foundation Classes (IFC) standard, to formally describe information and to facilitate information exchange. However, the current IFC schema contains limited entities to be used for defining road ITS components. This paper presents a semantic modeling approach for describing road ITS models. First, background information relevant to road ITS semantic modeling is given. Next, a semantic model of road intelligent transportation systems is presented, followed by an ITS case study, devised to validate the semantic model. The paper concludes with a summary and a discussion on a potential IFC schema extension to be employed for road ITS simulation platforms.

2. Knowledge sources for semantic modeling

For defining the semantic model of road intelligent transportation systems, properties of all physical and computational components of vehicular environments are to be formally described. In this section, sources that provide knowledge on the physical and computational components relevant to road ITS are analyzed with respect to semantic modeling. The knowledge sources are categorized into (i) network architectures, (ii) road ITS applications, (iii) intelligent road infrastructure, and (iv) communication networks and are briefly explained in the following subsections.

2.1 Network architectures

A vehicular ad-hoc network (VANET), representing the fundamental road ITS architecture, is a network paradigm based on peer-to-peer communications, i.e. V2X (vehicle-to-anything) communications. As a type of mobile ad-hoc networks, VANETs are self-forming networks with autonomous and intermittent connections, leading to frequent changes in ITS topology (Dixit et al., 2016). Road ITS elements that are connected through VANETs are referred to as "network nodes". To guarantee the integrity of data packet transmissions and communications between network nodes, different routing protocols and security standards are employed for vehicular ad-hoc networks. However, varying traffic densities and communication technologies pose challenges to the VANET deployment in ITS networks.

Merging VANETs with the Internet of Vehicles – the Internet of Things in vehicular environments – initiated the idea of employing underutilized resources of vehicles, i.e. on-board units, to decentralize computing processes and provide location-based services. Network nodes that were solely data consumers have become data producers as well; therefore, the cloud computing concept together with the VANET paradigm has created the vehicular cloud concept. Eltoweissy et al. (2010) have coined the term "autonomous vehicular clouds" as a group of vehicles that, by means of V2X communication, share on-board units and services with other authorized network nodes. Edge computing, vehicular cloud computing (VCC), and information-centric networking (ICN) are main characteristics of vehicular clouds that facilitate robust data sharing and cloud formation. An example of vehicular cloud formations and characteristics is depicted in Figure 1.

Advances in the automotive industry have led to the design of vehicles with various computational on-board capabilities, such as powerful computing units, several types of sensors, and different communication devices. Therefore, vehicles can absorb information from the environment, perform computational processes, and operate accordingly. As a result, all network nodes, including vehicles, are able to perform decentralized data processing, i.e. edge computing, to handle time-sensitive operations more efficiently, and to record data with local relevance temporarily (Atchison, 2018; Gerla et al., 2014). VCC is the mechanism used to access underutilized on-board units in the vicinity, combining resources to perform computing processes for location-based services and applications. In other words, VCC distributes computing burden between network nodes and lessens road ITS deployment costs by decreasing the number of centralized computing resources (Whaiduzzaman et al., 2014). Unlike VANET applications that mostly focus on traffic safety scenarios, e.g. collision avoidance, edge computing and VCC can be employed for cooperative and autonomous driving, hazard management, and infotainment applications (Eltoweissy et al., 2010; Gerla, 2012). ICN is a communication paradigm that places focus on the content of data packets by decoupling data packets from node IP addresses. Network nodes can send/receive data packets and translate packet contents with respect to several ICN architectures and messaging protocols that specify standard machine-readable naming and beacon exchanges (Ahlgren et al., 2012; Wan et al., 2014).

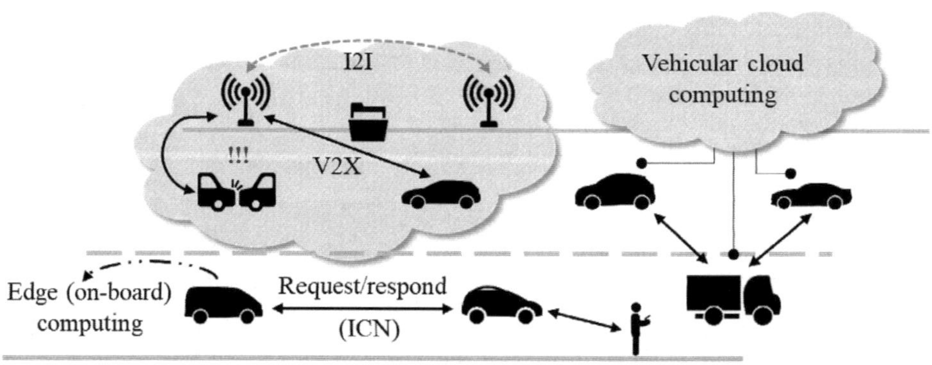

Figure 1: Example of vehicular cloud formations

Drawing from the above review of network architectures serving as a knowledge source for the semantic model proposed in this study, the vehicular cloud is recognized as the network architecture relevant to road intelligent transportation systems. The abovementioned properties of vehicular clouds are reflected in the semantic model as operations in network nodes. Moreover, communication scenarios are derived from the VANET topology and added to the semantic model.

2.2 Road ITS applications

Road ITS applications are designed to advance safe and convenient mobility scenarios, i.e. providing safety to ITS users and goods, decreasing adverse environmental impacts, and increasing efficient commutes with respect to energy consumption and travel time (Mirboland and Smarsly, 2018). As recommended by the European Telecommunications Standards Institute standard (ETSI EN 302 665), road ITS applications, with respect to the application categories, can be classified into "traffic efficiency", "road safety", and "other applications". Furthermore, with respect to application topics, road ITS applications can be grouped into "traffic and fleet logistics management", "telematics", "maintenance management", and "infotainment". Traffic and fleet logistics management applications comprise optimized commutes and traffic infrastructure control to avoid congestions and grant efficient travels. Telematics combine telecommunications and informatics for applications in vehicles and are developed to monitor the performance of vehicles ("intra-vehicle monitoring") as well as to report malfunctions to drivers or authorities. It should be noted that traffic and fleet logistics management and telematics applications overlap when a group of vehicles is considered for positioning and tracking scenarios. Maintenance management applications are based on continuous assessing and monitoring infrastructure and road conditions to provide road status information, detect structural damages, and notify drivers with detouring alerts in case of disasters or accidents. Finally, infotainment combines information and entertainment for applications in vehicles and grants passengers enjoyable time en route, providing access to Internet-based applications. Examples of different road ITS applications are listed in Table 1.

Table 1: Road ITS application groups and some examples

Application categories (ETSI EN 302 665)	**Application topics**	**Examples**
Traffic efficiency	Traffic and fleet logistics management	Optimized traffic signals, road traffic information, packet tracking systems, navigation, hazard warnings
Traffic efficiency, road safety	Telematics	Driver-assistant systems, autonomous driving, intra-vehicle monitoring, navigation and positioning
Road safety, other applications	Maintenance management	Damage detection of pavements, winter road services, disaster management
Other applications	Infotainment	Internet-based applications, multimedia libraries, gaming and news platforms

The semantic model proposed in this paper offers a generic view to map any application of road intelligent transportation systems. However, the focus is set on traffic and fleet logistics management applications, to provide a formal description of road ITS for traffic simulation platforms.

2.3 Intelligent road infrastructure

Road ITS applications use the data recorded and processed by network nodes. Therefore, road ITS applications are highly dependent on functional elements and on-board resources, i.e. ITS stations that together build the ITS architecture. Intelligent roads comprise ITS stations equipped with various types of devices that have sensing/actuating, computing and communication capabilities. ITS stations are of mobile or fixed type and, according to ETSI EN 302 665, can be further categorized into:

- Central ITS stations, also referred to as "control centers" or "base stations" (fixed).
- Personal ITS stations, i.e. smart devices, e.g. laptops, tablets, and smart phones (mobile).
- Roadside ITS stations, which comprise, e.g., traffic shields, cameras, and poles (fixed).
- Vehicle ITS stations, including all vehicle types, e.g. trucks, cars, and motorbikes (mobile).

Depending on the category, an ITS station may include different functional components and devices. It is assumed that all ITS stations comprise four main on-board units: Sensing unit, computing unit, communication unit, and power unit. The sensing unit contains sensing technologies relevant to traffic detection systems, e.g. micro-electro-mechanical systems (MEMS), inductive loops, radio-frequency identification (RFID), light detection and ranging (LIDAR) sensors, and automatic license plate recognition (ALPR) cameras, or sensor systems to detect environmental changes, such as pollution and temperature sensors. The computing unit comprises main processing and storage devices, while communication devices, e.g. radio transceivers, beacons, and Wi-Fi routers are parts of the communication unit. The power unit includes different power supply means, such as photovoltaic (solar) panels and piezoelectric transducers that may co-exist with electrical grids to deliver energy to ITS stations.

In addition, it is worth noting that roadside ITS stations may comprise actuators and control devices to change traffic signals and to control traffic flow on specific routes and road structures (e.g. bridges). Also, most roadside ITS stations provide gateways to the Internet and are therefore considered access points for vehicular clouds. In this paper, regardless of the underlying technology, intelligent road infrastructure is mapped into the semantic model primarily in terms of the abovementioned categories with sensing, computing, communication, and power units.

2.4 Communication networks

Advances in wireless network technologies have enabled integrating on-board wireless communication capabilities into vehicles. Therefore, vehicles can cooperatively connect to network nodes via V2X communications, i.e. cooperative-ITS (C-ITS) communications (Gerla, 2012). Wireless and cellular networks are leveraged for C-ITS communications, due to easy deployment and scalability needed for intelligent transportation systems and the ability to fulfil networking requirements in vehicular environments. According to the ETSI EN 302 636-3 standard, ITS communication (ITSC) networks are composed of external networks between ITS stations and internal networks in each ITS station. The architectures of both ITS external and internal networks are depicted in Figure 2 and are briefly described in the following paragraphs with respect to the knowledge relevant to the semantic model.

ITS external network architecture

The external network architecture includes an ITS domain and a generic domain, as shown in Figure 2. In the ITS domain, the ITS ad-hoc network represents wireless C-ITS communications between vehicle, personal, and roadside ITS stations. The ITS access network interlinks roadside and central ITS stations and provides communication between vehicle ITS stations through roadside ITS stations. In the generic domain, public access networks grant general data services and applications to public users, whereas private access networks provide secure access only to authorized groups of users.

ITS internal network architecture

The internal network in an ITS station interlocks functional networking components of the ITS station. A reference architecture for ITS station internal networks based on layered communication protocols is shown in Figure 3 (ETSI EN 302 665, ETSI TR 101 607). The reference architecture comprises six layers, which characterize different functionalities within ITS stations, and interfaces between layers.

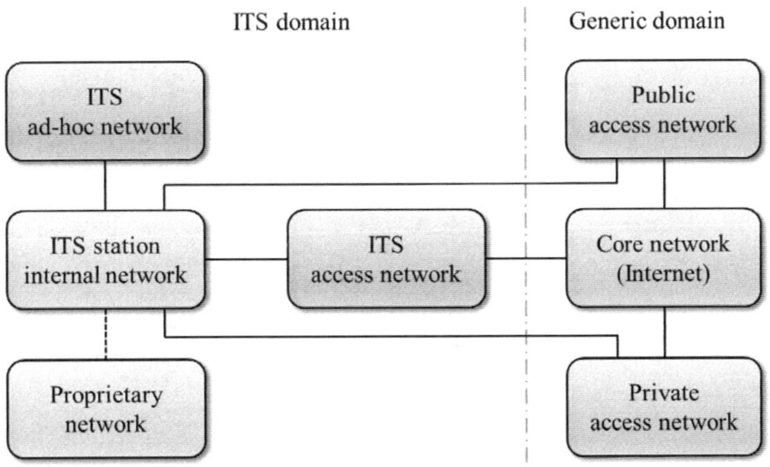

Figure 2: Road ITSC architecture – external (green and grey) and internal (orange) networks

The application layer contains standards for road safety, traffic efficiency, e.g. road hazard signaling and collision risk warning, and other applications. The facilities layer includes maintenance of applications, the decentralized environmental notification-based service, communication channels selection, and session supports. The networking and transport layer comprises one or more networking protocols (e.g. GeoNetworking), one or more transport protocols (i.e. dedicated ITSC transport protocols), and a layer management entity. The access layer contains station-internal and station-external interfaces, and specifications for V2X communications in 5.9 GHz frequency band (ITS-G5). Finally, having interfaces with all other layers, the management layer and the security layer contain functionalities that grant ITS station cross-layer and regulatory management as well as intrusion and authorization management, respectively.

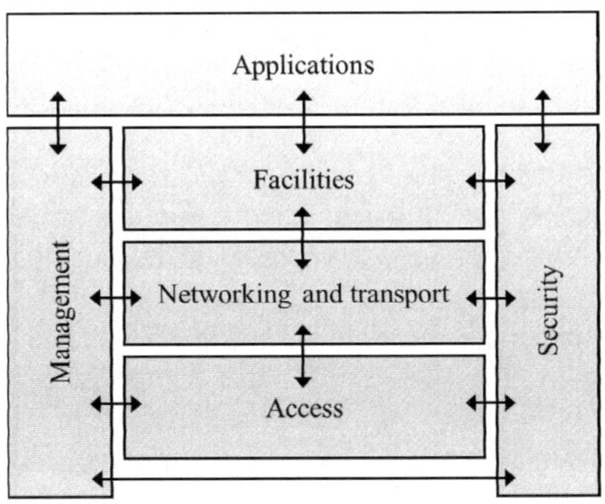

Figure 3: The layered reference architecture for ITS station internal networks

3. A semantic model of road intelligent transportation system

Upon analyzing the knowledge sources of road intelligent transportation systems elucidated in the previous section, Figure 4 presents an extract of the proposed semantic model developed from the aforementioned knowledge sources. The semantic model is shown in terms of a class diagram, in which, for the sake of clarity, attributes, methods, and multiplicities of associations are omitted. In the following paragraphs, main elements of the semantic model are described.

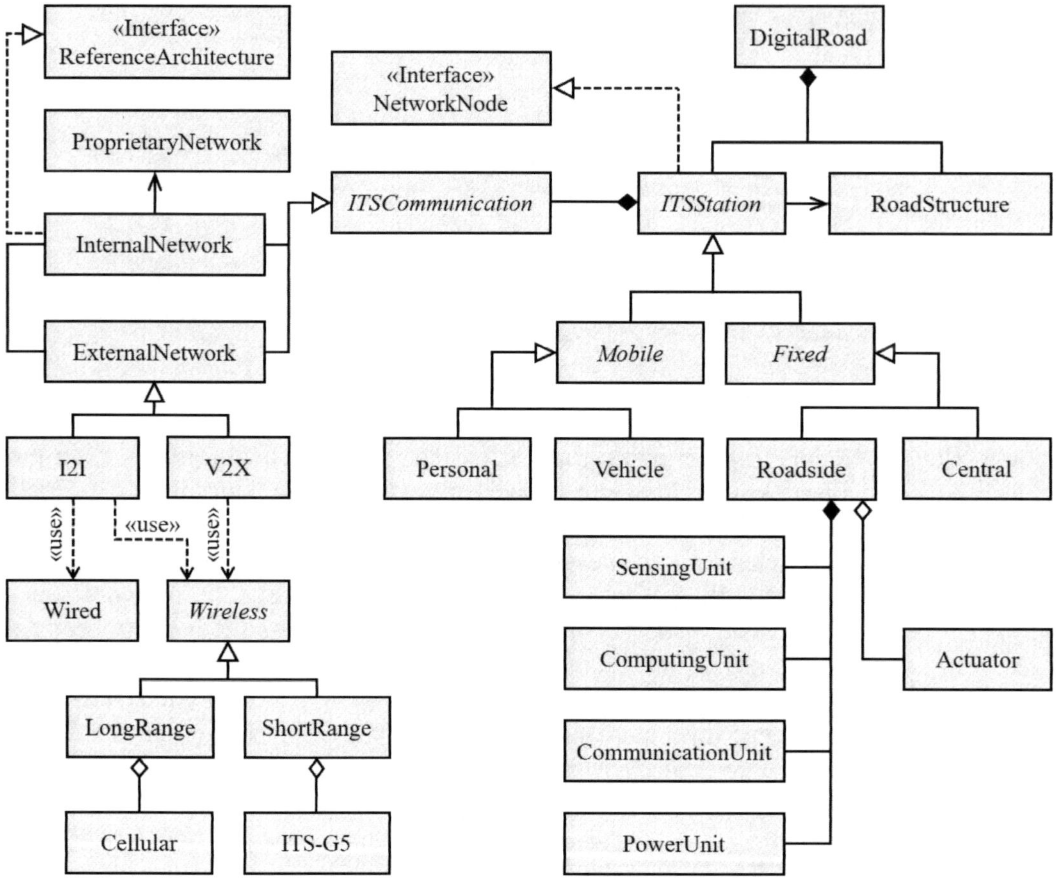

Figure 4: Semantic model of road intelligent transportation systems

The *DigitalRoad* class is composed of *RoadStructure* and *ITSStation* classes. The *RoadStructure* class represents the physical road structure including, e.g. pavement and resting areas. The abstract class *ITSStation* represents the core elements of intelligent road infrastructure. ITS stations, as mentioned previously, are categorized into two groups, depicted by the abstract subclasses *Fixed* and *Mobile*. Fixed ITS stations are of two types, *Central* and *Roadside*, and mobile ITS stations are categorized into *Vehicle* and *Personal* classes. The *SensingUnit*, *ComputingUnit*, *CommunicationUnit*, and *PowerUnit* depict ITS station on-board units and are shown in Figure 4 exemplarily for the *Roadside* class. ITS stations may have one or more control devices, such as *Actuator* devices.

The abstract class *ITSCommunication* represents communication networks in the ITS domain and is connected to the abstract class *ITSStation* with a composition relationship, since communication in the ITS domain is fully dependent on ITS stations. The abstract class *ITSCommunication* is a superclass of *InternalNetwork* and *ExternalNetwork*, which indicate communication within ITS stations and communication between ITS stations, respectively. The *InternalNetwork* class is defined based on the ITS station reference architecture introduced earlier. Therefore, the *InternalNetwork* class implements the *Reference Architecture* interface. Moreover, in internal networks of ITS stations, linked on-board units are recognized by the *ProprietaryNetwork* class. It is worth to note that proprietary networks comprise all on-board resources, e.g. sensors, beacons and transceivers, mechanical and/or electrical actuators, and several other devices, which are connected to the ITS station. The *ExternalNetwork* class comprises C-ITS and infrastructure-to-infrastructure (I2I) communications, shown by the *V2X* and *I2I* classes, respectively. I2I communication can be either wired or wireless, while V2X communication is solely wireless. The abstract class *Wireless* is a superclass of *LongRange* and *ShortRange* subclasses, which represent different wireless communication standards. An illustrative example of standards in each subclass is given by the *Cellular* and *ITS-G5* classes, respectively.

Case study

For validating the semantic model and, specifically, for better understanding the relationship between *ITSCommunication* and *ITSStation* classes, a scenario of vehicular cloud formation is considered as a case study. In the case study, communications in the ITS domain are employed for road safety and traffic management applications. As shown in Figure 5, it is assumed that an accident, rear-end collision, occurs in a section of a road, and ITS station external networks form a vehicular cloud to broadcast safety-related messages to other nodes.

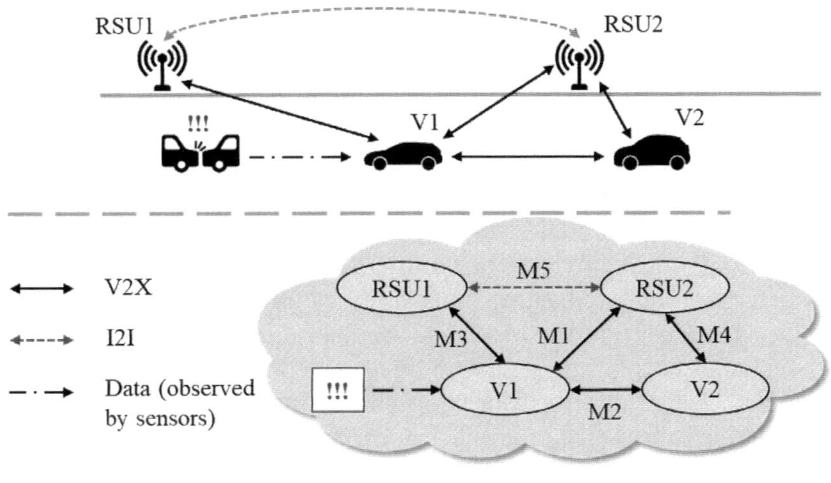

Figure 5: Vehicular cloud formation for road safety in the ITS domain

As can be seen from the scenario in Figure 5, vehicle ITS station *V1* broadcasts collision risk signals to ITS stations with potential interests, e.g. vehicles approaching and roadside units in the vicinity. *V1* sends a warning message (*M1*) to the roadside ITS station *RSU2* using ITS-G5 channels allocated for road safety messaging services. Meanwhile, *V1* utilizes Bluetooth wireless communication to inform vehicle ITS station *V2* with a collision risk message (*M2*). Using traffic management applications, *V1* sends a message (*M3*) to roadside ITS station *RSU1*, requesting the traffic status of an alternative route. *RSU2*, using 4G cellular communications, broadcasts congestion warnings to inform vehicles in farther distances. In response, *V2* asks for media footage of the accident via ITS-G5 (*M4*). In addition, the roadside ITS stations *RSU1* and *RSU2* communicate through 4G cellular communications to perform traffic safety-related actions, such as changing traffic lights (*M5*).

Figure 6 describes the semantic illustration of the scenario depicted in Figure 5 in terms of an object diagram as an instance of the proposed semantic model. The object diagram comprises four ITS station objects, messages shared among ITS stations (*M1*...*M5*), and the wireless communication standards employed for each communication.

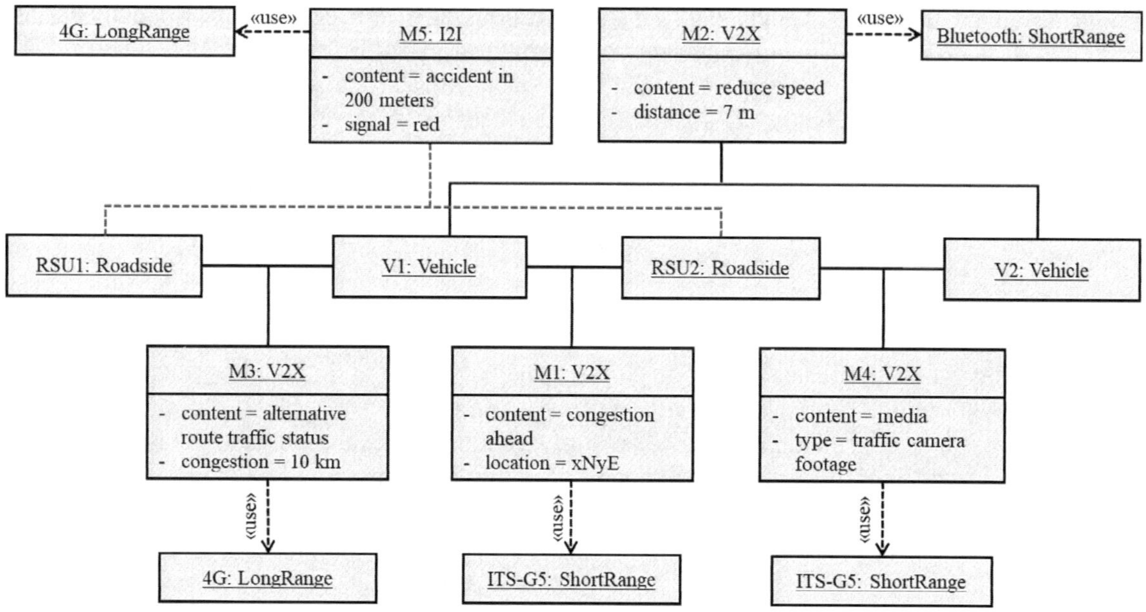

Figure 6: Object diagram of the scenario shown in Figure 5

Discussion of the results

As has been demonstrated in this section, the proposed semantic model is able to describe cloud formation scenarios with different numbers of ITS stations connected, various communication types involved, and different on-board units engaged. Moreover, data processing and computational models for various applications may be described using the semantic model, representing a means supporting formal descriptions of road intelligent transportation systems. In future work, the semantic model may be mapped into a standardized metamodel to describe road intelligent transportation systems on a standardized basis, preferably employing building information modeling as an increasingly used method in infrastructure modeling. When using the IFC standard as a formal basis, some entities defined in the IFC schema, such as *IfcCommunicationsApplicance*, may be used to describe road ITS components. However, due to a lack of entities to describe ITS-related infrastructure and components, the current IFC schema cannot be employed for fully mapping the proposed semantic model. Instead, an IFC extension is to be developed to consider all aspects covered by the semantic model of road intelligent transportation systems.

4. Summary and conclusions

To achieve a formal description of road intelligent transportation systems, a semantic model of road intelligent transportation systems has been developed. Knowledge sources for semantic modeling of road intelligent transportation systems have been analyzed. Associations and relationships between elements of intelligent road infrastructure and vehicular cloud infrastructure have been defined on a meta level using object-oriented modeling, and a scenario of vehicular cloud formation and data-sharing processes has been depicted for validating the proposed semantic model. The model is applicable for various road ITS use cases, and it can be used as a basis for designing ITS simulation platforms. In future work, extending the IFC schema is envisaged to facilitate standardized description of road intelligent transportation systems in terms of building information models.

Acknowledgements

This research is partially supported by the European Union through the European Social Funds (ESF) and by the Thuringian Ministry for Economic Affairs, Science and Digital Society (TMWWDG) under grant 2017 FGR 0068. The financial support is gratefully appreciated. Any opinions, findings, conclusions, or recommendations expressed in this paper are those of the authors and do not necessarily reflect the views of the aforementioned institutions.

References

Ahlgren, B., Dannewitz, C., Imbrenda, C., Kutscher, D. and Ohlman, B. (2012). A survey of information-centric networking. *IEEE Communications Magazine*, 50(7), pp. 26-36.

Atchison, L. (2018). *Edge Computing vs. Cloud Computing: Which One Is Right for Your Application?*. [online] New Relic Blog. Available at: https://blog.newrelic.com/technology/edge-computing-vs-cloud-computing-comparison/ [Accessed: February 2, 2019].

Boschian, V., Dotoli, M., Fanti, M. P., Iacobellis, G. and Ukovich, W. (2011). A Metamodeling Approach to the Management of Intermodal Transportation Networks. *IEEE Transactions on Automation Science and Engineering*, 8(3), pp. 457-469.

Datta, S.K., Costa, R.P., Haerri, J. and Bonnet, C. (2016). Integrating connected vehicles in Internet of Things ecosystems: Challenges and solutions. In: *Proc. of the 2016 IEEE 17th International Symposium on A World of Wireless, Mobile and Multimedia Networks*, Coimbra, Portugal, June 21, 2016.

Dixit, M., Kumar, R. and Sagar, A. K. (2016). VANET: Architectures, research issues, routing protocols, and its applications. In: *Proc. of the 2016 International Conference on Computing, Communication and Automation*. Noida, India, April 29, 2016.

Eltoweissy, M., Olariu, S. and Younis, M.F. (2010). Towards Autonomous Vehicular Clouds - A Position Paper (Invited Paper). In: *Proc. of the Second International Conference on Ad Hoc Networks*. Victoria, BC, Canada, August 18, 2010.

European Telecommunications Standards Institute (2010). Intelligent Transport Systems (ITS); Communications Architecture. ETSI EN 302 665 Standard (V1.1.1). ETSI, Sophia Antipolis, France.

European Telecommunications Standards Institute (2013). Intelligent Transport Systems (ITS); Cooperative ITS (C-ITS); Release 1. ETSI TR 101 607 Standard (V1.1.1). ETSI, Sophia Antipolis, France.

European Telecommunications Standards Institute (2014). Intelligent Transport Systems (ITS); Vehicular Communications; GeoNetworking; Part 3: Network Architecture. ETSI EN 302 636-3 Standard. ETSI, Sophia Antipolis, France.

Fernández-Isabel, A. and Fuentes-Fernández, R. (2015). Analysis of Intelligent Transportation Systems Using Model-Driven Simulations. *Sensors*, 15(6), pp.14116-14141.

Gerla, M. (2012). Vehicular Cloud Computing. In: *Proc. of the 11th Annual Mediterranean Ad Hoc Networking Workshop (Med-Hoc-Net)*, Ayia Napa, Cyprus, June 19, 2012.

Gerla, M., Lee, E., Pau, G. and Lee, U. (2014). Internet of vehicles: From intelligent grid to autonomous cars and vehicular clouds. In: *Proc. of the 2014 IEEE World Forum on Internet of Things (WF-IoT)*, Seoul, South Korea, March 6, 2014.

Ghariani, N., Elkosantini, S., Darmoul, S. and Ben Said, L. (2014). A survey of simulation platforms for the assessment of public transport control systems. In: *Proc. of the 2014 International Conference on Advanced Logistics and Transport (ICALT)*, Hammamet, Tunisia, May 1, 2014.

Legatiuk, D., Theiler, M., Dragos, K. and Smarsly, K. (2017). A categorical approach towards metamodeling cyber-physical systems. In: *Proc. of the 11th International Workshop on Structural Health Monitoring*. Stanford, CA, USA, September 12, 2017.

Mirboland, M. and Smarsly, K. (2018). Semantic modeling of road intelligent transportation systems. In: *Proc. of the Positioning and Navigation for intelligent transportation systems*, Berlin, Germany, November 15, 2018.

Wan, J., Zhang, D., Zhao. S., Yang, L.T. and Lloret, J. (2014). Context-aware vehicular cyber-physical systems with cloud support: architecture, challenges, and solutions. *IEEE Communications Magazine*, 52(8), pp. 106-113.

Whaiduzzaman, M., Sookhak, M., Gani, A. and Buyya, R. (2014). A survey on vehicular cloud computing. *Journal of Network and Computer Applications*, 40(2014), pp. 325-344.

State of the Art in Damage Information Modeling for Bridges

Mathias Artus, Christian Koch
Bauhaus-Universität Weimar, Germany
mathias.artus@uni-weimar.de

Abstract. The Bridge collapse in Genoa let us take a closer look at the health state of bridges. Inspection and maintenance is essential to ensure the serviceability and safety of bridges. Current inspection on site is often done manually on paper, and paper is the medium to exchange condition information between involved stakeholders. After damage registration or information exchange, the data is processed digitally. The repeated digitalization is an error prone process and leads to redundant work. A dedicated information model, called damage information model, could provide a solution to improve the information exchange. This present paper investigates the state of practice and research in damage information modeling for bridges. After analyzing bridge damage data, it reviews different norms, guidelines, and existing research papers. Analyzing different national practices and synthesizing available research results form the basis for the presented achievements and challenges in the field of damage information modelling.

1. Introduction

On 14th August 2018 43 people were killed by the collapse of the Ponte Morandi Bridge in Genoa. Carmelo Gentile, a structural engineering professor, had suggested to '[…] perform a […] computer study […]' before the collapse happened (Glanz et al., 2018). With a detailed damage information model, a computer simulation like that, could have been done easily. However, the current state of practice for inspection is paper based or relies on bridge management systems (BMS) (Caltrans, 2017; Bundesministerium für Verkehr, Bau und Stadtentwicklung, 2013). That means inspectors register defects and damages on site using paper and transfer the damage information to the BMS later in the office, which is an error prone practice. Furthermore, BMS store abstract data only, not considering any 3D models of the structure or damages. Instead, hand-made sketches, photos and textual descriptions are stored. This abstract data is difficult to understand without having a proper visualization. A damage information model (DIM) can support the inspection process and the later maintenance, to save money, to avoid errors and to help plan inspections and maintenance. This paper aims to identify significant damage types for bridges and to analyze the research that has addressed the information modeling of these types of damages.

Building Information Modeling (BIM) is the most common method to model buildings with a 3D-CAD model and additional information like material, processes and so on (Borrmann et al., 2018). The Industry Foundation Classes (IFC) represent a standard for implementing Open BIM providing a data format to share building information among several actors (ISO, 2013). Currently, BIM is being extended to the sector of civil engineering, e.g. Bridge Information Modeling (BrIM) (Costin et al., 2018). IFC-bridge, an implementation of BrIM, offers the possibility to model bridges with all their components (Lebegue, 2013). The current state of BIM and IFC allow to model damages on buildings with proxy elements and property sets, which might not be sufficient, as this approach lacks additional semantics, for example, damage types and taxonomies. Integrating and exchanging damage information in the context of BIM would support the operation and maintenance phase within the life-cycle of bridges.

2. State of practice

2.1 Bridge condition assessment

In Germany, the standard DIN 1076 regulates the inspection of all kinds of civil infrastructure (Deutsches Institut für Normung, 1999). Structures like bridges, tunnels, and similar, have to be inspected every 3 years. Within this interval the rough or plain inspection and the main in-depth inspection alternate. Inspectors have to inspect bridges within the range of the hands, to tap, to finger, and to take a close look. It is similar in California (USA) and Queensland (Australia). Both perform multiple types of inspection. The Unite States have a flexible period for inspection between 2 and 4 years (FHWA, 1988). Queensland defines an assessment score dependent inspection period between one and five years, e.g. intact bridges have a longer period than bridges with major deterioration (Department of Transport and Main Roads, 2016). For further information about guidelines of other countries, consider the paper of Hüthwohl et al. (Hüthwohl et al., 2018).

Independent from the country, it is necessary to register defects and damages for later assessment and maintenance planning. Modeling damages within a BIM context is a prerequisite to support the full life-cycle of built infrastructure. Aiming at modeling damage information it is important to know existing damage types and related parameters. To get an overview about damage types, an analysis of the German catalog of damages for civil engineering structures follows. The catalog of damages for civil engineering structures (Bundesanstalt für Straßenwesen, 2017) lists more than 500 types of damages. While grouping the damages related to components, the catalog lists damages of the same types several times, e.g. the superstructure and the substructure could have chloride penetration. This grouping is insufficient for later damage modeling, because a chloride penetration has the same parameters, independent from the component at which it occurs. Hence, all damages are grouped in categories, which are separated by semantics, for example material change, cracks, spalling, and divergences from specification/design and so on.

D = 3

S \ V	0	1	2	3	4
4	4.0	4.0	4.0	4.0	4.0
3	3.3	3.5	3.7	3.9	4.0
2	2.8	3.0	3.1	3.2	4.0
1	2.7	2.8	2.9	3.0	4.0
0	2.5	2.6	2.7	2.8	4.0

Figure 1: Matrix to calculate Z for D equal to 3 (see Haardt, 1999)

The condition assessment of bridges in Germany follows the algorithm developed by Haardt in 1999 (Haardt, 1999). Figure 2 shows an example for a bridge with 3 damages. Each single damage has its own assessment score within three categories: structural safety (S), road safety (V) and durability (D), like shown in step 1 of figure 2. The assessment scores within these categories range from zero to four. Using five matrices, a final assessment score (Z) is calculated. The Z-scores range from zero to four, too. Figure 1 shows an example of a matrix to calculate the Z-score of a damage. Assuming a damage has a D-score of three, S is equal to one and V equal to two, hence the final Z-score is 2.9. The inspector can decide to add a value of 0.1 to the calculated Z-value, due to a higher significance of the damage, or to subtract a value 0.1, due to a lower significance (Haardt, 1999).

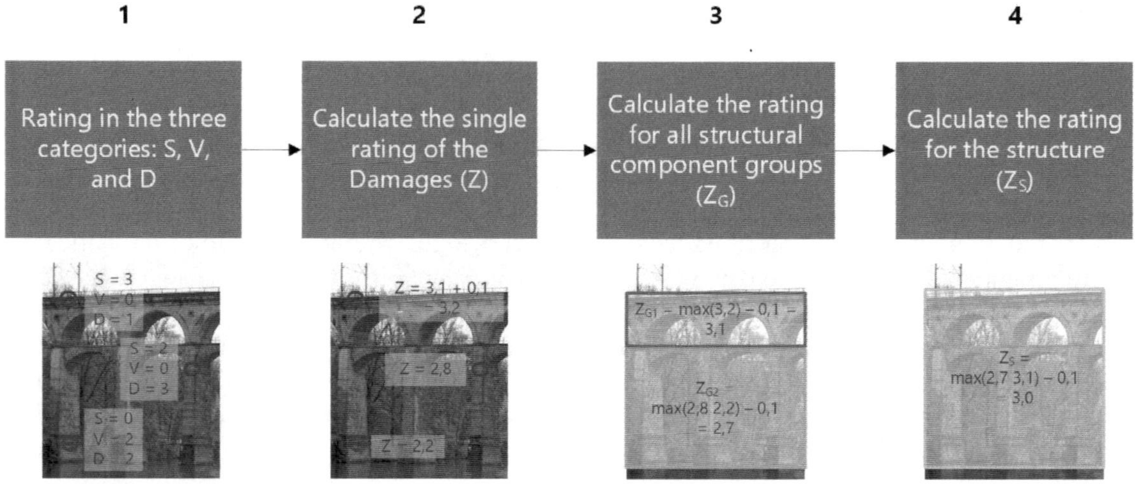

https://commons.wikimedia.org/wiki/Bridge#/media/File:Bietigheim-Bissingen_Viadukt_02.jpg

Figure 2: Bridge assessment process in Germany

The highest damage score Z from all damages within a component group, defines the score of the whole component group. In Germany, 14 component groups are defined, e.g. superstructure, substructure, prestressing, foundation, etc. Figure 2 shows only 2 component groups for simplicity. Depending on the amount of damages within the component group, the Z-score of the group can be increased or decreased by 0.1. Both condition ratings have a decrease of 0.1, because they have less than 5 or 3 damages, respectively. Finally, the score of the whole structure is the highest score of all component groups. The decrease in figure 1 emerges from the fact that less than 3 component groups are affected by damages. In conclusion, the damage with the highest Z-score leads to the assessment score of the entire bridge (Haardt, 1999).

2.2 Analysis of frequency and significance of damage types

To analyze data from practice, we defined 23 damage categories based on the German damage catalog (Bundesanstalt für Straßenwesen, 2017). The data used for the statistical analysis has been provided by the Thuringian Department of Building and Transportation (Thüringer Landesamt für Bau und Verkehr). The data covers 25 610 damages at 2 953 bridges. Figure 3 depicts the ten most often occurring damages. The x-axis displays the different categories, whereas the y-axis shows the amount of damages. The number above the bars show the amount of the damage occurrences. *Cracks* occur most often at bridges. Right after that follow *divergences from specification and design,* which summarize defects, for example, regarding the thickness of layers, dimensions of components or wrong component types. The third place are *joint damages*. This category includes expansion gaps, as well as mortar gaps. Next are *waste, pollution and other foreign bodies* e.g. garbage, vegetation or formwork residuals. Corrosion, chloride intrusion and carbonation are examples for *material changes*. That group has two sub groups: with and without loss of substance, e.g. corrosion can lead to a loss of substance. The subgroup *without loss of substance* takes place 6. Changes, which are visible at the surface of concrete, e.g. efflorescence, take place 7. Similar, however a bit different, are *enclosures of foreign bodies, coarse grain or voids* within concrete. The last two places cover the lack of components or parts and their state and functionality, e.g. fixed or loose. To define a damage model, it would be sufficient to start from the most frequent occurrences, namely cracks, divergences and joint damage.

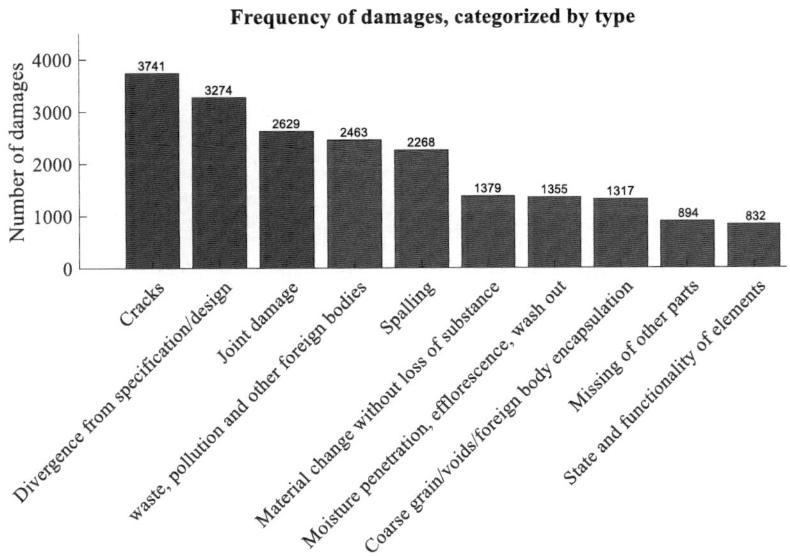

Figure 3: The ten most frequently occurring damage types (top three are red)

Beside the information about how often a damage occurs, it is interesting to know which influence has a damage on the overall assessment score of a bridge, e.g. cracks smaller as 0.2 mm in concrete are negligible for the structural integrity, and thereby for the assessment score, too. To answer which damage types are significant for the assessment score, it is necessary to consider the assessment algorithm, which is described above. Hence, to define the most significant damage types, the analysis only takes into account the damages with the highest Z-scores per bridge.

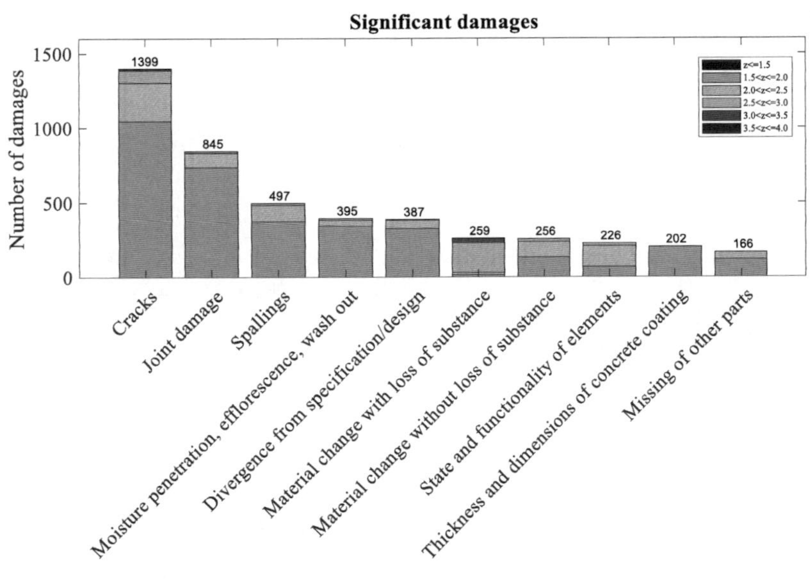

Figure 4: Significant damages with grouped Z-score

Figure 4 shows the result of the analysis on the significance of damage types. The x-axis lists the categories or types, whereas the y-axis shows the amount of damages within the category. The numbers on top of the bars show the amount of damages of the category. To give an overview about the Z-rating of the significant damages, the colors show six groups of damage Z-scores: lower than 1.5, between 1.5 and 2, between 2 and 2.5, between 2.5 and 3, between 3 and 3.5, as well as between 3.5 and 4. Some colors are not visible at the bars, e.g. blue. Two new categories are inserted into that graph: *Material change with loss of substance*, as well as the *thickness and dimensions of concrete coating*. As already described, the material change with loss of substance is mainly corrosion. Concrete coatings can be too thin or in a bad quality Material changes with loss of substance are interesting, because of the high ratio of Z-scores about 2.5 and above.

In conclusion, there are multiple damage categories, which are interesting to model, e.g. cracks, divergences from specification and design, spalling or joint damages. Future investigation on damage information modelling should care about multiple damage categories and focus on the most frequent and significant damage types.

3. State of research

The existing literature is systematically structured using two dimensions in order to form a two-dimensional matrix. Firstly, it is categorized according to eight damage types. Beside the six damage types with the most frequent occurrences, as discussed in section 2, two groups are added: *Other* and *Damages in general*. The category *Other* covers damage types aside from the top six, whereas *Damages in general* deals with literature that is concerned with a general approach to model damage information.

Secondly, the literature is structured according to the complexity of the modelled damage information. In this context, complexity refers to how much information is modelled at what detail, e.g. the concept only links raw data, it suggests an as-built model with damage parameters or it presents a comprehensive geometric and semantic information model for damages. Figure 5 illustrates these 3 complexity levels. Linked raw data are, for example, drawings, spread sheets, point clouds, textures, pictures, text or audio recordings, which are interlinked. The next category refers to a 3D as-built model of the bridge with damage parameters, e.g. crack width, spalling radius, corrosion depth etc. The highest complexity would be a geometric-semantic information model, which takes e.g. 3D damage model that includes relations to the bridge (component), influences on material data by this damage, repair recommendation, type of material for repair and so forth.

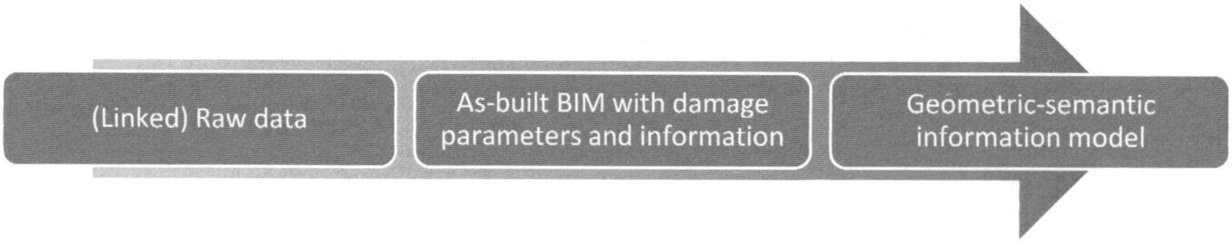

Figure 5: Complexity levels for DIM

3.1 Linked raw data

This section covers existing research approaches, which interlink raw data, e.g. point clouds, documents, pictures or others. In 2012, Adhikari et al. (2012) published a paper on automatic condition state prediction. The paper describes a method to automatically rate inspection results. An artificial neural network processes pictures of damages and predicts the rating for them. Even if the research does not show a data model, it deduces a first link between information: a damage has one or more pictures and a rating (Adhikari et al., 2012).

Matthew Torok (2014) worked on crack detection for post-disaster assessment. Besides photos, they use 3D-meshes for damage registration. Finally, the work stores the location of a damage. Even if there is no 3D as-built model, the position of a damage is the first parameter, which is important for further work. To evaluate the results, crack widths and depths are used. These parameters, damage position and dimension, are necessary for a comprehensive damage information model.

Every bridge is part of a particular environment. Thus, changes in the environment can affect the bridge condition, e.g. changes to the embankment can lead to impacts on the road safety. Due to this, Miyamoto et al. (2016) worked on the integration of environmental changes to a BIM database. After generating a 3D damage model of the embankment, the data is linked to a civil infrastructure information model.

Inspecting a bridge is time consuming and cumbersome. To address this issue, Omer et al. (2018) presented an approach that suggests inspecting bridges virtually via virtual reality (VR). Central for this is the acquisition of point clouds of the building. They use MATLAB (MathWorks, 1994) to process additional pictures that were taken on sight in order to highlight damages in the mesh. Finally, a head mounted display visualizes the point cloud with the highlighted damages. Again, this work shows some parameters of damages, like location and dimensions (Omer et al., 2018).

All of the work presented above lack 3D building models. They mainly collect independent data for visualization, simulation or planning.

3.2 As-built BIM with damage parameters

This section covers achievements that work with 3D models of the bridge and attach damage parameters and data. Sacks et al. (2016) describe an information delivery manual for bridge inspection. Central in the manual are parameters and semantics for bridges. After localizing damages, an algorithm groups them all by types, e.g. crack, spallings, scaling, efflorescence, corrosion or other. For that purpose, additional parameters are take, for example, the position. Upon this, a boundary shape representation is used to help visualizing damages (Sacks et al., 2016). However, further information, e.g. how to model the damage information, is not refined.

Sacks et al. (2018) extended their work on bridge inspection in 2018. Additionally to their information delivery manual, they published a model view definition. Every bridge element can have several element defects, whereas several element defects are part of a defect. Furthermore, every defect can be structural or not. Multiple damage types are specializations (child classes) of element defects and contain several parameters (Sacks et al., 2018). Even if the paper covers multiple damage types, there are still damage types, which are not covered, for example joint damages. Moreover, an inclusion of 3D damage models is missing.

During the construction process, defects, such as wrong dimensions of components or wrong placements, can lead to additional costs. Due to this, Hamledari et al. (2018) published a method on updating object data in IFC for as-built modeling. The idea is that every entity has a related type and a change in the parameters of an entity is done by changing the type with its parameters (Hamledari et al., 2018). This approach is comprehensible to some defects during constructions, e.g. installation of a wrong door. However, it is lacking links between defects.

In 2016, McGuire et al. (2016) developed a system to use damage information within structural analysis and for repair quantity estimation. Damage information from cracks, spallings and delamination have connections to bridge components. The paper also considers information about damage volumes. Last but not least, dimension parameters for the damages are defined

(McGuire et al., 2016). The next step would be a geometric model for the damages and links between damages.

Tanaka et al. (2018) started a work on damage information modeling in 2016. Based upon the IFC, they modeled degradations at bridges. Beside geometric information, images and measurements are part of the model. Additionally, Tanaka et al. integrated a time line to show the propagation of a damage. For this purpose, an extension of the IFC was necessary (Tanaka et al., 2016). However, the work lacks some data for a 3D model of a damage and relations between different damages. In 2018 Tanaka et al. extended their work with an automated data extraction from inspection reports (Tanaka et al., 2018).

3.3 Geometric-semantic information model

The section presents literature, which describes a damage model with geometric and semantic damage information, e.g. damage geometry, interlinking of damages, and effects of damages. Hamdan and Scherer (2018) published an information model for damages in 2018 that considers parameters and the geometry of damages. The information model contains some properties and documentation, too. Also, the decomposition of a damage into individual damages is suggested. What is missing is the relation between damages and influences on material parameters of the affected component. Furthermore, a definition of levels of detail or development is missing.

Hüthwohl et al. (2018) propose a second idea on modeling damages. Every damages is related to an inspection. Similar to (Sacks et al., 2018), Hüthwohl et al. disassemble a defect into several element defects and added several parameters. Additionally, the work contains data for inspection, e.g. time, type, inspector and weather. However, their approach lacks detailed 3D damage geometry and further semantic links and relations to represent damage histories.

3.4 Overview of the examined literature

Table 1 shows the summary of the literature examined. As clearly visible, several efforts have been made in the area of as-built BIM with damage parameters and information. However, so far only one research focuses on a more detailed model. None of the studies examined deals with links between damages, a level of detail or repair recommendations.

4. Already published achievements and remaining challenges

Damage information modeling is a growing branch in the entire architecture, engineering and construction society, mainly empowered by the research on automated bridge inspection. Bridge management systems (BMS) cover the first level of damage information modeling. These management systems link raw data about bridges (or other civil engineering structures) to the related bridge or other components. 3D models are currently not part of these systems. Scientists are on their way to overcome this issue. First attempts show damage information models that include relations between damages and the bridge or their components. Another achievement are the first ideas to visualize damages, e.g. by overlaying a texture upon a component. Data, which is related to damages, for example the inspection parameters and information, is part of publications as well. Finally, one publication enhances the information model with a 3D model of the damage and properties (Hamdan and Scherer, 2018).

Table 1: State of research overview

Damage type	(Linked) Raw data	As-Built BIM with damage parameters and information	Geometric-semantic information model
Cracks	Adhikari et al. (2012) Torok et al. (2014)	Sacks et al. (2018)	Hüthwohl et al. (2018)
Divergences from specification/ design		Hamledari et al. (2018)	
Joint damages			
Waste, pollution and other foreign bodies			
Spallings	Adhikari et al. (2012)	McGuire et al. (2016) Sacks et al. (2018)	Hüthwohl et al. (2018)
Moisture penetration, efflorescence, washout		Sacks et al. (2018)	Hüthwohl et al. (2018)
Other	Miyamoto (2016)	Sacks et al. (2018)	
Damages in general	Omer et al. (2018)	Sacks et al. (2016) Tanaka et al. (2016) Tanaka et al. (2018)	Hamdan and Scherer (2018)

Taking a close look at the current state of the art reveals the lack of investigation in damage types. Different damage types need different parameters, e.g. a crack might have a 3D geometric model whereas corrosion is maybe only a material defect on the surface. Future investigation should focus on necessary parameters depending on the damage type. Another area may deal with the relations for damages, e.g. some damages relate to a component of a bridge and other maybe relate to the whole bridge. Moreover, more often than not, damages relate to other damages. Normally, this is written in an inspection report, whereas a comprehensive damage model should be able to represent this via data relations within the information model. The current work mainly focuses on inspection. However, inspections are usually followed maintenance, construction monitoring or destruction. Damage information has at least relations to maintenance, for example the damage geometry helps calculate the amount of material for repair, structural damages or defects can deliver necessary information for destruction. Finally, a definition for levels of details for the damages is currently not being considerd. Think about a maintenance manager, he or she does not need all the information about every crack in detail, but may need the overall amount and location of cracks and the type of the related material. Hence, a definition of different levels of detail are important to make BIM applicable for the whole life cycle of bridges.

5. Conclusion

For safety and operations, it is important to keep bridges in secure conditions. Inspections are a key process to identify problems and weaknesses at bridges, as well as for repair and maintenance. Besides, BIM is a well-known and applicable concept to manage civil infrastructure and related processes. Using BIM over the whole bridge life cycle leads to the necessity of a damage information model. To define the needs of a damage model, this paper analyzed the state of practice and deduced damage categories from the German damage catalog.

Statistical data from Thuringia helped identify the most significant damage types, which delivered categories for the reviewed literature. Most of the existing research work deals with damage modeling in the way of linking different data together and take a 3D bridge model as the basis for all damages. Less effort exists in advancing damage models to geometric-semantic models with relations between single damages, level of detail or repair recommendations. If BIM shall be applicable within the field of inspection and maintenance, a geometric-semantic damage model is necessary. Future work should focus on this area allowing the usage of BIM data all over the life cycle.

With digital information about damages, e.g. crack geometry and position, an automated assessment calculation can be done maybe via an artificial neural network. Hence, a big part of assessment can be automated: take photos of the bridge, extract damage types and parameters with the usage of image processing, calculate the assessment of the damages, components, component groups and the whole bridge by using artificial neural networks or defined algorithms. If an assessment reveals critical structural issues, the content of the DIM can be used by engineers for calculations, simulations and helps to identify possible damage reasons or effects. Hence, it becomes cheaper and easier to analyse the bridge state and prevent collapses.

Last but not least, register as much information about damages as possible, offers possibilities for data analysis to improve design, inspection practices, assessment and maintenance concepts, by using technologies from the fields of data mining, machine and deep learning.

6. Acknowledgement

We thank the “Thüringer Landesamt für Bau und Verkehr” for their support with knowledge from practice in bridge inspection and statistical data about bridges in federal state of Thuringia in Germany.

References

Adhikari, R.S., Moselhi, O. and Bagchi, A. (2012), Automated Prediction of Condition State Rating in Bridge Inspection, in van Bronswijk, J.E.M.H., Maas, G.J. and van Gassel, F.J.M. (Eds.), International Symposium on Automation and Robotics in Construction, Eindhoven, The Netherlands, 26.06.2012 - 29.06.2012, International Association for Automation and Robotics in Construction (IAARC).

Borrmann, A., König, M., Koch, C. and Beetz, J. (Eds.) (2018), Building Information Modeling: Technology Foundations and Industry Practice, Springer International Publishing, Cham.

Bundesanstalt für Straßenwesen (2017), RI-EBW-Prüf Schadensbeispiele.

Bundesministerium für Verkehr, Bau und Stadtentwicklung (2013), Bauwerksprüfung nach DIN 1076 Bedeutung, Organisation und Kosten, available at: https://www.bmvi.de/SharedDocs/DE/Anlage/VerkehrUndMobilitaet/Strasse/dokumentation-bauwerkspruefung-nach-din-1076.pdf?__blob=publicationFile (accessed 8 August 2018).

Caltrans (2017), Caltrans Bridge Element Inspection Manual.

Costin, A., Adibfar, A., Hu, H. and Chen, S.S. (2018), Building Information Modeling (BIM) for transportation infrastructure – Literature review, applications, challenges, and recommendations, Automation in Construction, Vol. 94, pp. 257–281.

Department of Transport and Main Roads (2016), Structures Inspection Manual Part 3 - Structures Inspection Procedures.

Deutsches Institut für Normung (1999), DIN 1076: Ingenieurbauwerke im Zuge von Straßen und Wegen Überwachung und Prüfung No. 1076.

FHWA (1988), Revisions to the National Bridge Inspection Standards (NBIS), available at: https://www.fhwa.dot.gov/bridge/nbis/t514021.cfm (accessed 8 November 2018).

Glanz, J., Pianigiani, G., White, J. and Patanjali, K. (2018), Genoa Bridge Collapse: The Road to Tragedy, available at: https://www.nytimes.com/interactive/2018/09/06/world/europe/genoa-italy-bridge.html (accessed 27 September 2018).

Haardt, P. (1999), Algorithmen der Zustandsbewertung von Ingenieurbauwerken.

Hamdan, A.-H. and Scherer, J.R. (2018), A Generic Model for the Digitalization of Structural Damage, in Caspeele, R., Taerwe, L. and Frangopol, D.M. (Eds.), Life Cycle Analysis and Assessment in Civil Engineering: Proceedings of the Sixth International Symposium on Life-Cycle Civil Engineering (IALCCE 2018), 28-31 October 2018, Ghent, Belgium, Chapman and Hall/CRC, Milton.

Hamledari, H., Rezazadeh Azar, E. and McCabe, B. (2018), IFC-Based Development of As-Built and As-Is BIMs Using Construction and Facility Inspection Data. Site-to-BIM Data Transfer Automation, Journal of Computing in Civil Engineering, Vol. 32 No. 2.

Hüthwohl, P., Brilakis, I., Borrmann, A. and Sacks, R. (2018), Integrating RC Bridge Defect Information into BIM Models, Journal of Computing in Civil Engineering, No. 32, pp. 1–14.

ISO (2013), Industry Foundation Classes (IFC) for data sharing in the construction and facility management industries No. 16739:2013, available at: https://www.iso.org/standard/51622.html.

Lebegue, E. (2013), IFC-BRIDGE V2 Data Model, BuildingSmart Infrastructure Room, München.

MathWorks (1994), MATLAB, available at: https://www.mathworks.com/products/matlab.html (accessed 26 March 2019).

McGuire, B., Atadero, R., Clevenger, C. and Ozbek, M. (2016), Bridge Information Modeling for Inspection and Evaluation, Journal of Bridge Engineering, Vol. 21 No. 4, p. 4015076.

Miyamoto, K. (2016), A Framework for Data Coordination Method of Maintenance Data and 3D Conceptual Model on CIM Based Database.

Omer, M., Hewitt, S., Mosleh, M.H., Margetts, L. and Parwaiz, M. (2018), Performance evaluation of bridges using virtual reality, paper presented at European Conference on Computational Mechanics, 11. - 15.06.2018, Glasgow, available at: http://congress.cimne.com/eccm_ecfd2018/admin/files/filePaper/p1846.pdf (accessed 13 August 2018).

Sacks, R., Kedar, A., Borrmann, A., Ma, L., Brilakis, I., Hüthwohl, P., Daum, S., Kattel, U., Yosef, R., Liebich, T., Barutcu, B.E. and Muhic, S. (2018), SeeBridge as next generation bridge inspection. Overview, Information Delivery Manual and Model View Definition, Automation in Construction, Vol. 90, pp. 134–145.

Sacks, R., Kedar, A., Borrmann, A., Ma, L., Singer, D. and Kattel, U. (2016), SeeBridge Information Delivery Manual (IDM) for Next Generation Bridge Inspection, in University of Huddersfield (Ed.), International Symposium on Automation and Robotics in Construction, Vol. 33.

Tanaka, F., Hori, M., Onosato, M., Date, H. and Kanai, S. (2016), Bridge Information Model Based on IFC Standards and Web Content Providing System for Supporting an Inspection Process.

Tanaka, F., Tsuchida, M., Onosato, M., Date, H., Kanai, S., Hada, Y., Nakao, M., Kobayashi, H., Hasegawa, E., Sugawara, T. and Oyama, T. (2018), Bridge Information Modeling based on IFC for supporting maintenance management of existing bridges, 5-7.7.2018.

Torok, M.M., Golparvar-Fard, M. and Kochersberger, K.B. (2014), Image-Based Automated 3D Crack Detection for Post-disaster Building Assessment, Journal of Computing in Civil Engineering, Vol. 28 No. 5, A4014004.

Parametric Design and Isogeometric Analysis of Tunnel Linings within the Building Information Modelling Framework

Jelena Ninic[1*], Hoang Giang Bui[2], and Günther Meschke[2]
[1]Center for Structural Engineering and Informatics, University of Nottingham, United Kingdom
[2] Institute for Structural Mechanics, Ruhr University Bochum, Germany
*Jelena.Ninic@nottingham.ac.uk (Lead author email address)

Abstract. Both planning and design phase of large infrastructural project require analysis, modelling, visualization, and numerical analysis. To perform these tasks, different tools such as Building Information Modelling (BIM) and numerical analysis software are commonly employed. However, in current engineering practice, there are no systematic solutions for the exchange between design and analysis models, and these tasks usually involve manual and error-prone model generation, setup and update. In this paper, focussing on tunnelling engineering, we demonstrate a systematic and versatile approach to efficiently generate a tunnel design and analyse the lining in different practical scenarios. To this end, a BIM-based approach is developed, which connects a user-friendly industry-standard BIM software with effective simulation tools for high-performance computing. A fully automatized design-through-analysis workflow solution for segmented tunnel lining is developed based on a fully parametric design model and an isogeometric analysis software, connected through an interface implemented with a Revit plugin.

1. Introduction

The population explosion in developing countries connected with over-populated congested 'mega-cities' poses major challenges for urban mobility and air pollution. The use of underground transportation is an effective way to address these issues of mega-cities by effectively using underground space in highly congested urban areas while at the same time providing one of the most sustainable transport solutions in terms of CO2 emissions, energy consumption, and noise levels. Therefore, underground infrastructure is a key enabler for resource-efficient, low-carbon transportation for both people and goods in highly urbanised area. Mechanized tunnel construction, with the permanent support provided by precast segmental tunnel lining structures, has been proven as one of safest and most efficient construction technologies in terms of both costs and construction times, with minimal impact on the existing environment (Maidl, et al., 2012). In the last decades, the design and assessment of stability and robustness of the lining structure has been one of the key tasks to ensure a safe and durable tunnel structure design to withstand demanding use for 100 years and more.

Building Information Modelling (BIM) is a widely adopted concept for the design, construction and the management of buildings or industrial facilities over their entire lifecycle. However, in recent years, BIM is increasingly gaining attention also in large infrastructural projects, including urban mechanized tunnelling, where it has been used for tunnel design and construction management (Smith, 2014; Daller, et al., 2016). Some of the relevant, tunnelling-related BIM aspects recently addressed are interoperability using Industry Foundation Classes (IFC) (Koch, et al., 2017), multi-level modelling concepts (Borrmann, et al., 2015), collaborative design (Borrmann, et al., 2014), satellite-based settlement monitoring (Schindler, et al., 2016), and meta models for real-time design assessment (Ninic, et al., 2018).

Modern BIM tools have grown out of the infant stage as design tools for interactive object-based parametric design (Eastman, et al., 2008). In contrast to manual modelling of geometric details as in a generic 3D CAD approach, BIM tools allow for minimisation of direct modelling by using intelligent scripted parametric objects and algorithms with embedded knowledge about the relations between these objects. This is enabled by the extension of the BIM object-based concept with parametric modelling with embedded complex relations or intelligence between the models (Boeykens, 2012). This approach allows for automatic update of the complete model (object and constraints w.r.t. other objects) when object parameters are changed, which provides the basis for interactive design and analysis. Further enhancements of the design process are introduced by generative design, where a large number of design alternatives is generated based on input design constraints and parameters, such as materials, manufacturing methods, and cost constraints. The integration of parametric modelling and generative design within the BIM framework allows for an efficient generation of design alternatives, while the combination with other performance-based assessment methods guarantees effectiveness in generation of optimal solutions (Turrin, et al., 2011).

Another important aspect of the BIM framework is the systematic integration of assessment in the design models. In the tunnelling context, the design is evaluated using complex Finite Element (FE) simulations (Meschke, et al., 2014; Ninic, et al., 2019). In FE models, solid object is represented with trivariate polynomials of low order (usually one or two), while in design CAD models, these objects are commonly described with NURBS (Non-Uniform Rational B-splines). Therefore, to be utilised for the analysis in FE models, the CAD geometry has to be approximated using re-meshing techniques. Since FE analysis is sensitive to mesh refinement, several authors have tried to directly utilise the NURBS object definition for computationally efficient and higher-order numerical analysis by means of Isogeometric Analysis (IGA) (Breitenberger, et al., 2015; Philipp, et al., 2016) to alleviate this drawback. IGA, originally introduced by (Hughes, et al., 2005) is bridging the design process and analysis by direct use of the same shape function to represent the geometry in analysis. In addition, IGA offers additional advantages regarding the quality of the approximation, such as higher order and higher continuity of the computational mesh.

This paper presents a combination of emerging computing technologies in the area of parametric modelling and computational mechanics for the design assessment of segmented tunnel linings. Implementing an automated design-through-analysis workflow platform, we are facilitating the design process, contributing to modelling efficiency and at the same time reducing the possibility for human error. We present an extension of the recently introduced integrated SATBIM platform for information and numerical FE modelling of tunnel projects on different levels of detail (Ninic, et al., 2017; Ninic, et al., 2019), utilizing the advantages of higher-order geometry definition of the lining structure in the design software to generate higher-order and higher-continuity numerical models. By doing that, we provide a platform for the assessment and optimisation of tunnel design with high computational and modelling efficiency.

2. Methodology

The methodology for the presented integrated design-to-analysis workflow for segmented tunnel linings consists of i) fully parametric modelling of tunnel linings using the universal ring approach, ii) IGA computational framework and iii) reconstruction of the lining geometry for IGA analysis and automatic setup and extraction of computational IGA model. These three parts are briefly described in the subsequent sections.

2.1 Parametric modelling of tunnel structure

In the mechanised tunnelling process, the shield machine is digging directly into the ground, installing the precast segments at the back of the shield, so that they form the coating of the tunnel. Each ring is made of modular segments (from 4 to 10) and the narrowest spot on the segment ring is usually at the so-called key segment, which, as the last wedge element, closes and braces the ring. A complete segment ring is cone-shaped in order to accommodate curve radii from 150 m. The geometry of the entire ring and its individual segments as well as the arrangement of the joints and their sealing must be designed such that the can be easily moulded for the designed tunnel alignment. Hence, in order to have modular segments, the solution is to employ universal rings.

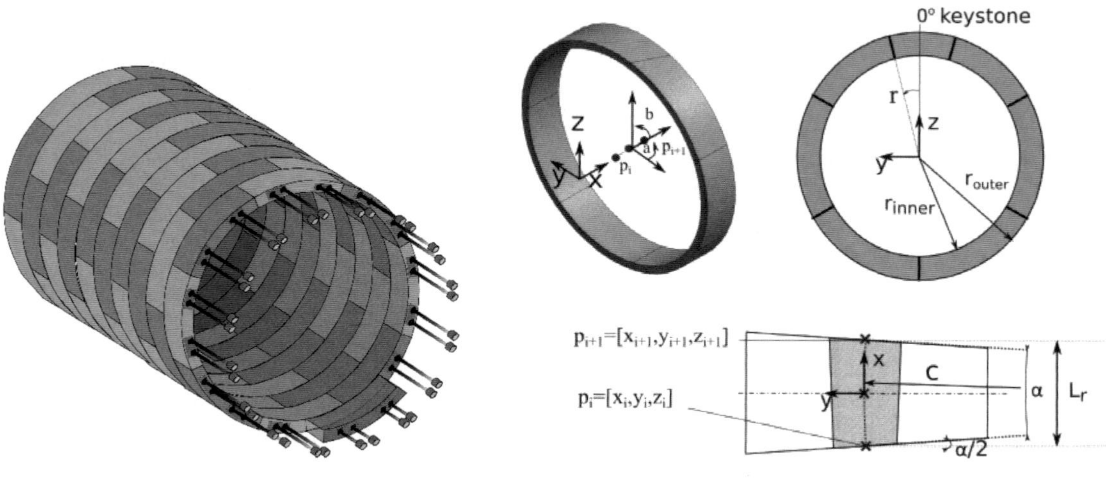

(a) (b)

Figure 1: (a) Segmented tunnel lining; (b) Geometry of the universal ring

A universal ring is characterized with the average ring length L_r, inner and outer radius of the ring (r_{inner} and r_{outer}), and the angle describing the tapered geometry of the ring α, which depend on the curvature c, the number of segments, and their divisions within the ring. The designed alignment of the tunnel is formed by adjusting the rotations of the rings.

Figure 2 outlines an algorithm for calculation of ring rotations, which leads to the best match between design and achievable tunnel alignment and enables the generation of the actual design model using the universal ring approach. Starting from the actual design alignment, imported as a CAD polyline, and based on the ring parameters, target points are created along the curve and ring rotations are determined based on the allowable ring rotations such that the actual ring positions have minimum discrepancy from the target design. For the calculations of the actual ring positions and $p_i(x_i, y_i, z_i)$, and spatial rotations (a, b), the following equations are derived:

$$x_i = x_{i-1} + L_r \cdot cos\left(a_{i-1} + \frac{\alpha}{2} \cdot cos(r_{i-1}) + \frac{\alpha}{2} \cdot cos(r_i)\right) \cdot cos\left(b_{i-1} + \frac{\alpha}{2} \cdot sin(r_{i-1}) + \frac{\alpha}{2} \cdot sin(r_i)\right),$$

$$y_i = y_{i-1} + L_r \cdot sin\left(a_{i-1} + \frac{\alpha}{2} \cdot cos(r_{i-1}) + \frac{\alpha}{2} \cdot cos(r_i)\right) \cdot cos\left(b_{i-1} + \frac{\alpha}{2} \cdot sin(r_{i-1}) + \frac{\alpha}{2} \cdot sin(r_i)\right),$$

$$z_i = z_{i-1} + L_r \cdot cos\left(a_{i-1} + \frac{\alpha}{2} \cdot cos(r_{i-1}) + \frac{\alpha}{2} \cdot cos(r_i)\right) \cdot sin\left(b_{i-1} + \frac{\alpha}{2} \cdot sin(r_{i-1}) + \frac{\alpha}{2} \cdot sin(r_i)\right) \quad (1)$$

$$\alpha = \arccos\frac{1 - L_r^2}{2c^2}\ ; \quad a_{n+1} = a_n + \frac{\alpha}{2}\cos(r_{i-1}) + \frac{\alpha}{2}\cos(r_i)\ ; \quad b_{n+1} = b_n + \frac{\alpha}{2}\sin(r_{i-1}) + \frac{\alpha}{2}\sin(r_i) \tag{2}$$

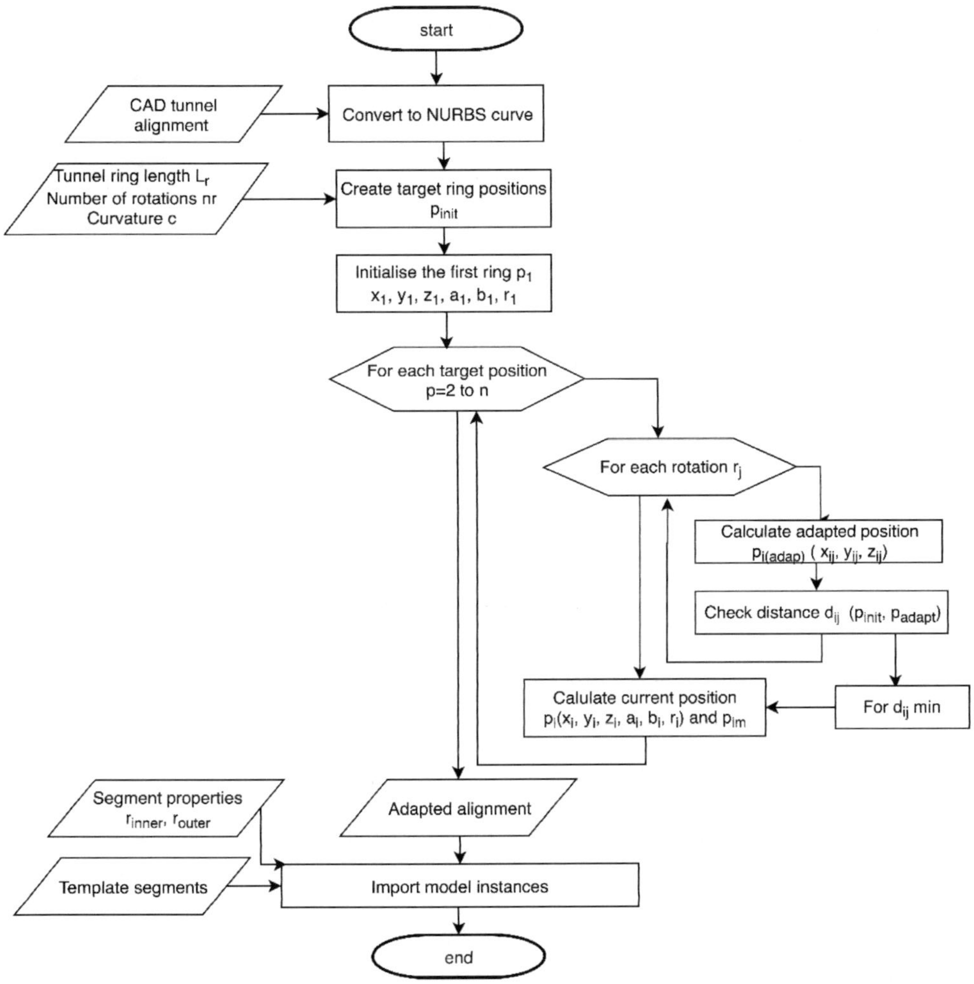

Figure 2: Algorithm for generation of the adapted tunnel alignment

Figure 3 (a) shows the calculated divergence of the calculated alignment from the actual design. The two curves nearly coincide, and for this particular example, the calculated discrepancy evaluated with root mean square error (RMSE) is 2.2 mm. The actual geometric-semantic design model of the segmented tunnel lining is shown in Figure 3(b).

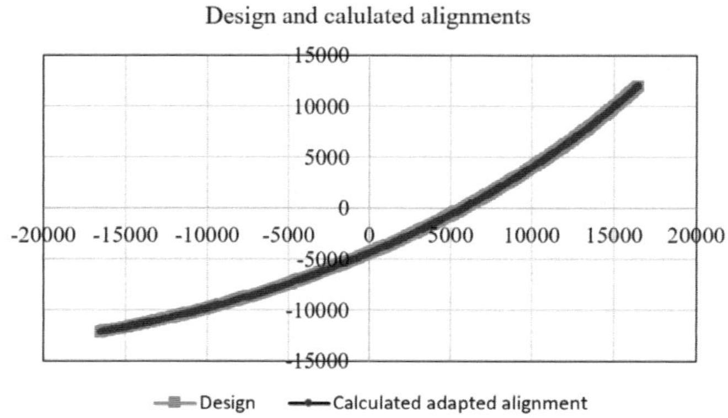

(a)

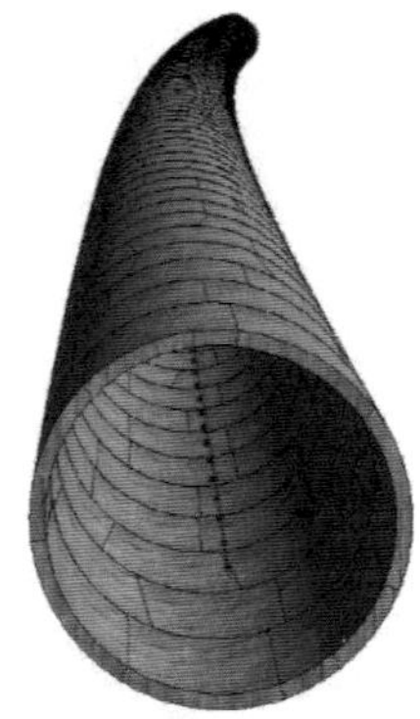

(b)

Figure 3: Evaluation of algorithm for generation of adaptive alignment

2.2 Isogeometric analysis (IGA): From NURBS geometry to NURBS basis functions

Univariate and multivariate NURBS geometries

Univariate B-spline functions can be used to construct a B-spline curve of order p by linear combination of piecewise rational polynomials. The geometry of the B-spline curve is defined as:

$$\boldsymbol{C}\,(\xi) \;=\; \sum_{i=1}^{n} N_i^p(\,\xi\,)\boldsymbol{P}_i \tag{3}$$

where $N_i^p(\,\xi\,)$ is the B-spline basis function of order p and $\boldsymbol{P}_i$ is the list of control points. The B-spline surface and volume are described as tensor products of two and three B-spline curves, respectively:

$$\boldsymbol{S}(\,\xi_1,\xi_2) = \sum_{i=0}^{n}\sum_{j=0}^{m} \boldsymbol{N}_i^p(\,\xi_1)\boldsymbol{N}_j^q(\,\xi_2)\boldsymbol{P}_{i,j} \tag{4}$$

$$\boldsymbol{V}(\,\xi_1,\xi_2,\xi_3) = \sum_{i=0}^{n}\sum_{j=0}^{m}\sum_{k=0}^{l} \boldsymbol{N}_i^p(\,\xi_1)\boldsymbol{N}_j^q(\,\xi_2)\boldsymbol{N}_k^r(\,\xi_3)\boldsymbol{P}_{i,j} \tag{5}$$

The B-spline basis can be generalized to the rational case by associating each control point $\boldsymbol{P}_i$ with the control weight w_I to form the projective control points in homogeneous coordinates. Then, the NURBS geometry is described by projecting the projective B-spline geometry as:

$$\widetilde{\boldsymbol{V}}\,(\xi) = \sum_{I=\{0,0,0\}}^{n,m,l} N_I(\,\xi\,)\boldsymbol{Q}_i\,, \quad where \quad \boldsymbol{Q} = \begin{bmatrix} w_i\boldsymbol{P}_I \\ w_i \end{bmatrix} \tag{6}$$

In 3D, the NURBS basis function is defined as:

$$R_{I(\,\xi)} = \frac{w_I N_I(\xi)}{\sum_{J=\{0,0,0\}}^{n,m,l} w_J N_J(\,\xi\,)} \tag{7}$$

It should be noted, that the B-Spline shape function can represented as a linear combination of *Bézier* shape functions of the same order as in (Borden, et al., 2011), which allows an more straightforward implementation similar to standard finite element models.

The computational analysis of the tunnel linings using isogeometric analysis is based upon the weak form of the initial boundary value problem,

$$\int_{\Gamma t}^{h} \delta\boldsymbol{u^h}\cdot\boldsymbol{t}\,dA \;+\; \int_{\Omega}^{h} \delta\boldsymbol{u^h}\cdot\boldsymbol{b}\,dV \;-\; \int_{\Omega}^{h} \delta\boldsymbol{\epsilon^h}\!:\boldsymbol{\sigma^h}\,dV \;=\; 0, \tag{8}$$

where $\boldsymbol{\sigma}^h$ is the stress tensor depending on the discretized displacement field $\boldsymbol{u}^h$, $\delta\boldsymbol{\epsilon}^h$ are the virtual strains obtained from the discretized test functions $\delta\boldsymbol{u}^h$, $\boldsymbol{t}$ are the boundary tractions and $\boldsymbol{b}$ the distributed volume forces. The system of algebraic equations resulting from Equation (8) is solved for the unknown displacements $\boldsymbol{u}$. To provide a seamless connection between the CAD-based geometry description and the analysis model, the spatial discretization of the displacements $\boldsymbol{u}$ and the test functions $\delta\boldsymbol{u}$ is based on the IGA approach, where the NURBS basis functions R_I (Equation (7)) are directly employed to approximate the displacement field:

$$\boldsymbol{u}^h(\boldsymbol{x}) = \sum_I R_I\left(\xi(x)\right)\boldsymbol{u}_I \qquad (9)$$

2.3 BIM-to-IGA

The main objective of integrated design-through-analysis workflows with IGA is to directly utilise the advantages of high-order geometry representations in design models to generate higher-order and higher-continuity numerical models, maximizing the computational and modelling efficiency. However, one of the biggest remaining challenges is the reconstruction of a solid model defined by boundary trimmed spline surfaces to obtain a parameterization suitable for IGA analysis (Al Akhras, et al., 2016). In the literature, different strategies have been proposed to solve this problem, such as use of tetrahedral meshes or swept volumes based on discrete volumetric harmonic functions (Martin, et al., 2009), variational approach to construct NURBS parameterization of swept volumes (Xu, et al., 2013), or a topologically equivalent solid bounded by (non-trimmed) B-spline surfaces (Xu, et al., 2013).

The geometry of tunnel segments exported in the ACIS (.sat) format is represented either with trivariate or trimmed NURBS, depending on the complexity of the segment geometry. For segments with parallel edges, the geometry is represented with trivariate NURBS surfaces (see Figure 4(a)), and for segments with inclined edges, such as keystone or neighbouring segments, NURBS surfaces are trimmed (see Figure 4(b)). In both cases, in order use the segment geometry for IGA analysis, the NURBS volumes needs to be reconstructed from surfaces according to Equation (6). Trivariate NURBS surfaces could be directly used for the generation of NURBS volumes by sweeping NURBS surfaces along the path using *Isogeometric_application* (see Section 3.1). However, a trimmed-NURBS boundary representation (BRep) is not suitable for the direct analysis using IGA, and therefore a method for NURBS reconstruction for tunnel linings along arbitrary alignments is proposed.

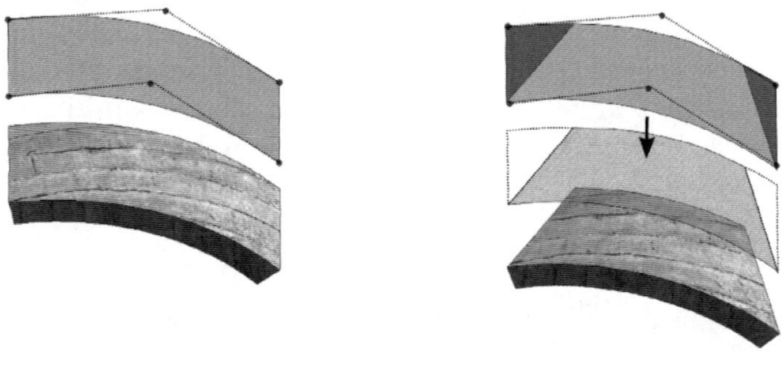

(a) (b)

Figure 4: (a) Trivariate NURBS surfaces; (b) Trimmed NURBS surfaces

The segment is constructed by sweeping a base surface along a tunnel alignment path with length of a ring L_r. The parametric segment is defined with the adaptive points (highlighted in red in Figure 5(a)), and the parameters r_{inner}, r_{outer}, α_{front}, α_{back}, β_{front} and β_{back}, where r, β and α, are the radius, arch length, and angle of the segment from the vertical axis, respectively. These parameters are used to reconstruct the trivariate NURBS definition of the segment as illustrated in Figure 5(a). The base surface is constructed as a bivariate NURBS, by defining control points $\boldsymbol{P}$ as a function of segment parameters. The bivariate NURBS is then swept along the path to generate NURBS volume as illustrated in Figure 5(b).

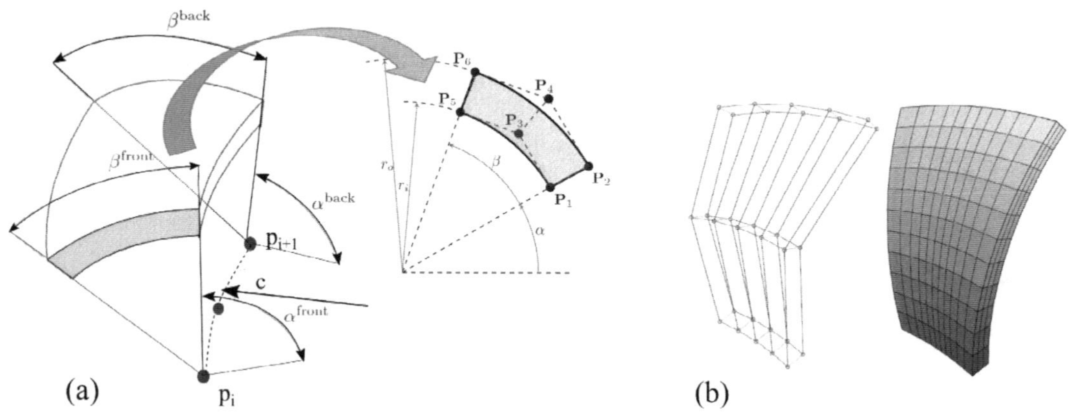

Figure 5:(a) Reconstruction of trimmed NURBS surfaces; (b) Trivariate NURBS volume

3. Implementation and Numerical examples

3.1 Implementation

The parametric model for the segmented tunnel lining has been developed using the industry-standard tools Revit and Dynamo (AUTODESK, 2017). For the generation of the universal rings, a parametric segment family was developed as described in Subsections 2.1 and 2.3. The instances of the parametric segment family are imported to the locations calculated using the methodology and algorithm presented in Subsection 2.1. The design model is then exported to ACIS (.sat) format, and the geometrical description of the segments is used to reconstruct the bivariate NURBS volumes using the methodology described in Subsection 2.3. Two alternatives for NURBS volume reconstruction are proposed. For a simple segment geometry with parallel edges of the individual segments, Trivariate NURBS surfaces are directly utilized to reconstruct the NURBS volume using *Isogeometric_application.*

If a more accurate representation of the curved segment geometry is required, which is characterized by a trimmed-NURBS BRep due to non-parallel edges according to the universal ring arrangement of segment joints, NURBS surfaces are reconstructed using same parametric rules used to generate the individual segments. For this purpose, a utility is developed in C++ with an interface to call it from Python. This utility reads in the geometrical description of the segment and performs the necessary geometric operations to form the NURBS volumes (see Section 2.3) exactly as computed from the parametric model in Subsection 2.1. It also supports the extraction of the surface information required for applying boundary conditions (load and interaction with soils), and setting the joint conditions using elastic springs between the segments.

The computational framework used for the implementation of IGA is the open source FE simulation software KRATOS (2017). KRATOS provides the necessary components to manage the components of the finite element model, such as the finite elements, boundary conditions, etc. Furthermore, it supports multiphysics simulations via a plugin mechanism, in which the *Isogeometric_application* is developed as a special plugin supporting IGA modelling and analysis.

3.2 Computational efficiency

The efficiency of the proposed framework compared to standard Finite Element analysis is demonstrated by means of the analysis of a segmented tunnel ring shown in Figure 6. In this example, a tunnel lining of 4.7 m outer radius and a thickness of 40 cm is assumed to be composed of 5 segments, which are connected using a surface joint model. The distance from the centre of the tunnel to the surface is 20 m, which accounts for an overburden of 15.3 m. The interaction between the soil and the tunnel is considered by means of nonlinear springs, and is characterized by the Variational Hyperstatic Reaction Method (Bui, et al., 2019). The nonlinear springs model and the loading conditions are illustrated in Figure 6(a). The resulting deformation of the lining from the earth pressure is shown in Figure 6(b). Although the joint opening is not adequately visible in the figure, it is measured to be in the range of 1° -2° between each segment.

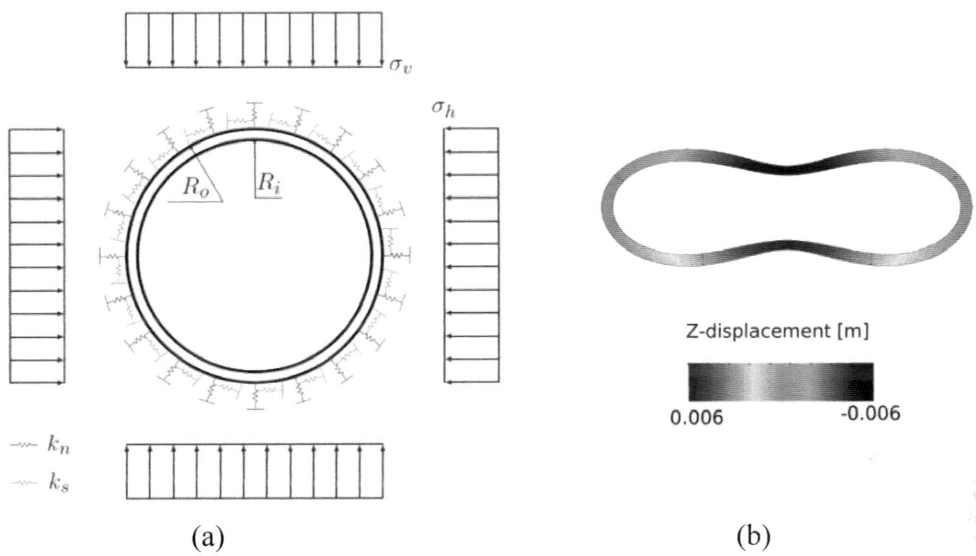

Figure 6: (a) Boundary conditions of the numerical model; (b) Deformation under earth pressure [400-fold magnification]

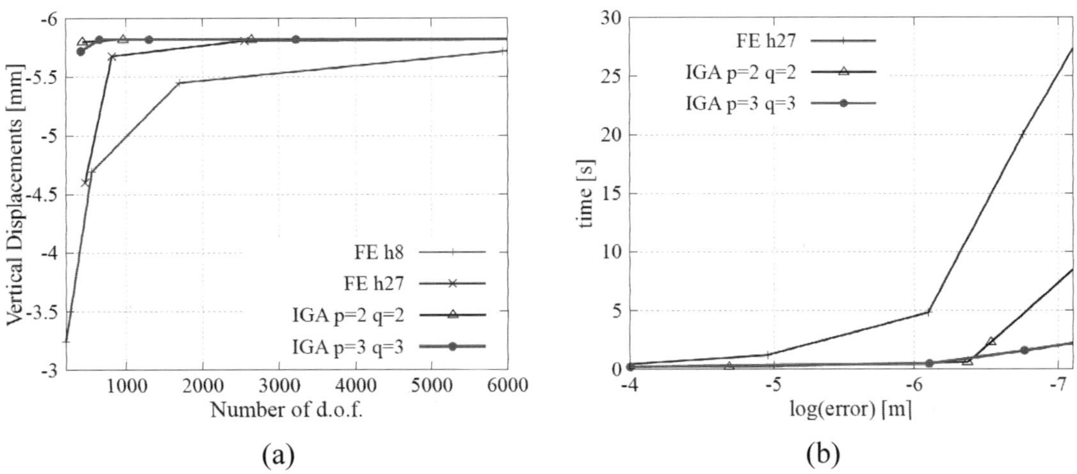

Figure 7: Comparison of performance of IGA and standard FE models: (a) Convergence of vertical displacement with mesh size, (b) Computational time required to reach a certain accuracy of the solution

The performance of the proposed methodology for the assessment of the tunnel lining design is verified against the performance of a standard FE model discretised using Lagrange basis function in terms of model size, i.e. the number of degrees of freedom (DOFs) required to reach a converged solution (setting the error tolerance for displacements to 10^{-7}). In Figure 7(a), it can be clearly observed that using IGA the solution is reached immediately, with only a very small number of DOFs (<500). In contrast, the FE solution shows the typical convergence behaviour depending on the polynomial degree of the shape functions. For linear interpolation functions, the solution does not even converge for the considered maximum model size of 6000 DOFs; for quadratic shape functions, approximately 3000 DOFs are needed. In Figure 7(b), FE and IGA are compared in terms of computational time needed to achieve the same accuracy of the numerical solution. The time is measured from start of the simulation until the end, without including the pre- and post-processing time. For IGA analysis, the time includes generating the NURBS mesh and computing the Bezier extraction operator. Figure 7(b) clearly shows that using IGA, high accuracy of the solution can be achieved without affecting the computational time. In other words, a sufficiently accurate numerical solution using a standard finite element model requires approximately 10 times more computational time than the IGA model.

3.3 Numerical example

In this example, we demonstrate how the proposed framework can be used for the efficient generation of the design and automated assessment of any arbitrary 3D tunnel structure.

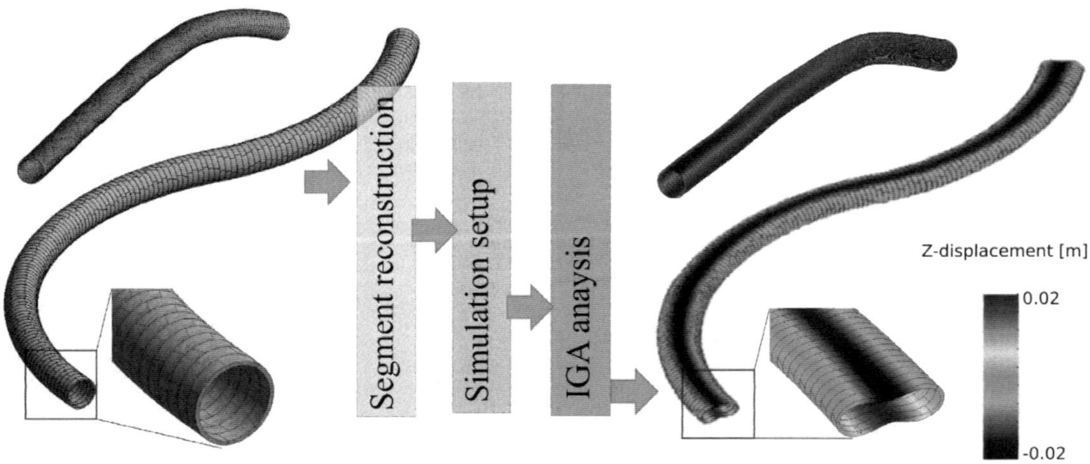

Figure 8: Automatized design-through-analysis workflow for the segmented tunnel linings

The only items defined by the user in the user-friendly interface are the designed tunnel alignment, the parameters defining the tunnel lining geometry, and the semantic parameters describing the lining and soil materials. The remaining workflow for generation of the optimal arrangements of tunnel rings, generation of the tunnel structure, and the reconstruction of the design geometry, simulation set-up and execution of IGA computational kernel, is fully automatized, with two "clicks"; one for start of the design and the other for the analysis. In the presented example, two tunnel alignments of approximately 300 m length are generated and analysed using the proposed concept. In both cases, the design-through-analysis workflow takes less than 10 min, considering the time needed for geometry generation, reconstruction and calculation of the model (which is approximately 3-4 minutes of the overall runtime).

4. Conclusions

In this paper, we demonstrated a systematic and versatile approach to efficiently generate a digital tunnel design model and analyse the tunnel lining in different practical scenarios. To this end, a BIM-based approach is developed, which connects user-friendly industry-standard BIM software with effective simulation tools, supporting high-performance computing and parallel simulation. Firstly, a fully parametric design model for the segmented tunnel lining is proposed. Secondly, a computational framework for the analysis of tunnel lining using high-order, high-continuity numerical representation by means of isogeometric analysis (IGA) is developed. Finally, an automatized design-through-analysis workflow solution for segmented tunnel lining is developed based on a fully parametric design model developed as a Revit plugin and an IGA B-Rep analysis software, connected through an interface implemented with the Revit plugin Dynamo. For the case of simplified lining geometry with straight segments, lining NURBS surfaces are directly utilised for the reconstruction of NURBS volumes, while for more complex geometry, where segment rings are described with trimmed NURBS surfaces, a reconstruction is required. The reconstruction procedure is not overly complicated and requires a few parameters, which are directly extracted from the design model. Overall, the prosed framework enables the investigation of tunnel alignment alternatives for very long sections in a user-friendly and computationally efficient way, reducing the manual modelling work substantially.

Acknowledgments

This project has received funding from the European Union's Horizon 2020 Research and Innovation Programme under the Marie Sklodowska-Curie grant agreement No 702874 "SATBIM - Simulations for multi-level Analysis of interactions in Tunnelling based on the Building Information Modelling technology". Financial support to the second author is provided by the German Research Foundation (DFG) in the framework of project C1 of the Collaborative Research Center SFB 837 "Interaction Modeling in Mechanized Tunnelling". This support is gratefully acknowledged.

References

Al Akhras, H., Elguedj, T., Gravouil, A. and Rochette, M. (2016). Isogeometric analysis-suitable trivariate NURBS models from standard B-Rep models. Computer Methods in Applied Mechanics and Engineering, Volume 307, pp. 256-274.

Arnau, O. and Molins, C. (2012). Three-dimensional structural response of segmental tunnel linings. Engineering Structures, 44(0), pp. 210-221.

AUTODESK. (2017). Autodesk Revit. [Online] Available at: http://www.autodesk.co.uk/products/revit-family/. [Accessed 10 January 2019].

Boeykens, S. (2012). Bridging building information modeling and parametric design. In: eWork and eBusiness in Architecture, Engineering and Construction: ECPPM . London: Taylor & Francis Group, pp. 453-458.

Borden, M., Scott, M., Evans, J. & Hughes, T. (2011). Isogeometric finite element data structures based on Bézier extraction of NURBS. International Journal for Numerical Methods in Engineering, Volume 87, pp. 15-47.

A. Borrmann, A., Flurl, M., Ramos Jubierre, J., Mundani, R.P. and Rank, E. (2014). Synchronous collaborative tunnel design based on consistency-preserving multi-scale models. Advanced Engineering Informatics, 28(4), pp. 499-517.

Borrmann, A., Kolbe, T.H., Donaubauer, A., Steuer, H., Jubierre, J.R.and Flurl, M. (2015). Multi-Scale Geometric-Semantic Modeling of Shield Tunnels for GIS and BIM Applications. Computer-Aided Civil and Infrastructure Engineering, 30(4), pp. 263-281.

Breitenberger, M., Apostolatos, A., Philipp, B., Wuechner, R. and Bletzinger, K. (2015). Analysis in computer aided design: Nonlinear isogeometric B-Rep analysis of shell structures. Computer Methods in Applied Mechanics and Engineering,, Volume 284, pp. 401-457.

Bui, H., Ninic, J. and Meschke, G., (2019). A Variationally Consistent Hyperstatic Reaction Method for Tunnel Lining Design. Journal for Numerical and Analytical Methods in Geomechanics. In preparation.

Dadvand, P., Rossi, R. and Oñate, E. (2017). Kratos Multi-physics. [Online] Available at: http://www.cimne.com/kratos/.[Accessed 1 March 2019].

Daller, J., Žibert, M., Exinger, C. and Lah, M. (2016). Implementation of BIM in the tunnel design – Engineering consultant's aspect. Geomechanics and Tunnelling, 9(6), pp. 674-683.

Eastman, C., Teicholz, P., Sacks, R. and Liston, K. (2008). BIM Handbook: A Guide to Building Information Modeling for Owners, Managers, Designers, Engineers, and Contractors. s.l.:Wiley & Sons.

Hughes, T., Cottrell, J. & Bazilevs, Y. (2005). Isogeometric analysis: CAD, finite elements, NURBS, exact geometry. Computer Methods in Applied Mechanics and Engineering, Volume 194, pp. 4135-4195.

Koch, C., Vonthron, A. and König, M. (2017). A tunnel information modelling framework to support management, simulations and visualisations in mechanised tunnelling projects. Automation in Construction, Volume 83, pp. 78-90.

Maidl, B., Herrenknecht, M., Maidl, U. and Wehrmeyer, G. (2012). Mechanised Shield Tunnelling. s.l.:Ernst und Sohn.

Martin, T., Cohen, E. and Kirby, R. (2009). Volumetric parameterization and trivariate B-spline fitting using harmonic functions. Computer Aided Geometric Design, 26(6), pp. 648-664.

Melendo, A., Coll, A., Pasenau, M., Escolano, E. and Monros, A. (2019). GiD: the personal pre- and postprocessor. [Online] Available at: http://www.gidhome.com/. [Accessed 1 March 2019].

Meschke, G., Freitag, S., Alsahly, A., Ninic, J., Schindler, S. and Koch, C. (2014). Numerical Simulation in Mechanized Tunneling in Urban Environments in the Framework of a Tunnel Information Model. Bauingenieur, 89(11), pp. 457-466.

Ninic, J., Bui, H., Koch, C. and Meschke, G. (2019). Computationally Efficient Simulation in Urban Mechanized Tunneling Based on Multilevel BIM Models. Journal of Computing in Civil Engineering, 33(3), pp. 04019007.

Ninic, J., Koch, C. and Stascheit, J. (2017). An integrated platform for design and numerical analysis of shield. Advances in Engineering Software, Volume 112, pp. 165-179.

Ninic, J., Koch, C. & Tizani, W., 2018. Meta models for real-time design assessment within an integrated information and numerical modelling framework. Lecture Notes in Computer Science, Volume 10863, pp. 201-218.

Philipp, B, Breitenberger, M., D'Auria, I., Wuechner, R. and Bletzinger, K.U. (2016). Integrated design and analysis of structural membranes using the Isogeometric B--Rep Analysis. Computer Methods in Applied Mechanics and Engineering, Volume 303, pp. 312 - 340.

Schindler, S., Hegemann, F., Koch, C., Koenig, M. and Mark, P. (2016). Radar interferometry based settlement monitoring in tunnelling: Visualisation and accuracy analyses. Visualization in Engineering, 4(1), p. 7.

Smith, S. (2014). Building information modelling – moving Crossrail, UK, forward. Proceedings of the Institution of Civil Engineers - Management, Procurement and Law, 167(3), pp. 141-151.

Turrin, M., von Buelow, P. and Stouffs, R. (2011). Design explorations of performance driven geometry in architectural design using parametric modeling and genetic algorithms. Advanced Engineering Informatics, 25(4), pp. 656-675.

Xu, G., Mourrain, B., Duvigneau, R. and Galligo, A. (2013). Analysis-suitable volume parameterization of multi-block computational domain in isogeometric applications. Computer-Aided Design, 45(2), pp. 395-404.

Xu, G., Mourrain, B., Duvigneau, R. and Galligo, A. (2013). Constructing analysis-suitable parameterization of computational domain from CAD boundary by variational harmonic method. Journal of Computational Physics, Volume 252, pp. 275-289.

Educational Facility Design with Graph Grammar Systems

E. Grabska, B. Strug, G. Ślusarczyk
Jagiellonian University, Poland
barbara.strug@uj.edu.pl

Abstract. This paper deals with graph grammar systems which are used to generate representations of complex designs. Space layouts of designs have their internal representations in the form of attributed graphs representing both topological structures and semantic properties. The system of graph grammars, which work in parallel on the common graph independently generating layouts of different design components, is proposed. The grammars of the system jointly generate a set of graphs representing design task solutions with required properties. The presented approach is illustrated through the example of designing kindergarten facilities.

1. Introduction

This paper deals with graph grammar systems that are a useful approach to coordinate the actions among generative subsystems involved in the generation of complex designs. The conceptual stage of the design related to layouts and arrangement of spaces in educational facilities are studied to illustrate the power of this approach in design automation.

Educational facilities are composed of many different design components based on various functional and organizational requirements. Designing such a facility requires thus integrating this expectations into one project. Hence there is a need for a formal model that would allow both to represent the structure of the whole design in an integrated way and to describe separately diverse aspects of the design process.

In this paper the externalization of early design solutions is made with the use of various visual editors in order to design layouts of spaces, express relations between their functional areas, and design space arrangements. All types of spaces are arranged using an appropriate equipment. The designer's drawings of space layouts are automatically transformed into their internal representations in the form of attributed graphs representing both topological structures and semantic properties of educational facilities (Grabska & Borkowski, 1996). Such graphs can be generated by a graph grammar (Rozenberg, 1999). The main problem of graph generation with graph grammars lies in the complexity and size (understood as the number of rules) of grammars needed in real world problems (that can be encountered in the domains of both engineering and design). Such grammars are also very difficult to define. Moreover, as the design of educational facilities has to encompass different components (a building with different zones, sports facilities, playground, recreational areas etc.) the grammar has to contain many unrelated or loosely related sets of productions.

It thus seems advantageous to use a number of simpler grammars, called a grammar system, cooperating in an effort to generate a design, instead of one complex grammar. A grammar system consists of a finite number of grammars which together influence (change) an environment by applying some operations to it. At a given moment the state of the system is described by the current environment (sub-environments). The system works by changing its state.

In our approach it is assumed that at any given time step there is only one graph being generated. The grammars of the proposed system work in parallel on the common graph independently generating solutions of subproblems. Each system grammar operates on this graph according to a communication protocol called the derivation mode. In case of educational facilities design the different elements of such a facility are designed independently with only occasional cooperation when common elements are being processed or common recourses are considered. The grammars of the system jointly generate a set of graphs representing design task solutions with properties specified by graph attributes. Grammar rules of the system are designed in a GraphTool framework (Ryszka & Grabska, 2013).

This approach can be seen as an equivalent of many "design teams" working on different parts of the same design. The only requirement here seems to be ensuring that no two teams work at the same time on the same part of the design, i.e. no two grammars operate on the same nodes of the current graph form. This problem is solved here by introducing a special set of labels which allow for activation of different system grammars at selected locations (Grabska et al., 2008).

The proposed generative method allows for a flexible approach to the design of complex facilities. Depending on the additional requirements some system grammars can be added or deleted from the design system thus representing the presence of some optional elements. The proposed system supports generation of alternative facilities models with various arrangement of spaces, which can be easily adapted to different needs of older and younger children. The presented approach is illustrated through the example of designing kindergarten facilities.

2. CP-graph Representation of Space Layouts

Usually the design process is started by the designer who formulates a set of design requirements on the basis of a design task. These requirements together with legal norms and standards constitute the design criteria for a given project. In our approach to design kindergarten facilities the visual editor (Grabska et al., 2009) supports the conceptual stage of the design by enabling the designer to browse the existing space layouts representing various arrangements of required areas. These layouts are composed of six possible types of areas representing spaces intended for a kindergarten building, yard, playgrounds, recreational areas, sports facilities, and parking lots.

Four possible layouts of kindergarten facilities are presented in Fig.1. The labels *Building, Yard, Playground, Recreation, Sport* and *Parking* denote the areas with specific purpose. The layout presented in Fig.1c contains two areas labeled *Playground*, as the one of them is planned for younger children, while the second one for older children.

If one of the presented designs satisfies the designer's requirements and expectations he can select it as an initial layout. Using the editor the designer can also modify any of the presented layouts or create a new one. The layout indicated by the designer becomes a starting point for the further development of a task solution.

Layouts of kindergarten facilities have their internal representations in the form of composition graphs (CP-graphs) (Strug et al., 2017). CP-graphs are labelled and attributed graphs, which represent both topological structures and semantic properties of educational facilities (Grabska & Borkowski, 1996). Nodes of these graphs represent different types of spaces, like a yard, playground, recreational area, spaces for playground facilities, and sports facilities. The type of a component represented by a node is determined by its label. Moreover nodes have attributes specifying properties of components assigned to them. To each node attributes specifying the length, width, area and the type of bedding of the corresponding component are assigned. Bonds assigned to nodes denote possible connections between layout components. Bonds are connected by edges representing spatial relations between components and labelled by the relation names.

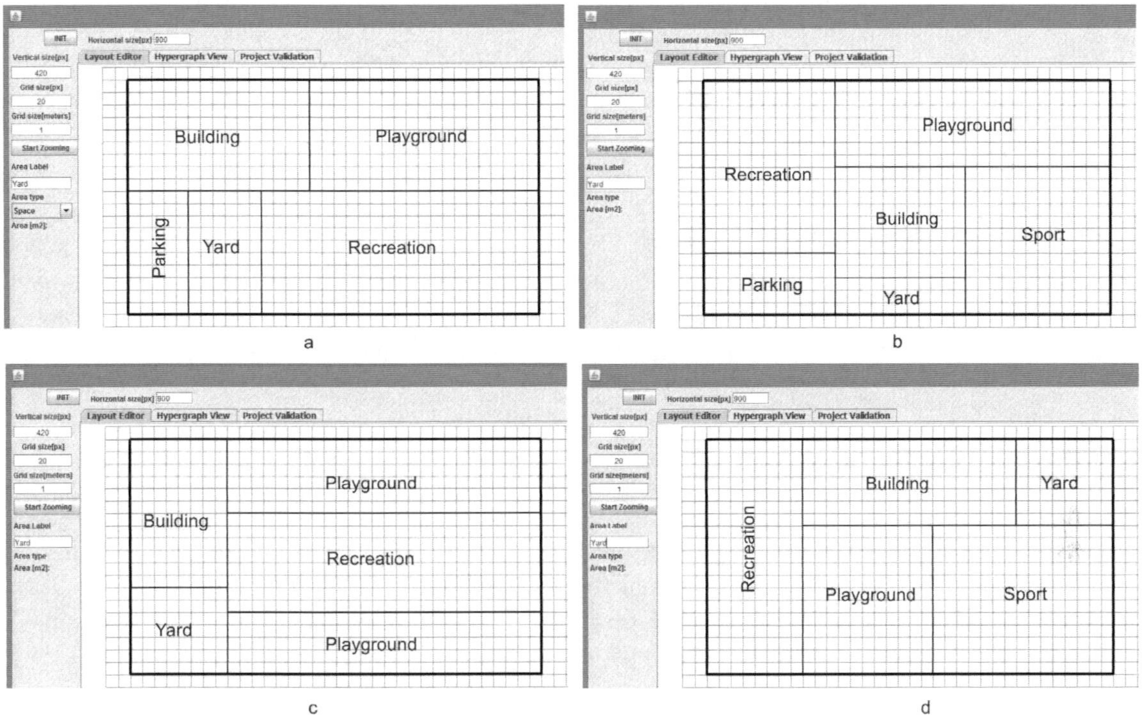

Figure 1: Four space arrangements of kindergarten facilities

The formal definition of a CP-graph is as follows.

Let Σ be a finite alphabet used to label object nodes, bond nodes and edges. Let A be a nonempty, finite set of attributes. For each attribute $a \in A$, let D_a be a fixed, nonempty set of its admissible values, known as the domain of a.

A CP-graph G is a tuple $G = (V, B, E, bd, s, t, lab, atr)$, where:

1. V, B, E are pairwise disjoint finite sets, whose elements are respectively called nodes, bonds and edges,
2. $bd: V \rightarrow 2^B$ is a function assigning sets of bonds to nodes in such a way that $\forall x \in B\ \exists!\ y \in V: x \in bd(y)$, i.e., each bond belongs to exactly one node,
3. $s, t: E \rightarrow B$ are functions assigning to edges source and target bonds, respectively, in such a way that $\forall e \in E\ \exists x, y \in V: s(e) \in bd(x) \wedge t(e) \in bd(y) \wedge x \neq y$,
4. $lab: V \cup B \cup E \rightarrow \Sigma$ is a labelling function,
5. $atr: V \cup B \cup E \rightarrow 2^A$ is an attributing function.

Each of the layouts of kindergarten facilities present or created in the visual editor has its CP-graph representation. Thus the CP-graph corresponding to the space layout selected by the designer becomes the starting graph for the system of grammars, which work in parallel on this graph jointly generating CP-graphs representing design task solutions.

CP-graphs representing space layouts presented in Fig. 1 are shown in Fig. 2. The CP-graph nodes representing different areas intended for a building, yard, playground, recreation, sport and parking are labeled as *BL, YR, PL, RC, SP*, and *PR*, respectively. Bonds assigned to nodes represent sides of areas and are drawn as small circles. The edges represent spatial adjacency between components. As the only one relation between components is considered, the edge labels are omitted.

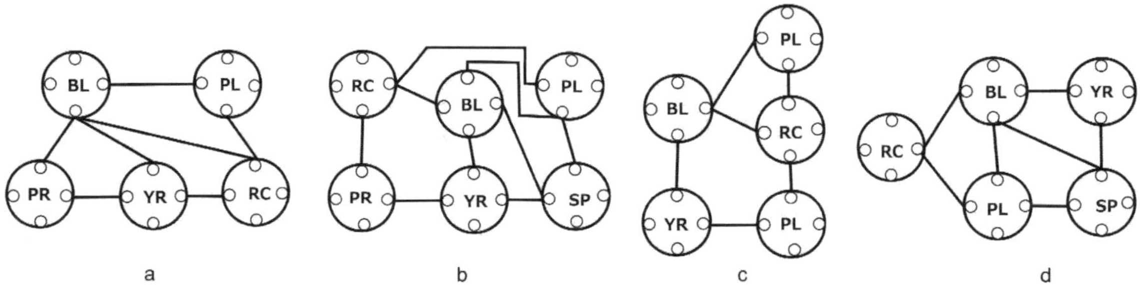

Figure 2: CP-graphs representing space layouts from Fig. 1

3. CP-graph Grammars

CP-graph representing structures of educational facilities designs are generated by CP-graph grammars. A CP-graph grammar is composed of a set of productions and an axiom being an initial CP-graph. In order to apply grammar rules some bonds of CP-graphs occurring in these rules are specified as external ones. Let $G = (V, B, E, bd, s, t, lab, atr)$ be a CP-graph. A partial function $ext: B \rightarrow \aleph$, where $\aleph$ is a set of integers, determines external bonds of G.

A CP-graph transformation rule is of the form $p = (l, r, sr)$, where l and r are attributed CP-graphs with the same number of different values of external bonds and sr is a set of functions specifying the way in which attributes assigned to nodes of l are transferred to the attributes assigned to nodes of r. Each attribute has a set of possible values, which are established during the rule application. The application of the rule p to a CP-graph G consists in substituting r for a CP-graph being an isomorphic image of l in G, replacing external bonds of the CP-graph being removed with the external bonds of r with the same numbers, and specifying values of attributes assigned to elements of r according to functions of sr. After inserting r into a host CP-graph all edges which were coming into (or out of) a bond with a given number in the CP-graph l, are coming into (or out of) bonds of r with the same number.

The formal definition of a CP-graph grammar is as follows.

Let N and T denote sets of non-terminal and terminal node labels, respectively.

A CP-graph grammar GG over N and T is a pair $GG = (P, S)$, where:

1. P is a finite set of productions of the form $p = (l, r, sr)$ satisfying the following conditions:

   – l and r are attributed CP-graphs such that the set of numbers defined for bonds of l by ext is the same as the set of numbers defined by ext for r, i.e., $set(ext(B_l)) = set(ext(B_r))$,

   – l contains at least one node with a label of N (i.e., $\exists v \in V_l: lab_l(v) \in N$),

2. S is an initial attributed CP-graph containing at least one node with a label of N, and called an axiom of GG.

The chosen rules of a CP-graph grammar, which generates CP-graph representations of building floor layouts, are shown in Fig. 3. Non-terminal labels of nodes start with a capital letter, while terminal labels are written in lower case letters. The rule $p1$ divides the floor area into a communication area represented by a node labelled Cmc, two play areas represented by nodes labelled as *Play*, a dining area (*Dining*), an area for bathrooms (*Bthrs*), an entrance, an utility room and a cloakroom. The productions *p2* and *p3* place one or two playrooms in each play area. The embedding transformation for all these productions is such that all edges which are connected in the host CP-graph with bond number *i* of the left-hand side of a production are replaced by edges connected with all bonds with number *i* on the right-hand side of this production. The way of determining the values of the attribute *area* for the nodes of the production right-hand side CP-graph in respect to the value of this attribute specified for the left-hand side CP-graph is shown for productions *p2* and *p3*. One of the possible floor layouts corresponding to a CP-graph generated by the presented CP-graph grammar is shown in Fig.4.

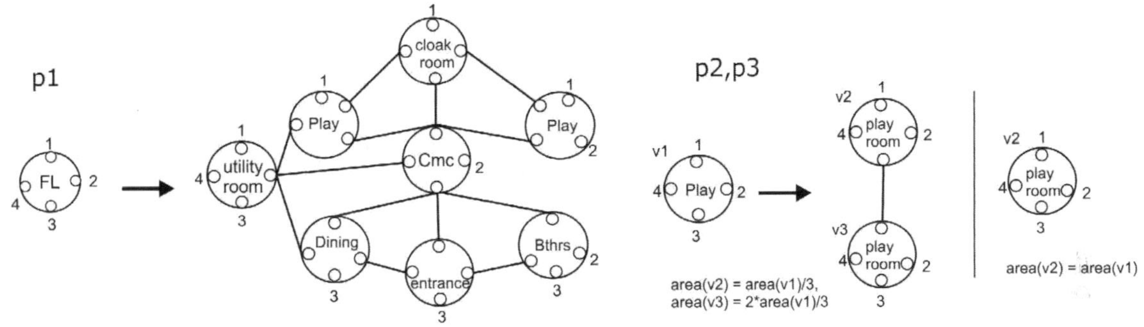

Figure 3: The chosen rules of a CP-graph grammar generating representations of floor layouts

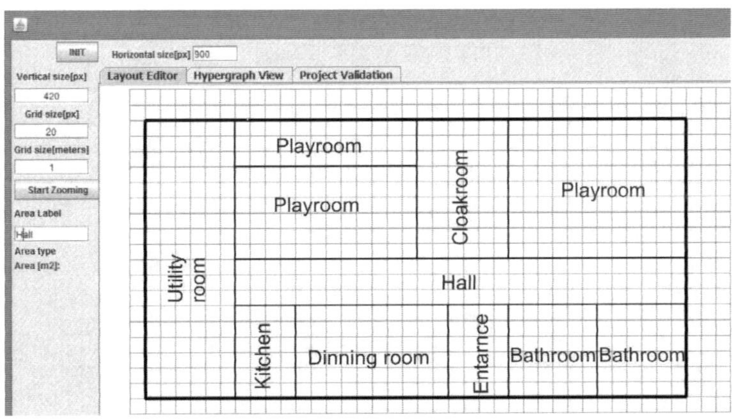

Figure 4: A floor layout corresponding to a CP-graph generated by the CP-graph grammar from Fig.3

In Fig. 5 twelve selected rules of a CP-graph grammar, which supports the user in designing various arrangements of playground facilities, are presented. The productions *p1* and *p2* generate arrangements of areas with bedding filled with grass (nodes labelled by *Lawn*), rubber mat (*Rubber*) and synthetic grass (*Synthetic*). The fourth type of area in the playground can be planted with trees (*Trees*). Productions *p3* and *p4* allow for generating an arbitrary number of trees, but at least two trees should be present. To production *p3* a variable, which specifies the maximum number of times this production can be applied, is attached. Productions *p10, p11* and *p12* enable us to obtain lawns on which there are paths, benches and/or shrubs. The number of benches and shrubs is generated in the same way as trees by means of productions *p3* and *p4*. Productions *p5* and *p6* generate arrangements of activity towers, swings, and spring rockers, which are located on rubber mats, while productions *p7* and *p8* generate arrangements of carousels, outdoor boards and play houses with sandpits, which are located on synthetic grass. Production *p9* is a context sensitive one, as its left-hand side CP-graph contains more than one node. This production allows us to place a bench between a sandpit and boards if this sandpit is to be located near outdoor boards. The area of spaces and the material used for different types of beddings are specified by graph attributes. Attributes allow also for selecting the right playground equipment for an appropriate age group (for children of age (3-4) and (5-6)). This selection should be taken into account for example when the equipment for the youngest children (age 3-4) is placed. Their equipment should be located close to the place where the kindergarten teachers are.

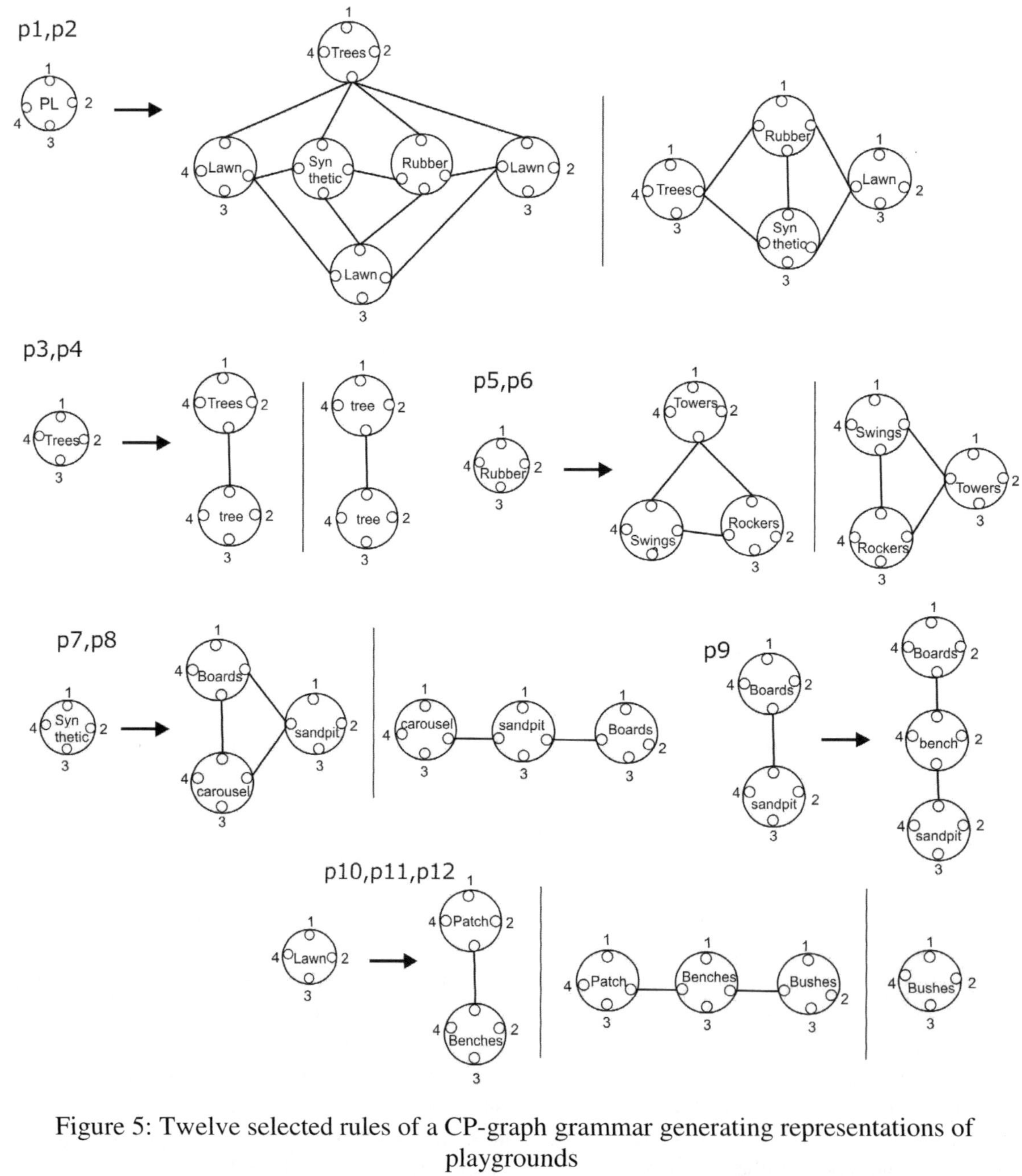

Figure 5: Twelve selected rules of a CP-graph grammar generating representations of playgrounds

Fig. 6 shows three examples of playground designs with equipment. The following categories of equipment are presented: activity towers (1, 3), swings (2, 7), spring rockers (6,8), carousel (9), outdoor tic-tac-toe board (5), and kids play house with sandpit (4).

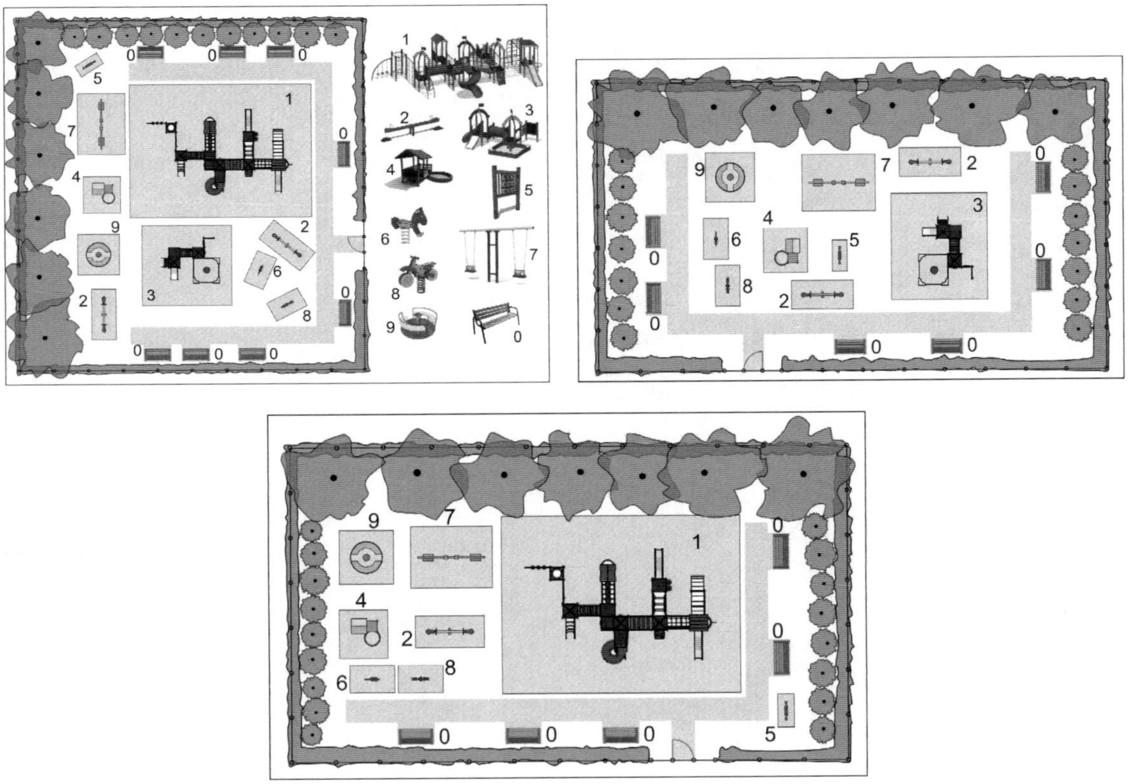

Figure 6: Three examples of playground designs with equipment

In Fig. 7a a recreation area arrangement, which corresponds to a CP-graph generated by CP-graph grammar supporting the design of various arrangements of trees, shrubs, flower beds, paths, bridges, benches and stones, is presented. A fragment of this arrangement and a corresponding subCP-graph are shown in Figs. 7b and 7c, respectively. The CP-graph nodes represent seven path segments, four flower beds, a tree, a bench, and a bridge.

The described CP-graph grammars are created with the use of *GraphTool*, which is an Integrated Development Environment providing tools necessary to define graphs, and graph transformation rules. It is implemented in the Java language as a plugin for the Eclipse framework, and is based on the EMF library (Eclipse Modeling Framework). By replacing CP-graph subgraphs in the way specified in CP-graph rules the *GraphTool* generates different CP-graphs representing possible arrangements of kindergarten facilities. The possibility of relating attributes of right-hand sides of CP-graph rules to attributes of their left-hand sides enables us to capture parametric modeling knowledge.

4. A Grammar System

As the kindergarten is actually a composition of different design components the design of each of them can be described by an independent grammar. Each of such grammars can be seen as an independent "design team" working on its own part of a design with minimal or no contact/interference/communication with other teams. Only when a given team does not know how to deal with a certain part of a design it can call another team – such an action is represented by triggering a specialized grammar able to solve a particular design subproblem (for example to design a part of a playground or to design a recreation area).

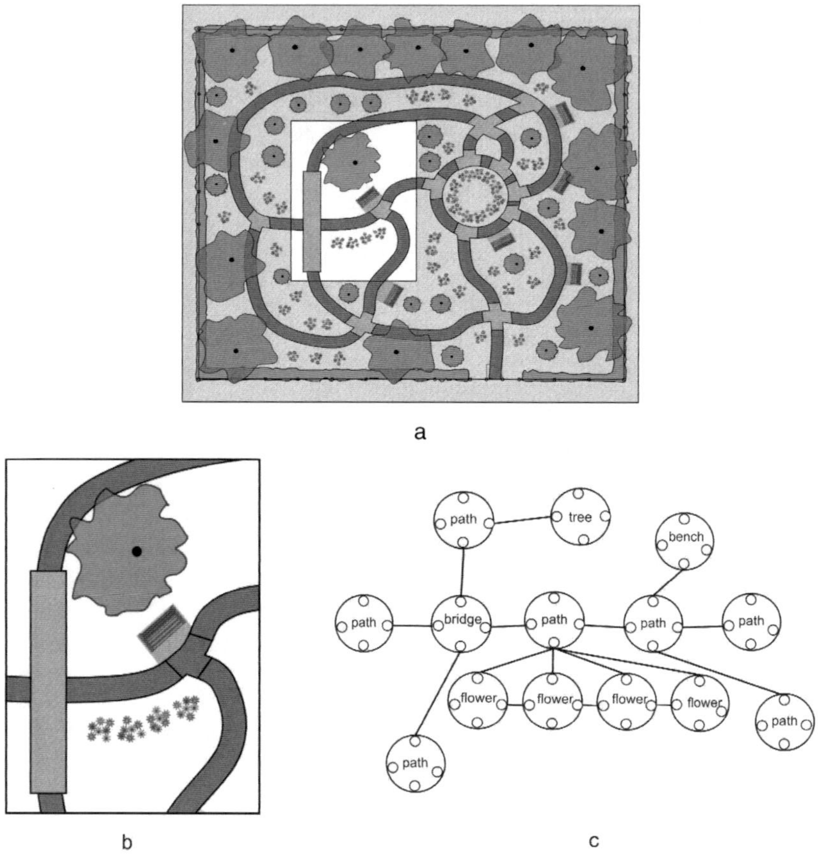

Figure 7: a) A recreation area arrangement, b) a fragment of this area, c) a CP-graph representation of this fragment arrangement

A family of grammars is called a grammar system. A grammar system consists of a finite number of grammars which can work together to change an environment by applying some operations to it. At a given moment the state of the system is described by the current environment (sub-environments). The system works by changing its state.

In general usually two types of grammar systems are distinguished: parallel communicating grammar systems (PC grammar systems) (Csuhaj-Varjú & Vaszil, 2001) and cooperating distributed grammar systems (CD grammar systems) (Csuhaj-Varjú, 2004). The main difference between these types of grammar systems consists in the way they work and communicate. In PC grammar systems each grammar operates on its own copy of the graph under derivation and they only exchange information when there is a specific request. In case of CD grammar systems the grammars operate on one common graph, one grammar at a time.

As in computer aided design domain a single object is usually developed, the CD grammar systems seem more appropriate here. They allow for a number of grammars to work together on one object. At any given time step there is only one graph being generated. Each system grammar operates on this graph according to a communication protocol called the *derivation mode*. There is a number of ways such a mode can be defined, for example it may allow a single grammar to perform a predefined number of steps or to work until no production of this grammar can be applied. The method of selecting which grammar should be used as the next "active" grammar is also important.

It has to be noticed that in case of CP-graph grammars the requirement that only one grammar can operate on a given temporary form seems too strong. Moreover in design systems it would be useful to allow more than one grammar to operate on the same common graph. The only requirement here seems to be ensuring that no two teams work at the same time on the same part of the design, i.e., no two grammars operate on the same nodes of the graph being derived.

Another aspect that has to be properly defined is a way of activating particular grammars. Such a method, called a *cooperation strategy*, may either be based on some predefined order - thus leading the system to operate under the control of an "external supervisor". Or, it can be based on dynamic activation of grammars related to the current state of a graph being derived. The way a given grammar works i.e. how long it performs its operations must also be defined. In this paper a so called *terminal derivation mode* is used, i.e. each grammar works as long as it contains a production that can be applied to a current graph.

An advantage of such an approach is the possibility to use grammars defined for different aspects of the design process. In case of adding some elements to the design it is enough to add a grammar to the grammar system. In case of a single grammar approach a grammar has to be redesigned to incorporate new production rules and new symbols. Moreover, it has to be noted that the use of a grammar system can lead to the reduction of computational costs, as different types of grammars can be used in one system. There exist different types of grammars. Context free grammars have lower computational cost than context sensitive grammars, but at the same time context sensitive grammars have higher expressive power. Yet in some cases context sensitive productions cannot be avoided. An example of such a production, which adds a bench only when a sandpit and a board are present, is depicted in Fig. 5 (production *p9*). In a single grammar adding just one context sensitive rule makes the whole grammar context sensitive. In case of a grammar system adding such a rule makes only one grammar to be context sensitive without affecting other grammar types and associated computational cost.

In the presented approach a CP-graph grammar system consists of a set of initial CP-graphs and a family of n (but at least two) CP-graph grammars, which communicate using a set of so-called *communication symbols*. This set is composed of all non-terminal labels of nodes occurring in axioms of the system CP-graph grammars. Each grammar has its own specific communication symbol, and therefore the number of communication symbols equals to the number of the system grammars.

Formally, a CP-graph grammar system defined over N and T is as a tuple

$GGS = (G_1, G_2, \ldots, G_n, C, S_0)$, where

- $G_i = (P_i, S_i)$, $(i=1 \ldots n)$ are CP-graph grammars such that each S_i is composed of only one node with a label of N,
- C is a set of communication symbols, such that $C \subset N$, is composed of all non-terminal labels occurring in grammar axioms and there are no identical communication symbols in axioms of different grammars.
- S_0 is a set of initial CP-graphs.

Nodes labelled with terminal, non-terminal and communication symbols will be called, terminal, non-terminal and communication nodes, respectively.

Each system grammar contains productions that have at least one node on the left side labelled by a non-terminal symbol. The nodes of the graph on the right side of the production can labelled by any symbol, terminal, non-terminal or communication one.

The non-terminal nodes can be intuitively understood as representing a part of a design that is not finished but a given grammar knows how to deal with it further. Taking this intuition further a communication symbol means that a particular grammar knows that some part of design is not finished but it is not "specialist" in this part and thus it "communicates" with other grammar that knows how to deal with this part. Terminal symbols represent part of a design that is considered to be finished.

The definition of a grammar system guarantees that if any grammar introduces a communication symbol into the graph, then at least one other grammar exists such that it contains an axiom node labelled by the same symbol. Thus communication symbols occurring in the derived graph allow for triggering appropriate system grammars.

For the kindergarten design, let $C = \{BL, PL, PR, YR, RC, SP\}$ and S_0 contain among other all of the CP-graphs representing initial space layouts depicted in Fig. 2. In this case after selecting an initial graph from S_0 a graph system can be run. Each of the labels of the initial graph triggers one grammar from the proposed CP-grammar system.

In Fig. 8 an example of the application of a grammar system is presented. In the first step the user selects an initial layout. In this case, the layout depicted in Fig. 1c and represented by the initial CP-graph depicted in Fig. 2c is selected. This CP-graph contains five nodes labelled with communication symbols: two of them are labelled by *PL*, and three nodes by *YR*, *BL* and *RC*, respectively. In the next step, four grammars from the grammar system are triggered by their respective symbols. For example the symbol *BL* triggers the grammar responsible for the design of the layout of the building. As there are two nodes labelled with the communication symbol *PL*, the grammar responsible for the design of the playground area is triggered twice. As the grammar is non-deterministic it allows us to obtain different designs in both areas. The productions can be selected either randomly or may be determined by attributes assigned to communication symbols (for example they may include a number or type of objects expected in a given area). It can be observed that by running the same process for a second time we may obtain a slightly different design but still following some basic structure.

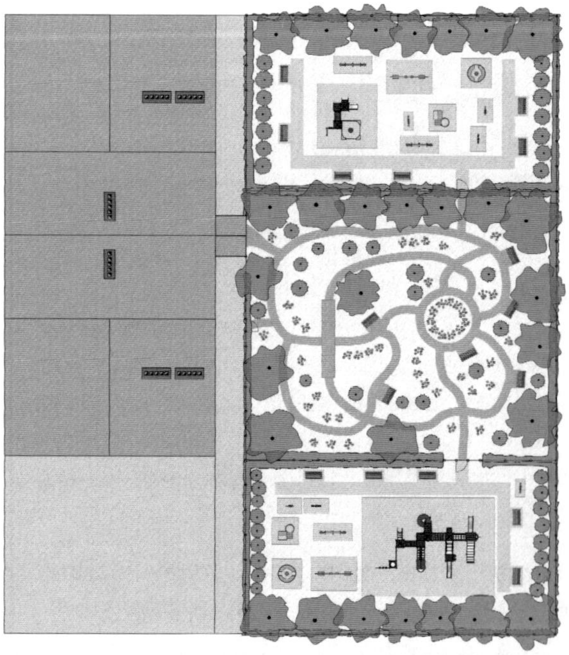

Figure 8: A design of kindergarten facilities corresponding to the CP-graph obtained using the proposed CP-graph grammar system

5. Conclusions

In this paper a graph grammar system, which supports the conceptual stage of designing layouts and arrangement of spaces in educational facilities is considered. The main advantage of such approach is the possibility of adding specialized grammars when a different type of space is required.

This system is equipped with a visual editor, where space layouts representing various arrangements of required areas are presented, and *GraphTool* supporting defining CP-graphs, CP-graph grammar rules, as well as applying them.

Up to now we have considered only one-storey kindergarten buildings. In case of designing higher buildings, the hierarchical CP-graphs will be used to represent their topological structure. In such a CP-graph each hierarchical node represents one floor and contains the CP-graph representing the space arrangement of this floor. At first the designer specifies for each floor the general arrangement of functional areas with places intended for stairs and lifts. These arrangements are represented by CP-graphs, which are further developed by a CP-graph grammar generating CP-graph representations of building floor layouts composed of specific rooms and relations among them.

In the next step of our research, we intend to define a control diagram for the whole graph grammar system. This will require adding "control" productions to the component graph grammars supporting verification of the selection of individual graph grammars in the process of generating complex projects.

The kindergartens presented in this paper are just one of the types of buildings illustrating the advantages of a graph grammar system in their design process. Designing hotel buildings with more demanding requirements is another example that would be worth considering in the framework of a graph grammar system.

References

Grabska, E., Borkowski, A. (1996). Assisting Creativity by Composite Representation. Artificial Intelligence in Design '96, Kluwer Academic Publishers, pp. 743-759.

Rozenberg, G. (1999). Handbook of Graph Grammars and Computing by Graph Transformations, vol.2 Applications, Languages and Tools, World Scientific, London.

Ryszka, I., Grabska, E. (2013). GraphTool - a new System of Graph Generation, ADVCOMP 2013, The Seventh International Conference on Advanced Engineering Computing and Applications in Sciences, ISBN: 978-1-61208-290-5, pp. 79-83.

Grabska, E., Strug. B., Ślusarczyk, G., Grabski W. (2008). Grammar-Based Distributed Design, in L. Rutkowski et al. (eds.), Computational Intelligence: Methods and Applications, EXIT, Warszawa, pp. 493-502.

Csuhaj-Varjú, E., Vaszil. Gy. (2001). On context-free parallel communicating grammar systems: Synchronization, communication, and normal forms. Theoretical Computer Science, 255, pp. 511-538.

Csuhaj-Varjú., E. (2004). Grammar systems: A short survey, Proceedings of Grammar Systems Week 2004, pp. 141-157, Budapest, Hungary.

Strug, B., Ślusarczyk, G., Grabska, E. (2017). A graph-based generative method for supporting bridge design, 24th EG-ICE International Workshop on Intelligent Computing in Engineering (EG-ICE 2017), Nottingham, pp. 294-302.

Grabska, E., Borkowski, A., Palacz, W., Gajek, Sz. (2009). Hypergraph System Supporting Design and Reasoning. In: Wolfgang Huhnt, ed., Computing in Engineering, EG-ICE Conference 2009, pp. 134-141.

Conformance Checking of IFC Models via Semantic BIM Reasoner

Muhammad Fahad, Nicolas Bus
Centre Scientifique et Technique du Batiment (CSTB), 06560 Valbonne, France
{fahad.muhammad, Nicolas.bus}@cstb.fr

Abstract. In the Building Information Modeling world, compliance checking of IFC models is an immense challenge. Many approaches such as Hard Coded Rule Checking, Query based Rule Checking, Rule Checking Approaches via dedicated rule languages (SWRL, Jess, N3Logic, etc., are being contributed to fulfil these requirements. In this paper, we present our research and development of Semantic BIM Reasoner (SBIM-Reasoner) tool for measuring and ensuring conformance of IFC models. SBIM-Reasoner implements multi-threading approach for embedding semantic querying and rule based approach for developing French building code compliance system. Various pre-processors (*IFC2RDF Converter, Geometry Extractor, Rule Evaluator*, etc.) run in different execution threads to build the underlying semantic repository providing faster rule checking and information retrieval from the triple store. When it finds non-compliant objects in the IFC model, it presents them to the end-user. With the knowledge graph over triplets, we have the freedom of extending our semantic IFC model, creation of newer vocabulary and formation of newer rules, concatenation of triplets to build rules with conditions and constraints over IFC data, dynamic reasoning over the triplets based on the initial data of IFC model, etc. We present encouraging results by various tests which were build using online IFC test models of various sizes and designs to test the performance of SBIM-Reasoner.

1. Introduction

Buildings must conform to the building regulations (commonly known as building codes) which are the policies and guidelines to identify the least acceptable level of security, hazards, accessibility, general welfare, etc. (Rebekka and Schultmann, 2014). Through building codes and standards, organizations accomplish their ultimate aim to guard public health, safety and general welfare as they relate to the construction and occupancy of buildings. For an example earthquake-resistant building codes verify building structures so that they can withstand during the seismic activity. The purpose of verifying models is to align several specialized indexations of building components at both sides, assuming that they deal with the same abstract concepts or physical objects, but according to their distinct representation prisms (Eastman et al., 2008). Building Code is vital to detect non-compliance elements in the IFC model (Thein, 2011) and to guarantee its quality and reliability in the entire life-cycle of Building Information Modeling (BIM). Many approaches and tools for the compliance checking of IFC models are being contributed to fulfil these requirements such as; *Hard Coded Rule Checking, Query based Rule Checking* and *Rule Checking via Dedicated Rule Languages* (Pauwels & Zhang, 2015). During our research for the French building codes compliance system, we investigated deeply whether which approach divulges more recompenses for the compliance checking of building codes. According to our exploration, a *hybrid approach* based on semantic querying for the information retrieval and building rule evaluator based on the semantic rule engine produces good results. Therefore, we have implemented a hybrid approach for French building code compliance system named *Semantic BIM Reasoner (SBIM-Reasoner)* which reasons compliance of building codes via semantic reasoning over RDF Triples. Building codes are implemented as SPARQL (2013) queries which run on the semantic repository to verify correctness and consistency of IFC objects in the building model. We use both forward chaining and backward chaining mechanisms (where appropriate) to build our semantic reasoner.

Several newer concepts, SPARQL rules (statements and materialization) are applied to enrich the underlying semantic repository as per demand of verification rules. Use of forward chaining mechanisms support the dynamic semantic verification for the future checks. We build several test cases comprise of different queries on different sizes of IFC models to evaluate our semantic approach. We discuss our experimental findings on many different analysis parameters; such as *number of RDF triples* in the RDF (turtle file) equivalent to IFC model, number of RDF triples in the semantic model (filtered turtle file) in the triple-store, estimated time taken by the *conversion pre-processor* and *geometric pre-processor*, etc. From the initial results, we conclude that SPARQL queries are flexible for retrieving data and perform validation in an optimized way giving better run-time as compared to the traditional approaches.

The rest of paper is organized as follows. Section 2 presents related work. Section 3 presents our research and development of Semantic BIM Reasoner and its different sub-components. Section 4 presents our experimental analysis via using online building models. Section 5 concludes this paper and shows our future directions.

2. Related Work

Many approaches and tools are being contributed to fulfil these requirements. Primarily Hard Coded Rule Checking mechanisms via MVDs are used where building codes are assimilated inside the application for the conformance checking of IFC models (Zhang et al., 2014). Tools such as Solibri Model Checking (Khemlani, 2009), IfcDoc (2012), etc. are contributed are examples of this approach. There are many drawbacks of mvdXML for extracting building views such as: lack of logical formalisms, solely consideration of IFC schema and MVD-based view constructors are not very flexible and dynamic (Mendes de Farias et al., 2016). The subset of the IFC schema needed to satisfy one or many Exchange Requirements of the AEC industry is called Model View Definition (MVD) and mvdXML is an open standard used to publish the concepts and associated rules (Chipman et al., 2016). It can be used with the BIM Server or IfcDoc tool developed by the buildingSMART International to read and write mvdXML and to provide a graphical user interface for defining all content within mvdXML. Due to the limitation of MVD and mvdXML, semantic web technologies have seen as an option which is regarded as a good compromise between development efforts and possibilities. Therefore Query based Rule Checking mechanisms are emerged, where BIM model is interrogated via conformance rules that are formalized directly into SPARQL queries. The contribution from Bouzidi et al. (2012) is regarded as Rule-checking by querying. They transform building model into RDF, create rules as SPARQL queries, and finally interpret query result to visualize the result. Recently Rule Checking Approaches via dedicated rule languages were developed for the rule-based inspection of IFC models for the conformance checking. Most recent contributions use rule languages such as; Wicaksono et al. (2013) based on SWRL rules (Horrocks, 2004), Pauwels et al. (2001) based on N3Logic rules (Berners-Lee, 2008) and M. Kadolsky et al. (2014). We have implemented a hybrid approach (SPARQL + Rule Engine) for French building code compliance system named Semantic BIM Reasoner (*SBIM-Reasoner*) which reasons compliance of building codes via semantic reasoning over RDF Triples. Our work is similar to these proposals as we also make advantage of semantic web technologies, but, we also consider geometric aspects, with focus on optimization and performance. We presented first version of our developed semantic reasoner which was without multi-threading approach (Fahad et al., 2017). This paper presents our optimized solution using multi-threading approach. We build several test cases comprise of different queries on different sizes of IFC models to evaluate our semantic approach. The only overhead is the conversion from an *IFC to RDF* and then storage of RDF triples into triple store which takes time. In a long run, once the triplestore is loaded with the data, querying is much faster to validate IFC models and detect inconsistent non-compliant IFC elements in the building model.

3. Multi-Threaded Semantic Approach for the Conformance Checking of BIM

The main contribution in this paper is about the research and development of *Semantic BIM Reasoner (SBIM-Reasoner)* tool for measuring and ensuring conformance of IFC models. The idea is to formulize building code rule as a SPARQL query and then execute it on the building model, which is formulated as triplestore via forward/backward chaining mechanisms, to check the possibility of non-compliant elements in the building model. Figure 1 illustrates the top level architecture of SBIM-Reasoner. *SBIM-Reasoner* implements multi-threaded approach for embedding semantic querying and rule based approach for developing French building code compliance system. The main thread gets desired IFC models as input and triggers the *Parallel Execution* of *Pre-Processsors* for the execution of different tasks. Primarily it has three pre-processors, i.e., IFC to RDF Converter, Geometry Extractor, and Semantic Preprocessor which has further sub-components named IfcOWL Ontology sub-graph, SPARQL Rules, SPARQL Queries and TripleStore. Finally rule evaluator executes queries over semantic repository to checking and report the conformance report of IFC objects.

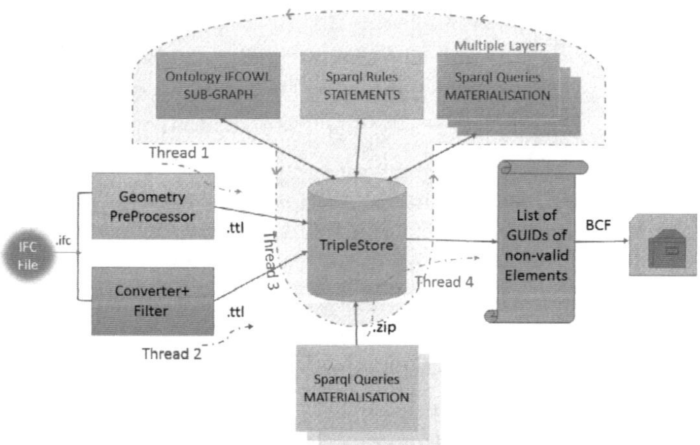

Figure 1: Top level architecture of SBIM-Reasoner

3.1 IFC2RDF Conversion Pre-processor

First thread executes conversion pre-processor to build the initial semantic repository based on RDF triples equivalently converted from an IFC model. Figure 2 shows partial RDF triples of an IfcDoor object. *IFC-to-RDF* is a set of reusable Java component that allows parsing IFC files and converts them into RDF graphs. Our implementation deploys modified version of IFC-to-RDF conversion plug-in provided by Pauwels & Oraskari (2012). After conversion, underlying RDF semantic model acts as a foundation stone to execute all the verification rules. We also need to apply filtration to get an RDF equivalent compact triple file to avoid several IFC elements, such as *Person, Address, Material-List,* etc. Therefore, the same thread did filtration to get only relevant RDF triples from the IFC model.

3.2 Geometric Pre-processor

Second thread executes geometric pre-processor to extract geometric related data from an IFC model. It employs *Geometry Render Engine* to extract geometric information and stores them as RDF triples in the semantic repository. Figure 2 illustrates the output triples corresponding to bounding box values of an IfcDoor object. Mainly there are two geometry render engine plugins available with the *BIM Server* named *IFCOPENSHELL* and *IFC Engine DLL*. These are helpful to extract geometry data about the IFC objects. The outputs of this preprocessor are the RDF triples which are formed from the extracted geometry data of relevant IFC objects. These two pre-processors are executed in parallel to gain time. The advantage of their parallel execution is that none of the threads wait for each other, their functionality is different so they can efficiently utilize the server processor to achieve their desired tasks. These threads propagate their results to the next thread. Once all RDF triples (i.e., Filtered RDF file of an IFC model and RDF triples corresponding to Geometry data) are generated by first and second threads, third thread gets and loads these RDF triples into the triple store for the fast querying, searching, and analyzing of RDF triples.

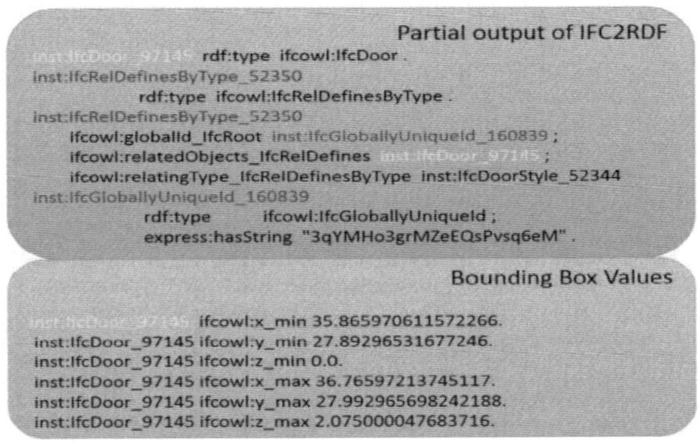

Figure 2: RDF triples corresponding to an IfcDoor object

3.3 Semantic Pre-processor

Third Thread executes to build the semantic repository (i.e., triplestore) with the output of previously discussed two pre-processors. It waits till it is triggered by the outputs of Converter thread and Geometry Extractor thread. It will not start until both the threads finish their execution completely and generate RDF triples. It uploads all the RDF triples to the triplestore. All types of inference and reasoning mechanisms for the semantic verification are applied over this semantic RDF repository to meet the requirements of compliance checking, and in addition to discover additional information that is not explicitly stated in the initial data of the IFC model. We have integrated both forward chaining and backward chaining mechanisms (where appropriate) to build our semantic repository. Several newer concepts, SPARQL rules (statements and materialization) are applied to enrich the underlying semantic repository as per the demand of verification rules. Use of forward chaining mechanisms support the dynamic semantic verification for the future checks. The following are its sub-components.

TripleStore – Stardog. Although IFC is an open standard; its complex nature makes information retrieval difficult from an IFC model when the size of IFC model grows. Therefore, we have used Stardog as a triplestore to build our semantic model so that querying semantic model is faster and gives a good run-time. When the application starts, an end-user provides an IFC model and the set of SPARQL queries which are the verification rules for checking code compliance of desired IFC model. As a result, our system converts an IFC file into filtered RDF model. It loads that converted-filtered IFC equivalent RDF into stardog. After RDF triples concerning geometry are added to capture geometrical information in the triplestore. Then the semantic model is enriched with IfcOWL basic vocabulary, i.e., sub-graph of IFC ontology. Then, it adds SPARQL rules into the triplestore. Finally, it executes our project specific forward chaining SPARQL queries which creates high level vocabulary and builds further RDF graphs over the existing triplets.

IfcOWL ontology sub-graph. As the standard IfcOWL ontology (Terkaj & Pauwels, 2014) has a very large set of IFC elements, therefore, we deal with the sub-graph to achieve better processing and querying performance.

SPARQL Rules – Statements. We have created a large set of SPARQL rules, i.e., statements. In fact, these statements are shortcuts overs the long chain of triplets to enable simplicity. For instance, we created '*intersects*' shortcut over the RDF triplets corresponding to bounded box values of IFC elements (see Figure 3). These statements promote readability, understandability and enable simplicity when creating SPARQL rules and queries. Otherwise the chain of triplets make things complex and ambiguous.

```
PREFIX rule: <tag:stardog:api:rule:>
[] a rule:SPARQLRule ; rule:content """
    IF {
        ?a ifcowl:x_min ?a_xmin . ?a ifcowl:x_max ?a_xmax .
        ?a ifcowl:y_min ?a_ymin . ?a ifcowl:y_max ?a_ymax .
        ?a ifcowl:z_min ?a_zmin . ?a ifcowl:z_max ?a_zmax .
        ?b ifcowl:x_min ?b_xmin . ?b ifcowl:x_max ?b_xmax .
        ?b ifcowl:y_min ?b_ymin . ?b ifcowl:y_max ?b_ymax .
        ?b ifcowl:z_min ?b_zmin . ?b ifcowl:z_max ?b_zmax .
        FILTER((?a_xmin <= ?b_xmax && ?a_xmax >= ?b_xmin) &&
        (?a_ymin <= ?b_ymax && ?a_ymax >= ?b_ymin) &&
        (?a_zmin + 0.1 <= ?b_zmax && ?a_zmax - 0.1 >= ?b_zmin)) .
    } THEN { ?a ifcowl:intersects ?b . } """ .
```

Figure 3: Intersect relation between two IFC objects

SPARQL Queries - Materialization. During the analysis of rules specification, we come across various types of vocabulary (introduced by regulatory texts) during building code compliance application. This vocabulary is composed of high level concepts present in business rules and regulation texts which are familiar by the stakeholders of BIM. There are two methods to build such vocabulary of newer high-level concepts, i.e.; via forwarding chaining and/or backward chaining. Based on the SPARQL rules, we have built SPARQL queries to introduce high level concepts based on the primary IFC vocabulary by using both forward and backward chaining where applicable. Figure 3 shows high level concepts *'intersects'* in our case study of building French code compliance via forward chaining. Backward chaining consists of ontology statements that align IFC concepts with regulatory concepts, whereas forward chaining consists of insert statements that create supplementary triplets. Forward chaining is a good at an implementation stage to save memory and CPU resources. From the machine point of view, backward chaining is processed each time a semantic query is submitted whereas forward chaining is executed each time the data changes. At this stage, this choice is a compromise between effective queries (forward chaining is more appropriate for complex and numerous queries) and model update frequency (backward chaining is more appropriate when data changes frequently). We can even say that it is a compromise between the amount of triplet (considering triplet generated by forward chaining statements) and the ontology complexity. Therefore, we have mixed both approaches backward and forward chaining to provide the optimal setting that minimizes response time and maximizes ontology consistence. With the help of these techniques, we have simplified several IFC patterns such as classifications, predefined types, properties, geometry, topology, etc.

3.4 Rule Evaluator - Compliance Checker

Fourth Thread executes rule evaluator also called compliance checker as it performs the fundamental task of evaluating building model against building codes. It waits till it is triggered by the outputs of third thread that builds semantic repository to fast access triples to fetch data and validate IFC models. It performs SPARQL queries over the semantic repository for the verification and code compliance of an IFC model. An end-user may apply SPARQL ASK and DESCRIBE queries to retrieve relevant information regarding the verification rules. Instead of using IfcDoc tool where there is no intermediate state and no explanation for the reason of non-compliance, we use SPARQL DESCRIBE Queries. The SPARQL DESCRIBE query does not actually return resources matched by the graph pattern of the query, but an RDF graph that "describes" those resources. It is up to the SPARQL query service to choose what triples are included to describe a resource. Therefore, SPARQL queries serve best by concatenating desired triplets for building verification rules to check the code compliance. Figure 5 shows an example of SPARQL query to detect whether an 'Alarm' is installed at some space in the building. This query is based on semantic rules *ifcowl:in and ifcowl:inStorey* which are also shown below the query. Once, it finds an IFC model which is not instatlled with an Alarm (in this example) or non-compliant objects in the IFC model (in other cases), it presents them to the end-user as inconsistent elements in the building model. With the knowledge graph over RDF triples, we have the freedom of extending our semantic IFC model, creation of newer vocabulary and formation of newer rules, concatenation of RDF triples to build rules with condition and constraints over IFC data, dynamic reasoning over the RDF triples based on the initial data of IFC model, etc.

```
SELECT ?name ?gid ?bld
WHERE
{
  ?bld a ifcowl:IfcBuilding ;
  ifcowl:gid ?gid ; ifcowl:oName ?name.
  FILTER NOT EXISTS {
          ?e ifcowl:in ?s . ?s ifcowl:inStorey ?st . ?st ifcowl:inStorey ?bld .
          ?e ifcowl:type ifcowl:IfcAlarmType } .
}

IF {
          ?agr ifcowl:relatedObjects_IfcRelDecomposes ?element1 .
          ?agr ifcowl:relatingObject_IfcRelDecomposes ?element2 .
} THEN {
          ?element1 ifcowl:inStorey ?element2 . }

IF {
       ?r ifcowl:relatedElements_IfcRelContainedInSpatialStructure ?element1 .
       ?r ifcowl:relatingStructure_IfcRelContainedInSpatialStructure ?element2
} THEN {
          ?element1 ifcowl:in ?element2 .   }
```

Figure 4: SPARQL Query build on several shortcuts

4. Implementation and Testing

The following sub-sections elaborate implementation and testing details of SBIM-Reasoner.

4.1 SBIM-Reasoner as a Semantic Service

We have developed *SBIM-Reasoner* as a semantic service inside a KROQI platform. As it is developed especially for the *French building code compliance*, therefore our web interface is also in French targeting French community. When the application starts, an end-user has to configure IFC input model by clicking under the synchronization button on the very first tab 'Maquette'. Then an end-user selects the set of rules to be verified on this input model by selecting/browsing their set of rules on the second tab 'Protocoles'. Then our web service starts by calling semantic reasoner which computes the set of rules and redirects to the result page

'Résultats'. Each of the rule is highlighted as green or red color depending on its status of compliance (see Figure 5a). When *SBIM-Reasoner* detects non-compliant objects (in case of red status), an end-user can further analyze them by clicking on the corresponding row. It displays the list of IFC non-compliant objects containing Name, GUID and Type of each IFC object (see Figure 5b). One can also export PDF and BCF files to analyze their results in detail.

Figure 5: (a) Final output of SBIM-Reasoner, (b) Showing details of inconsistent IFC objects

4.2 Experimental Finding on SBIM-Reasoner

We deployed SBIM-Reasoner service on a cluster kubernetes of 3 nodes (1 node = 1 VM), where each node has 4 vCPUs, 26 GB memory and type of Intel(R) Xeon(R) CPU @ 2.30GHz. We choose several IFC models (see Table 1.) from the online repository to test our *Semantic BIM Reasoner* such as; Chanteloup (17 Mb), AC9R1-Haus (4 Mb), BIM-EM (2 Mb), Candidat (29 Mb), HITOS (63 Mb), and LcD (32 Mb), etc.

Table 1: Size of an IFC model and corresponding number of triples

IFC model	IFC Size (Mb)	No of Triplets	
		RDF Equiv IFC	RDF – Filtered ttl
HITOS	62.5	5,054,202	205,631
AC9R1-Haus	4.4	490,961	10,982
BIM_EM	1.9	275,927	2,138
Candidat-23_04	28.9	694,709	132,115
Chanteloup	17.1	807,250	142,668
LcD	32.4	1627,750	132,845
Bat_CSTB	14.9	1047,216	13,973
Maq Test Checker	11.2	1,572,792	100,230
HAixFlowCtrl	13.1	1,970,366	21,549
Liberty_V3	12.2	1,760,207	86,545

These IFC models vary in size, number of IFC objects, free spaces, etc. We have also used four IFC models developed at our CSTB enterprise named Bat_CSTB (14.9 MB), HAixFlowCtrl (13.1 MB), Maquette Test Checker (11.2 MB) and Liberty (12.2 Mb). Tables 1 shows the size of these IFC models, the number of triples in the RDF equivalent to the original IFC model and the filtered model by IFC2RDF pre-processor. We took many different analysis parameters such as *number of RDF triples* in the RDF (turtle file) equivalent to IFC model, number of RDF triples in the semantic model (filtered turtle file) in the triple-store, estimated time taken by the *conversion pre-processor* and *geometric pre-processor*, etc. We have measured time taken by different *preprocessors* that produce desired output in Table 2. Our first version implementation is without multi-threading where pre-processors run sequentially. Our system gets input of an IFC model along with the rule set to be verified on the building model. It invokes conversion pre-processor, and loads the equivalent RDF triples into triple store. Then it runs the geometric pre-processor and gets the bounding box values (i.e., min/max values X, Y and Z coordinates) and updates the triple store with the geometric RDF triples. Finally Rule Evaluator runs the SPARQL queries to verify the compliance of building codes.

Table 2: Time taken by different Pre-Processors of SBIM-Reasoner

IFC model	IFC Size (Mb)	IFC-to-RDF Conversion (sec)	Geometry Extraction (sec)	Semantic Pre-Proc. (sec)	Rule Evaluator (sec)	Total (sec) version 1	Total (sec) Multi-Threading
HITOS	62.5	205	308	40	10	563	358
AC9R1-Haus	4.4	17	10	9	8	43	33
BIM_EM	1.9	16	10	7	7	40	30
Candidat-23_04	28.9	48	65	27	10	150	102
Chanteloup	17.1	41	31	18	10	100	69
LcD	32.4	97	103	31	9.5	241	144
Batiment_CSTB	14.9	40	27	11	9	87	60
Maq.Test Checker	11.2	32	19	8	8	67	48
HAixFlowCtrl	13.1	39	22	14	9	84	62
Liberty_V3	12.2	38	23	12	9	82	59

Later in our implementation which is the contribution of this paper, we adopted multi-threaded approach where geometric and conversion pre-processors run parallel to produce output RDF triples. In our test experiment, there are IFC models of various sizes and structures. An IFC model named HITOS is the largest building model which has 62.5 Mb size with 205,631 number of RDF triples and BIM_EM is the smallest building model which has 1.9 Mb size with only 2,138 number of RDF triples. When we see the time graph, we observe that *SBIM-Reasoner* took less than a minute by both the pre-processors to achieve their objectives when the size of IFC model is under 15 MB. But when the size of IFC model is 62 MB (in case of huge IFC model Hitos) then it took almost 3.4 minutes to convert and filter, and more than 5 minutes to extract geometry data. Here, we also mention that although pre-processors took time to build semantic model at the first time, but querying for the verification of IFC models are processed fast and a good run-time is achieved. On the other hand on traditional IFC model, it takes much time to verify each of the individual rule. In addition, we are not able to execute all types of rules as per our desire due to narrow scope of IFC tools available online. This is only with the semantic model that we are flexible enough to fetch any triplets and build rules according to our will for the verification of IFC models. We revealed encouraging results via several tests from the initial version of *SBIM-Reasoner*. The results of *SBIM-Reasoner* are checked manually to access the correctness of *SBIM-Reasoner* for each of the building models and they were 100% correct. On the basis of this analysis, we conclude that semantic model serves best for the verification of IFC models. We conclude that for such modules where execution can be done separately, multi-threading can benefit and gain time. It is highly visible when an IFC model is large (in the case of HITOS IFC model), parallel processing and CPU utilization reveals these pre-processors to execute simultaneously resulting the whole process take lesser time to achieve the whole functionality.

5. Conclusion

In the context of BIM when the question about the evaluation of an IFC model appears, the implementation of compliance checking of IFC models is vital to address. It is necessary to detection inconsistent and non-compliant IFC objects to ensure quality and reliability of an IFC model in the entire life-cycle of BIM. Compliance checking is an exhaustive process which cannot be done manually, in addition requires revolutionized advanced technology to process due to complex inherent nature of an IFC model itself. There are many techniques for the automatic verification of IFC models, but, still there are many open challenges. In this paper, we evaluated the idea to formulize building code rule as a semantic SPARQL query and then execute it on the building model to check the possibility of non-compliant elements in the building model. We have built a research prototype named *SBIM-Reasoner* which employs semantic approach for the building code conformance checking. We have tested and concluded that our approach based on semantic queries and rules can be easily extended, configured and deployed for the dynamic and changing BIM environment having broad spectrum of functionalities for the conformance checking of IFC models. We have also analyzed how multi-threaded approach can benefit our solution by comparing run-time of our two implementations with and without threading. We demonstrated several test models on *SBIM-Reasoner* and presented its efficiency and efficacy with empirical results. We conclude that the semantic model based on the semantic web technology is a good compromise between development efforts and opportunities. The graphical representation of RDF allows rules to be more intuitive and more efficient to reason and execute. Concatenation of triplets allows flexibility of making wide range of verification rules with condition and constraints at ease. SPARQL has a global scope with larger visibility of querying with the built-in functions and support of intermediate calculations for the validation of IFC models.On the basis of several analysis parameters, we have shown encouraging results by several tests on the *SBIM-Reasoner*. We have also found that multi-threading based approach served best and provided faster computation for the conformance checking of IFC models.

References

Building Smart, International home of openBIM, https://www.buildingsmart.org/standards/ [last access: jan 2019]

Bouzidi, K. R., Fies, B., Faron-Zucker, C., Zarli, A. and Thanh N. Le. (2012), "Semantic Web Approach to Ease Regulation Compliance Checking in Construction Industry", Future Internet, Special Issue Semantic Interoperability and Knowledge Building, 4 (3). pp. 830-851.

Chipman, T., Liebich, T., and Weise, M. (2016) "mvdXML specification of a standardized format to define and exchange MVD with exchange requirements and validation Rules," version 1.1 Final, Febrary 2016. Available at: http://www.buildingsmart-tech.org/downloads/mvdxml /mvdxml-1.1/final/mvdxml-1-1-documentation

Eastman, C., Teicholz, P., Sacks, R., and Liston, K. (2008). "BIM Handbook: A Guide to Building Information Modeling for Owners, Managers, Designers, Engineers, and Contractors," Hoboken, New Jersey, Wiley, 2008.

Fahad, M., Bus, N., Fies, B. (2014). "Semantic BIM Reasoner for the verification of IFC Models", eWork and eBusiness in Architecture, Engineering and Construction: ECPPM 2017, Denmark

Friedman-Hill, E. (2003). "Jess in Action: Rule Based Systems in Java," Manning Publications. ISBN 1-930110-89-8, 2003

Horrocks, I., Patel-Schneider, P.F., Boley, H., Tabet, S., Grosof, B., and Dean, M. (2004). "SWRL: A Semantic Web Rule Language Combining OWL and RuleML".

IfcDoc Tool (2012), available at: http://www.buildingsmart-tech.org/specifications/specification-tools/IfcDoc-tool/IfcDoc-help-page-section/IfcDoc.pdf [last access: jan 2019]

Kadolsky, M., Baumgärtel, K., and Scherer, R.J. (2014). "An ontology framework for rule-based inspection of eeBIM-systems," Procedia Engineering. vol. 85, pp. 293-301, doi:10.1016/j.proeng.2014.10.554.

Khemlani L. (2009). "Solibri model checker," AECbytes Product Review March 31, 2009

Berners-Lee, T., Connolly, D., Kagal, L., Scharf, Y., and Hendler, J. (2008). "N3Logic: A logical framework for the World Wide Web," Theory and Practice of Logic Programming. vol. 8 (3), pp. 249-269, doi:10.1017/S1471068407003213.

Mendes de Farias, T., Roxin, A., and Nicolle, C. (2016) "A Semantic Web Approach for defining Building Views," buildingSMART Summit Jeju, Korea.

Pauwels, P. and Oraskari, J. (2012) "IFC-to-RDF Converter" https://libraries.io/github/IDLabResearch/IFC-to-RDF-converter, [last access: jan 2019]

Pauwels, P. & Zhang, S. (2015). "Semantic Rule-Checking for regulation compliance checking: An overview of strategies and approaches". Proc. of the 32nd CIB W78 Conference, Netherlands.

Pauwels, P., Deursen, D. Van, Verstraeten, R., Roo, J. De, Meyer, R. De, Walle, R. Van de, and Campenhout, J. Van (2011). "A semantic rule checking environment for building performance checking," Automation in Construction. 20 (5), pp. 506-518.

Rebekka, J.S., and Schultmann F. (2014). "Building Information Modeling (BIM) for existing buildings—Literature review and future needs," Automation in construction, vol. 38, pp. 109-127, 2014, doi: 10.1016/j.autcon.2013.10.023

SPARQL Query Language for RDF (2013), http://www.w3.org/TR/rdf-sparql-query/ [last access: jan 2019]

Thein, V. (2011). Industry Foundation Classes (IFC), "BIM Interoperability through a Vendor-Independent File Format," A Bentley White Paper, September'11.

Terkaj, W., and Pauwels, P. (2014). "IfcOWL ontology file for IFC4". Available at: http://linkedbuildingdata.net/resources/IFC4_ADD1.owl [last access: jan 2019]

Wicaksono, H., Dobreva, P., Häfner, P., and Rogalski, S. (2013) "Ontology development towards expressive and reasoning-enabled building information model for an intelligent energy management system," Proc. of the 5th KEOD, pp. 38-47, SciTePress.

Zhang, C., Beetz, J. & Weise, M. (2014). "Model view checking: automated validation for IFC building models". In Mahdavi, ed. eWork and eBusiness in Architecture, Engineering and Construction: ECPPM'14.

Distributed manufacturer services to provide product data on the web

André Hoffmann[1], Anna Wagner[1], Tim Huyeng[1], Meiling Shi[1], Julian Wengzinek[2], Wendelin Sprenger[2], Christoph Maurer[3], Uwe Rüppel[1]

1: Institut für Numerische Methoden und Informatik im Bauwesen, Technische Universität Darmstadt, Darmstadt, Germany
2: Zentrale Technik, Direktion Digitalisierung und Software-Engineering (DS)-BIM.5D, Ed. Züblin AG, Stuttgart, Germany
3: Department Energy Efficient Buildings, Fraunhofer Institute for Solar Energy Systems ISE, Freiburg, Germany
hoffmann@iib.tu-darmstadt.de

Abstract. Digital planning methods are changing the needs of construction stakeholders. It should be as easy as possible to compare product data from different manufacturers and integrate them into the planning model without detours. Web technologies not only offer great potential to enhance existing ways of working, but also open up new business models for product manufacturers in the service and IOT domains. However, manufacturers have a legitimate interest to retain control over the disclosure of their product data. Therefore, it is often only available offline and on demand. Of technical interest are therefore solutions, in which a large part of the data autonomy and access control remains on the side of the manufacturer, but the project planner is allowed to search the product data of all manufacturers like an interconnected system. Frequently, such a searchability is ensured by a uniform data schema and storage of the data in a central storage location, a so-called data warehouse. Nonetheless, this stands in contrast to the natural interest of the manufacturer for data sovereignty. This paper focuses on systems that can replace centralized data storage with distributed data management on manufacturer-owned servers, without losing accessibility for planners. Manufacturers should have as much freedom of implementation as possible when establishing the security concept, modeling their data and integrating the proposed approach into their operating procedure.

1. Introduction

Information silos are a source of inefficiencies (Pala et al., 2016: 897); they result in existing solutions to problems not being found and used. Particularly in the relationship between manufacturer and customer, both sides are affected. On the one hand, the customer cannot identify whether an advertised product is better suited for a purchase than a comparable product based on the provided information. Under certain circumstances, this may lead to no or an insufficient solution being found. The manufacturer, on the other hand, loses a potential buyer.

In the construction industry, dismantling data silos of stakeholders is an important task. Currently, suppliers and specialist engineers from various disciplines exchange geometries in the form of 3D models enriched with semantic information (Pala et al., 2016: 900).

The quality of the data transfer although depends on the import module of the specialist engineer's proprietary software. The software interoperability often stands in contrast to the interest of the software developer, who supports proprietary formats that only allow further processing of the data with software applications from his own product catalog, if at all. One solution to exchange building data in an open and efficient way is the Industry Foundation Classes Standard (IFC). The IFC is supported by about 150 software applications worldwide to enable better work flows for the AEC industry[1]. Additionally, ontologies are examined in

[1] http://www.buildingsmart-tech.org/ (accessed: 01.04.2019)

numerous publications to integrate data models from various areas of engineering (Pauwels *et al.* 2017).

The flexibility and simplicity of the representation in the form of triples allow to model even complex interrelationships in a human- and machine-understandable way. Therefore, this technology presents at least a partial solution to the interoperability problem.

Another problem is the lack of a standardized dissemination process of the BIM objects. Manufacturers often rely on isolated solutions on their own websites or prefer the path of direct distribution. Centralized websites apparently lack manufacturer acceptance, which limits the number of products made available. However on bimobject.com, according to its web presence the "Worlds Leading BIM Content Platform", product families of about 1352 brands can be accessed[2].

In this paper, an approach to distribute product data on the Web without using a central platform and to leave the persistent product data on the side of the manufacturer is discussed. Each manufacturer hosts their own product data service, which is linked to other product data services by message exchange and passes on queries to all other service instances. Queries to the entire system can be directed to any of the manufacturer services, to guarantee independence from a central instance. The global data model is based on a product ontology and serves to compare and link product data.

Decentralization and the freedom to design the implementation of manufacturer services should increase the acceptance of manufacturers. A product ontology reduced to the essentials, which can be linked with domain-specific ontologies if required, should guarantee searchability and comparability.

2. Related Work

Architects and engineers have various central platforms at their disposal for the acquisition of BIM data. When researching the availability of BIM / CAD objects via open-access portals, the highly decentralized distribution of these objects was particularly noticeable. The number of large portals alone, in which objects of numerous manufacturers can be found, amounts to almost 20. If websites with manufacturer-specific content that are linked in the Autodesk BIM blog[3] are included in this estimate, more than 50 portals were identified. However, usually no information about the topicality and completeness of the content on the portals is available.

In addition, platforms often only offer strongly limited possibilities to filter the complete data base in search for specific objects. In most cases, such filtering is restricted to manufacturer of the object, some BIM object types and file formats. Manufacturer-specific pages usually offer a download of their entire library without allowing the user to select singular objects beforehand. Apart of object platforms, platforms to facilitate the exchange of product and other project data between suppliers and other parties involved in the construction process have already been proposed. Vortalway is conceived to be a central cloud solution into which other services can be integrated if required (Grilo and Jardim-Goncalves 2013). Their focus was primarily on mapping the bidding process in order to offer or request a service or a product. These also include ontologies at the conceptual level to solve the interoperability problem (He et al., 2018: 18).

---

[2] https://www.bimobject.com/en (accessed: 01.04.2019)

[3] https://blogs.autodesk.com/bimblog/revit-content-online-bibliotheken-mit-10-000en-familien-als-download-beitrag-wird-regelmasig-aktualisiert/ (accessed: 01.04.2019)

The networking of manufacturers to offer a service of common benefit is a research idea that already has tradition. A so-called virtual enterprise is "a temporary alliance of enterprises that come together to share skills or core competencies and resources in order to better respond to business opportunities, and whose cooperation is supported by computer networks" (Camarinha-Matos and Afsarmanesh 1999). Under this topic, the OSMOS API was proposed in the construction industry. The OSMOS API pursued a project-related approach of cooperation, but also relied on a centralized platform (Wilson *et al.* 2001).

This paper's content overlaps also with the field of Enterprise Application Integration, which aims to link applications on an internal or inter-company level in order to preserve resources and knowledge that were invested in existing applications for future purposes. A number of methods, architectural concepts and standards for fulfilling this goal are classified under as such Enterprise Application Integration (Arndt *et al.* 2009).

Furthermore, concepts for describing distributed semantic web architectures have been analyzed in the literature (Vdovjak *et al.* 2006). The hierarchical mediator architecture (see Figure 1) comes closest to the approach underlying this paper (Vdovjak et al., 2006: 44-51). The features provided in the theoretical concept could be simplified with knowledge of the existing data model.

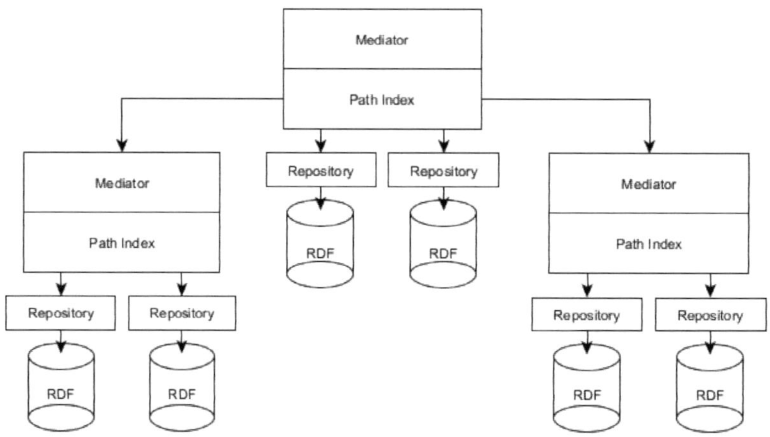

Figure 1: Hierarchical mediator architecture (adapted from Vdovjak *et al.* 2006: 45)

3. Concept

The basic idea of the approach presented in this paper is a network of manufacturer data services. Each of the data services provides product descriptions that contain information, which originated in the design and production phase and are therefore in the manufacturers' responsibility. Each data service can be integrated into a manufacturer's service infrastructure, for example via an API gateway that orchestrates requests and forwards them to the data service. The data service has two interfaces: a network and a query interface. The network API is used for communication with other manufacturer data services while the query API enables users and third-party systems to send queries to the entire network of manufacturer data services. The manufacturer data services exchange messages to answer queries like a related system. Thus, the same comparison and search possibilities of centralized platforms should be provided. In the context of distributed database systems, this property is referred to as network transparency (Özsu and Valduriez, 2011: 9).

The users and applicatons, that query the network, should not have to deal with the internal architecture and the exact location of the product data. To ensure this transparency, queries to one data service must be forwarded to all other data services relevant to the queries. This must be realized on horizontal and vertical level (see Figure 2). For query distribution on horizontal level, all data services that contain the desired product type must be queried, and the results of the query passed on to the user. On the other hand, parts of the affected queries must also be passed on vertically: Construction products consist of materials and parts from suppliers and should therefore be regarded as assemblies. Suppliers can themselves operate data services in which they provide information on their products. Ergo, queries about specific products can also refer to data stored on the suppliers' data services. In order for the data service to know which data services can be found at which addresses and what type of information they contain, a data catalog must exist that stores such information on each data service and must be synchronized if changes are made. The data service can be integrated into the manufacturer's own infrastructure to offer additional services. For example, the data can be preprocessed by a company's own web services depending on the use case. If, for example, a certain format is required, the web service responsible for processing sends the request to an interface to the overall system.

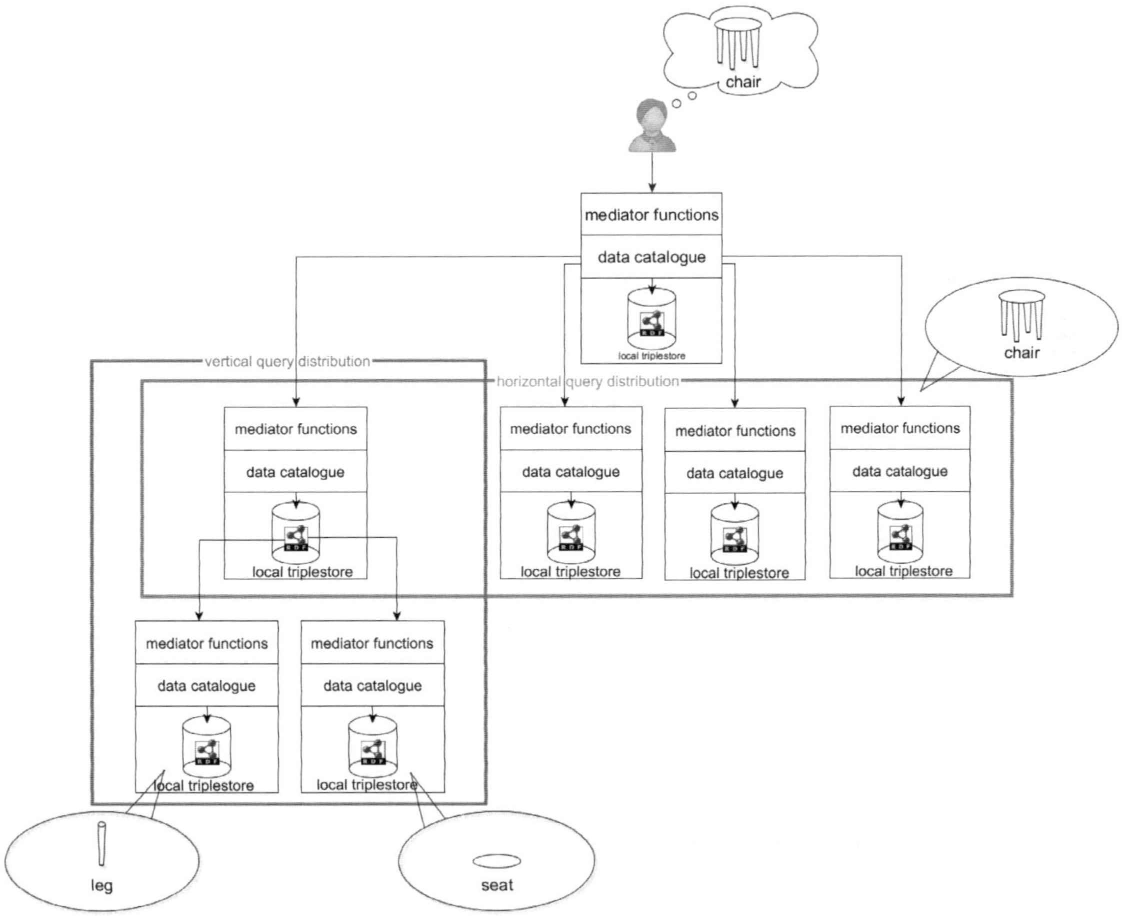

Figure 2: Vertical and horizontal query distribution

4. Data model

To enable communication of distributed and possibly not uniformly designed systems, machine-understandable data schemes are required. This also applies to the cross-platform product searches presented in this paper. It is therefore required for product data to be described using Building Product Ontology[4] (Wagner, A. 2019).

The BPO provides concepts for describing the basic structure of products, while additional information – such as the geometric description or classification of components, products and properties – is connected by other ontologies. For manufacturers, the property of BPO that products can be described in their composition in the form of components and assembly compounds is particularly interesting. Especially the latter enables manufacturers to reuse already existing descriptions of components that are parts of their products. For example, a manufacturer can link directly to the supplier's description of a screw or even complex components such as a door handle or window frame instead of remodeling it based on information received from suppliers in their own data environment.

Such linking functions by the property of the Semantic Web that all objects are occupied by a Unified Resource Identifier (URI) and can be accessed over this also from outside of the original graph to the objects either directly or by performing queries on the graph's database. In the BPO, the assembly connection relevant for this is implemented with the predicate bpo:consistsOf, which connects an assembly with any (also external) component and suggests that the component is installed as part of the product. An exemplary graph for the visualization of such a connection is shown in Figure 3.

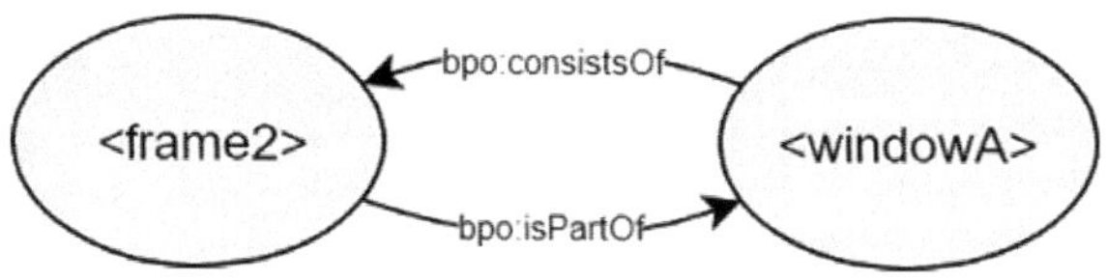

Figure 3: Example Relation between Products and Components

5. Dataservice: Components and processes

An data service consists of two functional components. One component is the so-called *query federator*, that applies the requested product data types to the data catalog to check which data service should be considered for querying. The *query federator* also forwards user queries to the corresponding data services identified in the previous step, and returns the summarized result to the user.

The second component is the *query responder*, which checks requests from other instances to identify whether data from suppliers is required to answer the requests and distributed the part of the query to all instances needed to fully describe the relevant product. The queries addressed to the APIs are formulated in the query language SPARQL. Alternatively, a format can be used that is transformed to a SPARQL query.

[4] https://w3id.org/bpo, accessed 31.05.2019

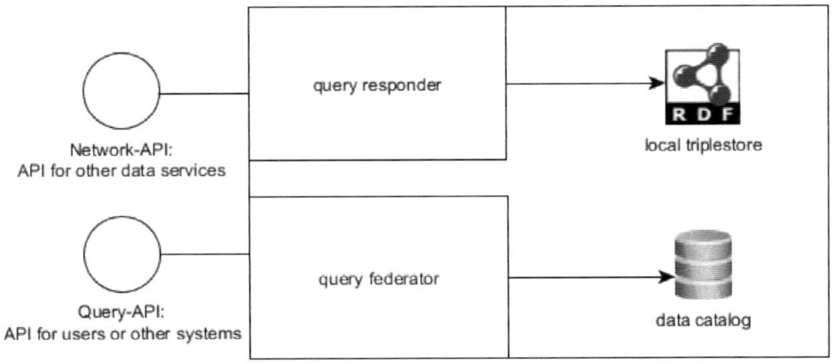

Figure 4: Architecture of a data service

5.1 Data catalog and synchronising

The data catalog is stored locally in each data service. It contains addresses of all data services and the product data types that are stored on them according to the buildingSMART Data Dictionary (bSDD). This metadata can be used to identify and request data services that are relevant for a query. If a new data service is added to the overall system or if a change is made to the product data types provided at a data service, a synchronization process must start. Such a process could be executed either traditionally by sending corresponding messages or - in case additional security is desired, that the data catalog is not manipulated and at every manufacturer the same – by implementing the data catalog synchronization with a blockchain. In essence, a blockchain is a chain of chronological blocks which is maintained by the nodes of a public or permissioned distributed network. By design, it is well suited for systems that require integrity, transparency and immutability (Wüst and Gervais 2018).

In this section the suitability of applying blockchain technology to data catalog synchronization will be analyzed. On implementing the data catalog which exists locally in distributed data services, following requirements must be fulfilled: First, data catalogs that are stored in distinct sites should be in a consistent state. That means changes in data catalog that are made locally must be synchronized in all other data services through the internet. In database management system these changes are documented as transaction logs. The synchronization process through multiple data services can be performed by the broadcast function of blockchain. Transaction logs will be wrapped up in a block and sent to all data services to synchronize; Second, unintended changes, including data altering with malicious intent and hardware breakdown, must be detected and avoided to guarantee data integrity. With suitable consensus mechanism manufacturer can give their approvals or rejections to a transaction log in data catalog so that unintended changes can be obviated; Third, information needs to be available when it is queried from outside of a data service. Blockchain is an art of distributed ledger that is maintained in every data service. If one data service falls down, queries can be sent to other data services. For the above mentioned reasons, blockchain is suitable to store an immutable record of transaction logs for distributed database (Sutton and Samavi 2017) (Aniello *et al.* 2017) that keeps the product data catalogs integral and available.

Apart from the requirements which are mentioned above, following aspects should also be taken into account. If multiple manufacturers update their catalogs simultaneously, all changes must be synchronized without high latency. Besides, executions – including meta data as author and timestamp – should be documented and traceable to avoid allegations in case of hostile alterations in the database. Furthermore, manufactures should only have writing access to their own product data catalog entries. To fulfill those requirements, a concept for deploying product data catalog synchronization with blockchain is presented (see Figure 5).

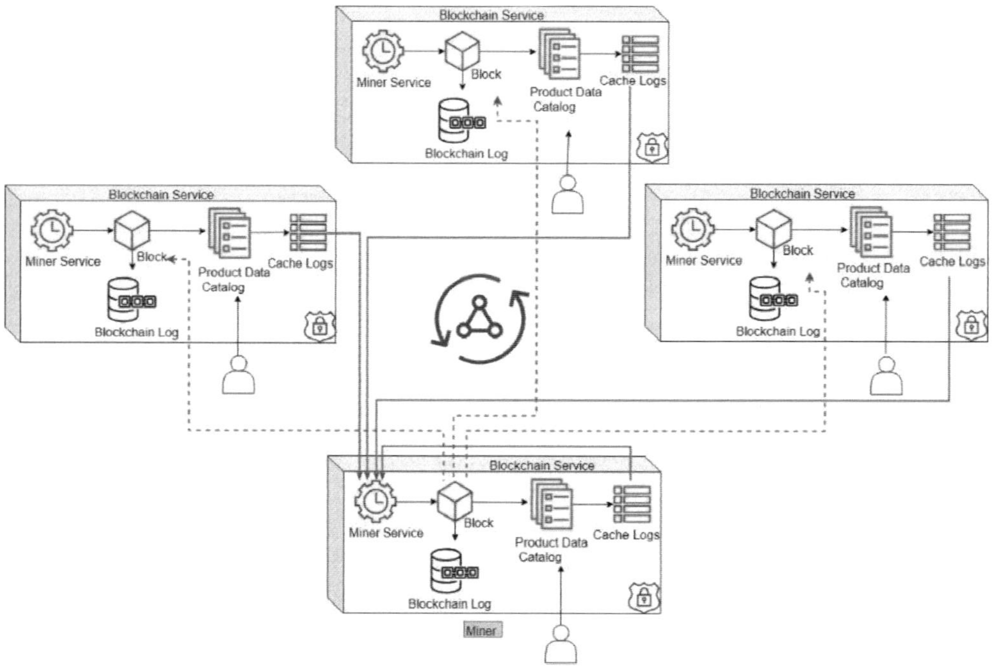

Figure 5: Concept for synchronization with blockchain

Similar to (Gaetani *et al.* 2017), we propose to use the mining rotation consensus to "mine" (generate) a block: First, a timespan will be defined to be round for generating one block. Each round, a miner is chosen by a pseudorandom generator. During the round, all executed transactions that are stored locally in "Cache Logs", including their timestamps, are sent to the "Miner Service" of miner this round. At the end of each round, the miner confirms all received transactions by signing with his digital private key and wrapping them with the cryptographic hash of the previous block as well as the timestamp of the round in a new block. Afterwards, a new hash is generated from this new block and is added to itself. After this mining process, the miner broadcasts the newly generated block to all nodes to verify its correctness. As soon as all nodes have confirmed the block with their individual digital cryptographic signature, the block can be appended to the original local blockchain "Blockchain Log" and execute the transaction logs in local "Product Data Catalog". The blockchain being maintained by a distributed instead of a centralized network also improves database security; if one node crashes or is attacked the transactions will not get lost. To ensure manufactures being restricted to edit their own product data catalog entries only, a smart contract can be applied. Smart contracts are part of the blockchain protocol and define who can update which entries in the product catalog.

5.2 Distributing queries vertically

The following section describes the algorithm for processing requests that require information about components originating from the supplier's data service. For example, queries of products may refer to specific properties that might be part of a subcomponent's description which is provided by the supplier's data service . To address the complete query, the part of the query that refers to the subproduct must be identified and processed accordingly. The results of both queries can be temporarily merged to answer the original query.

The separation can be realized by using the analogy of data model and data service structure. Products are linked to their subcomponents with the predicate bpo:consistsOf. In order to find queries that relate to several data service, a first step is to check whether the query can be answered completely by the data available on the current data service. If this is not the case, the query is shortened by the triples that use the object of the last bpo:consistsOf relationship as subject until the query can be resolved. The response of the shortened query is checked for references to other data services. Since Linked Data uses URIs as identifier for individual objects, the location of an object's description is stored in the data model. This allows the data service of a product to be identified directly from the result of a query.

The triples that could not be resolved in the original query can now be passed on to the referenced data services as a construct query. SPARQL construct queries allow the extraction of a subgraph that corresponds to the template specified within the query in the form of triples. The resulting subgraph of this construct query can be merged with the triples that match the solvable triples of the local triple store, forming a graph which has all information to answer the original incoming query. The complete process can be seen in Figure 6. The construct query itself is treated as an incoming query by the supplier data service, in which the same process is repeated. In this way, requests of this type are answered recursively by all concerned data services. The process only has to take place if the query is fed by the *query federator* of another data service. The module responsible for this is called *query responder*.

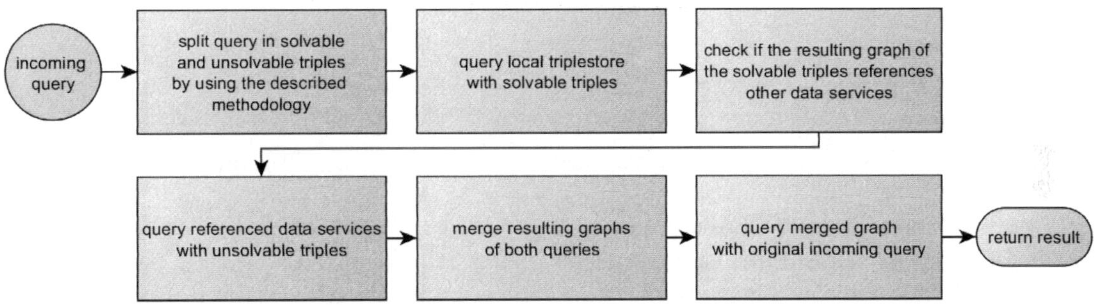

Figure 6: Algorithm to dissolve queries to subcontractors

5.3 Integration into the manufacturer's infrastructure

The presented service can be implemented with the help of a microservice architecture and can also be integrated into existing systems. Microservices are small processes that communicate with other processes via HTTP or a REST API (Dragoni *et al.* 2017). With microservices, a large application can be broken down into small applications that can be combined independently. These smaller applications can be used or replaced flexibly and organized as containers. Overall, the architecture of microservices is more complex than one of a monolithic system, but the scalability and flexibility of this approach outweigh the disadvantage. In the context of the presented work, flexibility is an advantage, since the presented decentralized data storage should be gradually integrated into existing manufacturer systems.

Of importance for the decentralized structure is a clear definition of interfaces between the individual services. Communication could be implemented via HTTP requests or other protocols and must be protected from external attacks.

One way of securing the individual services is an API gateway. Such gateways serve as entry points for a number of microservices, e.g., from manufacturers (see Figure 7). The gateway can authenticate a request with the help of an authentication service and distribute it to the corresponding services. As seen in Figure 7 microservices can also communicate with other services outside of their system. Therefore, it is recommended to use the API gateway from the other manufacture. If requests within one system occur, they can be processed either via the gateway or directly from service to service.

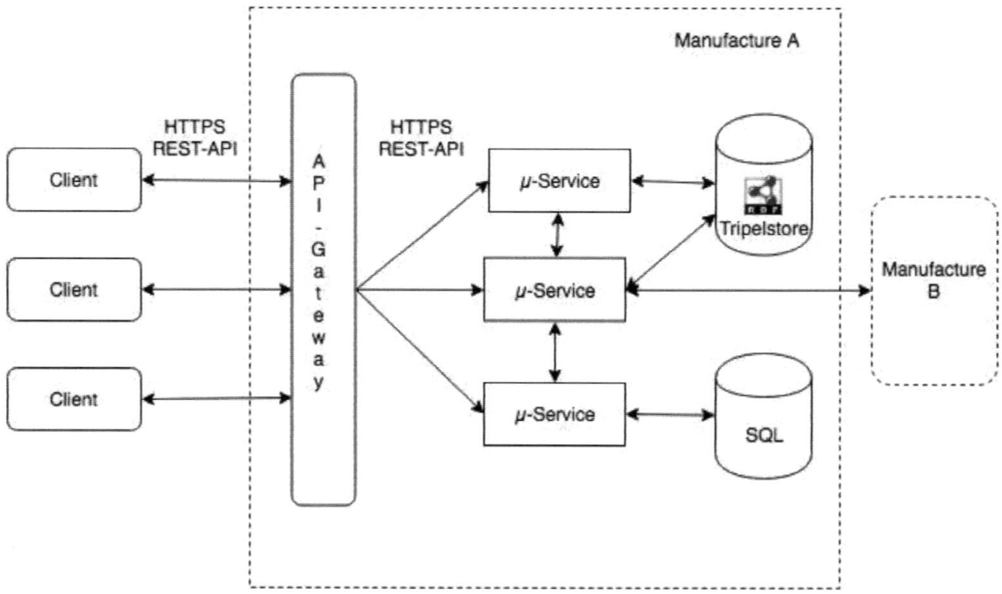

Figure 7: Micro-Service architecture, distribution via API gateways

Thanks to the microservice architecture, the integration of the dataservice into existing systems as well as maintenance and utilization for companies are simplified. Smaller companies, that cannot – or do not want to – provide all necessary services because of their internal structure, can also use and integrate other services. For example, computational services could be outsourced to a specialist who has optimized the specific service. Based on outsourcing processes, a new line of business can emerge, since high-performance services from other manufacturers could be used and the use of the service can be sold. However, data encryption must be ensured for enhancing acceptance and trust between individual stakeholders.

5.4 Authentification

An important component for increasing the confidence of manufacturers and users in micro-services is the authentication of partners. Since the concept proposed in this paper stores the data decentrally, it is essential to ensure unique identification. For this an authentication service is proposed, which can be outsourced to an own microservice if desired by the manufacturers.

This would enable central registration and prevent unwanted multiple logons to the various services and manufacturer instances. There are several possibilities for authentication: In addition to a single sign-on implementation, it is also possible to perform authentication with client certificates, API keys or a public and private keypair. Authorization can be connected to this service or can also be performed on any data service. Here, the individual manufacturers could assign rights to the respective users.

Another advantage of using microservices is the freedom of implementation. A free choice of programming languages as well as packages increases the potential to advance the manufacturers' own developments. In addition, the independent microservices can be deployed more easily and efficiently as containers. Current technologies, such as dockers, are available for this purpose (Stubbs *et al.* 2015).

6. Conclusion and Perspective

So far, parts of the functionalities have been implemented in an experimental manner in order to become familiar with the technologies and to gain an overview of the conceptual requirements for the architecture of the system. As a result of this effort, in the present paper, a concept for a distributed network of manufacturer services was presented, which enables stakeholders to search product data of all manufacturers as if it was a centralized system. One advantage of this decentralized data management is its reproduction of the natural distribution and thus guarantees manufacturers data autonomy. If interested, manufacturers can set up data services and integrate them into their own infrastructure. Thus, the overall system and the internal database of a manufacturer can grow modularly. Here, no single point of failure exists, since the entire network can be accessed via any manufacturer data service and all data services are to be regarded as equivalent. The hierarchical query processing results from the assembly structure of the product data model and, thereby, fits into the decentralized system architecture. Two sources of inefficiencies in the hierarchical mediator architecture should be mentioned (Vdovjak et al., 2006: 49-51), which also apply to the proposed approach: If, for example, a product is a subcomponent of more than one product, the information of the subcomponent is queried several times. Even if subcomponents refer to products that lie further up in the component hierarchy, inefficiencies can occur. The transition to a cooperative mediator architecture , which introduces additional communication channels between the data services, could create remedy here. The architecture of the communication channels could be justified by certain product data types on the data services and functional domains. In addition to the data services themselves, further microservices are to be created in the context of the research project SCOPE. Those services are to be understood as blueprints for various tasks in civil engineering and include, for example, processing routines for data from the BPO data model in planning software formats.

Acknowledgements

This work is part of the research project EnOB: SCOPE, founded by the German Federal Ministry for Economic Affairs and Energy (BMWi).

References

Aniello, L., Baldoni, R., Gaetani, E., Lombardi, F., Margheri, A. and Sassone, V. (2017). A Prototype Evaluation of a Tamper-Resistant High Performance Blockchain-Based Transaction Log for a Distributed Database. *2017 13th European Dependable Computing Conference (EDCC)*. pp. 151–154.

Arndt, C., Hermanns, C., Kuchen, H. and Poldner, M. (2009). *Best Practices in Der Softwareentwicklung*.

Camarinha-Matos, L.M. and Afsarmanesh, H. (eds.) (1999). The Virtual Enterprise Concept. *Infrastructures for Virtual Enterprises*. Boston, MA: Springer US.

Coelho, N. (2018). Security in Microservices Architectures.

Dragoni, N., Giallorenzo, S., Lafuente, A.L., Mazzara, M., Montesi, F., Mustafin, R. and Safina, L. (2017). Microservices: Yesterday, Today, and Tomorrow. In: Mazzara, M. and Meyer, B. (eds.). *Present and Ulterior Software Engineering*. Cham: Springer International Publishing, pp. 195–216.

Gaetani, E., Aniello, L., Baldoni, R., Lombardi, F., Margheri, A. and Sassone, V. (2017). Blockchain-based database to ensure data integrity in cloud computing environments. *Italian Conference on Cybersecurity (20/01/17)*.

Grilo, A. and Jardim-Goncalves, R. (2013). Cloud-Marketplaces: Distributed e-procurement for the AEC sector. *Advanced Engineering Informatics* **27**(2):160–172. doi: https://doi.org/10.1016/j.aei.2012.10.004.

He, D., Li, Z., Wu, C. and Ning, X. (2018). An E-Commerce Platform for Industrialized Construction Procurement Based on BIM and Linked Data. *Sustainability* **10**(8):2613. doi: https://doi.org/10.3390/su10082613.

Özsu, M.T. and Valduriez, P. (2011). *Principles of Distributed Database Systems*. 3rd ed. New York: Springer Science+Business Media.

Pala, M., Edum-Fotwe, F., Ruikar, K., Peters, C. and Doughty, N. (2016). Implementing commercial information exchange: a construction supply chain case study. *Construction Management and Economics* **34**(12):898–918. doi: https://doi.org/10.1080/01446193.2016.1211718.

Pauwels, P., Zhang, S. and Lee, Y.-C. (2017). Semantic web technologies in AEC industry: A literature overview. *Automation in Construction* **73**:145–165. doi: https://doi.org/10.1016/j.autcon.2016.10.003.

Stubbs, J., Moreira, W. and Dooley, R. (2015). Distributed Systems of Microservices Using Docker and Serfnode. *2015 7th International Workshop on Science Gateways*. pp. 34–39.

Sutton, A. and Samavi, R. (2017). Blockchain Enabled Privacy Audit Logs. In: d'Amato, C., Fernandez, M., Tamma, V., Lecue, F., Cudré-Mauroux, P., Sequeda, J., Lange, C., et al. (eds.). *The Semantic Web – ISWC 2017*. Springer International Publishing, pp. 645–660.

Vdovjak, R., Houben, G.-J., Stuckenschmidt, H. and Aerts, A. (2006). RDF and Traditional Query Architectures. In: Staab, S. and Stuckenschmidt, H. (eds.). *Semantic Web and Peer-to-Peer: Decentralized Management and Exchange of Knowledge and Information*. Berlin, Heidelberg: Springer Berlin Heidelberg, pp. 41–58.

Wagner, A., Rüppel., U. (2019). BPO: The Building Product Ontology for Assembled Products. *7th Linked Data in Architecture and Construction Workshop*. Lisbon: PT. in press.

Wilson, I., Harvey, S., Vankeisbelck, R. and Kazi, A.S. (2001). Enabling The Construction Virtual Enterprise: The Osmos Approach. *Journal of Information Technology in Construction*

6(Special issue Information and Communication Technology Advances in the European Construction Industry):83–110.

Wüst, K. and Gervais, A. (2018). Do you Need a Blockchain? *2018 Crypto Valley Conference on Blockchain Technology (CVCBT)*. pp. 45–54.

An automated approach for point cloud alignment based on density histograms

Jan Martens, Jörg Blankenbach
Geodetic Institute and Chair for Computing in Civil Engineering & Geo Information Systems, RWTH Aachen University, Germany
jan.martens@gia.rwth-aachen.de, blankenbach@gia.rwth-aachen.de

Abstract. Building Information Modeling is growing more relevant as digital models are not only used during the construction phase but also throughout the building's life cycle. The digital representation of geometric, physical and functional properties enables new methods for planning, execution and operation. Digital models of existing buildings are commonly derived from surveying data such as laser scanning which needs to be processed either manually or automatically throughout various steps. Aligning point clouds along a coordinate system's main axes is a common manual task benefitting subsequent manual and automated processing steps. With the intention of automating the alignment task, we hereby present an enhanced approach based on point density histograms. Our results show that this approach is computationally cheap, robust towards non-uniform point cloud resolutions and clutter as well as easy to integrate into existing BIM modelling software.

1. Introduction

The rise of Building Information Modeling (BIM) in recent years has led to a gradual paradigm shift in the AECO industry. With BIM providing a digital representation of all geometrical, physical and functional characteristics of buildings and constructions, it offers the opportunity of sharing information and tracking object states throughout the building life cycle. Therefore, object-oriented models, so called BIM models, are used. Up to now BIM has been predominantly used during the planning phase. However, solutions for using BIM during the execution and operation phase gain an increasing relevance. The benefits of using them e.g. for facility management (FM) or building preservation has earned BIM methods wide-spread interest. Problematically, creating BIM models from existing buildings without the existence of digital data or even digital models from planning is a costly procedure and requires trained staff. For this purpose, recent surveying techniques such as laser scanning or photogrammetry promise a lot of potential for as-is/as-built data capturing since they allow reality capturing with a high spatial resolution in a short period of time. However, laser scanning results in huge amounts of data in the form of point clouds which have to be analyzed for BIM modeling in a time-consuming process that is still characterized by much manual work. This has led to increased interest in techniques which either fully or partially automate the modeling process from point clouds.

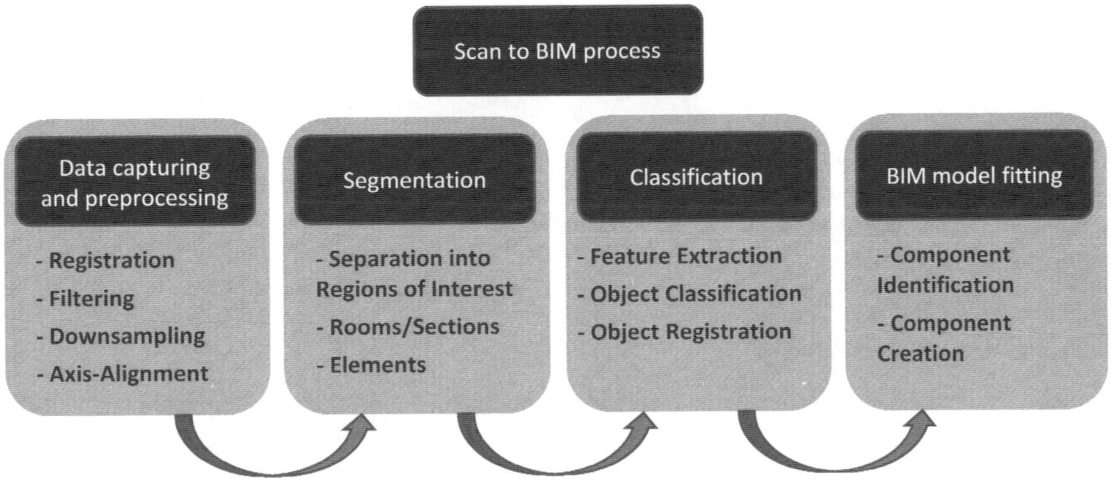

Figure 1: Stages of the "Scan to BIM"-process.

The process of automatic BIM model generation from point clouds (scan to BIM) can roughly be subdivided into the phases preprocessing, segmentation, classification and BIM model fitting as outlined in the adapted Figure 1 following Loges & Blankenbach (2017). Data preprocessing generally represents the point cloud processing step performed immediately after data capturing. The general goal of preprocessing is to denoise the point cloud by removing outliers, smoothing out noise and possibly downsampling and transforming it into a suitable format for later computations. Furthermore, this step can also be beneficial for manual modelling and visualization, as preprocessed data eases the modeling of structures, reduces the risk of potential errors and is generally more pleasant to deal with.

In this work, we focus on point cloud alignment, as it is most often the first operation done in manual modeling and carries great importance in automated reconstruction. Aligning a point cloud or pose normalization refer to rotating the point cloud such that at least one of the dominant building axes captured with it, is oriented along one of the global coordinate system axes. In the field of automation, the benefits of the alignment process lie in the fact that most data structures which ease point neighborhood lookups during point cloud processing such as voxel grids and octrees use boundary volumes oriented along the global coordinate system axes. Therefore, axis-aligned point clouds ensure optimal compactness and therefore usage of these structures. An example on how proper alignment reduces aliasing artifacts which might otherwise occur for voxel-based feature extraction is illustrated in Figure 2. Whereas in the aligned point cloud edges derived from the voxel-wise scatter values are clearly visible, edges in the unaligned point cloud are harder to identify and suffer from visible noise. This problem is commonly caused by planar surfaces which are not properly aligned with the axis-aligned voxels of the used grid.

Aside from benefits for data structures and some feature extraction techniques, many successful methods for segmentation and analysis make use of the Manhattan World assumption, which assumes structures contained in the point cloud to be oriented along a rectangular grid. Determining the global orientation of the grid and rotating the point cloud to match this grid thus represents an important precondition for such algorithms to work properly.

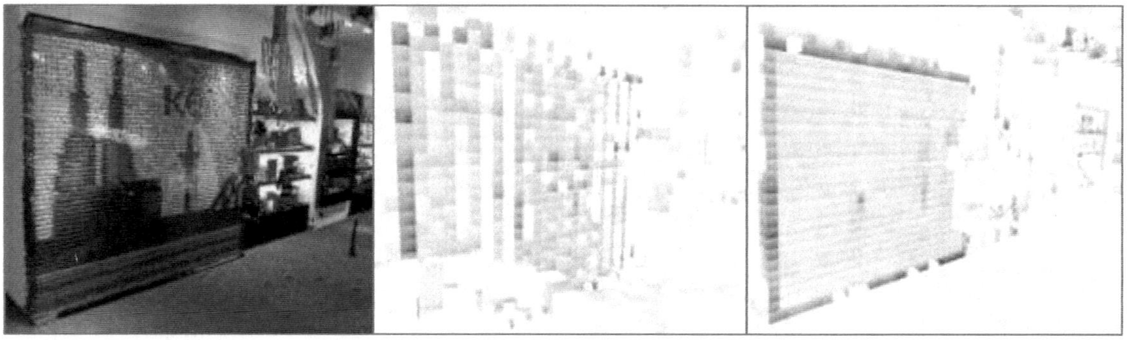

Figure 2: Impact of axis-alignment on voxel-based calculations. Left: Original point cloud. Center: Scatter values per voxel of un-aligned point cloud (contrast enhanced for visibility). Right: Scatter values per voxel of axis-aligned point cloud (contrast enhanced for visibility).

2. Related Work

The problem of pose normalization for 3D shapes and meshes has been extensively discussed in other works. However, publications in this field for point clouds are either sparse or concerned with solving different, related problems. Many works in the field of pose normalization commonly deal with alignment as a preprocessing step for shape matching or discuss it in context of feature extraction. Lian et al. (2010) defined a metric for 3D mesh rectilinearity which was dependent on the mesh's pose. Since their metric would measure the projected area of a mesh in relation to the total area, it could also be used to find suitable mesh orientations. An adaptation of their algorithm for point clouds does not exist though. Works done by Podolak et al. (2006), Paquet et al. (2000), Chaouch and Verroust-Blondet (2008) and Kazhdan et al. (2003, 2007) indicate that both symmetry and the presence of reflection planes help estimate correct rotation and object poses, however, laser scans of entire buildings rarely follow these assumptions.

Many of aforementioned works compared the pose normalization problem together with the principal component analysis (PCA). Most often the PCA is being used for feature extraction, but also represents a common way for calculating an object's principal axis. This is achieved by constructing the covariance matrix of a point set, followed by an eigenvalue decomposition of this matrix resulting in an orthogonal basis of principal axes. These principal axes, however, are often sensitive to noise and local sampling such that only the most dominant principal axis ends up being useful for shape alignment. In their publications, Kazhdan et al. (2007) compared multiple feature-based 3D pose retrieval methods for meshes using PCA as the baseline for evaluating their experiments. As pointed out and thoroughly discussed in their works, PCA does not represent a viable way of aligning objects along the axes of a global coordinate system. In context of point cloud processing, Okorn et al. (2010) used point density histograms for the segmentation of floor and ceiling planes and to estimate dominant orientations of cross sections of single rooms rather than entire point clouds. Aside from the limitation to single rooms which requires said rooms to be presegmented, this method requires the selected cross sections to be free of clutter. The method thus requires careful selection of a suitable cross section, limiting it even further to a handful of scenarios.

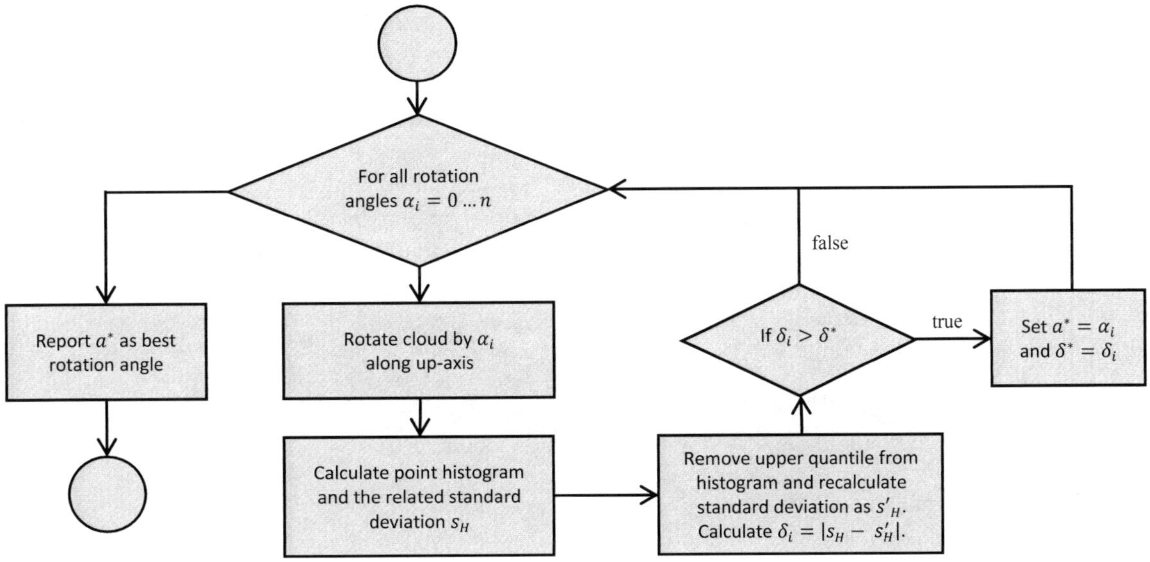

Figure 3: Workflow diagram of our point cloud alignment method.

Combining the ideas of both, symmetrical properties and dominant planes, Fu et al. (2008) presented an approach which would construct a convex hull from an input mesh and identify the dominant plane of the hull polygon. Due to the reliance on a convex hull, this method could be adapted for use with point clouds and furthermore indicates that the detection of planes in man-made structures plays an integral role in object alignment.

3. Methods

Our approach to point cloud alignment makes use of point density histogram to identify dominant wall segments, but contains multiple analysis steps shown in Figure 3. We initially start by defining a vector pointing "upwards" as our rotation axis and selecting an axis for alignment (which is oriented orthogonally to the upwards vector). This vector is typically chosen to be the global z-axis which is usually fixed in case of point cloud data captured with a terrestrial laser scanner in static mode. Afterwards, we incrementally rotate the point cloud and construct the density histograms. These histograms are created by counting the number of points falling into a specific range along the alignment axis. The shape of these histograms strongly depends on the chosen rotation, a behaviour explored further in Figure 3. As point densities are larger along planar surfaces such as walls, clearly identifiable peaks will emerge if a viable rotation angle for alignment has been chosen. Contrary, an unsuitable rotation angle results in a rather flat distribution in the density histogram. Based on this observation, the alignment problem is reduced to finding dominant peaks in the density histogram as their presence indicates that walls are aligned with the main axes. As a fast and robust metric for detecting histograms related to the desired rotation angle, the per-bin standard deviation s_H of the point distribution histogram is being calculated. Afterwards, the histogram bins falling into an upper quantile are being removed. In case of histograms related to suitable angles, this operation removes peaks and in consequence greatly reduces the standard deviation of the point density distributions. The difference δ_s between the original standard deviation s_H and the new standard s'_H deviation is used as an indicator for the desired histogram and therefore the desired rotation angle. The desired rotation angle in the search space thus maximizes the calculated difference δ_s of the standard deviations:

$$\delta_s = \max(|s_H - s'_H|)$$

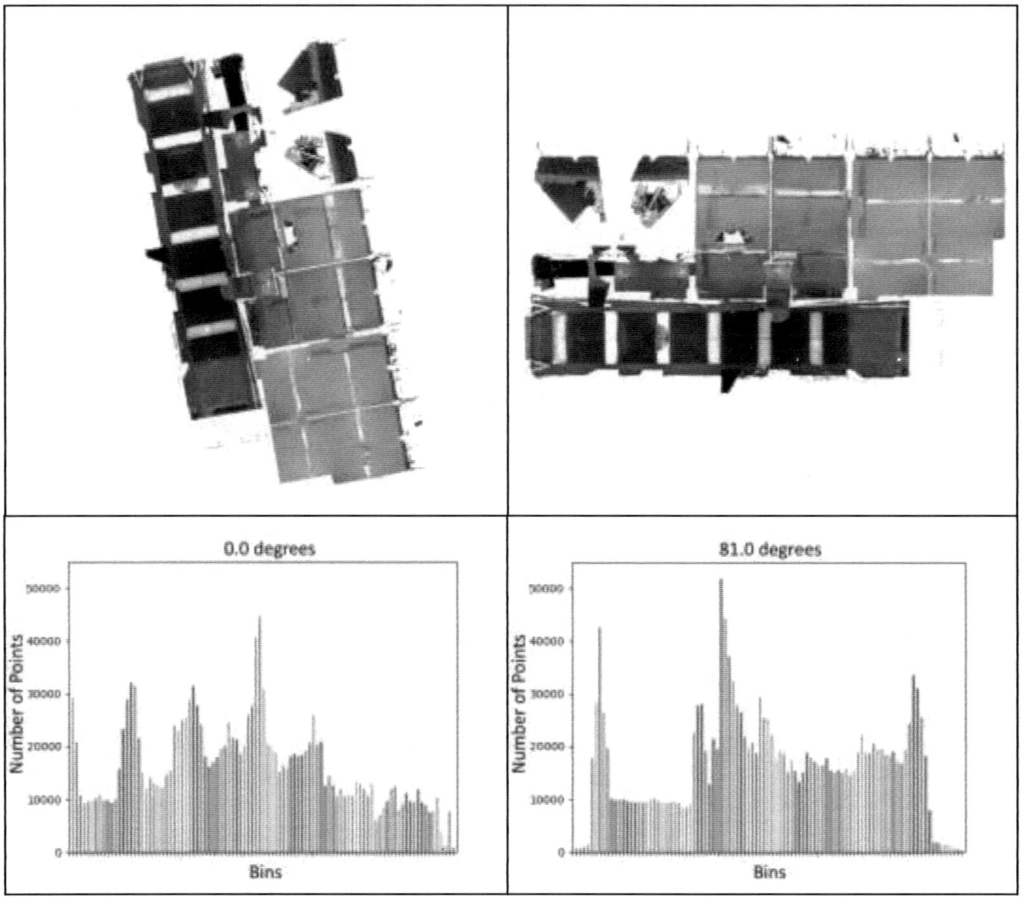

Figure 4: Comparison of density histograms for point cloud with 1,629,143 points. Left column: Top view of unaligned point cloud and correspong density histogram. Right column: Top view of aligned point cloud and correspong density histogram. Note how histogram peaks are more dominant in the aligned point cloud, with noticable flat regions.

Even though searching for the largest peak in the density histograms seems like a simpler option, we decided to use aforementioned method as it has proven to be more robust towards local point density variations and clutter. If desired, this alignment step may be repeated for the remaining axes. To ensure that the point cloud is still roughly located at the same position, all rotations are performed around the point cloud's centre of gravity.
The described algorithm depends on three parameters which are the resolution of the rotation angle, the number of histogram bins and upper quantile size.

In case of the number of histogram bins, it is advisable to choose their amount such that the resulting bin sizes roughly correspond to a wall's thickness. The size of the rotation angle increments on the other hand has an impact on the size of the search space and therefore on the algorithm's running time. In case of the point cloud with 1,629,143 points in Figure 4, we observed an overall execution time of around 8.408s for an angular resolution of 1 degree, but a significantly reduced execution time of 1.762s for an angular resolution of 5 degrees. The accuracy also depends on the upper histogram bin quantile, for which we found a value of 90% to be adequate for our experiments. In our example, removing this upper quantile from the histogram results reduces the overall standard deviation of the remaining histogram bins by 6,313.613 points.

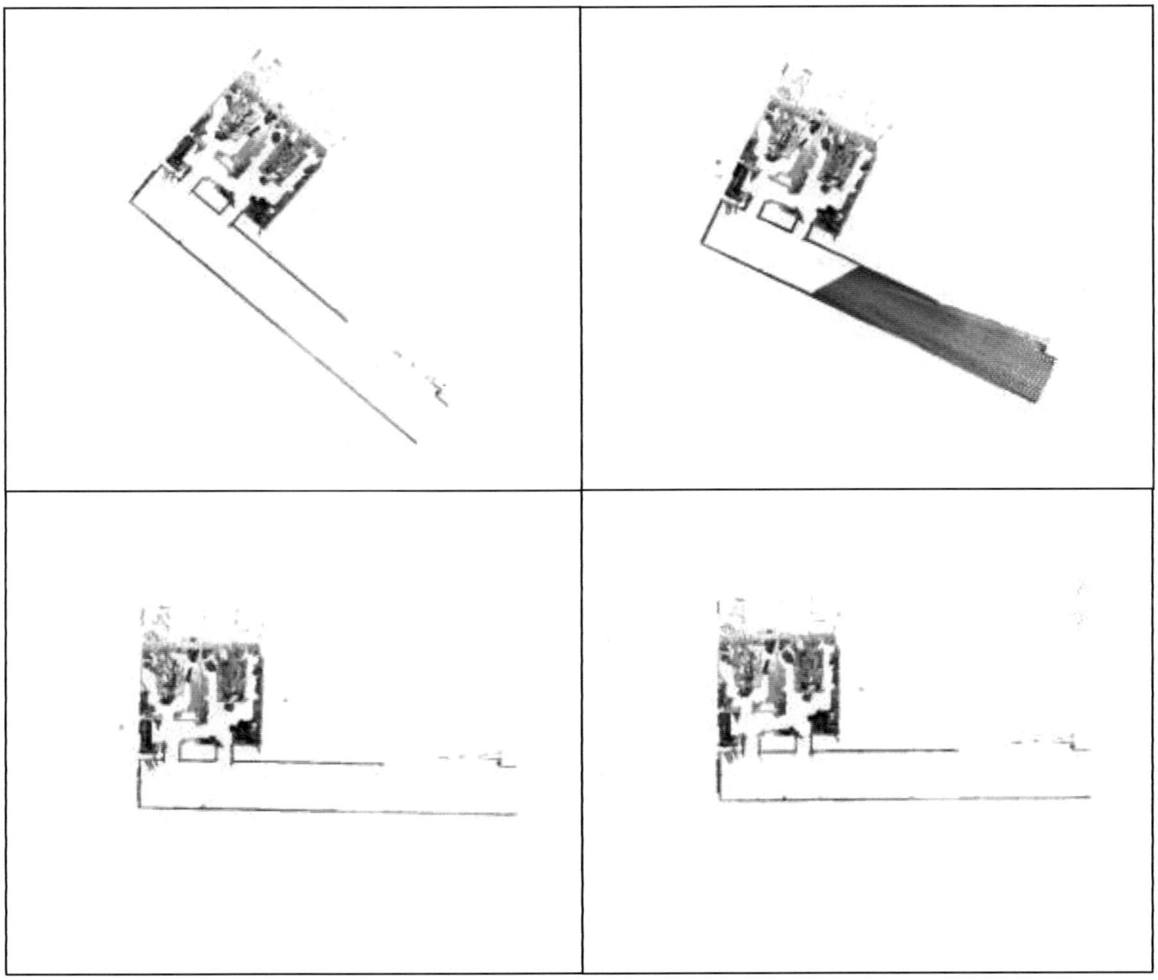

Figure 5: Top view of cross sections of original unaligned and axis-aligned point clouds. Top left: Original point cloud. Top right: The PCA-based alignment method is fast (approx. 0.116s), but fails to find the desired rotation angle. Alignment may even tilt the cloud, as apparent by the floor points which have been moved into the displayed cross section plane. Bottom left: Alignment with the histogram-based method. Using 10 bins results in a minor error. Bottom right: Using 100 bins for the histogram-based method provides excellent accuracy.

4. Results

We evaluated our method on various data sets (further examples shown in figure 6) and found that it performs desirably for evenly sampled point clouds. In direct comparison, it performs considerably better than an alignment based on the principal component analysis (PCA). For evaluation purposes, we implemented our algorithm and a PCA-based alignment algorithm as command line tools and subsequently embedded them both into Autodesk Revit as plugins, making them available inside a BIM-enabled modeling environment. It is important to point out that our experiments in Autodesk Revit were limited to 1,000,000 points due to API restrictions, while the command line tool has no such point count limits. Figure 5 displays the result of our algorithm in Autodesk Revit and compares it to the results of PCA-based alignment. As displayed in the figure, our method is capable of identifying the desired rotation angle even for point clouds where the PCA-based method struggles. Not only are point clouds being rotated as intended, but the algorithm is also capable of dealing with the uneven sampling mentioned earlier. Aligning subsampled point clouds also gives satisfactory results, meaning that accelerating the alignment by using subsampled data sets of the original point cloud is a viable option. Moreover, we found the algorithm capable of dealing with scans spanning along multiple floors. We also evaluated our method on point clouds acquired from different sensors with results being listed in Table 1. All show an uneven resolution with locally high point densities.

The PCA-based alignment method on the other hand merely calculates a local frame for a point cloud and aligns it with the global frame. This method is significantly faster in comparison, often finishing in less than a second, but delivers poor results as regions with high point densities will have a higher impact on the rotation. Another problem arises from laser scans where only one section of the building has been captured. In these cases, the scanned rooms have a bigger influence on the calculation of the principal axis than sparsely scanned corridors.

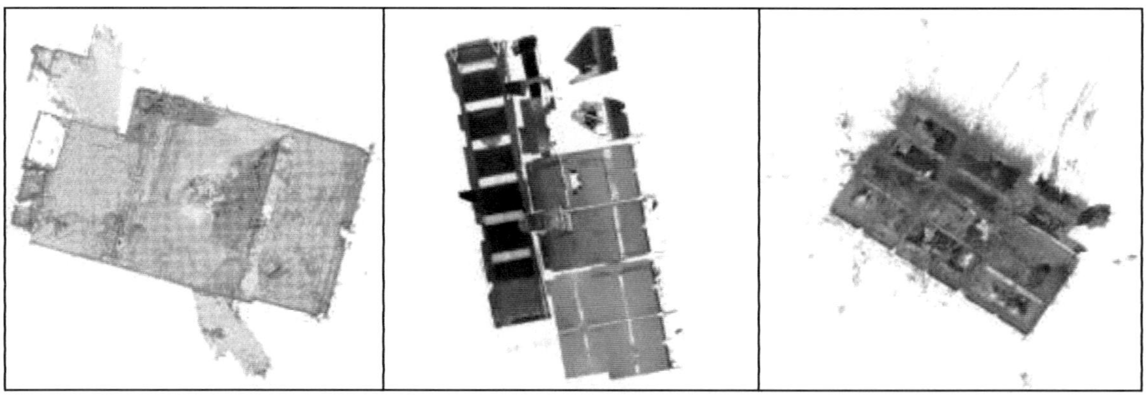

Figure 6: Visual comparison of point clouds used for evaluation (high-resolution versions of these images are shown in the appendix). Left: Single office captured with Google Tango device. Notice the low spatial resolution and rather even point distribution. Center: Multiple offices captured with Riegl VZ400 laser scanner. Overall scan resolution is high, and very dense close to the scanning device. Right: Point cloud reconstructed from image matching. Characteristics are the strong noise and fluctuation point densities.

Table 1: Execution times for PCA- and histogram-based algorithms with an angle resolution of 1° for various point clouds. The first cloud was acquired with a Google Tango device, while "Riegl1" and "Riegl2" have been captured with a geodetic laser scanner (Riegl VZ400); both show an uneven point distribution characteristic for TLS. The final cloud has been captured via image matching.

Point Cloud	Number of Points	Time (PCA) [s]	Time (Histogram) [s]
Tango	1,629,143	0.031	0.874
Riegl1	5,702,432	0.203	8.408
Riegl2 (original)	17,934,986	3.558	93.393
Riegl2 (Revit)	1,000,000	0.116	5.326
Image Matching	4,579,656	0.515	23.743

5. Conclusion and Outlook

We presented an enhanced method for the automated alignment of point clouds to a global coordinate system. Our method has proven to be fast and robust towards uneven sampling and delivers more precise results than the PCA-based method. Although we have already carried out extensive test runs with various point clouds of building, we intend to evaluate our method also with point clouds of engineering structures (e.g. bridges). With the algorithm being based on point density histograms, our brute-force algorithm could be optimized further by means of using more sophisticated optimization methods such as gradient descent, Monte Carlo methods or genetic algorithms. Large point clouds in particular would benefit from this extension. Modifying the algorithm to use histograms based on voxels rather than points might be an option to make it more robust towards densely sampled regions.

Interestingly, first trials of our command-line tool indicated that pose normalization with respect to multiple axes seems possible as well, with the alignment being performed successively for each axis. However, further evaluations need to be performed to verify this assumption. Aside from these technical aspects, an option for automated parameter selection would be useful to simplify user input and manual parameter selection.

6. References

Loges, S., Blankenbach, J. (2017), As-built Dokumentation für BIM – Ableitung von bauteilorientierten Modellen aus Punktwolken, Photogrammetrie – Laserscanning – optische 3D-Messtechnik: Beiträge der Oldenburger 3D-Tage 2017.

Okorn, B. E., Xiong, X., Akinci, B., Huber, D. (2010), Toward Automated Modeling of Flor Plans, Proceedings of the Symposium on 3D Data Processing, Visualization and Transmission.

Lian, Z., Rosin, P., Sun, X. (2010), Rectilinearity of 3D meshes, International Journal of Computer Vision.

Chaouch, M., Verroust-Blondet, A. (2008), A Novel Method for Alignment of 3D Models, IEEE International Conference on Shape Modeling and Applications, Proceedings.

Fu, H., Cohen-Or, D., Dror, G., Sheffer, A. (2008), Upright Orientation of Man-Made Objects, ACM Transaction on Graphics, Proceedings of SIGGRAPH.

Podolak, J., Shilane, P., Golovinskiy, A., Rusinkiewicz, S., Funkhouser, T., (2006), A Planar-reflective Symmetry Tranform for 3D Shapes, ACM Transactions on Graphics (TOG)

Kazhdan, M., Funkhouser, T., Rusinkievicz, S. (2003), Rotation Invariant Spherical Harmonic Representation of 3D Shape Descriptors, Symposium on Geometry Processing.

Kazhdan, M., (2007), An Approximate and Efficient Method for Optimal Rotation of 3D Models, IEEE Transaction on Pattern Analysis and Machine Intelligence.

Paquet, E., Rioux, M., Murching, A., Naveen, T., Tabatabai, A., (2000), Description of Shape Information for 2D and 3D Objects, Signal Processing: Image Communication.

7. Appendix

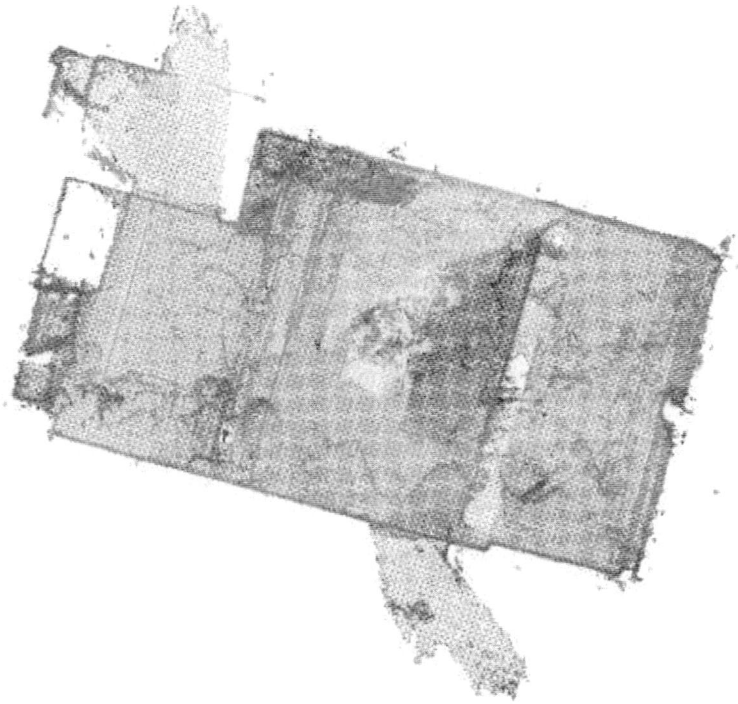

Figure 7: Point cloud acquired with Time-of-Flight camera of Google Tango device. Point distributions are even, but very coarse.

Figure 8: Point cloud reconstructed from multiple registered scans captured with a Riegl VZ400 laser scanner. The overall resolutions is very fine, but suffers from density fluctuations close to the scan positions.

Figure 9: Reconstructed point cloud created through image matching. Point densities vary greatly with points scattered along their respective surfaces. Heavy noise and low point densities in regions such as the ceiling are quite characteristic.

A Framework of a Multi-User Voice-Driven BIM-Based Navigation System for Fire Emergency Response

Hui Zhou, Mun On Wong, Huaquan Ying, Sanghoon Lee*
Department of Civil Engineering, The University of Hong Kong, Pok Fu Lam Road, Hong Kong
shlee1@hku.hk (*Corresponding author)

Abstract. Navigation support is of significant importance for fire evacuation and rescue due to the complexity of building indoor structures and the uncertainty of fire emergency. This paper presents a framework of a multi-user voice-driven building information model (BIM)-based navigation system for fire emergency response. Classes of the navigation system is first defined being consistent with the open BIM data standard (i.e. Industry Foundation Classes, IFC). A string-matching method is then developed to generate a navigation query from each voice navigation request based on the Levenshtein distance and Burkhard and Keller (BK)-tree of a fire navigation associated lexicon. With the semantic information of the location in the navigation query, the spatial geometric information of the location is extracted from the BIM model and visibility graph-based route plans for multiple users are generated. To deliver the route planning to building users in an intuitive and direct manner, patterns of different voice prompts will be designed to automatically broadcast the navigation route step by step. Finally, the proposed navigation system will be validated with virtual reality (VR) based experiment.

1. Introduction

Delayed evacuation service is more likely to cause a high proportion of emergency causalities and property losses, especially in residential and high-rise buildings (Purser and Bensilum, 2001). Navigation support is a crucial link in the chain of evacuation services to prepare routing plans and provide path-finding guidance for fire evacuation, rescuing trapped people and relocating dangerous goods. In practice, a static 2D route map is commonly used for navigation planning in case of a fire. However, it is not reliable in terms of effective and efficient navigation in fire emergencies with high uncertainty. Actually, extensive information about building facilities, occupants, fire and dangerous materials are required by first emergency responders for decision-making and response operations (Gökdemir, 2011). Building information model (BIM), as a comprehensive repository with structured building data, has been used in existing indoor navigation systems (Ivanov, 2017). For example, Lertlakkhanakul et al. (2009) developed a BIM-based system called "GongPath" for indoor pedestrian navigation. Lin et al. (2013) retrieved IFC BIM data to create a grid graph to support path planning in 3D indoor spaces, using the fast-marching method. However, their navigation systems or methods were generally designed for a given pair of locations. For the navigation in fire emergency response, a more comprehensive system including the determination of location information for the pair of origin and destination in each navigation query needs to be built.

Wang et al. (2015) built a web-based prototype of equipment maintenance in fire emergencies. The prototype was delivered to users by mobile devices where they can input their location information by finding and clicking the corresponding building components, which in turn may make an eye-off-road distraction for users. Another commonly used personal localization mechanism within existing navigation systems is based on sensing technologies. Yoon et al. (2016) developed a Wi-Fi-based system to track the movement of victims for localization and assessment. Cheng et al. (2017) created a Bluetooth-based sensor network to monitor information of temperature, smoke and signal strength for providing early alarm services and evacuation tracking. Rueppel and Stuebbe (2008) integrated wireless LAN (WLAN), ultra-wide-band (UWB), and radio frequency identification (RFID) techniques to develop a hybrid system to support indoor navigation in complex buildings. In such mechanisms, users are required to use mobile devices to scan the sensing tags or capture the signals delivered by position sensors. However, it may also cause dangers of eye-off-road distraction for responders on the path (Zhang et al., 2017). Moreover, sensor-based devices may be lacking in current buildings or be easily broken by fires or high temperatures, and the field of vision to find a sensor tag may be blurred by smoke. In addition, it is ignored that responders under emergencies can take an initiative to send evacuation or rescue queries with their location information using direct and prompt natural language speech. In regard to voice-based localization, Ivanov (2017) applied natural voice-based queries to retrieve relevant location data to develop a navigation system for visually impaired people. The navigation system was implemented with simulations in a 2D environment where a 2D escape route was generated as the only navigation assistance. However, such a route representation is not convenient enough for fire responders, especially for trapped occupants who may not be able to keep rational cognition and judgment under emergencies. To address these issues, voice-driven navigation queries and commands can be applied as a potential method because they are more natural and intuitive for users under fire emergencies. Moreover, scenarios for collaborative fire response among multiple users were seldom discussed in traditional fire emergency navigation systems.

Therefore, this paper aims to propose a framework for a multi-user BIM-based voice-driven navigation system for fire emergency response. Virtual Reality (VR) technology will be adopted to validate the proposed systems since it enables people to be immersed in the virtual environment (Zou et al., 2017). The rest of this paper is organized as follows. Classes of the proposed navigation system are defined in Section 2. Section 3 elaborates the two modules of the navigation system. Specifically, Section 3.1 presents the solutions to voice recognition and navigation query generation for voice navigation requests. Section 3.2 shows the developed approach of the BIM-based navigation model and the potential ways for voice navigation command generation among multiple users. Section 4 introduces the probable design of VR-based experimental validation for the proposed system. Finally, the paper is concluded in Section 5 and future research work is also presented.

2. Classes of the Proposed Navigation System

The classes of the proposed navigation system are composed of two aspects: users and facilities (as presented in Figure 1), for which objects are identified based on the information requirements for each module of the navigation system. The class of users contains objects of residential occupants, firefighters, and facility managers. For facilities, classes for building elements, transport elements, firefighting devices, hazardous materials, and embedded sensors are defined. The defined classes are identified by the attribute "ID" and have the general attribute "Location" or "Geometry Info", which refers to a 3D coordinate data in the global coordinate system of a building. Meanwhile, specific attributes are required for some classes. For the space and transport element classes, the attribute "Accessibility" is used to capture the information whether a space or transport element is accessible or not under emergency situations. The composite material information of each building element (e.g. fire resistance rating of composite materials) are specified in their attributes. For firefighting devices, the device type and quantities of devices are required. For hazardous materials, material information such as material type and toxicity, and the storage volume is defined within the system.

The semantics and topology relationships between the defined classes are consistent with those in the Industry Foundation Classes (IFC) schema, which is an open standard BIM data format, in order to use an IFC BIM model as a data hub of the proposed navigation system. In this paper, IFC4 is used as the base specification. Figure 2 presents the IFC data structure that supports the required information extraction for the defined classes. It is noted that most of the defined classes can be mapped with the IFC instances, with reference to IfcBuilding, IfcBuildingStorey, IfcSpace, IfcBuildingElement, IfcTransportElement, and IfcDistributionElement. However, the remaining classes such as the fire extinguisher in the firefighting device class and the hazardous material class, have no corresponding definitions in the IFC schema. In this case, the missing information is either stored in the database or added as an extension of IFC entity.

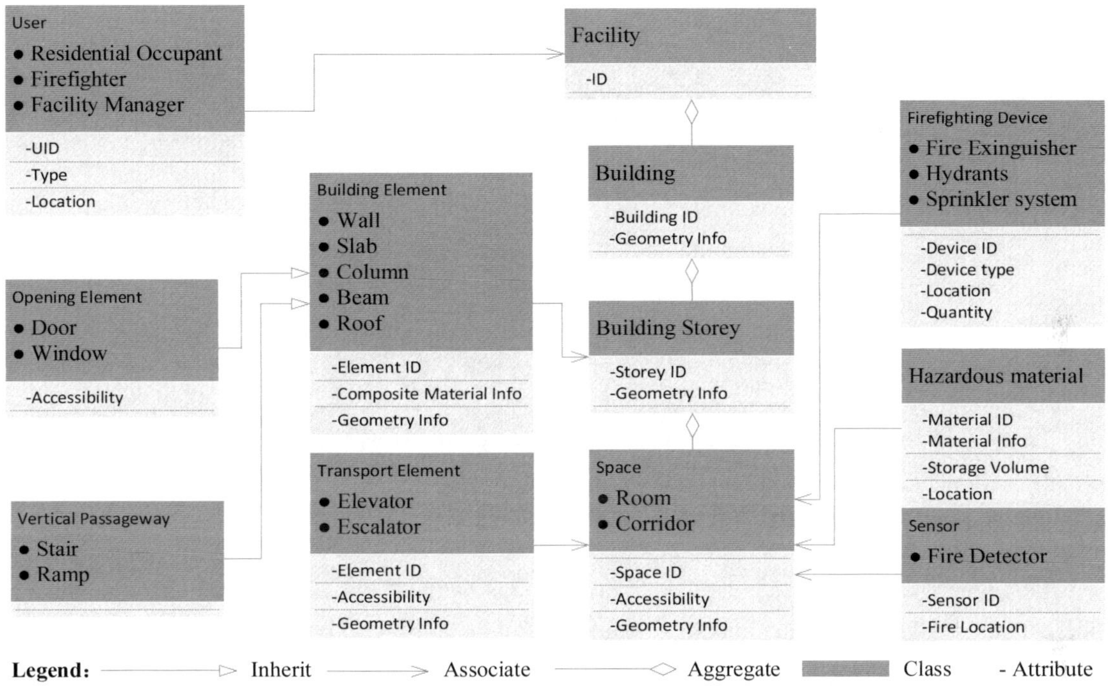

Figure 1: Classes definition of the proposed navigation system

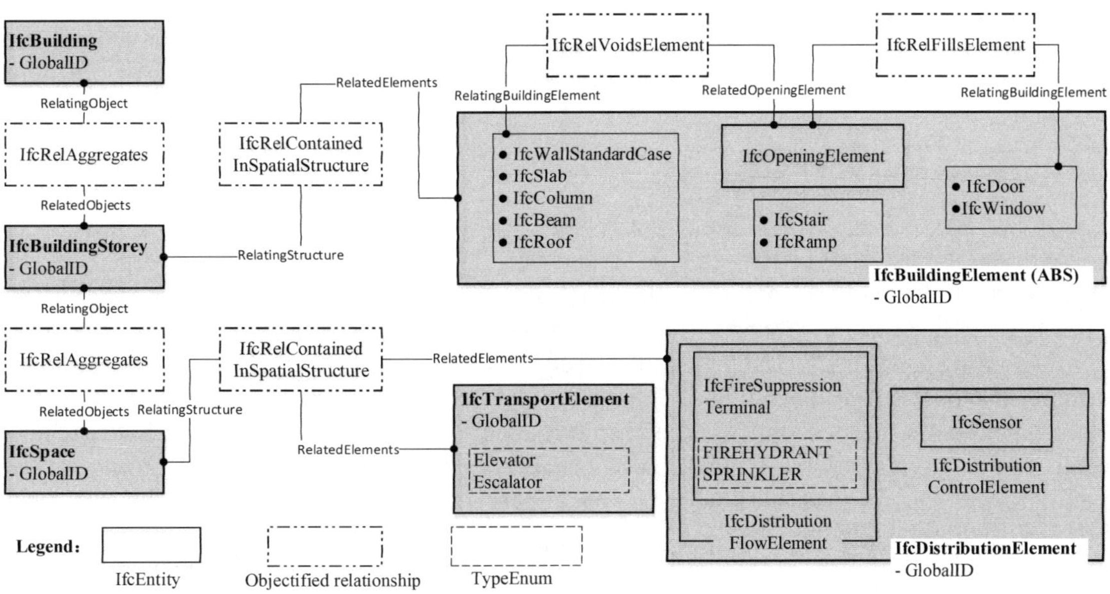

Figure 2: IFC data structure to support classes information extraction

3. The Framework of the Multi-User Voice-Driven BIM-Based Navigation System

The presented framework consists of two modules, as shown in Figure 3. The first module aims to recognize users' voice inputs and generate corresponding navigation queries. The second module is designed to retrieve the information required by each query from the BIM-based data hub and generate navigation models for different users. Details for each module are elaborated in the following sub-sections.

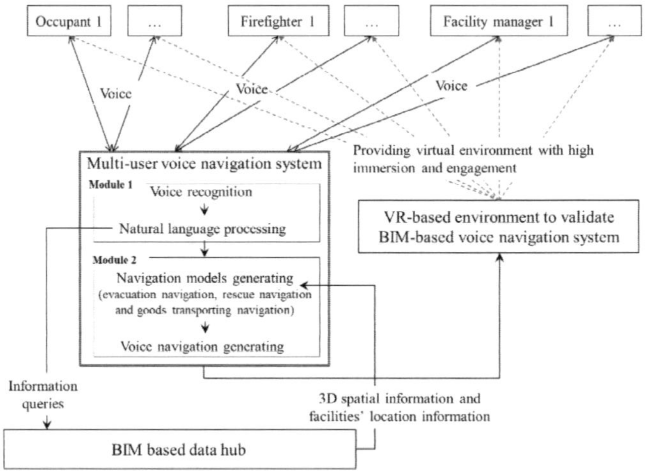

Figure 3: The framework of the multi-user voice-driven BIM-based navigation system

3.1 Module 1: Voice Recognition and Navigation Query Generation

3.1.1 Voice Recognition

Once a fire emergency occurs, users can communicate with the navigation system in natural English speech through mobile electronics which can record and play audio. The Google speech-to-text (STT) API (https://cloud.google.com/speech-to-text/) is then adopted to recognize and convert the audio streams received from users into sequences of words/sentences automatically. Based on its cloud storage, the Google STT API can provide synchronous voice recognition with significant accuracy (Harsur and Chitra, 2017; Këpuska, and Bohouta, 2017). The converted words/sentences are saved as .txt files and further used for navigation associated information extraction in Section 3.1.2. In this paper, it is hypothesized that effective network connectivity is available all the time to ensure real-time human-to-machine interaction.

3.1.2 Navigation Query Generation

To generate navigation queries from the recognized speeches, a fire emergency navigation-oriented lexicon is first constructed as a dataset for textual information processing. The predetermined vocabulary includes four categories: users, locations, request details, and interaction dialogs. Each category is composed of one to several sub-categories, which are further labelled under each category with a prefix of the category index, as shown in Table 1. Particularly, the location vocabulary represents the semantics of building components and is labelled sequentially according to the building components' relationships, which helps to enable more accurate indoor localization by organizing the location vocabulary from coarse to fine (e.g. from a building storey level to a space level).

Based on the constructed navigation-oriented lexicon, converted sentences are then input for detecting and extracting navigation-associated keywords using the string-matching approach based on "Levenshtein distance" (Levenshtein, 1966; Salehinejad et al., 2017). To reduce the search scope for each target word, the predefined navigation associated vocabulary is organized in the structure of a BK-tree (Burkhard and Keller, 1973). Concepts of the Levenshtein distance and BK-tree are briefly introduced as follows.

Table 1: Vocabulary context for the fire emergency navigation-oriented lexicon

Category (Index)	**Label: ID**	**Example words/phrases**
User (U)	-User Type: U01	Residential occupant, firefighter, facility manager
Location (L)	-Building storey: L01	Floor, level
	-Space: L02	Space, room, toilet
	-Building structure element: L03	Wall, column, slab, beam, roof
	-Opening element: L04	Door, window, exit
	-Vertical passageway: L05	Stair, ramp
	-Transport element: L06	Elevator, escalator, lift
	-Firefighting devices: L07	Fire extinguisher, hydrant, hose reel, sprinkler
	-Hazard material: L08	Oil, gas
	-Sensor: L09	Fire sensor, smoke sensor
	-Landmark: L10	Desk, statue, reception
Request Detail (RD)	-Action command: RD01	Walk, go, approach
	-The verb for request: RD02	Find, look for, search, relocate
	-Where adverb: RD03	On, in, inside, outside, at
	-Preposition for the position: RD04	From, to
Interaction Dialog (InD)	-Confirmation: InD01	Yes, no, yep, sure, okay

For two strings S_1 and S_2 with the lengths $|S_1|$ and $|S_2|$, respectively, $L(S_1, S_2)$ indicates the distance between the first i character of S_1 and the first j character of S_2 , such that

$$L(S_1^i, S_2^j) = \begin{cases} L(S_1^{i-1}, S_2^{j-1}), if\ S_1^i = S_2^j \\ 1 + L, \quad otherwise \end{cases} \tag{1}$$

Where

$$L = \min(L(S_1^{i-1}, S_2^j), L(S_1^i, S_2^{j-1}), L(S_1^{i-1}, S_2^{j-1})) \tag{2}$$

Specifically, $L(S_1^i, S_2^0) = i$ and $L(S_1^0, S_2^j) = j$, while S_k^0 represents an empty string. $L(S_1^i, S_2^j)$ is the minimum number of single-character operations (i.e. insertions, deletions, or substitutions) needed to match S_1^i and S_2^j.

An arbitrary element a is selected as the root of BK-Tree. $d(a, b)$ is defined as a distance function for each pair of elements of a set of objects. The m-th sub-tree branch is recursively built of all elements b such that $d(a, b) = m$. Figure 4(b) shows the constructed BK-tree of a set of navigation associated vocabularies with the word "floor" as the root. The number on edges indicates the Levenshtein distance between two strings. The root word can be determined more reasonably in accordance with the frequency of words used for indoor navigation.

A two-step approach is developed for the navigation query generation, based on principles of the Levenshtein distance and BK-tree. As shown in Figure 4(a), the first step extracts the associated information from converted sentences for navigation purpose. In detail, the sentences are first tokenized with word tags which represent their part of speech (POS) (e.g., noun, verb, preposition, etc.). Subsequently, noun phrases are extracted by predefined patterns (e.g. noun phrase: determiner + adjective + noun). Next step executes string matching based on the BK-tree word dictionary for nouns inside the extracted noun phrases. For a given word query, the distance D from the current root is first calculated. Then the words located in the Dth sub-tree branch are determined as the candidate list, while the sub-tree root is changed into the current root. Progressively, the target word can be detected when the distance from the query word to the current root equals to 0. For fuzzy string matching, a tolerance D_T is induced which means to search similar strings with the distance $D \pm D_T$ to the query string. As words in the BK-tree dictionary have been predefined with labels, the detected nouns can be organized accordingly. Word vocabulary of request detail is used to distinguish the current location from the navigation destination in each navigation request. For example, “from” can be connected with an origin, while “to” can be added before a destination. One example of the navigation query generation is illustrated in Figure 4(c).

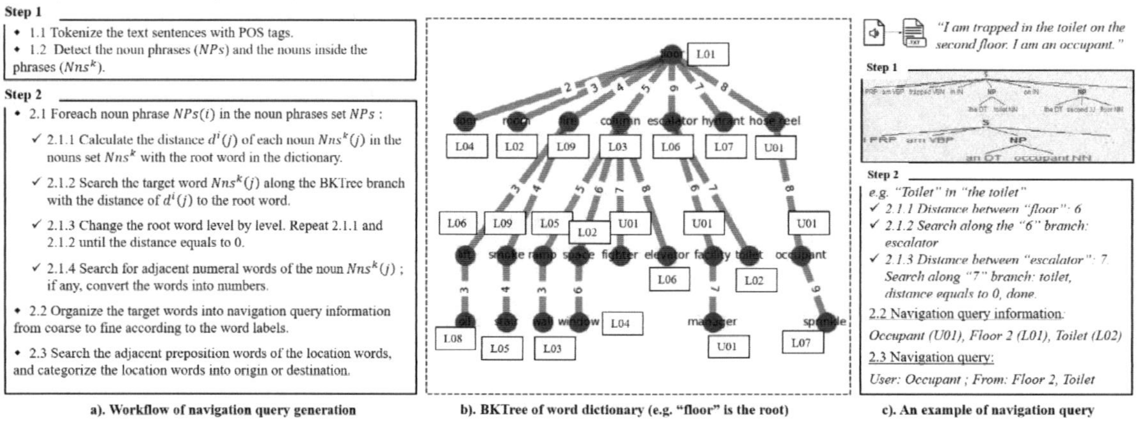

Figure 4: Diagram of navigation query generation

3.2 Module 2: Navigation Model and Voice Navigation Command Generation

3.2.1 BIM-based Navigation Model

Based on the semantic information of the origin and the destination in each navigation query, corresponding 3D spatial information and facilities’ location information are extracted from the BIM model or the developed database. Figure 5(a) presents the IFC data structure for extraction of the required data. IFC processing tools such as IFC Engine, IfcOpenShell, and xBIM Toolkit are available for IFC data extraction. For the network construction of the route map, the grid-based matrix method and the visibility graph (VG) method have been studied (Cheng et al., 2018). However, for the grid-based matrix method, discretized spaces represented in the $N \times N$ grid matrix increase the number of nodes on the planned route, which makes the method complex or even impossible to navigate users via voice prompts, as they may not be familiar with the building structure. The VG method is thus adopted in this paper as it can provide room-level details of buildings, which can avoid confusions or interpretation difficulties for voice navigation (Li et al., 2014). Dijkstra’s algorithm is used to dynamically plan the shortest route from the origin to the destination based on the graph. Figure 5(b) shows the workflow of the navigation model generation.

For navigation in high-rise buildings, stairs are represented by a walking line starts from one floor to another floor. For obstacles, it is hypothesized that users have the cognition of general furniture and can avoid them autonomously. Therefore, only conspicuous objects such as huge cupboards and reception corners need to be specifically considered. These obstacles can be simply represented as footprint polygons. Dangers in emergencies such as heat convection, toxicity, smoke coverage are considered as obstacles as well. To distinguish the risk level of approaching to obstacles, a buffer is built around the obstacle such as the dashed box in Figure 6 (b). If a buffer is created, the node in the visibility graph is also changed accordingly. Spaces are checked whether they are occupied by obstacles. If there are no obstacles, the visibility edge between the door and the space centroid is created. This indicates a navigation prompt for entering a space from a door and no guidance is needed for walking into an “empty” space. If obstacles exist, the connections between the vertices of obstacles or buffers and the doors are created. The accessibility of the graph nodes is changed in accordance with the dynamic information in fire emergencies, such as people distribution, fire and smoke spread trends, etc. Figure 6 presents an example of a BIM-based navigation for fire response in a sample building based on the proposed method.

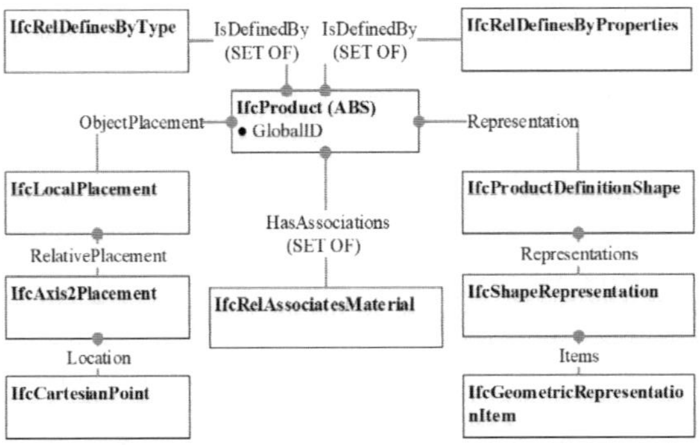

a) IFC data structure for extraction of the required data

- 1. Extract semantic, geometric and firefighting related information of building components
- 2. Extract semantic, geometric and firefighting related information for obstacles
- 3. Foreach floor (F_i):
  - 3.1 Calculate the spatial position of spaces (Ss^i), doors (Ds^i), obstacles (Os^i) and stairs (STs^i)
  - 3.2 Foreach space (S_j^i) in spaces (Ss^i):
    - 3.2.1 Check if any obstacle exist, if yes, create visibility graph of door-obstacle and door-to-door ; If no, create visibility graph of door-space and door-door
- 4. Extract the spatial position of the origin and destination in a navigation query
- 5. Check the accessibility of the nodes connected with the origin
- 6. Determine the next node with shortest distance to the origin
- 7. Repeat 5 and 6 until the destination is reached
- 8. Generate the route from the origin to destination

b) Workflow of the navigation model generation approach

Figure 5: Diagram of the navigation model generation

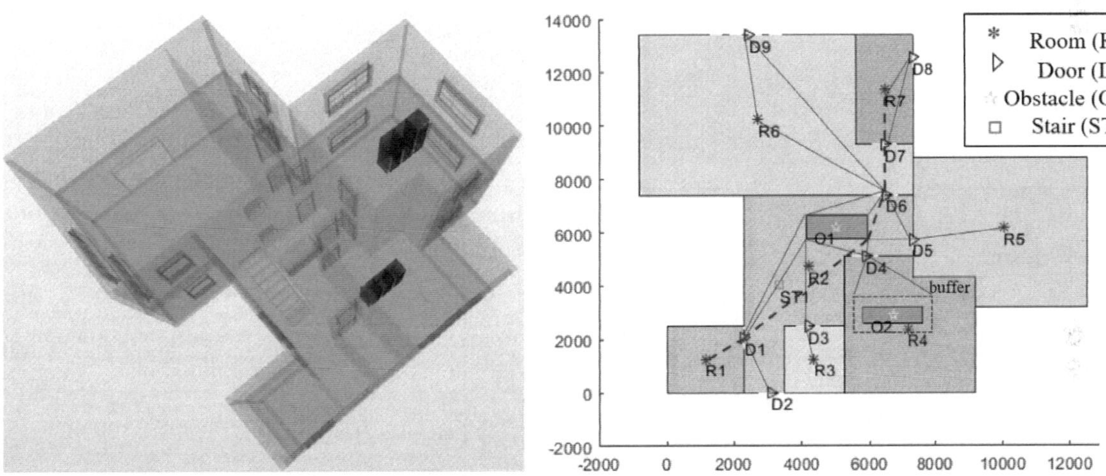

a). 3D transparent view of sample building

b). Navigation case on 1st floor (from R7-R1)

Figure 6: BIM-based navigation for fire response in a sample building

3.2.2 Voice Navigation Command Generation

Patterns of voice prompts for navigation to the route nodes are designed based on the types of graph nodes and their connections in the visibility graph (i.e. door-to-space, door-to-door, and door-to-obstacle). As shown in Figure 7, the voice prompt for navigation to a door could be "GO THROUGH THE" ith "DOOR ON THE LEFT" or "FRONT DOOR". The pattern is automatically determined for each route node, as the uniform word vocabulary for the semantic information of the location has been defined with unique labels in Module 1. The patterns for voice navigation to other locations such as spaces, obstacles, and stairs are also defined in the similar manner. Based on the designed navigation patterns, the optimal route from the origin to the destination is automatically translated into textual navigation commands with the support from the developed vocabulary in Module 1. Then, the text is input into a voice synthesizer tool called "eSpeak" to generate voice navigation commands.

As the navigation model is initially developed to enable multi-user navigation services, a communication mechanism between firefighters, facility managers, and residential occupants need to be predefined. Potential interactions could be rescue requests from the trapped people, hazardous materials relocation, and properties protection, etc. Figure 8 explains the potential interactions between multiple users with two navigation scenarios. The first scenario is that a trapped occupant sends a help request signal with his/her location to the navigation system which then delivers the message to firefighters and further plan the shortest route for rescue. Also, facility managers and residential occupants inform the navigation system of the locations of potential hazards and important properties in the building. This helps to update the building information in the navigation system and further plan shorter routes for users. Within these interactions, the navigation system requests users to confirm the query for the current location and ultimate destination, and it sends a message delivery confirmation to users. For such cases, sentences of general dialogs (e.g. your message is sent to firefighters) are defined and sent at the appropriate time.

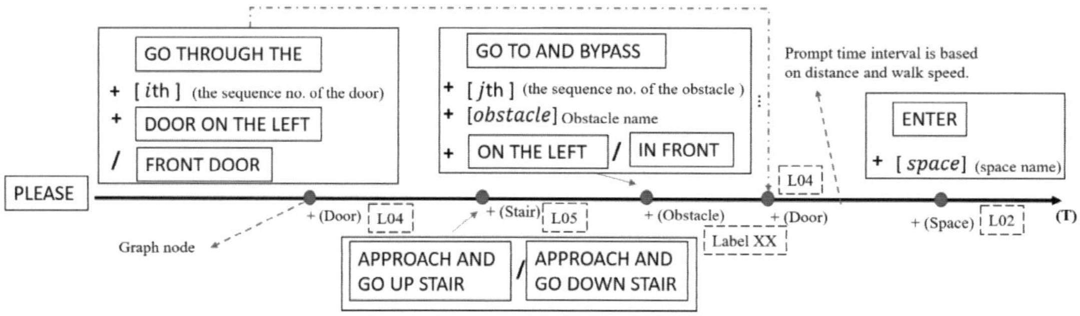

Figure 7: Voice prompt pattern for voice navigation command generation

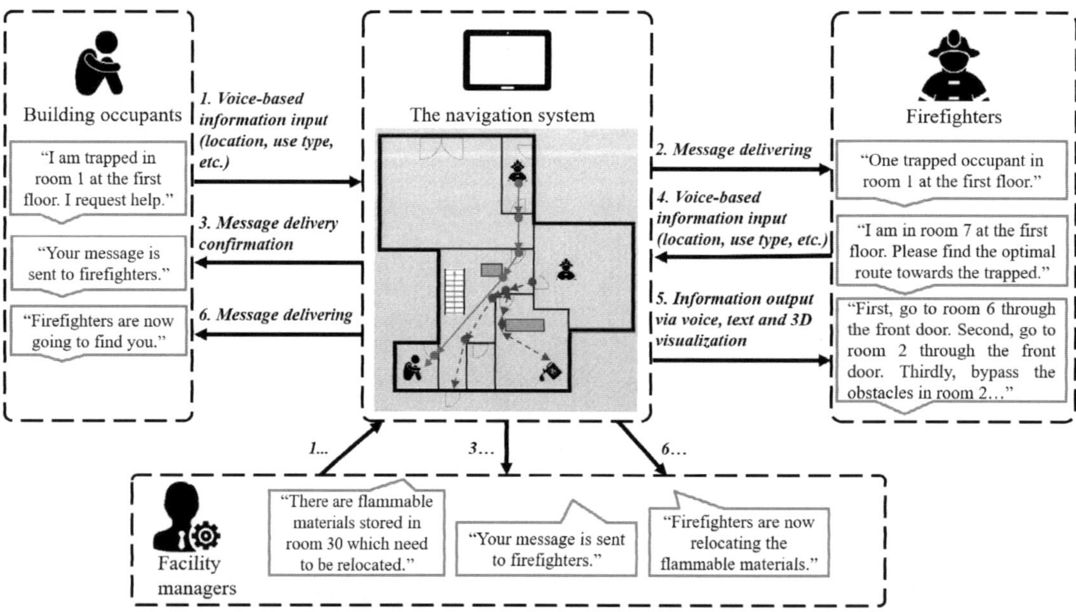

Figure 8: Multi-user voice-driven navigation cases with the assistance of the proposed system

4. VR-based Experimental Validation

Based on Modules 1 and 2, a multi-user BIM-based voice-oriented prototype for fire emergency navigation will be developed. Unity, a high-performance game development platform, will then be adopted to build a VR-based environment where people can be engaged in the fire emergency scenarios and interact with the navigation system as building users, as shown in Figure 9. To present full-scale immersive fire emergency scenarios, the VR-based environment will further be implemented in a CAVE system, as presented in Figure 9 (a).

The scenarios will be designed based on a preliminary study of potential reasons for several disastrous fire emergency cases in Hong Kong. Two groups of participants, namely the experimental group and the control group will be invited to finish designed tasks within the comparative experiment, assisted by the proposed navigation system or not, respectively. To realize voice navigation for multiple users, a multi-player High-Level API (HLAPI) as a Unity plug-in will be adopted for building the network of users' interaction. A Unity package named Tridify (https://www.tridify.com/) will also be used to ensure uniform coordinates between the VR environment and BIM models. Thus, the navigation system tested in the VR environment will further obtain the accurate position of participants in buildings through the tracking sensor.

a). VR-based fire emergency environment

Criteria	Sub- Criteria	Measurement
Navigation query generation	Recognition of user localization	Y/N
	Recognition of navigation destination	Y/N
BIM-based Navigation model generation	Fire recognition and localization	Y/N; Distance difference in 3D coordinates (m)
	Positioning of user	Distance difference in 3D coordinates (m)
	Positioning of navigation destination	Distance difference in 3D coordinates (m)
Voice navigation command generation	Distance judge between adjacent nodes	Distance difference in 3D coordinates (m)
	Direction guide between adjacent nodes	Right /wrong
	Navigation efficiency	Time from origin to destination (mins)
	Navigation clarity	Points in Likert scale

b). Evaluation criteria of the proposed navigation system

Figure 9: VR-based experimental validation of the proposed navigation system

To evaluate the performance of the proposed navigation system, assessment criteria will be built in terms of key module functions. Specifically, for navigation query generation, it can be assessed by whether the navigation system can recognize the semantic information of the users' locations and the navigation destinations. With regard to the BIM-based navigation model generation for multiple users, the proposed system will be tested to check whether it can recognize and localize the fire, users and navigation destinations based on the semantic information of locations in the navigation queries. For voice navigation command generation, the distance and direction guide between two adjacent nodes on the generated navigation route will be examined. Meanwhile, navigation efficiency and clarity are essential to the safe evacuation and rescue under fire emergencies. Figure 9 (b) illustrates the hierarchy of the evaluation criteria of the proposed navigation system. The corresponding measurement for each sub-criterion is also specified in Figure 9 (b). For instance, the time from the origin to the destination consumed by the experiment participants will be recorded to evaluate the navigation efficiency of the system.

5. Conclusions and Future Work

This paper proposes a framework of a multi-user voice-driven BIM-based navigation system for fire emergency response. This framework is expected to extend traditional BIM-based navigation approaches with intuitive voice-based localization and navigation prompt delivery. Specifically, a string-matching method is introduced to generate the navigation query from each voice navigation request based on the Levenshtein distance and BK-tree of a fire navigation associated lexicon. Approaches for dynamic route planning and intuitive navigation command generation for multiple users are proposed with the multi-user interaction definition and patterns of voice prompts. Therefore, the multi-user navigation system will be not only a navigation tool for planning the shortest route, but also an information sharing platform for involved participants to collaborate with each other. However, the approaches or algorithms involved in each module needs to be implemented with more fire emergency scenarios in real-world buildings. In addition, to avoid invalid voice input, the proposed navigation system hypothesizes that building users will only input navigation requests. For more general cases, sentiment analysis of the recognized voice information should be required. Moreover, deep learning methods for the navigation query generation and the voice navigation command generation can be integrated with the proposed system to ensure great efficiency in navigation services.

6. Acknowledgments

The work described in this paper was supported by a grant from Graduate Collaborative Research Awards funded by Universitas 21.

References

Burkhard, W.A. and Keller, R.M. (1973). Some approaches to best-match file searching. Communications of the ACM, 16(4), pp.230-236.

Cheng, M.Y., Chiu, K.C., Hsieh, Y.M., Yang, I.T., Chou, J.S. and Wu, Y.W. (2017). BIM integrated smart monitoring technique for building fire prevention and disaster relief. Automation in Construction, 84, pp.14-30.

Cloud Speech-to-Text. Accessed 30 March 2019, <https://cloud.google.com/speech-to-text/>.

Cheng, J.C., Tan, Y., Song, Y., Mei, Z., Gan, V.J. and Wang, X. (2018). Developing an evacuation evaluation model for offshore oil and gas platforms using BIM and agent-based model. Automation in Construction, 89, pp.214-224.

Gökdemir, N. (2011). Identification and representation of information items required for vulnerability assessment and multi-hazard emergency response operations. Middle East Technical University.

Harsur, A. and Chitra, M. (2017). Voice based navigation system for blind people using ultrasonic sensor. IJRITCC, 3, pp.4117-4122.

Ivanov, R. (2017). An approach for developing indoor navigation systems for visually impaired people using Building Information Modeling. Journal of Ambient Intelligence and Smart Environments, 9(4), pp.449-467.

Këpuska, V. and Bohouta, G. (2017). Comparing speech recognition systems (Microsoft API, Google API and CMU Sphinx). International Journal of Engineering Research and Applications, 7, pp.20-24.

Lertlakkhanakul, J., Li, Y., Choi, J. and Bu, S. (2009). GongPath: Development of BIM based indoor pedestrian navigation system, NCM 2009 - 5th International Joint Conference on INC, IMS, and IDC, pp. 382–388.

Levenshtein, V.I. (1966), February. Binary codes capable of correcting deletions, insertions, and reversals. In Soviet physics doklady, 10(8), pp. 707-710).

Li, N., Yang, Z., Ghahramani, A., Becerik-Gerber, B. and Soibelman, L. (2014). Situational awareness for supporting building fire emergency response: Information needs, information sources, and implementation requirements. Fire safety journal, 63, pp.17-28.

Lin, Y.H., Liu, Y.S., Gao, G., Han, X.G., Lai, C.Y. and Gu, M. (2013). The IFC-based path planning for 3D indoor spaces. Advanced Engineering Informatics, 27(2), pp.189-205.

Purser, D.A. and Bensilum, M. (2001). Quantification of behaviour for engineering design standards and escape time calculations. Safety science, 38(2), pp.157-182.

Rueppel, U. and Stuebbe, K.M. (2008). BIM-based indoor-emergency-navigation-system for complex buildings. Tsinghua science and technology, 13(S1), pp.362-367.

Salehinejad, H., Barfett, J., Aarabi, P., Valaee, S., Colak, E., Gray, B. and Dowdell, T. (2017), October. A convolutional neural network for search term detection. In 2017 IEEE 28th Annual International Symposium on Personal, Indoor, and Mobile Radio Communications (PIMRC) (pp. 1-6). IEEE.

Tashakkori, H., Rajabifard, A. and Kalantari, M. (2015). A new 3D indoor/outdoor spatial model for indoor emergency response facilitation. Building and Environment, 89, pp.170-182.

Tridify. Accessed 30 March 2019, <https://www.tridify.com/>.

Wang, S.H., Wang, W.C., Wang, K.C. and Shih, S.Y. (2015). Applying building information modeling to support fire safety management. Automation in Construction, 59, pp.158-167.

Yoon, H., Shiftehfar, R., Cho, S., Spencer Jr, B.F., Nelson, M.E. and Agha, G. (2016). Victim Localization and Assessment System for Emergency Responders, Journal of Computing in Civil Engineering, 30(2), pp. 1–14.

Zheng, Y., Liu, Y. and Hansen, J.H. (2017), June. Navigation-orientated natural spoken language understanding for intelligent vehicle dialogue. In Intelligent Vehicles Symposium (IV), 2017 IEEE (pp. 559-564). IEEE.

Zou, H., Li, N. and Cao, L. (2017). Emotional response–based approach for assessing the sense of presence of subjects in virtual building evacuation studies. Journal of Computing in Civil Engineering, 31(5), p.04017028.

Model-based interpretation of floor vibrations for indoor occupant tracking

Slah Drira[1,2], Yves Reuland[1], Ian F.C. Smith[1,2]
[1] Applied Computing and Mechanics Laboratory (IMAC), Swiss Federal Institute of Technology (EPFL) – Switzerland, [2] ETH Zurich, Future Cities Laboratory – Singapore
slah.drira@epfl.ch

Abstract. Information regarding occupant flows inside buildings is beneficial for applications such as thermal-load control, market research and security enhancement. Existing methodologies for occupant tracking involve data-driven techniques that rely either on radio-frequency devices, optical sensors or vibration sensors. Such data-driven techniques suffer from ambiguous interpretations, especially in presence of obstructions and varying floor rigidities. In this contribution, an occupant-tracking strategy using footstep-induced vibrations is outlined. The goal is to incorporate information from physics-based models in the interpretation of vibration measurements. Using error-domain model falsification (EDMF) a single occupant is localized using the vibrations resulting from footstep impacts and using various shoe types. EDMF is a multiple-model approach that provides a set of candidate locations from an initial population of possible footstep locations. Model responses that contradict footstep-induced vibration measurements are rejected through incorporating several sources of uncertainty from measurements and modeling. Occupant-trajectory identification is then performed based on the candidate-location set for each detected footstep using a sequential analysis that combines information from consecutive footsteps. A full-scale case study is used to evaluate the methodology. Model-based occupant tracking that includes structural information and takes into account systematic errors and model bias has the potential to identify accurately single occupant locations in a full-scale structure.

Keywords. Occupant tracking, Footstep-induced vibrations, Physics-based model data-interpretation, Error-domain model falsification, Sequential analysis, Trajectory identification.

1. Introduction

Sensing technologies, such as embedded and portable sensors, have been increasingly used to track occupants inside buildings. Indoor-occupant tracking information has the potential to improve understanding of occupant behavior. Thus, occupant security and comfort may be enhanced. Occupant tracking information might be useful for applications such as more informed fire rescue, market research, energy management (through thermal-load prediction) and increase information regarding patient locations for hospital and old-age accommodation facilities.

Most research on occupant detection and localization strategies involve intrusive equipment such as optical sensors (Erickson, Achleitner and Cerpa, 2013) and radio-frequency devices (Lazik *et al.*, 2015) to identify indoor occupant locations. Optical sensors, such as motion sensors and cameras, require large angles of coverage and clear lines of sight to localize indoor occupants precisely (Narayana *et al.*, 2015). Radio-frequency devices, such as radio-frequency beacons and smartphones, are sensitive to changing environmental conditions that make identification of occupant locations in buildings challenging (Bekkelien, Deriaz and Marchand Maillet, 2012; Lam *et al.*, 2016). Due to the intrusive nature of these devices, they might lead to disturbing indoor occupants. Thus, unobtrusive strategies are often preferred such as vibration sensors and smart flooring systems that use thousands of floor sensors (Serra *et al.*, 2014). Such systems thus rely on costly equipment that is not compatible with large full-scale applications.

In this paper, the use of sparsely distributed vibration sensors for occupant tracking is proposed in order to preserve the privacy of indoor occupants (Richman *et al.*, 2001). Ongoing research on vibration-based occupant tracking relies on processing and analyzing floor-vibration data induced by human footsteps using Time Difference of Arrivals (TDoA) for occupant localization (Lam *et al.*, 2016). TDoA requires a large number of sensors to provide accurate occupant detection and localization due to low signal-to-noise ratio of footstep-induced floor vibrations (Lam *et al.*, 2016). The dispersive nature of structures, varying floor rigidities and the presence of obstructions such as walls lead to uncertain localization estimation (Mirshekari *et al.*, 2018). Vibration-based data interpretation for occupant tracking using a physics-based model has been applied for a single occupant walking with one type of shoe (Reuland *et al.*, 2017; Drira *et al.*, 2019). Comparing vibration measurements with physics-based models have led to accurate identification of trajectories through identifying the location of successive footstep impacts (Drira *et al.*, 2019). However, possible trajectories were limited and additional uncertainty from varying shoe types has not been assessed.

In this paper, a strategy for tracking a single occupant based on comparing physics-based models of the structural behavior with floor-vibration measurements is presented. This approach has the potential to overcome the limitations that are related to varying rigidities of structural floors, obstructions as well as variation of the signal related to a person walking using various shoe types. Comparisons between model simulations and measurements are carried out using error-domain model falsification (EDMF), a model-based data interpretation (Goulet and Smith, 2013). EDMF incorporates multiple sources of uncertainties arising from measurements and simulations. EDMF has been successfully applied to more than fifteen full-scale systems (Smith, 2016) including structural identification (Goulet, Michel and Smith, 2013), fatigue life evaluation (Pasquier *et al.*, 2016) and post-seismic building assessment (Reuland, Lestuzzi and Smith, 2017).

This paper starts with a description of the model-based data-interpretation methodology for occupant tracking (Section 2). Application to a full-scale system is presented in Section 3 and conclusions are discussed in Section 4.

2. Model-based occupant tracking strategy

Based on floor-vibration measurements, the identification of possible trajectories of a single occupant is achieved through five steps: processing of footstep-event signals, simulation of footstep impacts at predefined locations, localization of footstep-impacts using EDMF, reduction of footstep-impact localization ambiguities using a sequential analysis and identification of occupant trajectories based on resulting footstep-impact locations. The model-based occupant-tracking strategy is graphically summarized in Figure 1.

To start, footstep-induced floor vibrations are decomposed using continuous wavelet transform (CWT) around the dominant frequencies of the structure (derived from prior ambient-vibration measurements) in order to better discern each footstep-event signal from ambient conditions. CWT is carried out with the Morlet wavelet as mother wavelet due to shape similarity with footstep-impact signals. Baseline levels of ambient vibration (decomposed at the same frequency range using CWT) are used to set thresholds, defined as three standard deviations (3σ) of ambient noise, for occupant detection. A footstep-event signal is extracted at each sensor location when exceedance of detection thresholds is achieved. In this study, the maximum difference in amplitudes (Δ_{amp}) of non-processed footstep-event signals are used as metrics for occupant tracking (see Figure 1).

For all potential occupant locations, footstep impacts are simulated using a finite-element model and the value of Δ_{amp} for simulated footstep-impact signals is derived. Occupant localization is performed using EDMF through comparing measurements with model simulations taking into account various sources of measurement and model uncertainties. Model uncertainties that may include model imperfections and unknown model parameters are estimated base on engineering judgment (Pasquier *et al.*, 2016; Pai, Nussbaumer and Smith, 2018). Measurement uncertainties include resolution and precision of the sensors as well as variability of footstep-induced floor vibrations (due to the natural variability of walking rhythm, occupant load distribution and shoe types) are quantified using prior measurements. Localization thresholds are computed based on combined uncertainties (that define the residual between measured and simulated responses) and a target reliability of identification (Goulet, Michel and Smith, 2013). For each footstep event, simulated model responses for all locations that do not contradict measurements form the candidate location set (CLS) (see Equation 1 in Figure 1).

Subsequently, the CLS related to each detected footstep event is subjected to a sequential analysis. Based on information from the previous footstep event, it is assumed that the distance of two successive footstep impacts cannot exceed a predefined distance, such as twice the length of a step (approximately 75 cm). As walking trajectories are not defined during measurement, a candidate location (CL) of footstep event $i+1$ is rejected when the distance with all CLs of footstep event i exceeds twice the pre-defined step length (see Equation 2 in Figure 1). Based on layout information of the full-scale case study, departure/arrival points are assumed to be pre-defined for a sake of simplicity. Starting from the first footstep event, CLs are grouped according to possible departures based on sequential analysis (see Figure 2). CLs that do not correspond to a possible departure are rejected.

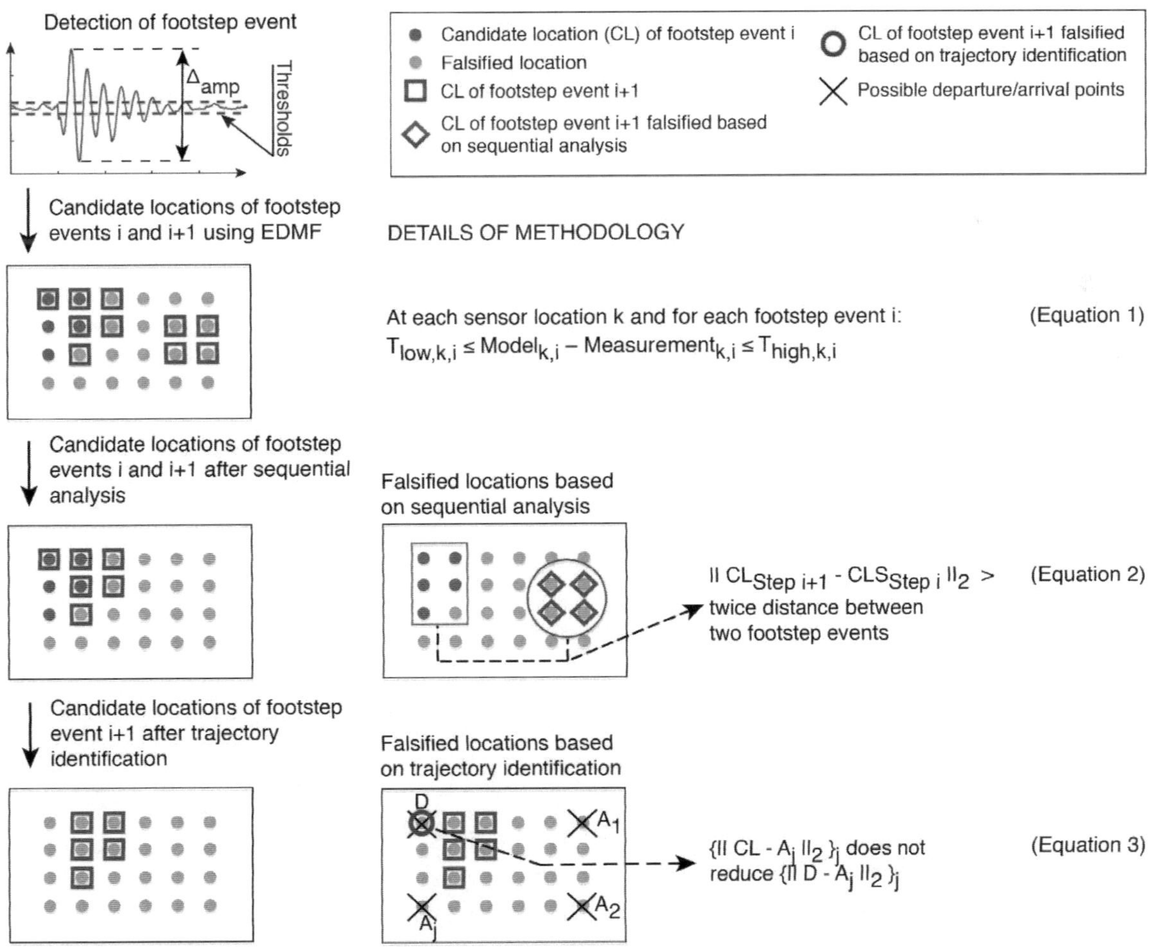

Figure 1: Measured signal of detected footstep-impact are compared with simulations. Location instances are falsified when the residual between simulations and measurements exceeds localization

thresholds ($T_{low,k}$ and $T_{high,k}$) at any sensor location. Based on information from the previous footstep event, sequential analysis reduces the population of the resulting CLS. A CL of footstep event $i + 1$ ($CL_{Step\ i+1}$ in Equation 2) is falsified when its distance with all CLs of footstep event i ($CL_{Step\ i}$ in Equation 2) exceeds twice the pre-defined step length. A CL that corresponds to a possible departure (D in Equation 3) is falsified when its distances with all possible arrivals (A_j in Equation 3) do not reduce the distance of the corresponding departure with all possible arrivals, respecting CLS of previous footstep events.

A trajectory identification is then performed based on the CLS (obtained after sequential analysis) of each detected step event. For trajectory identification, it is assumed that the occupant walks until reaching destination without backtracking. A CL that corresponds to a possible departure is rejected when the distance is not reduced with at least one possible arrival point. This analysis is again performed sequentially, as each CLS needs to contain locations for which the distance to at least one arrival point is reduced with respect to CLS of the previous footstep event (see Equation 3 in Figure 1).

3. Application to full-scale floor-slab

The model-based occupant-tracking strategy presented in Section 2 is tested on a part of a full-scale floor slab (approximately 950 m^2). The floor is a continuous reinforced-concrete slab supported by ten concrete columns as well as several reinforced-concrete walls (see Figure 2). The slab is supported by a uni-directional reinforced-concrete beam connecting the slab with the columns (see section A-A in Figure 2). The studied surface contains several masonry walls as well as separation walls made of plasterboard as shown in Figure 2. The floor-slab contains multiple structural elements, such as columns and beams that influence vibration measurements.

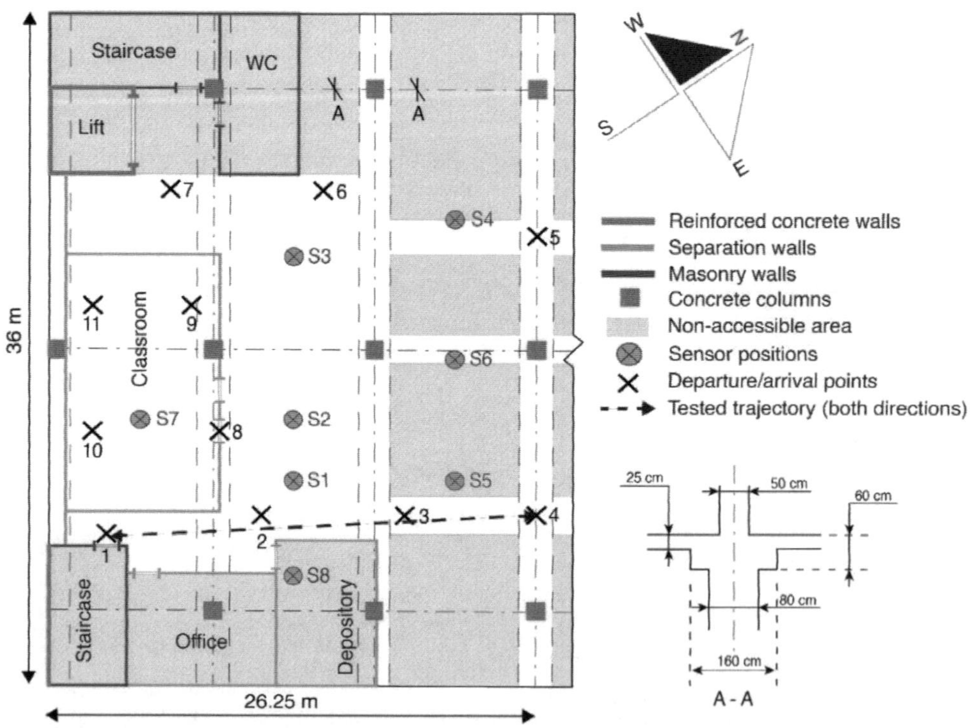

Figure 2: Occupant tracking is tested on a full-scale concrete slab. The slab contains eleven departure/arrival points for trajectories. Bi-directional trajectories of a single occupant between X1 and X4 are used for testing the presented methodology (see Figure 4).

Eight vibration sensors (Geophones SM-24 by I/O Sensor Nederland bv) are used to measure vertical velocity responses of the slab at a sampling rate of 1000 Hz (using an acquisition unit NI PCIe-6259). Vibration sensors are placed based on engineering judgment with the objective to cover to entire space providing clear measurements. Based on prior knowledge of the dynamical behavior of the structure sensor placement is done in order to capture higher natural modes (for example Sensors S2, S6, S7 and S8 in Figure 2) in addition to fundamental modes. In this case study, eleven departure/arrival points are assumed and define all possible trajectories (see Figure 2). The predefined departure/arrival points lead to 121 possible trajectories. Trajectories connecting points X1 and X4 are tested in both directions for model-based occupant tracking strategy. Measurements from a single occupant (approximately 90 kg) are taken using two types of shoes: hard-and-soft soled shoes. Although walking frequency is not fixed, it is naturally situated around 1.6 Hz.

Ambient-vibration measurements have revealed that vertical floor vibrations are contaminated by electrical instruments that operate at a fixed frequency of 50 Hz. Therefore, signal components at frequency range of [49-51] Hz are canceled out using a stop-band Butterworth filter to enhance signal-to-noise ratio of footstep events. Based on the ambient vibration measurements, fundamental vertical bending modes of the structure are found to be contained within the frequency range of [9-15] Hz. Using baseline levels of the ambient noise (see Section 2) and prior knowledge of walking frequency, each footstep-event signal of a walking occupant is detected and extracted successively from vibration measurements.

Model responses are simulated using a finite-element model of the slab. The dynamic responses of the slab generated by footstep impacts at various locations are simulated based on modal superposition. A time-history function describing the footstep-impact load is applied at all predefined locations that cover most of the accessible zones in Figure 2. Footstep-impact load function is described as a convex-shaped function that starts with non-zero slope and ends with zero slope. The input function is designed as a succession of two sine functions to illustrate events of heel contact (transmission of the full weight to the floor) and toe-off of the foot (Racic, Pavic and Brownjohn, 2009). Based on previous studies (Drira *et al.*, 2019), footstep full-weight duration (duration of the first sine function) is taken to be 0.1s and viscous damping ratio is taken to be 5% according to engineering heuristics.

Model simulations are prone to multiple sources of uncertainties that arise from unknown model parameters as well as model simplifications (such as idealized boundary conditions and omissions of separation walls and furniture). Model uncertainties resulting from model simplifications and omissions are estimated as a uniform distribution of [-30, +40] %. As the applied load function operates with low-frequency component that falls within the range of natural periods of the structure, low-frequency components of model simulations are highly affected (Drira *et al.*, 2019). Thus, velocity amplitudes are over-estimated leading to additional model uncertainties of up to [-40, 0] %.

Similar to modeling uncertainties, measurements are affected by multiple sources of uncertainties: limitations of sensor resolution and precision as well as variability of footstep-induced floor vibrations. This fluctuation of floor vibrations may result from natural variability of walking rhythm and impact force as well as the type of shoes worn by the occupant. Based on prior measurements of a person walking multiple trajectories along the same predefined locations using hard-and-soft-soled shoes, measurement uncertainties are found to be bounded by the interval [-45, 45] %. A uniform uncertainty distribution is assumed due to limited number of measurements and lack of more precise information about probability distribution.

Based on combined uncertainties, using Monte-Carlo sampling, and a target reliability of identification of 95 %, thresholds for each captured footstep event are estimated for occupant localization (Pasquier *et al.*, 2016; Pai, Nussbaumer and Smith, 2018). EDMF incorporates structural behavior of the floor slab, through footstep-impact simulations at predefined locations, to identify with a binary manner an estimate of occupant localization. For each footstep event, location instances for which residuals between model simulations and floor-vibration measurements are not compatible with the falsification thresholds are falsified. Combining information from each sensor location, remaining location instances define a CLS of each footstep event (see Figure 3,a for an example). Afterward, resulting CLS of each footstep event are subjected to sequential analysis and trajectory identification to infer candidate trajectories. A representation of the improvement over the CLS (squares) for the fifth footstep event of an occupant walking with hard-soled shoes from points X4 to X1 (see Figure 2) after sequential analysis and trajectory identification is shown in Figure 3. Based on the resulting CLS of the fifth footstep event (see Figure 3), only paths from departure point X4, except for arrival point X3, are candidate trajectories.

Sequential analysis reduces the ambiguity of CLS of each footstep event by verifying that the distance between two successive footstep events does not exceed a predefined distance (twice pre-defined step length). Taking into account information from previous footstep events, sequential analysis enhances the precision of CLS of each footstep event as shown in Figure 3,b. Assuming that all departure/arrival points are predefined and that occupants walk without backtracking until reaching destination, a trajectory identification is performed to further increase the precision of the resulting CLSs. A reduction in the size of the CLS related to a possible departure point is achieved when distances with all possible arrivals do not reduce the distance between the corresponding departure and all possible arrivals (see Figure 3,c).

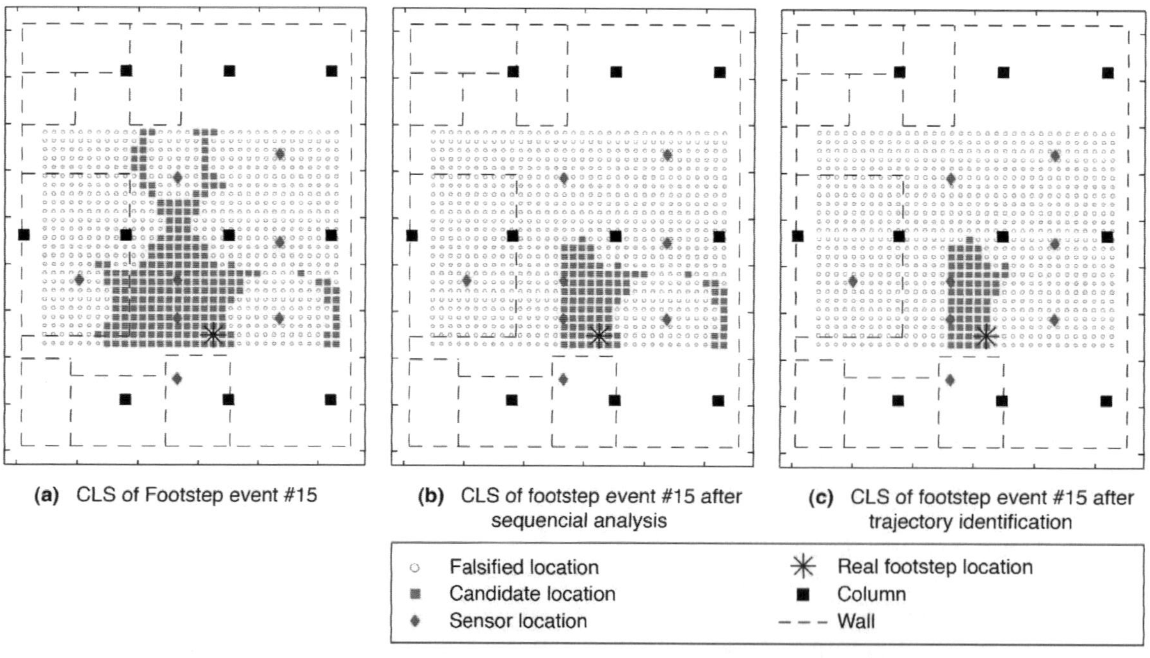

Figure 3: Candidate location set of footstep event #15; the precision of the candidate model set is enhanced based on (b) a sequential analysis and (c) subsequent trajectory identification. Information from previous footstep events (of the same trajectory) reduces the population of candidate locations (b). Candidate locations that do not reduce the distance between a departure and all possible arrivals are falsified (c).

Figure 4 illustrates examples of resulting CLSs (squares) of some footstep events that correspond to a tested trajectory of an occupant walking with soft-soled shoes from points X1 to X4 (see Figure 2). Circles correspond to falsified locations and real footstep locations (true occupant location) are represented with stars. CLS of the first captured footstep event needs to be compatible with the predefined departure points (see Figure 2), based on the same assumption than sequential analysis that verifies compatibility between subsequent step locations (see Equation 2 in Figure 1). CLs that are not compatible with a potential departure point are rejected (see footstep event #1 in Figure 4). Remaining departure points in Figure 4 are X1, X7, X9 and X11 (see Figure 2). Thus, CLs of the first footstep event are grouped based on corresponding departure points. Candidate trajectories starting from each starting point are updated with sequential analysis and trajectory identification using the information of all subsequent footstep events. CLs that verify the departure points X7, X9 and X11, illustrate the ambiguity resulting from model-based occupant localization. Measured floor vibrations are compatible with model simulations for all three departure points.

As can be seen in Figure 4, CLSs cover the true occupant locations for each footstep event. Thus, it is concluded that model-based occupant tracking provides accurate occupant localization results. However, for most footstep events precision of localization is low. Lack of precision of occupant localization may be due to the unknown parameter values of the finite-element model as well as treating the effect of shoe types as additional uncertainty source. Incorporating the existing obstructions such as separating walls and doors within trajectory identification may reduce the CLSs of footstep events and thus, will be studied in future development of the methodology.

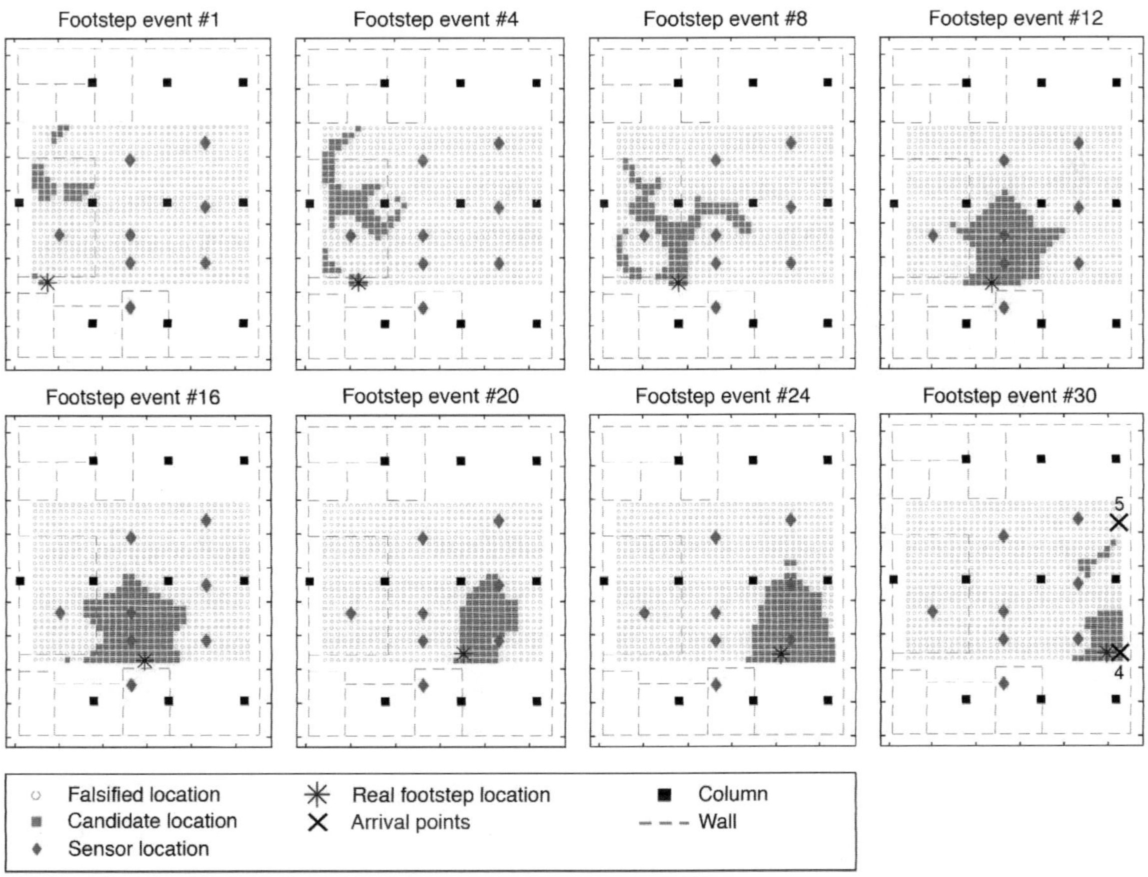

Figure 4: Candidate-location sets that are obtained using EDMF, sequential analysis and trajectory identification (see Figure 1) for an occupant walking with soft-soled shoes from X1 to X4 (see Figure 2).

Based on resulting CLSs and predefined departure/arrival points, candidate trajectories are identified and updated with information from CLS of each footstep-event. CLS of the first captured footstep event define the initial candidate trajectories. Only departure points that correspond to CLs are taken to be possible paths with the respect of all possible arrivals (see Figures 2 and 4). Exploring CLSs of remaining captured footstep events provides further information about trajectories that remain potential candidate trajectories. When a potential trajectory is achieved (reaching an arrival point) without exploring all CLS of captured footstep events, the corresponding trajectory is rejected. Once all CLSs of all captured footstep events are verified, candidate trajectories that do not end near arrival points are falsified. Based on CLS of the last captured footstep event (see footstep event #30 in Figure 4), only arrival point X4 leads to candidate trajectories. Table 1 summarizes the number of candidate trajectories at the first and the last detected footstep event of four-tested trajectories (see Figures 2 and 4).

Table 1: Number of candidate trajectories corresponding to first-and-last footstep events for four-tested trajectories (see Figure3).

Tested Trajectory	Candidate trajectories at footstep event #1	Candidate trajectories at the last footstep event
From X4 to X1; walking with hard-soled shoes (31 footstep events)	20 (out of 121)	3 (out of 121)
From X1 to X4; walking with hard-soled shoes (30 footstep events)	40	4
From X4 to X1; walking with soft-soled shoes (30 footstep events)	30	4
From X1 to X4; walking with soft-soled shoes (30 footstep events)	40	4

Starting from the first-footstep event, tested trajectories that relate points X1 and X4 of an occupant walking with hard-and-soft soled shoes (both directions) have led to a falsification of 66 % of possible initial candidate trajectories in worst cases (40 out of 121). Despite the lack of precision regarding the CLS of all footstep events, model-based occupant tracking provides a precise trajectory identification (approximately 97 %) with the correct trajectory is included in all cases.

Therefore, combining the knowledge of structural behavior with measurements and taking into account various sources of uncertainties, model-based occupant tracking has the potential to provide accurate and precise candidate trajectories of an occupant walking with different shoe types.

4. Conclusion

Model-based occupant tracking has been applied for an occupant walking with two types of shoes on a full-scale slab and leads to the following conclusions:

- Model-based occupant tracking (using error-domain model-falsification, EDMF) that includes structural information and takes into account systematic errors and model bias has the potential to identify accurately single occupant locations in a full-scale structure.

- Occupant tracking using sequential analysis and trajectory identification has the potential to provide precise occupant trajectories. For all case studies, a maximum of four candidate trajectories out of 121 have been identified.
- Model-based occupant tracking strategy can be applied to various types of shoes (sacrificing precision for accuracy) to identify accurately single occupant locations within a full-scale structure.

Future work includes studies of multiple occupants and automatic detection and correction for shoe type.

5. Acknowledgments

The authors acknowledge Tectus Dreamlab Pte Ltd and BBR Holdings Singapore for providing access to the full-scale floor slab to validate the model-based occupant-tracking strategy.

This work was funded by the applied computing and mechanics laboratory EPFL, the Singapore-ETH centre (SEC) under contract no. FI 370074011-370074016 and the Swiss National Science Foundation (SNSF) under contract no. 200020-169026.

References

Bekkelien, A., Deriaz, M. and Marchand Maillet, S. (2012) 'Bluetooth indoor positioning', *Master's thesis, University of Geneva.*

Drira, S. *et al.* (2019) 'Model-Based Occupant Tracking Using Slab-Vibration Measurements', *Frontiers in Built Environment*, 5, p. 63. doi: 10.3389/fbuil.2019.00063.

Erickson, V. L., Achleitner, S. and Cerpa, A. E. (2013) 'POEM: Power-efficient occupancy-based energy management system', in *Proceedings of the 12th international conference on Information processing in sensor networks*. Philadelphia, Pennsylvania, USA, pp. 203–216.

Goulet, J.-A., Michel, C. and Smith, I. F. C. (2013) 'Hybrid probabilities and error-domain structural identification using ambient vibration monitoring', *Mechanical Systems and Signal Processing*. Elsevier, 37(1–2), pp. 199–212.

Goulet, J.-A. and Smith, I. F. C. (2013) 'Structural identification with systematic errors and unknown uncertainty dependencies', *Computers & structures*. Elsevier, 128, pp. 251–258.

Lam, M. *et al.* (2016) 'Robust occupant detection through step-induced floor vibration by incorporating structural characteristics', in *Dynamics of Coupled Structures, Volume 4*. Springer, pp. 357–367.

Lazik, P. *et al.* (2015) 'ALPS: A bluetooth and ultrasound platform for mapping and localization', in *Proceedings of the 13th ACM conference on embedded networked sensor systems*. Seoul, South Korea, pp. 73–84.

Mirshekari, M. *et al.* (2018) 'Occupant localization using footstep-induced structural vibration', *Mechanical Systems and Signal Processing*. Elsevier, 112, pp. 77–97.

Narayana, S. *et al.* (2015) 'PIR sensors: Characterization and novel localization technique', in *Proceedings of the 14th international conference on information processing in sensor networks*. Seattle, Washington, pp. 142–153.

Pai, S. G. S., Nussbaumer, A. and Smith, I. F. C. (2018) 'Comparing Structural Identification Methodologies for Fatigue Life Prediction of a Highway Bridge', *Frontiers in Built Environment*. Frontiers, 3, p. 73.

Pasquier, R. *et al.* (2016) 'Measurement, data interpretation, and uncertainty propagation for fatigue assessments of structures', *Journal of Bridge Engineering*. American Society of Civil Engineers, 21(5), p. 4015087.

Racic, V., Pavic, A. and Brownjohn, J. M. W. (2009) 'Experimental identification and analytical modelling of human walking forces: Literature review', *Journal of Sound and Vibration*. Elsevier, 326(1–2), pp. 1–49.

Reuland, Y. *et al.* (2017) 'Vibration-based occupant detection using a multiple-model approach', in *Dynamics of Civil Structures, Volume 2*. Springer, pp. 49–56.

Reuland, Y., Lestuzzi, P. and Smith, I. F. C. (2017) 'Data-Interpretation Methodologies for Non-Linear Earthquake Response Predictions of Damaged Structures', *Frontiers in Built Environment*, 3, p. 43. doi: 10.3389/fbuil.2017.00043.

Richman, M. S. *et al.* (2001) 'Personnel tracking using seismic sensors', in *Unattended Ground Sensor Technologies and Applications III*, pp. 14–22.

Serra, R. *et al.* (2014) 'Human step detection from a piezoelectric polymer floor sensor using normalization algorithms', in *SENSORS, 2014 IEEE*, pp. 1169–1172.

Smith, I. F. C. (2016) 'Studies of sensor data interpretation for asset management of the built environment', *Frontiers in Built Environment*. Frontiers, 2, p. 8.

Knowledge-Based Target Selection in a Building Navigation System

Wojciech Palacz
The Faculty of Physics, Astronomy and Applied Computer Science,
Jagiellonian University, Kraków, Poland
wojciech.palacz@uj.edu.pl

Abstract. This paper is concerned with indoor navigation systems integrated with knowledge bases containing rich semantic data about buildings and their constituent spaces. Specifically, it is concerned with a system which utilizes graph models with labels, attributes and hierarchies storing semantic knowledge. That information can be used to describe navigation targets, as was shown in (Palacz et al., 2016). This paper continues that work and proposes a graphical user interface which allows for specifying complex target selection criteria.

1. Introduction

This paper is concerned with indoor pedestrian navigation systems. Their most obvious application is the case of a first-time visitor, who needs to get to a specific room in an unknown building while knowing only the number of this room. To help him in this task a navigation system needs a model of the building which allows for finding the optimal path between any two points, a way of determining the point where the visitor is currently standing, and a database containing numbers assigned to rooms in the building.

A room number is an example of a piece of semantic data attached to a particular space in a building. There are many more types of semantic data which are associated with buildings and their constituent areas. For example, knowledge about names of room occupants in an office building, about different room types in a university building (office room, lecture hall, laboratory, canteen, etc.), or about organizational units and which rooms are assigned to them.

Having this knowledge in its database makes the navigation system useful to people who already know the building and its room numbering scheme, but require a bit of help with finding targets described in terms of this additional semantic data. (Palacz et al., 2016) contains examples of such target descriptions. Some of them correspond to a single point/room (for example, "the coffee machine closest to my current position" or "the closest laboratory belonging to the Department of Organic Chemistry"), other to a set of points ("all office rooms belonging to the Department of Games").

The system proposed in (Palacz et al., 2016) uses graph-based data structures. Graphs are an obvious choice for any task related to path planning. All navigation systems use graphs with nodes representing places and edges representing costs of moving between them. This "cost" can mean a distance measured in kilometers, time required, expended liters of gasoline, or something else—this depends on what the navigation system is designed to optimize for. In our case, edges are labelled with time required by the average human to walk from one endpoint to the other.

Additional attributes and hierarchies are used to store semantic knowledge. For example, the models have hierarchies assigning nodes representing rooms as children of nodes representing functional areas of the building, as well as appropriate administrative departments. They also have attributes storing information about door labels ("room no 108"), about presence of specific equipment (e.g. big-format printers), and so on.

As an example of advanced target selection, (Palacz et al., 2016) discussed an algorithm which directs the user to rooms represented by graph nodes with a specific attribute, visiting them in the order determined by their position in the administrative hierarchy. That algorithm had to be implemented in the navigation application's code before the users could take advantage of it. While that approach is suitable for systems which support a few well-specified tasks, it does not scale and cannot be used in a general, multipurpose navigation system.

As the size and richness of the knowledge base grows, so does exponentially grow the number of target selection algorithms which can be envisioned. Implementing all of them in advance, on the remote chance that some user in the future will have a need for a particular one, is unfeasible. Therefore, this paper proposes extending the navigation application with a target selection GUI displaying available selection criteria. It will allow the user to choose those applicable to his current task, to combine them using boolean operators, and to arrange them into successive phases.

In order to be tightly aligned with the knowledge base the GUI has to be dynamically generated. Let us consider a building in which all rooms are assigned to the same department—in this case, including "administrative unit" among the selection criteria is unnecessary, maybe even confusing. It is also necessary to note that the graph model is extensible and may be modified rapidly. The navigation application has to be able to adapt its GUI to changes like updated labels or introduction of a new graph attribute.

2. Indoor Navigation Systems

The field of indoor navigation includes many research problems. The most obvious one is determining the current position of the user of a navigation system. In contrast to the outdoor systems, an indoor system cannot rely on satellite-based location methods, because they are unreliable inside buildings (Gilliéron et al., 2013).

Therefore, indoor systems usually determine their position by taking a fix on stationary devices installed in the building. Wi-Fi access points are often used in this role, because they are already present in nearly all contemporary buildings. An example of such a Wi-Fi-based system deployed on a university campus can be found in (Köbben et al., 2006).

Wi-Fi-based methods have rather low accuracy. In cases where more precision is required, a network of dedicated reference devices must be deployed. This network can use RFID tags, Bluetooth beacons, etc. The Meridian Platform (Aruba Networks, 2019) is a representative example of a commercially available, Bluetooth-based solution. It requires beacons which are placed no more than 10 meters apart and provides accuracy of about 4 meters.

A systematic review of different methods and sensors used for determining the user's location can be found in, e.g., (Pahlavan et al., 2002) or (Correa et al., 2017).

Another research problem concerns navigation maps. A navigation system needs a map of the building, and it needs to be some kind of a graph with nodes representing specific points in the building and edges representing available paths between these points. This map can be constructed manually by developers of the system, but this is time-consuming and can introduce errors.

Contemporary buildings are constructed using the BIM (Building Information Modeling) methodology. Thus, a computer-readable BIM model of the building must be available, often in the form of an IFC file (buildingSMART International, 2019). Using this model as a basis for navigation map is a much more attractive solution.

A BIM model can be compared to an object-oriented database. It is composed of IFC entities arranged in a hierarchical manner. Each entity includes a fixed number of attributes, defined in the IFC standard, and an arbitrary number of additional properties. There are three fundamental entity types: IfcObjectDefinition, IfcPropertyDefinition and IfcRelationship. They in turn have

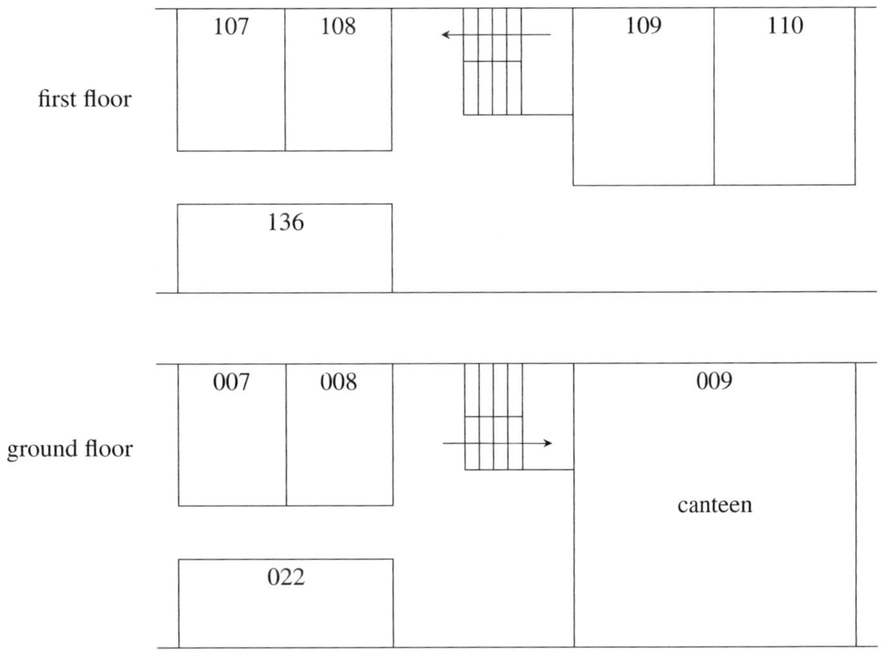

Figure 1: A fragment of a university building floor plan.

many subtypes: IfcBuildingStorey, IfcWall, IfcDoor, IfcOpeningElement, etc. Entities can be arranged in many different, complex ways, thus parsing an IFC file is a nontrivial task.

Systems which analyze BIM models in order to determine where human-accessible spaces are and how they are connected are described in, e.g., (Isikdag et al., 2013), (Tang et al., 2015) or (Xu et al., 2017). (Ferreira et al., 2018) presents a campus navigation system which integrates spatial data extracted from the BIM model with knowledge from other sources, which allows it to handle queries referring to university teachers, e.g. "how can I get to the Professor Smith's room?".

Location-based services (Sharma et al., 2017) are another area in the field of indoor navigation. Majority of theoretical research in this area focuses on privacy aspects; among practical applications, systems dedicated for museum environments are common.

For example, MusA (Rubino et al., 2013) combines roles of a navigation system and an electronic guide. This necessarily implies that its internal database contains not only information about spatial structure of the museum's building, but also about exhibits (names, descriptions, etc.). Its navigation module allows users to either select a single target point, or a path consisting of several points. A path can be specified manually, point by point, or chosen from the list of predefined thematic paths designed by museum's curators.

It is worth noticing that even when the internal database of the navigation system includes additional semantic data, the user usually cannot fully take advantage of it. For example, MusA knows descriptions associated with exhibits and can display them for the user, but cannot search these descriptions for particular keywords when the user is planning a path.

This paper attempts to propose a solution which gives the user a way of specifying navigation targets on basis of their semantic properties.

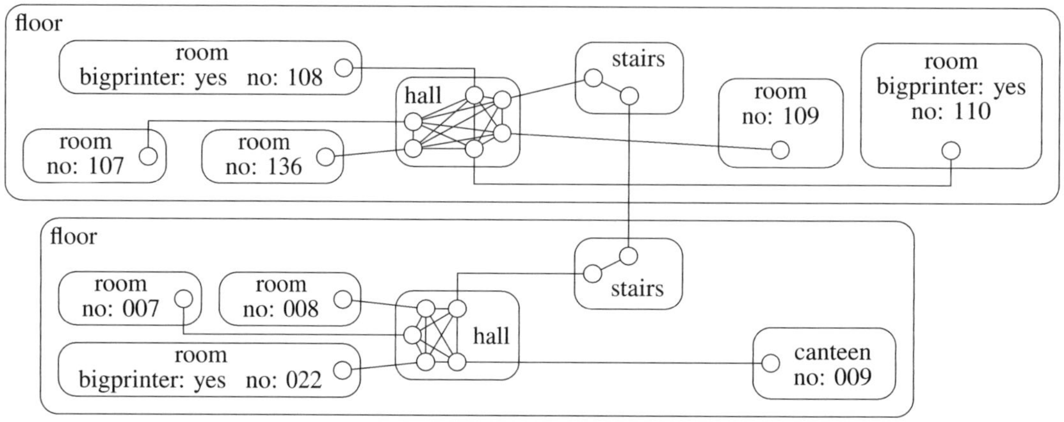

Figure 2: A view showing the spatial hierarchy (edge costs omitted).

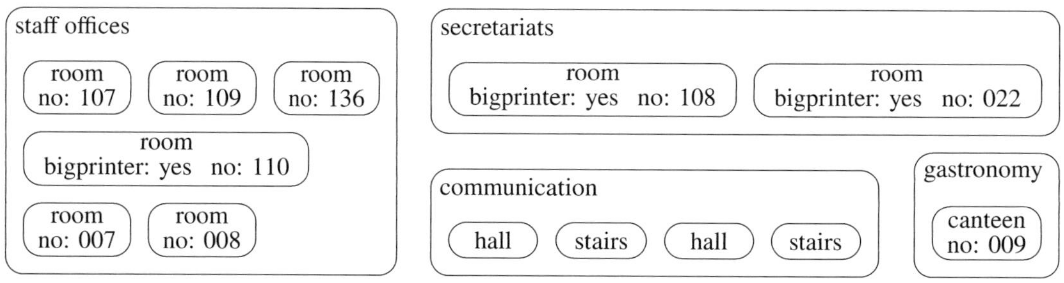

Figure 3: A view showing the functional hierarchy.

3. The Graph Model

Multi-hierarchical graphs proposed in (Palacz et al., 2016) are a result of research on design models presented in e.g. (Grabska et al., 2007, 2013; Strug et al., 2014). Ordinary flat graphs are often inadequate as models of structures encountered in real-world architectural design and engineering applications. Such complex structures are often hierarchical; therefore hierarchical graphs are proposed. They allow for separating components of modelled item from each other and for "hiding" some details in the lower levels of the hierarchy, while retaining the ability to specify relations between parts of different components.

The idea of multiple hierarchies was initially introduced in order to provide an additional spatial hierarchy, which was used to group stair segments and stair landings into staircases. It was necessary because staircases do not fit into the standard spatial hierarchy, which divides a building into separate floors, which are further divided into spaces (rooms, corridors, etc.).

In (Palacz et al., 2016) extra hierarchies were used to represent non-spatial relations between parts of the building. These relations could, in theory, be represented by appropriately labelled graph edges, but using graph hierarchies is more convenient when dealing with relations which by their inherent nature also are hierarchical.

Let us consider a small part of a university building as an example. Fig. 1 displays its floor plan, which includes several rooms belonging to two departments, a student canteen and a staircase. A multi-hierarchical graph which models this building has four hierarchies: spatial, vertical spatial, functional and administrative. A graph with many hierarchies is difficult to arrange on a diagram in a clear way, therefore views of different hierarchies are displayed in separate figures.

The standard spatial hierarchy (Fig. 2) groups together nodes representing spaces belonging

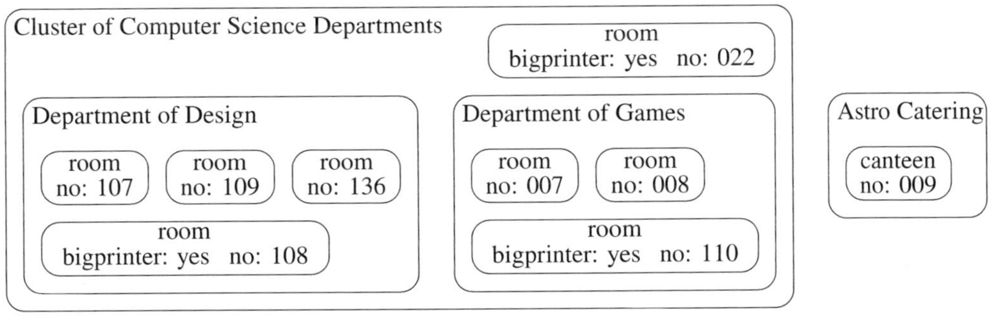

Figure 4: A view showing the administrative hierarchy.

to the same floor and places them inside a node representing that floor. It also contains nodes representing entry/exit points which are used to move between adjacent spaces. These nodes are connected by edges denoting accessibility. The cost of traversing a given edge (that is, time required to walk from one point to the other) is stored in that edge's attribute.

The functional hierarchy (Fig. 3) divides the building into functional areas. All corridors and stairs are assigned as children of the "communication" node, personal rooms of university employees as children of the "staff offices" node, canteens and other places where food can be bought are assigned to the "gastronomy" node, and so on.

The administrative hierarchy (Fig. 4) provides nodes corresponding to the administrative structure of the university (chairs, departments, etc.).

Nodes representing rooms take part in all hierarchies and are presented on all three views. For other nodes it varies, depending on what exactly do they represent. Halls, as common building areas which belong to no department, take part only in spatial and functional hierarchies. Parent nodes which group rooms usually correspond to immaterial entities which make sense only in context of a specific hierarchy, and thus take part only in that hierarchy.

In addition to hierarchies discussed above, the example graph model has node labels and attributes. They are used to store semantic data about building and its spaces, too. As can be seen in Figs. 2–4, information about types of spaces (room, hall, etc.), names given to grouping entities, room numbers and presence of big-format printers is represented.

4. Evolution of the Knowledge Base and Target Selection GUI

The navigation system proposed in (Palacz et al., 2016) requires both geometric data and semantic data. A single graph model which stores both is a considerable advantage. It provides the maximum possible degree of integration and eliminates the possibility of inconsistency between two separate databases. A graph is a well-known data structure, therefore developers charged with creating, updating and verifying building models should find that tasks straightforward.

Graphs are also easily extensible. Introducing a new attribute, assigning it to selected nodes and defining attribute values for these nodes does not require any changes in the formal definition of a multi-hierarchical graph. New node hierarchies can be easily introduced, too.

It seems probable that after deploying the navigation system, its users (i.e. students, lecturers and other staff) will propose new kinds of semantic data which should be included in the knowledge base. For example, they may wish to know canteen hours, or the number of seats in a lecture room (and if they have power sockets for laptops), or which equipment is installed in a laboratory.

To understand how this evolution of database contents may proceed we can look at Open-

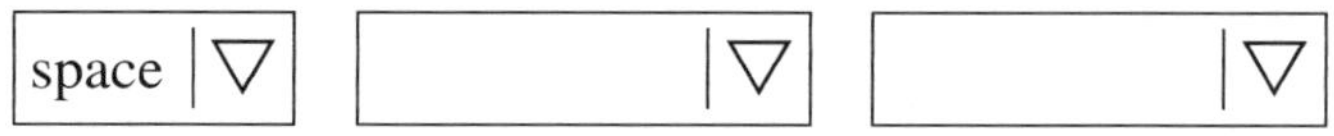

Figure 5: The initial state of the search form.

StreetMap (OSM), a well-known collaborative mapping project. OSM uses a topological data structure with three basic element types: points, polylines/polygons, and lists of elements. Each element usually has one or more tags, which are pairs consisting of a key and a value. For example, a hypothetical polygon could be be tagged with the "building=house", "addr:street=Apple Street" and "addr:housenumber=17" tags, which provide the type of object (a single-family house) and its semantic data. So, it should be clear that OSM tags are very similar to labels and attributes used in the multi-hierarchical graph model.

OSM is edited by volunteers, and each of them can invent their own tags. Nonetheless, the OSM community produced a common set of conventions describing which tags should be used for which purposes (OSM user community, 2019). This set of commonly used tags evolved over time. (Mocnik et al., 2017) describes this process and notes that it included introduction of new keys, but also refinement of existing tags. Consider the tag "building=residential", which is rather general—by introducing additional values "apartments", "detached", "terrace", etc. the map can be made more detailed. Currently there are several dozen frequently used keys, with no more than several dozen possible values per key (this does not include keys with free-form values, like "addr:street"). Let us assume that these upper limits will also hold for the graph model.

As was stated in the introduction, this paper aims to propose a GUI for specifying a navigation target by leveraging semantic data stored in the graph. This GUI needs to be able to adapt to unexpected changes in the knowledge base (introduction of new attributes or hierarchies, changes in attributes' value ranges).

The navigation system must analyse the graph model. It starts by using spatial hierarchy to find nodes corresponding to basic spaces and makes a list of their labels (which denote their types). Then it checks other hierarchies and makes another list, with labels of group nodes which contain found spaces. It also makes lists with attribute names and their values. Since text strings gathered on these lists will be displayed in the GUI, they must be human-readable and their meaning should be clear to an average user.

Look and feel of the GUI is similar to advanced search forms provided by electronic libraries. We start with an empty form (see Fig. 5). It provides three drop-down list widgets which allow us to specify which type of space we are interested in, and which simple condition this space must fulfill. Leaving all three of them in their initial state is technically allowed, but means that we want to visit any/all spaces in the building.

Widgets must be filled left-to-right. The middle drop-down list is used to specify is we want to check a specific attribute (after selecting its name the right list will offer a choice between values of this attribute) or a hierarchical relation (in that case the right list offers labels of group

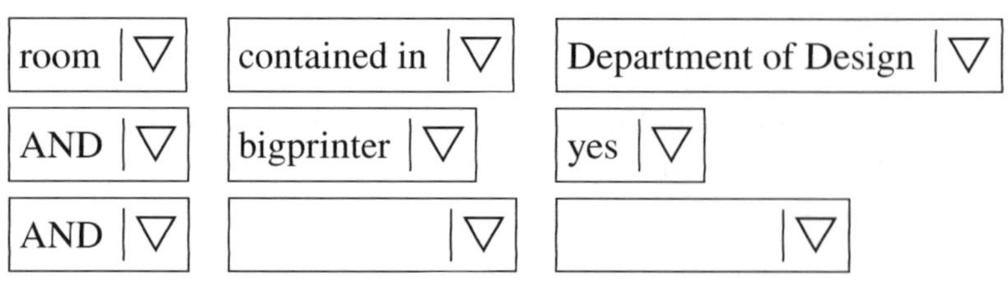

Figure 6: An example target description.

nodes). When all widgets are filled the form automatically extends, allowing us to specify another simple condition and combine it with the previous one. Fig. 6 shows an example which combines two conditions.

Constructed target description resolves to a set of spaces; it is worth noticing that this set may contain zero, one or more elements. In the case of multiple results, the navigation system will direct its user to the closest target, then ask if he wishes to continue onward to the next one, and so on until all targets are visited or the user commands it to stop.

Target descriptions can be chained together so that the system will guide the user to targets from the first set, then to targets from the second set (unless they were already visited in phase one), and so on.

5. Conclusion

This paper considered an indoor navigation system described in (Palacz et al., 2016), which uses a graph as its main data structure. The graph contains data required for path planning, as well as additional data which semantically describes rooms and other elements of a building. The semantic knowledge could be used to execute complex navigation tasks, but only by implementing a procedure which extracted and processed data appropriate to a given task.

To make the system more useful for ordinary users, this paper proposed a specialized graphical user interface. This GUI adjusts itself dynamically by taking into account types of semantic knowledge which are stored in the graph, and provides a point-and-click form which allows for describing navigation targets on the basis of their semantic properties. Form's complexity is about equal to the "advanced search" forms provided by online libraries and document repositories.

References

Aruba Networks (2019). The Meridian Platform. `https://meridianapps.com/`, accessed on June 1, 2019.

buildingSMART International (2019). IFC introduction. `https://www.buildingsmart.org/about/what-is-openbim/ifc-introduction/`, accessed on June 1, 2019.

Correa, A., Barcelo, M., Morell, A., & Vicario, J. L. (2017). Indoor positioning systems for mass market applications. *Sensors*, 17(8).

Ferreira, J. C., Resende, R., & Martinho, S. (2018). Beacons and BIM models for indoor guidance and location. *Sensors*, 18(12).

Gilliéron, P.-Y., Chazal, V., Flamm, M., von der Mühll, D., & Ruzicka-Rossier, M. (2013). Pedestrian navigation for the benefit of mobility. In A. Nait-Sidi-Moh, M. Bakhouya, J. Gaber, & M. Wack (Eds.), *Geopositioning and Mobility* chapter 7, (pp. 155–201). John Wiley & Sons.

Grabska, E., Łachwa, A., Ślusarczyk, G., Grzesiak-Kopeć, K., & Lembas, J. (2007). Hierarchical layout hypergraph operations and diagrammatic reasoning. *Machine GRAPHICS & VISION*, 16(1/2), 23–38.

Grabska, E., Ślusarczyk, G., & Gajek, Sz. (2013). Knowledge representation for human-computer interaction in a system supporting conceptual design. *Fundamenta Informaticae*, 124(1–2), 91–110.

Isikdag, U., Zlatanova, S., & Underwood, J. (2013). A BIM-oriented model for supporting indoor navigation requirements. *Computers, Environment and Urban Systems*, 41, 112–123.

Köbben, B., van Bunningen, A. H., & Muthukrishnan, K. (2006). Wireless campus LBS: Building campus-wide location based services based on WiFi technology. In E. Stefanakis, M. P. Peterson, C. Armenakis, & V. Delis (Eds.), *Geographic Hypermedia: Concepts and Systems* (pp. 399–408). Springer.

Mocnik, F.-B., Zipf, A., & Raifer, M. (2017). The OpenStreetMap folksonomy and its evolution. *Geo-spatial Information Science*, 20(3), 219–230.

OSM user community (2019). Map features. `https://wiki.openstreetmap.org/wiki/Map_Features`, accessed on March 25, 2019.

Pahlavan, K., Li, X., & Mäkelä, J.-P. (2002). Indoor geolocation science and technology. *IEEE Communications Magazine*, 40(2), 112–118.

Palacz, W., Ślusarczyk, G., Łachwa, A., Strug, B., Paszyńska, A., & Grabska, E. (2016). Towards knowledge-based building navigation with the use of a hierarchical graph model. In *Proceedings of the 23rd EG-ICE International Workshop* (pp. 301–311). Kraków, Poland.

Rubino, I., Xhembulla, J., Martina, A., Bottino, A., & Malnati, G. (2013). MusA: Using indoor positioning and navigation to enhance cultural experiences in a museum. *Sensors*, 13(12).

Sharma, L., Javali, A., Nyamangoudar, R., Priya, R., Mishra, P., & Routray, S. K. (2017). An update on location based services: Current state and future prospects. In *Proceedings of the 2017 International Conference on Computing Methodologies and Communication (ICCMC)* (pp. 220–224).

Strug, B., Grabska, E., & Ślusarczyk, G. (2014). Supporting the design process with hypergraph genetic operators. *Advanced Engineering Informatics*, 28(1), 11–27.

Tang, S. J., Zhu, Q., Wang, W. W., & Zhang, Y. T. (2015). Automatic topology derivation from IFC building model for in-door intelligent navigation. *The International Archives of the Photogrammetry, Remote Sensing and Spatial Information Sciences*, XL-4/W5.

Xu, M., Wei, S., Zlatanova, S., & Zhang, R. (2017). BIM-based indoor path planning considering obstacles. *ISPRS Annals of Photogrammetry, Remote Sensing and Spatial Information Sciences*, IV-2/W4, 417–423.

Adaptive feature-conserving compression for large scale point clouds

Felix Eickeler, André Borrmann
Chair of Computational Modelling and Simulation
Technical University of Munich, Germany
felix.eickeler@tum.de

Abstract. In this work we introduce a practical method for reducing big point clouds of buildings and infrastructure. The proposed method introduces bilateral filtering with a tailored set of evaluation functions, that will conserve as much information as possible. To determin the actual statistical parameters to perform this filtering and reason about our development, we investigate different point properties on a comprehensive dataset. The dataset contains artificial, photogrammetric and laser scanned point clouds and was made publicly available. We showcase our filtering method by preserving more information than voxel grid or density filters challenging even sparser photogrammetric datasets. Finally, we discuss some encoding strategies as well as the sweet spot between size and resolution.

1. Introduction

Point clouds are becoming a quasi-standard representation for capturing existing context, construction progress monitoring, as-built modeling and quality control. While previously only a topic of research, most recent real-world applications and software tools support fully automated workflows based on point cloud data. In tandem with the increasing number of implemented use cases, the instruments to generate suitable point clouds have improved as well. As sensors develop in precision and recording speed, they are adapted by the construction business and widely applied in planning and quality control. These sensors can capture point clouds of bigger construction sites, infrastructure in an adequate time frame and their point count can easily surpass multiple billion points.

For processing, the data is sliced or subsampled to manageable parts. Both strategies have downsides as slicing may lead to locality problems and merging issues and subsampling normally comes with the cost of precision or a change in the statistical point distribution. Our proposed method uses information about the domain to reduce the number of measures without sacrificing the properties of a high-density point clouds. Every point will be evaluated on the information gain of the point itself, using quantified relations between the different dimensions (locality, colour, orientation). We then use two approaches to optimize the data set: Grouping points with similar information (lossless compression), and we drop measures with low informational gain. To demonstrate the advantages, we benchmark the properties on multiple use cases built upon real world and synthetic data. All datasets are available under vision.cms.bgu.tum.de/eg_ice2019 (Eickeler 2019).

2. Related Work

Practitioners from the civil engineering industry mainly have two options when capturing as-is environments as point clouds - laser scanning and photogrammetric reconstruction. While both have advantages and disadvantages (Golparvar-Fard et al. 2011; Baltsavias 1999), the properties of the resulting point cloud can differ significantly. Laser scanners provide a fixed amount of measures per arc which leads to a radially decreasing point density. Most of the point clouds consist of multiple aligned scans (Boehler et al. 2003) creating a combined but locally inconsistent density: all points are created equal. In contrast, photogrammetric reconstructions are influenced by the number of images, parameter and colour gradients on the surfaces. Some surface materials with restless colouring are reconstructed with higher density and precision, which provides a natural grouping of points in regions of image diversity. Besides this distribution difference, the number of dimensions created by the recording device stands out the most. Original laser scan data consists of the three spatial properties - sometimes with an attached intensity, that encodes the strength of the signal that was the reflected by the hull. Some laser scanners attach colour information with a build-in camera device as a followup. The properties of the photogrammetric reconstruction can differ from one toolchain to another. Usually normals are estimated in the progress of dense reconstruction (Zheng et al. 2014; Schönberger et al. 2016) creating depth and normal maps. All usual properties and their common types are listed in Table 1.

Table 1: Encoded properties and their datatypes

Property	**Laser scan**	**Photogrammetric Reconstruction**
Spatial x, y, z	double	float
Orientation nx, ny, nz	-	float
Intensity i	float	-
Colour rgb	-	float / uint8[3]
Scalar field	-	-

Considering these properties, the memory consumption is respectively 28 bytes per point stored by a laser scanner. The same size is taken by several properties of the photogrammetric reconstruction. The size increases during processing due to the optimal Single Instruction Multiple Data (SIMD) memory alignment. Reducing the memory footprint has been in interest of research and work on reducing the consumption of the structure (Elseberg et al. 2013; Schnabel & Klein 2006). For large point clouds re-encoding the static part in a spatial structure results in huge memory saving but results in an increase of processing time.

Another way to reduce the memory consumption is filtering the point cloud. Traditionally the filtering methods are generalized methods, that will be applied to the recording point stream of scanners or simultaneous localization and mapping (SLAM) methods. Most methods such as bilateral or PDE based filtering (Han et al. 2017; Moorfield et al. 2015) try to optimize the cloud with respect to meshing performance. For Airborne Laser Scanning (ALS) a study was undertaken to compare different algorithms (Sithole & Vosselman 2005). The main goal of the examined filter types was not to reduce data, but to increase the signal-to-noise ratio (SNR). Filtering can be archieved by changing single properties of an outlier or by culling (removing) the point in question. Most of the laser scanners, as well as photogrammetric toolchains, employ multiple stages of filtering in the process of creating the merged point cloud.

If the original signal is not known, evaluating the SNR can be a challenge. The signal is a set of multidimensional measures along a surface with seemingly non-continuous behaviour. Divergent approaches have been taken to evaluate point clouds: While one approach is the evaluation of suitability in use cases (Rebolj et al. 2017), a second tries to evaluate a certain set of properties and their relations. Example for such analysis are the volumetric density or the number of geometric features (Haala et al. 2013; Angel Alfredo Martell 2017; Dyer 2001).

A recorded set of points can be compared to ground truth data that was generated by a more accurate procedure, such as rapid manufacturing or laser scanning (Tóth et al. 2013). A third approach benchmarks the toolchains and information density (Eickeler et al. 2018) by combining and trading between multiple criteria. As an extension, the cluster density (avg. nearest-neighbour-distance) was measured on multiple spatial cells. This lead to the introduction of density fields and is used to pre-align the clouds prior to a Iterative Closest Point Algorithm (Chen et al. 2017b). In a follow up the same authors use cluster density as criteria, while examining the deformation and the impact of density on a dataset containing bridges. Leading them to the conclusion that working on dense data rapidly increases the cost of recording and processing, but only adds a small plus at the detection rate (Chen et al. 2018).

Culling measures in an infrastructural context (and therefore addressing the same problem as this work) as well as redefining points by evaluating segments was analysed by Chen (Chen et al. 2017a) and therefore addressing the same problem as this work. In a first partitioning process segments are created and grown. Segments group points with the same direction (eigen values) together and extended by adding points in the vicinity of the point of origin (seed) and completed if a certain threshold is exceeded (Sampath & Shan 2010). For each segment two different key point indicators - smoothness and curvature - are evaluated and a local compression value is calculated. In a consecutive process, a voxel grid is used to reduce the number of measurements in each voxelated segment by this calculated factor. *Diverging* from this approach, we present a point-wise evaluation of informational gain and reduce the point cloud by grouping and culling points based on our evaluation model. Clusters are formed by similarity and frequency rather than eigen values.

3. Methods

The basic concept of our method is to evaluate each measurement on a point-by-point basis. We take multiple properties such as point normals, colours, and meta data into account. Based on our preceding analysis of our test dataset, we determin a weighting function and the statistical parameters for each property. These weighting is executed on each point of the cloud and based on their score the point is being kept or removed. For each measurement the score is revaluated as the filtering of the dataset progresses. This ensures that the removed point is always the lowest scoring one.

Taking this concept one step further, we cluster points of similar information content and try to increase the information density. This optimization will drop multiple points if their information content is marginal and add a new important point in between. Our algorithm merges certain points if their weights fall under a certain threshold. The information of the grouping is conserved by encoding the information in the length of the normal vector, without changing the memory layout of the point. In a similar way we compare the weights of a seeded set to their superset and calculate the roughness of the partitions. If the roughness is similar the information of the subset is encoded in the normal.

Datasets. Our test data is constructed of a set of synthetic and real captures. The synthetic consists of geometric primitive and simple construction and point clouds were extracted from multiple meshes. Per square unit we distributed measures with densities of $\log_{10}$ randomly on the containing triangles (Turk 1990) creating 10, 100, …, 1 000 000 $[points\ /\ square\ unit]$. The points spread is random (Mersenne Twister). For the real captures 3 captures were used: A photogrammetric reconstruction of a clock tower at the TU Munich, a photogrammetric reconstruction of a (advanced) construction site at [48°08'50.6"N 11°31'33.4"E] and laser scan of the same construction site that was taken in parallel. The photogrammetric reconstructions were created using the program colmap (Schönberger et al. 2016).

Table 2: Selection of used data sets. The sets shown a selection of the sets used in the evaluation. The datasets are publicly available (Eickeler 2019). The chosen datasets are border cases of the all data.

Point cloud	**Density NN5 [k / u²]**	**Nr. of measures [k]**	**Size [MB]**	**Properties**
Cube – D1K	9.70	0.006	0.2	xyz, n-xyz
Cube – D1M	304.92	6.000	164	xyz, n-xyz
Ape – D1K	9.72	0.012	0.3	xyz, n-xyz
Ape – D1M	298.15	12.462	349	xyz, n-xyz
Clock Tower	162.56	9.728	272	xyz, n-xyz, rgb
Construction Site – 1000px	58.91	8.813	235	xyz, n-xyz, rgb
Construction Site – 3000px	281.97	76.184	2 034	xyz, n-xyz, rgb
Construction Site – Laser S.	-	307.500	8 211	xyz, intensity

Concept. We use bilateral filtering to estimate the information content $I(\boldsymbol{p})$ for every point.

$$I(\boldsymbol{p}) = \sum\nolimits_{q \in ND} d(\boldsymbol{p},\boldsymbol{q}) \left(c + \frac{1}{|P|} \sum\nolimits_{a \in P} w_a(\boldsymbol{p},\boldsymbol{q})\right) \tag{1}$$

Where $\boldsymbol{p}$ is the point of interest and $\boldsymbol{q}$ part of ND the set k nearest neighbours. The w is a weighting function and $d(\boldsymbol{p},\boldsymbol{q})$, the eucledian distance between those measures. The last part consists of constant c and the sum of the weighted influence of properties of $\boldsymbol{p}$ and $\boldsymbol{q}$. The properties are evaluated by their dedicated function w_a. The constant was added since a minimal density is required by multiple guidelines and algorithms (GSA BIM Guide 2019). We propose following weighting functions:

$$w_d(\boldsymbol{p},\boldsymbol{q}) = H(d(\boldsymbol{p},\boldsymbol{q}) - c_{thr})\, \sigma_d \left[c_1 \left(\frac{d(\boldsymbol{p},\boldsymbol{q})}{d_{\ max}}\right)^3 - c_2 \left(\frac{d(\boldsymbol{p},\boldsymbol{q})}{d_{\ max}}\right)^2 + c_3 \left(\frac{d(\boldsymbol{p},\boldsymbol{q})}{d_{\ max}}\right) + c_4\right] \tag{2}$$

$$w_n(\boldsymbol{p},\boldsymbol{q}) = \frac{1}{\pi^2}\, \sigma_n\, cos^{-1}\left(\frac{\boldsymbol{p}_n \cdot \boldsymbol{q}_n}{|\boldsymbol{p}_n|\ |\boldsymbol{q}_n|}\right)^2 \tag{3}$$

$$w_{rgb}(\boldsymbol{p},\boldsymbol{q}) = \frac{1}{2^{bit}}\, \sigma_{col}\, d(\boldsymbol{p}_{rgb}, \boldsymbol{q}_{rbg}) \tag{4}$$

$$w_i(\boldsymbol{p},\boldsymbol{q}) = \ \sigma_i\ (\boldsymbol{p}_q - \boldsymbol{p}_{i)} \tag{5}$$

The space correlation is established by formula 2. We have chosen a polynomial of 3rd order for distance evaluation and use the euclidean distance as parameter. The use of this 3rd order emphasises sharp angles as well as far distance. The first term, the heaviside function enables thresholding to remove duplicates. All σ are individual constants for dampening the influence and should be chosen according to the specifications needed ($\sum \sigma = 1$).

The weight w_n evaluates the angle between the normal and the power of 2, we accentuate vivid change. Normal change has a great impact on the surface smoothness and the quality of the edges. Small normal changes may be due rough materials, greater changes hint interesting geometric features. In theory angles greater that 180 degrees are not covered, but as these angles cannot exists in photogrammetric reconstructions and no patch growing algorithm can generate such normals, this fact can be neglected. The colour weight, w_{rgb} is the normed distance in the colour-space. The factor 2^{bit} is needed since the colour range is not fixed and determined by the input point cloud. As alternative the intensity can be evaluated, since this measurement must be taken with care as multiple scans can target the same feature but record different intensities. This term is also used for all other properties that were encoded to the cloud.

After calculating I and removing the point based on the score, the algorithm reevaluate the points in the vicinity. Programmatically this is quite complicated since the lower scores might change drastically, and order can be cached beforehand. For optimizing the calculation, we can use a tree structure and start in multiple cells in parallel, before rearranging the point list. The number of filter cycles should not exceed 50% of the median for dense point clouds and even less for sparse point clouds.

4. Parameter extraction

This framework of formulas was defined by analyzing a broad set of point clouds. For our use we need to populate all statistical parameters and fit the model to our context. We used our *full set dataset* for the analysis, but only few examples are discussed. Two primitive sets and the high-res construction site are shown to mark the influence of density on the minimal, maximal and average distance (see Figure 1a-c). While on sparse data the reduction of the minimal distance is noticeable, the impact diminishes while using the datasets of medium or high density. This behavior does not differ using NN-2 or NN-10 (data online). For all further evaluation NN-5 was chosen to express a certain robustness and locality.

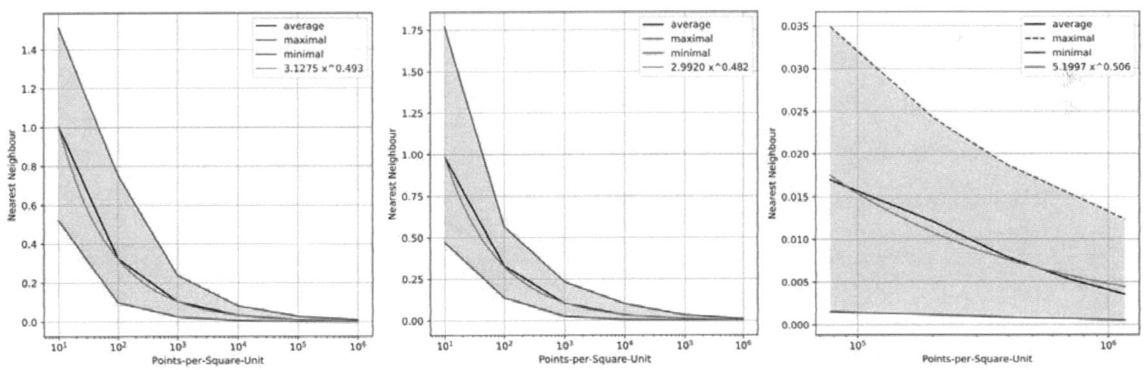

Figure 1 a-c: The plots show the influence of density on the minimal, maximal, average point-to-point distance. All plots were evaluated with NN-5. (a) The evaluation of the cube densities; (b) Displays densities of "Suzan"; (c) Shows our evaluation on the construction site, the maximal distance was replaced by a typical outlier filter;

The photogrammetric dataset shows equal properties, which is surprising since the toolchain does not guarantee an even distribution. The density was measured on the roof of the building (see Figure 2c). With the determined polynomial function one can estimate the density and parameters of photogrammetric toolchain before starting with the actual calculation.

For further analysis we create histograms of the existing point clouds. For all histograms a double peak can be observed (see Figure 2e-j). The fitted hull curve is based on a double gaussian distribution, and perfectly frames our data. The shape of the distribution does not change with higher density: The first peak can be explained as the influence of the angles on the density, close to the edge the density increasing because of the angular change. If the euclidian distance between the points increases, this influence gets diminished and the histogram of the synthetic examples are uniform. While this seems counter intuitive, these are properties of the nearest neighbour search combined with the influence of planar and almost planar surfaces. In the photogrammetric reconstruction, the peaks melt together and many of the measurements are at lower end. The reason for the faster, rising edge roots in the used reconstruction toolchain, where the maximal resolution is limited by the input image. The flat response of the second gaussian is the outcome of the applied photo consistency function during the dense point cloud creation. As shown in earlier research, the lack of features on rather smooth walls such as concrete tend to have lower density values (Eickeler et al. 2018). This effect flattens the response and shifts the peak to the right. However interestingly the median and the mean still have a similar distance.

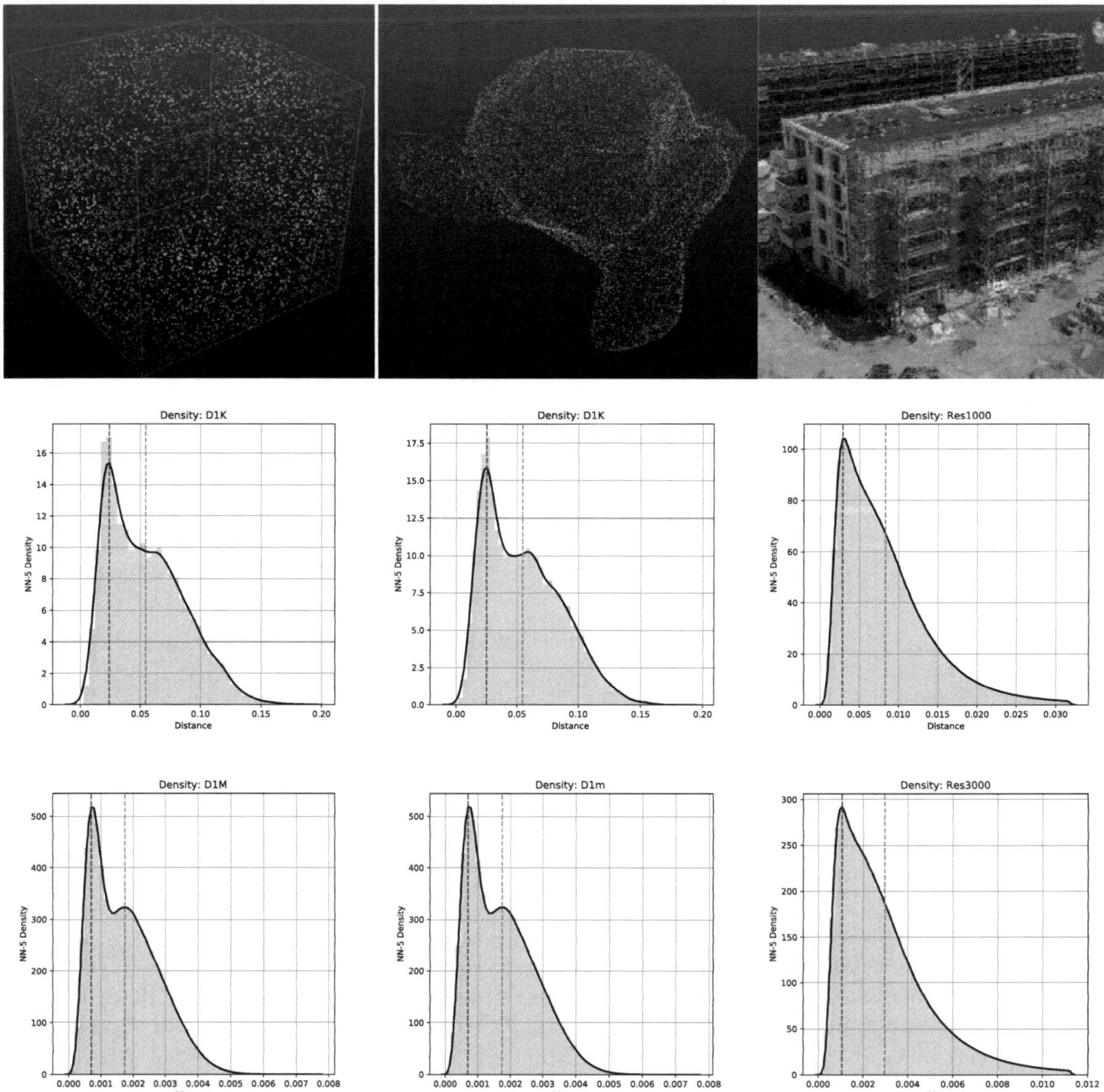

Figure 2 a-j: Histograms of the selected datasets. The data is arranged column wise, and shows an image of the dataset, the selected lower and higher resolution. The histograms show similar properties, with 2 gaussian peaks. While the scale changes the distribution is similar.

For determining good parameters for c_1 to c_4 we need also to take the contextual properties of our filtering into account. With increasing distance, points become more valuable since we want to guarantee a certain deterministic minimal space distribution. We also want to balance the first gaussian peak as an indicator for geometric turbulence and therefore higher information density. Based on our chosen dataset of this work, we determin: $c_1 = 8.76$, $c_2 = 9.82$, $c_3 = 3.09$, $c_4 = 0.02$. The dampening parameter: $\sigma_d = 0.1$, $\sigma_n = 0.7$, $\sigma_{rgb} = 0.2$, $\sigma_i = 0.2$.

5. Implementation & Evaluation

The filtering was implemented in C++ featuring the Point Cloud Library (PCL) and tinyply. While removing measurements from the cloud the information content needs to be recalculated. Because the needed nearest neighbour search is very costly, a dynamic tree structure is optimal. We were able to achieve similar results and good performance by recalculating a static tree structure after removing a random set of spatial unrelated, lower scoring points. This might not lead to the highest scoring point cloud, but we achieved over 98% of the total score on our test data with lower density. For our real-world data, some colours, intensities and normal were not available and their information context was set to 0. Since we used our own quality criteria to filter the cloud, these same criteria cannot be used to evaluate the performance of our filtering. As an alternative benchmark, we discuss multiple properties of the filtered point clouds to ensure the effectivity of our approach.

In Figure 3a we are visualizing the effect of the filtering to our dense cube. The dense cube was filtered by 80% of the orignial density leaving 120 k measures. The filtering has two properties: (1) The surfaces are reduced to equidistant density. (2) At the edge of the cube the information content is greatest and more points are preserved.

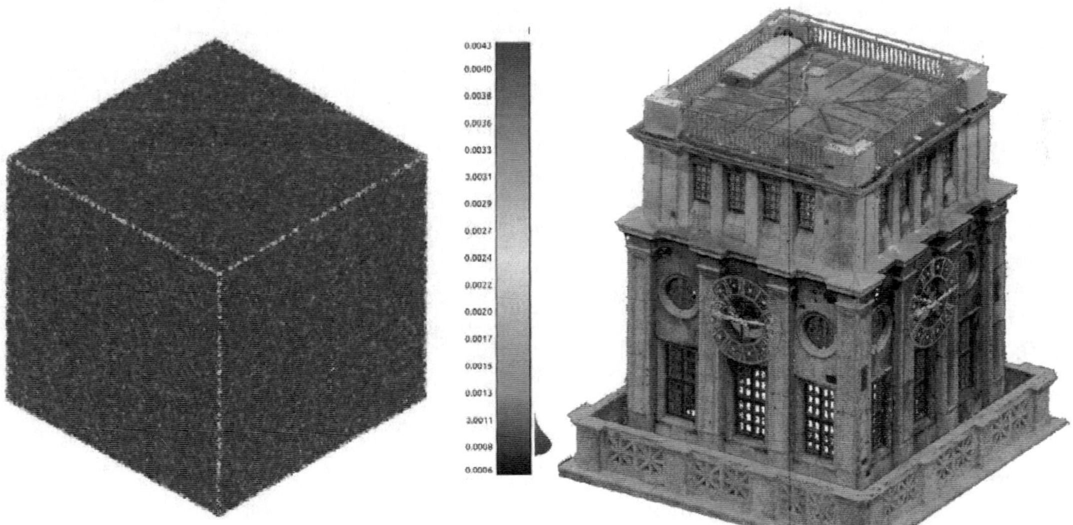

Figure 3 a,b: (a)Visualization of the information content – edges score higher than points in the plane. After reduction a non-uniform distribution(green-blue) forming. (b) The dashed line drawn upon the clocktower indicates the crossing of the original | filtered point cloud.

As a showcase of colour filtering we are visualizing the information content of the clock tower data (Figure 3b). This photogrammetric reconstruction has high density and features intresting colouring on the old copper plating. The points are again reduced by 80%, reducing the binary filesize from 260 MB to 60 MB. The figure is split by a fine line, inidicating the crossing of the orignal and the filtered cloud.

In the clocktower cloud the texture quality was conserved by the increase in the local density. Overall the original data, the standard deviation of the density was increased by 15%. On features that have both, a normal and a colour change the information content is high. This can be observed at the contact points of the roof plating. The original score of I was 12 975 which was improved to 16 778. The filtering of the clocktower without parallelization or optimizations took around 28 min (~10 million points). Further analysis was undertaken to determine the information gain compared to a lower valued reconstruction. We compared the construction site data with two settings of our dense reconstruction pipeline. The underlying geometry and the camera positions were kept constant while the resolution of the depth and normal maps were increased (1000px to 3000px). Additionally, we filtered the high-density dataset to contain the same number of points as the original low-resolution point cloud. The filtering increased the contrast by a vast amount. One example of these results is shown in Figures (14-17).

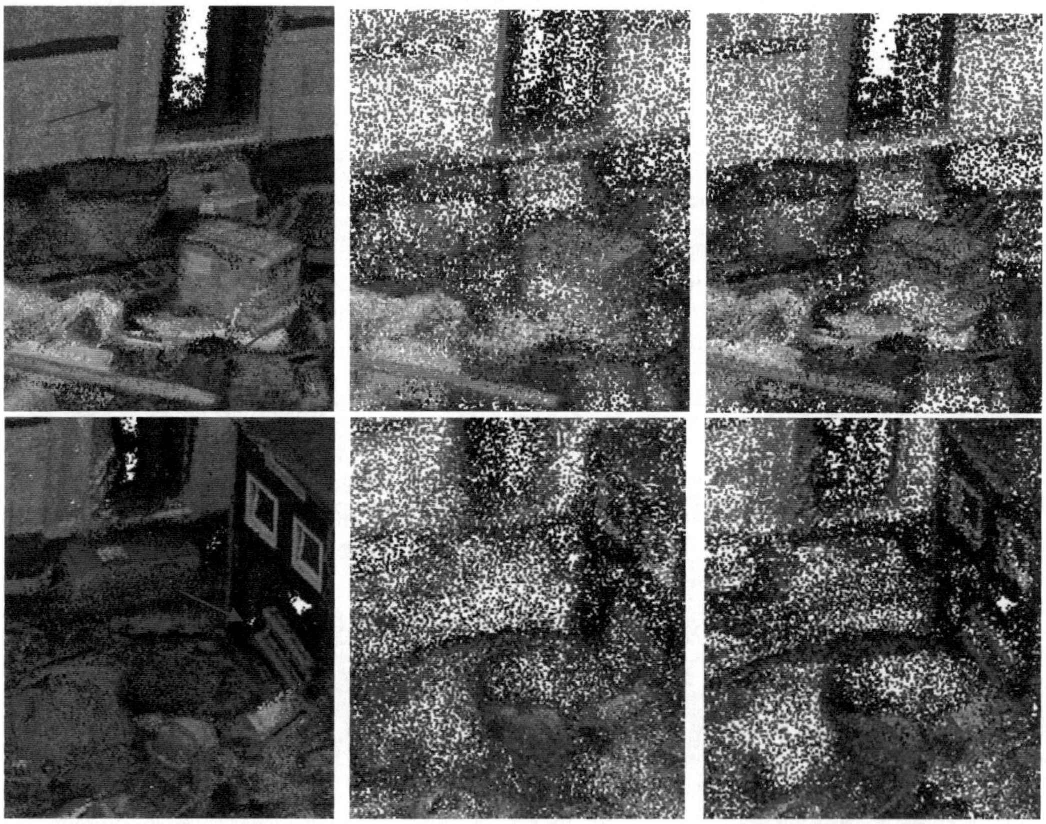

Figure 4 a-f: Dataset "construction site": (a, d) high-res, (b, e) low-res; (c, f) filtered point cloud. The arrows indicate preserved features. Compared to the low-res reconstruction the filtered cloud shows higher geometric contrast.

Grouping: The second part of the filtering is the grouping of points of similar properties. The amount of grouping heavily depends on the grouping parameters provided. By using the weights w_a for grouping the elements below a certain threshold, every parameter that delivers a constant first derivative can be filter points on planes easily. On the point cloud with a higher density the results are basically the same as culling with different parameters. The algorithm behaves as if the eucledian distance in $\boldsymbol{d(p,q)}$ to 1.

For the roughness, the distance to the best fitting plane is evaluated. If the superset estimates the same roughness as the subset the points are grouped, and the roughness is saved. We achieved good results by creating a subset from the median. The grouping and the roughness are encoded as the length of the normal vector. We used the first bit to keep the information steady and then encoded the weight by big endian notation in the first 2 bytes and the roughness in the following. While further processing such a point cloud, we faced some problems with existing software. Some of our day-to-day software normalized the vectors before evaluation, others when writing results to a file. In both cases the normals were replaced and the information was lost. The altered point cloud may show different behaviour in a certain set of evaluation algorithms and should not be used for further analysis.

6. Conclusion

We previously showed that we can preserve geometry and colour by selective density variations. Our proposed method shows multiple improvements over the classical filtering approaches of large-scale datasets. Nonetheless employing the filtering increases the complexity of the tool chain and the actual speed up needs to be researched on a case by case basis. While the filtering of small point clouds is relatively fast, its complexity is of $n\ log(n)$ and therefore can get computational expensive. This is the same for most of the algorithms used in the analysis which may be more expensive or less parallelizable. As grouping can be achieved with less extra effort, we would love to recommend it over culling the limitations of the encoding as normal length is not feasible. The determination of the roughness contains the same limitations.

Another impressing fact is that the increase of the minimal resolution is only marginal with the addition of points on surfaces. Adding more points will result in a reduction of error rather than rising the minimal spatial resolution (see figure 1a-c). Practitioners should use historical data or available data sets to evaluate their sweet spot between resolution and effort. As with most recording, if the properties are not completely known, resolution is king. As shown in this work reducing the amount of data in a second step can be done effectively with filtering. However, this does not apply to captures of bigger datasets as the effort is increasing manifold. Before recording, users should ask the question: "what is the statistical error that I can accept" rather than "what are the smaller features that I want to capture". Naturally the trade of for increasing the resolution of the capture gets worse. The most important part of our filtering model is, that there is no filtering by property. As speciality of bilateral filtering we can apply our method without influencing the latter analysis. This is in stark contrast to the family of PCA based methods, as they will reinforce the later PCA used Recognitions algorithms and change the parameters practitioners are using on smaller, unfiltered samples.

7. Outlook

The focus of the discussion is mainly on the evaluation of speed increase and data reduction opposed to the quality loss. Most operations on points are rather cheap if they are performed on single points but putting them to a bigger scale soon reaches computational limits. One of the limitations is the data throughput and splitting strategies for big data sets. With modern technologies there are certain improvements that should be discussed: First and most importantly, the encoding of the point cloud can be improved. The choice of floats and their non-linear accuracy over their range maybe suboptimal. Another improvement can also be made by encoding the normal vector with radians leaving 4 bytes of information for local functions. All improvements need to be adapted to the availability of extended SIMD instructions which opens the possibility to further enhance the throughput of points.

Following up this discussion, a smart process of annotation of points, facets and volumetric elements needs to be developed. The encoding of semantic data on grouped or single points should be researched thoughtfully. Many formats have domain specific solution, such as geodetic information encoded in **.las* files, that could be generalized.

References

Angel Alfredo Martell 2017, *Benchmarking structure from motion algorithms with video footage taken from a drone against laser-scanner generated 3D models*. Available from: https://robotik.informatik.uni-wuerzburg.de/telematics/download/MSc_Angel_Martell.pdf [22 February 2018].

Baltsavias, EP 1999, 'A comparison between photogrammetry and laser scanning', *ISPRS Journal of Photogrammetry and Remote Sensing*, vol. 54, 2-3, pp. 83–94.

Boehler, W, Vicent, MB & Marbs, A 2003, 'Investigating laser scanner accuracy', *The International Archives of Photogrammetry, Remote Sensing and Spatial Information Sciences*, vol. 34, Part 5, pp. 696–701.

Chen, J, Tang, P & Xiong, W 2018, 'Characterizing Point Cloud Data Density for Spatial Change-Based Maintenance Planning of Civil Infrastructure Systems'. *Construction Research Congress 2018. Construction Information Technology,* eds C Wang, C Harper, Y Lee, R Harris & C Berryman, American Society of Civil Engineers, Reston, pp. 776–785.

Chen, J, Zhang, C & Tang, P 2017a, 'Geometry-Based Optimized Point Cloud Compression Methodology for Construction and Infrastructure Management' in *Computing in Civil Engineering 2017,* pp. 377–385.

Chen, M, Wang, S, Wang, M, Wan, Y & He, P 2017b, 'Entropy-Based Registration of Point Clouds Using Terrestrial Laser Scanning and Smartphone GPS', *Sensors (Basel, Switzerland)*, vol. 17, no. 1.

Dyer, CR 2001, 'Volumetric Scene Reconstruction from Multiple Views' in *Foundations of Image Understanding,* ed LS Davis, Springer US, Boston, MA, pp. 469–489.

Eickeler, F 2019, *Dataset EG-ICE 2019,* Lehrstuhl für Computergestützte Modellierung und Simulation. Available from: http://vision.cms.bgu.tum.de/eg_ice2019.

Eickeler, F, Borrmann, A & Mistre, A 2018, 'Defining quality metrics for photogrammetric construction site monitoring' in *Proc. of the 12th European Conference on Product and Process Modelling, Copenhagen, Denmark*.

Elseberg, J, Borrmann, D & Nüchter, A 2013, 'One billion points in the cloud–an octree for efficient processing of 3D laser scans', *ISPRS Journal of Photogrammetry and Remote Sensing*, vol. 76, pp. 76–88.

Golparvar-Fard, M, Bohn, J, Teizer, J, Savarese, S & Peña-Mora, F 2011, 'Evaluation of image-based modeling and laser scanning accuracy for emerging automated performance monitoring techniques', *Automation in Construction*, vol. 20, no. 8, pp. 1143–1155.

Haala, N, Cramer, M & Rothermel, M 2013, 'QUALITY OF 3D POINT CLOUDS FROM HIGHLY OVERLAPPING UAV IMAGERY', *ISPRS - International Archives of the Photogrammetry, Remote Sensing and Spatial Information Sciences*, XL-1/W2, pp. 183–188.

Han, X-F, Jin, JS, Wang, M-J, Jiang, W, Gao, L & Xiao, L 2017, 'A review of algorithms for filtering the 3D point cloud', *Signal Processing: Image Communication*, vol. 57, pp. 103–112.

Moorfield, B, Haeusler, R & Klette, R 2015, 'Bilateral Filtering of 3D Point Clouds for Refined 3D Roadside Reconstructions' in *Computer analysis of images and patterns. 16th international conference, CAIP 2015, Valletta, Malta, September 2 - 4, 2015; proceedings,* eds G Azzopardi & N Petkov, Springer, Cham, pp. 394–402.

Rebolj, D, Pučko, Z, Babič, NČ, Bizjak, M & Mongus, D 2017, 'Point cloud quality requirements for Scan-vsBIM based automated construction progress monitoring', *Automation in Construction*, vol. 84, pp. 323–334.

Sampath, A & Shan, J 2010, 'Segmentation and Reconstruction of Polyhedral Building Roofs From Aerial Lidar Point Clouds', *IEEE Transactions on Geoscience and Remote Sensing*, vol. 48, no. 3, pp. 1554–1567.

Schnabel, R & Klein, R 2006, 'Octree-based Point-Cloud Compression', *Spbg*, vol. 6, pp. 111–120.

Schönberger, JL, Zheng, E, Frahm, J-M & Pollefeys, M 2016, 'Pixelwise View Selection for Unstructured Multi-View Stereo' in *Computer vision - ECCV 2016. 14th European conference, Amsterdam, The Netherlands, October 11-14, 2016 : proceedings,* eds B Leibe, J Matas, N Sebe & M Welling, Springer, Cham, pp. 501–518.

Sithole, G & Vosselman, G 2005, 'Filtering of airborne laser scanner data based on segmented point clouds', *International Archives of Photogrammetry, Remote Sensing and Spatial Information Sciences*, vol. 36, part 3

Tóth, T, Rajťúková, V & Živčák, J 2013, *Comparison of optical and laser 3D scanners,* IEEE.

Turk, G 1990, 'Generating Random Points in Triangles. Graphics Gems' in , ed AS Glassner, Academic Press Professional, Inc, San Diego, CA, USA, pp. 24–28. Available from: http://dl.acm.org/citation.cfm?id=90767.90772.

Zheng, E, Dunn, E, Jojic, V & Frahm, J-M (eds.) 2014, *Patchmatch based joint view selection and depthmap estimation*.

Metamodeling wireless communication in cyber-physical systems

Kay Smarsly, Theresa Fitz and Dmitrii Legatiuk
Bauhaus University Weimar, Germany
kay.smarsly@uni-weimar.de

Abstract. With recent developments in embedded sensing technologies, cyber-physical systems, materializing Industry 4.0 concepts, are increasingly implemented in civil engineering to advance structural health monitoring (SHM) and control applications. Recent studies have shown the potential of metamodels enabling information integration and interoperability between different platforms and technologies, while metamodeling of cyber-physical systems has been scarce. In this study, a metamodel for describing cyber-physical systems, putting emphasis on communication issues, is proposed and implemented into a SHM and control system. The metamodel is mapped into the Industry Foundation Classes (IFC) data schema that is standardized for describing structures compliant to the principles of building information modeling (BIM). Finally, the metamodel proposed in this study is validated by IFC-compliant, BIM-based example modeling and implementation of a cyber-physical system designed to monitor and control a laboratory test structure.

1. Introduction

Through the Internet of Things concept and the progress made in Industry 4.0 technologies, cyber-physical systems applied in the field of structural health monitoring (SHM) and control evolve by achieving higher degrees of interconnection (Rajkumar et al. 2010), by cognitive automation (Ibanez et al. 2019), and by shifting the process of data collection and processing into cloud-based applications (OGC 2019). Cyber-physical systems integrate mechanical and electrical components in intelligent networks realizing computational and physical processes (Lee 2008). The term "intelligent" denotes the embedment of algorithms and data processing capabilities into nodes forming networks, such as sensor networks for SHM and control, in which sensor data, e.g. temperature data or acceleration data for building automation or structural control, is automatically recorded, processed, exchanged, and stored. To distinguish computational and physical processes, the architecture of cyber-physical systems is structured into a physical domain and a cyber domain. The physical domain comprises physical processes as well as mechanical and electrical components controlling physical processes. The cyber domain encompasses networking and computational processes to evaluate sensor data originating from physical processes and to control actuators that manipulate the physical domain (Legatiuk & Smarsly 2018).

Networking processes, including wireless communication in cyber-physical systems, must provide reliable information exchange between the physical domain and the cyber domain to establish a sound basis for system automation (Wollschläger et al. 2017). State-of-the-art approaches towards synchronized, reliable, and efficient communication between individual system components are, e.g., Ethernet time-sensitive networking and telecommunication based on fifth-generation (5G) telecom networks. To integrate all individual system components, multiple sensing, processing, and communication technologies must be coupled. Coupling of various technologies accounts for the complexity of cyber-physical systems and renders unified and semantic information modeling a prerequisite for implementing cyber-physical systems.

Semantic modeling, or metamodeling respectively, encompasses methods for platform-independent and technology-independent information modeling following the syntax and semantics defined by modeling languages (Hitzler et al. 2009). Metamodels contain information about the structure and the functionalities of a family of systems and are origins to derive models describing individual systems of specific purposes, such as SHM and control (Legatiuk et al. 2017). To enable system documentation and information exchange with respect to the rapid advancements in sensing technologies and the complexity of cyber-physical systems, metamodels are needed (Lee 2015, Fitz et al. 2019). In civil engineering, technology-independent semantic descriptions of structures and of structural components using open building information modeling (BIM) are well-established. The standard ISO 16739:2013 "Industry Foundation Classes (IFC) for data sharing in the construction and facility management industries" specifies a metamodel for describing building information including building components, construction schedules, and facility management services on a formal basis (ISO 16739:2013).

Cyber-physical systems for SHM and control are integral parts of modern, automated structures that are, in current engineering practice, typically modeled using BIM. For incorporating information describing cyber-physical systems into BIM models, recent research of Theiler et al. (2018) has shown that describing information related to SHM and control is not yet fully possible using the current IFC standard. To fully describe information related to monitoring and control, the IFC standard needs to be extended. In this paper, a metamodel to describe cyber-physical systems for SHM and control is presented. The focus is set on describing communication-related information as a subset of monitoring-related information including communication technologies, such as communication protocols and technical devices for coupling different communicating system components. To describe and document cyber-physical systems for SHM and control conjointly modeled with structures being monitored, the metamodel is mapped into the IFC schema extended by Theiler & Smarsly (2018).

To develop and to validate the metamodel and the extended IFC schema, this paper is structured as follows. In Section 2, the principles of metamodeling as well as different metamodeling approaches are introduced, followed by a description of the metamodel. Subsequently, the metamodel is mapped into the IFC schema extended by components related to monitoring and control, presented in Section 3. Modeling capabilities added to the current version of the IFC standard to describe communication in cyber-physical systems are highlighted. In Section 4, to investigate the descriptive capacities of the metamodel and of the extended IFC schema, a prototype cyber-physical system for monitoring and control of a test structure is setup and described by an IFC-compliant BIM model. The results of the study are summarized and an outlook on future work is given in Section 5.

2. Metamodeling communication-related information

Metamodeling comprises methodologies for describing the meaning (i.e. the semantics) of information to cast human knowledge into machine-processable formats (Hitzler et al. 2009). For describing cyber-physical systems, a variety of object-oriented modeling languages standardized, e.g., by the Object Management Group (OMG), by the Open Geospatial Consortium (OGC), or by the International Standardization Organization (ISO) may be used. In this section, the principles of metamodeling are illuminated and three metamodeling approaches frequently used in computing in civil engineering are introduced: (i) approaches based on Unified Modeling Language (UML), developed and maintained by OMG, (ii) the Sensor Web Enablement (SWE) framework of OGC, and (iii) the data modeling language EXPRESS standardized in ISO 10303-11. Subsequently, information for describing cyber-physical systems for SHM and control are formalized and compiled in the metamodel. The focus is put on metamodeling information that describes communication technologies and components referred to as communication-related information.

2.1 Metamodeling approaches relevant to metamodeling cyber-physical systems in civil engineering

UML-related approaches

Established by OMG, the Model-Driven Architecture (MDA) standard is a widely used realization of model-driven development subsuming software and systems engineering approaches based on technology-independent metamodels (Favre 2010, OMG 2014). To develop metamodels that remain stable as technology evolves, the MDA metamodeling approach starts with a platform-independent model (PIM) describing functionalities and behavior of systems. In subsequent metamodeling steps, the PIM is converted into a platform-specific model (PSM) and into a working implementation.

For technology-independent and platform-independent metamodeling, OMG has established a variety of special-purpose and multi-purpose modeling languages, such as UML, the Common Warehouse Metamodel (CWM), the System Modeling Language (SysML), and the Software & System Process Engineering Metamodel (SPEM). To comply with the MDA principle of creating reusable and extendable models, the OMG modeling languages are translatable into each other because of a common meta-metamodel, termed Meta Object Facility (MOF), defining syntax and semantics (OMG 2016). Meta-metamodels serve as models for different modeling languages as the basis for automated mapping of metamodels and models defined in different modeling languages. The OMG format for automated mapping of models is an XML-based interchange format, XML Metadata Interchange (XMI), for standardizing XML document formats and schemas (OMG 2015).

The UML modeling (and metamodeling) approach is widely applied in the field of computing in civil engineering because UML offers a broad wealth of notations and modeling constructs to describe architecture and behavior of computational systems. In UML, two semantical categories are distinguished, (i) structural semantics and (ii) behavioral semantics (OMG 2017). Structural semantics, materialized in classes, relationships, and data types are used to describe system architectures. Based on structural semantics, behavioral semantics, e.g. implemented through activity diagrams, state machine diagrams, and sequence diagrams, can be used to express interaction sequences for describing communication processes in cyber-physical systems for SHM and control.

Extension mechanisms included in the ULM standard enable UML to be adapted for further domains by creating UML "dialects", so-called "profiles", that remain in semantic compliance to MOF (Fuentes et al. 2004). To create UML profiles describing a specific domain, the number of available UML modeling constructs may be restricted and constraints can be added to restrict the way in which a metamodel can be used.

The SWE framework of OGC

The key idea of the SWE framework is to make data of sensor systems online accessible through interfaces and protocols following well-defined standards (OGC 2019). To provide metamodeling capabilities for geospatial systems, a selection of UML modeling constructs is reused according to the principles of UML profiles. As a result, the seven OGC standards forming the SWE framework provide UML notations (and XML notations) for describing sensor networks, sensors, sensor observations, and measurements that are as well relevant to metamodeling cyber-physical systems for SHM and control. However, for communication-related information, graphical notations or exhaustive XML encodings have not been standardized within the SWE framework.

The data modeling language EXPRESS

Another data modeling language, and a metamodel that provides computer-interpretable descriptions of semantic information, is EXPRESS and the graphical notation EXPRESS-G. Though the graphical notational capacities of EXPRESS-G are limited compared to UML, EXPRESS is of gaining importance for information modeling in civil engineering. The IFC specifications forming the basis for open BIM are formally described using EXPRESS and EXPRESS-G. In conjunction with the "Standard for the Exchange of Product Model Data" (STEP) in ISO 10303-21, EXPRESS models are used to realize consistent exchange, storage, archiving, and transformation of building information (ISO 10303-21:2016, ISO16739:2013, ISO10303-11:2004).

Summary

In summary, UML possesses the most comprehensive range of metamodeling capabilities of the modeling languages introduced herein. The wide scope and notational variety for structural and behavioral modeling render a UML-based metamodeling approach applicable to many modeling purposes. On the other hand, it should be emphasized that information modeling using EXPRESS along with the IFC standard to describe buildings and infrastructure is gaining attention in research and practice. For the above reasons, the UML modeling capabilities are used as a formal basis to develop the metamodel for describing communication-related information in cyber-physical systems.

2.2 A metamodel for describing communication-related information in cyber-physical systems

To formally describe communication-related information in cyber-physical systems, components of cyber-physical systems for SHM and control are characterized and communication-related information is defined. Subsequently, the information related to monitoring and communication is compiled in a metamodel using UML class diagrams.

Communication-related information is a subset of monitoring-related information describing communication technologies applied in cyber-physical systems. Communication technologies metamodeled in this study encompass, e.g., communication protocols, routing of communication (including origins and destinations of communication processes), transmission media, and technical devices employed to realize sensor communication. The metamodel presented in Figure 1 essentially shows UML classes to describe cyber-physical systems, with elements describing communication-related information, shaded in gray, primarily stemming from the mathematical theory of communication proposed by Shannon (1948) and from reviews of wireless communication standards, such as ZigBee, Wi-Fi and MQTT frequently applied in wireless sensor networks (Fahmy 2016).

As reflected in the gray-shaded elements of Figure 1, communication systems include (i) transmitters, (ii) transmission media, (iii) receivers, and (iv) data units, which are transformed into (v) electrical signals. Data units are initiated by (vi) information sources (i.e. sensor nodes) making observations (i.e. temperature, acceleration) and are processed at (vii) destinations of communication systems (i.e. other sensor nodes, base stations, or computer systems). Two processes involved in communication are encoding on the transmitter side of communication systems and decoding on receiving system components. Encoding and decoding are performed in compliance with syntax and semantics defined by communication protocols. As nodes of wireless sensor networks for cyber-physical systems are spatially distributed, autonomous devices, power consumption, and resource management are important criteria in choosing suitable communication protocols and network topologies.

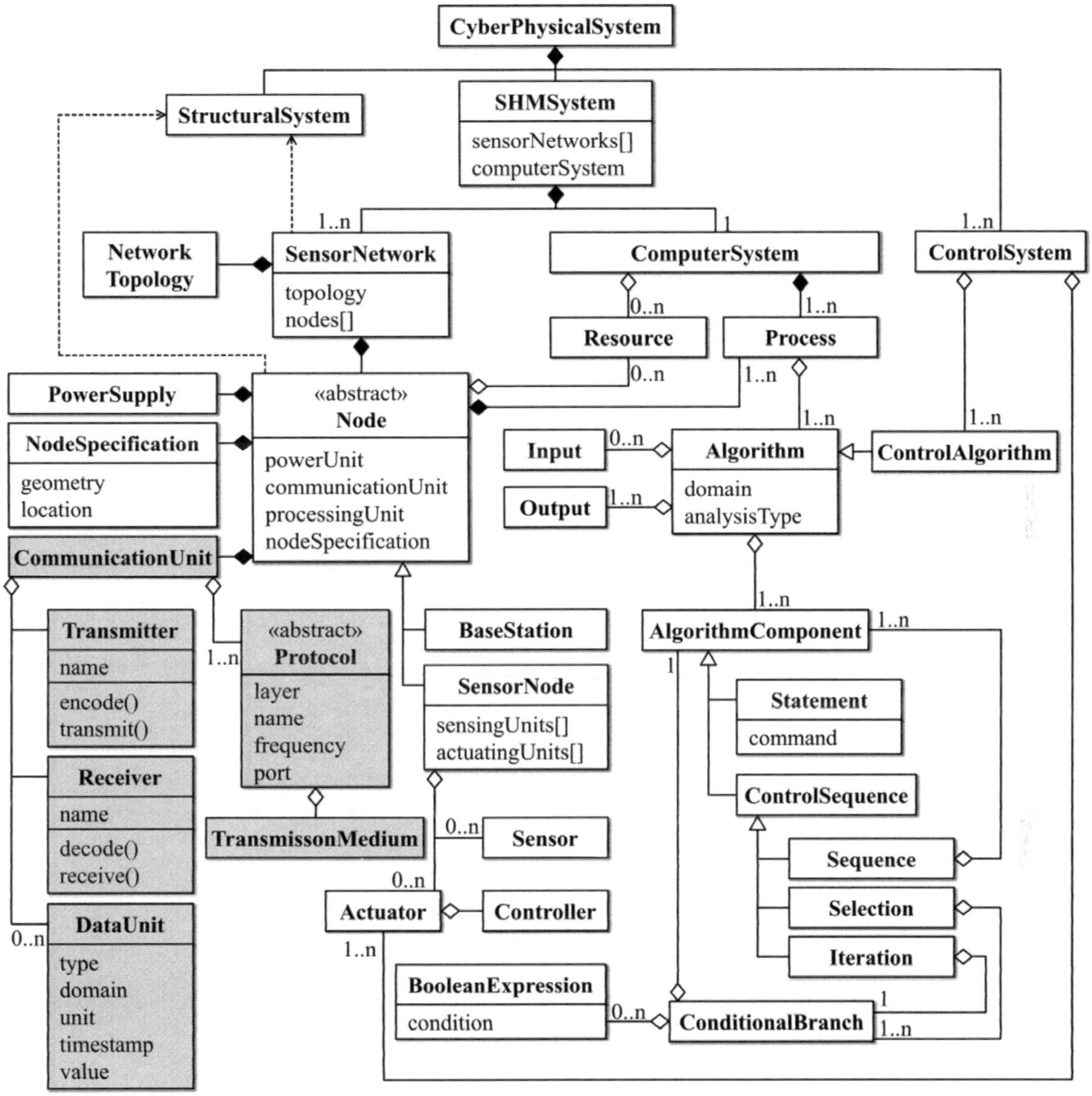

Figure 1: Metamodel of cyber-physical systems for SHM and control including control-related elements (red) and communication-related information (gray)

From the metamodel shown in Figure 1, it can be seen that cyber-physical systems are composed of a computer system and of one or more sensor networks. In sensor networks, two types of nodes are distinguished. Both, sensor nodes and base stations, possess power units, processing units, and communication units similar to computer systems. To formally describe communication-related information, communication units are modeled in terms of aggregations of transmitters, receivers, data units describing raw or preprocessed data, and communication protocols that are, dependent on the transmission media and characterized by multiple attributes and methods. To account for the variety of communication protocols applicable to cyber-physical systems for SHM and control, the protocol class is defined as an abstract class.

3. BIM-based description of cyber-physical systems

In this section, for describing cyber-physical systems for SHM and control on the basis of open BIM, the metamodel is mapped into the IFC schema. For mapping, entities and objectified relationships of the IFC schema standardized in ISO 16739:2013 and of the IFC schema extension "IFC Monitor" proposed by Theiler and Smarsly (2018) are taken as a basis. Entities to describe cyber-physical systems, sensor networks, and sensor nodes are provided according to the UML classes shown earlier in the metamodel. By the objectified relationship *IfcRelAggregates*, sensor nodes are semantically connected to a communication unit termed *IfcCommunicationsAppliance*. As can be seen from Figure 2, *IfcCommunicationsAppliance* entities together with *IfcDistributionPort* and *IfcDistributionSystem* entities form the basis for describing communication-related information. *IfcCommunicationsAppliance* entities have ports, e.g. used as transmitters and receivers for communication, as being part of *IfcDistributionSystem* entities that can be determined to signal or data transmission or to communication in general.

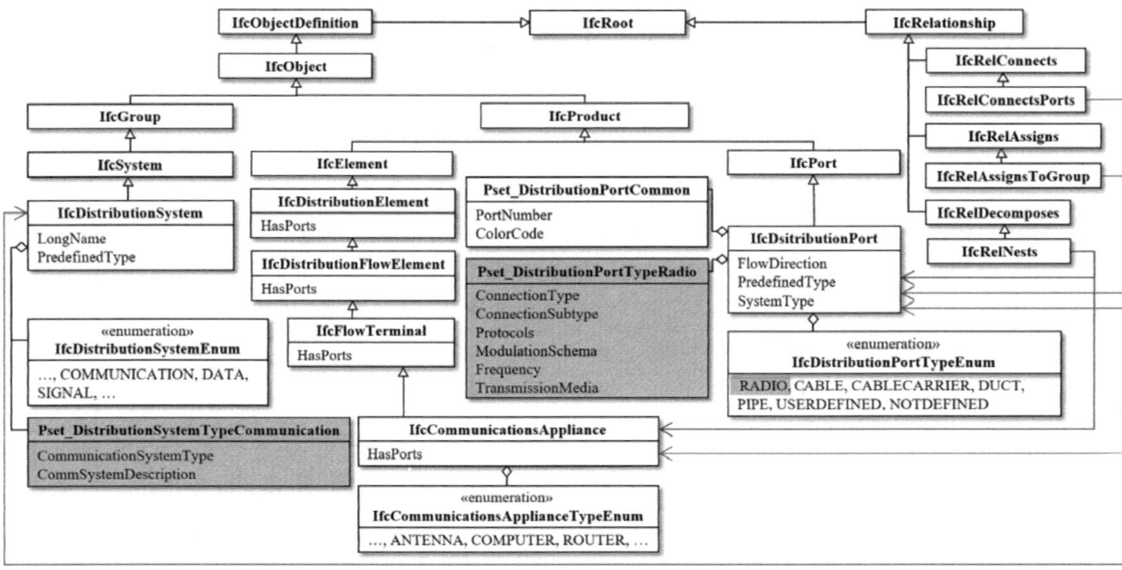

Figure 2: Extract of the extended IFC schema (shaded in gray) for describing communication in cyber-physical systems

To describe *IfcDistributionPort* entities of type "radio" for wireless communication and *IfcDistributionSystem* entities of type "communication" in more detail, the property sets shaded in gray are proposed. *IfcDistributionSystem* entities of type "communication" represent communication systems that are specified by the property set *Pset_DistributionSystemTypeCommunication*. To connect communication ports of different communication units being components of sensor nodes, base stations, and computer systems, the system type predefined by the IFC schema must conform to the *CommunicationSystemType* attribute of *IfcDistributionSystem*. Besides the *SystemType* attribute, *IfcDistributionPort* entities are characterized by the attribute termed *PredefinedType*, such as "radio" for wireless communication ports, and the *FlowDirection* attribute to distinguish between transmitting and receiving ports. To describe transmitters, receivers, and the communication protocols applied in the cyber-physical system, the property set Pset_*DistributionPortTypeRadio* extending the IFC schema is proposed according to the metamodel developed earlier.

4. Example modeling of a prototype cyber-physical system

In this section, to validate the metamodel and the descriptive capacities of the extended IFC schema, a prototype cyber-physical system for monitoring and control of a laboratory test structure is designed. Both the cyber-physical system and the test structure are described through an IFC model that implements the metamodel mapped into the IFC schema.

The wireless prototype cyber-physical system is composed of two wireless sensor nodes of type Raspberry Pi 3 Model B+ (Raspberry Pi Foundation 2017) that are, via Wi-Fi, connected to a computer system in star topology. As shown in Figure 3, sensor node "n1" has two acceleration sensors attached that are fixed to the middle of the first and third story of the test structure. Sensor node "n2" is connected to an actuator controlling the electrical valve of a tuned liquid column damper situated on the top story of the test structure. The test structure is composed of five aluminum slabs of dimensions 300 mm × 200 mm × 15 mm (length × width × thickness) resting on four 20 mm × 2 mm aluminum columns. The story height is 300 mm and the plate-to-column connections are fully fixed. The base plate and columns are clamped on a solid block at the base of the structure. In the left of Figure 3, structural components of the test structure are modeled using a conventional BIM software tool.

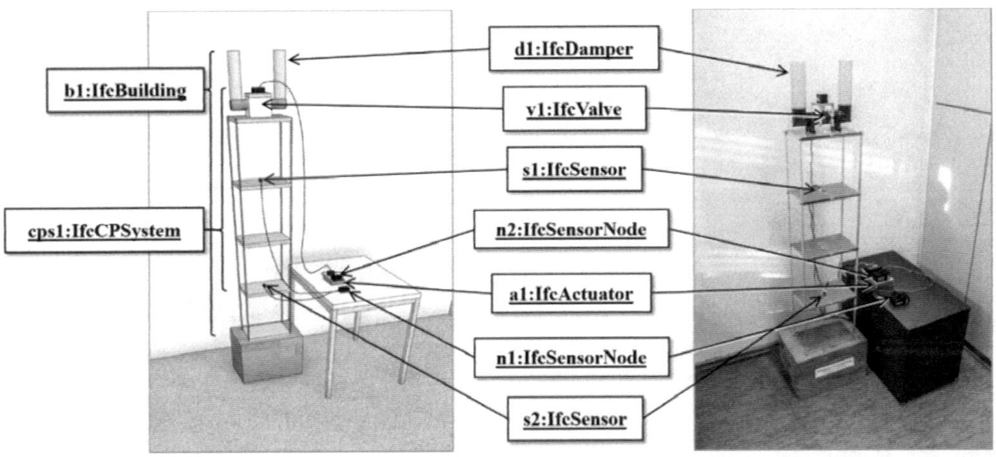

Figure 3: BIM model (left) and physical implementation (right) of the prototype cyber-physical system

To complement the BIM-based structural description of the test structure by monitoring-related and communication-related information, the extended IFC schema is used for manual post-processing of the BIM model. In Figure 4, the IFC model describing the prototype cyber-physical system for SHM and control including monitoring-related information originating from the IFC Monitor extension (shaded in gray) and communication-related information (shaded in blue) is shown. The *IfcDistributionPort* entities representing transmitters and receivers of the sensor nodes and of the computer system are, by means of the *IfcRelAssignsToGroup* relationship, semantically connected to an *IfcDistributionSystem* entity of type communication not shown in Figure 4.

As a result, by describing and implementing the prototype cyber-physical system and the test structure, the metamodel is shown to be suitable for describing and maintaining information related to cyber-physical systems using the extended IFC schema. In the laboratory tests, the cyber-physical system designed upon the metamodel developed in this study is used successfully to measure and to process acceleration data for controlling structural responses of the test structure exposed to manual excitations.

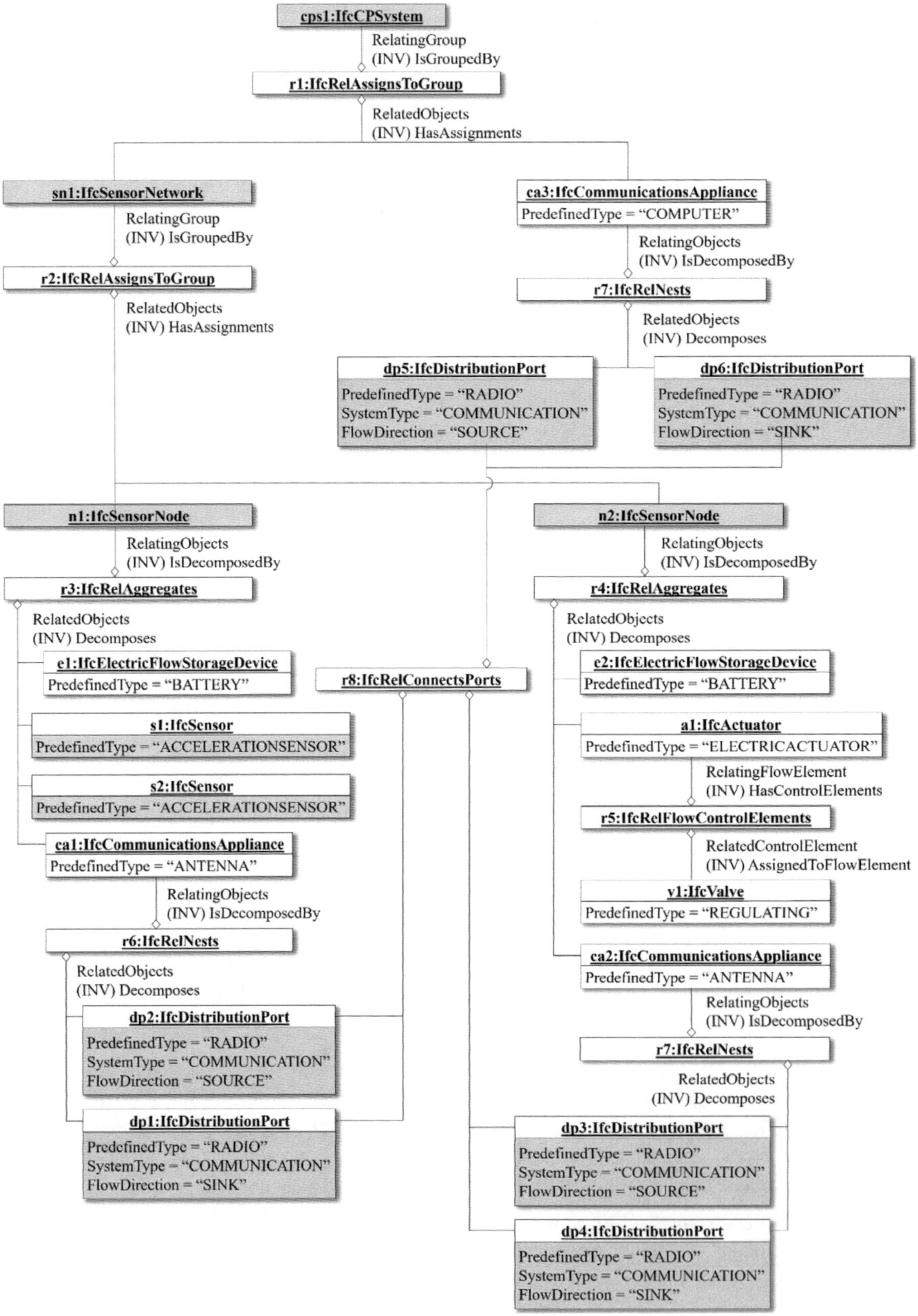

Figure 4: IFC model of the prototype cyber-physical system (communication-related information shaded in blue)

5. Summary and conclusions

Cyber-physical systems for SHM and control are of increasing importance for operating and maintaining civil infrastructure. Because of the technological heterogeneity of cyber-physical systems composed of sensing, actuating, and processing devices, metamodeling methods facilitating documentation and optimization of cyber-physical systems are needed. In this paper, a metamodeling approach towards formally describing cyber-physical systems with focus on communication has been proposed and applied to a prototype cyber-physical system for SHM and control.

To enable the BIM-based description of cyber-physical systems, monitoring-related and communication-related information has been formalized in the metamodel using UML class diagrams. Subsequently, the metamodel has been mapped into the IFC schema extended by IFC entities for describing monitoring-related and communication-related information. For validating the metamodeling approach, the metamodel has been used to exemplarily describe and setup a prototype cyber-physical system for monitoring and control of a laboratory test structure. In laboratory tests, the prototype cyber-physical system has successfully been used to measure and to process acceleration data and to automatically control the structural response to external loads.

As an outcome of this study, it has been demonstrated that cyber-physical systems for SHM and control can be described following the principles of open BIM in compliance with the IFC standard. In future work, both the metamodel and the extension of the IFC schema may be enhanced by formal semantic representations of sensor data and control sequences, which cannot yet be adequately described using the IFC standard.

6. Acknowledgements

The authors express their sincere appreciation to the German Research Foundation (DFG) for the support through grant SM 281/7-1 and grant SM 281/9-1. Major parts of this work have been conducted in the "Structural Health Monitoring Laboratory", sponsored by the European Union through the European Fund for Regional Development (EFRD) and the Thuringian Ministry for Economic Affairs, Science and Digital Society (TMWWDG) under grant 2016 FGI 0009, whose support is gratefully acknowledged. Any opinions, findings, conclusions, or recommendations expressed in this paper are those of the authors and do not necessarily reflect the views of DFG, EFRD, or TMWWDG.

References

Fahmy, H. M. A. (2016). Wireless sensor networks. Concepts, applications, experimentation and analysis. Springer, Singapore.

Favre, L. (2010). Model driven architecture for reverse engineering technologies: Strategic directions and system evolution. Engineering Science Reference, Hershey, NY, USA.

Fitz, T., Theiler, M. and Smarsly, K. (2019). A metamodel for cyber-physical systems. Advanced Engineering Informatics, 41(2019), 100930.

Fuentes-Fernández, L. and Vallecillo-Moreno, A. (2004). An Introduction to UML Profiles. UPGRADE - The European Journal for the Informatics Professional, 5(2), pp. 6-13.

Hitzler, P., Krötzsch, M. and Rudolph, S. (2009). Foundation of Semantic Web Technologies. Chapman & Hall/CRC, Boca Raton, FL, USA.

Ibanez, S., Fitz, T. and Smarsly, K. (2019). A semantic model for wireless sensor networks in cognitive buildings. In: Proceedings of the ASCE International Conference on Computing in Civil Engineering, Atlanta, GA, USA, 06/17/2019 (submitted).

International Organization for Standardization (ISO) (2016). ISO 10303-21:2016 – Industrial automation systems and integration – Product data representation and exchange – Part 21: Implementation methods: Clear text encoding of the exchange structure. Geneva, Switzerland.

International Organization for Standardization (ISO) (2013). ISO 16739:2013 – Industry Foundation Classes (IFC) for data sharing in the construction and facility management industries. Geneva, Switzerland.

International Organization for Standardization (ISO) (2008). ISO 10303-11:2004 – Industrial automation systems and integration – Product data representation and exchange – Part 11: Description methods: The EXPRESS language reference manual. Geneva, Switzerland.

Lee, E. A. (2015). The past, present, and future of cyber-physical systems: A focus on models. Sensors, 15(3), pp. 4837–4869.

Lee, E. A. (2008). Cyber Physical Systems: Design Challenges. In: 11th IEEE Symposium on Object Oriented Real-Time Distributed Computing, Orlando, FL, USA, 05/05/2008.

Legatiuk, D. and Smarsly, K. (2018). An abstract approach towards modeling intelligent structural systems. In: Proceedings of the 9th European Workshop on Structural Health Monitoring 2018, Manchester, United Kingdom, 07/10/2018.

Legatiuk, D., Theiler, M., Dragos, K. and Smarsly, K. (2017). A categorical approach towards metamodeling cyber-physical systems. In: Proceedings of the 11th International Workshop on Structural Health Monitoring, Stanford, CA, USA, 09/12/2017.

Object Management Group (OMG) (2017). OMG Unified Modeling Language (OMG UML). Version 2.5.1, Needham, MA, USA.

Object Management Group (OMG) (2016). OMG Meta Object Facility (MOF) Core Specification. Version 2.5.1. Needham, MA, USA.

Object Management Group (OMG) (2015). XML Metadata Interchange (XMI) Specification. Needham, MA, USA.

Object Management Group (OMG) (2014). Model Driven Architecture (MDA). MDA Guide rev. 2.0. OMG Document. Needham, MA, USA.

Open Geospatial Consortium (2019). The OGC's Sensor Web Enablement (SWE) Initiative. Wayland, MA, USA, Available at: http://www.opengeospatial.org/domain/swe (Accessed on: 01/14/2019).

Rajkumar, R., Lee, I., Sha, L. and Stankovic, J. (2010). Cyber-Physical Systems: The Next Computing Revolution. In: Proceedings of the 47th Design Automation Conference, Anaheim, CA, USA, 06/13/2010.

Raspberry Pi Foundation (2017). Raspberry Pi 3 Model B+. (Product data sheet), Available at: https://static.raspberrypi.org/files/product-briefs/Raspberry-Pi-Model-Bplus-Product-Brief.pdf (Accessed on: 01/15/2019).

Shannon, C. E. (1948). A mathematical theory of communication. The Bell System Technical Journal, 27(3), pp. 379-423

Theiler, M. and Smarsly, K. (2018). IFC Monitor – An IFC extension for modeling structural health monitoring systems. Advanced Engineering Informatics, 37, pp. 54-65.

Theiler, M., Dragos, K. and Smarsly, K. (2018). Semantic description of structural health monitoring algorithms using building information modeling. In: The 25th International Workshop on Intelligent Computing in Engineering, Lausanne, Schweiz, 06/10/2018.

Wollschläger, M., Sauter, T. and Jasperneite, J. (2017). The Future of Industrial Communication: Automation Networks in the Era of the Internet of Things and Industry 4.0. IEEE Industrial Electronics Magazine, 11(1), pp. 17-27.

System-Based Resilience Assessment of Networked Transportation Systems in Metropolitan Areas: Case of Greater Los Angeles

Eyuphan Koc[1], Barbaros Cetiner, M. ASCE[2], Jisu Lee[3], Anya Nutakki[4] , Lucio Soibelman, F. ASCE[5], Ertugrul Taciroglu[6]

[1] Ph.D. Student, Sonny Astani Department of Civil and Environmental Engineering, University of Southern California, Los Angeles, California 90089. E-mail: ekoc@usc.edu

[2] Ph.D. Candidate, Department of Civil and Environmental Engineering, University of California Los Angeles, Los Angeles, CA 90095. E-mail: bacetiner@ucla.edu

[3] Transportation Modeler, Southern California Association of Governments, 900 Wilshire Blvd., Ste. 1700, Los Angeles, CA 90017. E-mail: leej@scag.ca.gov

[4] Undergraduate Researcher, Department of Computer Science, University of California Los Angeles, Los Angeles, CA 90095. E-mail: nutakki@usc.edu

[5] Professor, Sonny Astani Department of Civil and Environmental Engineering, University of Southern California, Los Angeles, California 90089. E-mail: soibelman@usc.edu

[6] Professor, Department of Civil and Environmental Engineering, University of California Los Angeles, Los Angeles, CA 90095. E-mail: etacir@ucla.edu

Abstract

One essential aspect of urban resilience is the ability of the transportation networks to maintain mobility and accessibility during the immediate aftermath, as well as in the long-term recovery, of an extreme event. Despite the critical nature of transportation services, the infrastructure inventory in many developed countries are in poor condition. For example, transportation infrastructure in the United States has repeatedly been graded poorly by American Society of Civil Engineers as it is aged and in need of a major retrofit or replacement effort. It is well established that topology-based approaches in transportation resilience abstract out network supply and travel demand relationships as well as fundamental traffic assignment concepts such as flow under capacity constraints. On the other hand, system-based approaches that are more promising in generating actionable policy insights lack the granularity enabled now by the recent advances in data and modeling, omit the scale of analysis required in metropolitan areas, and ignore formal considerations of the hazard itself which makes studies prone to simplistic what-if assumptions. To address such shortcomings, a preliminary framework intended to couple seismic hazard analysis with transportation network analysis is designed and deployed in a Greater Los Angeles Area case study where the impacts of a 7.3M scenario earthquake are investigated.

Introduction

Transportation networks are critical to the mobility of people and goods and are the backbone of the layered and interdependent network of civil infrastructures that facilitate everyday life. Due to their nature, they are exposed to a number of stressors including numerous natural and man-made hazards. In the case of natural hazards (e.g., earthquakes, hurricanes, etc.), the post-disaster functionality of transportation systems determine how rapidly the disaster-stricken area can recover (Chang, 2003). In the seismic regions of the US, transportation networks are especially vulnerable because of the current poor conditions of a significant portion of their bridges (ARTBA, 2018). As a result, resilience assessments of transportation systems have been a major research focus.

Research in this area is broadly categorized into two main categories of approaches: topology-based and system-based. Topology-based approaches are based on the graph-theoretic (nodes and edges) representation of transportation systems and quantify resilience in terms of network centrality based metrics such as betweenness centrality. Despite being practical in terms of data and modeling requirements, topology-based approaches often abstract out essential supply and demand relationships in the network (e.g., fundamental capacity-flow relationship). This makes them unable to generate actionable policy insights. For example, similar values of betweenness centrality in the abstract network may represent very different consequences in terms of how many travelers are affected and how large the total increase in travel time will be, depending on the demand and the availability and travel times of alternative routes in the real network (Mattsson and Jenelius, 2015). System-based methods founded on network supply and demand relationships are more promising in capturing the adverse impacts of hazard-induced disturbances on the transportation networks and their users. However, most system-based investigations of transportation resilience lack the granularity enabled now by the recent advances in data and modelling (road network and mobility data, software to simulate large scale models, etc.). There is also a tendency to test and validate approaches in small-scale networks omitting the scale of insights required by policymakers in metropolitan areas. Moreover, many studies analyze resilience via simple assumptions regarding the hazard without incorporating an understanding of the cause of failures (Khademi et al., 2015). The data and modelling needs in this area of research are discussed in detail in recent papers published by the authors (Koc et al., 2019; Cetiner et al., 2019) calling for holistic and coupled assessments of seismic hazards and the transportation disruptions caused by them. In this study, deploying a framework to address identified gaps, the authors investigate the transportation disruption resulting from a 7.3M earthquake affecting the Greater Los Angeles metropolitan area.

Background

By 2050, approximately 70% of human population will be living in cities (United Nations, 2018). Despite the well-known economic benefits of urban settlements, cities are known to be vulnerable to natural and man-made hazards due to their high concentration of people, capital and infrastructure. Many cities will face increasingly complex resilience challenges due to, for example, expected increases in the frequency and severity of extreme weather events, threats of terrorism, and risks due to active seismic faults near urban areas. The root of its definition originating from ecological resilience, urban resilience refers to *"the ability of an urban system - and all its constituent socio-ecological and socio-technical networks across temporal and spatial scales- to maintain or rapidly return to desired functions after a disturbance, to adapt to change, and to quickly transform systems that limit current or future adaptive capacity"* (Meerow et al., 2016). In this definition, an urban system is characterized by its governance networks, networked material and energy flows, urban infrastructure and form, and socio-economic dynamics (Dicken, 2007). Among these constituents, civil infrastructure systems are the lifelines that supports the lives, interactions, and dynamics of urban dwellers; one of the defining attributes of urban dwellers is mobility. It is argued that transportation is the most significant lifeline, because disturbance to transportation imposes extra burden on the other lifelines (Hopkins et al., 1991).

Mobility is an immediate functional need in the aftermath of and during the recovery from disasters. Therefore, one essential aspect of urban resilience is the ability of the urban transportation networks to maintain mobility and accessibility during the immediate aftermath, as well as in the long-term recovery, of an extreme event. Despite the critical nature of transportation services, the infrastructure inventory in many developed countries is in poor condition. For example, transportation infrastructure in the United States has repeatedly been graded poorly by American Society of Civil Engineers as it is aged and in need of a major retrofit or replacement effort (ASCE, 2017). The presently poor condition of the transportation infrastructure is exacerbating the risk together with the backdrop of impending natural hazards. Large metropolitan areas that are already vulnerable to natural hazards (e.g., earthquake risk in the Greater Los Angeles Area, storm surge risk in Southeast US, etc.) are especially challenged due to the increasing exposure triggered by mentioned factors. These developments necessitate a quantified assessment of transportation resilience in metropolitan areas. This information is crucial for urban policy-making towards enhanced resilience in the long-run (Noulas et al., 2012, Brockmann et al., 2006), and for emergency response planning for a potential extreme event (Schneider et al., 2013, Aschenbruck et al., 2004, Song et al., 2014, Uddin et al., 2009, Lu et al., 2012).

Meanwhile, scalable urban mobility data and large scale travel models are increasingly available from both conventional and novel sources (Census Transportation Planning Products (CTPP), and mobility data from social media and smartphones, etc. (Jurdak et al., 2015, Song et al., 2010, Gonzalez et al., 2008)). Particularly, government initiatives for the development of large scale travel demand models by metropolitan planning organizations (MPOs), State Departments of Transportation, etc. create a unique opportunity for resilience research. Despite the availability of data and models, comprehensive investigations of resilience in the nexus of mobility are scarce.

Previous efforts have particularly fallen short in two major dimensions. First, there is a lack of utilization of explicit and holistic road network models of large metropolitan areas. This shortcoming results in an over-simplified physical abstraction of the transportation networks when they could explicitly be modeled (e.g., modeling freeways or major arterials only and neglecting surface streets), and does not allow realistic hazard simulations to be incorporated into the analyses. Second, the potential costs of mobility perturbation to communities have not been studied from a user-centric resilience perspective. In other words, mobility perturbations and impacts on travelers are not known at a high geographical resolution. These capability gaps impede the assessment of the burden urban dwellers have to bear as they recover from a disruption and prevents economic impact analyses and policy-making to focus on particularly vulnerable communities/segments within the larger urban ecosystem.

As such, there is a need for improved methodologies. To address the shortcomings of the literature in the area, these new methodologies need to be scalable in order to go beyond assessing the engineered resilience of an infrastructure component to assessing the resilience of transportation in metropolitan areas to enable actionable insights. New methodologies also need to incorporate formal considerations of the disruptive event (e.g., earthquake, flash flood, etc.) and identify direct damages based on infrastructure inventory data as well as state-of-the-art hazard analysis procedures. Moreover, they should incorporate the human stakeholders of the urban environment in order to quantify the mobility disturbance from a user-centric standpoint.

Methodology

The authors designed the preliminary framework on Figure 1 that couples seismic hazard analysis with transportation network analysis to achieve a high granularity, comprehensive resilience assessment while addressing the shortcomings discussed in the previous section.

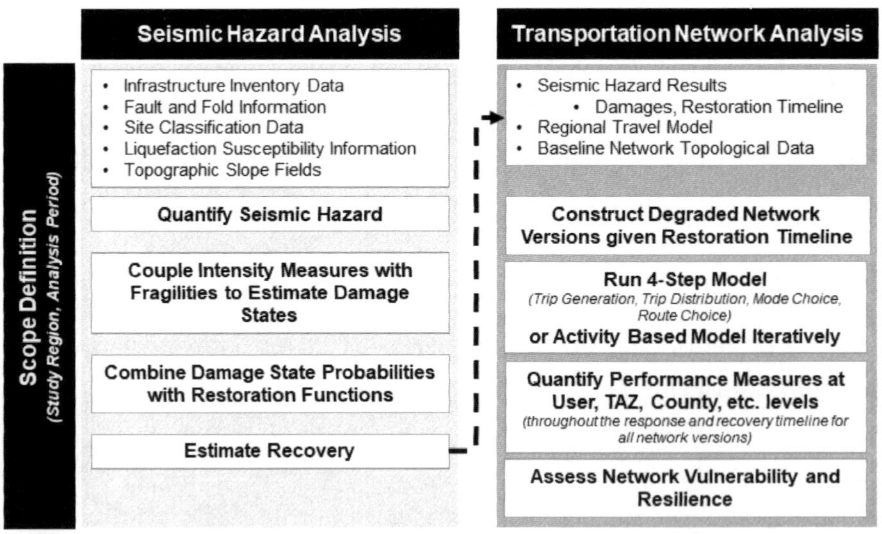

Figure 1: Preliminary framework for vulnerability and resilience assessments in metropolitan networks.

Seismic hazard analysis procedure of the framework begins with a scope definition (study region, analysis period) and a collection of datasets that provide infrastructure inventory data, fault and fold information, site classification, liquefaction susceptibility and topographic slope fields. Taking these datasets as inputs, seismic hazard analysis consists of three principal components: (i) quantifying deterministic seismic hazard governing an urban transportation network, (ii) coupling the intensity measures (IMs) resulting from the seismic hazard with component fragility functions to estimate the damage state probabilities, and (iii) combining the damage state probabilities with restoration functions to calculate the downtime of network components.

In simplest terms, deterministic scenario event for a region is identified as the event with the highest contribution to the IMs resulting from probabilistic seismic hazard (Cornell, 1968). For ground shaking due to earthquakes, this is typically performed by identifying the mode of the deaggregation plot for PSH (Bazzurro and Cornell, 1999) for 1-second spectral acceleration (S_{a1}) (Shafieezadeh et al., 2012). Once, the governing event is identified, then using the source information for the event and the site characteristics for all locations within the study region, S_{a1} at each site is computed using a ground motion prediction equation (Boore et al., 2014). These IM values are then coupled with fragility functions for the system components within the affected areas. For a set of IMs, the probability of a network component being in a damage state (P_j^k) is calculated as

$$\mathrm{P}_j^k = \begin{cases} \Pr(D^k \geq \mathrm{ds}_j) - \Pr(D^k \geq \mathrm{ds}_{j+1}) & j = 1,2,3,4, \\ \Pr(D^k \geq \mathrm{ds}_5) & j = 5. \end{cases} \tag{1}$$

For a set of IMs, expected downtime ($\mathrm{E}[D^k]$) is defined with respect to P_j^k using the recovery function for each damage state (RC_j) as in

$$\mathrm{E}[D^k] = \sum_{n=1}^{5} \mathrm{P}_j^k \cdot RC_j \tag{2}$$

where k is the index for IMs, j is the index for damage states, D^k is the damage state of network component due to IM_k, ds_1: no damage, ds_2: slight damage, ds_3: moderate damage, ds_4: extensive damage, and ds_5: complete damage states (Kiremidjian et al. 2006).

Physical damage and downtime findings are conveyed to transportation analysis and used to construct multiple network versions (pre-disaster baseline, post-disaster degraded versions). Given these network topologies (network supply), analysis includes (1) running a travel demand model iteratively; (2) quantifying network functionality indicators such as travel times, distances etc. at desired spatial resolutions and throughout the disaster timeline including response and recovery; (3) carrying out resilience assessment given functionality indicators.

Resilience of a system is analytically defined as

$$R = \frac{1}{h}\int_{h}^{h+t} Q(t)dt \tag{3}$$

where t is the instant in which the disruption occurs and h is the investigated time horizon and Q(t) is an indicator of functionality. In other words, resilience is quantified as the area under the functionality curve with respect to 100% functionality throughout the investigated time horizon (See Figure 2). For transportation networks, several functionality indicators are proposed in the literature with system total travel time (Vehicle Hours Traveled: VHT) and total travel distance (Vehicle Miles Traveled: VMT) being common to most system-level indicators (Frangopol and Bocchini, 2011). Delay, as quantified by a volume-delay function (e.g., Bureau of Public Roads function), or average speed can also be used as network functionality indicators. The framework assesses resilience based on this definition of resilience for transportation systems.

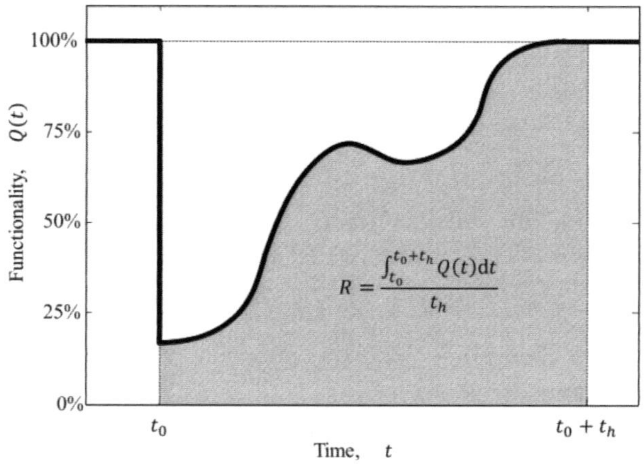

Figure 2. Network resilience curve adopted from Frangopol and Bocchini (2011).

Implementation of the transportation network analysis facet of the framework is based on a trip-based regional travel model developed by Southern California Association of Governments (SCAG). The trip-based model is developed periodically by SCAG--the metropolitan planning organization formed by the voluntary association of six Southern California counties including Los Angeles, Orange, Ventura, Riverside, San Bernardino and Imperial and it provides a common foundation for transportation planning and decision making by SCAG as well as other participating organizations (SCAG, 2016). The most recent version of the model is used by the authors with socioeconomic data from 2016. The model is highly granular and accommodates a holistic transportation network enabling a wide range of analyses including investigations of expansion projects, highway pricing strategies, introduction of new types of transportation services, etc. In accordance with the framework demonstrated above, the authors leveraged the model to determine the pre-disaster condition of the regional transportation network (baseline) as well as its condition in a post-disaster setting (day 30 after the earthquake).

Figure 3. The level-of-detail of the underlying network model in SCAG RTDM. Red lines indicate network links.

Case Study

The authors deploy the framework mentioned above in a Greater Los Angeles Area case study. For this study, by disaggregating the PSH results for a return period of 975 years, the seismic event that has the greatest contribution to PSH results was identified as the M_w 7.3 earthquake caused by a rupture of the Palos Verdes Connected fault system at an epicentral distance 1.4 km off the Ports of Los Angeles and Long Beach. Using this event as the scenario earthquake, the ground shaking associated with the earthquake rupture was quantified by taking into consideration the relevant source, path (Boore et al., 2014) and site effects (Wald and Allen 2007). The damage to bridges in the study area was computed using the fragility functions developed for HAZUS (FEMA 2003). For computing the bridge functionalities 30 days after the scenario earthquake, recovery functions in HAZUS were used. A total of 55 bridges were determined to have a functionality level below 75% and deemed insufficient for operation.

The damage assessment results, i.e. closure of 55 bridges in study region on day 30 after the earthquake, are modeled in the SCAG RTDM (Regional Travel Demand Model) network by editing the network topology on TransCAD. The links that correspond to these bridges are deleted while ensuring connectivity of the remaining links around them. With the revised network, the trip-based model is run again to quantify the resulting mobility disturbance under fixed demand conditions. The comparison of baseline and post-disaster results reveals worsening network functionality indicators (delays, total distance/time traveled, etc.) due to the functionality loss induced by direct damages and paves the way for quantifying resilience. Table 1 presents the system-level travel time and distance functionality indicators (VMT and VHT) for baseline and day 30 model runs presented together with absolute differences and percent changes. It also presents disaggregated results for every county. Expectedly, VMT and VHT surge due to earthquake damage and Los Angeles County suffers the highest functionality loss. A striking result is that system TTT (total travel time) quantified as VHT increases by more than 20% throughout the SCAG region despite the relatively localized impact of the scenario earthquake with bridge closures mostly concentrated along three freeway routes (110, 710 and 405).

Utilizing the granular results generated by the SCAG RTDM, the authors also publish results online at the Tier 1 TAZ (Traffic Analysis Zone) level which is a zoning breakdown that divides the study region into more than 4,000 zones (https://arcg.is/1908zK). High granularity results and visualizations shared online enable local insights such as the identification of neighborhoods that experience more surface street traffic due to nearby highway link closures. Analytics in this context could go a step further to investigate emissions related externalities induced on neighborhoods, and open doors to environmental justice and transportation equity discussions. These research directions will be considered in authors' future work.

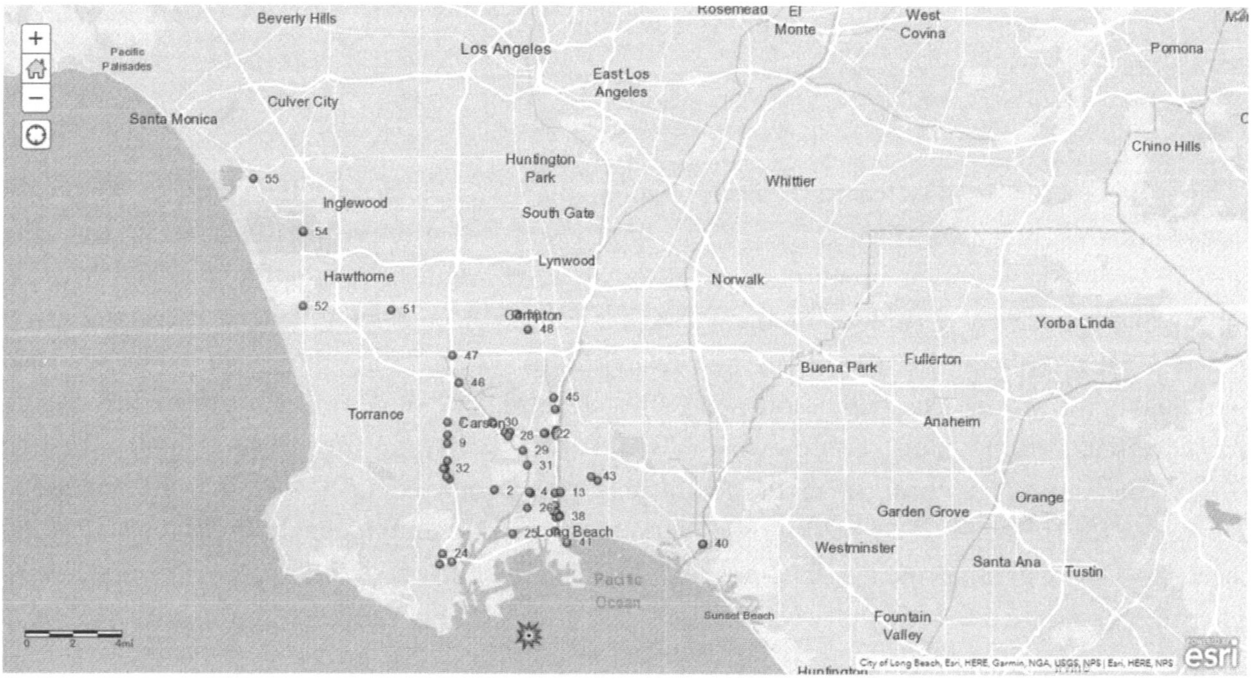

Figure 4. Bridges deemed closed on day 30 (red circles) after the scenario earthquake (epicenter marked with red/yellow star) according to the damage assessment.

Delays as quantified by the conventional BPR function are also quantified. Delay for the L&MDV class increase by as much as 71% where Los Angeles County experiences an 87.1% increase in delays.

Vehicle Miles Traveled (VMT) (miles)	Baseline	Day 30	Difference	% Change
VMT L&MDV	441,337,712	464,257,322	22,919,610	5.19%
VMT HDT	33,252,067	33,877,722	625,655	1.88%
VMT TOTAL (L&MDV+HDT)	**474,589,779**	**498,135,044**	**23,545,265**	**4.96%**
VMT by County (L&MDV+HDT) (miles)				
VMT Imperial	6,022,112	5,950,718	(71,394)	-1.19%
VMT Los Angeles	235,509,163	255,404,060	19,894,897	8.45%
VMT Orange	81,289,401	84,044,612	2,755,210	3.39%
VMT Riverside	64,087,908	64,101,547	13,639	0.02%
VMT San Bernardino	66,827,791	67,452,134	624,343	0.93%
VMT Ventura	20,853,404	21,181,974	328,570	1.58%

Vehicle Hours Traveled (VHT 1,000 hours)	Baseline	Day 30	Difference	% Change
VHT L&MDV	12,555	15,288	2,733	21.77%
VHT HDT	715	811	96	13.37%
VHT TOTAL (L&MDV+HDT)	**13,270**	**16,098**	**2,829**	**21.32%**
VHT by County (L&MDV+HDT) (1,000 hours)				
VHT Imperial	113,199	112,009	(1,189)	-1.05%
VHT Los Angeles	7,259,160	9,511,524	2,252,363	31.03%
VHT Orange	2,318,305	2,688,612	370,307	15.97%
VHT Riverside	1,465,415	1,533,608	68,193	4.65%
VHT San Bernardino	1,537,662	1,648,862	111,199	7.23%
VHT Ventura	538,659	566,336	27,677	5.14%

Table 1: System-level functionality indicators (VMT and VHT) for the pre-disaster baseline network and the degraded day 30 network. Results presented together with absolute differences and percent changes. L&MDV stand for light and medium weight vehicles (<8500 pounds in gross weight) and HDT stands for heavy-duty trucks.

Vehicle Hours Delayed (1,000 hours)	Baseline	Day 30	Difference	% Change
Delay L&MDV	2,651	4,551	1,900	71.66%
Delay HDT	144	215	72	50.05%
Delay TOTAL (L&MDV+HDT)	**2,795**	**4,766**	**1,972**	**70.55%**

Delay by County (L&MDV+HDT)	Baseline	Day 30	Difference	% Change
Delay Imperial	3	2	(0)	-2.17%
Delay Los Angeles	1,768	3,313	1,544	87.31%
Delay Orange	519	787	267	51.46%
Delay Riverside	188	247	59	31.30%
Delay San Bernardino	225	305	81	35.88%
Delay Ventura	92	112	21	22.60%

Table 2: Delays quantified per the conventional BPR function, presented for the study region as well as disaggregated to the county level.

Discussion and Conclusions

The framework designed by the authors to investigate transportation system resilience incorporates formal seismic hazard analysis procedures enriched by inventory data as well as a large-scale travel demand model. This coupled approach shows promise in addressing many shortcomings in the area mentioned in the earlier sections. The granularity of the analyses allows highly detailed visualizations related to the changing mobility pattern of the region.

One limitation of the case study is the conventional fixed demand assumption that ignores the potential travel behavior impacts of worsening network functionality. Travelers may chose to stay home, shift their demand to less congested times in the day, etc. Authors' investigation of resilience in metropolitan transportation systems has not focused on the post disaster travel behavior. However, SCAG's RTDM utilized in this study has sophisticated trip generation and trip distribution components that pave the way to study travel behavior. Moreover, this paper only presents network analysis results for two network versions, baseline and day 30 after scenario earthquake. The authors will publish results relating to the entire disaster timeline until full recovery in their future work. This way, a more comprehensive set of results demonstrating the pace of recovery will be obtained.

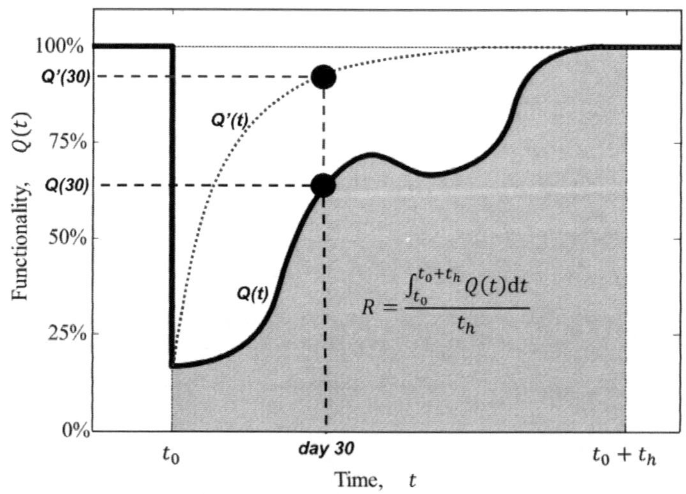

Figure 5. Network resilience curve adapted from Frangopol and Bocchini (2011) and revised. Dashed red line indicates faster recovery path achieved through implementation of resilience tactics.

Based on the resilience definition of Frangopol and Bocchini (2011), resilience is quantified—with respect to the continuous black line showing *Q(t)* on Figure 5—as the remaining functionality in the network following the disturbance stemming from direct physical damages to the infrastructure (e.g., bridge closures due to structural damages). This conceptualization of resilience is similar to the *static resilience* definition by Rose and Dormady (2018) which refers to *using remaining resources efficiently to maintain function*. In other words, static resilience in this context refers to the system-level indicators quantified by the user-equilibrium traffic assignment results under the new network supply conditions in the degraded network. Authors also intend to investigate *dynamic resilience* defined by Rose and Dormady which is characterized as *investing efficiently in repair and reconstruction in order to reestablish capacity as quickly as possible to regain function*. We indicate the improved recovery curve that may be achieved through *dynamic resilience* as *Q'(t)* on Figure 5. Some of the resilience tactics to achieve the faster recovery curve could be allocating resources to rapidly open critical corridors (e.g., I 405) to service or shifting heavy duty truck traffic to less congested time periods in the day to compensate for less desirable congestion levels due to the hazard.

The framework is currently being developed further to incorporate other hazards such as tsunamis and hurricanes. Moreover, the authors are focusing on advancements to the HAZUS inventories that have well-known limitations such as the use of archetype structures and a general lack of site-specific and structure-specific details. For this purpose, an image-based modeling approach is currently being integrated into the overarching framework to carry out more informed fragility analysis.

References

1. ARTBA, 2018 Bridge Report, <https://www.artbabridgereport.org/> (Nov. 25, 2018).
2. Aschenbruck, N., Frank, M., Martini, P., and Tolle, J. (2004). "Human mobility in manet disaster area simulation-a realistic approach." Local Computer Networks, 2004. 29th Annual IEEE International Conference on, IEEE, 668–675.
3. Bazzurro, P., and Cornell, C. A. (1999). "Disaggregation of seismic hazard." Bulletin of the Seismological Society of America, 89(2), 501–520
4. Boore, D. M., Stewart, J. P., Seyhan, E., and Atkinson, G. M. (2014). "NGA-West2 Equations for Predicting PGA, PGV, and 5% Damped PSA for Shallow Crustal Earthquakes." Earthquake Spectra, Earthquake Engineering Research Institute, 30(3), 1057–1085.
5. Brockmann, D., Hufnagel, L., and Geisel, T. (2006). "The scaling laws of human travel." Nature, 439, 462–465.
6. Cetiner, B., Koc, E., Soibelman, L., Taciroglu, E., Jisu, E., Nutakki, A. (2019). A Granular Simulation of Bridge Closures due to a Southern California Scenario Earthquake and its Effects on the Disruption and Recovery of Freight Traffic to and from Ports of Los Angeles and Long Beach. *Proceedings of the ASCE International Conference on Sustainable Infrastructure 2019 (accepted).*
7. Chang, S. E. (2003). Transportation planning for disasters: An accessibility approach. *Environment and Planning A*, 35(6), 1051–1072.
8. Cornell, C. A. (1968). "Engineering seismic risk analysis." Bulletin of the seismological society of America, The Seismological Society of America, 58(5), 1583–1606.
9. Dicken, P. (2007). Global shift: Mapping the changing contours of the world economy. SAGE Publications Ltd.

10. Federal Emergency Management Agency (FEMA). (2003). Hazus–MH 2.1 Earthquake Model Technical Manual. Washington D.C.
11. Frangopol, D., and Bocchini, P. (2011). "Resilience as Optimization Criterion for the Rehabilitation of Bridges Belonging to a Transportation Network Subject to Earthquake." Structures Congress, 2044–2055.
12. Gonzalez, M. C., Hidalgo, C. A., and Barabasi, A.-L. (2008). "Understanding individual human mobility patterns." Nature, 453, 779–782.
13. Hopkins, D. C., Lumsden, J. L., & Norton, J. A. (1991, August). Wellington's Lifelines in Earthquake Project: An Outline of a Major Review. *Lifeline Earthquake Engineering,* (pp. 774-804).
14. Jurdak, R., Zhao, K., Liu, J., AbouJaoude, M., Cameron, M., and Newth, D. (2015). "Understanding human mobility from Twitter." PloS one, 10, e0131469.
15. Khademi, N., Balaei, B., Shahri, M., Mirzaei, M., Sarrafi, B., Zahabiun, M., and Mohaymany, A. S. (2015). Transportation network vulnerability analysis for the case of a catastrophic earthquake. *International Journal of Disaster Risk Reduction*, 12, 234–254.
16. Kiremidjian, A., Moore, J., Fan, Y. Y., Basoz, N., Yazali, O., and Williams, M. (2006). Highway Demonstration Project. PEER Report 2006/02, Berkeley, CA.
17. Koc, E., Cetiner, B., Soibelman, L., Taciroglu, E. (2019). System-Based Vulnerability and Resilience Assessment in Mega-Scale Transportation Systems: Towards Data and Model-Driven Methodologies. *Proceedings of the ASCE International Conference on Computing in Civil Engineering 2019 (accepted).*
18. Lu, X., Bengtsson, L., and Holme, P. (2012). "Predictability of population displacement after the 2010 Haiti earthquake." Proceedings of the National Academy of Sciences, 109, 11576–11581.
19. Mattsson, L. G., and Jenelius, E. (2015). Vulnerability and resilience of transport systems - A discussion of recent research. *Transportation Research Part A: Policy and Practice*, 81, 16–34.
20. Meerow, S., Newell, J. P., and Stults, M. (2016). "Defining urban resilience: A review." Landscape and Urban Planning.
21. Noulas, A., Scellato, S., Lambiotte, R., Pontil, M., and Mascolo, C. (2012). "A tale of many cities: universal patterns in human urban mobility." PloS one, 7, e37027.
22. Rose, A., and Dormady, N. (2018). "Advances in Analyzing and Measuring Dynamic Economic Resilience." SSRN Electronic Journal, 2, 1–8
23. Schneider, C. M., Belik, V., Couronné, T., Smoreda, Z., and González, M. C. (2013). "Unravelling daily human mobility motifs." Journal of The Royal Society Interface, 10, 20130246.
24. Shafieezadeh, A., Ramanathan, K., Padgett, J. E., and DesRoches, R. (2012). "Fractional order intensity measures for probabilistic seismic demand modeling applied to highway bridges." Earthquake Engineering & Structural Dynamics, John Wiley & Sons, Ltd, 41(3), 391–409.

25. Song, C., Qu, Z., Blumm, N., and Barabási, A.-L. (2010). "Limits of predictability in human mobility." Science, 327, 1018–1021.
26. Song, X., Zhang, Q., Sekimoto, Y., and Shibasaki, R. (2014). "Prediction of human emergency behavior and their mobility following large-scale disaster." Proceedings of the 20th ACM SIGKDD international conference on Knowledge discovery and data mining, ACM, 5–14.
27. Southern California Association of Governments (2016). SCAG Regional Travel Demand Model and Model Validation. <http://www.princeton.edu/~alaink/Orf467F16/SCAG_RTDM_2012ModelValidation.pdf> (Nov. 25, 2018).
28. Uddin, M. Y. S., Nicol, D. M., Abdelzaher, T. F., and Kravets, R. H. (2009). "A post-disaster mobility model for delay tolerant networking." Winter Simulation Conference, Winter Simulation Conference, 2785–2796.
29. United Nations DESA, Department of Economic and Social Affairs. (2018). <https://www.un.org/development/desa/en/news/population/2018-revision-of-world-urbanization-prospects.html> (Mar. 1, 2019).
30. Wald, D. J., and Allen, T. I. (2007). "Topographic Slope as a Proxy for Seismic Site Conditions and Amplification." Bulletin of the Seismological Society of America, GeoScienceWorld, 97(5), 1379–1395.

Knowledge-based Registration for Reliable Correlated Change Detection on High-pier Curved Continuous Rigid Frame Bridge

Zhe Sun[1], Ying Shi[2], Wen Xiong[2], Pingbo Tang[1,*]
[1] Arizona State University, the United States
[2] Southeast University, China
zsun43@asu.edu

Abstract. Change detection on continuous rigid frame bridges is challenging due to its complex shapes. Accurate and effective change analysis is necessary to not only locate the changes but also investigate the root causes behind. Registration of 3D imageries collected at different times for structural change analysis, however, is an obstacle even with the help of advanced registration algorithms. This study proposed a knowledge-based registration approach that segments point clouds into structural elements for recovering the correlated torsional and bending behaviors of connected bridge elements. The proposed approach uses the joint equilibrium condition between structural elements as domain knowledge to guide the selection of correspondences for point cloud registration and element-level change detection. Besides, the approach iterates the correspondence locating process until change detection results comply with the joint equilibrium condition. The results indicate that the proposed knowledge-based registration approach provides more reliable correlated change detection results than using the Iterative Closest Point (ICP) algorithms.

1. Introduction

Curved bridges have the advantages of great adaptability of roads and aesthetically pleasing shapes widely used in transportation systems (Pahlavan *et al.*, 2015). The continuous rigid frame bridge can adjust the force of the bridge reasonably and avoid setting up bearings (Li, Yang, and Yang, 2015; Zong *et al.*, 2016). Designers, therefore, favor the bridge design of curved continuous rigid frames in practice. However, change detection on such bridges for revealing potential structural failures is challenging. Because of the horizontal curvatures, a complicated bending-torsion coupling interaction occurs in bridge components under vertically asymmetrical loads. Such coupling interactions often result in a higher force and displacement demands in curved bridges compared to straight bridges (Feng *et al.*, 2018). Also, developing spatial changes on structural elements of bridges can be indicators of structural defects and possible structural deteriorations (Kalasapudi *et al.*, 2018). Accurate and effective change analysis is thus necessary to not only locate the changes due to torsional and bending behaviors of the bridge elements but also investigate the root causes behind. Such analysis also supports decision making during future inspection and maintenance over the service life of bridges.

However, the current practice of bridge inspection still heavily rely on the judgment of field bridge engineers and tedious inspection works require large amounts of manual surveying (Hüthwohl, Lu and Brilakis, 2016). Terrestrial laser scanning (TLS) provides the potential for acquiring accurate geometric information of bridges and give a quantitative estimation of the as-is conditions (Meral, 2011). Recent studies revealed the potential of using point cloud data collected by laser scanners at different times for detecting spatial changes of bridge structures over the years (Tang and Akinci, 2012; Kalasapudi *et al.*, 2018). Using acquired 3D data for supporting bridge inspection by aligning two point clouds captured from different times and visually comparing the differences is essential for change detection (Kasireddy and Akinci, 2015). Such aligned process is the "registration" of two point cloud datasets into one common coordinate system. However, conventional registration approach by simply aligning raw point clouds not only requires a significant amount of human efforts (i.e., select control points, extract

2D features, and so on) but also challenging in terms of accuracy and computational efficiency. Analyzing changes of large-span bridges from 3D point clouds, which may contain billions of points, becomes more challenging (Kasireddy and Akinci, 2015). Unreliable or inaccurate registration of 3D laser scanning datasets of a bridge collected at different times can lead to incorrect detections of spatial changes and eventually leading to unreliable condition assessment of bridge structures (Kalasapudi, Tang and Turkan, 2017).

Structural deteriorations on bridges follow specific patterns depending on the structure type and designed loading capacity (Law, Silcock, and Holden, 2018). Previous studies have claimed the potential of using similar deformation patterns as knowledge for supporting reliable change detection (Zong *et al.*, 2016). Changes on connected bridge elements are correlated and should follow the same deformation patterns according to fundamental structure theorem (Xu, Yang, and Neumann, 2018). Besides, certain bridge elements contain different structural characteristics in terms of deformation. Girders on a curved continuous rigid frame bridge should suffer both bending and torsion due to the curvature and other causes (i.e., concrete shrinkage, prestress losses, and so on) (Feng *et al.*, 2018; Mangalathu *et al.*, 2018). Plus, girders and piers on such bridge are rigidly connected and do not allow relative rotation. Piers on such bridge will have lateral displacement triggered by the torsion of the connected girders (Yuan and Harik, 2010). Such structural engineering knowledge help not only determines correspondences on different datasets for accurate element-level registration and deformation analysis but also validate the change detection results using the moment equilibrant theorem.

Registration is a process that aligns two point clouds. Global registration is an alignment method to align multiple three-dimensional shapes in arbitrary initial positions (Gelfand *et al.*, 2005). Existing studies reveal the potential of applying advanced registration algorithms for global change detection with a limited explanation on the detected spatial changes (Antova, 2015; Zheng *et al.*, 2016; Kalasapudi *et al.*, 2018). Others have discussed and examined the potential of applying the non-rigid registration method for revealing spatial transformations of local correspondence (Bosché, 2010; Ma *et al.*, 2017). Some studies examined an automated method for bridge element segmentation (Lu and Ioannis, 2018; Lu, Brilakis and Middleton, 2018). Other studies developed automatic skeleton detection algorithms for object detection (Han and Lee, 2013; Saha, Borgefors and Sanniti di Baja, 2016). Structure engineers, however, spend efforts in experimental testing and finite element modeling for understanding bridge failure modes (Barbato and Conte, 2006; Conte and Zhang, 2007; Moaveni and Conte, 2014). However, limited research has considered the fundamental structural theorem when registering two datasets with partially overlapped points for change detection.

This study proposed a structural engineering knowledge-based registration approach that firstly segments point clouds into structural elements for recovering the torsional and bending behaviors of structural elements. The proposed approach uses the joint equilibrium condition between structural elements as domain knowledge to guide the selection of correspondences for point cloud registration and element-level change detection. Besides, the approach iterates the correspondence locating process until a finely registered scan. In the end, the approach correlates the detected changes for validating the change detection results and assessing structural system behaviors

2. Methodology

The proposed research has two objectives: 1) Establish a registration method using joint equilibrium condition between structural elements as domain knowledge for reliable 3D point clouds registration to detect element-level deformations; 2) Validate the correlated change detection results using structural engineering knowledge (equilibrium condition at the joints between/among structural elements). The proposed research then examined the established knowledge-based registration method for spatial change detection by using a prestressed concrete curved continuous rigid frame bridge as a case in China.

Structural deterioration knowledge is the information associated with particular structural deformation patterns of bridges. Besides, deformation patterns of adjacent girders and pier connected at a joint should follow specific structure rules depending on the boundary condition (i.e., bending-torsion coupling scenario occurred at rigid frame bridges). The proposed knowledge-based registration method uses joint equilibrium condition between structural elements as domain knowledge with bridge inspection experiences to help support reliable change detections. The pipeline of the proposed knowledge-based registration approach shown in Figure 1 below.

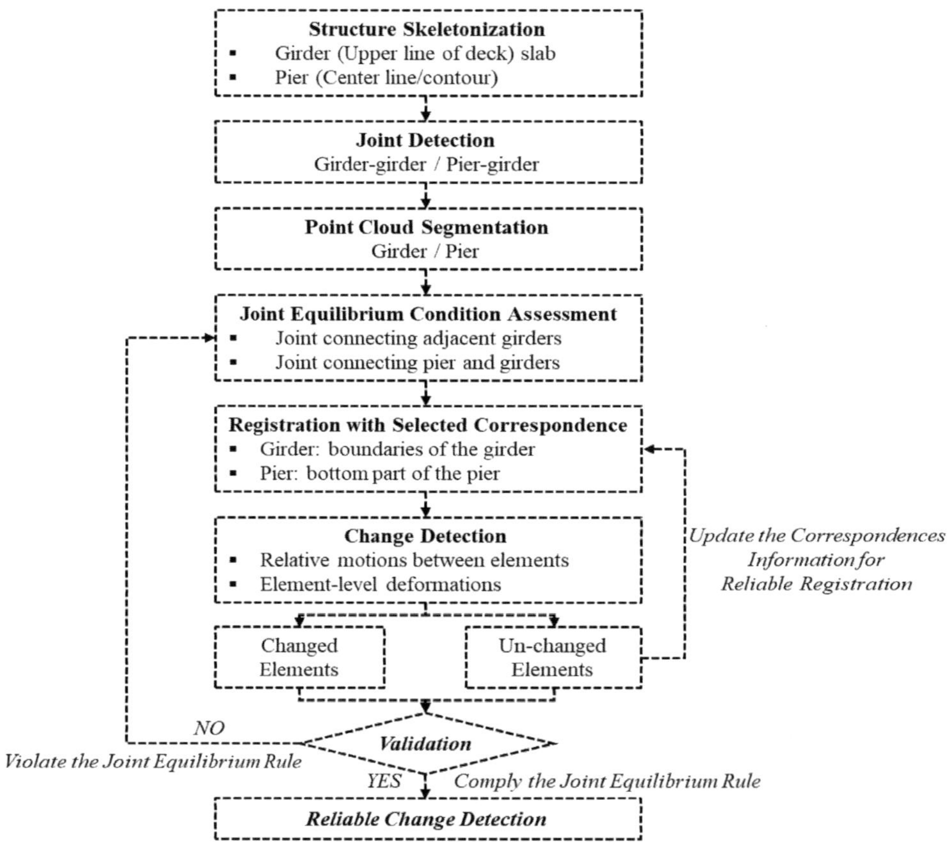

Figure 1: Structural Engineering Knowledge-based Point Cloud Registration Workflow

The proposed method first segments point clouds into structural elements for recovering the correlated torsional and bending behaviors of connected bridge elements. Often, the local deformations could be "overwhelmed" by rigid body motions at the structure level when conducting element-level change analysis with global registration method. The authors first conducted structure skeletonization to extract skeletons of the upper (girder) and the lower part (pier) of the bridge. For the upper part of the bridge, the authors draw a polyline based on the centreline of the bridge from the top view. Based on the polyline (path), the authors define the distance along the path between two orthogonal sections in order to create multiple orthogonal sections along the polyline (the distance must be small in order to get more orthogonal sections in order to represent the shape of the bridge better). As for the pier, the authors extract the contour of each pier on its side view. After skeletonization of the bridge, the authors identify joints based on the contours of piers and orthogonal sections. Then, the authors isolate the pier from the superstructure and segment each span for preparation of local registration.

The authors then assess the joint equilibrium condition at joints that connecting adjacent girders and pier based on the boundary condition. As a rigid frame bridge, the superstructure and substructure are rigidly connected at joints to act as a continuous unit. The joints connecting structure elements are rigid connections which transfer bending moment, axial forces, and shear forces. Besides, such rigid connections do not allow relative rotations between connected structural elements. However, boundaries of girders and the bottom part of piers tend to have relatively small deformations, even the girders and piers are experiencing bending and torsional behaviors. The authors first decided to use boundaries of girders and the bottom part of piers as correspondences for local registration to detect deformations of girders and piers. Next, the proposed method will conduct a local registration on each span and pier segmented from the previous step between different datasets. During the registration, a point-pair method has been used based on the correspondences selected according to the joint equilibrium condition assessment. For instance, Figure 2 shows the selected correspondence (four points) at the left end of a girder for registration of the third span. The authors conducted a Cloud-to-cloud (C2C) distance calculation for change detection.

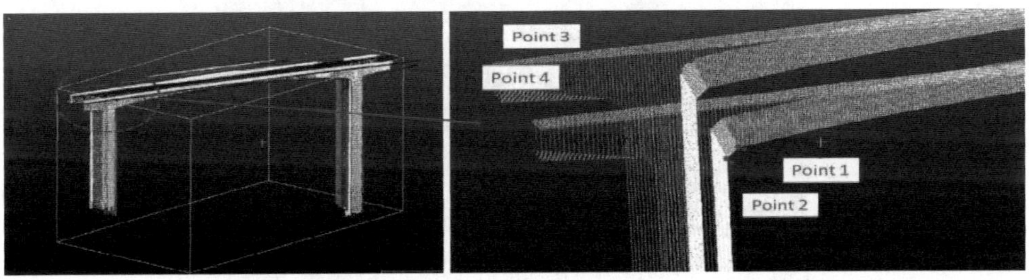

Figure 2: Selected Correspondence at Both Ends of a Girder

At last, the proposed method correlates and validates the change detection results of girders and piers according to the joint equilibrium condition at the joints between structural elements. If the correlated change detection results do not comply with the joint equilibrium condition, the proposed method will update the correspondences by using unchanged segments from the change detection results for another iteration of change detection. The method will iterate the correspondence updating and registration process until change detection results comply with the joint equilibrium condition.

3. Case Study: Inspection of a Curved Continuous Rigid Frame Bridge in China

The studied bridge is at Anhui Province, China, which has extremely mountainous and complex terrain conditions. The bridge has a total length of 1,010 m, including a six-span main bridge of 612m (66m + 4*120m + 66m). The main bridge uses the prestressed concrete continuous rigid frame with high hollow thin-walled piers (83m). The authors collected 3D point cloud data for the Bridge in China in 2017 and 2018 by using the FARO Focus S 350 laser scanner (37 scans for 2017; 31 scans for 2018). The authors performed the registration for each 3D laser scanning dataset by using Cloud-to-Cloud (C2C) registration through *SCENE* (FARO, 2019) and manually remove the redundant data (i.e., trees, cars, and so on) by using the segmentation tool in *CloudCompare* (Girardeau-Montaut, 2019). Due to the size of the point cloud data, the authors proposed a skeleton-based segmentation method to 1) isolate the upper part (deck), and the lower part of the bridge (pier) based on the joint detected within the skeleton that represents the bridge topology; and 2) segment each span into one individual part based on the joint for local registration preparation.

3.1 Structural skeletonization and joint detection

The authors first manually draw a polyline (appears in red) along the center line of the bridge from the top view of the point cloud (see Figure 3). *CloudCompare* then automatically generated multiple orthogonal sections along the polyline based on the defined width between sections (the distance along the polyline between two orthogonal sections are equal). After the generations of several sections, the authors ask *CloudCompare* to extract the corresponding cloud slices of each generated sections. Then, the authors rotate the point cloud to the side view of the bridge and try to extract the 2D contour of each pier by using the "Cross Section Segmentation" tool in *CloudCompare*.

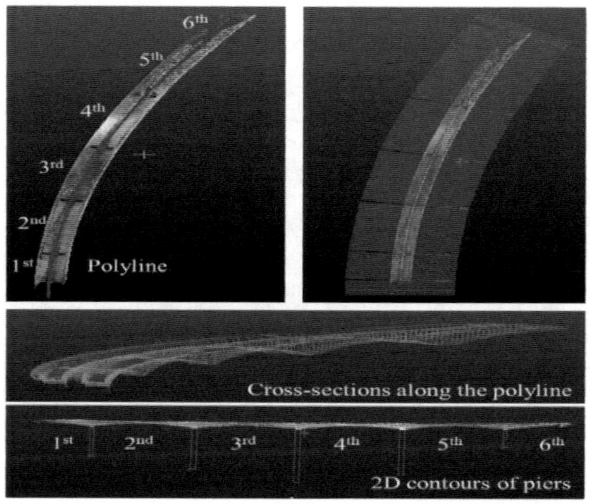

Figure 3: Skeleton Extraction of the Bridge

3.2 Point cloud segmentation

Though existing research has applied automated algorithms for point cloud segmentation (Lu and Ioannis, 2018), the focus of this study is not in the same direction. The point cloud segmentation process includes two steps: 1) isolate the upper and lower part of the bridge; and 2) segment each span into individual elements. The author first manually identified the joints connecting the cross sections of the upper part and the 2D contour of piers and use that joint in order to isolate the upper and lower part of the bridge (blue: upper part of the bridge; red: lower part of the bridge). The authors use the segmentation tool in *CloudCompare* to complete the segmentation process. Then, the authors segmented each span into individual parts. This segmentation uses the cross sections generated according to the polyline mentioned in the last section (see Figure 4).

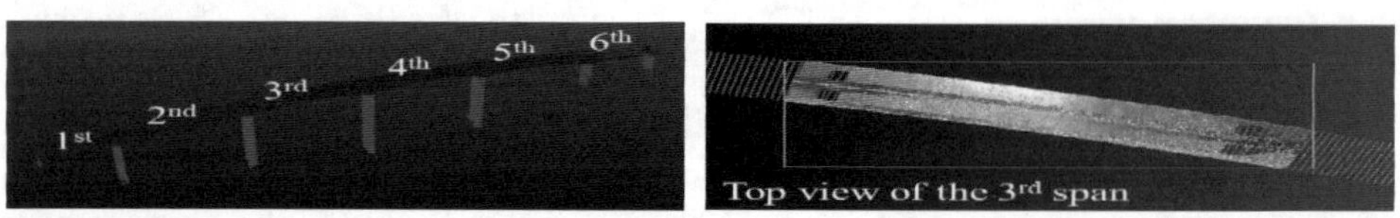

Figure 4: Point Cloud Segmentation (Girder/Pier; Span by Span)

3.3 Registration

Local deformations of structure elements are critical to be used for investigating changes of internal forces and assessing changes of bridge condition. The proposed knowledge-based registration method is a non-rigid local registration that integrates structural engineering knowledge for local deformations at the structure element level. Such a knowledge-based registration method could help revealing local deformations of the bridge elements (girders and piers) and eliminate the errors caused by other registration methods (i.e., ICP). The authors use correspondences that are established based on existing local features. Moreover, the authors selected these features at locations where deformations are unlikely to occur (both ends of girders and bottom of piers) based on bridge engineering knowledge.

According to the point cloud, the points are much denser in the 2nd, 3rd, and the 4th span of the studied bridge. The authors then examined the proposed local registration method in the 2nd, 3rd, and the 4th span of the studied bridge. Also, the authors registered these three spans globally (registration without segmentation of individual spans) by using the traditional registration algorithms (ICP) for comparison.

In the proposed knowledge-based registration process, the authors registered each span between the two-year point clouds (i.e., register the girder of the 3rd span from the 2017 dataset to the same girder in 2018 dataset). To get better registration results, the authors manually select the corresponding points at both ends of the girder (the authors assume both ends of a girder tend to have relatively small deformations than the mid-span based on basic structural engineering knowledge) (see Figure 5).

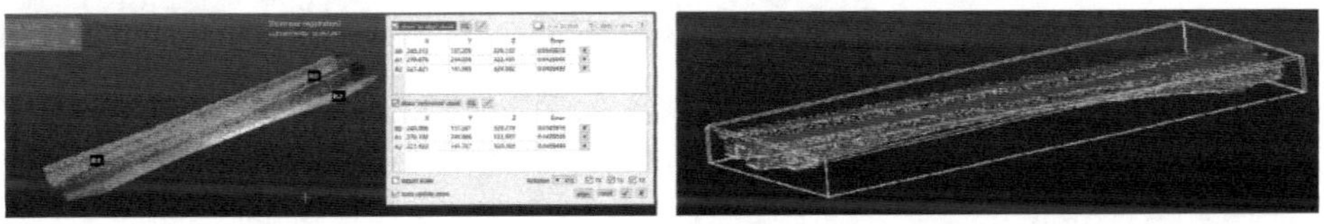

Figure 5: Knowledge-based Local Registration – Girder (i.e., the 3rd Span)

By using the Iterative Closest Point (ICP) registration method, the authors registered the whole three spans from the 2017 dataset to the same spans in 2018 dataset by using the traditional registration algorithms (ICP) (see Figure 6).

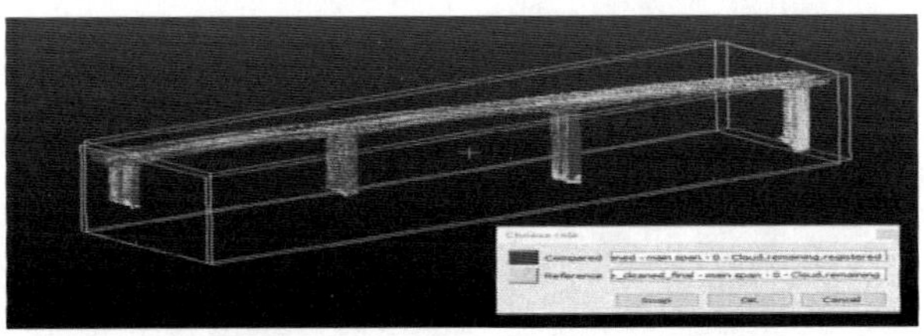

Figure 6: Registration using the Iterative Closest Point (ICP) (the 2nd, 3rd, and 4th Span; yellow: 2017 point cloud; red: 2018 point cloud)

4. Change Detection Results and Discussion

The preliminary research findings suggest that the established knowledge-based registration method has the potential of accurate detections of structural changes on curved continuous rigid frame bridges. Such method resolves the difficulties of aligning the deformed structure with its original shape when finding correspondences for change detection during conventional rigid and non-rigid registration approach. Besides, change detection results show the detected spatial changes obey the fundamental structure theorem between each bridge elements and aligned with the documented deficiencies in the inspection report.

4.1 Change Detection – Knowledge-based Local Registration on Girders and Piers

The authors compute a Cloud-to-cloud (C2C) distance between the registered point cloud (2018) and the reference point cloud (2017). Results (see Figure 7) indicate the girders of the studies three spans are all suffered bending and torsion, and the piers are undergoing lateral displacement. According to the *Right-hand Rule*, the vector of the torsion can have two elements that are along the x (lateral direction) and y (longitudinal direction) directions of the bridge. Plus, the change detection results indicate the pier connecting the 2nd and the 3rd span of the bridge is undergoing lateral displacement (see Figure 8). The maximum lateral displacement occurred at the top of the pier, whereas the bottom of the pier has no displacement. The results help explain a bending-torsion coupling scenario where the torsion of the girders is balancing the moment of the high pier connected.

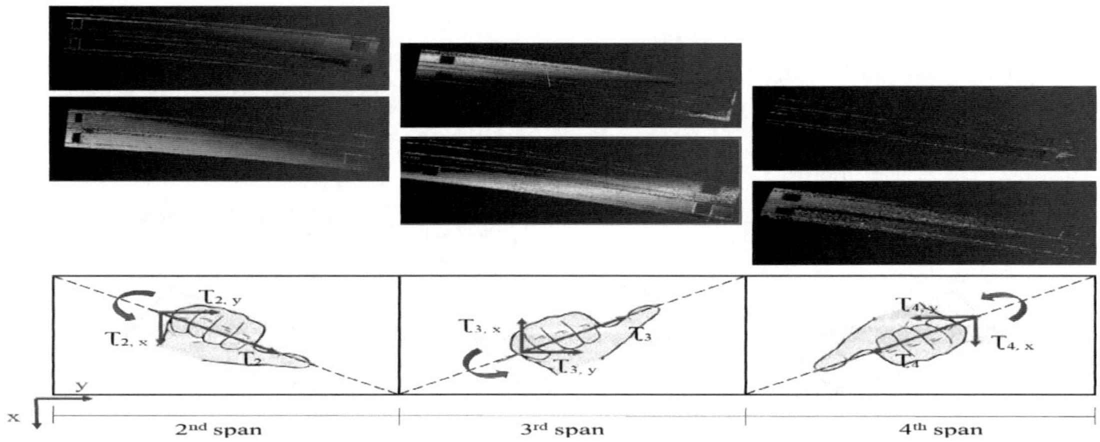

Figure 7: Knowledge-based Local Registration – Girder (top view of the bridge)

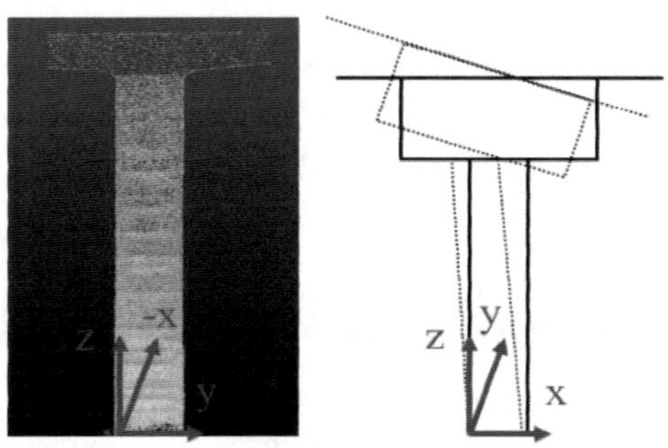

Figure 8: Lateral Displacement of Piers (i.e., Pier Connecting the 2nd and 3rd Span)

The authors also checked the bending status of each spans to determine the direction (upward, downward) of the bending. For girders of each span, the authors select three points (joints connecting the deck and pier) from each dataset to fit a plane horizontally, then calculate the distance (***d***) from the vertex (***point C***) of this span to the fitted plane (***plane***$_{1,2,3}$). Then, the authors compared the difference between the distances (***Δd***) calculated from the 2017 and the 2018 datasets to determine the direction of bending on this span (see Figure 9).

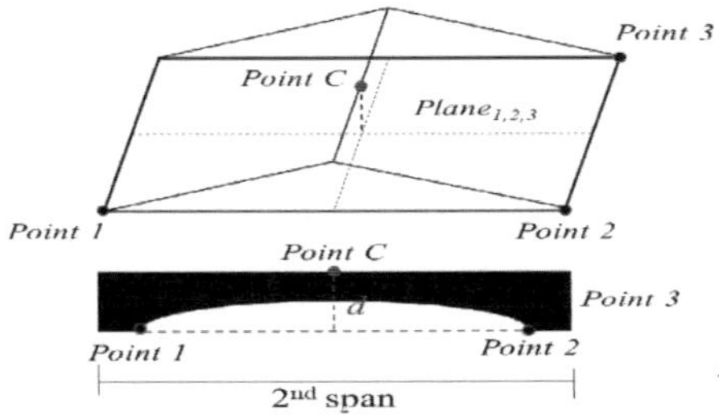

Year	Distance (***d***)		
	2nd Span	3rd Span	4th Span
2017	6.68	6.05	6.65
2018	6.58	6.90	6.38
Δd	-0.10	+0.85	-0.27

$$\Delta d = d_{2018} - d_{2017} = d_{c\text{-}Plane1,2,3}' - d_{c\text{-}Plane1,2,3}$$

Figure 9: Distance Calculation for Determining Direction of Bending

Results (see Figure 10) indicates that the 2nd and the 4th span are suffered downward bending, whereas the 3rd span is bending upward. Plus, the authors found that the piers within this three-span are undergoing displacement in the longitudinal direction (y direction) of the bridge. The results indicate the consistency of the bending and torsional behaviors of connecting girders and high piers at the joints.

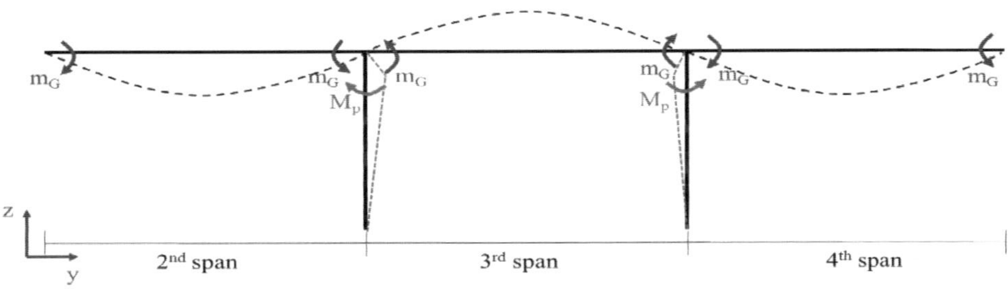

Figure 10: Bending of the Studied Bridge

4.2 Change Detection – Rigid Local Registration using ICP Algorithm on Girders and Piers

The authors compute a Cloud-to-cloud (C2C) distance between the registered point cloud (2018) and the reference point cloud (2017). Results (see Figure 11) indicate the girders of the studies three spans are all suffered only bending. However, the pier connecting the 2nd and the 3rd span of the bridge is undergoing lateral displacement (x-direction). The registration results indicate that the girders of the bridge are suffered to bend, whereas no displacement in the lateral direction should appear on the pier. Deformations shown from the registration results show inconsistency between girders and pier and do not align with the documented deficiencies in the inspection report.

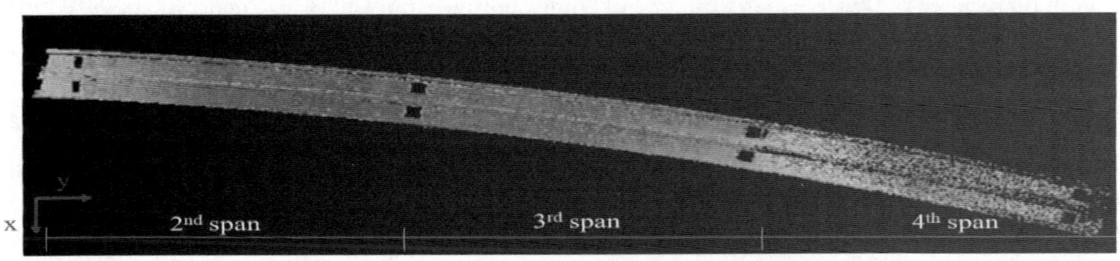

Figure 11: Registration Using Iterative Closest Point (ICP) – Girder (top view of the bridge)

5. Conclusion and Future Research

Due to the curvature of the studied bridge, the center of the gravity of the bridge is not on the bridge, which often reflects in the coupling of bending and torsion. Moreover, since the studied bridge is a rigid frame bridge, the joint connecting the girder and pier is fixed, which allows force and moment transfer. In other words, the torsion of the bridge must balance the bending of the pier in the lateral direction of the bridge. Moreover, the bending moment of the studied bridge in the three spans are also balanced by the longitudinal bending of the piers according to the joint analysis.

Most current research focuses on the use of "nearest" neighbor search (NNS) to compare two clouds, which effectively calculates the closest (or most similar) points. Direct comparison of two partially overlapping point clouds of the same object and measuring the changes between them could be hard with some popular computer methods (i.e., ICP). It is thus vital to understand small size changes of specific objects for interpreting deformations and require a subtler analysis of the measured scene. Besides, structure engineering knowledge specifies possible correlated deformations among connected bridge element, which is valuable information for validating the change detection results and support further registration. The proposed method does not only guide accurate local registration but also offers a potential for adjusting and supporting the planning of bridge inspection. This study reveals the fact that the traditional registration approach or register using the control network fixed on the job site might not be appropriate for understanding the structural behaviors of curved continuous rigid frame bridges. Moreover, the proposed method shows the potential of analyzing local deformations of bridge elements for assessing potential bridge failures.

Acknowledgment

This material is based on work supported by the science and technology project on transportation construction by the U.S. National Science Foundation (NSF) under Grant No. 1454654 and the Ministry of Transport of the People's Republic of China (Project No. 2013318223380, 2014318J14250). The supports are gratefully acknowledged.

References

Antova, G. (2015) 'Registration Process of Laser Scan Data in the Field of Deformation Monitoring', *Procedia Earth and Planetary Science*. Elsevier B.V., 15, pp. 549–552. DOI: 10.1016/j.proeps.2015.08.096.

Barbato, M. and Conte, J. P. (2006) 'Finite element structural response sensitivity and reliability analyses using smooth versus non-smooth material constitutive models', *International Journal of Reliability and Safety*, 1(1/2), p. 3.DOI: 10.1504/ijrs.2006.010688.

Bosché, F. (2010) 'Automated recognition of 3D CAD model objects in laser scans and calculation of as-built dimensions for dimensional compliance control in construction', *Advanced Engineering Informatics*, 24(1), pp. 107–118. DOI: 10.1016/j.aei.2009.08.006.

Chen, H. and Zheng, S. (2015) 'Seismic Response of Ultra High-pier Railway Bridge under Spatially Varying Site Conditions of Earthquake Excitations', *Journal of Highway and Transportation Research and Development*, 9(2), pp. 61–68. DOI: 10.3969/j.

Conte, J. P., and Zhang, Y. (2007) 'Performance-Based Earthquake Engineering: Application to an Actual Bridge-Foundation-Ground System', *In 12th Italian national conference on earthquake engineering, Pisa, Italy* ., pp. 1–18. Available at: http://jaguar.ucsd.edu/publications/Conference Proceedings/ANIDIS_Conte_Keynote_Paper_with_Header.pdf.

FARO (2019) *SCENE 2019*. Available at: https://www.faro.com/products/construction-bim-cim/faro-scene/.

Feng, R., Wang, X., Yuan, W. and Yu, J. (2018) 'Impact of seismic excitation direction on the fragility analysis of horizontally curved concrete bridges', *Bulletin of Earthquake Engineering*. Springer Netherlands, 16(10), pp.

4705–4733. DOI: 10.1007/s10518-018-0400-2.

Gelfand, N., Mitra, J. N., Guibas, J. L. and Pottmann, H. (2005) 'Robust Global Registration', in *Eurographics Symposium on Geometry Processing*, pp. 156–160. DOI: 10.1016/0167-4781(89)90095-X.

Girardeau-Montaut, D. (2019) *CloudCompare - 3D point cloud and mesh processing software Open Source Project*. Available at: http://www.cloudcompare.org/.

Han, S. and Lee, S. (2013) 'A vision-based motion capture and recognition framework for behavior-based safety management', *Automation in Construction*. Elsevier B.V., 35, pp. 131–141. doi: 10.1016/j.autcon.2013.05.001.

Hüthwohl, P., Lu, R. and Brilakis, I. (2016) 'Challenges of bridge maintenance inspection', *16th International Conference on Computing in Civil and Building Engineering*, (July).

Kalasapudi, V. S., Tang, P. and Turkan, Y. (2017) 'Computationally efficient change analysis of piece-wise cylindrical building elements for proactive project control', *Automation in Construction*. Elsevier, 81(May), pp. 300–312. DOI: 10.1016/j.autcon.2017.04.001.

Kalasapudi, V. S., Tang, P., Xiong, W. and Shi, Y. (2018) 'A multi-level 3D data registration approach for supporting reliable spatial change classification of single-pier bridges', *Advanced Engineering Informatics*. Elsevier, 38(June), pp. 187–202. DOI: 10.1016/j.aei.2018.06.010.

Kasireddy, V. and Akinci, B. (2015) 'Challenges in Generation of As-is Bridge Information Model: A Case Study', *32nd International Symposium on Automation and Robotics in Construction*. DOI: 10.22260/ISARC2015/0037.

Law, D. W., Silcock, D. and Holden, L. (2018) 'Terrestrial laser scanner assessment of deteriorating concrete structures', *Structural Control and Health Monitoring*, 25(5), pp. 1–15. DOI: 10.1002/stc.2156.

Li, J., Yang, Y. and Yang, Z. (2015) 'Long-span continuous rigid frame bridge construction control', (Icadme), pp. 1316–1320.

Lu, R., Brilakis, I., and Middleton, C. R. (2018) 'Detection of Structural Components in Point Clouds of Existing RC Bridges', *Computer-Aided Civil and Infrastructure Engineering*, (July). DOI: 10.1111/mice.12407.

Lu, R. and Ioannis, B. (2018) 'Detection of Key Components of Existing Bridge in Point Cloud Datasets', in, pp. 111–115.

Ma, J., Zhao, J., Jiang, J. and Zhou, H. (2017) 'Non-rigid point set registration with robust transformation estimation under manifold regularization', *31st AAAI Conference on Artificial Intelligence, AAAI 2017*, pp. 4218–4224. DOI: http://0-dx.doi.org.wam.leeds.ac.uk/10.1097/BRS.0b013e31823a012e.

Mangalathu, S., Choi, E., Park, H. C. and Jeon, J.-S. (2018) 'Probabilistic Seismic Vulnerability Assessment of Tall Horizontally Curved Concrete Bridges in California', 32(6). DOI: 10.1016/j.foreco.2015.09.026.

Meral, C. (2011) 'Evaluation of laser scanning technology for bridge inspection', *Measurement*, (March). Available at: http://idea.library.drexel.edu/bitstream/1860/3451/1/Meral, Cihan.pdf.

Moaveni, B. and Conte, J. P. (2014) 'System and Damage Identification of Civil Structures', in *Encyclopedia of Earthquake Engineering*, pp. 1–9. DOI: 10.1007/978-3-642-36197-5_70-1.

Pahlavan, H., Zakeri, B., Amiri, G. G. and Shaianfar, M. (2015) 'Probabilistic Vulnerability Assessment of Horizontally Curved Multiframe RC Box-Girder Highway Bridges', *Journal of Performance of Constructed Facilities*, 30(3), p. 4015038. DOI: 10.1061/(ASCE)cf.1943-5509.0000780.

Saha, P. K., Borgefors, G., and Sanniti di Baja, G. (2016) 'A survey on skeletonization algorithms and their applications', *Pattern Recognition Letters*. Elsevier Ltd., 76, pp. 3–12. DOI: 10.1016/j.patrec.2015.04.006.

Tang, P. and Akinci, B. (2012) 'Automatic execution of workflows on laser-scanned data for extracting bridge surveying goals', *Advanced Engineering Informatics*. Elsevier B.V., 26(4), pp. 889–903. DOI: 10.1016/j.aei.2012.07.004.

Xu, X., Yang, H. and Neumann, I. (2018) 'Deformation monitoring of typical composite structures based on terrestrial laser scanning technology', *Composite Structures*. Elsevier Ltd, 202, pp. 77–81. DOI: 10.1016/j.compstruct.2017.11.049.

Yuan, P. and Harik, I. E. (2010) 'Equivalent Barge and Flotilla Impact Forces on Bridge Piers', *Journal of Bridge Engineering*, 15(5), pp. 523–532. DOI: 10.1061/(ASCE)BE.1943-5592.0000080.

Zheng, L., Yu, M., Song, M., Stefanidis, A., Ji, Z. and Yang, C. (2016) 'Registration of long-strip terrestrial laser scanning point clouds using RANSAC and closed constraint adjustment', *Remote Sensing*, 8(4). DOI: 10.3390/rs8040278.

Zong, Z., Xia, Z., Liu, H., Li, Y. and Huang, X. (2016) 'Collapse Failure of Prestressed Concrete Continuous Rigid-Frame Bridge under Strong Earthquake Excitation: Testing and Simulation', *Journal of Bridge Engineering*, 21(9), p. 4016047. DOI: 10.1061/(ASCE)BE.1943-5592.0000912.

Fault-Tolerant Variable Speed Limit Control for Freeway Work Zone

Shuming Du, Saiedeh Razavi
McMaster University, Hamilton, Ontario, Canada
dus5@mcmaster.ca

Abstract. Freeway work zone can easily lead to traffic congestion which has detrimental effects on travel time and safety. By using the detected traffic states near work zone area, variable speed limit (VSL) control system has been widely studied to improve traffic mobility and safety. However, occurrence of sensor fault can cause traffic state deviation and system degradation. Therefore, this study presents a fault-tolerant VSL control system for freeway work zone. A traffic flow model was first designed to analyze the traffic dynamics. Then a sliding mode controller for VSL was designed based on the previous study. By comparing the estimated traffic states from Kalman filter with the observed states from the observer, the developed fault diagnosis can detect the sensor fault and reconfigure the controller. The proposed system was evaluated under a realistic freeway work zone environment in traffic simulator SUMO. The results show the proposed system can achieve fault tolerance and improve traffic mobility and safety under fault-free and sensor-fault scenarios.

1. Introduction

With the aging of road infrastructure, a large number of work zones are setup up for highway maintenance projects such as road reconstruction, resurfacing and rehabilitation. Despite the long term benefit from road maintenance projects, work zones with lane closure in these projects exacerbate traffic congestion and increase the safety risk near work zone area. In 2014, around 888 million hours delay, 90 thousand crashes and 600 fatalities occurring in US are attributed to work zones (FHWA, 2014). To reduce the impacts of freeway work zone, variable speed limit (VSL) control system has been studied. By dynamically changing the speed limits upstream of a work zone bottleneck, VSL control system can restrict the traffic inflow or improve the traffic homogenization so as to improve traffic mobility and safety.

To design the VSL control system, a number of approaches have been developed. By using the detected traffic density near work zone area, the proportional-integral (PI) feedback VSL controller was designed by Carlson et al. (2011) to regulate the mainline traffic flow. This method was also applied to multiple bottlenecks (Iordanidou et al., 2017). The model predictive control method was developed to improve the performance of VSL control system using macroscopic model and microscopic model respectively (Hegyi et al., 2005; Du et al., 2017). Although the improved system performance with reduced travel time and safety risk is shown by using VSL systems in the abovementioned studies, the potential sensor fault is not considered. The implementation of such VSL systems is mainly based on an assumption that accurate traffic state measurement is available. However, in reality, the stationary sensors such as loop detectors, video cameras and magnetic sensors suffer from different types of sensor faults. Approximately 40% of the traffic data is missing due to the sensor malfunction in California (Rajagopal et al., 2007). Therefore, without consideration of the sensor fault, the performance of VSL control system can be highly unpredictable and it may cause safety issues with an improper VSL control scheme.

In the case of sensor faults, the redundancy of the control system is exploited to achieve the fault tolerance and maintain the system performance. Two types of redundancies, physical redundancy and analytical redundancy, are commonly utilized in control systems (Blanke et al., 2006). Since the physical redundancy demands additional components to be installed, it is hardly affordable to use such fault tolerance due to its extra cost in a large scale system like freeway in this study. However, the analytical redundancy is analyzed and extracted from the mathematical system model, whereby the dependability of a system is improved with little additional cost. Therefore, the analytical redundancy is mainly discussed and studied.

Various studies have developed traffic data imputation methods to overcome the issue of traffic sensor faults. A tensor decomposition based method was developed to recover the missing traffic data (Tan et al., 2013). By training the model using a deep learning algorithm, Duan et al. (2016) presented a well-trained model for traffic data imputation. However, these traffic imputation approaches are implemented offline and cannot recover the missing data in real time. Since VSL control systems require real-time traffic state estimation or imputation when sensor fault occurs, it is difficult to incorporate offline imputation methods in the design of VSL control system. Many online imputation methods were also proposed. The corrupted traffic data is estimated using the linear regression model (Chen et al., 2003). Iterative multiple imputation method was developed to predict the missing traffic data pattern via a calibrated regression model (Henrickson et al., 2015). Zhang and Zhang (2016) proposed two multivariate forecasting methods based on regression models to forecast the missing traffic data. Nevertheless, large historical data samples are required to calibrate the abovementioned regression models before being used to recover the missing data online. However, when there is a work zone, particularly a short-term work zone, set up in the freeway, such historical traffic data is normally not available. Consequently, it is also difficult to apply aforementioned online imputation methods to VSL control system for freeway work zone.

To overcome the impacts of sensor faults, this study presents a fault-tolerant VSL control system for freeway work zone. Two main contributions are made: 1) maintain the VSL control performance with the occurrence of sensor faults; 2) achieve sensor fault diagnosis online using the observer-based method without the requirement of large historical data samples. Therefore, the developed system has the following objectives: 1) accurately estimate the traffic states using stationary sensors and probe sensors; 2) develop a VSL controller based on the previous study; 3) design a fault diagnosis scheme to achieve fault detection and model reconfiguration; 4) evaluate the designed system using a realistically simulated freeway work zone environment in traffic simulator SUMO.

The rest of this paper is organized as follows. The system framework is first described. Based on the designed traffic flow model, a sliding mode controller is introduced for VSL control. Then Kalman filter is employed to estimate the traffic states. After the design of the observer, fault diagnosis scheme is discussed. Afterwards, the developed system is evaluated with analytical results. Finally, conclusions and future work are discussed.

2. Methodology

The framework of the designed fault-tolerant VSL control system is shown in Figure 1. The sliding mode controller is designed to generate the speed limit signal in order to track the traffic state reference and improve traffic condition near work zone area. Then this speed limit signal is incorporated in the traffic flow model to affect the evolution of the traffic states. With traffic measurements from stationary sensors and probe sensors, Kalman filter is employed to improve the accuracy of the traffic states estimation. Traffic measurements are also sent to the designed observer to generate the observed traffic states as the redundant information. Then both estimated traffic states from Kalman filter and observed traffic states from the observer are fed into the fault diagnosis to detect whether a sensor fault occurs and reconfigure the controller accordingly. The details of each component in Figure 1 are presented in the following sections.

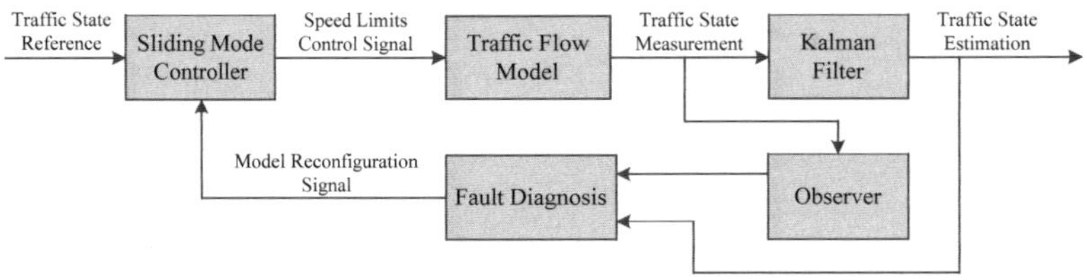

Figure 1: System Framework

2.1 Traffic Flow Model

The layout of freeway work zone with lane closure is shown in Figure 2. The mix traffic flow with conventional and connected vehicles moves towards the right side. Connected vehicles used in this study have the ability to transmit their positions and speeds during the travel while conventional vehicles do not have the communication ability. The driver behavior between conventional vehicles and connected vehicles is assumed to be the same. Traffic states are detected using stationary sensors and probe sensors. Stationary sensors are installed at fixed locations to detect traffic states and connected vehicles are utilized as probe sensors. In the case of stationary sensors, two traffic sensors TS 1 and TS 2, which are located immediate upstream of the work zone and within work zone area respectively, are used. It can be seen that congestion can easily occur when traffic demand exceeds the work zone capacity.

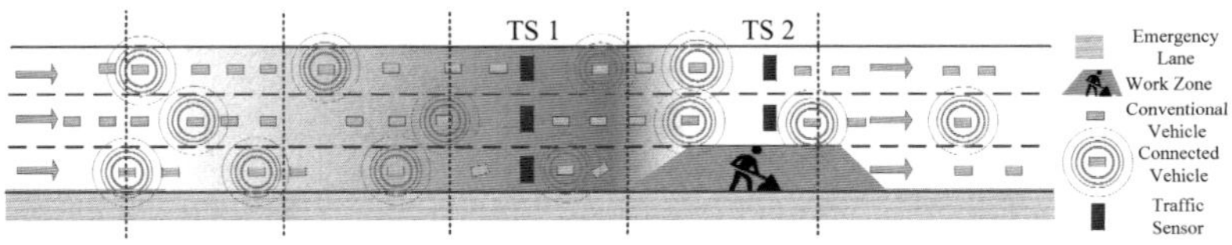

Figure 2: Layout of Freeway Work Zone Area

To analyze the traffic dynamics near work zone area, the layout of freeway work zone area is partitioned into multiple segments as shown in Figure 3.

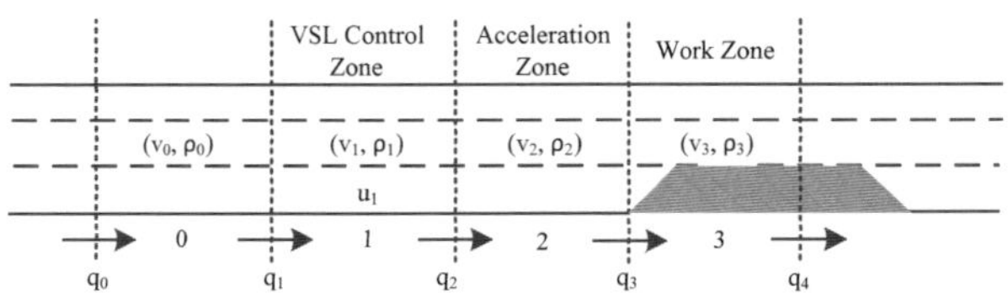

Figure 3: Segments of Freeway Work Zone Area

The traffic flow rate q_i and q_{i+1} are the inflow and outflow for segment i. The length of each segment, average speed and density in segment i are expressed as L_i, v_i and ρ_i respectively. Traffic sensor TS 1 and TS 2 are located inside acceleration zone and work zone respectively. One speed limit sign is installed at the beginning of the VSL control zone to control vehicle speed within VSL control zone. Another speed limit sign is installed at the start of the acceleration zone to allow vehicles to accelerate and travel through the work zone area with maximum free flow speed. In this study, we assume no congestion happens downstream of the work zone.

Based on the conservation law (Daganzo 1994), the evolution of traffic density is derived as

$$\rho_i(k+1) = \rho_i(k) + \frac{\Delta T_s}{L_i}[q_i(k) - q_{i+1}(k)], i = 0,1,2,3 \quad (1)$$

where ΔT_s is the sample time interval and k stands for the discrete time step k. Since the objective of VSL controller is to control the traffic density of the acceleration zone (Du and Razavi, 2019), traffic flow q_2, q_3 and q_4 are obtained in Equation (2) under the assumption of triangular fundamental diagram

$$\begin{cases} q_2(k) = \min\{v_1(k)\rho_1(k), \dfrac{\omega\rho_j u_1(k)}{u_1(k)+\omega}, \omega(\rho_j - \rho_2(k))\} \\ q_3(k) = \min\{v_2(k)\rho_2(k), \beta C^b\} \\ q_4(k) = v_3(k)\rho_3(k) \end{cases} \tag{2}$$

where ω and ρ_j represent the backward wave speed and jam density respectively. $u_1(k)$ is the speed limit of VSL control zone. C^b is the work zone bottleneck capacity which equals to 2/3 of full road capacity C as one of three lanes is closed shown in Figure 3. The capacity drop phenomenon occurs when a queue forms upstream of the work zone (Hall et al., 1992; Chung et al., 2007). This can further decrease the work zone bottleneck capacity C^b. Therefore, a capacity drop factor β is introduced when capacity drop occurs.

As we can see, the impact of speed limits on traffic flow is reflected by the term $q_2^u(k) = \omega\rho_j u_1(k)/[u_1(k)+\omega]$. When $v_1(k)\rho_1(k) < q_2^u(k)$, traffic demand is lower than the work zone capacity C^b and vehicles can travel through the work zone area with free flow speed. Therefore, VSL controller is not needed to restrict the traffic flow with speed limits. On the other hand, when $\omega(\rho_j - \rho_2(k)) < q_2^u(k)$, the VSL controller cannot restrict the traffic flow. This conflicts with the stability of VSL controller discussed in the sliding mode controller section. Therefore, the evolution of traffic density $\boldsymbol{x}(k)$ is derived as

$$\boldsymbol{x}(k+1) = \boldsymbol{A}(k)\boldsymbol{x}(k) + \boldsymbol{B}(k)\boldsymbol{u}(k) + \boldsymbol{\varepsilon}(k) \tag{3}$$

where $\boldsymbol{u}(k)$ is the system input and $\boldsymbol{\varepsilon}(k)$ is the system process noise which is assumed to be Gaussian noise of zero mean and covariance $\boldsymbol{Q}(k)$. $\boldsymbol{A}(k)$ and $\boldsymbol{B}(k)$ are system matrices. More specifically, Equation (3) can be rewritten as

$$\begin{bmatrix} \rho_2(k+1) \\ \rho_3(k+1) \end{bmatrix} = \begin{bmatrix} 1-\dfrac{\Delta T_s}{L_2}v_2(k) & 0 \\ \dfrac{\Delta T_s}{L_3}v_2(k) & 1-\dfrac{\Delta T_s}{L_3}v_3(k) \end{bmatrix} \begin{bmatrix} \rho_2(k) \\ \rho_3(k) \end{bmatrix} + \begin{bmatrix} \dfrac{\Delta T_s}{L_2}q_2^u(k) \\ 0 \end{bmatrix} + \begin{bmatrix} \varepsilon_1(k) \\ \varepsilon_2(k) \end{bmatrix} \tag{4}$$

$$\begin{bmatrix} \rho_2(k+1) \\ \rho_3(k+1) \end{bmatrix} = \begin{bmatrix} 1 & 0 \\ 0 & 1-\dfrac{\Delta T_s}{L_3}v_3(k) \end{bmatrix} \begin{bmatrix} \rho_2(k) \\ \rho_3(k) \end{bmatrix} + \begin{bmatrix} \dfrac{\Delta T_s}{L_2}(q_2^u(k) - \beta C^b) \\ \dfrac{\Delta T_s}{L_3}\beta C^b \end{bmatrix} + \begin{bmatrix} \varepsilon_1(k) \\ \varepsilon_2(k) \end{bmatrix} \tag{5}$$

Equation (4) and (5) are derived under without capacity drop and with capacity drop scenarios respectively. The average speed $v_2(k)$ and $v_3(k)$ are detected by connected vehicles.

Meanwhile, the stationary sensors TS 1 and TS 2 can be used to detect the traffic flow. Thus the measurement equation is derived as

$$\boldsymbol{y}(k) = \boldsymbol{C}(k)\boldsymbol{x}(k) + \boldsymbol{\zeta}(k) \tag{6}$$

where $y(k)$ is the measurement vector and $\zeta(k)$ is the measurement noise assumed to be Gaussian noise of zero mean and covariance $\boldsymbol{R}(k)$. Specifically, Equation (6) is written as

$$\begin{bmatrix} \frac{q_3(k)}{v_2(k)} \\ \frac{q_4(k)}{v_3(k)} \end{bmatrix} = \begin{bmatrix} 1 & 0 \\ 0 & 1 \end{bmatrix} \begin{bmatrix} \rho_2(k) \\ \rho_3(k) \end{bmatrix} + \begin{bmatrix} \zeta_1(k) \\ \zeta_2(k) \end{bmatrix} \tag{7}$$

where traffic flow $q_3(k)$ and $q_4(k)$ are detected by the stationary sensor TS 1 and TS 2.

By combining Equation (3) and (6), the traffic flow model is established.

2.2 Sliding Mode Controller

The sliding mode controller, which is a non-linear control strategy for VSL control, can generate switching control signal to drive the traffic state to the desired equilibrium state with certain convergence rates. The objective of the designed controller is to stabilize the traffic density ρ_2 at the bottleneck critical density $\rho_c^b = C^b / v_f$ where v_f is the free flow speed. Through this stabilization, the capacity drop is avoided and the maximum flow rate can be achieved. The designed controller is based on the previous study (Du and Razavi, 2019).

The desired equilibrium state ρ_c^b is first designed on the sliding surface as:

$$s(k) = c[\rho_c^b - \rho_2(k)] \tag{8}$$

where c is a constant nonzero parameter. The reaching process, which is designed as Equation (9) is utilized to drive the traffic state towards the surface (Gao et al., 1995).

$$s(k+1) = s(k) - \Delta T_s \eta \operatorname{sgn}(s(k)) - \Delta T_s q s(k) \tag{9}$$

where both η and q are positive constant parameters. The term $\Delta T_s q s(k)$ can make the traffic state move towards the surface at exponential convergence rate, while the term $\Delta T_s \eta \operatorname{sgn}(s(k))$ can make the traffic state converge to equilibrium state with finite time steps.

Therefore, the traffic density $\rho_2(k+1)$ can be derived from the perspective of the controller design by combining the Equation (8) at time step k+1 with Equation (9). On the other hand, the traffic density $\rho_2(k+1)$ can also be obtained from the perspective of the traffic dynamics in Equation (3) which contains the control signal $u_1(k)$. Thus combining these two densities $\rho_2(k+1)$ gives a function g of speed limit control signal $u_1(k)$ as

$$u_1(k) = g(\rho_2(k), v_2(k), s(k)) \tag{10}$$

The stability of the designed controller is guaranteed with the condition that $\eta > 0, q > 0$ and $2 - \Delta T_s q \gg 0$ which is proved in the previous study (Du and Razavi, 2019). Also, different convergence rates should be designed for with and without capacity drop scenarios. The reason is that the major consideration for VSL controller under different scenarios is different (Du and Razavi, 2019). A quick response is needed when there is no capacity drop, while an overshoot issue should be avoided when capacity drop occurs.

To apply the speed limit control in real world, three speed constraints are considered: 1) only discrete speed limits between maximum legitimate speed limit $v_{\max}$ and minimum speed limit

v_{min} with the increment speed Δv are displayed; 2) the continuous speed limit is rounded up to its closed discrete speed limit; 3) the maximum speed difference is limited to Δv_{max} between two consecutive control time step.

2.3 Kalman Filter for Traffic State Estimation

Kalman filter is a dynamic estimation algorithm with time update and measurement update (Bar-Shalom et al., 2001). The following update equations are used to estimate traffic states

$$\boldsymbol{x}(k+1|k) = \boldsymbol{A}(k)\boldsymbol{x}(k) + \boldsymbol{B}(k)\boldsymbol{u}(k) \tag{11}$$

$$\boldsymbol{P}(k+1|k) = \boldsymbol{A}(k)\boldsymbol{P}(k)\boldsymbol{A}(k)^{\mathrm{T}} + \boldsymbol{Q}(k) \tag{12}$$

$$\boldsymbol{K}(k) = \boldsymbol{P}(k+1|k)\boldsymbol{C}(k)^{\mathrm{T}}(\boldsymbol{C}(k)\boldsymbol{P}(k+1|k)\boldsymbol{C}(k)^{\mathrm{T}} + \boldsymbol{R}(k))^{-1} \tag{13}$$

$$\boldsymbol{x}(k+1) = \boldsymbol{x}(k+1|k) + \boldsymbol{K}(k)(\boldsymbol{y}(k) - \boldsymbol{C}(k)\boldsymbol{x}(k+1|k)) \tag{14}$$

$$\boldsymbol{P}(k+1) = (\boldsymbol{I} - \boldsymbol{K}(k)\boldsymbol{C}(k))\boldsymbol{P}(k+1|k) \tag{15}$$

With the one step prediction of state $\boldsymbol{x}(k+1|k)$ and state covariance $\boldsymbol{P}(k+1|k)$, the filter gain $\boldsymbol{K}(k)$ is updated. By incorporating the error between the measurements and one step prediction, the state $\boldsymbol{x}(k+1)$ along with the state covariance $\boldsymbol{P}(k+1)$ at next time step are updated. Then this recursive process is performed to update and estimate the traffic density with new measurements at each time step.

2.4 Observer

The observer can provide the redundant traffic state to achieve fault tolerance. It can be seen that traffic density $\rho_2(k)$ is critical to the design of sliding mode controller. Consequently, a faulty traffic sensor TS 1, which can provide the measurement of $\rho_2(k)$ via the detection of traffic flow, can greatly affect the VSL control. Therefore, the observer should provide the observed traffic density $\rho_2^o(k)$ when traffic sensor TS 1 fails.

Observability. When TS 1 fails, Equation (6) is modified as $\rho_3(k) = \boldsymbol{C}^o(k)\boldsymbol{x}(k) + \zeta_2(k)$ where $\boldsymbol{C}^o(k) = [0 \quad 1]$ and $\zeta_2(k)$ is the Gaussian noise with zero mean and variance $R_2(k)$. Then the observability matrix $\boldsymbol{O}_{\text{no,drop}}$ and $\boldsymbol{O}_{\text{drop}}$ for without capacity drop and with capacity drop scenarios respectively are derived as

$$\boldsymbol{O}_{\text{no,drop}} = \begin{bmatrix} 0 & 1 \\ \dfrac{\Delta T_s}{L_3} v_{n+2}(k) & 1 - \dfrac{\Delta T_s}{L_3} v_3(k) \end{bmatrix}, \boldsymbol{O}_{\text{drop}} = \begin{bmatrix} 0 & 1 \\ 0 & 1 - \dfrac{\Delta T_s}{L_3} v_3(k) \end{bmatrix} \tag{16}$$

When $v_2(k) \neq 0$, $\boldsymbol{O}_{\text{no,drop}}$ has full rank. Accordingly, traffic density $\rho_2(k)$ is observable when capacity drop does not occur, while $\rho_2(k)$ is non-observable with capacity drop.

Observer Design. In the case of the scenario without capacity drop, since $\rho_2(k)$ is observable, the observed density $\rho_2^o(k)$ can be obtained using the Kalman recursive algorithm which acts as an observer instead of a filter. By replacing $\boldsymbol{C}(k)$, $\boldsymbol{y}(k)$ and $\boldsymbol{R}(k)$ in Equation (13)-(15) with $\boldsymbol{C}^o(k)$, $\rho_3(k)$ and $R_2(k)$ respectively, the Kalman recursive process is performed using

Equation (11)-(15) to obtain the observed $\rho_2^o(k)$. When capacity drop occurs, the recursive process cannot be used as $\rho_2(k)$ is non-observable. However, the error of one-step prediction does not diverge with capacity drop. Therefore, an open loop estimator with one-step prediction using Equation (11) is utilized to obtain the observed traffic density $\rho_2^o(k)$.

2.5 Fault Diagnosis

The observer-based method is employed to design the fault diagnosis. By utilizing the observer discussed in Section 2.4, the designed fault diagnosis can detect the sensor fault, and then reconfigure the VSL controller when a fault occurs. This study focuses on the stationary sensor fault, specifically traffic sensor TS 1 which is critical to the design of VSL controller. There are different types of sensor faults. For example, the fault with the detection of zero flow rate is the leading fault among the malfunctions in loop detectors (Chen et al., 2003). Therefore, the malfunction TS 1 of zero flow rate is mainly considered in this study.

The residual between the estimated density $\hat{\rho}_2(k)$ and the observed density $\rho_2^o(k)$ is analyzed to achieve fault detection. The residual r_d for traffic density $\rho_2(k)$ is derived as

$$r_d = \frac{\left|\hat{\rho}_2(k) - \rho_2^o(k)\right|}{\lambda \rho_c^b} \tag{17}$$

where λ is a constant parameter. When there is no sensor fault, the estimated $\hat{\rho}_2(k)$ will be closed to the observed $\rho_2^o(k)$. Then a small residual can be obtained. However, a sensor fault can cause a large residual due to the abnormal deviation of $\hat{\rho}_2(k)$. Therefore, a threshold τ is determined as a comparison to achieve fault detection. λ and τ are selected considering model uncertainties and noises.

After the detection of a sensor fault, the fault diagnosis can reconfigure the controller. Without sensor fault, the estimated density can be used in the design of VSL controller. However, when a sensor fault occurs, the estimated density will greatly deviate from the actual density. To maintain the control system performance, the fault diagnosis can reconfigure the controller by replacing the estimated density with the observed density.

3. Experiment and Results

The developed fault-tolerant VSL control for freeway work zone was evaluated on a 4.8 km (3 mi) freeway segment of I-15S in California, US. A work zone was set up from State PM (postmile) 40.2 to State PM 37.6 on July 22, 2016. This freeway segment with the work zone is shown in Figure 4. The blue line represents the simulated freeway segment, while the red line shows part of the work zone where one of three lanes was closed. The freeway network was built in traffic simulator SUMO. The microscopic model was calibrated and validated using realistic traffic measurements from California freeway database (PeMS, 2016).

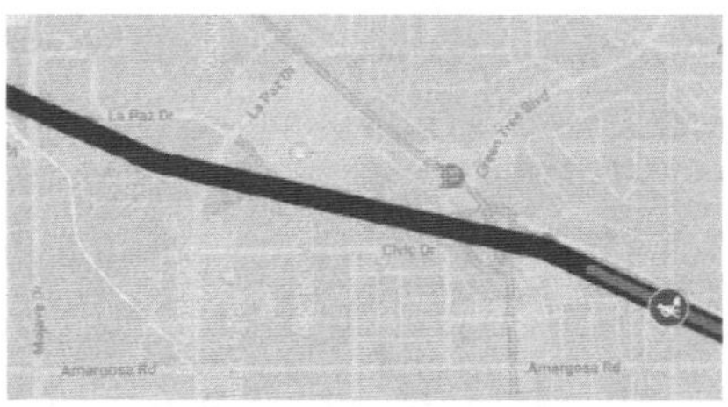

Figure 4: Freeway Network with Work Zone

With the built traffic network, the fundament diagram was calibrated. The road capacity C, jam density ρ_j, the critical density ρ_c^b, free flow speed v_f, backward propagating wave speed ω, capacity drop factor β are calibrated as 4800 veh/h, 270 veh/km, 35 veh/km, 108 km/h, 21 km/h and 0.94 respectively. Without the loss of generality, the length of each segment is selected same as 500 m. The method proposed in this study can potentially be extended to different lengths of segments. According to the realistic traffic data statistics analysis (Bekiaris-Liberis, et al., 2016), the standard deviation of the noises of stationary sensors and probe sensors were selected as 25 veh/h and 3 km/h respectively. The connected market penetration rate was chosen as 20%. The speed limits $v_{\max}$, $v_{\min}$, Δv and $\Delta v_{\max}$ were 113 km/h (70 mi/h), 16 km/h (10 mi/h), 8 km/h (5 mi/h) and 16 km/h (10 mi/h) respectively. For the controller, two sets of parameters $c_1 = 2, \eta = 6, q_1 = 15$ and $c_1 = 10, \eta = 50, q_1 = 90$ were selected for without capacity drop and with capacity drop scenarios respectively. The 15 s sample time interval and 30 s control time interval were selected. $\lambda = 2$ and $\tau = 0.5$ were chosen. Different combinations of λ and τ were tested in this study to find the appropriate value, whereby a fault can be accurately detected without a false alarm.

The developed fault-tolerant control system was evaluated under three scenarios: 1) without control; 2) with fault-tolerant control but no sensor fault occurs; 3) with fault-tolerant control but TS 1 fails during the simulation. The simulation was first run for 5 minutes as the warm-up period with low traffic demand. This 5-minute traffic data was discarded. Then 1 h simulation was conducted. During this 1 h simulation, an average low demand 1500 veh/h was first generated until the time 400 s, then there was an average high demand 3600 veh/h lasting for 1100 s, followed by low demand 1500 veh/h for the rest 2100 s. An artificial sensor fault occurred at the time step 1200 s under scenario 3.

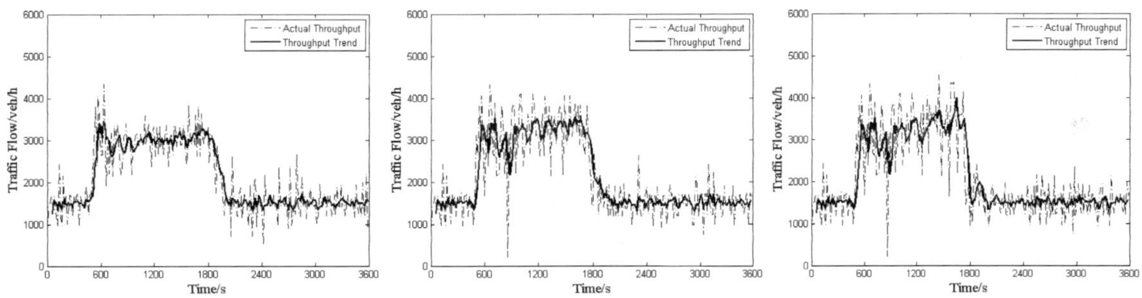

a) b) c)

Figure 5: Work Zone Throughput under a) Scenario 1; b) Scenario 2; c) Scenario 3

The work zone throughputs under three scenarios are illustrated in Figure 5. The actual throughput in dash line is collected by TS 2 every sample time inteval, while the throughput trend in solid line is presented using moving average technique. Without VSL control, the capacity drop occurs in Figure 5a with a throughput of about 3000 veh/h during the high demand. In contrast, throughputs under scenario 2 and 3 stay around 3200 veh/h which is the work zone capacity under high demand. Though the throughput slightly drops for a short time near time step 900 s due to the initiation of VSL, the overall throughput succesfully maintains at the work zone capacity. The similar performance between Figure 5b and 5c after 1200 s when the sensor fault occurs shows the effectiveness of fault-tolerant control.

The residual and traffic density at acceleration zone under scenario 2 and 3 are presented in Figure 6 and 7 respecitvely. It can be seen that the developed system shows the ability to achieve density estimation and fault tolerance. Under scenario 2, the residual stays below the threshold all the time without false alarm. The density estimation is compared with the ground truth measurement from the simulator in Figure 6b. An accurate density estimation is achieved with the RMSE of 3.9 veh/km. In Figure 7a, the residual exceeds the threshold at the time step 1200 s when the sensor fails. Then the density estimation greatly deviates from the measurment in Figure7b. However, the observed traffic density in blue line comes into effect and replaces the corrupted density estimation. Thus the fault tolerance can be achieved.

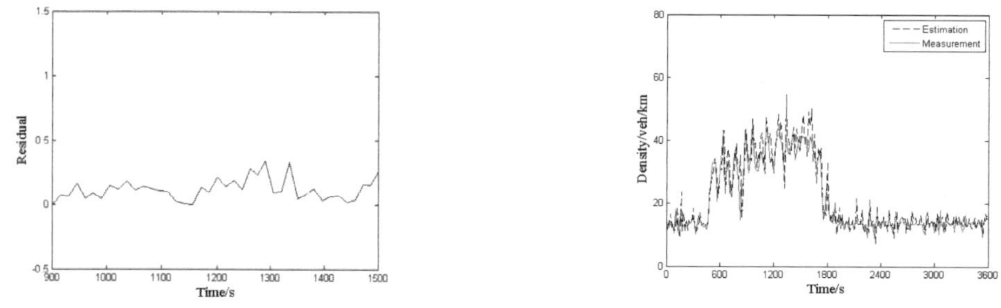

a) b)

Figure 6: Under Scenario 2 a) Residual; b) Density at Acceleration Zone

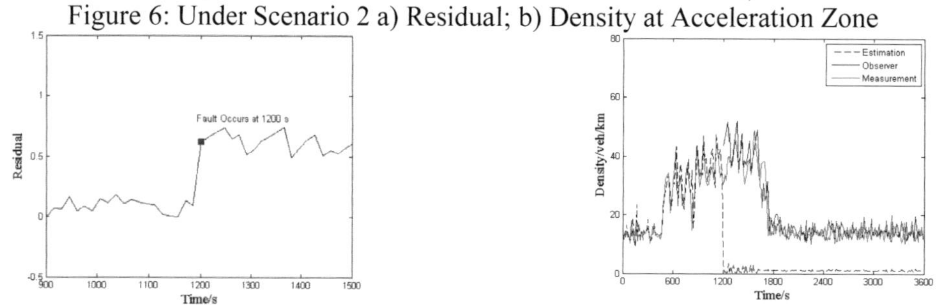

a) b)

Figure 7: Under Scenario 3 a) Residual; b) Density at Acceleration Zone

Table 1: Permance Measurment

Scenario	Travel Time T/min	Improvement/%	Time-to-collision p/%	Improvement/%
1	2.30	-	4.43	-
2	2.11	8.26	0.42	90.5
3	2.10	8.70	0.41	90.7

The travel time T and probablity of time-to-collision p are presented in Table 1. Only the travel time upstream of the work zone is considered. 1.5 s is used as the minimum time to avoid the collision (Genders and Razavi, 2016). Table 1 shows the developed system can not only improve the mobility and safety by around 8% and 90% respectivly near work zone area, but also achieve fault tolerance with the similar system performance under scenario 3.

The results indicate that the developed fault-tolerant VSL control system can avoid the capacity drop phenomenon occuring near freework zone area and improve the mobility and safety at the same time. More importantly, the system can achieve fault tolerant control and maintain the system performance with the presence of a sensor fault.

4. Conclusions and Future Work

To ensure the effectiveness of VSL control and avoid system degradation when a sensor fault occurs, a fault-tolerant VSL control system for freeway work zone is developed in this study. Accurate traffic density estimation is achieved by employing Kalman filter. Meanwhile, the sliding mode controller for VSL control can avoid the capacity drop and improve traffic mobility and safety for freeway work zone. Furthermore, the developed fault diagnosis can not only detect a sensor fault but also reconfigure the controller accordingly. The designed fault-tolerant VSL control shows the ability to consistently improve the traffic condition near freeway work zone area even with a sensor fault.

In this study, only the stationary sensor fault is considered. However, the faults of connected vehicles such as the communication delay and corrupted samples can also affect the VSL control performance. Probe sensor faults will be considered in the future. Meanwhile, the impacts of different connected vehicle market penetration rates will also be studied. Mobile applications as another type of probe sensors will be considered for fault detection as well.

References

Bar-Shalom, Y., Li, X. R. and Kirubarajan, T. (2001). *Estimation with Applications to Tracking and Navigation: Theory, Algorithms, and Software*. New York: Wiley.

Bekiaris-Liberis, N., Roncoli, C. and Papageorgiou, M. (2016). Highway Traffic State Estimation with Mixed Connected and Conventional Vehicles. *IEEE Trans. Intell. Transp. Syst.*, 17(12), 3484–3497.

Blanke, M., Kinnaert, M., Lunze, J. and Staroswiecki, M. (2006). *Diagnosis and Fault-Tolerant Control*. 2nd ed. Berlin: Springer.

Carlson, R. C., Papamichail, I. and Papageorgiou, M. (2011). Local Feedback-based Mainstream Traffic Flow Control on Motorways Using Variable Speed Limits. *IEEE Trans. Intell. Transp. Syst.*, 12(4), 1261–1276.

Chen, C., Kwon, J., Rice, J., Skabardonis, A. and Varaiya, P. (2003). Detecting Errors and Imputing Missing Data for Single-Loop Surveillance Systems. *Transp. Res. Rec.*, (1855), 160–167.

Chung, K., Rudjanakanoknad, J. and Cassidy, M.J. (2007). Relation Between Traffic Density and Capacity Drop at Three Freeway Bottlenecks. *Transp. Res. Part B Methodol.*, 41, 82–95.

Daganzo, C. F. (1994). The Cell Transmission Model: A Dynamic Representation of Highway Traffic Consistent with the Hydrodynamic Theory. *Transp. Res. Part B Methodol.*, 28(4), 269–287.

Du, S., Razavi, S. and Genders, W. (2017). Optimal Variable Speed Limit Control under Connected Work Zone and Connected Vehicle Environment. In *Proc.,34th Int. Symp. Automat. Robotics in Construction*, *June 2017*, Taibei, Taiwan: IAARC.

Du, S. and Razavi, S. (2019). Variable Speed Limit for Freeway Work Zone with Capacity Drop Using Discrete-Time Sliding Mode Control. *J. Comput. Civ. Eng.*, 33(2):04019001.

Duan, Y., Lv, Y., Liu, Y.L. and Wang, F. (2016). An Efficient Realization of Deep Learning for Traffic Data Imputation. *Transp. Res. Part C Emergin Technol.*, 72, 168–181.

FHWA (2014). Work Zone Management Program. [Viewed 1 March 2019]. Available from: https://ops.fhwa.dot.gov/wz/resources/facts_stats.htm.

Gao, W., Wang, Y. and Homaifa, A. (1995). Discrete-time Variable Structure Control Systems. *IEEE Trans. Ind. Electron.*, 42(2), 117–122.

Genders, W. and Razavi, S. (2016). Impact of Connected Vehicle on Work Zone Network Safety through Dynamic Route Guidance. *J. Comput. Civ. Eng.*, 30(2):04015020.

Hall, F. L., Hurdle, V. F. and Banks, J. H. (1992). Synthesis of Recent Work on the Nature of Speed-flow and Flow-occupancy (or density) Relationships on Freeways. *Transp. Res. Rec.*, 1365, 12–18.

Hegyi, A., De Schutter, B. and Hellendoorn, J. (2005). Optimal Coordination of Variable Speed Limits to Suppress Shock Waves. *IEEE Trans. Intell. Transp. Syst.*, 6(1), 102–112.

Henrickson, K., Zou, Y. and Wang, Y. (2015). Flexible and Robust Method for Missing Loop Detector Data Imputation. *Transp. Res. Rec.*, (2527), 29–36.

Iordanidou, G. R., Papamichail, I., Roncoli, C. and Papageorgiou, M. (2017). Feedback-based Integrated Motorway Traffic Flow Control with Delay Balancing. *IEEE Trans. Intell. Transp. Syst.*, 18 (9), 2319–2329.

PeMS. (2016). Caltrans Performance Measurement System. [Viewed 1 March 2019]. Available from: http://pems.dot.ca.gov.

Rajagopal, R.. and Varaiya, P. (2007). Evaluating the Health of California Loop Sensor Network. Transportation Research Board, Washington DC.

Tan, H., Feng, G., Feng, J., Wang, W., Zhang, Y.J. and Li, F. (2013). A Tensor-based Method for Missing Traffic Data Completion. *Transp. Res. Part C Emergin Technol.*, 28, 15–27.

Zhang Y. and Zhang Y. (2016). A Comparative Study of Three Multivariate Short Term Freeway Traffic Flow Forecasting Methods With Missing Data. *J. Intell. Transp. Syst.*, 20(3), 205-218.

Towards Registration of Construction Drawings to Building Information Models using Knowledge-based Extended Geometric Hashing

Maciej Trzeciak, André Borrmann
Technical University of Munich, Germany
maciej.trzeciak@tum.de

Despite the increasing adoption of BIM technologies, construction drawings are still excessively used in the industry. Many leading AEC figures predict the coexistence of 3D models and 2D drawings for at least a decade. Very often, these two are managed – and in particular for the more advanced design stages – developed separately from each other which puts their consistency at severe risk. In current practice, the deviation detection between drawings and 3D models is a manual, cumbersome, and erroneous process. To overcome this issue, the need for automation emerges. In this paper, we explore this problem and propose a robust drawing-to-model registration system which provides a basis for subsequent consistency verification. It translates the 2D-3D matching problem into the 2D-2D one by cutting a 3D model into sections and measuring similarity between them and the construction drawing. At the core of the proposed approach is geometric hashing, which we extend to further automate the registration process. We propose to build two geometric hash tables which are being matched against each other while measuring similarity. In order to reduce the matching ambiguity – which is the drawback of the proposed extension – we estimate the minimal number of bases to be randomly sampled in the presence of outliers by using the random sample consensus. Moreover, we decrease the burden of building hash tables by reducing the bases – in which features are described – to line segments. We demonstrate the applicability of the proposed system in a case study and provide experimental results.

1. Introduction

The construction industry is currently in a transition period in which drawing-based practices are slowly being replaced by model-based ones, which implies the coexistence of construction drawings and digital 3D models. According to many leading figures in the AEC industry, the intense use of technical drawings in the design and construction of buildings will continue for at least a decade despite the increasing adoption of BIM technologies. In particular, drawings will prevail for a number of years as the legally binding documents for the actual construction processes on site, but also for approval processes by permission authorities. This is also reflected by the recently published international standard ISO 19650 that defines the concept of information containers composed of models and the associated drawings (ISO, 2018). Most of the exchange information requirements (EIR) documents and the associated contracts demand the consistence of the models and the drawings handed over at a certain point in time (data drop) (ISO/DIS, n.d.). In many cases, checking the consistency is part of the approval processes for passing one of the quality gates (Preidel *et al.*, 2017). However currently, these checks must be done manually as no automated methods exist.

Commercial BIM design applications allow to derive drawings that are fully consistent with the created BIM model. However, due to the established processes of the industry, construction drawings and BIM models are subsequently managed separately from each other. Even worse, in many cases they are developed further and refined independently from one another. Therefore, the need for automated verification of consistency between BIM models and the corresponding construction drawings persists. This paper does not question the well-documented value of model-based design and construction (Sacks *et al.*, 2019). However, it respects the reality of the coexistence of models and drawings for many years to come. More specifically, it connects to today's established working practices where drawings form the major basis of information exchange, even if BIM models are created by individual stakeholders. In this paper, we introduce a robust method for the registration of construction drawings to BIM models, which provides the basis for consistency verification and deviation detection.

In a broader sense, shape registration is a task of aligning two shapes in a shared coordinate system (Shao *et al.*, 2011). More specifically, the positioning of a 3D model against an image is known as the model-to-image registration (Jung *et al.*, 2016), co-registration (Avbelj *et al.*, 2015), or 3D-to-2D registration (Wunsch and Hirzinger, 1996). Generally, most registration problems can be divided into three steps: (1) Feature extraction – where distinctive features are derived from two objects to be matched; (2) Matching – which measures the degree of similarity between the two sets of extracted features and (if necessary) establishes the explicit correspondences between them; (3) Transformation – which transforms the matched features so that they align in a shared coordinate system; The researches related to the matching step focus mainly on either feature-based shape matching or matching topology.

We propose a registration system, tailored specifically to the drawing-to-model matching problem in the construction industry, which focuses on feature-based shape matching. The idea of this approach is similar to the one used in view-based 3D model retrieval domain (Tangelder and Veltkamp, 2008; Liu, 2012), in which two 3D models are defined to be similar if they look similar from different views based on the shape of the object in these views. Accordingly, the 2D-3D matching problem is translated into the 2D-2D one.

The ultimate objective of our method is that a given drawing (subsequently called a query drawing) is supposed to be placed (translated, rotated, scaled) in the three dimensional space of a BIM model such that the cross-section derived at the corresponding plane (subsequently called a model section) is the most similar to the query drawing. Before this, however, we derive model sections and measure their level of similarity to the query drawing by comparing the extracted features. For the most similar model section, we establish explicit correspondences to the query drawing and align the drawing to the model section.

At the core of the proposed matching algorithm is geometric hashing. We decrease the burden of building hash tables by reducing the space of bases to line segments. Furthermore, we propose to extend the original geometric hashing algorithm in such a way that the matching process is fully automated. To this end, we propose to build two geometric hash tables which are being matched against each other while measuring similarity between a model section and the query drawing. In order to reduce the matching ambiguity – which is the drawback of the proposed extension – we propose to estimate the minimal number of bases to be randomly sampled in the presence of outliers by using the random sample consensus - RANSAC (Fischler and Bolles, 1981).

The paper has the following structure. Section 2 describes our model-to-drawing registration system, including feature extraction, similarity measure and matching methods, correspondence establishment, and alignment. Section 3 contains a case study for a standard 3-story residential building along with results. We conclude this paper with Section 4 devoted to discussion.

2. Drawing-to-model registration system – methodology

The drawing-to-model registration system focuses on feature-based shape matching and uses knowledge-based extended geometric hashing as the method for measuring similarity and correspondence establishment between a query drawing and a set of cross-sections (in this paper, we name them model-sections) derived from a 3D BIM model. The overview of these steps is shown in Figure 1. We will walk through them in detail in the next sections.

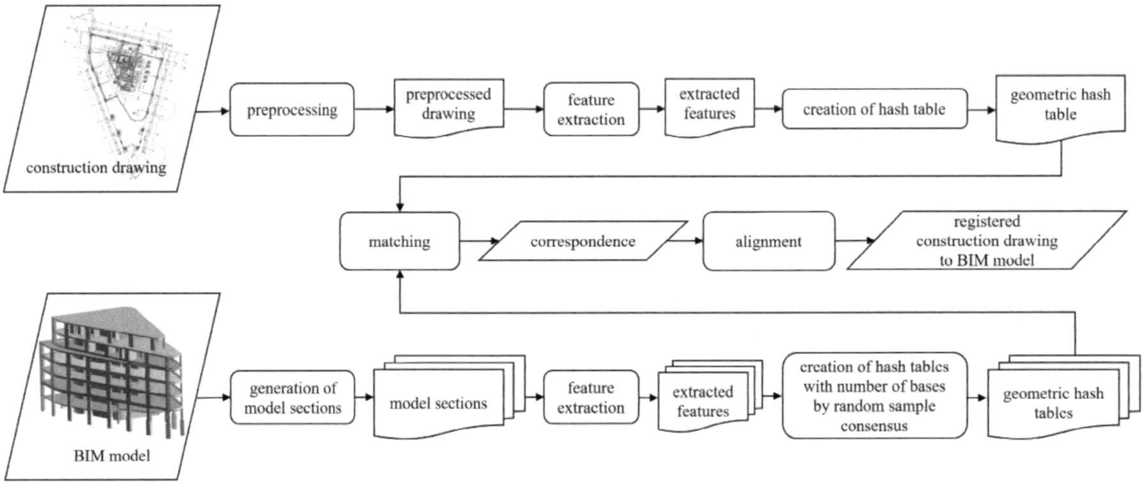

Figure 1: High-level pipeline for the drawing-to-model registration system.

2.1 Generation of model sections

We translate the 2D-to-3D matching problem into 2D-to-2D by cutting the 3D model. In this paper, we use horizontal planes in such a way, that each of them is located above each building level so that it reflects the engineering practice of deriving floor plans at 1.20 m. above a building level. Accordingly, we reduce the number of potential model sections (the discretization of solution space) to be compared with the query drawing significantly. In case of the drawings showing the vertical cross-section of a building, we propose to cut the 3D model vertically and at uniformly distributed distances.

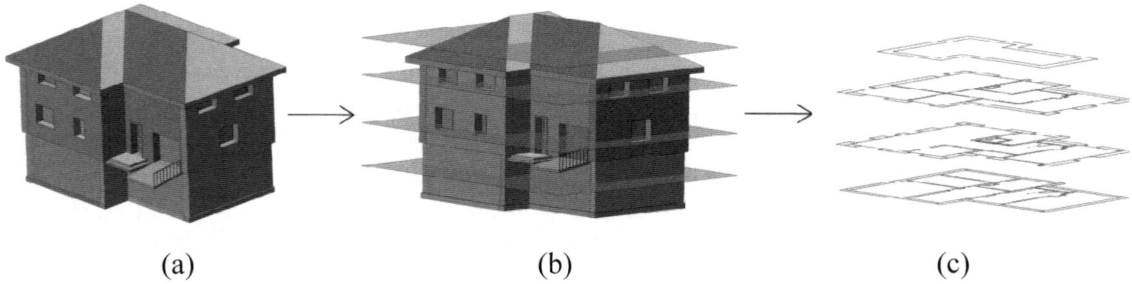

Figure 2: In our system, the 2D-to-3D matching problem is translated into 2D-to-2D by cutting a BIM model (a) using planes as shown in (b). As a result, the solution space is reduced to separate 2D model sections (c).

In case of the drawings of facades, we propose to create orthographic projections of all the sides of the BIM model. Moreover, since BIM models are comprised both of geometry and semantics, we are able to select the types of building elements that we use for matching. For example, elements as doors and windows are shown in construction drawings as icons conforming to engineering standards and not as their pure orthographic projections, and as such, they are not good candidates for the shape-based assessment of similarity by our system.

As shown in Figure 3, the shapes of a floor plan and a model section derived from the same level appear rather similar to a human, however they inevitably differ from each other in details. The purpose of the left one is to convey engineering design and therefore, they are richer in explicit and additional descriptions (hatch patterns, fills, dimensional lines, descriptions) than

BIM models, mainly due to conforming to engineering standards. For example, the building elements such as thermal insulation, concrete columns or walls cut by a plane are filled in with hatch patterns, explicit dimensional lines are drawn, the symbols of certain types of building elements such as doors or windows are agreed icons and differ from their orthographic projections. In addition, what might not be seen instantly from Figure 3 is the fact that the orientation and the scale of the presented drawing and model section are already correct. In a real scenario, the descriptor responsible for measuring similarity must be invariant to rotation, translation and scaling if this process is supposed to be automated and the correspondence properly established. Moreover, construction drawings very often contain additional details not present in BIM models due to the fact that the modeling of all details in 3D is not yet sufficiently efficient.

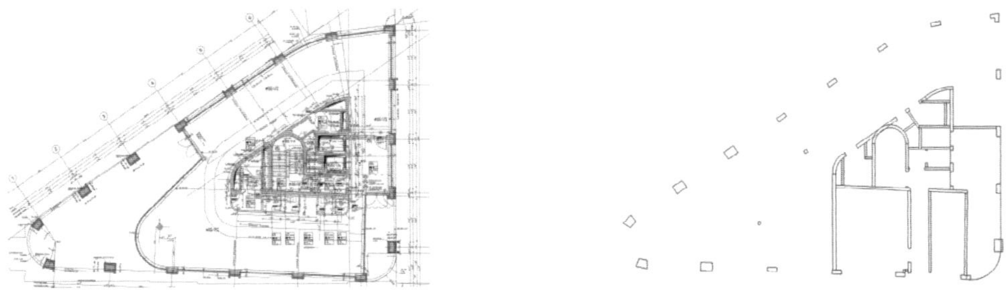

Figure 3: Visual comparison of a construction drawing and its pure section derived from an IFC model at the same level.

Having this in mind, the proposed concept is to measure the commonality of construction drawings and the model sections. The more they have in common, the more similar they are. We extract a unique fingerprint (a unique set of features) occurring in each model section and we find this unique set in the query drawing. In other words, we find the common part of the two sets of features – one set belonging to a model section and the other belonging to the query drawing. We repeat this process for each model section, and the section with the greatest common part is then proposed as the best match. It is then used for the subsequent explicit establishment of correspondence and the alignment.

2.2 Feature extraction

Since the model sections and the floor plan are in vector-based representations, we query them in such a way that we extract their features and segment lines. We do not use methods for detection of key-points or lines from raster images (e.g. Hough line transform).

In building engineering, corner points are the dominant type of features since construction drawings are mainly comprised of straight segments. Accordingly, for each derived 2D model section we extract key-point features as corner points, here understood as the start, end, and intermediate points defining polylines, and as the start and end points of single segment lines whose overlapping points (duplications) are later filtered out. Due to the fact that we propose to build hash tables using segment-wise bases, and not all the possible combinations of bases of key-point features, we extract a set of line segments described by their start and end points.

In a similar vein, we extract the same key-point features and segment lines from the query drawing. In the core of the proposed methodology is the measure of the common part between the model sections and the query drawing. Since the model sections, by definition, contain only elements cut by a plane, and not projected onto the plane, it makes sense to look for these elements in the query drawing. In the engineering convention, such lines cut by a plane are the thickest, and therefore, we first query the thickest lines in the query drawing, and based on them, we extract the key-point features and line segments. The line segments are ordered sets of points and for each line segment, two bases are later taken into consideration (start-end-point basis and end-start-point basis), which is necessary for unambiguous alignment in a further step of the proposed solution.

2.3 Similarity measurement using geometric hashing

In order to find the common part of two sets of features, the descriptor must be able to partially match objects. By partial matching we mean finding a shape whose part is similar to a part of another shape, which in this case, translates to finding the matching features between two sets. Moreover, it must be tailored for specific purpose of matching many model sections to a query drawing within reasonable time. Accordingly, we do not need descriptors setting up the explicit correspondence for each model section and the query drawing, for example such as presented in (Belongie *et al.*, 2002). Additionally, translation, scaling, and rotation invariances are required simply due to the fact that models and drawings are described in arbitrary coordinate systems. Therefore, in the proposed approach, there is a need to provide the descriptor which supports partial matching and provides fast scores for the common part.

We have decided to match shapes between the corresponding building elements in 2D and 3D, and not – for example – to match the grid systems of drawings and 3D models. From our experience, grid systems are very rarely exported to IFC models, and therefore, matching based on the grids would impose a severe prerequisite. Instead, we provide a general solution to the existing problem which works without major prerequisites and thus, without barriers in its application.

As such, we propose and extend *geometric hashing* which was originally developed as an object recognition technique in computer vision (Wolfson and Rigoutsos, 1997). The general procedure and ideas behind it can be found in the original paper and we skip this part due to the page limit. Geometric hashing consists of two stages – preprocessing and recognition.

Preprocessing phase

In our case, the preprocessing stage turns the features described in segment-wise bases extracted from a query drawing into a hash table. The naïve solution would be to describe the features (n stands for the number of the features) in all their combinations ($C_{n,k}$ – combinations without repetition, with $k = 2$, because a basis consists of an ordered pair of points), which yields the quadratic function as shown in equation 1. The equation shows asymptotic number of naïve bases using all combinations of key-point features needed to build a geometric hash table:

$$C_{n,k} = \binom{n}{k} = \frac{n!}{k!\,(n-k)!} = \frac{n(n-1)}{2} = O(n^2) \qquad (1)$$

We reduce the basis space, however, to segment-wise bases (B_m), meaning that each straight segment becomes a basis. This reduces the number of bases in which a hash table is built to a linear function (see equation 2), as each segment line increases the number of bases by 1 (or in case of query drawings, each segment line increases the number of bases by 2):

$$B_m = 1m = O(m) \qquad (2)$$

Recognition phase

Since the hash table of the query drawing is built with the features described in all segment-wise bases, in order to compare the similarity to a model section, we need to sample one corresponding basis in the model section, and count the number of matching features by accessing entries of the hash table built on the query drawing. In other words, the task comes down mainly to finding a corresponding segment line between the model section and the query drawing. The model section whose basis has the most corresponding features (and thus the greatest common part) is therefore the most similar to the query drawing. In the ideal situation, this task would be trivial if the query drawing and the model section did not have any outliers or noise. We could randomly sample a basis, describe all the features in this basis, and the model section with the highest number of corresponding features would be the most similar to the query drawing. Our model sections, however, do contain outliers because, for example, they are composed of the cross-sections of individual building elements (see an example in Figure 4 which shows a part of a model section comprised of two walls marked in green and blue). Consequently, not all of the line segments between the query drawing and the model section overlap, and those which do not, are considered as outliers (an outlier can be seen in Figure 4 marked with a yellow arrow, whereas the green arrow shows an inlier). Another example where outliers occur is a drawing which consists of building elements not modelled in the BIM model, and therefore not appearing in the derived model sections. Accordingly, there is a need to estimate how many bases need to be sampled from the model section in order to select at least one error-free basis corresponding to the query drawing.

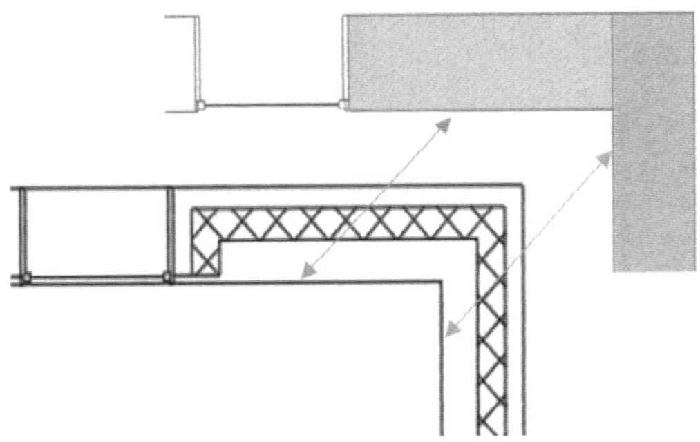

Figure 4: Corresponding segment lines between a model section (at the top) and a query drawing (at the bottom). The presented part of the model section is mainly comprised of two cross-sections of two building elements marked with the green and blue fills. Using a green arrow, we mark an example of bases which correspond with each other (inliers), whereas in yellow, we mark an example of bases which do not correspond with each other (outliers).

The naïve number of the sampled bases would equal to all of the segment-wise bases (as in the preprocessing stage executed on the query drawing). This, however, would increase the burden of building another full hash table, and what is worse, it would increase the matching ambiguity due to redundant bases. In order to reduce these drawbacks, we propose to estimate the minimal number of bases to be randomly sampled in the presence of outliers by using the random sample consensus so that at least one inlier is sampled. Having estimated the minimal number of sampled bases, we describe all the features in these bases and store them in another hash table which is being matched against the hash table of the query drawing. By doing this, we provide the full automation of the recognition phase (and thus the automation of the drawing-to-model registration). The major difference to the original geometric hashing is that the native procedure urges the user to choose an arbitrary basis in the to-be-recognized image, whereas we propose to build another hash table by storing the features described in a certain number of sampled bases (in which there is at least one inlier) estimated by RANSAC, and to match these two hash tables against each other. As a result, the matching bases between the model section and the query drawing can be determined.

Accordingly, we model the outliers as a random variable, and having assumed a certain outlier rate (ϵ), we sample k bases with very high probability (p) to select at least one (r) inlier basis. The number of trials (k) is computed as shown in equation 3 (Fischler and Bolles, 1981).

$$k = \frac{\log(1-p)}{\log(1-(1-\epsilon)^r)} \tag{3}$$

2.4 Correspondence establishment

Geometric hashing does not solve for explicit correspondence between all corresponding features (Belongie *et al.*, 2002). Instead it uses the features to vote for a specific basis. As a consequence, the explicit correspondence in our proposed system can be automatically established only between most voted bases from each hash table.

In our modified version, we simultaneously vote for bases in two hash tables. At the end, there is one basis in each hash table (in case of no redundant bases have been sampled in the recognition phase) that is most voted and we establish the correspondence between them. We do not explicitly recover all the feature-to-feature correspondences. Instead, we use the two corresponding bases between a drawing and a model section in 2D to align them.

2.5 Determination of alignment

Having found two corresponding bases, we align them in the following way: (1) The corresponding segment lines are viewed as vectors and the difference in scale between a model-section and the drawing is determined by the quotient of the norms of these vectors; (2) The translation vector is calculated between the middle points of the corresponding segment lines; (3) The rotation angle is calculated using the formula for the vector-vector dot product, where the corresponding segment lines are seen are vectors. Having calculated the above parameters, the drawing is accordingly scaled, translated and rotated.

3. Test case

We demonstrate the applicability of the proposed system in a case study of a standard 3-story residential building. Our prototype operates on IFC-based BIM models, and construction drawings in the DXF format. The geometric hashing algorithm and its extension has been programmatically implemented from scratch based on the original paper and extended as described in the previous section. IFC and DXF readers, viewers, and scientific computing libraries are free-license packages. The visualization of the BIM model and the floor plan can be seen in Figure 5. The BIM model was created using a commercial BIM modeling tool. The floor plan was then derived and modified to conform to engineering standards using this tool. Ultimately, the model and the floor plan were exported to the IFC and the DXF data formats.

We cut the IFC-based BIM model horizontally at 4 different levels (shown in Figure 6a) in such a way that the horizontal cutting plane is located at 1.20m above each floor level, which translates to the following building levels: -1.30m, 1.20m, 4.00m and 6.20m. The corresponding model sections are shown in Figure 6 b-e. The model sections are comprised of all the instances of parent type IfcProduct. The dimensions of the BIM model (and thus model sections) are stored in meters, whereas the dimension of the floor plan are stored in millimetres.

Figure 5: Visualization of a BIM model as a standard 3-story residentail building, and its corresponding floor plan portraying the ground floor derived at 1.20m level.

In case of the floor plan, we first filter all the geometric primitives, select those with the highest stroke width and build a geometric hash table for all the extracted key-point features described in all the extracted bases (segment lines). Next, for each model section, we extract its key-point features and segment lines and build a geometric hash table. We calculate the number of randomly sampled bases with the probability for selection at least one error-free base ($p = 0.99$) and outlier rate ($\epsilon = 0.9$). In such a case, the number of sampled bases is equal to k = 44, which reduces the number of bases used to build the hash tables around 4-7 times in case of model sections b, c and d presented in Figure 6. In all the cases, we quantize the coordinates of features stored in the hash tables by a bin of size 0.24.

(a) (b) (c) (d) (e)

Figure 6: An IFC-based BIM model horrizontally cut at 4 different levels – figure a. Figues from b to e present the corresponding model sections.

3.1 Experimental results

We match the hash tables of each model section against the hash table of the query drawing. In Figure 7, we show the 3 most voted bases for each model section. The model section derived at level +1.20 is most voted, and within this level, there are two bases with a very high score. This level is also marked in green on the right side of the figure.

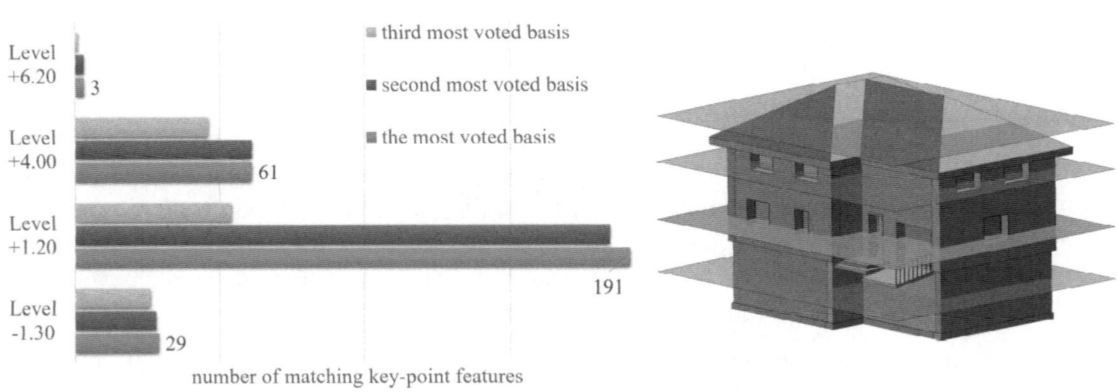

Figure 7: Results obtained after matching the geometric hash table of the query drawing against all the geometric hash tables of the model sections. The first three most voted bases are presented.

The most voted basis at level +1.20 and the most voted basis from the query drawing are then proposed for setting up the correspondence, which is shown in Figure 8 on the left hand side.

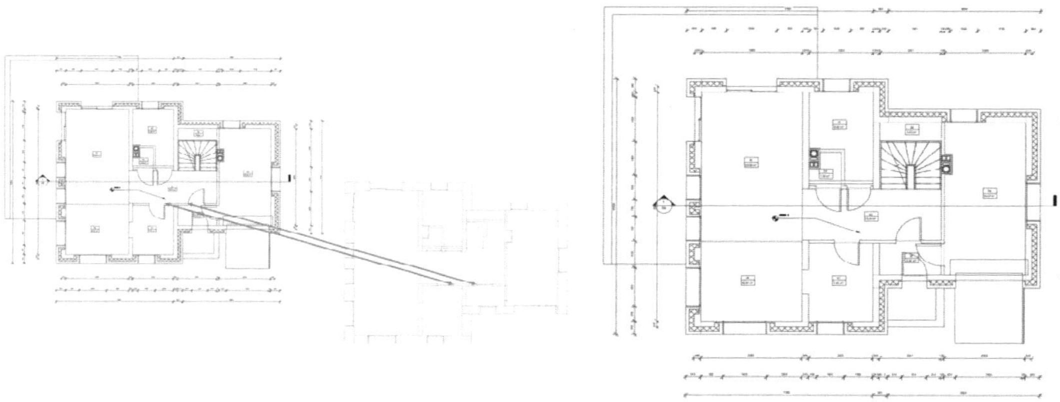

Figure 8: Left: The two corresponding bases between the query drawing and the most voted model section. Right: Aligned query drawing and model section.

4. Conclusions and future work

In this paper, we propose a robust feature-based shape matching method for the registration of construction drawings to BIM models with the extended geometric hashing at its core. We test this method in a case study of a standard 3-story residential building. The early experimental results are promising when it comes to measuring similarity with level-wise accuracy between floor plans in vector-based formats and BIM models using key-point features and segment line bases. The proposed reduction of basis space to segment lines reduces the burden for building hash tables due to its linear (and not quadratic) complexity.

The proposed extension of geometric hashing allows to cast votes simultaneously in two hash tables and therefore, it is possible to automatically establish the correspondence between two most voted bases. The results show that this method correctly attributes the query drawing to one of the model sections, and correctly indicates two corresponding bases which allows to establish the explicit correspondence. As +1.20 level shows, however, the proposed random-sample-consensus-based sampling of bases for model sections in the presence of outliers returned 2 inliers (1 redundant basis). Any redundant basis causes the matching ambiguity while setting up the explicit correspondence between two bases as the margin between the first and the second most voted bases is very little. In the future, in such situations, we propose to measure the similarity between the two registered objects by establishing more corresponding features and calculating the distance between them (for example using the L2 distance function). Moreover, it must be noted that the more similar the model sections are to the query drawing (fewer outliers), the more corresponding key-point features can be matched. In our case, the prototype operates on IFC models, whose pure cross-sections are comprised simply by cutting individual building elements which make the model section be prone to outliers (in comparison to the corresponding construction drawing). Additionally, such parameters as the outlier rate and the bin size need to be tuned on more real projects, as they drive the performance of this system, which we could not show in this paper due to its page limit.

There are many other cases in which our registration system could be tested as well. Matching drawings of details which contain elements not necessarily modeled in BIM models (for example - highly detailed steel connections), matching vertical cross-sections or projections of facades are use cases which could be tested. In all of these cases, the derivation mechanism for model sections presented in this paper must be extended so that it returns good 2D candidates for comparison to the query drawing. The derivation mechanism is potentially the biggest limitation in the proposed system because it is hard-coded for specific cases (horizontal model-sections for floor plans, vertical models-sections for cross-sections and so on). Also, in case of drawings which are not comprised of mainly straight segment lines, we would have to extend the types of features that are supposed to be matched because the fewer key-point features extracted, the less confident the system is. Therefore, the second major limitation of the proposed system is its non-consideration of curved geometric primitives which limits the applicability of this system in certain cases with more advanced geometry.

Overall, the proposed registration system shows promising results in building engineering for further automation of both the registration process and its subsequent consistency verification which could be used, for example, in the verification of consistency between construction drawings and BIM models at quality gates in approval process by authority.

Acknowledgements

This work is supported by ALLPLAN GmbH and Nemetschek Group. The authors would like to gratefully thank these companies for making this research possible.

References

Avbelj, J., Iwaszczuk, D., Müller, R., Reinartz, P. and Stilla, U. (2015), "Coregistration refinement of hyperspectral images and DSM: An object-based approach using spectral information", *ISPRS Journal of Photogrammetry and Remote Sensing*, Vol. 100, pp. 23–34.

Belongie, S., Malik, J. and Puzicha, J. (2002), "Shape matching and object recognition using shape contexts", *Pattern Analysis and Machine Intelligence, IEEE*, Vol. 24 No. 24.

Fischler, M.A. and Bolles, R.C. (1981), "Random sample consensus: a paradigm for model fitting with applications to image analysis and automated cartography", *Communications of the ACM*, Vol. 24 No. 6, pp. 381–395.

ISO (2018), *Organization and digitization of information about buildings and civil engineering works, including building information modelling (BIM): Information management using building information modelling -- Part 1: Concepts and principles* No. ISO 19650-1:2018, available at: https://www.iso.org/standard/68078.html (accessed 2019-03).

ISO/DIS (n.d.), *Information container for data drop: Exchange specificaton -- Part 1: Container* No. ISO/DIS 21597-1, available at: https://www.iso.org/standard/74389.html (accessed 2019-05).

Jung, J., Sohn, G., Bang, K., Wichmann, A., Armenakis, C. and Kada, M. (2016), "Matching Aerial Images to 3D Building Models Using Context-Based Geometric Hashing", *Sensors (Basel, Switzerland)*, Vol. 16 No. 6.

Liu, Q. (2012), *A Survey of Recent View-based 3D Model Retrieval Methods*, available at: http://arxiv.org/pdf/1208.3670v1.

Preidel, C., Daum, S. and Borrmann, A. (2017), "Data retrieval from building information models based on visual programming", *Visualization in Engineering*, Vol. 5 No. 1, pp. 1–14.

Sacks, R., Eastman, C.M., Lee, G. and Teichlz, P. (2019), *BIM Handbook: A Guide to Building Information Modeling For Owenrs, Designers, Engineers, Contractors, and Facility Managers,* Third Edition, Wiley.

Shao, T., Xu, W., Yin, K., Wang, J., Zhou, K. and Guo, B. (2011), "Discriminative Sketch-based 3D Model Retrieval via Robust Shape Matching", *Computer Graphics Forum*, Vol. 30 No. 7, pp. 2011–2020.

Tangelder, J.W.H. and Veltkamp, R.C. (2008), "A survey of content based 3D shape retrieval methods", *Multimedia Tools and Applications*, Vol. 39 No. 3, pp. 441–471.

Wolfson, H.J. and Rigoutsos, I. (1997), "Geometric hashing: an overview", *IEEE Computational Science and Engineering*, Vol. 4 No. 4, pp. 10–21.

Wunsch, P. and Hirzinger, G. (Eds.) (1996), *Registration of CAD-Models to Images by Iterative Inverse Perspective Matching.*

Input Feature Optimization for ANN Models Predicting Daylight in Buildings

C-L. Lorenz, A. B. Spaeth, C. Bleil De Souza, M. Packianather
Cardiff University, Wales, U.K.
lorenzc4@cardiff.ac.uk

Abstract. Artificial Neural Networks (ANNs) were used as prediction models to explore design solutions for the atrium design of a school building. To this end, a solution space of 165 design variants was generated via parametric modeling. This paper details the process of extracting and selecting the input features required for ANN training in order to predict the DA and sDA metric. The feature selection undertaken in this study mainly consisted of two steps: Firstly, a computationally less extensive machine learning model was used to rank the input features according to their relevance in predicting daylight levels. Secondly, ANNs were trained applying sequential forward selection. The proposed method is investigated in terms of achievable improvements to prediction accuracy, reduceable training time and the feasibility of the method.

1. Introduction

Access and exposure to daylight not only regulates the circadian rhythm but is vital to reducing fatigue (Figueiro *et al.*, 2017) and has been shown to improve well-being, work performance and students' performance in schools (Maesano and Annesi-Maesano, 2012; Veitch, Christoffersen and Galasiu, 2013). In recent years, the Daylight Factor (DF), a standard metric for assessing daylight in buildings, came under scrutiny for its unsuitability as a design driver, given that it considers neither orientation nor climate (Reinhart, Mardaljevic and Rogers, 2013). In its stead, climate-based metrics were introduced (Reinhart and Walkenhorst, 2001) and have only recently been adopted into European and British building standards (EN 17037:2018). Of particular interest in this paper was the Daylight Autonomy (DA) metric, which quantifies the percentage of occupied hours in a year, in which a threshold of 300 lux can be met with daylight. However, compared to point-in time daylight factor calculations, the annual simulation for climate-based metrics is more time consuming, making it inherently more difficult to assess design options as an integral part of the design process (Jones and Reinhart, 2019).

Research has introduced Artificial Neural Networks (ANNs) as surrogate energy simulation software in order to improve the feasibility of performance-driven design investigations (Nguyen, Reiter and Rigo, 2014). The benefits of such ANN-based models include their instantaneous response rate (once trained) and high accuracy, under the condition that ANN models are trained with sufficient performance data, an appropriate model selection and parameter settings (Zhao and Magoulès, 2012). Such models have been found to be particularly useful for automated building control, where an immediate response is required (Hu and Olbina, 2011). Their use further extends to the modeling of large design solution spaces in order to solve design problems with numerous design variables (Machairas, Tsangrassoulis and Axarli, 2014). In general, ANNs present a promising avenue in research as a mature technology that works well with noisy data (i.e. simulation data) and can operate with various types of input and output (i.e. real, discrete, Boolean), the relationship between which need not be known (Mckee, Schulz and Caruana, 2006). Such research has laid the groundwork of this paper, as we applied ANN-based modeling to efficiently predict daylight for the solution space of a building design. More specifically, this study trained ANNs to predict climate-based metrics to explore design variants for the central atrium of a school building. Within that context, this paper focused on the selection and optimization of input features.

1.1 ANN-based Daylight Predictions

In the field of daylight design, ANNs have been used as prediction models for luminous efficacy (Lopez and Gueymard, 2007), sky luminance and sky irradiance (Pattanasethanon, Lertsatitthanakorn and Atthajariyakul, 2008; Janjai and Plaon, 2011), and horizontal internal illuminance levels (Kazanasmaz, Gunaydin and Binol, 2009). The ANN models relied on historic data as training data, which constituted an obstacle in terms of the time and the effort required to generate the training data. The need of data to be collected over a longer period of time - e.g. around 3 months as in Kazanasmaz et al. (2009) - also undermines the feasibility of applying ANNs in the first place. One line of research has circumvented this problem by applying ANNs in the optimization of building design, thereby training the ANN models on data extracted from a fraction of simulations required as part of the optimization process. Magnier and Haghihat (2010) showed that simulation-based ANNs could be used to pass performance results to the fitness function of a Genetic Algorithm to considerably reduce simulation time. In further optimization studies, ANNs were used to predict electric energy consumption and visual comfort (Wong, Wan and Lam, 2010; Kim, Jeon and Kim, 2016). Concerning climate-based metrics, Zhou and Liu (2015) were able to predict the specific illuminance range of the UDI (Useful Daylight Illuminance). The studies undertaken typically predict hourly or point-in-time daylight levels. Thus, annual culminative predictions of the DA metric has been understudied. The potential for predicting DA metric was introduced in the authors' previous work (Lorenz *et al.*, 2018) and is reinvestigated for a more complex design scenario. The input features so far had been selected empirically. As a result, the need for a robust, automated and replicable method of improving the input feature selection was identified.

1.2 Input Feature Selection and Optimization

Input features, also known as predictor variables, make up the training data which is passed to ANN models in order to facilitate supervised, unsupervised and reinforcement type learning. Input feature selection refers to the reduction of the dimensionality of training data by selecting a subset of input features. An objective function is commonly used as selection criterium to minimize the predictive error and thereby identify an optimal or suboptimal subset of input features. Such input feature selection methods have been shown to improve prediction accuracy and identify the minimum number of features needed (Marcano-Cedeño *et al.*, 2010; Özşen, 2013).

As exhaustive search methods are computationally expensive, two other common methods of input feature selection are Sequential Forward Selection (SFS), and Sequential Backward Selection (SBS). SFS is a bottom-up approach that starts with an empty set of features to which features are iteratively added (Whitney, 1971). Its counterpart, SBS starts from the complete set from which features are iteratively removed (Marill and M. Green, 1963). Inevitably, both methods inhibit a nesting problem, whereby potentially important features, once removed, cannot be re-introduced. To ensure that important features would be kept alive, mixed method approaches were introduced (Pudil, Novovi and Kittler, 1994). A comparative evaluation of methods is given in (Zongker and Jain, 1996). As forward-based methods have been shown to be faster than backward-based methods, this paper works with a forward-sequential approach in combination with a machine learning algorithm, which was used to determine the sequence of input features.

2. Research Methodology

The different steps to developing, optimizing and validating ANN models are illustrated in Figure 1. The ANNs were employed to predict daylight for a design solution space. As such, performance data was collected from selected samples of the design solution space. The performance data was extracted from daylight simulations and recorded features describing the design changes and the corresponding daylight results. While a majority of data was used for training the ANN models, a part of it was retained for validation of the models.

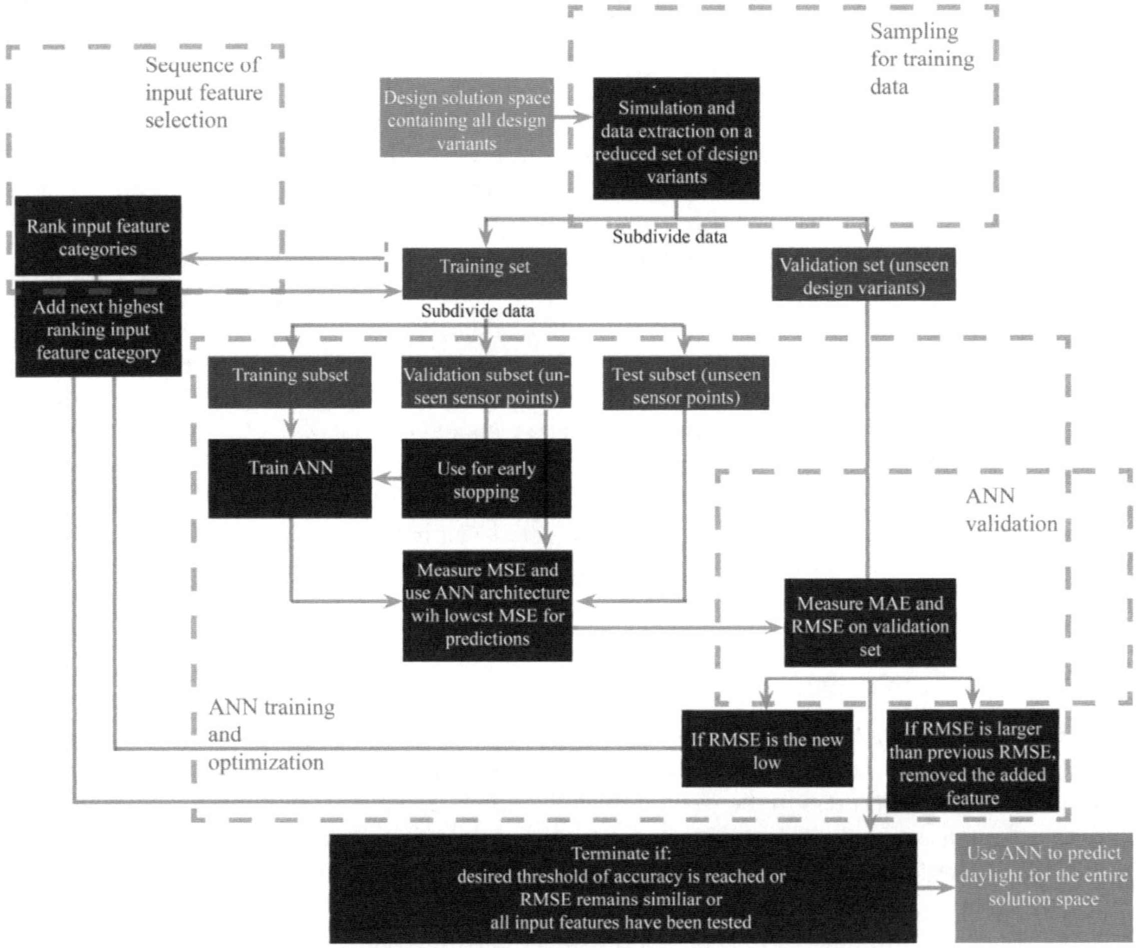

Figure 1: ANN model development and validation

Once a training set had been generated, bagged decision trees, a machine learning technique, were used to determine a sequence for the forward-sequential selection of features. Thus, the ANN models were first trained with the input features that showed the highest impact as predictors. The training data set was again subdivided into a training subset, a validation subset and a test subset at the ratio of 65:25:15. The validation subset was used for early stopping to avoid overfitting and the test subset was used to estimate prediction accuracies on new cases. Both subsets were also used to assist in the optimization of the network architecture. Each network architecture was trained ten times with the initial weight settings and distribution of samples across the subsets varying in each training run. The network architecture with the lowest error across ten training runs was used for predictions, and the output of all ten networks was averaged to improve generalization.

The predictions were validated against the simulations withheld from training. In the case of insufficient accuracy, another training feature was added to the training set and the optimization of network architecture, and validation was repeated. There are several options for terminating the training cycle: once a desired threshold of accuracy is reached, once the accuracy converges for a number of training cycles, once all input features have been tested, or a combination of the three. In this study we tested all input features to allow for a more wholistic evaluation of the method. However, if the aim is not to find an optimal subset of features but to identify the minimum number of input features required to reduce the training time, the first two options of termination better serve the purpose.

2.1 Design Solution Space and Design Variables

The exploration of design solutions was done for the central atrium of a school-building in Hamburg (Figure 2). As a first design variable, the atrium base dimension was reduced from 225m^2 to 56,25m^2, thereby splaying the atrium well walls in obtuse angles between 90 and 79°. With a second design variable, the atrium well was slanted, changing the orientation between north and south. 9 possible solutions were specified for the slant of the atrium well, modifying its splay angles between 58 and 104°. This resulted in a 9 by 6 matrix of 54 possible design variants for the atrium well geometry. As the third design variable, 3 possibilities were specified for the window-to-wall ratios (WWR) across floor levels of the 6-storey building. The WWR was reduced from the ground to higher floor levels in order to increase the reflected light and daylight levels on the ground floor (Samant, 2017). In a first option, the WWR distribution was set to 50% -6th floor, 60% - 5th floor, 70% - 4th floor, 80%- 3rd floor, 90% - 2nd floor and 100% - ground floor. In a second option, the WWR distribution was set to 20% -6th floor, 35% - 5th floor, 50% - 4th floor, 65%- 3rd floor, 80% - 2nd floor and 100% - ground floor. Lastly, in a third option, the WWR distribution was set to 20% -6th floor, 30% - 5th floor, 40% - 4th floor, 50%- 3rd floor, 60% - 2nd floor and 100% - ground floor. The entire solution space thereby contained 162 design variants for the central atrium.

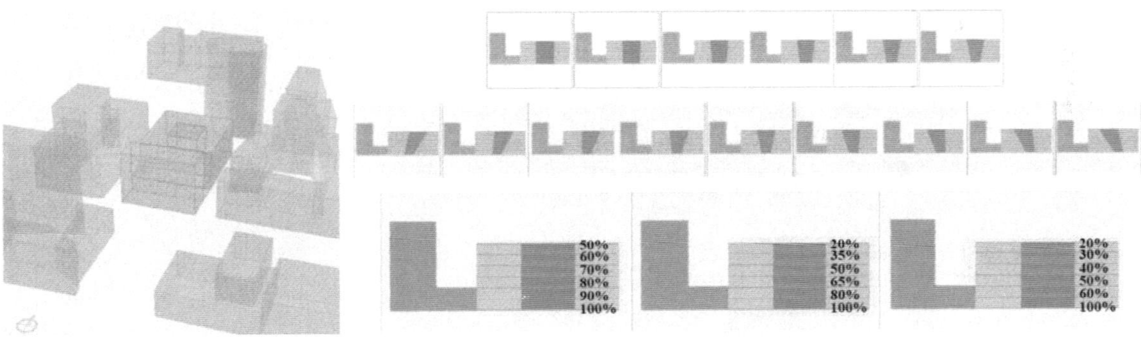

Figure 2: To the left: The school building and surrounding buildings. To the right, from top to bottom: 6 variants for a reduced atrium base dimension, 9 variants for the atrium well orientation, 3 variants for the WWR distribution across floor levels (the atrium well is highlighted in dark blue)

2.2 Daylight Simulation and Data Extraction

From the solution space of 162 variants, a reduced set of 36 variants were selected to provide training data and another 21 variants were selected for validation of ANN accuracy. The architectural models were built in Grasshopper, and daylight simulation on the selected variants were run in Diva – a radiance-based and validated software (Mohsenin and Hu, 2015). DA was calculated for sensor points at a work-plane height of .8 m above floor level and the sensor points were spaced in .6 m distance of each other. The input features were extracted for every sensor point and passed to the input layer of the network model (Figure 3). The corresponding DA levels were passed to the output layer of the network for it to undergo supervised training. As shown in Figure 3, 26 input features in total were extracted from the simulation model and grouped according to categories. This was done for the next step, in which a sequence for feature selection was determined.

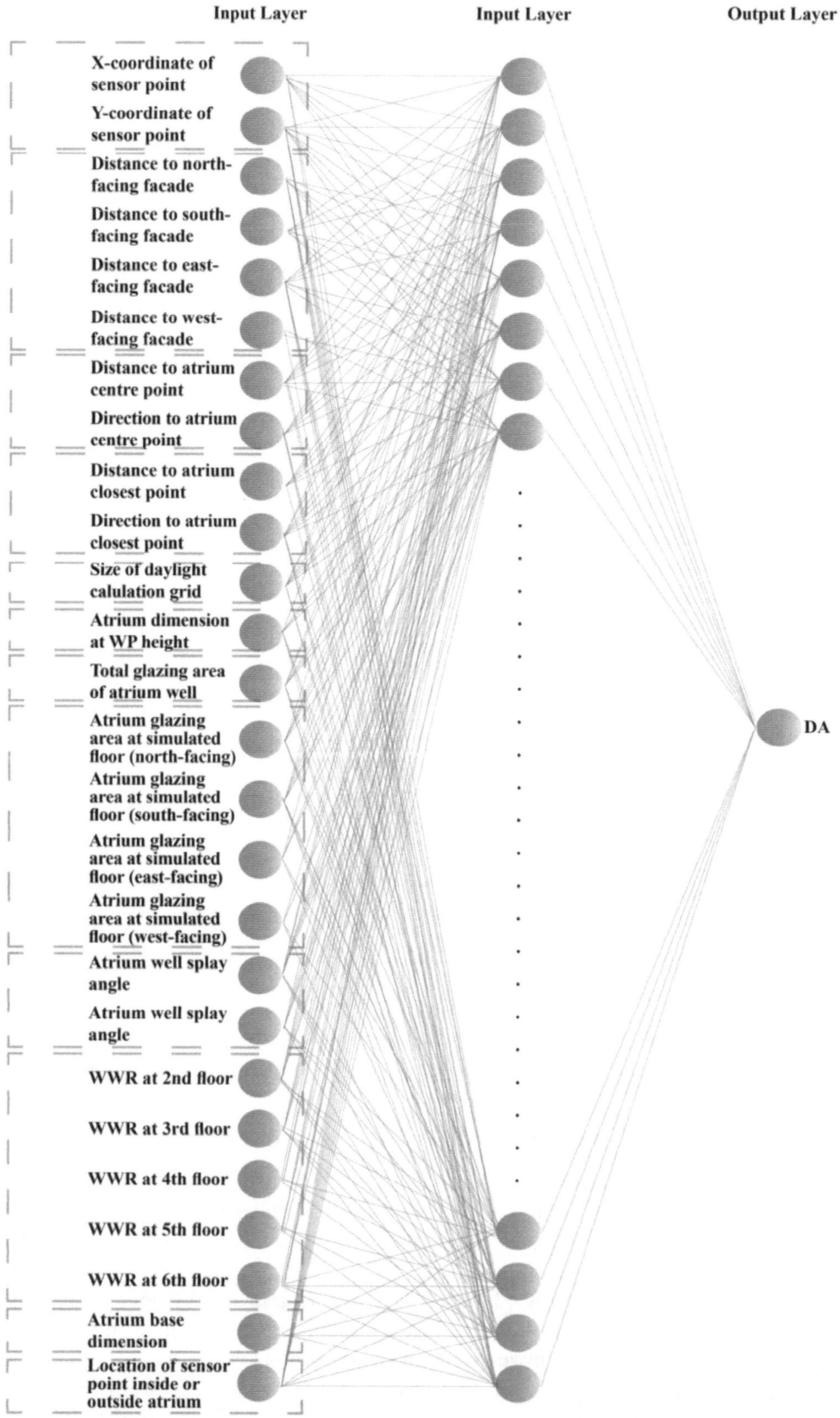

Figure 3: Representation of ANN model as a construct of neurons with an input layer, hidden layer and output layer. The extracted input features are passed to the input layer of the model and the daylight performance data (in DA) to the output layer. A suitable number of hidden neurons needs to be identified as these effect the ANN training time and prediction accuracy.

2.3 Ranking of Input Feature Categories

In order to rank the input feature categories according to their impact as predictors, the training data set was passed to machine learning (ML) models for fitness approximation. Although ANNs can be trained to identify significant features, this was not done due to their increased computation time. Among the tested ML techniques were linear regression models, fine, medium and coarse trees, boosted tree ensembles, liner, quadratic, cubic, fine Gaussian support vector machines and Gaussian Process Regression models. Bagged decision trees showed the lowest root mean squared error (RMSE) and superior performance compared to the other models. Additionally, the computation time was low, with approximation taking around four minutes. Hence, they were selected to identify a feature selection sequence.

From the data set that was passed to the bagged trees model, every input feature category was individually removed and the corresponding variance in RMSE was measured. The features were then ranked according to the variance they inflicted on the error, with those features causing the largest variance ranked highest. The RMSE during approximation on the training data set and resulting sequence of input feature categories is given in Table 1.

Table 1: Ranking of input feature categories according to variance in prediction error

Input Feature Category	Sequence Order	RMSE	Input Feature Category	Sequence Order	RMSE
Distance and direction to atrium closest point	1	1.19	X-, Y-coordinates of sensor points	7	.87
Distance to facade	2	.99	Glazing area at simulated floor level	8	.85
Distance and direction to atrium centre point	3	.96	Glazing area across all floors	9	.84
WWR	4	.90	Atrium base dimension	10	.84
Location of sensor point inside or outside atrium	5	.90	Atrium dimension at WP height	11	.84
Atrium well spay angles	6	.89	Daylight calculation grid size	12	.84

2.4 Sequential Feature Selection and Validation

The ANN models were trained starting from a data set with one input feature category. Once trained, the ANN model was used to predict the DA metric for the 21 retained variants and predictions were compared to the simulated DA. Two measures were used: the mean absolute error (MAE) and the root mean square error (RMSE). The MAE, which gives the absolute difference between the simulated and predicted values, was chosen for its ease of interpretation. The RMSE was selected as it weighs larger errors more heavily and is a commonly used measure of accuracy. The RMSE was observed for each added input feature and its minimization was used as the objective function to optimise the selection. As long as the RMSE reached a new low, one additional input feature category was added to the training data set. If the RMSE worsened, the last added feature was removed before adding the next feature in the sequence. In this way, all input features were added to the training data set at some point in a forward-sequential manner. The results discuss the observed errors in accuracy for every added feature.

2.5 ANN Training

Back-propagation ANN models were employed in conjunction with the Lavenberg-Marquardt algorithm. The training parameters were set to an initial mu of 1, a mu decrease factor of .8 and mu increase factor of 1.5. The training was run for 200 epochs, during which the connection strengths between neurons were adjusted to minimise the mean squared error (MSE) on the training data set. The training data set was again divided into a subset of training, validation and test data in order to ensure robustness of the trained networks through cross-validation and early stopping. The maximum number of validation failures was set to 6. Ten network architectures with 38 to 40 neurons in the hidden layer were trained and tested with said settings and the network architecture with the lowest MSE on the training, validation and test subset was used for predictions. This was done to ensure that a network optimised architecture was used to evaluate the input features.

3. Results

The MSE on the training data set (36/162 simulations with 150.706 sensor point data samples) and the RMSE and MAE on the validation set (21/162 sim with 87.850 sensor point data samples) were recorded at each training stage of the sequential search. Figure 4 shows the MSE during feature selection (for the sequence refers back to Table 1). Figure 5 shows the MAE obtained on the validation set and Figure 6 the RMSE. The minimum achieved error has been highlighted in red. The sequence at which an added input feature category was again removed from the training data has been highlighted in yellow.

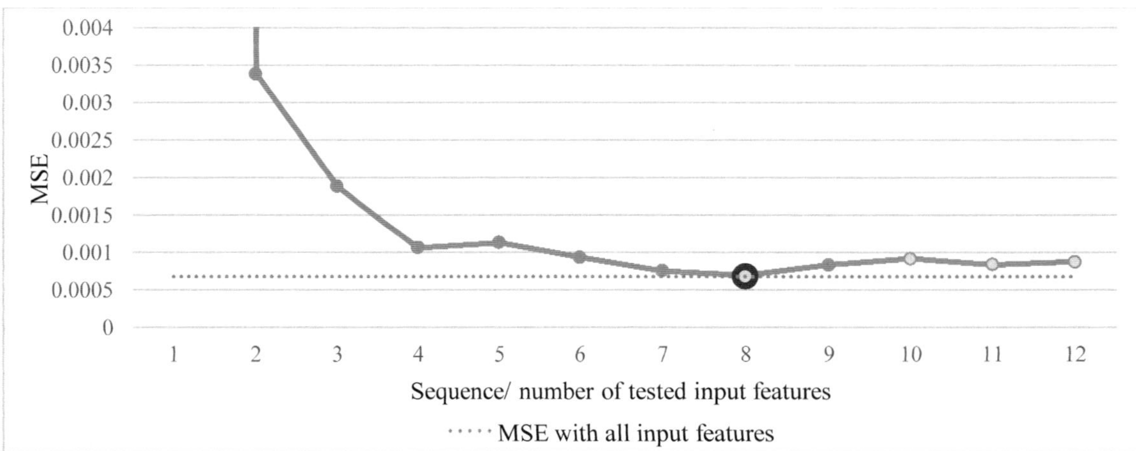

Figure 4: MSE on the training data set after every added input feature category

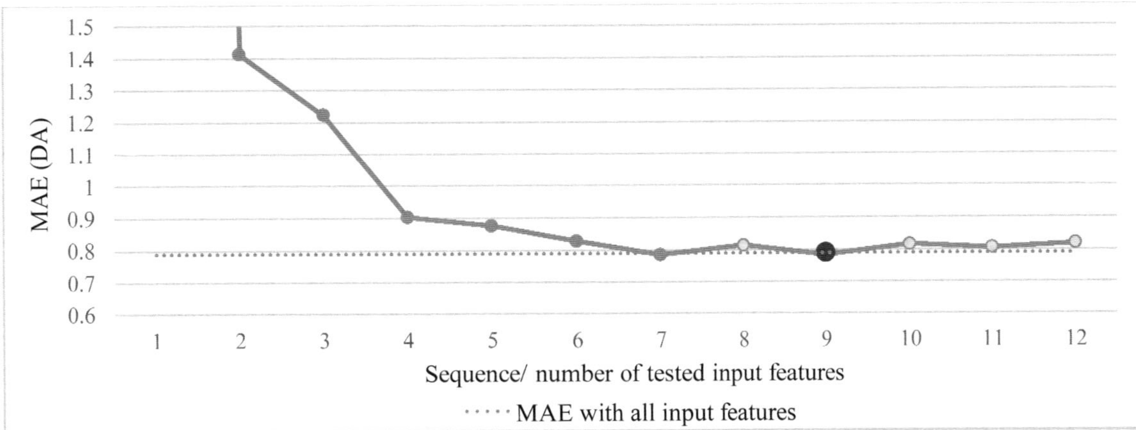

Figure 5: MAE on the training data set after every added input feature category

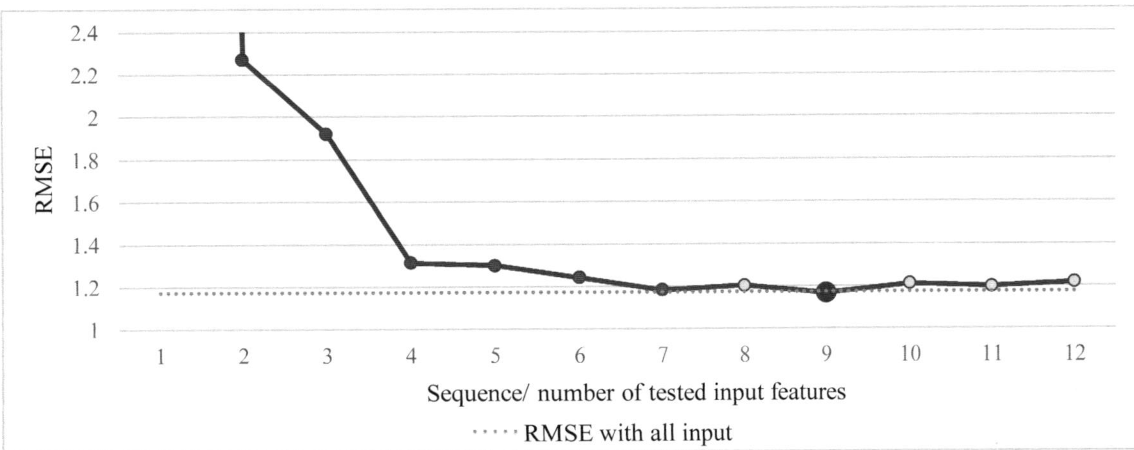

Figure 6: RMSE on the training data set after every added input feature category

The MSE dropped below 0.01 after including six input features (which include distance and direction to atrium closest point, distance to façade, distance and direction to atrium center point, WWRs, location of sensor points inside or outside atrium, and atrium well spay angles). The MAE and RMSE remained in the similar range after the 7th input feature category, the sensor point identifiers, were added as training data. The lowest MSE was reached after adding the 8th input feature describing glazing areas on the simulated floor level. The MAE and RMSE however increased, resulting in the feature being removed from the feature set. Consecutively, the MAE and RMSE reached their minimum at .78 MAE and 1.16 RMSE. In comparison, the ANNs trained with all input features showed marginally higher errors of .79 MAE and 1.17 RMSE. Although this shows that the input feature selection could not result in a significant improvement of accuracies, it highlights that not all input features are needed and overall training time can be reduced.

In fact, training time of the 'optimal' feature set with 8 added and one removed input feature category (19 individual features) including network optimization took 04:33 (hh:mm), whereas the training and optimization of the model that included all input features was 05:55. Taking a more minimal approach, the training with 7 added feature categories (18 individual features) was 03:01. Predictions on the validation set were made in less than 1 second.

Inadvertently, due to nature of the selection process, it lacks in feasibility compared to a trial and error approach validating an empirically selected feature set. The above outlined time savings can therefore only truly be achieved if: a) the selected input feature subset is extracted and trained for a larger data set, b) the feature subset holds validity for a new or similar design scenario, or c) the same input features would be selected with a smaller and thereby less computationally expensive network architecture of fewer hidden neurons. This however would still need validation. The training times as measured here were taken on a 2.6 GHz Intel Core i9 processor.

The prediction accuracy converged around .8 DA MAE, meaning that this was, on average, the absolute difference between the simulated and predicted DA. The simulated DA range from 0 to 88%, with 1% referring to 1% of occupied hours in a year. A difference of .8 DA can therefore hardly be interpreted and constitutes a negligible error. The RMSE, which converged around 1.2%, supports this finding and shows a high accuracy of ANNs in predicting the DA metric.

In order to achieve above-mentioned accuracies, data was extracted from a total of 57/162 simulations for training and validation. As daylight simulations took approximately 3 hours per design variant, a total of 315 hours of simulations were bypassed through ANN predictions. Given that the process relied on a small sample size of 13% for validation, 16,4% when including the validation subset within the training data, the results may vary. However, increasing the validation set within the ANN-integrated workflow would require a larger number of simulations to be run, thereby reducing the achievable time-savings.

4. Conclusion and Recommendations for Future Research

Overall, the following conclusions for ANN-based daylight predictions can be drawn:

a) On average, prediction accuracies of around .8 DA mean absolute error (MAE) were achieved. These accuracies could be maintained as the number of input features increased.

b) The MSE on the training data set did not directly correlate with the MAE and RMSE on the validation data set, as the prediction accuracies could improve (lower MAE and RMSE) even though the ability of the network to fit the data decreased (higher MSE).

d) Having superfluous input features did not significantly lower accuracies (e.g. calculation grid size and atrium dimension at WP height). It did however increase training time. On the other hand, too few input features (e.g. before sequence 4), though requiring less training time, compromised prediction accuracies.

e) Using the proposed method, accuracies barely improved compared to the empirically selected full set of input features. However, the training time for the ANN models could be reduced by around 50% without significantly compromising the accuracies.

The paper proposes a viable method for selecting input features useful for predicting daylight in buildings. Additionally, the study investigated in how far improvements could be achieved. Although, in terms of accuracy, those were marginal in this study, the selection method may prove more valuable in larger and more complex solution spaces with a larger number of variables. A downside of the proposed method is that it remains computationally expensive, as it requires multiple training runs with already computationally demanding ANN models. It would therefore be useful to evaluate the results of feature selection using smaller and more feasible network architectures, or completely rely on computationally less expensive ML models for feature selection. A comparison to alternative feature selection methods is recommended, as well as the application of the proposed method on more complex solution spaces.

References

Figueiro, M. G., Steverson, B., Heerwagen, J., Kampschroer, K., Hunter, C. M., Gonzales, K., Plitnick, B. and Rea, M. S. (2017) 'The impact of daytime light exposures on sleep and mood in office workers', *Sleep Health*. National Sleep Foundation., 3(3), pp. 204–215. doi: 10.1016/j.sleh.2017.03.005.

Hu, J. and Olbina, S. (2011) 'Illuminance-based slat angle selection model for automated control of split blinds', *Building and Environment*. Elsevier Ltd, 46(3), pp. 786–796. doi: 10.1016/j.buildenv.2010.10.013.

Janjai, S. and Plaon, P. (2011) 'Estimation of sky luminance in the tropics using artificial neural networks: Modeling and performance comparison with the CIE model', *Applied Energy*. Elsevier Ltd, 88(3), pp. 840–847. doi: 10.1016/j.apenergy.2010.09.004.

Jones, N. L. and Reinhart, C. F. (2019) 'Effects of real-time simulation feedback on design for visual comfort', *Journal of Building Performance Simulation*. Taylor & Francis, 12(3), pp. 343–361. doi: 10.1080/19401493.2018.1449889.

Kazanasmaz, T., Gunaydin, M. and Binol, S. (2009) 'Artificial neural networks to predict daylight illuminance in office buildings', *Building and Environment*, 44, pp. 1751–1757. doi: 10.1016/j.buildenv.2008.11.012.

Kim, W., Jeon, Y. and Kim, Y. (2016) 'Simulation-based optimization of an integrated daylighting and HVAC system using the design of experiments method', *Applied Energy*. Elsevier Ltd, 162, pp. 666–674. doi: 10.1016/j.apenergy.2015.10.153.

Lopez, G. and Gueymard, C. A. (2007) 'Clear-sky solar luminous efficacy determination using artificial neural networks', *Solar Energy*, 81(7), pp. 929–939. doi: 10.1016/j.solener.2006.11.001.

Lorenz, C.-L., Packianather, M., Spaeth, A. B. and Bleil de Souza, C. (2018) 'Artificial Neural Network-Based Modelling for Daylight Evaluations', in *Symposium on Simulation for Architecture + Urban Design*. Delft. The Netherlands.

Machairas, V., Tsangrassoulis, A. and Axarli, K. (2014) 'Algorithms for optimization of building design: A review', *Renewable and Sustainable Energy Reviews*, 31(1364), pp. 101–112. doi: 10.1016/j.rser.2013.11.036.

Maesano, C. and Annesi-Maesano, I. (2012) *Impact of Lighting on School Performance in European Classrooms*. Paris. Available at: http://velcdn.azureedge.net/~/media/com/articles/pdf/light and performance_whitepaperfinal 1.pdf (Accessed: 29 August 2017).

Magnier, L. and Haghighat, F. (2010) 'Multiobjective optimization of building design using TRNSYS simulations, genetic algorithm, and Artificial Neural Network', *Building and Environment*. Elsevier Ltd, 45(3), pp. 739–746. doi: 10.1016/j.buildenv.2009.08.016.

Marcano-Cedeño, Quintanilla-Domínguez, J., Cortina-Januchs, M. G. and Andina, D. (2010) 'Feature selection using Sequential Forward Selection and Classification applying Artificial Metaplasticity Neural Network', *IECON 36th Annual Conference on IEEE Industrial Electronics Society*, pp. 2845–2850. doi: 10.1109/IECON.2010.5675075.

Marill, T. and M. Green, D. (1963) 'On the effectiveness of receptors in recognition systems', *Information Theory, IEEE Transactions on*, 9, pp. 11–17. doi: 10.1109/TIT.1963.1057810.

Mckee, S. A., Schulz, M. and Caruana, R. (2006) 'Efficiently Exploring Architectural Design Spaces via Predictive Modeling', in *Asplos International Conference on Architectural Support for Programming Languages and Operating Systems*. CA, USA, pp. 195–206.

Mohsenin, M. and Hu, J. (2015) 'Assessing daylight performance in atrium buildings by using Climate Based Daylight Modeling', *Solar Energy*, 119, pp. 553–560. doi: 10.1016/j.solener.2015.05.011.

Nguyen, A.-T., Reiter, S. and Rigo, P. (2014) 'A review on simulation-based optimization methods applied to building performance analysis', *Applied Energy*, 113, pp. 1043–1058. doi: 10.1016/j.apenergy.2013.08.061.

Özşen, S. (2013) 'Classification of sleep stages using class-dependent sequential feature selection and artificial neural network', *Neural Computing and Applications*, 23(5), pp. 1239–1250. doi: 10.1007/s00521-012-1065-4.

Pattanasethanon, S., Lertsatitthanakorn, C. and Atthajariyakul, S. (2008) 'An accuracy assessment of an empirical sine model , a novel sine model and an artificial neural network model for forecasting illuminance / irradiance on horizontal plane of all sky types at Mahasarakham , Thailand', 49, pp. 1999–2005. doi: 10.1016/j.enconman.2008.02.014.

Pudil, P., Novovi, J. and Kittler, J. (1994) 'Floating search methods in feature selection', *Pattern Recognition*

Letters, 15(November), pp. 1119–1125.

Reinhart, F, C., Mardaljevic, J. and Rogers, Z. (2013) 'Dynamic Daylight Performance Metrics for Sustainable Building Design', *The journal of the illuminating Engineering Society of North America*, 3(1), pp. 7–31. doi: 10.1582/LEUKOS.2006.03.01.001.

Reinhart, C. F. and Walkenhorst, O. (2001) 'Validation of dynamic RADIANCE-based daylight simulations for a test office with external blinds', *Energy and Buildings*, 33(7), pp. 683–697. doi: 10.1016/S0378-7788(01)00058-5.

Samant, S. (2017) 'Atrium and its adjoining spaces: a study of the influence of atrium façade design Swinal Samant Atrium and its adjoining spaces: a study of the influence of atrium faç ade design', *Architectural Science Review*, 54(4). doi: 10.1080/00038628.2011.613640.

Veitch, J. A., Christoffersen, J. and Galasiu, A. D. (2013) *Daylight and View through Residential Windows : Effects on Well-being, Residential dayligting and well-being.*

Whitney, A. W. (1971) 'A Direct Method of Nonparametric Measurement Selection', *Computers, IEEE Transactions on*, 20, pp. 1100–1103. doi: 10.1109/T-C.1971.223410.

Wong, S. L., Wan, K. K. W. and Lam, T. N. T. (2010) 'Artificial neural networks for energy analysis of office buildings with daylighting', *Applied Energy*. Elsevier Ltd, 87(2), pp. 551–557. doi: 10.1016/j.apenergy.2009.06.028.

Zhao, H. X. and Magoulès, F. (2012) 'A review on the prediction of building energy consumption', *Renewable and Sustainable Energy Reviews*. Elsevier Ltd, 16(6), pp. 3586–3592. doi: 10.1016/j.rser.2012.02.049.

Zhou, S. and Liu, D. (2015) 'Prediction of Daylighting and Energy Performance Using Artificial Neural Network and Support Vector Machine', *American Journal of Civil Engineering and Architecture, Vol. 3, 2015, Pages 1-8*, 3(3A), pp. 1–8. doi: 10.12691/AJCEA-3-3A-1.

Zongker, D. and Jain, A. (1996) 'Algorithms for Feature Selection: An Evaluation', in *Proceedings of 13th International Conference on Pattern Recognition*. Vienna, Austria, pp. 18–22.

Combining airborne images and open data to retrieve knowledge of construction sites

Katrin Jahr[1], Dorota Iwaszczuk[2], André Borrmann[1]
[1]Technical University of Munich, Germany
[2]Technical University of Darmstadt, Germany
katrin.jahr@tum.de

Abstract. Construction site planning is based on both explicit knowledge, as retrieved from regulations, and implicit knowledge, arising from experience. To retrieve and formalize rules from implicit knowledge, past construction projects can be analyzed. In this paper, we present an image analysis pipeline to retrieve information on past construction sites from airborne images. We fuse machine learning based image analysis with georeferencing and openly available geospatial data to retrieve a detailed description with true dimensions of the construction site at hand.

1. Introduction

The digitization of the AEC (Architecture, engineering, construction) industry offers various new possibilities for designing, planning, and monitoring buildings. In recent years, many research projects focused on using methods of computer-aided engineering, such as building information modelling or structural simulations, to facilitate and enhance the planning process. However, as of now, not many of the advantages of using digital support are carried on after structural designing is concluded. Specifically, construction site layout planning (CSLP) is still mostly realized based on planner's experience and rules of thumb, if at all. Using scientifically proven digital support tools offers significant potential for improvement regarding planning accuracy and time efficiency.

A large set of information, traditionally acquired in late planning stages, must be considered during site equipment (SE) planning. To reduce planning efforts and prevent repetitive re-planning phases due to changes in construction design or construction methods, SE planning is usually conducted only after decisions on design and construction have been finalized (without in-depth information on required equipment). To address this issue and enable efficient CSLP, several semi-automatic solutions have been proposed in previous research. Key point to formulating these planning algorithms is extensive domain knowledge, both explicit and implicit. Explicit knowledge can be retrieved from regulations, guidelines, and local boundary conditions. However, in practice, numerous SE variants might be applicable for each construction project. To support the decision, implicit knowledge is vital. Implicit knowledge arises from expert knowledge and practical experience and is hard to extract and formulate in a strict, logical, and computable manner. Executing companies dread competitive disadvantages, and often hesitate when asked to give out delicate information on design decision on past construction sites. Therefore, we propose gathering information by analyzing large numbers of aerial photographs containing construction sites.

In this paper, we present an image analysis pipeline for retrieving information on past construction sites. We fuse information retrieved from convolutional neural networks for image analysis on airborne images with georeferencing and external data sources to retrieve a detailed description of the construction site at hand. The applicability of our approach is presented in a case study.

2. Related work

Image analysis, as part of computer vision, is a heavily researched topic, that got even more attention through recent advances in autonomous driving and machine learning related topics. For effective and efficient image analysis and object recognition, machine learning algorithms have been increasingly used during the last decades. In 2012, the convolutional neural network (CNN) "AlexNet" (Krizhevsky, Sutskever, and Hinton, 2012) achieved a top-5 error of 15.3% in the prestigious ImageNet Large Scale Visual Recognition Challenge (Russakovsky et al., 2015). These results were surprisingly accurate at the time, proving the advantages of using CNN. On this account, the software industry shifted towards using CNN for all machine learning based image processing tasks (LeCun, Bengio, and Hinton, 2015).

Image analysis on construction sites, on the other hand, is a rather new topic. Since one of the key aspects of machine learning is the collection of large datasets, current approaches focus on data gathering. Tajeen and Zhu (2014) present an image dataset containing numerous annotated images of construction equipment, however centering on excavation phase (excavator, loader, dozer, roller and backhoe) and images taken from ground. Kropp, Koch, and König (2018) detect indoor construction elements based on similarities, focusing on radiators. In the scope of automated construction progress monitoring, Han et al. published an approach for Amazon Turk based labelling (Han and Golparvar-Fard, 2017). Bügler et al. (2017) combined photogrammetric methods and video analysis to assess the progress of earthworks. To this end, they created point clouds to measure the volume of excavated soil and detected truck dumpers on images using foreground detection. Jahr, Braun, and Borrmann (2018) use an artificial intelligence approach to detecting formwork elements on UAV imagery of construction sites.

3. Methodology

To generalize implicit knowledge from airborne images, we propose an image analysis pipeline utilizing machine learning algorithms, georeferencing, as well as data retrieval (see Figure 1). In a first step, we detect construction sites by using an object detection algorithm on the airborne images. If at least one construction site is detected, an instance segmentation algorithm is used to detect individual elements of the construction. In this paper, we concentrate on detecting tower cranes, as they highly affect construction progress. To enable georeferencing, surveying information on the images is required. To be able to estimate element dimensions, the images are orthorectified. Additional information relevant to the construction site, such as building dimensions, property lines, or neighboring constructions, can be retrieved by georeferencing the image and linking it to spatial information retrieved from the cadastral map or other geoinformation services, such as OpenStreetMap or city models. Finally, all information retrieved is stored in a database for reliable data management and access.

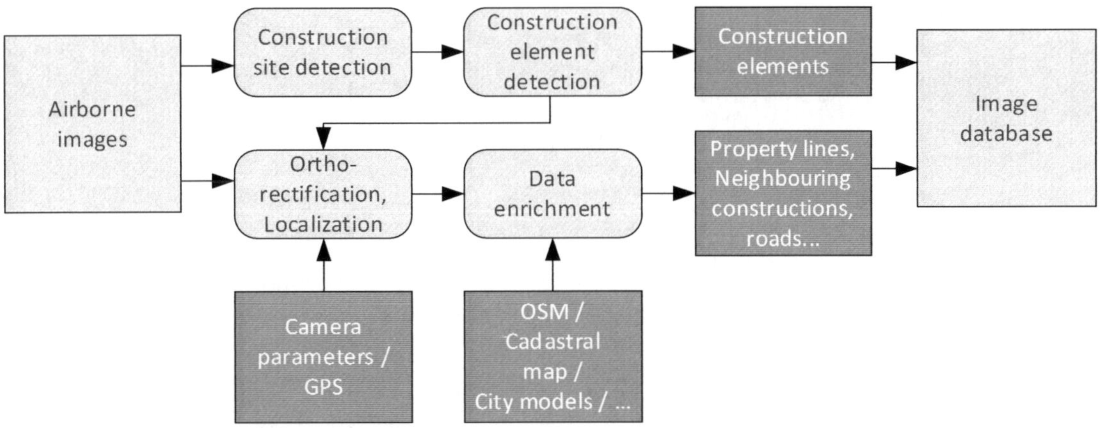

Figure 1: Image analysis pipeline: In a first step, airborne images are scanned for construction sites. If any were found, individual construction elements are detected. To retrieve correct dimensions, the images are orthorectified and georeferenced. Additional data sources are used to add context.

3.1 Image analysis on airborne images

To evaluate the photographs, we use two different CNNs: the first network detects construction sites on airborne images, the second network segments the resulting cropped images.

Image analysis using convolutional neural networks. There are different tasks to be solved by image processing algorithms. Well known tasks include classification, where classes of single-object images are recognized; object detection, where several objects in one image may be classified and localized within the image; and image segmentation, where individual pixels are classified (Rusk, 2015). In this paper, we focus on object detection and instance segmentation using CNNs.

CNNs are structured in locally interconnected layers with shared weights (see Figure 2). Each layer comprises multiple calculation units, or neurons. The neurons of the first layer (input layer) represent the pixels of the analyzed image, the last layer (output layer) comprises the predictable object classes. Between input and output layer, any number of hidden layers can be arranged. To adapt to different problem domains, such as recognizing construction site elements, CNNs are trained. During training, the connections between certain neurons are increased, while the connections between other neurons are reduced—the weights connecting consecutive layers are weighted. The training is usually carried out using supervised backpropagation, meaning the network is fed with exemplary input-output pairs (Rusk, 2015). The expected output, viz. correct solution, for each input is called ground truth. To train a CNN towards reliable predictions, a significant amount of training data is required, which has to be prepared in a preprocessing step. To accelerate the training processes, weights of previously trained CNNs can be used. To adapt pretrained CNNs, usually the last layers are replaced with layers representing the new problem domain before training with new data.

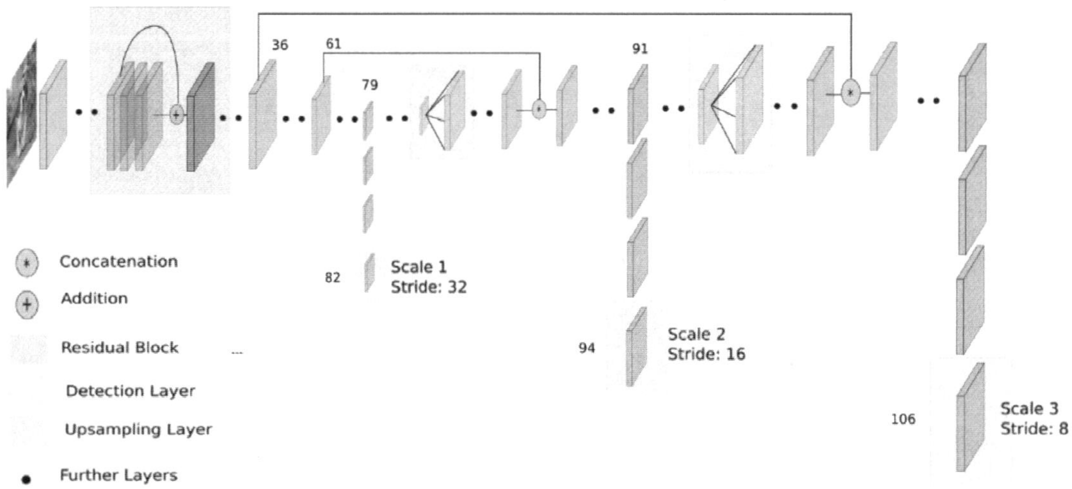

Figure 2: Layered structure of YOLOv3 (slightly modified from https://towardsdatascience.com/yolo-v3-object-detection-53fb7d3bfe6b)

Detecting construction sites using convolutional neural networks. To collect information on construction sites, first, they have to be localized. The task to classify and localize objects on images containing several objects of different types is called object detection (Rusk, 2015). To solve this task, algorithms usually predict rectangular areas (bounding boxes) with high probabilities of object occurrences, as well as the corresponding object class. To measure the performance of an algorithm, the intersection of union between prediction and correct solution is examined. Acknowledged measures include precision (How many of the predictions are correct?), recall (How many relevant items are predicted?) and mAP (mean average precision, calculated from recall and precision).

In this paper, we used an "you only look once" network (YOLOv3, see Figure 2) in Darknet framework (Redmon & Farhadi, 2018). YOLOv3 is a single shot detector, which enables reasonable prediction rates with very fast training and prediction times compared to other leading algorithms. YOLOv3 divides the input image in a grid, where each cell predicts only one object. Predictions of objects of varying sizes are enabled by a feature pyramid network—YOLOv3 makes predictions at three different scales for each location. To predict the bounding box of the detected object, YOLOv3 uses anchor boxes with dimensions tailored to the specific problem domain.

Segmenting construction elements using convolutional neural networks. As exact information on the whereabouts and dimensions of the site equipment is desired, each equipment has to be detected as precisely as possible. We want to know the exact shape of the object rather than its bounding box. Therefore, we need an instance segmentation algorithm that labels images pixelwise and is able to distinguish not only between several classes, but between several objects of the same class.

A very capable algorithm for instance segmentation is Mask R-CNN (He, Gkioxari, Dollár, and Girshick, 2017). Mask R-CNN predicts instance masks for detected objects in two stages: firstly, it uses a RoI (region of interest) Align network to locate bounding boxes and classes for possible objects. Secondly, a semantic segmentation model is used to determine the exact object outlines within the bounding box. Since only one object should be contained in each bounding box, a binary classifier mapping the pixels 1/0 is sufficient—1 representing the presence, 0 the absence of an object.

3.2 Orthorectification of images

Aerial images are not only source of information about the captured scene regarding the content but can also deliver information about localization of the objects and metric information. To be able to measure and localize objects in aerial images, the following information is needed:

- Exterior orientation parameters for each image (position and orientation of the camera during acquisition)
- Interior orientation parameters of the camera (obtained in the calibration process)
- Meshed digital Surface Model (DSM) generated from the images itself, if stereo pairs are provided, or DSM from another source.

Georeferencing. Determining the exterior orientation of the camera in the world coordinate system is called georeferencing. This can be done either by using ground control points (GCPs), or by using the GNSS (global navigation satellite system) position together with inertial measurement unit (IMU) and system calibration for camera orientation (direct georeferencing). Direct georeferencing has the advantage that the manual effort of measuring the GCPs is avoided. The accuracy of the direct georeferencing depends on the quality of the GNSS signal and can vary from few decimeters to few meters (Pfeifer, Glira, and Briese, 2012).

Ground Sample Distance. To estimate true dimensions in aerial photographs, the distance between two pixels on ground (Ground Sample Distance, GSD) must be known. In traditional aerial photogrammetry, images are acquired using nadir view. Assuming a locally flat Earth surface and knowing flight altitude, sensor size and camera constant (focal length), the GSD can be calculated. The altitude is determined relatively to the reference surface and not the terrain (Figure 3). Therefore, changes in the terrain height and presence of other objects (e.g. high buildings) lead to varying GSD. Furthermore, the flight altitude does not remain constant over the whole flight campaign, as well as vertical acquisition geometry not always can be ensured. Accordingly, only approximate GDS can be indicated. Modern aerial photogrammetric camera systems use a combination of nadir and oblique view cameras, delivering additional views on building facades and other 3D objects. GSD in oblique images, however, cannot be determined.

Orthophoto. During orthorectification, aerial images in central projection are transformed into orthogonal projection in order to unify the GSD and allow direct measurements in the images (Figure 4). For each cell of the DSM mesh, the corresponding part of the image is identified and transformed onto the DSM. The resulting mesh is then ortho-projected on a regular grid created on the reference surface with defined GSD. We orthorectify not only the color image, but also obtained labels.

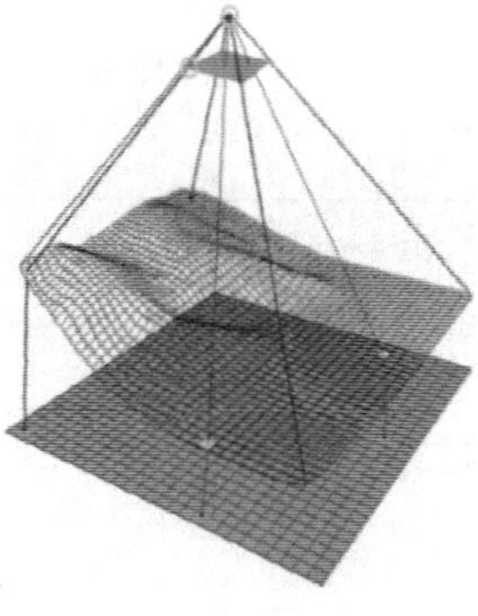

Figure 3: Flight altitude, terrain height and reference surface

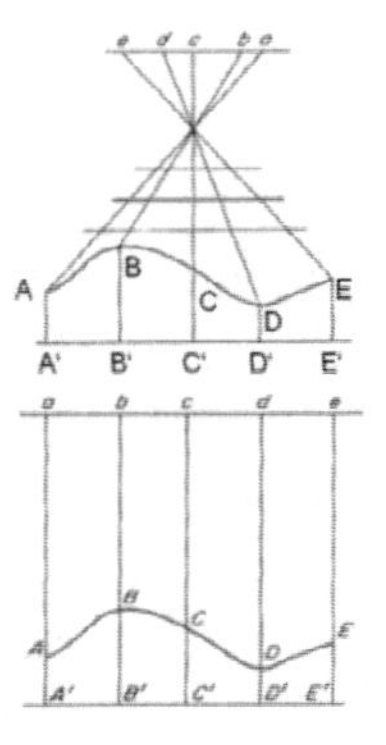

Figure 4: Orthorectification of a central projection

3.3 Additional sources and data enrichment

Surrounding amenities and conditions of construction sites pose big influences on the site equipment. For example, neighboring buildings might influence tower crane positions and minimum dimensions to ensure safe operation without interference; access roads are highly relevant for material supply and will influence construction roads and storage area positioning. If the location of a construction site has been determined through georeferencing the image, the information on that construction site can be enriched using spatial information on the surrounding amenities. Spatial information is available from different sources, e.g. cadastral maps. Cadastral maps show property lines and ownerships and may include additional information such as parcel numbers and existing structures.

A wide selection of digital geodata is available on OpenStreetMap[1] (OSM). OSM aims to collect and provide data under an open license. The geodata provided includes, inter alia, roads, parks, building outlines, and amenities such as fire hydrants and post boxes. While the data can be viewed as map representation, several APIs are available for data access, of which Overpass API is currently well maintained. Overpass works with queries either in xml or in its native language, Overpass QL. In this paper, we used the Overpass API with Overpass QL to retrieve information on neighboring buildings and roads.

Additional 3-dimensional information could be retrieved from city models. Depending on the model's Level of Detail (LoD), buildings are represented as 3D blocks (base area and height) or with increasing detailing, such as roof shape, window areas and even interior construction. City models are widely available. For storing and exchanging city models, the open standard CityGML, among other data models, might be used.

4. Case study

The presented image analysis steps were implemented individually to prove the proposed approach. The results are presented in the following sections.

4.1 Generating ground truth data for image analysis

To create ground truth data for both CNNs, we used airborne images provided by the German Aerospace Center (DLR) (Kurz et al., 2012). The aerial photographs were not commissioned for this paper, but rather repurposed from other applications, therefore not leading to additional data recording efforts. The images were gathered in Germany, both by airplane and helicopter. In total, approximately 4.500 high resolution images with varying image sizes have been sighted and labeled. In a first step, we extracted manually all images that contain construction sites within the construction phase (characterized by the use of tower cranes; visible material storage; first construction elements have been erected. See Figure 5). Subsequently, to generate the object detection dataset, we added bounding boxes for all construction sites using the labeling platform "Labelbox"[2]. We translated the labels from Labelbox format to YOLO format and split the data in training, testing and validation data set (Table 1).

Table 1: Number of images used for training, testing and validation, and number of construction sites

Images total	Number of construction sites	Training (70%)	Testing (20%)	Validation (10%
4443	1727	1209	345	173

[1] https://www.openstreetmap.org
[2] https://labelbox.com/

To prepare the segmentation dataset, we used images of tower cranes taken by UAVs, and images taken by hand cameras (mostly from below) (Figure 6). Additionally, we further processed images from the object detection dataset. We added a margin around the construction site bounding boxes to ensure that all relevant information is contained (especially tower cranes reaching outside construction field) and cropped along the labels. Corresponding image areas for neighboring construction sites with overlapping bounding boxes are contained in both crops. We again used Labelbox to add polygonal labels for all tower cranes. For training the Mask R-CNN network, we decided to use the COCO data format. In this case, too, we split the data in 70% training data, 20% testing data and 10% validation data.

Figure 5: Samples for cropped images containing construction sites

Figure 6: Samples for hand held camera and UAV images of tower cranes

4.2 Training CNNs for object detection and instance segmentation

Object detection with YOLOv3. For training the construction detection network, we use a YOLOv3 architecture in Darknet (Redmon and Farhadi, 2018). To better adapt the network to the construction site dataset, we regenerated the anchor sizes. To that end, we used k-means clustering on the aggregate of bounding boxes in the construction site dataset. The resulting 9 clusters for bounding box width and length, normalized on the respective image size (see Figure 7), are used as length and width of the anchors.

To reduce training time and retrieve better results with our limited data set, we use the pretrained weights of the Darknet53 network. Training for 1000 epochs took approximately 10h on an Nvidia DGX-1. Examples for resulting bounding boxes are depicted in Figure 8. While bounding boxes for smaller construction sites are very well predicted, the CNN is not yet sufficiently adapted for larger construction sites. When sighting the dataset, it gets apparent, that smaller construction sites are predominant in residential areas and make up for a majority of the dataset. To a broader variety of construction sites, the training dataset is currently expanded further. Another step to improve the object detection algorithm entails more extensive preprocessing of the data.

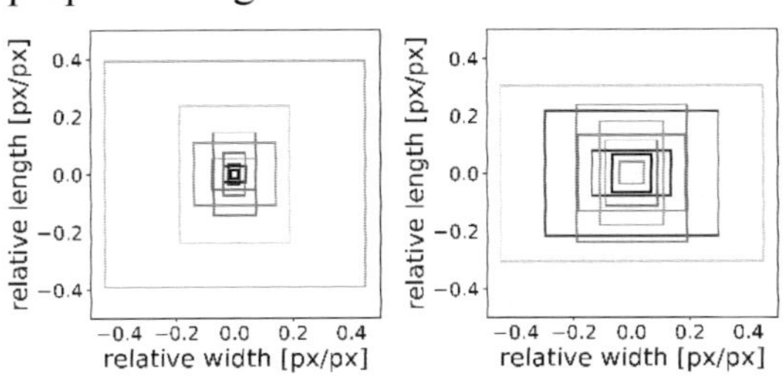

Figure 7: Original YOLOv3 anchor boxes (left) and construction site anchor boxes (right)

Figure 8: Examples for resulting bounding boxes from validation set

Tower crane segmentation with Mask R-CNN. For image segmentation, we used Mask R-CNN in Keras with TensorFlow backend (He et al., 2017). We used pretrained weights from the COCO Dataset (Lin et al., 2014). Mask R-CNN adjusted very fast to the tower crane dataset, leading to low loss after few epochs (Figure 9). Examples for resulting instance bounding boxes and masks are depicted in Figure 10. Object bounding boxes are predicted reliably, while, in some cases, masks tend to disconnections. To improve the predictions, the training data set is increased continuously.

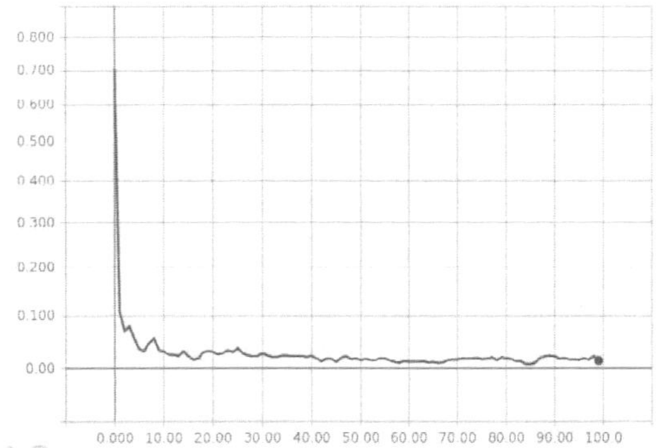

Figure 9: Loss for training Mask R-CNN on tower crane dataset

Figure 10: Examples for resulting masks (in red) from validation set.

4.3 Georeferenced information

In Figure 11, we present results for orthorectification. First, the DSM was generated (left) and then the orthophoto was calculated (right). Here, the seamline dividing the areas covered by color information from two images cuts a tower crane into two parts, which makes it difficult to detect tower cranes directly in the orthophoto. Therefore, cranes were labeled in original aerial images (Figure 12, left) and the labels were orthoprojected on the DSM (Figure 12, right). As we see in Figure 11, crane 1 is not present in the DSM at all, and from crane 2 only the tower of the crane is mapped in the DSM. This is because the crane structure is not easy to reconstruct from images. As a very thin structure, cranes do not provide many points in the point cloud. Points that are detected are on much higher level than the surrounding, therefore many algorithms detect those points as outliers and remove them from DSM. In addition, cranes may move during data acquisition, which leads to further difficulties in the reconstruction. The remedy for this situation is using true orthophotos based on high-density and high-accuracy point clouds, which contain entire tower cranes. True orthophotos, however, require high overlaps between the images (80% in flight direction and 60% between the image stripes). Here not only the difficult geometry of the crane must be considered, but also its dynamic behavior. This aspect should be a subject of our future investigations. Currently, we select for orthorectification labels which are located close to the image center and orthorectify labels object-wise, which means that we prevent seamlines splitting the labels.

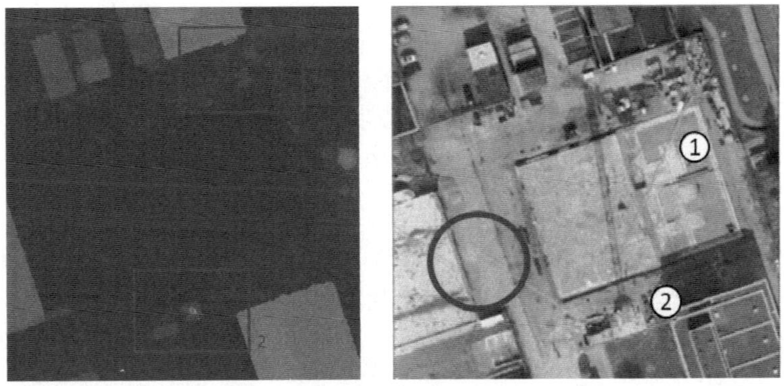

Figure 11: Difficulties with orthorectification of cranes: DSM (left); orthophoto sections with cranes (right)

Figure 12: Orthorectification and georeferencing of labels: aerial image with labeled tower crane (left); orthorectified and georeferenced labels stored as GeoTIFF (right)

4.4 Data enrichment using Overpass API

To retrieve surrounding amenities to the construction site in question from OSM, we used Overpass API. Using the GPS coordinates of the construction's outer corners, we queried adjacent roads and footways as well as neighboring buildings. Overpass API returns the queried data text based (i.e. as json or xml). For monitoring the results, we used Overpass turbo[3] (Figure 13). Overpass turbo is a web-based tool able to run Overpass API queries. The results are shown as interactive map, where further information on the queried nodes can be retrieved. The additional data collected from OSM is added to the information retrieved from the images.


```
<meta osm_base="2019-04-12T11:05:02Z"/>
  <way id="26775855">
    <nd ref="293694475"/>
    <nd ref="293694476"/>
    <nd ref="293694477"/>
    <nd ref="2368200281"/>
    <nd ref="293694475"/>
    <tag k="addr:city" v="Braunschweig"/>
    <tag k="addr:country" v="DE"/>
    <tag k="addr:housenumber" v="35"/>
    <tag k="addr:postcode" v="38106"/>
    <tag k="addr:street" v="Franz-Liszt-Straße"/>
    <tag k="building" v="university"/>
    <tag k="building:levels" v="3"/>
    <tag k="operator" v="TU Braunschweig"/>
  </way>
  <way id="26776014">
    <nd ref="429587899"/>
    <nd ref="293696352"/>
    <tag k="access" v="permissive"/>
```

Figure 13: Neighboring elements (footways, highways, buildings) of the construction site as retrieved by Overpass API. Left: XML scheme, right: Visualization using Overpass turbo, queried elements are marked with blue outlines.

[3] https://overpass-turbo.eu/

5. Summary

In this contribution, we presented an image analysis pipeline capable of detecting construction sites as well as construction elements on airborne images. To gain further information on the situation on site, we retrieve real dimensions of the construction field and tower cranes by orthorectifying the images. Further data sources can be used to enrich the information. Using the overpass API, we retrieve information on the site's surroundings from OpenStreetMap. In the end, we gained a knowledge database for construction sites in Germany, which will be dynamically extended. Next steps include the extension with further construction site elements such as containers or vehicles, connection to city models to retrieve 3D information and the advancement of available algorithms using the knowledge database for solving the CSLP.

References

Bügler, M., Borrmann, A., Ogunmakin, G., Vela, P. A., & Teizer, J. (2017). Fusion of Photogrammetry and Video Analysis for Productivity Assessment of Earthwork Processes. *Computer-Aided Civil and Infrastructure Engineering*, *32*(2), 107–123. https://doi.org/10.1111/mice.12235

Han, K. K., & Golparvar-Fard, M. (2017). Potential of big visual data and building information modeling for construction performance analytics: An exploratory study. *Automation in Construction*, *73*, 184–198. https://doi.org/10.1016/j.autcon.2016.11.004

He, K., Gkioxari, G., Dollár, P., & Girshick, R. (2017). Mask R-CNN. *Proceedings of the IEEE International Conference on Computer Vision*, 2961–2969.

Jahr, K., Braun, A., & Borrmann, A. (2018). Formwork detection in UAV pictures of construction sites. *Proc. of the 12th European Conference on Product and Process Modelling, Copenhagen, Denmark.*

Krizhevsky, A., Sutskever, I., & Hinton, G. E. (2012). Imagenet classification with deep convolutional neural networks. *Advances in Neural Information Processing Systems*, 1097–1105.

Kropp, C., Koch, C., & König, M. (2018). Interior construction state recognition with 4D BIM registered image sequences. *Automation in Construction*, *86*, 11–32. https://doi.org/10.1016/J.AUTCON.2017.10.027

Kurz, F., Meynberg, O., Rosenbaum, D., Türmer, S., Reinartz, P., & Schroeder, M. (2012). Low-cost optical camera system for disaster monitoring. *Int. Archives of the Photogrammetry, Remote Sens. and Spatial Information Sci*, *39*, B8.

LeCun, Y., Bengio, Y., & Hinton, G. (2015). Deep learning. *Nature*, *521*(7553), 436–444. https://doi.org/10.1038/nature14539

Lin, T.-Y., Maire, M., Belongie, S., Hays, J., Perona, P., Ramanan, D., … Zitnick, C. L. (2014). Microsoft COCO: Common objects in context. *European Conference on Computer Vision*, 740–755.

Pfeifer, N., Glira, P., & Briese, C. (2012). Direct georeferencing with on board navigation components of light weight UAV platforms. *International Archives of the Photogrammetry, Remote Sensing and Spatial Information Sciences*, *39*(B7), 487–492.

Redmon, J., & Farhadi, A. (2018). Yolov3: An incremental improvement. *ArXiv Preprint ArXiv:1804.02767*.

Rusk, N. (2015). Deep learning. *Nature Methods*, Vol. 13, p. 35. https://doi.org/10.1038/nmeth.3707

Russakovsky, O., Deng, J., Su, H., Krause, J., Satheesh, S., Ma, S., … Fei-Fei, L. (2015). ImageNet Large Scale Visual Recognition Challenge. *International Journal of Computer Vision*, *115*(3), 211–252. https://doi.org/10.1007/s11263-015-0816-y

Tajeen, H., & Zhu, Z. (2014). Image dataset development for measuring construction equipment recognition performance. *Automation in Construction*, *48*, 1–10. https://doi.org/10.1016/J.AUTCON.2014.07.006

Convolutional Long Short-Term Memory Model for Recognizing Postures from Wearable Sensor

Junqi Zhao, Esther Obonyo
Pennsylvania State University, U.S.
eao4@psu.edu

Abstract. This research investigates the feasibility and viability of applying Deep Neural Networks (DNN) to improve performance with respect to posture recognition based on multi-channel motion data from Wearable Sensors (WS). The authors use the recognition of posture that can be linked to risk of Musculoskeletal Disorder (MSD)- among construction workers as the testbed. The proposed approach is based on the use of a DNN model integrating Convolutional Neural Network (CNN) and Long short-term memory (LSTM) that can achieve automated feature engineering and sequential pattern detection. The model performance was evaluated using datasets collected from four construction workers. The proposed model outperformed baseline CNN and LSTM models. Under the personalized modelling approach, it improved recognition performance by 3% from the benchmark Machine Learning models; the improvement is 2% for generalized modelling approach. The proposed model achieves high-performance posture recognition, which facilitates the MSD prevention in construction through monitoring injury-related postures.

1. Introduction

The authors explore the feasibility and viability of using DNN to improve performance in the recognition of motion data from multi-channel Wearable Sensor (WS) – this data can be treated as high-dimensional data streams (Plötz and Guan 2018). It has been demonstrated that Deep Neural Networks (DNN) models can increase performance in the recognition of objects from high-dimensional data streams. Successful deployments have been in application domains such as Computer Vision, Speech Recognition, and Natural language Processing (Plötz and Guan 2018). Building environment examples include the use of DNN models in the automated objects detection, ranging from pipeline cracks for structure health monitoring (Cheng and Wang 2018) to workers' behaviour monitoring (Xiaochun Luo et al. 2018b). There is an opportunity to deploy DNN models to the detection of awkward postures that compound the risk of workers developing musculoskeletal disorders (MSD) (Zhao and Obonyo 2018). Examples of closely related work research done by Chen et al. (2017) and Ryu et al. (2018). This study focuses specifically on the extent to which DNN-based models can be used to achieve high posture recognition performance using motion data from WS.

An ideal solution is one that can be used to improve the accuracy with respect to the recognition of awkward posture without increasing the computational effort. The use of Machine-Learning (ML)-based models in detecting MSD-related posture from WS output has the advantages of robustness in challenging deployment contexts and ease of data processing (Chen et al. 2017, Ryu et al. 2018, Zhao and Obonyo 2018). It is important to note that conventional ML-based models use the "sliding-window-based analysis pipeline" (Plötz and Guan 2018). The main problems associated with the use of this approach include: i) heuristic engineering biases, ii) ignoring the sequential patterns, and iii) isolation of feature engineering and selection, as well as model optimization. These problems result in the model's performance being sub-optimal. The authors contend that this challenge can be addressed through leveraging DNN's deep hierarchical architecture - more specifically the Convolutional Neural Network (CNN) and the Recurrent Neural Network (RNN). CNN can extract rich features from raw output without manual feature engineering while the Recurrent Neural Network (RNN) can be used to improve the recognition of temporal patterns (Plötz and Guan 2018). It has been demonstrated that the use of a deep hybrid model that integrates the CNN and RNN can result in improved performance with respect to detecting workers' activities from videos (Ding et al. 2018). In the subsequent sections, this research investigates the feasibility of adapting and replicating this approach to posture recognition that can be linked to the risk of MSD among construction workers. The remainder of the paper is organized as follows. Section 2 briefly reviews the research background. Section 3 describes the proposed DNN model configuration and model test. The test result and discussion are reported in Section 4. The conclusion and further work summarized in Section 5.

2. Theoretical Background

2.1 Posture-based MSD Assessment and Prevention

Epidemiological studies have established that physical factors pose the highest risks for MSD (Nunes and Bush 2012). Workers in labor-intensive sectors such as construction routinely adopt awkward working postures. This exposes them to a high risk of developing MSD. Some of these efforts directed at addressing this problem through the development of more proactive safety management practices have focused on the use of emerging wearable sensor technologies to monitor the posture adopted by the targeted workers. Such efforts are at times leverage ergonomics rules to facilitate the monitoring of repetitive awkward postures. Common ergonomic rules include "Rapid Entire Body Assessment" (Hignett and McAtamney 2000), Ovako Working Posture Analyzing System (OWAS) and its extension (Kivi and Mattila 1991), and the ISO 11226:2000 (Normalizacón 2000). The use of such rules in construction relies on the visual assessment of superintendents – these tend to suffer from subjective biases.

2.2 Posture Capture in Construction

Vision-based sensing and wearable sensing techniques present an opportunity for motion data collection in a more effective and efficient way, compared to manual inspection (Wang et al. 2015). Vision-based sensing has exceptionally high accuracy and often comes with powerful analytical tools for assessing both body posture and internal joint load (Han and Lee 2013). However, the vulnerability to occlusion and lighting conditions, as well as data processing complexity (Ding et al. 2018, Hanbin Luo et al. 2018) limits its application to construction sites.

Wearable sensors, particularly the Inertial Measurement Units (IMU), are more applicable to the constraints of working in a construction job site. IMU capture streaming motion data in a non-intrusive, robust, and cost-effective manner (Wang et al. 2015). The raw IMU sensor output can be used to detect awkward posture without the need for a total reconstruction of a 3D human body model. Such advantages are brought by the ML-based posture recognition models. The robustness and flexibility of IMU sensors make them appropriate for use on the construction job site.

2.3 DNN for Posture and Activity Recognition

Conventional ML-based models suffer from three main problems when used in pattern recognition tasks (Plötz and Guan 2018). Firstly, heuristic feature engineering, which manually crafts features, is a time-consuming and biased feature construction process. Secondly, it separates sliding windows, isolates the consecutive sample data and assumes that the time-series motion data are static, which neglects any existing sequential patterns. Thirdly, it separates feature engineering and selection from model tuning during the training process, resulting in sub-optimal performance.

DNN models can address some of these challenges. They have been used successfully in pattern recognition tasks in Computer Vision and Speech Recognition (Plötz and Guan 2018). The multi-layer CNN can automatically extract rich features with increasing complexity from raw data, reducing the bias in manual feature engineering. The RNN has the advantage in capturing sequential patterns. The integration of the CNN and RNN leverages the learning capabilities from both extremely complex features and sequential patterns directly from input data. This ultimately improves the performance of the models.

The use of Computer Vision and DNN for posture recognition in construction research is an emerging area. Zhang et al. (2018) used multilayer CNN to extract view-invariant features from a single video camera for awkward working posture recognition, which significantly improved the model's generality. Hanbin Luo et al. (2018) eliminated the need for reconstructing complex 3D human body models in their posture recognition system, that was developed using a pre-trained CNN model (VGG-16). Ding et al. (2018) deployed the RNN with pre-trained CNN model (Inception V3) to further capture the sequential patterns from the video frames. The resulting hybrid model outperformed the state-of-the-art heuristic feature engineering approaches with respect to activity recognition. In other efforts, it was demonstrated that DNN models can be used detect the misuse of Personal Protective Equipment from multiple workers in the same video scene (Fang et al. 2018a, Fang et al. 2018b). The CNN-based classifier (ResNet-50) can also be used to detect construction equipment, materials, and workers, and recognize interactive construction activities (Xiaochun Luo et al. 2018a). Xiaochun Luo et al. (2018b) demonstrated the feasibility of using the CNN model to detect objects from surveillance cameras. These breakthroughs have been made possible because of two key factors: i) the existence of a robust CNN architecture (such as VGG-16, Inception, and ResNet-50) for automated feature extraction from images and videos; ii) RNN for capturing sequential patterns. Notwithstanding these developments, environmental constraints and the insufficient data for training deep model continue to limit the real-life deployment and scaling of DNN models that use data from vision-based sensing (Ding et al. 2018, Hanbin Luo et al. 2018).

This paper explores the possible strategies for addressing these challenges based on the use of data captured using Wearable IMU sensors. The proposed approach treats motion data from multiple sensor channels that has been segmented into windows of the same dimension as 2D "images." This "trick" enables one to apply DNN models to WS output. A simple DNN model was first introduced into wearable sensing-based posture recognition in an effort to find discriminative features (Plötz and Guan 2018). On-going research work has achieved promising recognition performance (Ordóñez and Roggen 2016, Zeng et al. 2014). The DNN-based models have shown high-performance in recognizing human daily activities and postures from WS output. However, there is no universal, pretrained, and ready-to-use deep model architecture for different scenarios (Plötz and Guan 2018). It is, therefore, necessary to investigate how one can configure a DNN-based model for use in the recognition of construction workers' posture.

3. DNN-based Model Development and Test

The DNN models were implemented using Keras (TensorFlow GPU backend). The model development, training, and testing were done on a Windows 10 PC (Intel Core i7-7700 CPU@ 2.8 GHz, 16GB RAM, NIVIDA GeForce GTX 1060 GPU@16GB RAM). The authors experimented with the use of a DNN-based posture recognition model, which combines CNN and Long short-term memory (LSTM) into a Convolutional-LSTM Network (CLN). The LSTM extends the conventional RNN's ability to capture longer temporary patterns. The CLN was evaluated using both non-recurrent CNN and non-convolutional LSTM as baseline models. The difference between CLN and CNN is the topology of fully connected dense layers, the CLN uses LSTM units as dense layers. The LSTM model uses raw sensor output without features learned from CNN. In this case, the difference in model performance can be attributed to the architecture of the model – the performance is not driven by optimization, pre-processing or ad hoc customization (Ordóñez and Roggen 2016).

3.1 Components in DNN-based Model Architecture

A CLN model example using one-layer CNN and one-layer LSTM is shown in Figure 1.

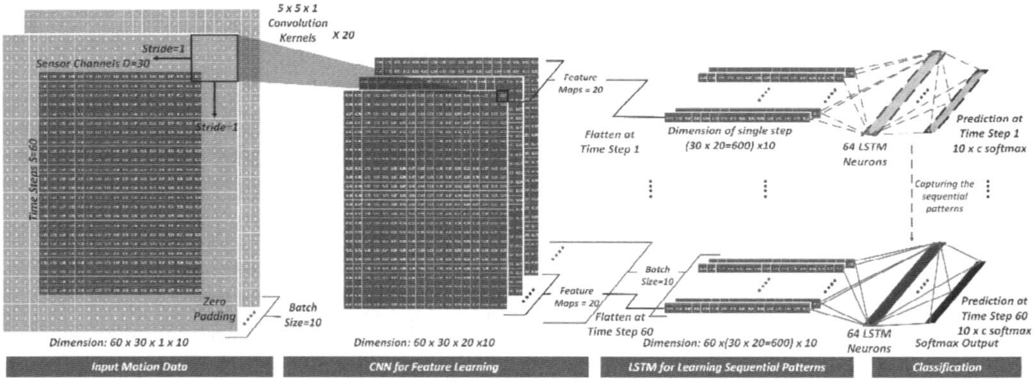

Figure 1 Simple CLN Model Example

Model Input: Model input is segmented by a sliding window. The raw sensor output is normalized for each channel. After segmentation, it can be treated as a 2D image of "S" by "D" (e.g. 60 by 30 in Figure 1), where S is timesteps, and D is the number of sensor channels in a window. All sensor channels are treated as one layer, resulting in an input depth of 1-layer.

Batch and Epoch: The entire dataset for the DNN is divided into multiple (non-overlapping) groups of equal size. One can then feed each group into the model for training. Each group is also referred to as a **batch** (e.g. 10 in Figure 1) for effective model training. One **epoch** of training means all batches of training data pass both forward and backward through the model for once. Multiple epochs can be used for parameter optimization when training data is limited.

Convolutional Layer: A convolutional layer computes the output that is connected to the local region of each sample in the input. The **stride** (e.g. 1 by 1 in Figure 1) quantify the movements of the convolutional kernel along with the vertical or horizontal direction. **Zero-padding** of the input data avoids losing information on the border of 2D input. The reference to "n" convolutional kernels, identifies the number of feature maps (e.g. 20 in Figure 1). This creates an additional dimension of **depth** for the convolutional layers. A **Flatten Layer** is used to establish a full-connected dense layer. It converts each sample's feature maps into a one-dimensional vector representing one sample to be classified.

LSTM Layers: Flattening the CNN output ignores temporal dependencies between different time steps. LSTM can address this problem. Figure 1 shows only the feature maps along the depth dimension are flattened. The vertical time step dimension is reserved for capturing the sequential pattern. Each slice over the time step has a dimension of 600 (features) × 10 (batch size). Samples in a batch fully connect with 64 neurons in LSTM layer. The LSTM neurons are then fully connected with the ***softmax*** layer. This is used to predict the class of each sample in a batch. The LSTM gives a prediction for every time step "t" in sequence. However, the memory of LSTM units tends to become more informed with more time steps pass. This is because the activation information in LSTM neurons at each time step is passed on to the next. This implies that the more time steps LSTM neurons have "seen", the more informative the model can be (Ordóñez and Roggen 2016). Class probability distribution at the last time step "T" is used as a recognition result, when the full sequence in the window have been observed.

Fully-Connected Layer: In the non-recurrent CNN model, all elements in the vector generated by Flatten Layer will connect with neurons in a subsequent fully-connected layer. The last fully-connected layer has an equal number of neurons to the number of class labels. The ***softmax*** function is used to deliver a class probability distribution of samples in the batch. Each sample can be classified by the class label with the highest probability.

3.2 Model Architecture

CLN Model: The proposed CLN model uses four convolutional layers to extract complex features. Each layer has 64 kernels with a size of 5 by the number of sensor channels, 1×1 stride, and zero-padding. Karpathy et al. (2015) and Ordóñez and Roggen (2016) recommend the use of a two-layer LSTM. Each LSTM layer has 128 units. The output from the LSTM is used by the softmax layer for prediction. This model can be expressed as $\boldsymbol{C(64) - C(64) - C(64) - C(64) - RL(128) - RL(128) - Sm}$ (Pigou et al. 2018), where the $\boldsymbol{C(n_c)}$ denotes a convolutional layer with n_c features, $\boldsymbol{RL(n_r)}$ denotes a recurrent LSTM layer with n_r units, $\boldsymbol{Sm}$ is the softmax classification. The hyperbolic tangent function was used in the proposed model to activate neurons in each layer of CNN and LSTM.

Baseline Models: The baseline CNN model was developed by substituting the LSTM layers with two 128-unit dense layers in CLN. The CNN model can be expressed as $\boldsymbol{C(64) - C(64) - C(64) - C(64) - D(128) - D(128) - Sm}$, where $\boldsymbol{D(n_d)}$ denotes a dense layer with n_d units. The baseline LSTM model can be represented as $\boldsymbol{RL(128) - RL(128) - Sm}$. It uses normalized sensor output in each window as model input – it does not use feature engineering.

3.3 Data Collection and Preparation

Four subjects were recruited from nearby construction projects. Five IMU sensors (Mbinet Lab Meta Motion C) were deployed at the hardhat, upper arm, chest center, right thigh, and right calf (Figure 2) by sticking on cloth. After acquiring the workers' consent using Institutional Review Board (IRB)- approved protocols, each subject was asked to perform their routine tasks for 30 minutes. Their activities were recorded for cross-referencing. The data collected are summarized in Table 1.

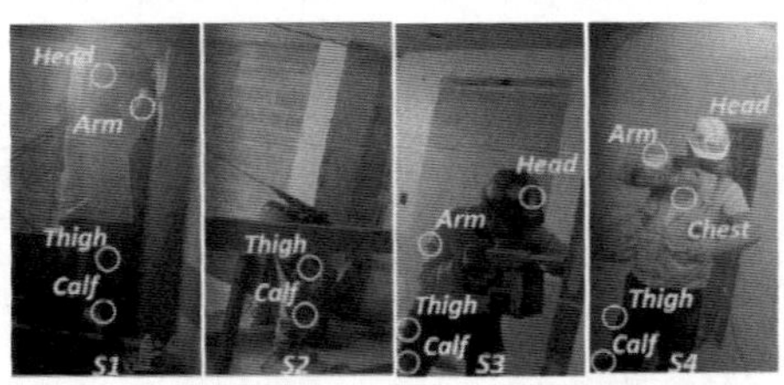

Figure 2. Subjects Working with Sensors (the sensors blocked are not circled)

The output was down-sampled to 40 Hz from all the sensors' channels for S2, S3, and S4. The data for S1 was collected at 25 Hz and down-sampled to 20 Hz. Each record was labelled with video reference. This research used a 1-second window with 50% overlap for segmentation. Each window was labelled using the majority label in the window.

Table 1 Description of Field Dataset (Detailed description provided in Appendix 1)

Subjects	Activities Labels with Proportion	Label Explanation
S1 Masonry	BT (14.7%), KN (2.0%), LB (12.3%), OW (7.2%), ST (52.4%), WK (3.4%)	BT-Static bending and minor movement with bending, and short-term pick up. KN-Kneel on one leg and both legs OW-Overhead Work with one arm or both arms SQ- Squatting, ST-Standing, LB-Literal Bend. NULL-transit movements. The posture data without video reference (due to block) was not labelled, resulting in labelled postures not adding up to 100%
S2 Demolition	BT (72.9%), NULL (4.3%), ST (12.5%), WK (9.1%)	
S3 Electrician	BT (13.6%), KN (46.7%), NULL(15.0%), SQ (3.0%), ST (22.0%)	
S4 Electrician	BT (12.3%), ST (71.5%), WK (12.3%)	

3.4 Set-up for the Model Training and the Model Implementation

Dataset Splitting for Model Training and Testing: Stratified random shuffle was used to split the dataset. This ensured that the same class distribution was maintained in both train and test data. 8:2 ratio is the recommended "rule of thumb" for splitting the datasets in related studies (Ordóñez and Roggen 2016). This set-up was used to fully train the DNN models. The ratio used for the training and validation was set at 9:1 (higher than the recommended ratio). The splitting was repeated five times using different random state. This minimized bias in dataset splitting and improved the reliability of model evaluation.

Model Performance Evaluation Metric: The construction workers' postures are highly unbalanced between classes. This reflects the natural human postures. The classification accuracy is insufficient for measuring model performance - a naive model would achieve high accuracy by classifying every sample as the majority class. The authors used the Macro F1-score to account for this imbalance. The F1-score for each label was acquired using the harmonic mean of Precision and Recall. By giving equal weights to the majority and minority labels when evaluating overall performance for all labels, the model can be trained to achieve high-performance for recognizing all postures. The Macro F1-score is calculated in Equation (1) using an unweighted average. "N" in the equation denotes the number of class labels. High Macro F1- scores reflect high classification performance.

$$\text{Macro F1} = \frac{1}{N}\sum_i 2\,\frac{\text{Precision}_i \times \text{Recall}_i}{\text{Precision}_i + \text{Recall}_i} \qquad \text{Equation (1)}$$

Checkpoint in Model Training: The model performance does increase consistently after every epoch during the training process. The models were trained until their performance ceased to improve. This occurred after *300 epochs*. The model training checkpoint was set to save the trained model with improved performance in an "overwritten" way. It saved the DNN models with the best performance after all epochs. A dropout operation (50%) was used before fully-connected layers to control model overfitting.

4. Result and Discussion

4.1 Model Performance Evaluation

The evaluation was based on the use of conventional ML-based models as the benchmark on the same dataset. The features used in the benchmark models were the same as the authors' previous experiments (Zhao and Obonyo 2018). Classification algorithms in ML-based models include Support Vector Machine (SVM), K-Nearest-Neighbour (KNN), Naive Bayes (NB), Decision Tree (DT), and Random Forest (RF) as an ensemble model. The differences between DNN and ML models are features constructed and classification models used. The ML models were implemented using Scikit-learn (Pedregosa et al. 2011). Results are given in Table 2.

Table 2 Performance Evaluation of Deep Architectures (Macro F1 Score as a metric)[1]

Models	S1	S2	S3	S4
CLN	**0.872**	**0.784**	**0.898**	0.846
CNN	0.872	0.783	0.891	0.771
LSTM	0.826	0.772	0.880	**0.855**
Best Benchmark	0.869	0.664	0.840	0.823

The recognition model's performance for each subject reflects the "personalization" capabilities of the proposed approach, which can be used to capture individual posture idiosyncrasy (Plötz and Guan 2018). Table 2 shows the proposed CLN model consistently outperformed the benchmarking models by an average of 3%. However, CNN and LSTM models were outperformed by the benchmarking model for S4 and S1. This supports the hypothesis that the CLN model can leverage the advantages from both the CNN and LSTM layers. The result is consistent with previous work which integrated CNN and RNN models in vision-based (Ding et al. 2018) and WS-based (Ordóñez and Roggen 2016) studies.

Confusion matrixes are constructed to assess model errors (Appendix 2). LSTM models make most classification errors when distinguishing postures between bent, working overhead, and standing (S1). The models also make errors in recognizing transitional postures (S2 and S3). This may be due to the lack of convolutional layers, which limits the LSTM models in learning complex features. The sequential patterns alone are not enough for effective postures recognition. The authors contend that proper feature engineering can be used to improve the models' performance. The proposed CNN model's low performance for S4 stems from the high recognition errors associated with walking posture. This may be caused by data imbalance. S4 contains least postures types and an imbalanced postures distribution. The imbalanced dataset may lead to the overfitting for majority postures and low performance for recognizing minority.

Improved recognition performance contributes to the reliability of posture-based MSD risk assessment. The frequency of awkward postures can be detected more accurately, which enhances the validity of MSD risk level assessment using OWAS. The recognition accuracy greatly influences the ease with which postures can be detected continuously (Ordóñez and Roggen 2016). Improved accuracy can help avoid problems such as false alarm and missing real-time posture assessment. In subsequent research efforts, the authors will investigate these potential improvements further.

4.2 Analysis of Model Generalization

The use of the deep learning model makes it possible for one to generalize deployment of the author's proposed posture recognition approach to new individuals (Plötz and Guan 2018). Datasets S2 and S4 were downsampled to 20 Hz and combined with S1 as S5[2]. The generalized models used were based on the architecture described in Section 3.2 (see the 4 convolutional

[1] The detailed evaluation result of models is provided in Appendix 3 and Appendix 4.

[2] S2 was not used as it did not contain sensor output from arm.

layers in Figure 4). As shown in Table 3, the CLN model consistently outperformed the baseline DNN models. The best benchmarking model's performance also improved by over 2%. This supports the hypothesis that CLN model can successfully extract common subject-invariant features from different subjects. The observations also indicate that the performance of the model was better than what is observed when the heuristic features engineering approach is used. The baseline performance for DNN models was higher than that for the generalized approach (compare Table 2 and Table 3). This can be attributed to increased training data size.

Table 3 Performance Evaluation of Generalized Model (Macro F1 Score)

	CLN	CNN	LSTM	Benchmark (SVM[3])
S5	0.852	0.813	0.827	0.835

The generalized models' confusion matrices (Figure 3) depicts how the CLN model improves the benchmarking model (SVM). CLN and SVM give a comparable performance in recognizing common postures from multiple subjects (BT, KN, ST, WK). The CLN model exhibited a more superior performance when the recognized postures were limited to only one subject (LB, NON, OW, SQ). The CLN outperformed the benchmarking model by 28% when detecting transitional postures (NULL). This may be explained by the CLN's ability to capture sequential data patterns and identify dynamic postures. The results also show that the CLN model can be used to effectively detect an individual's unique postures even where there is less data.

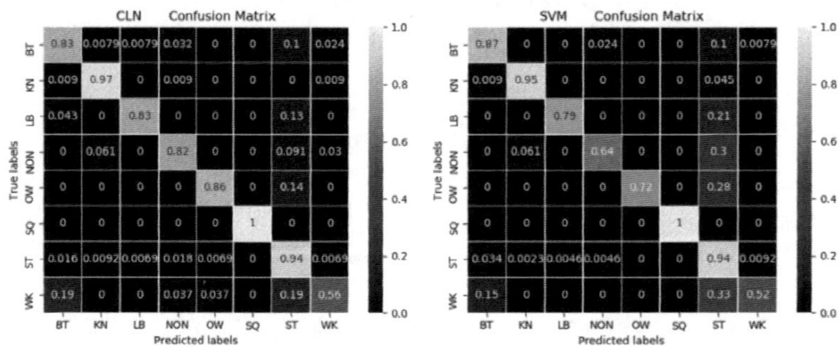

Figure 3 Confusion Matrices for CLN and Benchmarking SVM

4.3 Analysis of Fusing Multi-Sensor Channels

The output from different sensor channels was fused directly based on an assumption that they were similar to pixels in images. The validity of this assumption was assessed using the CLN model's performance when fusing different sensor channels on the S5 dataset. It was established that modifying the convolutional kernel sizes can allow the direct fusion. The performance increased by 1.9% when fusing two types of channels. These findings suggest fusing motion data across channels is an appropriate strategy for proposed CLN model. Accelerometers contribute more to increased recognition performance. Table 4 shows that the model using data from the accelerometer resulted in superior performance than that based on data from the gyroscope. These findings are consistent with observations form Ordóñez and Roggen (2016).

Table 4 Performance Evaluation of Fusing Multi-Sensor Channels (Macro F1 Score)

	Accelerometers	Gyroscopes	Accelerometers+ Gyroscopes
Convolutional Kernel	20Hz*15channels	20Hz*15channels	20Hz*30channels
CLN Performance	0.836	0.592	0.852

[3] The benchmarking model is SVM with 90 features selected using Recursive Feature Elimination.

4.4 Analysis of Hyperparameter

Convolutional layers' depth influences DNN models' ability to learn complex features. The authors compared the performance of baseline CNN model with varying depths using dataset S5. The goal was to evaluate influences from convolutional layers without considering the influence of the LSTM layers.

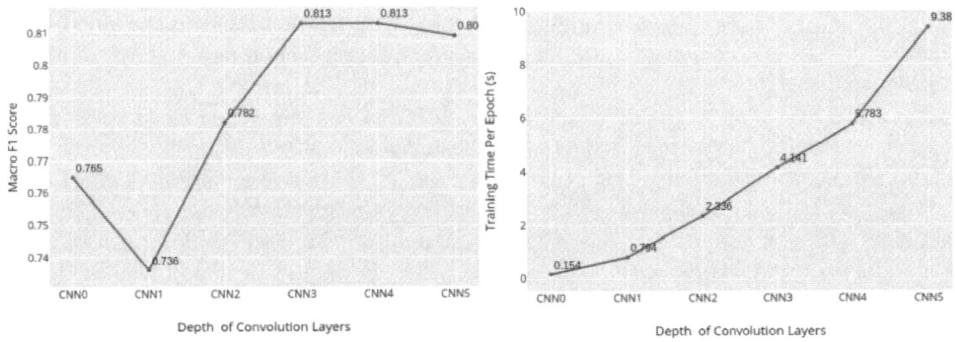

Figure 4 Analysis of Convolutional Layer Depth

As shown in Figure 4, increasing the depth of the convolutional layer from one to three significantly improves the model's performance. There is a plateau when convolutional layer depth reaches four, after which the model's performance starts to decrease. Without the convolutional layers, the tested CNN model becomes a Multilayer Perceptron (MLP) model ($\boldsymbol{D(128) - D(128) - Sm}$). The CNN model's performance is no better than the MLP model when only one convolutional layer is used. These results suggest that the convolutional layers can be used to extract features effectively as long as the optimal depth has been identified. The improper feature representation from one shallow convolutional layer can have an adverse impact on the model's performance. As show in Figure 4, too deep of an architecture can decrease the model's performance. Besides the problem of overfitting, the deep architecture can also result in a "varnishing gradient" problem, that is, when the model's performance decreases because of the architecture becoming too complex. Additionally, the model training time increases significantly when it goes deeper. It is necessary to tune the depth for balancing complexity and performance.

5. Conclusion and Future Work

The proposed use of a CLN model can improve the performance of recognizing construction workers' postures based on the use of data obtained from wearable IMU sensors. The consistently high-performance of the CLN model supports that the author's position that: i) the integrated CLN model can take advantage both CNN and LSTM models' power to further improve the DNN-based model performance; ii) an automated feature extraction approach can reduce engineering bias in the heuristic feature engineering process, thus resulting in improved recognition performance.

The CLN model can capture both the "subject-invariant" common features and unique features of a specific subject. This outcome cannot not be easily achieved when using the heuristic feature engineering approach. The CLN model can be a promising approach to balance generalization and personalization (Plötz and Guan 2018). This is an important goal in ML-based posture recognition. The CLN model can also be applied directly to output from WS. The deployed CLN model can learn complex features directly from the raw sensor output. CLN model performance tends to increase with more sensor channels. However, it is recommended to tune the convolutional layer depth as a hyperparameter for DNN-based models. The learning power may not be fully leveraged in shallow and overly deep models.

The authors have extended the application of DNN-based models beyond vision-sensing to multi-channel motion sensing data. The proposed approach was validated using the need for accurate posture recognition in MSD risk assessment based on the use of data derived from WS. In subsequent efforts, the authors will refine the DNN models' hyperparameters and deploy ensembled DNN models for performance improvement. The developed model will be reconfigured for deployment on mobile devices in real-time. The authors will also investigate the CLN performance on "unseen" subject's data.

References

Chen, J., Qiu, J. and Ahn, C. (2017) Construction worker's awkward posture recognition through supervised motion tensor decomposition. Automation in Construction, 77, pp. 67-81.

Cheng, J. C. and Wang, M. (2018) Automated detection of sewer pipe defects in closed-circuit television images using deep learning techniques. Automation in Construction, 95, pp. 155-171.

Ding, L., Fang, W., Luo, H., Love, P. E., Zhong, B. and Ouyang, X. (2018) A deep hybrid learning model to detect unsafe behavior: integrating convolution neural networks and long short-term memory. Automation in Construction, 86, pp. 118-124.

Fang, Q., Li, H., Luo, X., Ding, L., Luo, H. and Li, C. (2018a) Computer vision aided inspection on falling prevention measures for steeplejacks in an aerial environment. Automation in Construction, 93, pp. 148-164.

Fang, Q., Li, H., Luo, X., Ding, L., Luo, H., Rose, T. M. and An, W. (2018b) Detecting non-hardhat-use by a deep learning method from far-field surveillance videos. Automation in Construction, 85, pp. 1-9.

Han, S. and Lee, S. (2013) A vision-based motion capture and recognition framework for behavior-based safety management. Automation in Construction, 35, pp. 131-141.

Hignett, S. and McAtamney, L. (2000) Rapid entire body assessment (REBA). Applied Ergonomics, 31(2), pp. 201-205.

Karpathy, A., Johnson, J. and Fei-Fei, L. (2015) Visualizing and understanding recurrent networks. arXiv preprint arXiv:1506.02078.

Kivi, P. and Mattila, M. (1991) Analysis and improvement of work postures in the building industry: application of the computerised OWAS method. Applied Ergonomics, 22(1), pp. 43-48.

Luo, H., Xiong, C., Fang, W., Love, P. E., Zhang, B. and Ouyang, X. (2018) Convolutional neural networks: Computer vision-based workforce activity assessment in construction. Automation in Construction, 94, pp. 282-289.

Luo, X., Li, H., Cao, D., Dai, F., Seo, J. and Lee, S. (2018a) Recognizing Diverse Construction Activities in Site Images via Relevance Networks of Construction-Related Objects Detected by Convolutional Neural Networks. Journal of Computing in Civil Engineering, 32(3).

Luo, X., Li, H., Cao, D., Yu, Y., Yang, X. and Huang, T. (2018b) Towards efficient and objective work sampling: Recognizing workers' activities in site surveillance videos with two-stream convolutional networks. Automation in Construction, 94, pp. 360-370.

Nunes, I. L. and Bush, P. M. (2012) Work-related musculoskeletal disorders assessment and prevention. in Ergonomics-A Systems Approach: InTech.

Ordóñez, F. J. and Roggen, D. (2016) Deep convolutional and lstm recurrent neural networks for multimodal wearable activity recognition. Sensors, 16(1), pp. 115.

Pedregosa, F., Varoquaux, G., Gramfort, A., Michel, V., Thirion, B., Grisel, O., Blondel, M., Prettenhofer, P., Weiss, R. and Dubourg, V. (2011) Scikit-learn: Machine learning in Python. Journal of machine learning research, 12(Oct), pp. 2825-2830.

Pigou, L., Van Den Oord, A., Dieleman, S., Van Herreweghe, M. and Dambre, J. (2018) Beyond temporal pooling: Recurrence and temporal convolutions for gesture recognition in video. International Journal of Computer Vision, 126(2-4), pp. 430-439.

Plötz, T. and Guan, Y. (2018) Deep Learning for Human Activity Recognition in Mobile Computing. Computer, 51(5), pp. 50-59.

Ryu, J., Seo, J., Jebelli, H. and Lee, S. (2018) Automated Action Recognition Using an Accelerometer-Embedded Wristband-Type Activity Tracker. Journal of construction engineering and management, 145(1), pp. 04018114.

Wang, D., Dai, F. and Ning, X. (2015) Risk Assessment of Work-Related Musculoskeletal Disorders in Construction: State-of-the-Art Review. Journal of construction engineering and management, 141(6), pp. 04015008.

Zeng, M., Nguyen, L. T., Yu, B., Mengshoel, O. J., Zhu, J., Wu, P. and Zhang, J. (2014) Convolutional neural networks for human activity recognition using mobile sensors. in 6th International Conference on Mobile Computing, Applications and Services: IEEE. pp. 197-205.

Zhang, H., Yan, X. and Li, H. (2018) Ergonomic posture recognition using 3D view-invariant features from single ordinary camera. Automation in Construction, 94, pp. 1-10.

Zhao, J. and Obonyo, E. (2018) Towards a Data-Driven Approach to Injury Prevention in Construction. in Advanced Computing Strategies for Engineering. EG-ICE 2018,Cham: Springer International Publishing. pp. 385-411.

Appendix

Appendix 1 Description of Collect Dataset

Subjects	Tasks	Collected Data	Used Data	Dataset Size
S1 Masonry	Bricklaying	30.75min @25Hz @30 channels	30.27min @20Hz@30 channels	33260 rows by 30 columns .CSV file 6.54 MB
S2 Demolition	Ground Guardrail Installation	30.64min @50Hz@30 channels	30.27min @40Hz@24 channels[4]	65200 rows by 24 columns .CSV file 10.0 MB
S3 Electrician	Ground Electrical Conduit Installation	26.94min @50Hz@30 channels	18.50min @40Hz@30 channels	44080 rows by 30 columns .CSV file 8.51 MB
S4 Electrician	Wire Pulling	28.48min @50Hz@30 channels	18.50min @40Hz@30 channels	51960 rows by 30 columns .CSV file 10.0 MB

Appendix 2 Performance Evaluation of Deep Architectures

		Model Setup			Model Setup
		Ave_F1	**Epoch_time (s)**	**Exe_time (s)**	
S1	CLN	0.872	3.096	1.137	20Hz*30Channels 333 examples in test dataset
	CNN	0.872	2.400	0.730	
	LSTM	0.826	0.682	1.339	
	Best Benchmark	0.869			
S2	CLN	0.784	3.821	1.385	40Hz*24Channels 326 examples in test dataset
	CNN	0.783	2.563	1.056	
	LSTM	0.772	1.272	1.974	
	Best Benchmark	0.664			
S3	CLN	0.898	3.006	2.750	40Hz*30Channels 220 examples in test dataset
	CNN	0.891	2.097	0.324	
	LSTM	0.880	1.070	1.185	
	Best Benchmark	0.840			
S4	CLN	0.846	3.600	2.251	40Hz*30Channels 260 examples in test dataset
	CNN	0.771	2.356	0.330	
	LSTM	0.855	1.997	2.894	
	Best Benchmark	0.823			

[4] The arm sensor came across malfunction during data collection, the six channels from arm sensor was not considered.

Appendix 3 Performance Evaluation of Benchmarking ML-based Models. FF represent full features, SF represents features selected through Recursive Feature Elimination

		Ave_F1		Train Time (s)		Test Time (s)		Key Model Parameters Setup
		FF	SF	FF	SF	FF	SF	
SVM	S1	0.858	0.811	2.912	0.077	0.278	0.007	Kernel: Radial Basis Function Kernel Coefficient: 1/features Multi-Class: One-vs-one Penalty Parameter C: 1
	S2	0.633	0.606	1.307	0.338	0.098	0.026	
	S3	0.826	0.786	1.924	0.033	0.181	0.003	
	S4	0.820	0.809	1.286	0.103	0.088	0.009	
KNN	S1	0.836	0.807	0.053	0.003	0.702	0.014	K: 7[5] Distance Metric: Euclidean Weight: uniform weight
	S2	0.664	0.582	0.038	0.011	0.485	0.100	
	S3	0.785	0.779	0.038	0.005	0.362	0.007	
	S4	0.830	0.799	0.054	0.010	0.697	0.048	
NB	S1	0.568	0.680	0.026	0.002	0.005	0.000	Prior probabilities: classes proportion
	S2	0.622	0.592	0.036	0.008	0.004	0.001	
	S3	0.720	0.758	0.021	0.004	0.002	0.000	
	S4	0.726	0.773	0.050	0.004	0.009	0.010	
DT	S1	0.776	0.707	2.042	0.060	0.001	0.000	Criterion: Gini index Min Samples for Split: 2 Max Depth: No limits Max Leaf Nodes: No limits
	S2	0.643	0.549	0.813	0.360	0.001	0.000	
	S3	0.779	0.667	0.713	0.023	0.001	0.000	
	S4	0.760	0.778	0.920	0.085	0.001	0.000	
RF	S1	0.869	0.782	4.181	0.513	0.011	0.007	Ensemble Method: Bootstrap Number of Estimators: 100 Estimator: DT Estimator Setup: Same as DT
	S2	0.648	0.600	2.564	1.107	0.009	0.007	
	S3	0.840	0.794	1.859	0.262	0.008	0.006	
	S4	0.822	0.823	1.918	0.483	0.008	0.006	

[5] Parameter tuning from cross-validation.

Appendix 4 Confusion Matrix for DNN Models on Each Subject. For each subject, all the three DNN models used are those giving median performance among the five trained models with stratified shuffle splitting

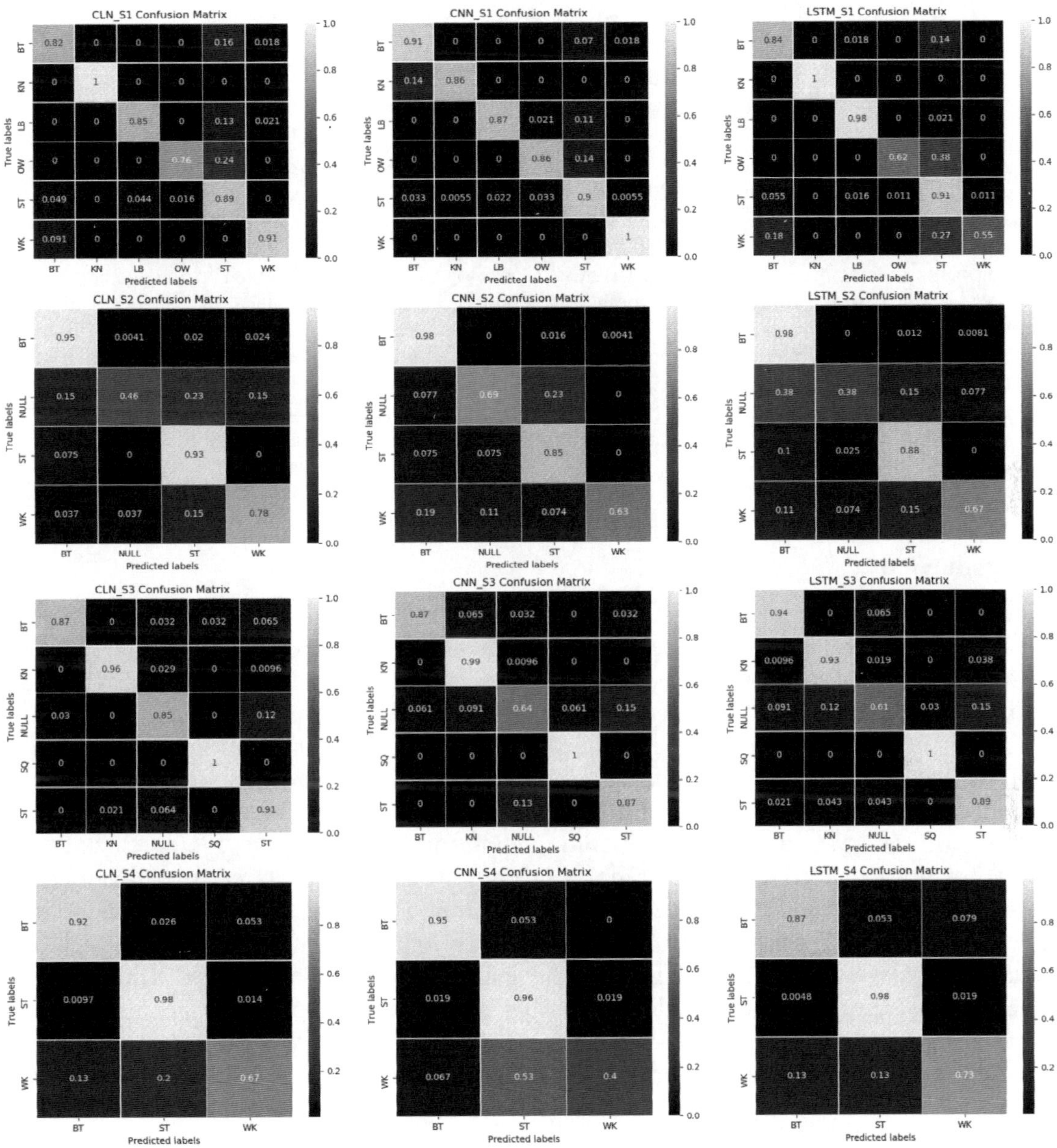

Skills Assessment for Robotics in Construction Education

Fopefoluwa M. Bademosi, Ralph Tayeh, Raja R.A. Issa
University of Florida, USA
mofoluwaso@ufl.edu

Abstract. The construction industry is considered one of the least digitized industries around with most of its processes being repetitive and labor-intensive. However, recently, the industry has witnessed an upsurge in the volume of new technologies implemented in practice. One prospective opportunity for innovative technologies in construction is the implementation of robotics and automation technologies. With these disruptive technologies being implemented in the industry, there is a need to improve pedagogic methods to address the changing demands of the workforce and equip new employees with the abilities required to drive construction robotics processes. The principal purpose of this research is to examine the current applications of robotics technologies in the construction industry in order to identify the foundational knowledge, skills, and abilities (KSAs) construction students must possess to perform in the future workforce successfully. This paper presents the background of construction robotics, the research framework and initial assessment of essential KSAs.

1. Introduction

In recent years, the architecture, engineering, construction, and operations (AECO) industry has witnessed an increase in the volume of new technologies implemented in practice, and the development of innovative technological solutions has evolved to make an impact on the industry as a whole. One prospective opportunity for innovative technologies in construction is the implementation of robotics and automation, which is the application of autonomous machines that carry out construction tasks and operations automatically through intelligent programming and controls (Kamaruddin et al. 2016). Robotics has been introduced into the construction industry as a solution to its productivity problem since the 1960s (Bock 2007). Presently, many advanced technologies are being employed in the field of construction robotics, such as unmanned aerial systems, laser scanning, virtual and augmented reality, autonomous and robotic systems, additive manufacturing, and mobile computing (Oesterreich and Teuteberg 2016). Some of these technologies have already been widely applied while some are just emerging into the market. Consequently, construction companies are increasingly incorporating these advanced construction technologies integrated with a central platform of connected building information modeling (BIM) on construction projects (Oesterreich and Teuteberg 2016).

With these disruptive technologies being implemented in the AECO industry, there is a need to improve the pedagogic methods in training and education to address the changing demands of the workforce. Furthermore, in the face of troubling skilled labor shortages, it is crucial for new recruits to join the construction workforce with the skills and exposure to technologies to drive construction robotics processes and higher levels of precision in construction. Therefore, it is imperative to teach construction robotics and automation to AECO students in institutions of higher learning in order to expose them to advanced construction technologies and equip them with the necessary inter-disciplinary skills and abilities required to thrive in the workforce of the industrialized era. The primary purpose of this research is to identify and examine the current applications of robotics technologies in the construction industry in order to identify the essential knowledge, skills, and abilities (KSAs) construction students must possess to perform in the future workforce successfully. Therefore, the two main objectives of this study are to:

1. Identify the current technology trends and applications of robotics and automation in the construction industry.
2. Determine the perceived critical construction robotics KSAs required to perform construction robotics tasks in the industry.

2. Literature Review

With most of its processes being monotonous and labor-intensive, the construction industry remains one of the least digitized industries around. The industry still operates traditionally, resulting in relatively low productivity when compared to other industrial sectors. The industry calls for more efficient construction companies, effectual and practical construction processes, and advanced construction methods to productively contend for relevance under the pressure of growing urbanization, globalization, technological innovations, and industry competition in the twenty-first century (World Economic Forum 2016). One of the primary problems the construction industry is facing is the stagnant levels of productivity (Barbosa et al. 2017). According to the Bureau of Labor Statistics (2018), the productivity levels in the construction have been on a decline for the past few years when compared to other mature industries, such as the manufacturing industry. The adoption of modern, innovative technologies and processes is very critical for the industry, as an improvement in productivity will have a significant impact on the global economy. Another major challenge associated with the construction industry is the skilled labor shortages, which has sustained a recurrent cyclic trend for the past thirty years (Karimi et al. 2018).

A promising opportunity to improve the productivity, safety, and quality aspects of the construction industry lies in the implementation of innovative robotics and automation technologies Construction robots are intelligent machines operated by smart controls with a variable range in levels of sophistication, and are generally intended to enhance speed and boost the precision of construction processes (Buswell et al. 2007). Construction automation is the application of automated and computerized techniques in construction to perform mechanical operations aimed at reducing time, labor intensity, and risk of exposure to harm, while at the same time preserving and even enhancing the quality of the finished products (Hewitt and Gambatese 2002). Both the terms robotics and automation have been broadly recognized in the construction industry and customarily describe mechanization, unmanned processes, and robotization of construction tasks and processes (Kamaruddin et al. 2016). Therefore, the definition of construction robotics and automation can be synthesized as the application of autonomous machines that carry out construction tasks and operations automatically through intelligent programming and controls.

2.1 Construction Robotics Technologies

The progression in digital technology encountered in several mature industries over the past decade has transformed these industries, thus leading them into a new technological era identified as the Fourth Industrial Revolution, also known as the era of industrialization (Schwab 2017). The term of Industry 4.0 has been used as a concept to describe new developments in manufacturing, and it has been deemed reasonable to use the Industry 4.0 technology as a benchmark to identify the advanced technologies ushering in the era of digitization and industrialization in the construction industry (Oesterreich and Teuteberg 2016). To present the Industry 4.0 technologies in construction effectively, Oesterreich and Teuteberg (2016) completed a content analysis review of several articles. The review method required a broad search of articles by applying the keywords 'Industry 4.0' and 'construction.' The results of the study by Oesterreich and Teuteberg (2016) comprised almost all the leading-edge topics in construction robotics, besides laser scanning. In addition, some of the technologies identified are similar or belong to the same technical sphere. Accordingly, similar technologies are grouped, and the final identified construction robotics technologies are listed in Table 1.

Table 1. Trends in current construction robotics research

Construction robotics technologies	
Reality computing technology	Laser Scanners
	Rovers
	Unmanned Aerial Systems
Simulation technology	Augmented Reality
	Mixed Reality
	Virtual Reality
Automation technology	Additive Manufacturing
	Autonomous Vehicles
	Prefabrication and Modularization
	Robotics systems
Smart Technology	Artificial Intelligence
	Big Data
	Cloud computing
	Cyber-Physical Systems
	Human-Computer Interaction
	Internet of Things (IoT)
	Radio-Frequency Identification

2.2 Applications of Robotics Technologies in Construction

Significant efforts to automate aspects of the construction process and enhance efficiency in the industry have been prevalent since the nineteenth century, as seen in the various manifestation of large and technologically complex construction like long-span bridges (Romero et al. 2014). Construction activities that employed the use of pieces of machinery as an alternative to human labor were new modes of mechanization in construction. By the end of 1970, robotic equipment with the abilities to lay masonry blocks were developed, and by late 1980, there was a growing demand for construction robots in Japan (Kamaruddin et al. 2016). From the review of current literature, it is observed that the range of application of construction robotics and automation technologies is extensive, spanning over all the different phases of the lifecycle of construction projects. These technologies can be implemented post-construction for maintenance and operation activities, until eventual deconstruction. However, the level of robotics and automation technologies implementation differs significantly throughout the different stages of construction, with the actual construction phase being the most prevalent. Some of the current applications of robotics technologies in construction research are shown in Table 2. These applications were selected as a result of focused and organized review of current literature within the last year that showcase state-of-the-art construction robotics technologies and applications.

2.3 Robotics and Automation in Construction Education

The new era of digitization in construction offers immense benefits for the construction industry, the environment, and the economy. The technological disruption of the AECO industry calls for a change in the pedagogic methods in AECO education to address the future of work. The advent of construction robotics technology such as prefabrication, 3D printing, robotic arm systems, big data, and predictive analysis and IoT should influence construction education. It is critical for institutions of higher learning to introduce these new technologies and processes into construction education, to equip students adequately with the knowledge and skills required to thrive in the workforce of the industrialized era. Furthermore, in the face of troubling skilled labor shortages, it is crucial for employees to be equipped with the necessary abilities and exposure to technologies to drive construction robotics processes and higher levels of precision in construction as they join the workforce.

Although research in construction automation and robotics has become well established over the years, transferring the knowledge gained in these fields through classroom teaching has not gained as much traction (Bayne 2015). Furthermore, there is a lack of a collective establishment of fundamental KSAs relevant to the implementation of construction robotics within existing research. As these technologies continue to evolve and continue to make significant advancement in the industry, developing and recruiting young talent will be vital for accelerating innovation and should be a high priority for the industry. Integrating robotics and automation in the broad AECO curriculum will be a significant and viable solution to the growing demand for a strong robotics talent pipeline. This research is a primary action in establishing the essential KSAs necessary to meet workplace job-task performance requirements related to construction robotics in order to develop skilled talent for the future workforce.

3. Methodology

3.1 Framework

To identify the essential KSAs required for construction robotics competency, three primary phases were developed for this study, with each being built upon by a subsequent phase. Figure 1 shows these phases as literature review, semi-structured interviews, and Delphi study. This research is on-going and this paper presents the preliminary results for the first phase, which has been completed.

Literature Review

The first phase of the research was an extensive review of literature on construction robotics and automation. Information on construction robotics technologies was gathered through a comprehensive evaluation of academic literature to establish a foundation for the general knowledge for this study. The especially relevant conference proceedings explored include The American Society of Civil Engineers (ASCE), Construction Research Congress (CRC), The

Institute of Electrical and Electronics Engineers (IEEE), International Symposium on Automation and Robotics in Construction (ISARC), the ASCE Computing Division Computing Workshops, and The Joint Conference on Computing in Construction (JC3) conference series. The journals searched were the Automation in Construction Journal, Journal of Computing in Civil Engineering, Journal of Construction Engineering and Management, Journal of Information Technology in Construction (ITCon), and Journal of Educational Technology. Several academic papers on current construction robotic technologies implemented in the construction industry, with a focus on the United States, were evaluated. Furthermore, the literature review assisted in the preliminary identification of essential KSAs required to meet performance requirements related to construction robotics tasks in the industry. This phase has been completed, and the results are presented in this paper.

Table 2. Current trends in the applications of construction robotic technologies

Authors	Robotics technologies	Construction applications
Wang and Zhang (2019)	Robotic crawler and arm system	Nail and screw recycling
Agnisarman et al. (2019)	Micro aerial vehicles Autonomous robotic systems Unmanned aerial systems Remotely operated vehicles	Routine inspection and maintenance
Camacho et al. (2018)	Additive manufacturing (Robotic 3D printing)	Fabrication of building elements
Zhang et al. (2018)	Mobile robot 3D printers	On-site fabrication of concrete structure
Goessens et al. (2018)	Unmanned aerial systems	Transporting, handling and laying masonry in masonry construction
Kim et al. (2018)	Automated robotic excavator	Earthwork processes
Chen et al. (2018)	Automated robots Robotic 3D printing Digital fabrication	Construction tasks automation
Louis and Dunston (2018)	Internet of Things	Real-time and automated decision-making in repetitive construction operations
Bogue (2018)	Robotic systems Unmanned aerial systems Autonomous ground vehicles Robotic 3D printing	Bricklaying Glazing installation Surveying Project progress monitoring Stockpile and inventory logistics Health and safety assessment Excavation and earthmoving operations Building and infrastructure construction
Lee et al. (2018)	Robotic arm systems	Maintenance work for high-rise building Curtain wall building façade cleaning

Semi-Structured Interviews

The next step in this research is to conduct one-on-one interviews with construction industry and educational professionals considered to be subject matter experts (SME) in robotics and automation. The interviews will be semi-structured to permit deeper investigating and consequently collect a large quantity of data, as the interviewees will be encouraged to examine the research topic and share their opinions based on their experiences. The industry professional expertise solicited in the semi-structured interviews is essential in providing an understanding of the application of robotics and automation technologies in their respective companies. In addition, educators who have been at the forefront of construction robotics research and have introduced construction robotics to students in their classrooms will be sought after. The interviews will establish a baseline for categorizing the vital KSAs considered necessary for construction robotics proficiency. The interview participants will be offered the chance to take part in the subsequent Delphi phase. The findings of the interview will be used to support and cross-validate the findings of the literature review.

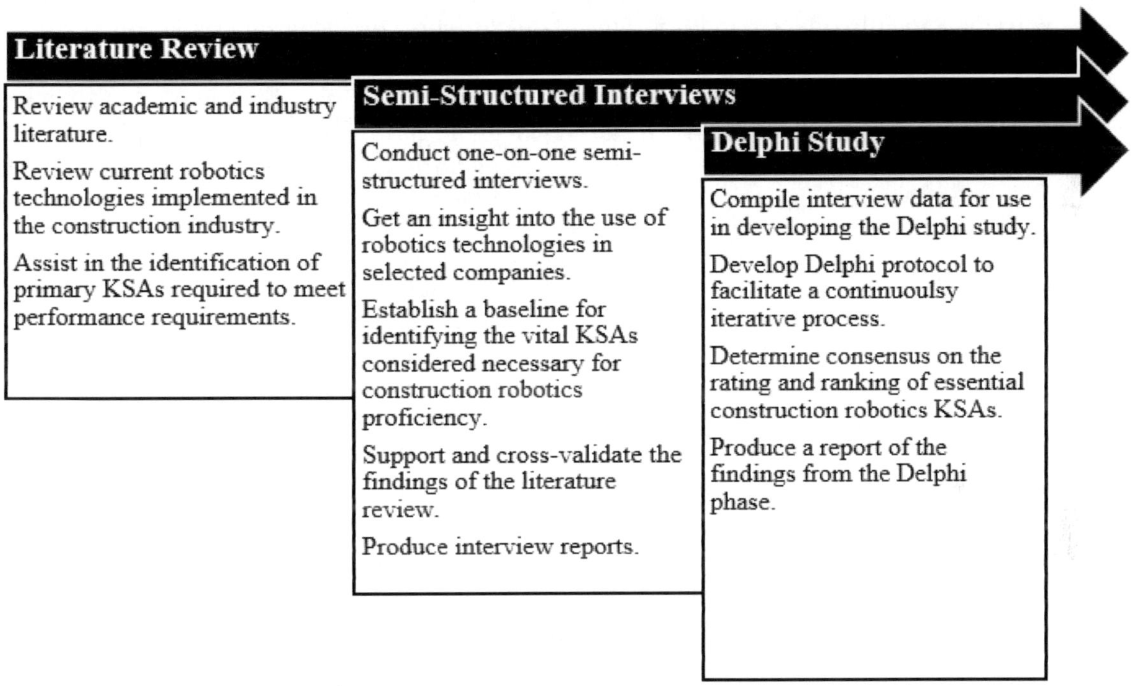

Figure 1: Research Methodology Phases

Delphi Study

The third and final phase of the research will involve the development and execution of a Delphi study with participants from the SME pool identified during the interview phase. During the interview phase, possible involvement in a Delphi study will be discussed with the SMEs and the expectations regarding their participation, time commitment and anticipated outcomes of the Delphi study will be clearly outlined. The list of participants who agree to participate will be created as they are being interviewed and upon completing the informed consent forms. The Delphi study itself will be conducted in multiple stages of development. The Delphi study for this research will be conducted in three iterations. During the first round, a preliminary list of the required construction robotics KSAs will be generated, and the first round will serve as an open discussion among the Delphi panelists to expand the preliminary list and determine the relevance and applicability of each item on the list. Consensus evaluation will be conducted throughout the second and third rounds. At the end of the Delphi study, a final report will be generated to present the perceived important KSAs related to construction robotics according to their ratings and rankings.

4. Results

4.1 Initial Assessment of Construction Robotics KSAs

A content analysis based review technique was employed to develop a preliminary list of the essential construction robotics KSAs. Given the absence of an established framework for determining construction robotics KSAs, several research articles were reviewed to corroborate the implementation of construction robotics technologies and applications, and the research development process and technical requirements associated with them. Inferences were then made by systematically identifying specific characteristics in the articles. The techniques required the review of several publications, from which results were drawn and highlighted in Table 3. The content analysis-based review was carried out in two parts to achieve a systematic review of literature from 2009 to 2019, as shown in Figure 2. A thorough exploration of literature using the Google Scholar search engine using various keywords such as automation, robotics, robotic technologies, construction, construction education, and robotic skills was completed in Phase 1.

Phase 1 resulted in the identification of 53 related articles mostly from the Automation in Construction journal, the International Journal of Advanced Research in Computer Science, the Journal of Computing in Civil Engineering, and the Journal of Information Technology in Construction. The contents of these articles were reviewed and screened in Phase 2 in order to extract publications that were deemed irrelevant to the study. Upon completion of the screening procedure, 34 articles were selected for further analysis. While this two-phase search and review method may not deliver the maximum amount of publications eligible to be evaluated, it adequately presents a substantial volume of significant research, from which this research could extrapolate conclusions and advance to the next phase of the research. From the articles selected for further examination at the end of Phase 2, 29 publications facilitated the development of the preliminary list of the essential KSAs required to perform construction robotics related tasks.

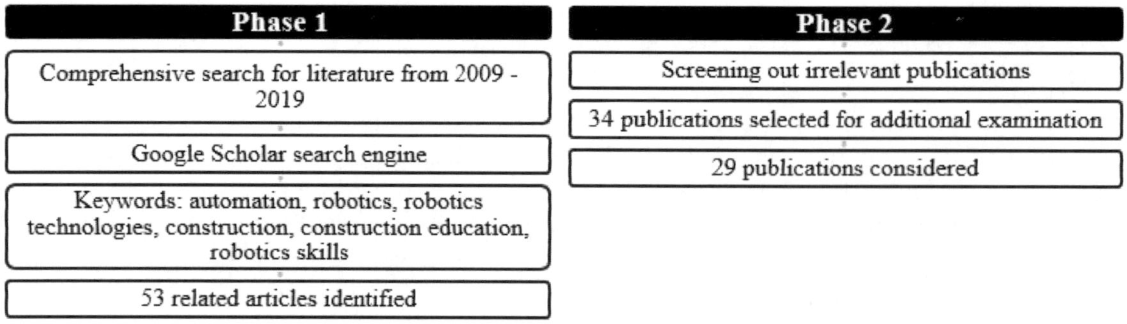

Figure 2: Content Analysis Based Review Method

From the literature review and content analysis based review, the fundamental KSAs that were required to complete the job tasks highlighted in the articles were extracted based on a broad mention in multiple applications, aimed at capturing the complex dynamics of the technologies and processes. These identified KSAs can be broken down into two major categories: computing KSAs and computer science KSAs, as shown in Table 3. The preliminary list will be expanded on and validated during the semi-structured interview phase of this research. After which, the list will be further evaluated during the Delphi study phase where the panel will reach a consensus on the essential KSAs.

Table 3. Identification of foundational construction robotics skills

KSA category	KSAs
Computing skills	Building information modeling
	Cloud computing
	Collaborative environments
	Electronic communications
	Parametric design
	Programming
	Specialized engineering software
Computer science skills	Algorithms and computational complexity
	Automated reasoning in artificial intelligence
	Big data analytics
	Computational mechanics
	Computer graphics
	Database concepts (computer-based databases)
	Data structures
	Geometric modeling
	Knowledge systems for decision support
	Machine learning
	Object representation and reasoning
	Optimization and search

5. Conclusions

Robotics and automation have been employed in the construction industry for several decades. However, very few research studies have tried to uncover the shift in robotics technologies. Through a systematic review of conference proceedings and journal articles, this research assesses and highlights some of the current technology trends and applications of automation and robotics in the construction industry, uncovering the focal point of construction robotics research. In addition, through a two-phase content analysis based review method, this research provides insight into the perceived critical construction KSAs required to perform construction robotics tasks in the industry. Additional systematized review and evaluation of the list of construction robotics KSAs will be accomplished through a series of one-on-one semi-structured interviews with construction industry and education professionals followed by a rigorous three-round, consensus-building Delphi study.

6. Future Study

Upon completion of the study, a significant area of future research is the development of a construction robotics competency benchmark and performance assessment framework to assist educators and industry professionals in cultivating talent and advance innovations in construction robotics. The research priorities are as follows:

1. Develop a model of student learning objectives for construction robotics training and education curricula with the integration of effective assessment measures.
2. Benchmark the desired student learning outcomes and career-specific competency in developing talent in construction robotics.
3. Evaluate the possibilities of integrating construction automation and robotics in construction education curriculum.
4. Guide the development of a training course to ensure the proposed competency benchmark and performance assessment framework provide meaningful outcomes to educators for developing and assessing the competency of students.
5. Test and validate the developed competency benchmark and performance assessment framework.

The developed skills benchmark is expected to make significant contributions to construction robotics curricula, training development, and competency cultivation in academia, as well as industry.

References

Agnisarman, S., Lopes, S., Madathil, K. C., Piratla, K., and Gramopadhye, A. (2019). A survey of automation-enabled human-in-the-loop systems for infrastructure visual inspection. Automation in Construction, 97, 52-76.

Barbosa, F., Woetzel, J., Mischke, J., Ribeirinho, M. J., Sridhar, M., Parsons, M., and Brown, S. (2017). Reinventing construction: A route to higher productivity. McKinsey Insights Report, McKinsey and Company.

Bayne, S. (2015). Teacherbot: Interventions in automated teaching. Teaching in Higher Education, 20(4), 455-467.

Bock, T. (2007). Construction robotics. Autonomous Robots, 22(3), 201-209.

Bogue, R. (2018). What are the prospects for robots in the construction industry? Industrial Robot: An International Journal, 45(1), 1-6.

Bureau of Labor Statistics (2018). A closer look: construction industries. Retrieved October 31, 2018, from https://www.bls.gov/lpc/

Buswell, R. A., Soar, R. C., Gibb, A. G., and Thorpe, A. (2007). Freeform construction: mega-scale rapid manufacturing for construction. Automation in construction, 16(2), 224-231.

Camacho, D. D., Clayton, P., O'Brien, W. J., Seepersad, C., Juenger, M., Ferron, R., and Salamone, S. (2018). Applications of additive manufacturing in the construction industry–A forward-looking review. Automation in Construction, 89, 110-119.

Chen, Q., de Soto, B. G., and Adey, B. T. (2018). Construction automation: Research areas, industry concerns and suggestions for advancement. Automation in Construction, 94, 22-38.

Flick, U. (2018). An introduction to qualitative research. Sage Publications Limited.

Goessens, S., Mueller, C., and Latteur, P. (2018). Feasibility study for drone-based masonry construction of real-scale structures. Automation in Construction, 94, 458-480.

Hewitt, M.M. and Gambatese, J.A. (2002). Automation consideration during project design. International Symposium on Automation and Robotics in Construction (ISARC), Washington, DC.

Kamaruddin, S. S., Mohammad, M. F., and Mahbub, R. (2016). Barriers and impact of mechanization and automation in construction to achieve better quality products. Procedia-Social and Behavioral Sciences, 222, 111-120.

Karimi, H., Taylor, T. R., Dadi, G. B., Goodrum, P. M., and Srinivasan, C. (2018). Impact of skilled labor availability on construction project cost performance. Journal of Construction Engineering and Management, 144(7), 04018057.

Kim, J., Lee, S. S., Seo, J., and Kamat, V. R. (2018). Modular data communication methods for a robotic excavator. Automation in Construction, 90, 166-177.

Lee, Y. S., Kim, S. H., Gil, M. S., Lee, S. H., Kang, M. S., Jang, S. H., and Han, C. S. (2018). The study on the integrated control system for curtain wall building façade cleaning robot. Automation in Construction, 94, 39-46.

Louis, J. and Dunston, P. S. (2018). Integrating IoT into operational workflows for real-time and automated decision-making in repetitive construction operations. Automation in Construction, 94, 317-327.

Oesterreich, T. D. and Teuteberg, F. (2016). Understanding the implications of digitisation and automation in the context of Industry 4.0: A triangulation approach and elements of a research agenda for the construction industry. Computers in Industry, 83, 121-139.

Romero, J. A., Lozano-Guzmán, A. A., Betanzo-Quezada, E., and López-Cajún, C. S. (2014). Robotics and road transportation: A review. In International Conference on Intelligent Robotics and Applications (pp. 467-478).

Schwab, K. (2017). The fourth industrial revolution. Crown Business.

Wang, Z., Li, H., and Zhang, X. (2019). Construction waste recycling robot for nails and screws: Computer vision technology and neural network approach. Automation in Construction, 97, 220-228.

World Economic Forum (2016). Shaping the future of construction: A breakthrough in mindset and technology. World Economic Forum. Cologny, Switzerland.

Zhang, X., Li, M., Lim, J. H., Weng, Y., Tay, Y. W. D., Pham, H., and Pham, Q. C. (2018). Large-scale 3D printing by a team of mobile robots. Automation in Construction, 95, 98-106.

4D Simulation Considering Adjusted Schedules for Safety Planning in Hydroelectric Projects

Michel Guévremont, P.Eng.,[1] and Amin Hammad, Ph.D.[2]

[1] Scheduling Advisor, Hydro-Québec, 855 Sainte-Catherine St. East, Montréal, QC, Canada H2L 4P5; Ph.D. Student, Concordia Institute for Information Systems Engineering, Concordia Univ., 1515 Sainte-Catherine St. West, Montréal, QC, Canada H3G 2W1 (corresponding author). Email: guevremont.michel@hydro.qc.ca

[2] Professor, Concordia Institute for Information Systems Engineering, Concordia Univ., 1515 Sainte-Catherine St. West, Montréal, QC, Canada H3G 2W1. Email: amin.hammad@concordia.ca

ABSTRACT The construction industry is known for numerous and severe accidents. For the hydroelectric industry, nine dominant critical risks have been identified in the construction phase. This paper aims to develop a 4D simulation technique to minimize potential accidents at different phases of a project considering different 4D levels of development (4D-LOD). The proposed method integrates safety planning with 4D simulation in the hydroelectric industry. Specific risks for this industry include working near water and live energy sources. Statistical analysis of historical safety issues impacting schedules is used to identify potential safety risks. Then, 4D simulation is used to visualize construction operations at low and then high 4D-LOD. As a predictive tool, 4D simulation scenarios can be evaluated in relation to the number of risky activities considering their periods and zones, which can be prioritized and visualized. Case studies are presented to support the method involving subprojects of powerhouses.

KEYWORDS: 4D simulation, safety, BIM, hydroelectric company

1. Introduction

The construction industry is known for dangerous projects and being the source of numerous and severe accidents. Leite (2018) mentioned that construction remains the second most hazardous industry especially due to the dangerous combination of pedestrian workers and heavy construction vehicles and machinery, such as dump trucks, dozers, and rollers. In construction projects of new facilities and maintenance projects of old ones, safety risks are a major concern for hydroelectric companies. The industry involves fast-paced projects, which can lead to a lack of planning and scheduling. In the hydro-electrical industry, the nine most critical risks in worksites are observed as patterns as shown in Figure 1: (1) moving vehicles, (2) energy sources (e.g. induction), (3) working-at-heights, (4) lifting operations, (5) water presence, (6) confined spaces, (7) excavations and unstable grounds and rocks, (8) unstable or falling objects and (9) dangerous goods or substances. These risks will be described in detail in Section 3. To handle these risks, the general intentions at the feasibility, construction or operation phase (in decreasing order of impact) are to: eliminate the risk, reduce the risk (substitution), isolate employees from the risk (engineering controls), modify the methods (administrative controls) and protect the employees with the personal protective equipment (PPE). PPE can include boots, helmet, face mask, working gloves, visibility vest, fire resistant suit, ear plugs, respiratory masks, etc.

As mentioned by Leite et al. (2016), although the benefits of the simulation modeling to the construction industry are widely acknowledged (such as visualization), large-scale adoption is still challenging because of existing barriers, such as budgetary constraints, insufficient training, uncertain effectiveness, cultural issues and limited expertise. Safety can be an integrated aspect of normal operations and considered in early planning and scheduling. 4D simulation provides spatio-temporal representations of objects based on scheduling and space planning. The 4D simulations presented in this paper are more than an animation as the schedule integration is linked with the 3D model. 4D simulation is helpful for detecting safety risks. Objects such as workspaces, equipments (e.g. vehicles) and materials are prepared in the 3D model and later manually linked with the schedule in the 4D simulation. This paper aims to develop a 4D simulation technique to minimize potential accidents at different phases (e.g. early in the pre-feasibility or in the construction phase) of a project considering different levels of development (4D-LOD). The objective is to provide a method for integrating safety planning in adjusted schedules for enhanced 4D simulation in the context of the hydro-electrical industry. The developed method integrates 3D modeling and visualization techniques of safety simulation that were validated in actual construction projects. The safety context can be continuously evaluated with the 4D simulation and it will be shown in the case studies. The paper first explores the related work in the next section. Then, the 4D simulation method specific to safety planning is described. This is followed with case studies where the method has been tested. The 4D simulation general process was described in Guevremont (2017) and the 4D-LOD of such 4D simulation are described in Guevremont and Hammad (2019).

Figure 1: Pictograms of nine critical risks in hydroelectric powerhouses

2. Related Work

2.1. Safety Planning with 4D Simulation

Limited research considered 4D simulation for safety in a general manner. Most previous efforts focused on the use of sensors or modeling equipment and related worker proximity risks. Hammad et al. (2012) listed spatial information related to prevention program for safety. They included protection against falling (guardrail and safety net), housekeeping and means of access (storage area and temporary access), scaffolding and shoring, confined spaces and tanks, electricity with overhead or proximity of power lines, reserved work spaces and proximity for heavy machinery, and barriers and fences for trenches and excavations. They tested the guardrails and collision prevention with 4D models. Guo et al. (2012) demonstrated the use of game technologies for improving construction safety training. The results of their interviews and questionnaire survey about tower cranes, mobile cranes and pile drivers indicated five important aspects of safety performance with advanced technologies: the ability of recognizing operations, the ability to identify safety problems, the possibility of preventing safety problems, the ability to improve collaboration among operators, and the ability to improve operations' processes. Dawood et al. (2014) evaluated the use of 4D simulation in health and safety training to spot safety hazards (e.g. missing railings, obstruction, poor storage, etc.) and the way users interacted with the 4D model. They concluded that 4D simulation approaches can improve users' engagement and affect their abilities to spot health and safety hazards. Hazards were modeled and linked with the project schedule to emulate an evolving construction environment. Teo et al. (2016) looked at the safety aspect of BIM to determine a safety index and enhance safety performance. From a survey, they evaluated contractors, architectural, engineering and surveying firms about their safety practices and mentioned the potential of BIM in improving safety with hazard identification, pre-project planning, clash detection, location tracking, conformance to performance standards and regulations, safety monitoring using actual construction site data, and safety simulation. The system they developed has rule checking, hazard checking, control measures, safety evaluation and planning, and monitoring. Guo et al. (2017) reviewed 78 articles on the use of visualization for construction safety management. They found that visualization technology, such as 4D simulation, can improve safety management by aiding safety training, job hazard area (JHA) identification and onsite safety monitoring and warnings. They focused on the automatic identification of falls from height, spatial collision, layout of protection guards, and measures for potential structural collapse. Zou et al. (2017) reviewed risk management through BIM and BIM-related technologies. They mentioned the latest efforts with automatic rule checking for working-at-heights and also described the lack of human factor testing. Specifically about 4D simulation, they wrote that the benefits for risk management are facilitating early risk identification and communication for improving construction management. Zhou and Ding (2017) developed pictograms for hazard energy involved in deep excavation of metro stations, such as radiant, heat, optical, electrical, gravitational, vibrational, explosive, chemical, potential and strain energies. Cheng et al. (2018) developed a model to improve evacuation performance in case of accidents to prevent serious fatalities and financial losses. To minimize the total evacuation time, they considered evacuation model input, simulation environment modeling, agent definition, simulation, comparison, environment sensing (emerging accidents, herding behavior, communication) and dynamic escape path planning. Synchro Software (2019) included safety management in 4D simulation with features, such as highlighting design risks, communicating residual safety issues at the time of procurement, adding early input for safety of construction workers at the pre-construction phase, and handover of maintenance safety regimes and facility management planning. In the construction phase, they created specific visual methods, visual toolbox, site inductions and VR safety training. They also considered different safety events such as crush points, body positioning, confined spaces, equipment, falls, fire, hoisting and rigging, ladders, line of fire, signage, tools, falling objects, PPE, lockout-tag out and sharp edges. As a general limit, the previous works listed above has provided great advancement for safety in simulation but lacked the scheduling impact adjustments and considerations.

2.2. Adjusting Schedules for Safety

Benjaoran and Bhokha (2010) inserted safety measures in schedules and 4D models for working-at-height hazards. Their integrated system for safety proactively raised awareness about edges and boundaries of columns, beams, slabs and walls. Zhang and Hu (2011) developed principles and a methodology for structural safety analysis in 4D simulation for temporary structures. Their safety analysis calculated indicators, forecast and warning; therefore enabling adjustment of values such as workspaces for tower cranes. Their model uses a first level with rough bounding boxes and a second level with detailed bounding boxes. They generated the child boxes (2nd level) to avoid conflict and collisions. Kim and Teizer (2014) developed a rule-based system that automatically plans temporary scaffolding systems to minimize code compliance problems, inefficiencies and waste of procuring and managing material. Their system recognizes geometric and non-geometric conditions that can be utilized in communication, billing of materials and scheduling simulation. Interior and exterior scaffolding placement is based on schedule tasks, building objects, and work faces. Their geometric reasoning tied building objects (faces) to work faces and its performance was assessed with correctly identified, false positives and false negatives. Zhang et al. (2015) developed 4D simulation with automatic addition of fall protective systems (posts, railings, guardrails) at concrete slab edges by detection of holes. They added fall hazard detection and prevention to BIM-based models. They observed the benefits of their automated modeling approach, such as short time requirements, little safety related knowledge, ease of updates and low 3D-LOD. Choe and Leite (2017) developed a three-phase general research process to generate work periods and work zones safety scores from risky activities. From accident types and sources of injury, they conducted a case study to test and verify the data they used with Synchro. It included general safety knowledge, and site-specific temporal and spatial information. They mentioned that visual safety materials can enhance safety communication among project participants. They aimed at answering which activities are dangerous (risk quantification), when and where risky activities are planned (safety schedule) and how risky activities can be effectively communicated (safety 4D simulation). They identified the most dangerous days when the most activities were planned simultaneously in work zones and visualized work zone risk with colors. They discussed that the method can help safety managers develop a safety planning systematically (macro-level site-specific safety planning and micro-level safety practices), and that the safety 4D simulation can increase safety communication among project participants. Leite (2018) mentioned that it is important to integrate safety planning and project schedules to create more effective site-specific safety plans. She brought the safety schedule aspect in 4D simulation including prioritizing risky activities. However, she did not mention what are the risky activities and how to prioritize them based on other elements than concurrent activities, number of workers, occupation types and zoning plan. She also mentioned that the challenge lies on automating safety information representation. To increase project planning performance, Germain and Drouin (2019) suggested a model to introduce safety measures early in the feasibility phases of a project life cycle. They considered safety impacts on planning and scheduling of a mega project with categorization of safety events, lessons learned from past projects, performance analysis and negative patterns. The extension of this work could include the ranking and causes of the negative patterns. The abovementioned works suggested including safety activities in the project schedule (manually, with rule-based algorithms or automatically) and eventually in the 4D simulation. However, they did not rank the risk patterns in the context of 4D simulation for hydroelectric projects.

3. Method

The planned evolution of safety culture in companies could perhaps be summarized with 4 steps: (1) no interest (reactive), (2) must do (viewed as a constraint to manage risks), (3) want to do (viewed as a continuous process driven by management and politics), and (4) value in the ADN of employees. In step 1, safety is not important and employees just do not want to get caught. In step 2, the safety is still reactive and the company does the safety essential only after events. In this step, the company uses systems in place to manage risks. In the 3rd step, safety is a continuous process driven by management and corporate values of safety at work. In step 4, safety is a value in the backbone of the company and employees. To support the safety culture evolution related by the 4 steps above, Table 1 shows the nine most critical risks patterns for hydroelectric powerhouse related work along with examples of specific items considered in the

4D simulation and their representation. Intangible benefits of these efforts are to raise employee's awareness of critical risks to save lives, prevent accidents and near-misses and to enhance planning and working methods. The safety features exposed in Table 1 must be evaluated at multiple periods during the course of a project and inserted into the schedule.

Table 1: Generic hazard representation for 4D safety simulation of hydroelectric projects

Modeling generic risks patterns in hydro-electrical facility	**Item considered in 4D model (general and *specific* hazards)**	**Representation in 4D model**
(1) Moving vehicle	Eliminating or minimizing back-up areas with identification on ground; planning of parking areas; showing speed limit signs	Prism on ground with texture; Delimited areas for back-up of vehicles; delimited zones for pedestrians crossings
(2) Energy sources	Identifying limitations of crane paths; *water power risks safety procedure in spillway chute area; identifying existing transmission lines; mapping minimal safe distance from source; visualizing induction objects or zone*	Colored (yellow) prisms for aerial lines and spillway chute zones and red prisms for crane boom areas; cylinders around transmission lines for minimal safety distance for work zone (prohibited red zone) and work zone under temporary instructions (yellow zone at 3 m for < 125 kV, at 5 m if between 125 kV and 55 kV, at 8 m if between 250 kV and 550 kV and at 12 m if > 550 kV); induction represented on objects (yellow color)
(3) Working at heights/falling hazard	Safety nets and plates (wood or steel) under work zone enabling superposed work	Warning prism in zone or safety object modeling (plates or nets); risk zone highlighted; handrails in concrete and in stair cases; inspection of platforms
(4) Lifting objects	*Turbine-generator components, Valves with cranes*; adjacent and underneath work zones	Colored moving object and colored adjacent and underneath work zones with bounding box (prism) and text for lifting procedure
(5) Working near water	*Boat, nautical safety rescue crew and divers*	Boat representation, warning zone with prims when water is in proximity (e.g. 2 m) and text indicators for required safety measures; show timing for diving framework
(6) Confined spaces	*Valve room, pit area, electricity change under overhead cranes*, manholes, access shaft, pipes, *chimney*, reservoir, silo, caisson, piles, sewer, tank	Zone highlighted with bounding boxes (colored prism) and text indicator for adequate procedure (e.g. text for PPE)
(7) Unstable grounds and excavation	Slopes at a maximum of 45 degrees, protecting vertical rock with consolidation (rock bolts and meshing), unstable ground/rocks	Colored slopes and colored consolidation; roads to a minimum distance of 3 m of slope abutment for travelling and parking
(8) Unstable objects	*Turbine-generator, valves and gates at height*	Coloring object and/or highlighting proper safety zone perimeter (e.g. underneath, in proximity); avalanche fences; safety cables and locks; drop cones can be shown at high 4D-LOD; Bounding boxes are used at lower 4D-LOD. Another way to show a visual reminder to the 4D user is to use a specific color code for dangerous objects at height (e.g. highlight object itself or nearby objects).
(9) Dangerous goods	Management program for asbestos, silica and lead (e.g. silica fumes when cutting concrete); painting and epoxy coatings installation	Colored bounding box (red prism) for preventive hose with spray or shelters for workers with masks

The proposed method integrates safety planning with 4D simulation in the hydroelectric industry is shown in Figure 2. Hereafter are specific safety comments about the steps of the proposed method:

(1) Statistical analysis of historical safety issues impacting schedules are used to identify potential safety risks.

(2) From the analysis at step (1) emerges negative safety patterns. As a predictive tool, 4D simulation scenarios can be evaluated in relation to the number of risky activities considering their work periods and zones, which can be prioritized and visualized. With the dynamic nature of the construction jobsites, this can help choosing a feasible scenario considering the context of the operations. The general 4D simulation method is explained in Guevremont and Hammad (2018). Safety should be part of the normal operations and can be evaluated at the planning process for temporal and spatial considerations. It must be considered from the planning and scheduling normal process in the lifecycle of a project. Examples of negative patterns include minimal safety distances (e.g. with water presence), workspaces with temporary measures, dedicated work zones for energized areas or lifting areas, inspection of scaffolding, platforms and cranes, and requirements of workers adapted individual PPE (e.g. flotation vest, gas detectors).

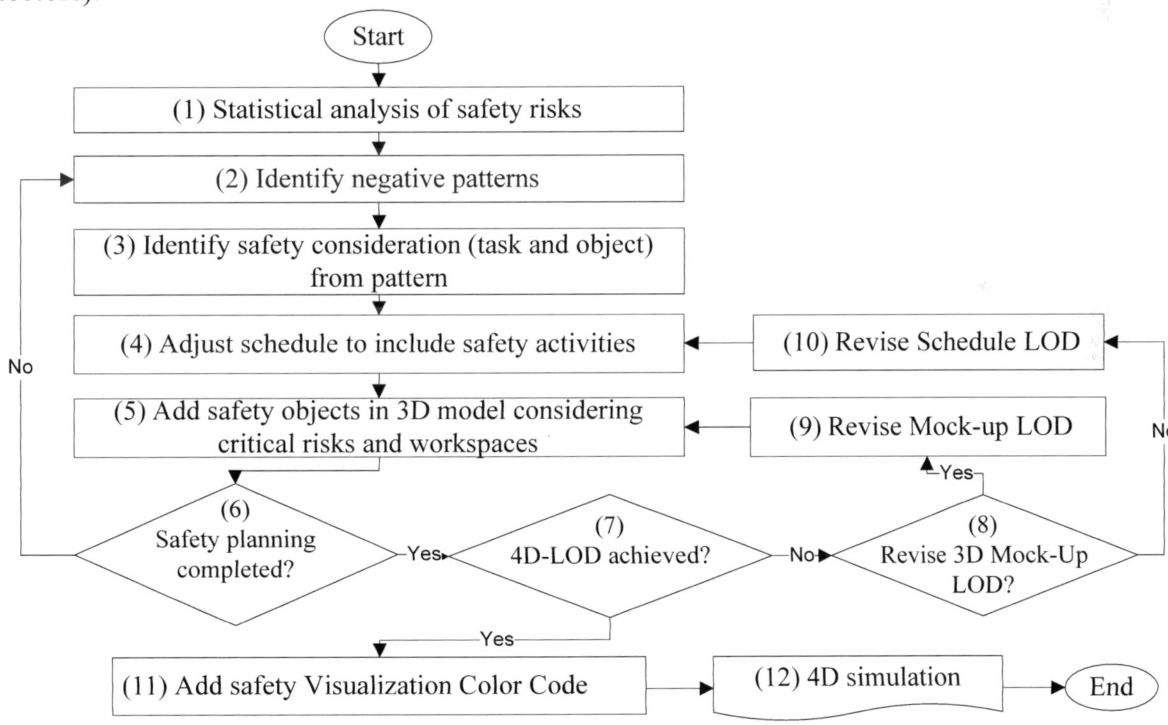

Figure 2: Safety 4D simulation flow chart

(3-4) From the safety patterns emerge considerations and mitigation with tasks and objects. The schedule can include information in specific codes to consider safety aspects such as type of workspace, dimensions of workspace, shape control in relation to 4D-LOD, etc. Schedule activities that are not represented in the 3D model can be questioned. In the schedule, steps of installation or dismantling of equipment with sequencing and worker's trades involved can be represented as identified per the worker's safety code. Work must be planned considering safety including access, co-activity, site setup, safety rules and their impact on the schedule. Fast tracking impact can be evaluated considering safety. The 9 patterns described in Table 1 can be evaluated for consideration, prioritized and included in the schedule. Dangerous construction activities are identified and mitigation measures are added to the schedules with new activities.

(5-6) A complete 4D simulation considering safety could visualize items such as: moving equipment with required safety measures such as padlocks, storage areas added for good site conditions, spreading of skid-proof materials. These safety considerations could be useful for safety managers to review or audit a specific construction site. 4D simulation can integrate the critical risks considering the development of time with 3D models to include Planning for Safety (PfS) in 4D for workspaces (equipment, staff and storage).

(7-10) Early adjustments of 4D-LOD can be a useful and proactive tool for planning. Characteristics of the schedule such as lags can impact 4D-LOD's and visual output of the 4D simulation. A low 4D-LOD or a mix of different 4D-LOD's in simulations can typically include numerous lags, generating numerous concurrent activities, and consequently being insufficient for proper 4D safety simulation planning, and hence, could justify a higher 4D-LOD to be more useful. Bounding box technique is usually at low 4D-LOD (A or B) while objects are used at higher 4D-LOD (C, D or E). The bounding box is a preliminary stage. Color coding starts with bounding box technique and depends on 4D-LOD. 4D simulation is used to visualize construction operations at a high 4D-LOD (D or E). The description of the different 4D-LOD's is described in details in Guevremont and Hammad (2019). Modeling equipment movement (i.e. translations and rotations) with respect to assigned safety workspaces and workers' workspaces can help planning the critical activities to meet the commissioning dates while considering detailed and safe operations.

(11) The safety aspect of alternative construction methods can be evaluated in the planning process considering potential spatiotemporal conflicts of workspaces in the 4D simulation. At the design phase, the construction method is detailed to include timing considerations for the sequence of activities. These activities with physical issues are included in the 4D simulation with the bounding-box techniques, and color codes are used to illustrate workers hazards such as dangerous sources of energy, elevated work issues, fall of objects, movement of vehicles, access issues and co-activity of multiple contracts, projects or trades. A construction method could be scored according to a 4D audit considering safety. With the dynamic nature of the construction jobsites, this can help the choice of a scenario in the context of feasibility or for the operations.

(12) From a requirements analysis, safety elements are considered in 4D simulations of hydro-electrical projects for measurement, training and communication. They can measure the proximity of a road to an object (with a virtual arrow on the ground), identify the speed limits (with signs), identify back-up areas (with floor delimitations), identify areas without pedestrians (with signs, cones and barriers), identify walkways in pre-defined areas (with white lines in the floor) and the perimeter of the construction site (with a fence). This can affects the reasoning to help workers in training. With the intent of preventing accidents, the communication output and share of this 4D simulation to other people can help visual training to safety department experts and field personnel to enhance the timing of their safety planning, and thus, to avoid field issues. This reinforces that the project challenges are not only technical demanding but need a good socio-technological integration of people, processes and technologies and a good collaboration with projects stakeholders. The identification and analysis of the risks helps project owners eliminate the root cause of hazards as required by safety regulations.

4. Case Studies

Case studies presented in this section are from a utility in the province of Quebec and are used to illustrate efficiency of the proposed method in powerhouse projects involving different subprojects such as concreting, turbine-generator installation, overhead cranes and valves dismantling and steel deck obstruction. Hydroelectric projects are complex and generate multiple safety risks, which appear and disappear during the course of a project. The case studies used visualization for elements (object themselves or safety mitigation) presented in the method from risky activities in adjusted project schedule considering safety. The project schedules of Figure 3 and 4 have been adjusted to include specific risk patterns listed in Table 1 as described hereafter. This has proven useful for visual inspection and safety planning with the virtual model. Colored indicators are enabled for obstructions (potential conflicts or risks) or safety evaluation with green, yellow and red values. Safety index with density of work obtained from the schedule and are exposed considering time and space in the 4D simulation. A poor index result could require enhancement of 4D-LOD in specific zones. In addition to the field personnel and management team, safety teams from the site or the main office have been engaged early on these case studies with early communications to help identify safety items to be planned for the respective projects. In the feasibility phase, Figure 3 is related to safety measures in rehabilitation projects. Figure 3(a) demonstrates a 4D-LOD B with risk pattern 1 for a safety zone. The safety zone is related to an electricity type (i.e. DC to AC) switch between two types of overhead cranes inside a powerhouse and workers workspaces. Figure 3(b) presents a 4D-LOD D with a safety analysis of bridge deck obstruction including an automated label for access of vehicles (risk pattern 1) from the left shore to the powerhouse. This case involved working at heights on superior deck rehabilitation (dismantling shown in red with two cranes for the lift) and in proximity of upstream water, representing risk patterns 3, 4, 5 and 8. The downstream concrete work involves shelters and masks (PPE) for workers when cutting and using silica fumes (risk pattern 9).

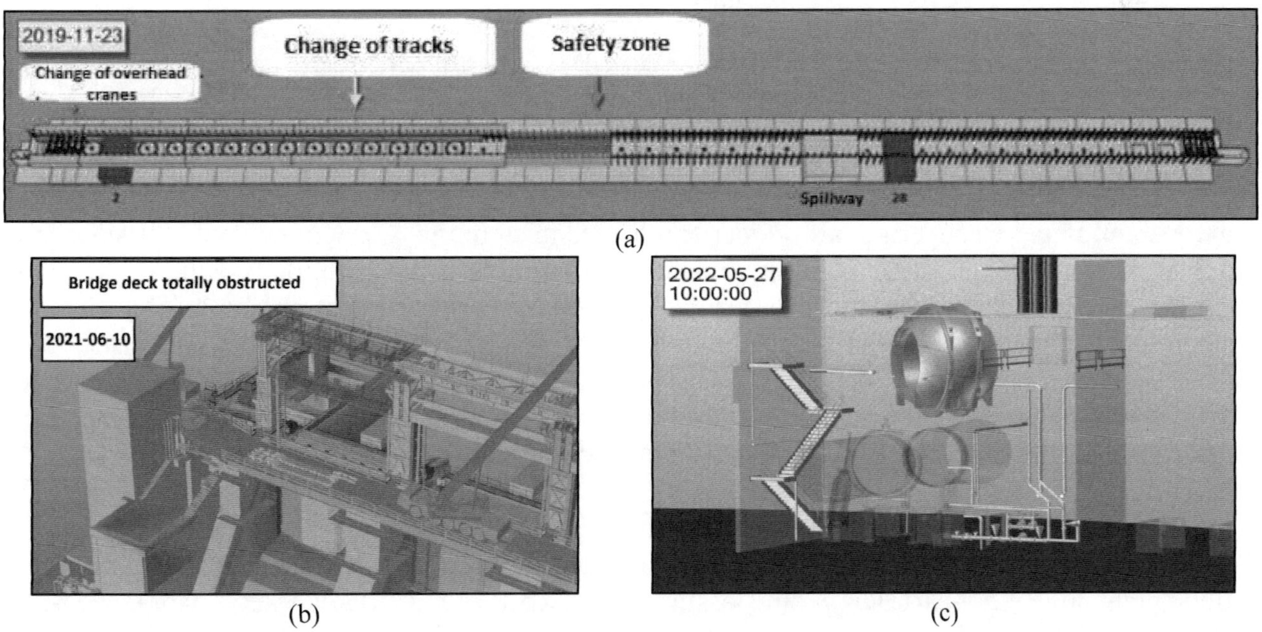

Figure 3: Safety measures for rehabilitation projects (a) 4D-LOD B with risk pattern 1, (b) 4D-LOD D with risk patterns 1, 3, 4, 5, 8 and 9, (c) 4D-LOD E with risk patterns 2, 3, 4, 6 and 8.

Figure 3(c) presents a 4D-LOD E with highlighted colors for safety of moving heavy objects (risk pattern 4 and 8) inside a powerhouse (e.g. lifting an eyelid valve) and stairs with handrails protective systems (risk pattern 3). This work is performed in a small room (risk pattern 6) and with live pipes and electricity (risk pattern 2). Specific durations considering safety are included in the project schedule for these risk patterns. Figure 4 is related to safety measures in the construction phase for new facilities. Figure 4(a) shows concrete pours in a new hydroelectric powerhouse at 4D-LOD C. Specifically, safety related precautions that must be considered at the time of mobilisation are displayed. Actions include guardrails installation as per the regulation code to prevent falls from heights (risk pattern 3) and avalanche fences installation prior to concreting activities at these high locations (risk pattern 8). Other colours show pouring of concrete in magenta and anchor installation in cyan (risk pattern 7) to secure existing rock faces. Figure 4(b) shows a 4D-LOD D for risk pattern 1 with identified safety back-up areas in a powerhouse (red floor) for vehicles. Further, it includes safety considerations for lifting turbine-generator parts (risk patterns 4 and 8) enabling them to move to their respective pits (risk pattern 6).

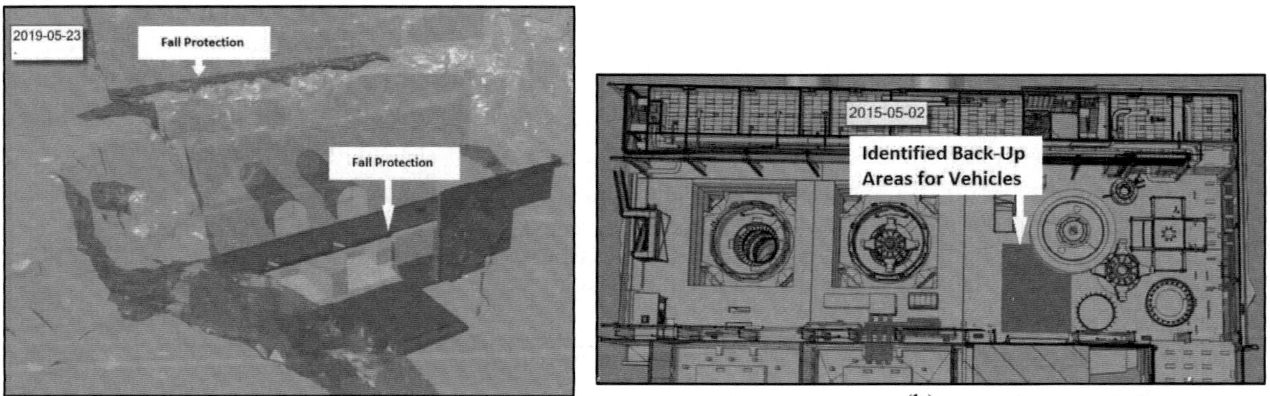

(a) (b)

Figure 4: Safety measures for new facilities (a) 4D-LOD C with risk patterns 3, 7 and 8, (b) 4D-LOD D with risk patterns 1, 4, 6 and 8.

5. Summary and Conclusion

Safety should be the concern of all project employees in a company where safety is considered as a value. 4D simulation can help communicate and share this value with the integration of safety elements and aspects in the course of normal operations. This paper has shown a 4D simulation technique to minimize potential accidents at different phases (e.g. pre-feasibility or construction) of a project and considering different levels of development (4D-LOD). This method has been useful for integrating safety planning with 4D simulation in the context of the hydro-electrical industry. The identification of potential risks ahead of the construction phase can be used as a preventive safety training tool for a safer work place. The identification and analysis of the risks will help project owners eliminate the root cause of hazards as required by safety regulations. This included enhanced planning techniques for enabling proper inspection timing of temporary safety elements (e.g. scaffolding) and assigning of work zones and workers' workspaces. In addition, the 4D simulation has been used as a jobsite tool for daily operations decision-support to protect workers from different hazards and sources of energy for the new facilities. Adjustments to the schedule were updated and considered as input for revised 4D simulation.

Future work includes studying the impact of safety on the critical path of project schedules and 4D simulation.

References

Benjaoran, V. and Bhokha, S. (2010). An Integrated Safety Management with Construction Management Using 4D CAD Model, Safety Science. 48, pp. 395-403.

Chen, J.C.P., Tan, Y., Son, Y., Mei, Z., Gan, V.J.L. and Wang, X. (2018). Developing an Evacuation Evaluation Model for Offshore Oil and Gas Platforms Using BIM and Agent-Based Model, Autom. in Constr. 89, pp. 214-224.

Choe, S. and Leite, F. (2017). Construction safety planning: Site-specific temporal and spatial information, Automation in Construction. 84, pp. 335-344.

Dawood, N., Miller, G., Patacas, J. and Kassem, M. (2014). Construction health and safety training: the utilisation of 4D enabled serious games, J. of Information Technology in Construction. 19, pp. 326-335.

Germain, C. and Drouin, N. (2019). Introduce Safety Measures in Earlier Phases of the Project Life Cycle to Increase Success of Project, In: 63rd Int. Conf. of the Assoc. for the Adv. of Cost Eng. Conf., New Orleans, USA.

Guevremont, M. (2017). Virtual construction management. In: Proceedings of the 61st International Conference of the Association for the Advancement of Cost Engineering, Orlando, USA.

Guevremont, M. and Hammad, A. (2018). Multi-LOD 4D Simulation in Phased Rehabilitation Projects. In: Proc. of the 17th Int. Conf. on Computing in Civil and Building Engineering, Tampere, Finland.

Guevremont, M. and Hammad, A. (2019). Defining Levels of Development for 4D Simulation of Major Capital Construction Projects, In: Mutis, I., Hartmann, T. (Eds.). Advances in Informatics and Computing in Civil and Construction Engineering, Springer Nature Switzerland, pp. 77-83.

Guo, H., Li, H., Chan, G. and Skitmore, M. (2012). Using Game Technologies to Improve the Safety of Construction Plant Operations, Accident Analysis and Prevention. 48, pp. 204-213.

Guo, H., Yu, Y. and Skitmore, M. (2017). Visualization Technology-Based Construction Safety Management: A Review, Automation in Construction. 73, pp. 135-144.

Hammad, A., Zhang, C., Setayeshgar, S. and Asen, Y. (2012). Automatic generation of dynamic virtual fences as part of BIM-based prevention program for construction safety. In: Wint. Sim. Conf., Berlin, Germany.

Kim, K. and Teizer, J. (2014). Automatic Design and Planning of Scaffolding Systems Using Building Information Modeling, Advanced Engineering Informatics. 28, pp. 66-80.

Leite F. (2018). Automated Approaches Towards BIM-Based Intelligent Decision Support in Design, Construction, and Facility Operations. In: Smith I., Domer B. (Eds.). Advanced Computing Strategies for Engineering. EG-ICE 2018. Lect. Notes in Computer Science, vol 10864. Springer, Cham.

Leite. F., Cho, Y., Behzadan, A., Lee, S., Choe, S., Fang, Y., Akhavian, R. and Hwang, S. (2016). Visualization, Information Modeling and Simulation Grand Challenges in the Construction Industry, Journal of Computing in Civil Engineering. 04016035.

Synchro software (2019). Website: https://www.synchroltd.com/. accessed March 2019.

Teo, A.L.E., Ofori, G., Tjandra, I. K. and Kim, H. (2016). Design for safety: theoretical framework of the safety aspect of BIM system to determine the safety index, Construction Economics and Building. 16(4), pp. 1-18.

Zhang, J.P. and Hu, Z.Z. (2011). BIM- and 4D-Based Integrated Solution of Analysis and Management for Conflicts and Structural Safety Problems during Construction: 1. Principles and Methodologies, Aut. Constr. 20, pp. 155-166.

Zhang, S., Sulankivi, K., Kiviniemi, M., Romo, I., Eastman, C.M. and Teizer, J. (2015). Bim-Based Fall Hazard Identification and Prevention in Construction Safety Planning, Safety Science. 72, pp. 31-45.

Zhou, C. and Ding, L.Y. (2017). Safety barrier warning system for underground construction sites using Internet-of-Things technologies, Automation in Construction. 83, pp. 372-389.

Zou, Y., Kiviniemi, A. and Jones, S. (2017). A review of risk management through BIM and BIM-related technologies, Safety Science. 97, pp. 88-98.

AUTHOR INDEX